Fodor's 4th Edition

P9-DJU-811

India

The Guide for All Budgets, Completely Updated, with Many Maps and Travel Tips

Where to Stay, Eat,
and Explore

On and Off
the Beaten Path

When to Go,
What to Pack

Post-it® Flags,
Web Sites, and More

Fodor's Travel Publications • New York, Toronto, London, Sydney, Auckland
www.fodors.com

Fodor's India

EDITOR: Diane Mehta

Editorial Contributors: Beatrice Aranow, Christine Cipriani, Laura Kidder, Deborah Kaufman, Soumya Battacharya, Michael W. Bollom, Scott Carney, Vaihayasi Pande Daniel, Gaye Facer, Jayanth Kodkani, Shanti Menon, Kavita Milner, Keith Snodgrass, R. Edwin Sudhir, Ami Trivedi

Editorial Production: Taryn Luciani

Maps: David Lindroth, *cartographer;* Rebecca Baer, Bob Blake, *map editors*

Design: Fabrizio La Rocca, *creative director;* Guido Caroti, *art director;* Jolie Novak, *senior picture editor;* Melanie Marin, *photo editor*

Cover Design: Pentagram

Production/Manufacturing: Angela L. McLean

Cover Photo (the Blue City, Rajasthan, Jodhpur): Andrea Pistolesi

Copyright

Fourth Edition

ISBN 0–676–90224–3

ISSN 1079–6444

Important Tip

Although all prices, opening times, and other details in this book are based on information supplied to us at press time, changes occur all the time in the travel world, and Fodor's cannot accept responsibility for facts that become outdated or for inadvertent errors or omissions. So **always confirm information when it matters,** especially if you're making a detour to visit a specific place.

Special Sales

Fodor's Travel Publications are available at special discounts for bulk purchases for sales promotions or premiums. Special editions, including personalized covers, excerpts of existing guides, and corporate imprints, can be created in large quantities for special needs. For more information, contact your local bookseller or write to Special Markets, Fodor's Travel Publications, 280 Park Ave., New York, NY 10017. Inquiries from Canada should be directed to your local Canadian bookseller or sent to Random House of Canada, Ltd., Marketing Department, 2775 Matheson Boulevard East, Mississauga, Ontario L4W 4P7. Inquiries from the United Kingdom should be sent to Fodor's Travel Publications, 20 Vauxhall Bridge Road, London SW1V 2SA, England.

PRINTED IN THE UNITED STATES OF AMERICA

10 9 8 7 6 5 4 3 2 1

CONTENTS

Maps

ON THE ROAD WITH FODOR'S

THE MORE YOU KNOW before you go, the better your trip will be. India's most fascinating small museum (or its spiciest restaurant or its most beautiful temple) could be just around the corner from your hotel, but if you don't know it's there, it might as well be on the other side of the globe. That's where this book comes in. It's a great step toward making sure your next trip lives up to your expectations. As you plan, check out the Web as well. Guidebooks have been helping smart travelers find the special places for years; the Web is one more tool. Whatever reference you consult, be savvy about what you read, and always consider the source. Images and language can be massaged to make places appear better than they are. And one traveler's quaint is another's grimy. Here at Fodor's, and at our on-line arm, Fodors.com, our focus is on providing you with information that's not only useful but accurate and on target. Every day Fodor's editors put enormous effort into getting things right, beginning with the search for the right contributors—people who have objective judgment, broad travel experience, and the writing ability to put their insights into words. There's no substitute for advice from a like-minded friend who has just come back from where you're going, but our writers, having seen all corners of India, are the next best thing. They're the kind of people you'd poll for tips yourself if you knew them.

Soumya Bhattacharya is editor (Features and Opinion) of *Hindustan Times*, Calcutta. He has worked in London, Delhi, and Calcutta and travelled widely in Europe and Southeast Asia. But Calcutta is the only city in which he says he can find his way home blindfolded.

Michael W. Bollom has eight years of experience traveling, living, and working in India. Having studied Hindi literature, researched Indian political economy, and worked in development, he now teaches history and economics at the American Embassy School in New Delhi, a city in which he indulges his passion for eating out.

Scott Carney is a freelance writer based out of New York City, but has lived and traveled extensively in India. With aspirations toward a Ph.D. he has conducted research on Rajput folklore in Chittorgarh and Udaipur. Formerly a senior editor of *Manhattan Style*, his work appears in a variety of publications, including *India Today*.

A granddaughter of Estonian and Indian freedom-fighters, **Vaihayasi Pande Daniel** was born in Montréal, grew up in Baltimore, married a Tamil Christian, and has lived in India since 1976. Peripatetic tendencies draw her (and her two young daughters) all over India and elsewhere, but she prefers Bombay to any other place in the world. The assistant managing editor at rediff.com's New York-based publication *India Abroad*, she earlier managed rediff's travel site and now writes on travel and current affairs for this popular Indian news service.

Gaye Facer, a Canadian-born writer and literary agent, has been based in New Delhi since 1997. She teaches Drama at the American Embassy School, and founded "Shakti Creative Agency" to promote literary and literacy partnerships between South Asian and Western publishers. She indulges in trekking adventures in the Himalayas, as well as yoga and massage in the spa culture that's burgeoning in northern India. She also attributes much of the exuberant hospitality she finds all over India to her intrepid companion and dessert critic—her 10-year-old daughter Emma.

Jayanth Kodkani, assistant editor at a newspaper in India, has lived in Bangalore all his life, watching it grow from a lazy garrison town to a booming metropolis. He itches for more time to roam the beaches of Goa and Karnataka. Writing for Fodor's, he says, gave new life to his inner tourist, helping him appreciate nooks and crannies he hadn't otherwise stopped to contemplate.

Editor **Diane Mehta** was raised in Bombay by a Gujarati Jain father and a Jewish mother, and has spent her adult life in the New York area. She has traveled extensively throughout India, from Kerala's rugged backwaters to the serene lake city of Udaipur. She is also editor of *Escape to the Wine Country* and *Fodor's London, Ireland,* and *the South*.

Kavita Milner is a freelance travel writer and features journalist with a penchant for little-known places. She has lived in the historic cities of Mysore and Calcutta, and now works for the World Bank in Chennai, India. She enjoys trekking in the mountains and forests of the south, and has written on destinations from Scotland to Australia.

Keith Snodgrass, who wrote the chronology, lived in India and Pakistan for a year and a half, and has studied the history of South Asia. He currently produces programming on India for teachers and the general public in the Seattle area, and teaches at the University of Washington.

R. Edwin Sudhir, a senior journalist with a leading English daily, has settled in his native Bangalore after living for several years in Maharashtra. For Fodor's he toured temples and heritage sites all over South and East India, in addition to braving urban sprawls, and was reminded that no matter how much you see in this country, there's always more to be seen.

For their kind assistance in preparing this edition, we'd like to thank the commendable Jet Airways; the Government of India Tourist Office, New York; Nosh Nalavala, editor and publisher of *Traveler's India;* and Prakash Swamy of the News India Group, New York. Thanks also to the Taj Group of Hotels, particularly Jodi Dell Leblanc in New York, Saleem Yousuff at the Ambassador Hotel (Delhi), Sonal Bakshi at the Taj Palace (Delhi), T. Murugan Rajan at the Taj Coromandel (Madras), Gitesh Aggarwal at Fisherman's Cove (Madras), Dinaz Madhukar and Genevieve Mathias D'Cunha at the Taj Malabar (Cochin), and Shankar Menon at the Taj Garden Retreat (Kumarakom). Special thanks, too, to the Casino Hotel Group in Kerala; Dr. Venu V, District Collector of Kannur in North Kerala; Rajini Chopra of the Oberoi Hotels Group; and Francis Wacziarg and Aman Nath of the Neemrana Hotels Group; Miriya Chacko and Bradford Zak at Ananda in the Himalayas; Tenduf La and Sherab Tenduf at the Windamere Hotel Darjeeling; Nadir Rashid, Yawar Rashid, and Bano Rashid at the Jehan Numa Place Hotel Bhopal; and GS Chahal Madhya Pradesh Tourism also have our thanks and appreciation.

Don't Forget to Write

Keeping a travel guide fresh and up-to-date is a big job. So we love your feedback—positive and negative—and follow up on all suggestions. Contact the India editor at editors@fodors.com or c/o Fodor's, 280 Park Avenue, New York, New York 10017. And have a wonderful trip!

Karen Cure
Editorial Director

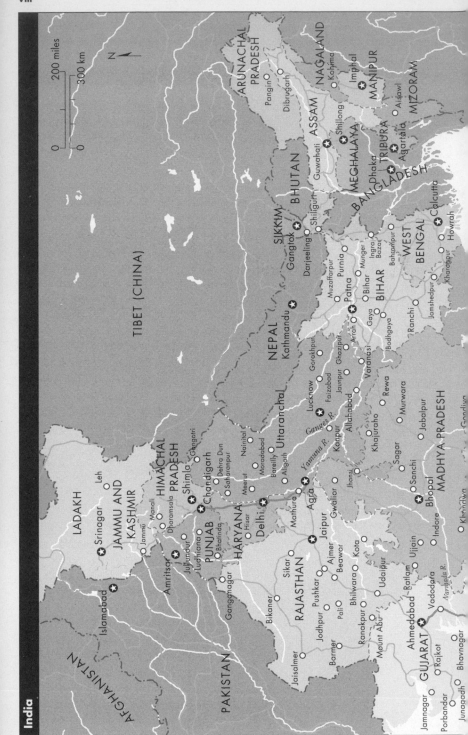

India

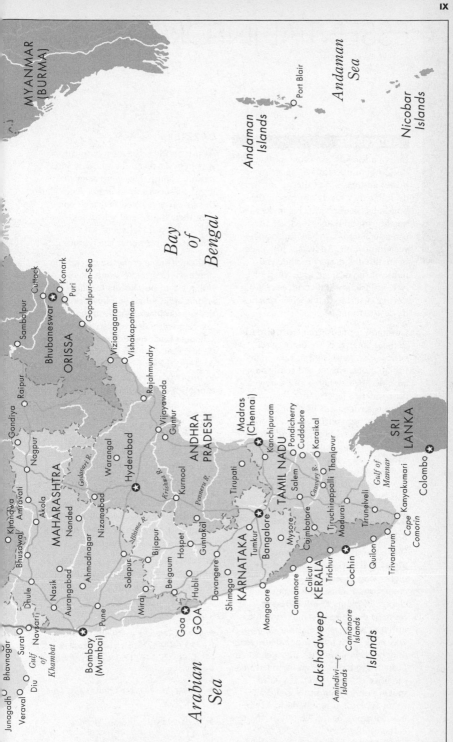

ESSENTIAL INFORMATION

Indian addresses are often haphazard. Building numbers may appear in postal addresses, but they aren't very useful as they rarely appear on the buildings themselves. This makes neighborhood names—which are often included in urban addresses—very important. Addresses for places in small villages may include the name of the nearest large town or big city. In India, postal codes play a big part in ensuring that a letter reaches its destination.

Common terms for the word "road" in local languages are *marg, galli, rasta, salai, peth, sarani.* Like many Indian cities, streets and roads have an older, British name and a newer, post-Independence name. Residents often refer to roads by their old names or use abbreviated versions of cumbersome names. In Bombay, for instance, Netaji Subhash Chandra Marg is still called by its old, easy-to-remember name of Marine Drive and Jay Prakash Road is referred to as J. P. Road.

AIR TRAVEL

BOOKING

When you book **look for nonstop flights** and **remember that "direct" flights stop at least once.** Try to avoid connecting flights, which require a change of plane. **Check different routings and airports,** and look into different airports. Note that on your way *back* from India a departure tax may be payable in cash upon check-in rather than having been included in the price of your ticket. If you're moving on to Bhutan, Nepal, Pakistan, Sri Lanka, Bangladesh, Myanmar (Burma), or the Maldives, the tax is Rs. 300; otherwise, it's Rs. 500. For more booking tips and to check prices and make on-line flight reservations, log on to www.fodors.com.

CARRIERS

At this writing, the airline industry was in great turmoil and many international companies were re-evaluating their service to southern Asia. Call the air carriers listed below to confirm their flights and schedules, or work with a travel agent who's knowledgeable about the region.

Although some domestic carriers don't sell their tickets outside of India, try to **buy tickets for flights within India when you buy tickets to the subcontinent.** Within India, flights are frequently delayed, so **don't schedule back-to-back domestic flights.** Competition has forced Indian Airlines, the national domestic carrier, to improve its service and become more timely—with some success. (You can book tickets and buy air passes for Indian Airlines at Air-India offices abroad, even if you're not flying to the subcontinent on Air-India.) More service-oriented than Indian Airlines are the private carriers, Jet Airways and Sahara Airlines. Domestic flights cost about 50% more than train trips in first-class, air-conditioned cars—if a tight budget is a bigger concern than a tight itinerary, consider taking the train.

➤ FROM NORTH AMERICA: **Air France** (800/237–2747). **Air-India** (☎ 212/751–6200). **Delta** (☎ 800/241–4141). **Northwest** (☎ 800/447–4747). **United** (☎ 800/328–6877).

➤ FROM THE U.K.: **Air-India** (☎ 01753/684–828). **British Airways** (☎ 0345/222–111). **United** (☎ 0800/888–555).

➤ FROM AUSTRALIA: **Qantas** (☎ 13–1313).

➤ WITHIN INDIA: **Indian Airlines** (☎ 11/569–6950 or 11/569–6327 in India). **Jet Airways** (☎ 925/866–1205 or 866/835–9538 in North America; 208/970–1525 in the U.K.; 612/9244–

2132 in Australia; 11/685–3700 in India). **Sahara Airlines** (☎ 818/990–9733 in North America; 208/897–1164 in the U.K.; 2/9299–1818 in Australia; 11/332–6851 in India).

CHECK-IN & BOARDING

Most carriers require you to check in two hours before your scheduled departure time for domestic flights and 2½ to 3 hours before international flights. Always **ask your carrier about its check-in policy.**

Assuming that not everyone with a ticket will show up, airlines routinely overbook planes. When everyone does, airlines ask for volunteers to give up their seats. In return, these volunteers usually get a certificate for a free flight and are rebooked on the next flight out. If there aren't enough volunteers, the airline must choose who will be denied boarding. The first to get bumped are passengers who checked in late and those flying on discounted tickets, so **get to the gate and check in as early as possible,** especially during peak periods. Always **bring a government-issued photo ID to the airport;** even when it's not required, a passport is best.

Security in Indian airports is tight, and procedures (searches and scans, equipment checks, having you identify your luggage on the tarmac before you board) require considerable time. **Check in at least two hours before a flight within India.** Golf clubs aren't allowed in the cabin; neither are pocket knives or other sharp implements. Be sure that batteries are charged and installed in flashlights, cameras, tape and CD players, and computers; you may be asked to turn such equipment on to prove it's what it appears to be. Note that on some flights, you may be asked to dispose of extra batteries or those in such equipment (computers aside) for safety reasons.

CUTTING COSTS

The least expensive airfares to India must usually be purchased in advance and are non-refundable. It's smart to **call a number of airlines,** and when you are quoted a good price, **book it on the spot**—the same fare may not be available the next day. Always

check different routings and look into using different airports. Travel agents, especially low-fare specialists (☞ Discounts & Deals), are helpful.

Consolidators are another good source. They buy tickets for scheduled international flights at reduced rates from the airlines, then sell them at prices that beat the best fare available directly from the airlines, usually without restrictions. Sometimes you can even get your money back if you need to return the ticket. Carefully read the fine print detailing penalties for changes and cancellations, and **confirm your consolidator reservation with the airline.**

Children under 12 and students ages 12 to 26 (with a valid ID) qualify for discounts on most domestic airlines. Indian Airlines's Discover India pass gives you 15 days of unlimited travel within the country for US$500; a 21-day package costs US$750. The India Wonderfare pass offers a week of unlimited travel within the north, south, east, or west of India for US$300. (On the southern route, there's a surcharge of $100 for Port Blair in the Andaman Islands.) There's a tax of US$10 for each flight you make using a pass. If you buy your pass at a travel agent representing Indian Airlines abroad, be sure to have it endorsed upon arrival in India. It's easier if you pay for the pass in foreign currency, though you can pay in rupees upon arrival if you furnish an exchange receipt.

Jet Airways offers 15-day (US$500) and 21-day (US$750) Visit India passes. These also require you to pay a tax of US$10 per flight. You can buy the passes on arrival in India or at Jet Airways agents abroad.

➤ CONSOLIDATORS: **Cheap Tickets** (☎ 800/377–1000). **Discount Airline Ticket Service** (☎ 800/576–1600). **Unitravel** (☎ 800/325–2222). **Up & Away Travel** (☎ 212/889–2345). **World Travel Network** (☎ 800/409–6753).

ENJOYING THE FLIGHT

For more legroom, **request an emergency-aisle seat.** Don't sit in the row in front of the emergency aisle or in front of a bulkhead, where seats may not recline. If you have dietary concerns, **ask for special meals when booking.** These can be vegetarian, low-cholesterol, or kosher, for example. On long flights, try to maintain a normal routine, to help fight jet lag. At night, **get some sleep.** By day, **eat light meals, drink water** (not alcohol), and **move around the cabin** to stretch your legs. For additional jet-lag tips consult *Fodor's FYI: Travel Fit & Healthy* (available at bookstores everywhere).

FLYING TIMES

Flying time to either Delhi or Bombay is 16 hours from New York, 18 hours from Chicago, 20 hours from Los Angeles, 8 hours from London or Amsterdam, and 14 hours from Sydney.

HOW TO COMPLAIN

If your baggage goes astray or your flight goes awry, complain right away. Most carriers require that you **file a claim immediately.**

➤ AIRLINE COMPLAINTS: U.S. Department of Transportation **Aviation Consumer Protection Division** (✉ C-75, Room 4107, Washington, DC 20590, ☎ 202/366–2220, WEB www.dot.gov/airconsumer). **Federal Aviation Administration Consumer Hotline** (☎ 800/322–7873).

RECONFIRMING

Within India delays and cancellations are frequent. **Reconfirm all flights 72 hours before departure and again right before leaving for the airport.** Ticket or no ticket, you may lose your seat if you don't confirm well in advance; confirming once more just before your flight may save considerable frustration.

AIRPORTS

India's major international gateways are Indira Gandhi International Airport in Delhi and Mumbai International Airport in Bombay.

➤ AIRPORT INFORMATION: **Indira Gandhi International Airport** (☎ 11/565–2011). **Mumbai International Airport** (☎ 22/836–6700).

BUS TRAVEL

Bus travel isn't recommended within India, especially at night. If you do take buses, try to travel on privately run air-conditioned coaches and stick to popular routes.

BUSINESS HOURS

India has numerous secular and religious holidays that shut the commercial world down. A little research on these will go a long way toward ensuring that your travel within the country is relatively free of delays.

BANKS & OFFICES

Most banks are open weekdays 10 to 2 and Saturday 10 to noon. International airports and some top hotels have 24-hour currency-exchange facilities, and the major American Express branches have extended hours for check-cashing. Post offices are generally open Monday through Saturday 10 to 5.

GAS STATIONS

Gas stations are usually open daily from 6 AM to 10 PM. In larger cities, some stay open 24 hours.

MUSEUMS & SIGHTS

Most museums are closed on Monday. Site museums (adjoining archaeological monuments) are normally closed on Friday.

PHARMACIES

Pharmacies are usually open daily from 9:30 to 8, though in cities there are some 24-hour establishments. In some places you can also buy medicine from the 24-hour pharmacies at large hospitals. (Note that in India pharmacies are called "chemists.")

SHOPS

Outside the four major metropolitan areas (Bombay, Delhi, Calcutta, and Madras), many shopkeepers close their establishments for an afternoon siesta.

CAMERAS & PHOTOGRAPHY

Ask before you snap. Photography isn't permitted in airports, on airplanes, at some government buildings, at military sites (including some bridges), and at certain religious sites and events. Some women and tribal peoples may also object to having their pictures taken. Other people may ask for money before allowing you a snapshot; carry a bit of change for such moments. If someone asks you to send a copy of the photo, don't say yes unless you intend to keep the promise.

The *Kodak Guide to Shooting Great Travel Pictures* (available at bookstores everywhere) is loaded with tips for memorable snapshots.

➤ PHOTO HELP: **Kodak Information Center** (☎ 800/242–2424).

EQUIPMENT PRECAUTIONS

Don't pack film and equipment in checked luggage, where it is much more susceptible to damage. X-ray machines used to view checked luggage have become much more powerful and therefore are much more likely to ruin your film. Always **keep film and tape out of the sun.** Carry an extra supply of batteries, and **be prepared to turn on your camera or camcorder** to prove to security personnel that the device is real. Always **ask for hand inspection of film,** which becomes clouded after repeated exposure to airport X-ray machines, and **keep videotapes away from metal detectors.** Dust can be troublesome in India, so keep gear under wraps when it's not in use.

CAR RENTAL

Renting a car and driving yourself around India isn't recommended. The rules and road conditions are probably like nothing you've ever experienced, so taking taxis or hiring a car and driver (☞ Car Travel) are better choices. If you must get behind the wheel yourself, there are reliable rental agencies in India's major cities. Rates in Bombay begin at $54 a day and $326 a week for an economy car with unlimited mileage.

➤ MAJOR AGENCIES: **Alamo** (☎ 800/ 522–9696; 020/8759–6200 in the U.K., WEB www.alamo.com). **Avis** (☎ 800/331–1084; 800/879–2847 in Canada; 02/9353–9000 in Australia; 09/525–1982 in New Zealand; 0870/ 606–0100 in the U.K., WEB www.avis. com). **Budget** (☎ 800/527–0700; 0870/156–5656 in the U.K., WEB www.budget.com). **Dollar** (☎ 800/ 800–6000; 0124/622–0111 in the U.K., where it's affiliated with Sixt; 02/9223–1444 in Australia, WEB www. dollar.com). **Hertz** (☎ 800/654–3001;

800/263–0600 in Canada; 020/8897– 2072 in the U.K.; 02/9669–2444 in Australia; 09/256–8690 in New Zealand, WEB www.hertz.com). **National Car Rental** (☎ 800/227–7368; 020/ 8680–4800 in the U.K., WEB www. nationalcar.com).

CUTTING COSTS

To get the best deal, **book through a travel agent who will shop around.**

INSURANCE

When driving a rented car you are generally responsible for any damage to or loss of the vehicle as well as for any property damage or personal injury that you may cause. Before you rent, see what coverage your personal auto-insurance policy and credit cards provide.

REQUIREMENTS & RESTRICTIONS

Your own driver's license is not acceptable in India—you need an International Driver's Permit. In North America you can get one of these from the American or Canadian automobile associations; in the United Kingdom, contact the Automobile Association or Royal Automobile Club.

SURCHARGES

Before you pick up a car in one city and leave it in another, **ask about drop-off charges or one-way service fees,** which can be substantial. Note, too, that some rental agencies charge extra if you return the car before the time specified in your contract. To avoid a hefty refueling fee, **fill the tank just before you turn in the car,** but be aware that gas stations near the rental outlet may overcharge.

CAR TRAVEL

Driving in India isn't for the faint of heart. Traffic is incredibly multifarious: slow-moving cyclists, bullock carts, cows, and even camels or elephants share the road with speeding, honking, quick-to-pass, ready-to-brake-for-animals vehicles of all shapes and sizes. Barring a few principal routes, Indian roads are a mess, especially during monsoons. Speed limits, set according to road conditions, are often ignored. Road signs, when they exist, are usually in Hindi or the local language.

In rural areas, two-way roads are often only one-lane wide, so vehicles frequently dodge oncoming traffic for hours on end. Some roads also serve as innovative extensions to farms, with grain laid out to dry on the pavement or sisal rope strung over the route so that vehicles tramp the grain down. British-style left-side driving creates one more challenge to many motorists. Bottom line: **hire a car and driver or a taxi rather than take to the road yourself.**

EMERGENCY SERVICES

Outside of some places where traffic police patrol the highways, there aren't any emergency services to speak of. If your car breaks down, you have few options aside from flagging down a ride to the nearest service station.

GASOLINE

Gas stations are full service, but the only people who expect tips are the attendant who wipes your windshield and the man who provides "free" air. At this writing, 1 liter of gas costs Rs 31. Plan to pay with cash as few stations—or petrol pumps, as they're called—accept credit cards.

Leaded fuel and diesel are readily available. Unleaded fuel or petrol is harder to find, particularly on secondary highways. When tanking up for a long journey, **choose a busy pump along a major highway.** Smaller stations often sell adulterated gas.

HIRED CARS WITH DRIVERS

Hiring a car and driver is affordable by Western standards; just be sure to **establish terms, rates, and surcharges in advance.** Shorter trips are generally priced by kilometer. Figure Rs. 6 to Rs. 10 per kilometer for a non–air-conditioned Ambassador—a hefty, roomy car designed by the British in the 1950s. In some locations, a higher rate gets you a diesel Sumo jeep or an air-conditioned Cielo, Contessa, or Audi; yet more cash gets you a Toyota, a minivan, or a Mercedes-Benz. On longer trips one price usually covers a certain number of hours and kilometers; beyond that you pay extra. Add to this a halt charge of Rs. 100 to Rs. 200 per night for overnight trips. Some companies

also charge a driver's fee for an eight-hour day.

Arrange a car and driver only through a licensed, government-approved operator or, for a bit more money, through your hotel. Be sure to **discuss your itinerary up front.** Roads in some areas—wildlife sanctuaries for example—require a Jeep; better to iron out all the details than miss sights because you don't have the appropriate vehicle. On long journeys, **decide in advance where and when you'll stop for tea or meal breaks.** The dare-devil road maneuvers that are the norm in India can be unsettling. **Ask the driver to travel slowly,** or have the operator inform the driver of this request.

CHILDREN IN INDIA

Bringing your kids to India may seem daunting, but children love it here. India is like a giant circus, with color, chaos, and a side show every minute. Kids are warmly welcomed everywhere except, perhaps, in the stuffiest of restaurants, and most Indians will bend over backward to help you with a child-related need. In fact, so much affection is lavished on children here—everyone wants to pick them up, pinch their cheeks, talk to them—that your little ones may even get perturbed.

Involve your youngsters as you plan your trip: Remember to schedule some sightseeing activities of particular interest to the little ones. If you are renting a car, don't forget to **ar-range for a car seat** when you reserve. For general advice about traveling with children, consult *Fodor's FYI: Travel with Your Baby* (available in bookstores everywhere).

FLYING

If your children are 2 or older, **ask about children's airfares.** As a general rule, infants under 2 not occupying a seat fly at greatly reduced fares or even for free. When booking, **confirm carry-on allowances** if you're traveling with infants. In general, for babies charged 10% of the adult fare you are allowed one carry-on bag and a collapsible stroller; if the flight is full, the stroller may have to be checked or you may be limited to less.

Experts agree that it's a good idea to use safety seats aloft for children weighing less than 40 pounds. Airlines set their own policies: U.S. carriers usually require that the child be ticketed, even if he or she is young enough to ride free, since the seats must be strapped into regular seats. Do **check your airline's policy about using safety seats during takeoff and landing.** And since safety seats are not allowed everywhere in the plane, get your seat assignments early.

When reserving, **request children's meals or a freestanding bassinet** if you need them. But note that bulkhead seats, where you must sit to use the bassinet, may lack an overhead bin or storage space on the floor. Flights to India usually have plenty of children on them, so request a bassinet early and reconfirm. Also some airlines don't offer vegetarian children's meals; if that's important to you, check on it as well.

LODGING

Most hotels in India allow children under a certain age to stay in their parents' room at no extra charge or for a nominal charge, but others charge for them as extra adults. **Confirm the cutoff age for children's discounts.**

PACKING FOR CHILDREN

Bring a bag of amusements to keep kids busy on the long international flight and on trips within India—books, coloring books, crayons, and other quiet toys. During takeoffs and landings your youngster's ears may hurt; keep a pacifier, earplugs, and a bottle of milk, water, or juice—with a straw—at the ready.

Indian cities don't have much sidewalk space for strollers, but such a conveyance is a clean, safe, comfortable place to park your toddler. **Pack all necessary medicines as well as rash creams, zinc oxide, sunscreen, diapers, and diaper wipes.** Clean bathrooms are also hard to come by in both cities and the countryside, so **carry toilet paper and moist towelettes with you at all times.**

Although the major brands of disposable diapers as well as Nestlé; instant baby cereals are available in most cities, they can be hard to find. Powdered milk produced by such companies as Amul and Nestlé; is readily available. Bottled mineral water and packaged snacks—potato chips, cookies, chocolate bars, fruit juices, and soft drinks—are sold throughout India. Though not nutritious, such snacks are often preferable to food that may be spicy or not entirely hygienic. If you're heading out for a day of sightseeing, ask your hotel staff if they can pack a lunch for your child. A small hot pot or kettle can be useful for making instant soup or noodles; you may want to bring a few packages of these with you.

Pack cool, loose, easy-to-wash clothes. If you'll be taking any air-conditioned trains, bring a few pieces of warm clothing, as the cars get cold. Leggings help protect against mosquitoes in the evening, hats shade youthful faces from the sun, and rubber slippers or sandals are always practical. If you plan to travel by car **bring a portable car seat.** Choose accommodations that are air-conditioned or have rooms equipped with mosquito netting to protect your child from mosquito bites. **Pack plenty of insect repellant as well as a 3-square-ft piece of soft cloth netting** (available in fabric stores), which you can drape over a carriage or car seat to shield your child from insects.

SIGHTS & ATTRACTIONS

Places that are especially appealing to children are indicated by a rubber-duckie icon (🦆) in the margin.

COMPUTERS ON THE ROAD

If you plan to bring a laptop to India, **carry a spare battery and spare adapter.** New batteries and replacement adapters are expensive and hard to find. Never plug your computer into a socket before asking about surge protection—some hotels don't have built-in current stabilizers, and extreme electrical fluctuations can short your adapter or even destroy your computer. IBM sells a pen-size modem tester that plugs into a phone jack and tells you whether or not the line is safe to use; this gadget is invaluable in India, where phone lines aren't always reliable and can harm your modem.

CONSUMER PROTECTION

Whenever shopping or buying travel services in India, **pay with a major credit card,** if possible, so you can cancel payment or get reimbursed if there's a problem. If you're doing business with a particular company for the first time, **contact your local Better Business Bureau and the attorney general's offices** in your state and (for U.S. businesses) the company's home state as well. Have any complaints been filed? Finally, if you're buying a package or tour, always **consider travel insurance** that includes default coverage (☞ Insurance).

➤ BBBs: **Council of Better Business Bureaus** (✉ 4200 Wilson Blvd., Suite 800, Arlington, VA 22203, ☎ 703/276–0100, ℻ 703/525–8277, ⓦ www.bbb.org).

CUSTOMS & DUTIES

When shopping, **keep receipts** for all purchases. Upon reentering the country, **be ready to show customs officials what you've bought.** If you feel a duty is incorrect or object to the way your clearance was handled, note the inspector's badge number and ask to see a supervisor. If the problem isn't resolved, write to the appropriate authorities, beginning with the port director at your point of entry.

IN AUSTRALIA

Australian residents who are 18 or older may bring home $A400 worth of souvenirs and gifts (including jewelry), 250 cigarettes or 250 grams of tobacco, and 1,125 ml of alcohol (including wine, beer, and spirits). Residents under 18 may bring back $A200 worth of goods. Prohibited items include meat products. Seeds, plants, and fruits need to be declared upon arrival.

➤ INFORMATION: **Australian Customs Service** (Regional Director, ✉ Box 8, Sydney, NSW 2001, Australia, ☎ 02/9213–2000, ℻ 02/9213–4000, ⓦ www.customs.gov.au).

IN CANADA

Canadian residents who have been out of Canada for at least seven days may bring home C$750 worth of goods duty-free. If you've been away fewer than seven days but more than 48 hours, the duty-free allowance drops to C$200; if your trip lasts 24–48 hours, the allowance is C$50. You may not pool allowances with family members. Goods claimed under the C$750 exemption may follow you by mail; those claimed under the lesser exemptions must accompany you. Alcohol and tobacco products may be included in the seven-day and 48-hour exemptions but not in the 24-hour exemption. If you meet the age requirements of the province or territory through which you reenter Canada, you may bring in, duty-free, 1.14 liters (40 imperial ounces) of wine or liquor *or* 24 12-ounce cans or bottles of beer or ale. If you are 19 or older you may bring in, duty-free, 200 cigarettes and 50 cigars. Check ahead of time with the Canada Customs Revenue Agency or the Department of Agriculture for policies regarding meat products, seeds, plants, and fruits.

You may send an unlimited number of gifts worth up to C$60 each duty-free to Canada. Label the package UNSOLICITED GIFT—VALUE UNDER $60. Alcohol and tobacco are excluded.

➤ INFORMATION: **Canada Customs Revenue Agency** (✉ 2265 St. Laurent Blvd. S, Ottawa, Ontario K1G 4K3, Canada, ☎ 204/983–3500 or 506/636–5064; 800/461–9999 in Canada, ⓦ www.ccra-adrc.gc.ca).

ENTERING INDIA

If you're entering India with dutiable or valuable articles, you must stop at customs and mention this; officials may ask you to fill in a Tourist Baggage Re-Export Form (TBRE), as such articles must be re-exported when you depart. You'll have to pay a duty on anything listed on the TBRE that is not being re-exported. Depending on the attitude of the customs official, you may have to list your laptop computer, camera or video equipment, and mobile phone on a TBRE form.

You may bring the following into India duty-free: personal effects (clothing and jewelry); cameras and up to five rolls of film; binoculars; a portable musical instrument; a radio or portable tape recorder; a tent and camping equipment; sports equipment (fishing rod, a pair of skis, two tennis rackets); 200 cigarettes or 50 cigars or 250 grams of tobacco; 1 liter of liquor each; and gifts not exceeding a value of Rs. 4,000 (about US$80). You may *not* bring in dangerous or addictive drugs, firearms, gold coins, gold and silver bullion or silver coins not in use, Indian currency, or plants.

LEAVING INDIA

Rupees aren't allowed out of India; you must exchange them before you depart. Foreign-exchange facilities are usually in the same airport halls as the check-in counters—note that you'll have no access to these facilities once you pass through immigration.

All animal products, souvenirs, and trophies are subject to the Wildlife Protection Act of 1972. The export of ivory (unless you can prove it's antique) and skins made from protected species isn't allowed, and such items aren't allowed *into* many other countries, including the United States, anyway. Export of exotic birds, wildlife, orchids, and other flora and fauna is forbidden as well.

In general items more than 100 years old cannot be exported without a permit from the Archaeological Survey, which has offices in many cities including Delhi, Bombay, Calcutta, Bhubaneswar, Madras, and Bangalore. Reputable shops will provide you with the necessary permit or help you procure it.

IN NEW ZEALAND

Homeward-bound residents 17 or older may bring back $700 worth of souvenirs and gifts. Your duty-free allowance also includes 4.5 liters of wine or beer; one 1,125-ml bottle of spirits; and either 200 cigarettes, 250 grams of tobacco, 50 cigars, or a combination of the three up to 250 grams. Prohibited items include meat products, seeds, plants, and fruits.

➤ INFORMATION: **New Zealand Customs** (Custom House, ✉ 50 Anzac Ave., Box 29, Auckland, New Zealand, ☎ 09/300–5399, ℻ 09/359–6730, WEB www.customs.govt.nz).

IN THE U.K.

From countries outside the European Union, including India, you may bring home, duty-free, 200 cigarettes or 50 cigars; 1 liter of spirits or 2 liters of fortified or sparkling wine or liqueurs; 2 liters of still table wine; 60 ml of perfume; 250 ml of toilet water; plus @145 worth of other goods, including gifts and souvenirs. If returning from outside the EU, prohibited items include meat products, seeds, plants, and fruits.

➤ INFORMATION: **HM Customs and Excise** (✉ St. Christopher House, Southwark, London, SE1 OTE, U.K., ☎ 020/7928–3344, WEB www.hmce.gov.uk).

IN THE U.S.

U.S. residents who have been out of the country for at least 48 hours (and who have not used the $400 allowance or any part of it in the past 30 days) may bring home $400 worth of foreign goods duty-free. U.S. residents 21 and older may bring back 1 liter of alcohol duty-free. In addition, regardless of your age, you are allowed 200 cigarettes and 100 non-Cuban cigars. Antiques, which the U.S. Customs Service defines as objects more than 100 years old, enter duty-free, as do original works of art done entirely by hand, including paintings, drawings, and sculptures.

You may also mail or ship packages home duty-free: up to $200 worth of goods for personal use, with a limit of one parcel per addressee per day (except alcohol or tobacco products or perfume worth more than $5); label the package PERSONAL USE and attach a list of its contents and their retail value. Do not label the package UNSOLICITED GIFT or your duty-free exemption will drop to $100. Mailed items do not affect your duty-free allowance on your return.

➤ INFORMATION: **U.S. Customs Service** (✉ 1300 Pennsylvania Ave. NW, Room 6.3D, Washington, DC 20229, WEB www.customs.gov; inquiries ☎ 202/354–1000; complaints c/o ✉ 1300 Pennsylvania Ave. NW, Room 5.4D, Washington, DC 20229; registration of equipment c/o Office of Passenger Programs, ☎ 202/927–0530).

DINING

The restaurants we list are the cream of the crop in each price category. An ✗🏨 icon indicates a hotel whose restaurant warrants a trip of its own.

Bombay and Delhi are in financial leagues of their own, so the chapters on those cities have their own dining charts. For the rest of India, dining categories are as follows. (The major cities are Agra, Bangalore, Bombay, Calcutta, Jaipur, Madras, Pune, and Varanasi.)

CATEGORY	MAJOR CITIES*	OTHER AREAS*
$$$$	over Rs. 500	over Rs. 350
$$$	Rs. 350– Rs. 500	Rs. 250– Rs. 350
$$	Rs. 150– Rs. 350	Rs. 100– Rs. 250
$	under Rs. 150	under Rs. 100

*per person for a dinner entrée

MEALTIMES

Restaurants in cities normally stay open until 11 PM or midnight. In other areas, expect an earlier dinner unless you're staying in a luxury hotel. Coffee shops in urban luxury hotels are often open 24 hours. Unless otherwise noted, the restaurants listed in this guide are open daily for lunch and dinner.

RESERVATIONS & DRESS

Reservations are always a good idea: we mention them only when they're essential or not accepted. Book as far ahead as you can, and reconfirm as soon as you arrive in that city. We mention dress only when men are required to wear a jacket or a jacket and tie.

WINE, BEER & SPIRITS

Dry days—when alcohol isn't available anywhere in the country—are observed on January 26, August 15, October 2, and certain festival dates. Some states observe additional dry days; others prohibit everything but beer. Gujarat is always dry. As a foreigner you may apply to the Gujarat Tourism Development Corporation for a permit that allows you to buy alcohol in the state; hotels also sell them for Rs. 100. The Government of India Tourist Office abroad can also issue a three-month liquor permit allowing you to carry liquor into Gujarat.

DISABILITIES & ACCESSIBILITY

India has a large population of people with disabilities, but in a country with so many fundamental problems, the needs of these people aren't a high priority. Luxury hotels have ramps for those using wheelchairs or walkers, but few bathrooms are designed for use by people with disabilities. Also, except for a few international airports, disembarkation from planes is via staircase. There are very few sidewalks in India, and no such thing as the pedestrian right of way.

RESERVATIONS

When discussing accessibility with an operator or reservations agent, **ask hard questions.** Are there any stairs, inside *or* out? Are there grab bars next to the toilet *and* in the shower/tub? How wide is the doorway to the room? To the bathroom? For the most extensive facilities meeting the latest legal specifications, **opt for newer accommodations.**

➤ COMPLAINTS: **Aviation Consumer Protection Division** (☞ Air Travel) for airline-related problems. **Civil Rights Office** (✉ U.S. Department of Transportation, Departmental Office of Civil Rights, S-30, 400 7th St. SW, Room 10215, Washington, DC 20590, ☎ 202/366–4648, FAX 202/366–9371, WEB www.dot.gov/ost/docr/index.htm) for problems with surface transportation. **Disability Rights Section** (✉ U.S. Department of Justice, Civil Rights Division, Box 66738, Washington, DC 20035-6738, ☎ 202/514–0301 or 800/514–0301; 202/514–0383 TTY; 800/514–0383 TTY, FAX 202/307–1198, WEB www.usdoj.gov/crt/ada/adahom1.htm) for general complaints.

TRAVEL AGENCIES

In the United States, the Americans with Disabilities Act requires that travel firms serve the needs of all travelers. Some agencies specialize in working with people with disabilities.

➤ TRAVELERS WITH MOBILITY PROBLEMS: **Access Adventures** (✉ 206 Chestnut Ridge Rd., Scottsville, NY 14624, ☎ 716/889–9096, dltravel@prodigy.net), run by a former physical-rehabilitation counselor. **Flying Wheels Travel** (✉ 143 W. Bridge St., Box 382, Owatonna, MN 55060, ☎ 507/451–5005 or 800/535–6790, FAX 507/451–1685, WEB www.flyingwheelstravel.com).

Smart Travel Tips A to Z

DISCOUNTS & DEALS

Be a smart shopper and **compare all your options** before making decisions. A plane ticket bought with a promotional coupon from travel clubs, coupon books, and direct-mail offers or on the Internet may not be cheaper than the least expensive fare from a discount ticket agency. And always keep in mind that what you get is just as important as what you save.

DISCOUNT RESERVATIONS

To save money, **look into discount reservations services** with toll-free numbers, which use their buying power to get a better price on hotels, airline tickets, even car rentals. When booking a room, always **call the hotel's local toll-free number** (if one is available) rather than the central reservations number—you'll often get a better price. Always ask about special packages or corporate rates.

When shopping for the best deal on hotels and car rentals, **look for guaranteed exchange rates,** which protect you against a falling dollar. With your rate locked in, you won't pay more, even if the price goes up in the local currency.

➤ AIRLINE TICKETS: ☎ **800/AIR–4LESS.**

➤ HOTEL ROOMS: **Players Express Vacations** (☎ 800/458–6161, WEB www.playersexpress.com). **Steigenberger Reservation Service** (☎ 800/223–5652, WEB www.srs-worldhotels.com). **Travel Interlink** (☎ 800/888–5898, WEB www.travelinterlink.com). **Turbotrip.com** (☎ 800/473–7829, WEB www.turbotrip.com).

PACKAGE DEALS

Don't confuse packages and guided tours. When you buy a package, you travel on your own, just as though you had planned the trip yourself. Fly/drive packages, which combine airfare and car rental, are often a good deal.

ELECTRICITY

Black outs—lasting anywhere from 30 minutes to 12 hours—are a part of everyday Indian life, particularly in summer when the load is high. Storms also play havoc with electricity. In addition, low-voltage electricity and surges are problems. Carry a flashlight at all times, and consider packing a small, battery-operated, hand-held fan.

To use electric equipment from North America, **bring a converter and adapter.** The electrical current in India is 220 volts, 50 cycles alternating current (AC); wall outlets take plugs with two round prongs.

If your appliances are dual-voltage (as are most laptop computers) or British in origin, you'll need only an adapter. Don't use 110-volt outlets marked FOR SHAVERS ONLY for high-wattage appliances such as hair dryers.

EMBASSIES

➤ AUSTRALIA: (✉ No. 1/50 G Shantipath, Chanakyapuri, New Delhi, ☎ 11/688–8223 or 11/688–5556).

➤ CANADA: (✉ 7/8 Shantipath, Chanakyapuri, New Delhi, ☎ 11/687–6500).

➤ NEW ZEALAND: (✉ 50 N. Nyaya Marg, Chanakyapuri, New Delhi, ☎ 11/688–3170).

➤ UNITED KINGDOM: (✉ Shantipath, Chanakyapuri, New Delhi, ☎ 11/687–2161).

➤ UNITED STATES: (✉ Shantipath, Chanakyapuri, New Delhi, ☎ 11/419–8000).

➤ INDIAN EMBASSIES ABROAD: **Australia** (✉ 3-5 Moonah Pl., Yarralumla, Canberra, ☎ 26/273–3999 or 26/627–33774). **Canada** (✉ 10 Springfield Rd., Ottawa, ☎ 613/744–3751 or 613/744–3752). **New Zealand** (✉ 180 Molesworth St., Wellington, ☎ 4/473–6390 or 4/473–6391). **United Kingdom** (✉ India House, Aldwych, London, ☎ 71/836–8484). **United States** (✉ 2107 Massachusetts Ave. NW, Washington, DC, ☎ 202/939–7000).

EMERGENCIES

Delhi's 24-hour East-West Medical Center has a referral list of doctors, dentists, pharmacists, and lawyers throughout India. Its staffers can arrange treatment wherever you are in the country, and it's the only clinic in India recognized by most international insurance companies. Note you must pay the center when you receive assistance—credit cards are accepted—and than apply for reimbursement by your insurance company later.

Meera Rescue, based in Delhi with branches in Bombay and Goa, is an extremely professional evacuation service recognized by international insurance companies. Meera evacuates from anywhere in the country to hospitals in major cities, as well as overseas if necessary; it's open 24 hours. Like East-West, you must pay Meera and be reimbursed by your insurance company later.

➤ CONTACTS: **East-West Medical Center** (✉ 38 Golf Links, New Delhi 110003, ☎ 11/462–3738, 11/469–9229, 11/469–0429, or 11/469–8865; FAX 11/469–0428 or 11/463–2382; WEB www.eastwestrescue.com). **Meera Rescue** (✉ 112 Jor Bagh, New Delhi 110003, ☎ 11/465–3100 or 11/465–3170, FAX 11/461–8286), WEB www. meera-rescue.com).

ETIQUETTE & BEHAVIOR

If you're invited to a traditional Indian home, **observe the prevailing seating rules.** Men often sit separate from women. Sometimes, when the menfolk entertain a foreign visitor (even a woman), the women of the house shy away or don't emerge; they may not speak English, or may be mildly xenophobic. In some homes, shoes are taken off before entering; here too, inquire, or watch what the family does.

Numerous customs govern food and the partaking of meals. In many households, you arrive, sit and talk, and then have your meal; after you eat the evening is over. Don't be surprised if the woman of the house serves her guests but doesn't join the gathering. Don't protest, and don't follow her into the kitchen—in orthodox Hindu homes the kitchen is frequently off-limits—just accept her behavior as the tradition of this particular home. When you eat in remote areas, you may not be given utensils; **eat only with your right hand,** as the left is considered unclean. (Left-handers can use utensils, though left-handedness in general is considered curious.) If you want a second helping or are buying openly displayed food, don't help yourself with your hands; this act

pollutes the food. **Let your host or vendor serve you.**

BEGGING

Many Westerners are upset by the number of beggars who beseech them for spare rupees, motioning from hand to mouth to indicate that they have nothing to eat. The grimy faces of tiny waifs in particular will pull on your heartstrings. If you give a beggar money, a dozen more will immediately spring up, and you'll be forced to provide for all; it can also be difficult to get the first beggar off your tail. Moreover, beggars aren't always as destitute as they look; your contribution may well support a drug habit or prolong the abuse of a child. If you want to contribute, **donate to a legal charity** or **pass out candy to the child beggars** you encounter.

BUSINESS ETIQUETTE

Indians aren't a very formal people, and this carries over into the world of business. Rarely do Indians wear suits to meetings, though ties are now popular. Executives greet each other by shaking hands; occasionally, a woman executive may prefer not to do this. Business cards are de rigueur.

Indians are gracious hosts and will often foot the bill for business lunches or dinners. Unless he or she is invited, do not bring your spouse to a business dinner.

SACRED SITES

Religious monuments demand respect. With all of India's faiths, you must **remove your shoes before entering a shrine,** even if it appears to be in ruins. All religions ask that you **don't smoke, drink alcohol, or raise your voice** on the premises. Some temples and mosques are off-limits to travelers who don't practice the faith; **don't try to bribe your way inside.** Women visiting sacred places should dress modestly and cover their heads before entering a Sikh temple or a mosque. Cameras and video cameras are sometimes prohibited inside houses of worship. On rare occasions, a Hindu or Muslim festival involves animal sacrifice, which may upset you or your child; do a little research on what festivals involve ahead of time.

Some Hindu and Jain temples don't allow any leather products inside their shrines, including wallets, purses, shoes, belts, and camera cases. Many temples also expect you to **purify yourself by washing your hands and feet in a nearby tap or tank before you enter.** In Sikh temples, don't point your feet toward the Holy Book or step over anyone sitting in prayer or meditation. Play it safe in both Hindu and Sikh temples: if you sit on the floor, **sit cross-legged or with your feet tucked beneath you.** In some shrines, the sexes are separated; look around (or follow instructions) and let the situation govern what you do. **Step into the courtyards of mosques with your right foot first.**

Many well-meaning travelers commit an unforgivable sacrilege when they visit a Buddhist monastery. You're welcome to spin any prayer wheel, but just as you must circumambulate the interior and exterior of a monastery, *stupa,* or *mani* wall in a clockwise direction, you must **spin prayer wheels clockwise only.** Inside the monastery, cushions and chairs are reserved for lamas (monks), so sit on the steps outside or on the floor. If you meet a *rimpoche* (head lama) or a respected monk, it's polite not to turn your back on him when you leave. Also **remove your hat and lower your umbrella** in the confines of a monastery and in the presence of a lama.

GAY & LESBIAN TRAVEL

Although India is a sexually conservative society, there's a growing awareness and acceptance of homosexuality in major cities. Still, gay and lesbian travelers should keep their sexual preference to themselves. No hotel will object to two people of the same sex sharing a room, but **don't display your affection in public.** Note that Indian men and boys commonly walk hand in hand as a sign of friendship.

➤ GAY- & LESBIAN-FRIENDLY TRAVEL AGENCIES: **Different Roads Travel** (✉ 8383 Wilshire Blvd., Suite 902, Beverly Hills, CA 90211, ☎ 323/651–5557 or 800/429–8747, FAX 323/651–3678, lgernert@tzell.com). **Kennedy Travel** (✉ 314 Jericho Turnpike, Floral Park, NY 11001, ☎ 516/352–4888 or 800/237–7433, FAX 516/354–

8849, WEB www.kennedytravel.com). **Now Voyager** (✉ 4406 18th St., San Francisco, CA 94114, ☎ 415/626–1169 or 800/255–6951, FAX 415/626–8626, WEB www.nowvoyager.com). **Skylink Travel and Tour** (✉ 1006 Mendocino Ave., Santa Rosa, CA 95401, ☎ 707/546–9888 or 800/225–5759, FAX 707/546–9891, WEB www.skylinktravel.com), serving lesbian travelers.

HEALTH

No vaccination certificate or inoculations are required to enter India from the United States, Canada, or the United Kingdom unless you're coming via Africa, in which case, you'll need proof of inoculation against yellow fever. Immigration officials don't normally ask to see an international health certificate, but it's smart to have one in case you need medical attention. See your doctor about obtaining one, and **talk to your doctor about vaccinations three months before departure** in any case. The Centers for Disease Control and Prevention posts a list of recommended vaccinations for the Indian subcontinent on its Web site; these include hepatitis and typhoid fever.

In areas where malaria and dengue—both carried by mosquitoes—are prevalent, use mosquito nets, wear clothing that covers the body, apply repellent containing DEET, and use spray for flying insects in living and sleeping areas. **Consider taking antimalaria pills,** as malaria is common even in the big cities. There's no vaccine to combat dengue.

Bring a medical kit containing aspirin or its equivalent, diarrhea medication, moist towelettes, antibacterial skin ointment and skin cleanser, antacids, antihistamines, dandruff shampoo, adhesive bandages, antibiotics, a water-purification kit, and plastic strip thermometers.

ALTITUDE SICKNESS

An adverse reaction to low oxygen pressure, altitude sickness can be deadly. If your urine turns bright yellow, you're not drinking enough water. To minimize high-altitude misery, **drink lots of water, eat foods high in carbohydrates, and cut back**

on salt. Stop and rest immediately if you develop any of the following symptoms: nausea, loss of appetite, extreme headache or lightheadedness, unsteady feet, sleeplessness. If resting doesn't help, head for lower ground immediately.

FOOD & DRINK

Drinking water and fresh fruit and vegetables are often contaminated by fecal matter, which causes traveler's diarrhea. **Watch what you eat**—stay away from uncooked or cold food and unpasteurized milk and milk products. **Avoid raw vegetables and fruit,** even those that have been peeled. Raw produce served at luxury hotels is mostly hygienic, but many buffets and salad bars soak produce in an iodine preparation to kill parasites; ask the waiter about this before you indulge. If you're dying for fresh fruit or vegetables, cut and peel your own, choosing varieties with thick skins.

Stay away from pork products outside luxury hotels; **make sure that all meats are thoroughly cooked.** It's not necessary to go vegetarian, and to do so would mean missing out on some delicious dishes; just **choose restaurants with care, and eat hot foods while they're hot.** A little bit of personal hygiene can also go a long way in preventing stomach upsets. **Wash your hands before you eat anything, and carry moist towelettes.** These are readily available in large cities; Fresh Ones is a common brand.

Know that locally popular, worn-looking restaurants often serve the safest food. Such restaurants often can't afford refrigeration, so the cooks prepare food acquired that day—not always the case with the upscale places. Some hotel chefs buy in bulk and, thanks to temperamental electricity, a refrigerator may preserve more than just foodstuffs. Stomach upsets often are due as much to the richness and spice of Indian cuisine as to the lack of hygiene. Many hotel restaurants cook Indian dishes with quite a bit of oil, which can trigger Delhi Belly. **If you have a sensitive stomach, ask the chef to use less oil.** Fried foods from street vendors often look delicious, but inspect the oil: if it looks as old as the pot, it could be rancid.

Mild cases of intestinal distress may respond to Immodium A-D (known generically as loperamide) or Pepto-Bismol (a little weaker), both available over the counter. Paregoric, another antidiarrheal agent, requires a doctor's prescription in India. Drink plenty of purified water or tea—chamomile is a good folk remedy for diarrhea. In severe cases, rehydrate yourself with a salt-sugar solution (½ tsp. salt and 4 tbsp. sugar per quart/liter of water).

Drink only water that has been bottled or boiled for at least 20 minutes; avoid tap water, ice, fruit juices, or drinks to which water has been added. **Turn down offers of "filtered" or "aqua-guard" water;** it may have been filtered to take out particles but not purified to kill parasites. **Buy bottled water from a reputable shop;** Bisleri, Kinley (a Coca-Cola product), or Aquafina (a Pepsi product) are widely available, reputable brands. **Check that the cap hasn't been tampered with.** Bottles are sometimes refilled with tap water. Soft drinks, in bottles or cans, and packaged fruit juices are other safe, readily available options. Always **keep at least one bottle of water in your hotel room** for brushing your teeth as well as for drinking.

MEDICAL PLANS

No one plans to get sick while traveling, but it happens, so **consider signing up with a medical-assistance company.** Members get doctor referrals, emergency evacuation or repatriation, hot lines for medical consultation, cash for emergencies, and other assistance.

➤ MEDICAL-ASSISTANCE COMPANIES: **International SOS Assistance** (✉ 8 Neshaminy Interplex, Suite 207, Trevose, PA 19053, ☎ 215/245–4707 or 800/523–6586, FAX 215/244–9617; ✉ 12 Chemin Riantbosson, 1217 Meyrin 1, Geneva, Switzerland, ☎ 4122/785–6464, FAX 4122/785–6424; ✉ 331 N. Bridge Rd., 17-00, Odeon Towers, Singapore 188720, ☎ 65/338–7800, FAX 65/338–7611, WEB www.internationalsos.com).

PESTS & OTHER HAZARDS

All Indian cities are heavily polluted. Regulations and devices were introduced in 1995, but most vehicles still use leaded gas or diesel fuel. People with breathing problems, especially asthma, should **carry the appropriate respiratory remedies.** India's heat can dehydrate you, and dust can irritate your throat, so **drink plenty of liquids.** Dehydration will make you weak and more susceptible to other health problems.

If you travel into forested areas during or right after a monsoon, **protect yourself against leeches** by covering your legs and carrying salt. Don't wear sandals. If a leech clings to your clothing or skin, dab it with a pinch of salt and it will fall off. If itching persists, apply an antiseptic; infection is rare.

For bedbugs, buy a bar of Dettol soap (available throughout India) and use it when you bathe to relieve itching and discomfort. If you're staying in an unknown, perhaps dubious hotel, **check under the mattress** for bedbugs, cockroaches, and other unwanted critters. Use Flit, Finit, or one of the other readily available spray repellents on suspicious-looking furniture and in mosquito-infested rooms. Tortoise coils, or *kachua,* and Good Knight are fairly effective at "smoking" mosquitoes away; these are either plugged into the wall or lit with a match and placed under a bed or table. On the road, **treat scratches, cuts, or blisters at once.** If you're trekking, save the bottle and cap from your first bottled water so you can refill it with water that you purify yourself.

Send your clothes to be laundered only through decent hotels. *Dhobi,* or washerman's itch—that is, scabies—can be picked up from poorly washed clothes. It's better to **wash your clothes yourself** and send them out for ironing, or give them directly to a reliable dry-cleaner. Definitely wash all underwear and lingerie yourself.

SUN EXPOSURE

Beware of overexposure even on overcast days. To avoid sunburn, **use a sunscreen** with a sun-protection factor of at least 24. To play it safe, **wear a wide-brimmed hat.** If you plan to travel above 10,000 ft, use zinc oxide, lip balm with sunblock, and sunglasses that block ultraviolet rays. When you're on snowy terrain, remember that UV rays reflect from below.

➤ HEALTH WARNINGS: **National Centers for Disease Control and Prevention** (CDC; National Center for Infectious Diseases, Division of Quarantine, Traveler's Health Section, ✉ 1600 Clifton Rd. NE, M/S E-03, Atlanta, GA 30333, ☎ 888/232–3228 or 877/394–8747, FAX 888/232–3299, WEB www.cdc.gov).

HOLIDAYS

India's fixed national holidays are January 26 (Republic Day), August 15 (Independence Day), October 2 (Gandhi's birthday), and December 25 (Christmas). Endless festivals enliven—and shut down—different parts of the country throughout the year.

INSURANCE

The most useful travel-insurance plan is a comprehensive policy that includes coverage for trip cancellation and interruption, default, trip delay, and medical expenses (with a waiver for preexisting conditions).

Without insurance you will lose all or most of your money if you cancel your trip, regardless of the reason. Default insurance covers you if your tour operator, airline, or cruise line goes out of business. Trip-delay covers expenses that arise because of bad weather or mechanical delays. Study the fine print when comparing policies.

If you're traveling internationally, a key component of travel insurance is coverage for medical bills incurred if you get sick on the road. Such expenses are not generally covered by Medicare or private policies. U.K. residents can buy a travel-insurance policy valid for most vacations taken during the year in which it's purchased (but check preexisting-condition coverage). British and Australian citizens need extra medical coverage when traveling overseas.

Always **buy travel policies directly from the insurance company**; if you buy them from a cruise line, airline, or tour operator that goes out of business you probably will not be covered for the agency or operator's default, a major risk. Before making any purchase, **review your existing health and home-owner's policies** to find what they cover away from home.

➤ TRAVEL INSURERS: In the U.S.: **Access America** (✉ 6600 W. Broad St., Richmond, VA 23230, ☎ 800/284–8300, FAX 804/673–1491, WEB www.etravelprotection.com). **Travel Guard International** (✉ 1145 Clark St., Stevens Point, WI 54481, ☎ 715/345–0505 or 800/826–1300, FAX 800/955–8785, WEB www.travelguard.com).

➤ INSURANCE INFORMATION: In the U.K.: **Association of British Insurers** (✉ 51–55 Gresham St., London EC2V 7HQ, U.K., ☎ 020/7600–3333, FAX 020/7696–8999, WEB www.abi.org.uk). In Canada: **RBC Travel Insurance** (✉ 6880 Financial Dr., Mississauga, Ontario L5N 7Y5, Canada, ☎ 905/791–8700, 800/668–4342 in Canada, FAX 905/816–2498, WEB www.royalbank.com). In Australia: **Insurance Council of Australia** (✉ Level 3, 56 Pitt St., Sydney NSW 2000, ☎ 02/9253–5100, FAX 02/9253–5111, WEB www.ica.com.au). In New Zealand: **Insurance Council of New Zealand** (✉ Level 7, 111–115 Customhouse Quay, Box 474, Wellington, New Zealand, ☎ 04/472–5230, FAX 04/473–3011, WEB www.icnz.org.nz).

LANGUAGE

Hindi is the national language, but India isn't truly unified linguistically; most states and countless smaller areas have their own tongues. The country functions in English alongside Hindi, however, so barring rural areas you aren't likely to experience a language barrier.

LODGING

Secure all room reservations before arrival, especially during peak season (September to March) and in the major cities and popular tourist destinations such as Agra, Kerala, and Goa. School holidays have Indians vacationing in April, May, and early June; for a few days in October or November (for Diwali or, in eastern India, Durga Puja); and for 10 days between Christmas and the New Year. Reservations are extra-difficult during these times.

The lodgings we review are the cream of the crop in each price category. Unless otherwise noted, rooms in all hotels have private bathrooms. We always list facilities, but we don't specify whether they cost extra: when pricing rooms, always **ask what's included and what costs extra.** An ✕🍽 icon indicates a hotel whose restaurant warrants a trip of its own.

Assume that hotels operate on the **European Plan** (EP, with no meals) unless we specify that they use either the **Continental Plan** (CP, with a Continental breakfast), **Breakfast Plan** (BP, with a full breakfast), **Modified American Plan** (MAP, with breakfast and dinner), or are **all-inclusive** (including all meals and most activities).

Room rates are skyrocketing in business-oriented cities such as Bangalore, Bombay, Calcutta, Delhi, and Madras. Urban hotels rarely have off-season discounts, though some international chains have incentive programs for frequent guests. In other areas, hotels may be seeking guests, so you may be able to negotiate your price. When you reserve, **ask about additional taxes** and service charges, which increase the quoted room price.

Delhi is in a financial league of its own, so the chapter on that city has its own lodging chart. For the rest of India, dining categories are as follows. (The major cities are Agra, Bangalore, Bombay, Calcutta, Jaipur, Madras, Pune, and Varanasi.)

CATEGORY	MAJOR CITIES*	OTHER AREAS*
$$$$	over Rs. 8,000	over Rs. 4,000
$$$	Rs. 5,000– Rs. 8,000	Rs. 2,500– Rs. 4,000
$$	Rs. 2,000– Rs. 5,000	Rs. 1,500– Rs. 2,500
$	under Rs. 2,000	under Rs. 1,500

for a standard double room, excluding taxes and service charge

GOVERNMENT LODGING

The national and state governments, the public works department, and the forestry department manage inexpensive accommodations throughout India. Most of these facilities are poorly maintained, and government employees and officials receive priority booking, which means you can be thrown out upon the unexpected arrival of a VIP even if you have a reservation. Some states, however—particularly Madhya Pradesh, Maharashtra, and Kerala—run fairly competent hotels and often provide the best lodgings in remote destinations. For more information contact the tourist office in the capital of the state you plan to visit.

HERITAGE HOTELS

The Indian government has an excellent incentive program that encourages owners of traditional *havelis* (mansions), forts, and palaces to convert their properties into hotels or bring existing historic hotels up to government standards. Many of these official Heritage Hotels—noted in reviews throughout this guide—are well outside large cities. Their architecture and decor are authentically Indian, not Western. If this type of lodging appeals to you, **contact the Government of India Tourist Office for a list of Heritage Hotels.** There are more than 60 such establishments in Rajasthan; about 15 in Gujarat; and one or two in Madhya Pradesh, Himachal Pradesh, Kerala, and other states.

HOSTELS

No matter what your age, you can **save on lodging costs by staying at hostels.** In some 4,500 locations in more than 70 countries around the world, Hostelling International (HI), the umbrella group for a number of national youth-hostel associations, offers single-sex, dorm-style beds, and, at many hostels, rooms for couples and family accommodations. Membership in any HI national hostel association, open to travelers of all ages, allows you to stay in HI-affiliated hostels at member rates; one-year membership is about $25 for adults (C$26.75 in Canada, @9.30 in the U.K., AUS$30 in Australia, and NZ$30 in New Zealand); hostels run about US$10–$25 per night. Members have priority if the hostel is full; they're also eligible for discounts around the world, even on rail and bus travel in some countries.

➤ ORGANIZATIONS: **Hostelling International—American Youth Hostels** (✉ 733 15th St. NW, Suite 840, Washington, DC 20005, ☎ 202/783–6161, FAX 202/783–6171, WEB www.hiayh.org). **Hostelling International—Canada** (✉ 400–205 Catherine St., Ottawa, Ontario K2P 1C3, Canada, ☎ 613/237–7884; 800/663–5777 in Canada, FAX 613/237–7868, WEB www.hostellingintl.ca). **Youth Hostel Association of England and Wales** (✉ Trevelyan House, 8 St. Stephen's Hill, St. Albans, Hertfordshire AL1 2DY, U.K., ☎ 0870/8708808, FAX 01727/844126, WEB www.yha.org.uk). **Youth Hostel Association Australia** (✉ 10 Mallett St., Camperdown, NSW 2050, Australia, ☎ 02/9565–1699, FAX 02/9565–1325, WEB www.yha.com.au). **Youth Hostels Association of New Zealand** (✉ Level 3, 193 Cashel St., Box 436, Christchurch, New Zealand, ☎ 03/379–9970, FAX 03/365–4476, WEB www.yha.org.nz).

HOTELS

Many luxury urban hotels offer a mind-boggling range of room options. Some call their least expensive quarters "superior," their more expensive ones "deluxe," and, again, their top ones "superior." There may be still other, more exclusive rooms on club or executive floors. The cheapest rooms in *any* establishment often really are the worst. Rooms in the next class up, however, might be delightful. Before you reserve, **request a list of room classifications and descriptions.**

India's tourism department approves and classifies hotels based on a rating system of five stars (the fanciest) to no stars (no frills). The ratings are based on the number of facilities and on hotel and bedroom size. Hotels without pools or those that serve only vegetarian food—including some historic, charming, comfortable properties—don't qualify for five-star status but are often just as luxurious as those that do. The rating system also fails to take service and other important intangibles into account. Although these ratings can be misleading, tour operators often use them, so **ask what a star-rating means** when booking.

In small towns, opt for the best room in the best hotel. If the room or bathroom still looks doubtful, tip the bellboy to have it re-cleaned in front of you. Regardless of where you stay, inspect your room before checking in, even if you have a prior reservation. Examine the door lock, the air-conditioner, the curtains, and the bathroom and its plumbing. Be sure the room has candles, matches, and sufficient bed linen. Confirm that renovations aren't taking place nearby.

➤ TOLL-FREE NUMBERS: **Best Western** (☎ 800/528–1234, WEB www.bestwestern. com). **Choice** (☎ 800/221–2222, WEB www.choicehotels.com). **Comfort** (☎ 800/228–5150, WEB www.comfortinn. com). **Days Inn** (☎ 800/325–2525, WEB www.daysinn.com). **Holiday Inn** (☎ 800/465–4329, WEB www.basshotels. com). **Hyatt Hotels & Resorts** (☎ 800/233–1234, WEB www.hyatt.com). **Inter-Continental** (☎ 800/327–0200, WEB www.interconti.com). **Marriott** (☎ 800/228–9290, WEB www.marriott. com). **Nikko Hotels International** (☎ 800/645–5687, WEB www.nikkohotels. com). **Oberoi Hotels** (☎ 800/562–3764 in the U.S. and Canada, 800/1234–0101 in the U.K. and western Europe, WEB www.oberoihotels.com). **Quality Inn** (☎ 800/228–5151, WEB www.qualityinn.com). **Renaissance Hotels & Resorts** (☎ 800/468–3571, WEB www.renaissancehotels.com). **Sheraton** (☎ 800/325–3535, WEB www. starwoodhotels.com).

➤ INDIAN HOTEL CHAINS: **Ashok Hotels** (reserve through a travel agent or Ashok Sales Office, ✉ Jeevan Vihar, 3rd floor, 3 Sansad Marg, New Delhi 110001, ☎ 11/332–4422, WEB reservation@theashokgroup.com). **Clarks** (✉ U.P. Hotels, 1101 Surya Kiran, 19 Kasturba Gandhi Marg, New Delhi 110001, ☎ 11/331–2367 or 11/372–2596, WEB clark@bol.net.in or www.hotelclarkindia.com). **Taj Group** (☎ 800/458–8825 in the U.S., 800/282699 in the U.K.). **Welcomgroup** (✉ A-9 U. S. O. Rd., Qutab Institutional Area, New Delhi, ☎ 11/614–3199 or 11/614–5352, WEB mail@welcomgroup.com).

MAIL & SHIPPING

Airmail letters and postcards take a week to 10 days to reach most destinations from India. Postal delays are caused by holiday rushes (during Diwali and the Christmas season) and strikes.

EXPRESS-MAIL SERVICES

Express mail is known as "speed post" in India. There are speed-post centers all over the country; they're generally open from 9 to 5. It costs Rs. 425 to send a letter or parcel of 250 gms or less to Australia, Canada, New Zealand, the United Kingdom, or the United States. Every additional 250 gm will cost Rs. 100 for U.S. and Canadian destinations and Rs. 75 for destinations in Australia, New Zealand, or the United Kingdom. You can send a package weighing as much as 35 kg by speed post.

Private couriers and parcel companies—Airborne Express, Blue Dart, DHL, UPS—operate in India as well. A letter sent through such a service takes about three working days to reach Australia, Canada, New Zealand, the United Kingdom, or the United States. Rates are marginally higher than speed-post rates.

POSTAL RATES

Airmail letters (weighing 10 grams) to the United States, Canada, South Africa, or Europe cost Rs. 11; airmail postcards cost Rs. 7. Airmail letters to Australia and New Zealand run Rs. 9 and postcards cost Rs. 6. Aerograms to anywhere in the world are Rs. 8.50.

RECEIVING MAIL

To receive mail in India, **have letters or packages sent to an American Express office.** Mail is held at these offices for 30 days before it's returned to the sender; it can also be forwarded for a nominal charge. To retrieve your mail, show your American Express card or American Express Travelers Checks plus one piece of identification, preferably a passport. This service is free to AmEx cardmembers and traveler's-check holders; others pay a fee.

SHIPPING PARCELS

You can send parcels home "surface air lifted," a special service provided by the Indian postal department that's cheaper than airmail. A letter or parcel of 250 gms or less costs Rs. 310 to Canada or the United States, Rs. 420 to the United Kingdom, and Rs. 440 to Australia or New Zealand.

MONEY MATTERS

India is cheaper than most destinations when it comes to shopping, eating at independent restaurants, and staying in comfortable lodgings. That said, the increasing cost of gasoline has led to fare hikes of about 50% for planes, trains, hired cars with drivers, taxis, and auto-rickshaws. Moreover, travel is on the rise here, so room rates at resorts in places like Goa and in deluxe urban hotels are comparable to those elsewhere in the world. Many top hotels and some airlines charge foreigners U.S.-dollar prices that are substantially higher than the rupee prices paid by Indians.

A cup of tea from a stall costs about US5–10¢, but in top hotels it can cost more than $1. A 650-ml bottle of beer costs about US$1 in a shop, $4 without taxes in a top hotel. A 5-km (3-mi) taxi ride in Delhi is supposed to cost about US$1.50 (though it rarely does). Throughout this book, we quote admission fees for adults, which in India are usually the same as those for children. For information on taxes, *see* Taxes.

ATMS

There aren't that many cash machines in India. Still, if you think you'll need cash from your bank account or cash advances through your credit card, **make sure that your bank and credit cards are programmed for ATM use in India** before you leave home.

CREDIT CARDS

American Express isn't widely accepted in India, and Discover isn't accepted at all. In this book we use the following abbreviations: **AE,** American Express; **DC,** Diner's Club; **MC,** MasterCard; **V,** Visa.

CURRENCY

The units of Indian currency are the *rupee* and the *paisa*—100 paise equal one rupee. Paper money comes in denominations of 2, 5, 10, 20, 50, 100, 500, and 1,000 rupees. Coins are worth 5, 10, 20, 25, and 50 paise, 1 rupee, 2 rupees, and 5 rupees. At this writing, the rate of exchange was approximately US$1 = Rs. 48; @1 = Rs. 69; C$1 = Rs. 30; AUS $1 = Rs. 25; NZ$1 = Rs. 20.

CURRENCY EXCHANGE

India has strict rules against importing or exporting its currency. The currency-exchange booths at the international airports are always open for arriving and departing overseas flights. When you change money, remember to get a certain amount in small denominations to pay taxi drivers and such. **Reject torn, frayed, taped or soiled bills,** as many merchants, hotels, and restaurants won't accept them, and it's a hassle to find a bank to get them exchanged.

Always **change money from an authorized money-changer and insist on receiving an encashment slip.** Some banks now charge a nominal fee for this slip, which you'll need if you want to pay hotel bills or travel expenses in rupees, and again if you want to reconvert rupees into your own currency upon departure from India. Don't be lured by illegal street hawkers who offer you a higher exchange rate.

For the most favorable rates, **change money at banks.** Although ATM transaction fees may be higher abroad than at home, ATM rates are excellent because they're based on wholesale rates offered only by major banks. India's state-run banks can take forever to cash traveler's checks; if possible, save time and use an American Express office or the foreign-exchange service at your hotel. Rates will be slightly lower, but you'll save irritation and time. Rates are also unfavorable in airports, at train and bus stations, in restaurants, and in stores.

➤ EXCHANGE SERVICES: **International Currency Express** (☎ 888/278–6628 for orders, WEB www.foreignmoney. com). **Thomas Cook Currency Services** (☎ 800/287–7362 for telephone orders and retail locations, WEB www. us.thomascook.com).

TRAVELER'S CHECKS

Traveler's checks are best exchanged in major cities as soon as you need more cash. Most merchants, whether urban or rural, don't accept them. Lost or stolen checks can usually be replaced within 24 hours. To ensure a speedy refund, buy your own traveler's checks—don't let someone else pay for them. The person who bought the checks should also make the call to request a refund. Don't leave traveler's checks in your hotel room, and keep the counterfoil with the check numbers separate from the checks.

PACKING

Delicate fabrics don't stand up well to Indian laundering facilities except at deluxe hotels. Although dry-cleaning is available at all top hotels in major cities, the cleaning fluid can be harsh. Plain cottons and cotton/synthetic blends are coolest in summer and easiest to wash; in general, **avoid synthetic fabrics that don't breathe.** Pack a hat; the sun is strong. Sensible footwear is necessary—a pair of rubber sandals and comfortable walking shoes. Hiking boots, though comfortable, may be inappropriate for Indian travel; they're hot and and are difficult to unlace when you want to remove your shoes to enter religious spots.

Most important, **dress modestly.** Only children can get away with short shorts. Men should wear comfortable jeans or longer shorts. T-shirts are fine, but the male topless look should be left to wandering *sadhus* (Hindu ascetics). To deter undesired attention and command more respect, women should **avoid tight or sheer tops and those with plunging necklines** and **stick to long skirts or lightweight slacks regardless of the weather.** To visit sacred sites, women must wear a below-the-knee skirt or dress or neat pants. Travel in a Muslim community calls for even more discretion: women should consider wearing a *salwar kameez*, the popular Indian outfit of a long tunic over loose pants gathered at the ankle. (A cotton one is inexpensive, comfortable, and flattering.) Bathing suits should be conservative. All that said, India is not a dressy society. If you attend an upscale function (barring weddings), men can wear a standard business suit; women can wear a dress or skirt and blouse with flats or low heels.

A money pouch or belt is especially useful for Indian travel as are medical and hygienic supplies (including towelettes and a hand-sanitizing liquid); a sewing kit; a lock and key for each piece of luggage; a high-power, impact-resistant flashlight; and spare batteries (unless they're a popular size). Good sanitary napkins are sold in India, but tampons are substandard; plan accordingly. For bird-watching or wildlife-spotting, bring binoculars. Sports enthusiasts should bring their own tennis or golf balls, which are expensive in India. Smokers should carry their own cigarettes, cigars, and pipe tobacco; low-nicotine cigarettes aren't readily available. Scotch lovers may want to bring a bottle of their favorite brand. You might also consider carrying a portable electric kettle (with the right plug attachments and voltage converters) as well as instant beverages and soup or noodle packets.

Bring an extra pair of eyeglasses or contact lenses in your carry-on luggage, and if you have a health problem, **pack enough medication** to last the entire trip, or have your doctor write you a prescription using the drug's generic name—brand names vary from country to country. **Don't put prescription drugs or valuables in luggage to be checked:** It might go astray. To avoid problems with customs officials, carry medications in their original packaging.

If you visit in monsoon season, bring a collapsible umbrella. In winter, bring a sweater or a light jacket for cool evenings, and **if you plan to spend time in the Himalayas, bring a warm wardrobe.** Plan to triple layer: the first layer (long johns) should be made of synthetic fabrics or silk that carry moisture away from the skin (cotton soaks up perspiration and keep you wet). Wool, fleece, or a synthetic fabric knitted into thick pile make a good second layer. Bring a down vest if you anticipate extremely cold weather. For the third layer, opt for a well-made, oversize windbreaker or lightweight parka insulated with a small amount of down and made of Gore-Tex (or an equivalent fiber like Zepel or VersaTech); such material not only allows moisture to escape but is waterproof—not merely water-repellent. Bulky down parkas are advisable only for winter excursions or a climb into higher altitudes. A pair of lined Gore-Tex over-pants is indispensable when you're thrashing through wet underbrush.

Most adventure-travel firms supply sleeping bags for their clients. If you're roughing it on your own, choose a lightweight sleeping bag with an outer shell. You don't need a bag designed for an assault on a mountain peak unless that's the trip you've planned. A down bag guaranteed to keep you warm at 15°F (a fairly low temperature in the Himalayan trekking season) is adequate. If you plan to take overnight trains, consider a sleeping-bag liner. On any outdoor adventure, long or short, **assemble a day pack for your sweater, camera, moist towelettes, and plastic water bottle.** Trekkers should also pack out their nonbiodegradable garbage and bury biodegradable refuse away from water sources. Use a trekking agency that carries kerosene for cooking.

Check *Fodor's How to Pack* (available in bookstores everywhere) for more tips.

CHECKING LUGGAGE

You are allowed one carry-on bag and one personal article, such as a purse or a laptop computer. Make sure that everything you carry aboard will fit under your seat or in the overhead bin. Get to the gate early, so you can board as soon as possible, before the overhead bins fill up.

If you are flying internationally, note that baggage allowances may be determined not by piece but by weight—generally 88 pounds (40 kilograms) in first class, 66 pounds (30 kilograms) in business class, and 44 pounds (20 kilograms) in economy.

Airline liability for baggage is limited to $1,250 per person on flights within the United States. On international flights it amounts to $9.07 per pound or $20 per kilogram for checked baggage (roughly $640 per 70-pound bag) and $400 per passenger for unchecked baggage. You can buy additional coverage at check-in for about $10 per $1,000 of coverage, but it excludes a rather extensive list of items, shown on your airline ticket.

Before departure, **itemize your bags' contents** and their worth, and label the bags with your name, address, and phone number. (If you use your home address, cover it so potential thieves can't see it readily.) Inside each bag, **pack a copy of your itinerary.** At check-in, **make sure that each bag is correctly tagged** with the destination airport's three-letter code. If your bags arrive damaged or fail to arrive at all, file a written report with the airline before leaving the airport.

PASSPORTS & VISAS

When traveling internationally, **carry your passport** even if you don't need one (it's always the best form of ID) and **make two photocopies of the data page** (one for someone at home and another for you, carried separately from your passport). If you lose your passport, promptly call the nearest embassy or consulate and the local police.

ENTERING INDIA

Unless you hold an Indian passport or are a citizen of Nepal or Bhutan, you need a visa to enter India. This applies to children and infants as well. A standard, multiple-entry tourist visa costs US$60 for Americans, A$30 for Australians, CAN$62 for Canadians, NZ$90 for New Zealanders, and £30 for U.K. citizens. You must **arrive in India within six months of the date your visa is issued.** If you need to extend your visa, go to the Foreigners' Regional Registration Office in one of the major cities or any of the Offices of the Superintendent of Police in the District Headquarters. (Note that travelers to certain parts of the Himalayas need special permits. Bring extra passport photographs; you may need them for these permits.)

You can obtain a visa through the mail by paying additonal postal costs, but this takes up to a month. To prevent delays **get your Indian visa in your home country** through the Indian embassy or a consulate or through your travel agent or tour operator. If you're traveling on business or as a student, you made need a different visa; be sure to check. The Indian government operates a Web site that provides visa information and the appropriate forms.

➤ VISA INFORMATION: WEB http://passport.nic.in/vspassport/welcome.html.

PASSPORT OFFICES

The best time to apply for a passport or to renew is in fall and winter. Before any trip, check your passport's expiration date, and, if necessary, renew it as soon as possible.

➤ AUSTRALIAN CITIZENS: **Australian Passport Office** (☎ 131–232, WEB www.dfat.gov.au/passports).

➤ CANADIAN CITIZENS: **Passport Office** (☎ 819/994–3500; 800/567–6868 in Canada, WEB www.dfait-maeci.gc.ca/passport).

➤ NEW ZEALAND CITIZENS: **New Zealand Passport Office** (☎ 04/494–0700, WEB www.passports.govt.nz).

➤ U.K. CITIZENS: **London Passport Office** (☎ 0870/521–0410, WEB www.ukpa.gov.uk) for fees and documentation requirements and to request an emergency passport.

➤ U.S. CITIZENS: **National Passport Information Center** (☎ 900/225–5674; calls are 35¢ per minute for automated service, $1.05 per minute for operator service; WEB www.travel.state.gov/npicinfo.html).

REST ROOMS

Traditional Indian toilets are covered holes in the ground. In many bathrooms you'll see a faucet, a small hand-held shower head, and/or a bucket with a beaker or other small vessel; Indians use these to rinse, bidet-style, after using the toilet. Hands are always washed elsewhere. Outside of hotels and some restaurants, clean public rest rooms are hard to find and are best avoided. On long road journeys finding any public rest room—let alone a clean one—is difficult. Be on the look out for a decent hotel or opt for the outdoors.

Nicer hotels and restaurants provide toilet paper, but you can't depend on this, as most Indians don't use the stuff (they use their left hand, which is why this hand is considered unclean). **Keep toilet paper with you at all times;** it's readily available in pharmacies and grocery stores in large cities. **Never throw anything in a toilet;** India's septic systems can't handle it. In many bathrooms you'll find sanitary bags, which you can use, close, and place in the trash bin.

SAFETY

Avoid leaving unlocked suitcases in your hotel room, and unless your room has a safe, **never leave money, traveler's checks, passports, or jewelry in a hotel room.** Don't even leave personal items—cosmetics, perfume, after-shave—strewn about. Avoid wandering around late at night, especially in smaller towns where shutters close early, and avoid road journeys after dark. As anywhere, never leave suitcases unattended in airports or train stations.

India has no tourist police. The most visible policemen are traffic cops, clad in white and khaki; they can usually help out, even with a non-traffic problem (though taxis are in their jurisdiction). Otherwise, look for a regular policeman, clad in khaki.

LOCAL SCAMS

Avoid strangers who offer their services as guides or money-changers. In crowds, **be alert for pickpockets—** wear a money belt, and/or keep your purse close to your body and securely closed. Be careful, too, when you use credit cards; when dining out, you can ask that the machine be brought to your table to make sure the card isn't used to make an impression on more than one form. If you travel by train, **don't accept food or beverages from a fellow passenger.** Foreigners who accept such generosity sometimes ingest drug-laced refreshment and are robbed once the drug takes effect. In train stations, **ignore touts who tell you that your hotel of choice is full or has closed;** they hope to settle you into a place where they get a kickback for bringing in business.

WOMEN IN INDIA

It doesn't take much imagination to figure out the people, places, and things a lone woman should avoid: traveling late at night, seedy areas of town, down-in-the-heels hotels, touts volunteering their services, over-friendly strangers, bars, deserted beaches or other areas, jostling crowds of men. If you **dress conservatively,** you can prevent some unwanted attention. Also, **never get into a taxi or auto-rickshaw if a second man accompanies the driver.** If you find yourself in a tricky situation—a taxi driver demanding a king's ransom, a hawker plaguing you, a stranger following you—head straight for a policeman or at least threaten to do so, which often works just as well. Don't hesitate to **protest loudly if you're harassed.**

Chain-lock the door to your hotel room, as staffers often knock quickly and then come right in. If your train companions seem suspicious, attempt to switch your seat for one near other women. Better yet, when reserving your ticket, **request a berth in one of the "ladies compartments," which exists on some long-distance trains.**

SENIOR-CITIZEN TRAVEL

To qualify for age-related discounts from Western chain hotels, **mention your senior-citizen status when you reserve,** not when you check out.

➤ EDUCATIONAL PROGRAMS: Elderhostel (✉ 11 Ave. de Lafayette, Boston, MA 02111-1746, ☎ 877/426–8056, FAX 877/426–2166, WEB www.elderhostel. org). Interhostel (✉ University of New Hampshire, 6 Garrison Ave., Durham, NH 03824, ☎ 603/862–1147 or 800/733–9753, FAX 603/862–1113, WEB www.learn.unh.edu). Folkways Institute (✉ 14600 S.E. Aldridge Rd., Portland, OR 97236-6518, ☎ 503/ 658–6600 or 800/225–4666, FAX 503/ 658–8672, WEB www.folkwaystravel. com).

SHOPPING

Shop around; prices vary tremendously. Learn the going price of an item or class of goods at a fixed-price government emporium, then hit the rest of the retail trail. Note that government-approved shops aren't the same as government-run shops; the quality of goods is usually assured in government-approved shops, but prices aren't fixed. Bargaining is expected in bazaars. **Offer one-third the stated price,** then settle for about 60%.

Check wares for damage, defects, or tears before making a purchase. **Carefully count—in front of the shop owner—the money being paid for a purchase and any change you receive.** Also be sure to **verify your bill before signing a credit-card slip. Don't buy items made of wild animal skins or ivory;** technically such goods are

illegal, and poaching is decimating India's wildlife. Besides, you may not be allowed to bring these items into your own country anyway.

WATCH OUT

Be careful when buying jewelry, leather goods, and silk items. Fakes abound: a string of pearls might be made of plastic, a silver necklace of white metal. In popular shopping areas such Rajasthan, **beware of drivers or touts who want to take you to a certain store,** particularly an alleged friend's or relative's store. These hucksters get a commission. You'll feel pressure to buy from the moment you arrive at the shop, and you'll pay a higher price (to cover the commission) if you do.

Before you purchase any item that a shopkeeper claims is 100 years old, **ask for an export permit.** A reputable shopkeeper will have the permit or help you procure it. If he refuses, the item is a fake or hasn't been approved by the government for export.

STUDENTS IN INDIA

➤ IDs & SERVICES: Council Travel (CIEE; ✉ 205 E. 42nd St., 15th floor, New York, NY 10017, ☎ 212/822– 2700 or 888/268–6245, FAX 212/822– 2699, WEB www.councilexchanges.org) for mail orders only, in the U.S. **Travel Cuts** (✉ 187 College St., Toronto, Ontario M5T 1P7, Canada, ☎ 416/979– 2406 or 800/667–2887 in Canada, FAX 416/979–8167, WEB www.travelcuts. com).

TAXES

AIRPORT

You may have to pay an airport departure tax when you leave India (increasingly, this tax is included in the price of airline tickets). If you're moving on to Bhutan, Nepal, Pakistan, Sri Lanka, Bangladesh, Myanmar (Burma), or the Maldives, the tax is Rs. 300; otherwise, it's Rs. 500.

HOTEL

India levies a 10% expenditure tax on any room costing more than Rs. 1,200 (about US$32). The hotel industry is lobbying to reduce these taxes, as they can increase the cost of a hotel room by 30%. You should also expect an additional sales tax on food and beverages; the percentage varies from state to state.

TELEPHONES

Many Indian businesses have a series of phone numbers instead of just one, as networks can get congested. If a number reads "562/331701 through 562/331708," for example, you can reach the establishment using any number between 331701 and 331708. Also, the number of digits in Indian phone numbers varies, even within one city.

Phones in India are often out of service, and numbers change frequently. To verify the status of a phone or get a new number, dial ☎ 197. In big cities 197 operators speak English; in small towns and rural areas ask a local to help with the verification.

AREA & COUNTRY CODES

The country code for India is 91. **In India, when dialing a long-distance number listed in this book, add 0 before the area code.** The country code is 1 for the U.S. and Canada, 61 for Australia, 64 for New Zealand, and 44 for the U.K.

CELLULAR PHONES AND PAGERS

Since standard phone service is erratic, cell phones are extremely useful. Indian cell phones work on the GSM standard, so those designed for the American standard won't work. Cell service is available in more and more parts of the country, and in many cities you can rent a cell phone for a day or a week from a luxury hotel or the airport. Luxury hotels can also provide you with a pager.

DIRECTORY & OPERATOR ASSISTANCE

For local phone numbers, dial 197. For long-distance numbers within India, dial 183. Speak slowly, but don't be surprised if the operator just hangs up on you; India is modernizing its phone system, and the operator may not even have the latest number. If you're not calling from an International Subscriber Dialing (ISD) facility, dial 186 to reach an international operator.

INTERNATIONAL CALLS

International calls can be subject to long delays, but most hotels, airports, and post offices are connected to the computerized International Subscriber Dialing (ISD) system, which eliminates the need for an operator. You just dial 00, followed by the country code, the area code, and the number. Remember that hotels add an enormous surcharge to international calls and faxes; in addition, they sometimes charge a fee per call made on your calling card. Find out what the charges are before you dial. To avoid the surcharge, make your calls at an ISD offices (even then, the price will be around US$3 a minute to most places). There are no reduced-rate calling hours for international calls.

LOCAL CALLS

A local call normally costs between Rs. 1 and Rs. 5. Some deluxe hotels have coin-operated public phones that take Rs. 1 coins or special tokens available at the reception desk.

LONG-DISTANCE CALLS

Domestic long-distance calls are expensive. You can make them quickly through a computer system called Subscriber Trunk Dialing (STD), which is available in most hotels, at specially designated public phones, and at private ISD/STD offices, easily spotted by their bright-yellow signs. The system carries no surcharge, though most hotels will add their own.

LONG-DISTANCE SERVICES

AT&T, MCI, and Sprint access codes make calling long distance relatively convenient, but you may find the local access number blocked in many hotel rooms. First ask the hotel operator to connect you. If the hotel operator balks, ask for an international operator, or dial the international operator yourself. One way to improve your odds of getting connected to your long-distance carrier is to travel with more than one company's calling card (a hotel may block Sprint, for example, but not MCI). If all else fails, call from a pay phone.

➤ ACCESS CODES: **AT&T USADirect** (☎ 000116 or 000117). **MCI Call USA** (☎ 000126 or 000127). **Sprint Express** (☎ 000136 or 000137).

PUBLIC PHONES

To use a public phone, dial the number, then deposit the required coin (phone cards aren't prevalent in India) once the connection is made. The time limit is three minutes, and can be extended to six. The dial tone sounds, but often after you dial the number you'll hear a pulsing tone for a few seconds before the ring cuts in. If you use an ISD/STD facility, there's no time limit—a meter records the duration of your chat, and you pay the the required amount.

When using an STD booth, **check the meter reading before you pay** to see that the time on the slip matches the actual time used on the phone, and that the number recorded on the slip matches the number you dialed. Rates for domestic calls decrease by 50% after 7 PM and 75% after 10:30 PM.

TIME

India is 5½ hours ahead of Greenwich Mean Time, 10½ hours ahead of Eastern Standard Time, 13½ hours ahead of Pacific Standard Time, 4½ hours behind Sydney time, and 7½ hours behind Auckland time.

TIPPING

India runs on tips, and waiters, room-service attendants, housekeepers, porters, and doormen all expect to receive one. Some hotels include in their bills a service charge of 10%, which is also an appropriate amount to leave the waiter in any restaurant. You won't go wrong if you tip your room valet Rs. 20 per night. Bellboys and bell captains should be paid Rs. 10 per bag. For room service, tip 10% of the bill. Tip the concierge about Rs. 5 if he gets you a taxi. Train-station and airport porters should be paid Rs. 5–Rs. 10 per bag, depending on the weight; set the rate before you let him take your bags. Taxi drivers don't expect tips unless they go through a great deal of trouble to reach your destination; in such a case Rs. 10–Rs. 15 is fair. If you hire a car and driver, tip the driver about Rs. 50–Rs. 100 per day, depending on the distance traveled. Tip local guides Rs. 40 for four hours, Rs. 80 for a full day.

TOURS & PACKAGES

Because everything is prearranged on a prepackaged tour or independent vacation, you spend less time planning—and often get it all at a good price.

BOOKING WITH AN AGENT

Travel agents are excellent resources. But it's a good idea to collect brochures from several agencies as some agents' suggestions may be influenced by relationships with tour and package firms that reward them for volume sales. If you have a special interest, **find an agent with expertise in that area**; the American Society of Travel Agents (ASTA; ☞ Travel Agencies) has a database of specialists worldwide.

Make sure your travel agent knows the accommodations and other services of the place being recommended. Ask about the hotel's location, room size, beds, and whether it has a pool, room service, or programs for children, if you care about these. Has your agent been there in person or sent others whom you can contact?

Do some homework on your own, too: local tourism boards can provide information about lesser-known and small-niche operators, some of which may sell only direct.

BUYER BEWARE

Each year consumers are stranded or lose their money when tour operators—even large ones with excellent reputations—go out of business. So **check out the operator.** Ask several travel agents about its reputation, and try to **book with a company that has a consumer-protection program.** (Look for information in the company's brochure.) In the United States, members of the National Tour Association and the United States Tour Operators Association are required to set aside funds to cover your payments and travel arrangements in the event that the company defaults. It's also a good idea to choose a company that participates in the American Society of Travel Agents' Tour Operator Program (TOP); ASTA will act as mediator in any disputes between you and your tour operator.

Remember that the more your package or tour includes the better you can predict the ultimate cost of your vacation. Make sure you know exactly what is covered, and **beware of hidden costs.** Are taxes, tips, and transfers included? Entertainment and excursions? These can add up.

➤ TOUR-OPERATOR RECOMMENDATIONS: **American Society of Travel Agents** (☞ Travel Agencies). **National Tour Association** (NTA; ✉ 546 E. Main St., Lexington, KY 40508, ☎ 859/226–4444 or 800/682–8886, WEB www.ntaonline.com). **United States Tour Operators Association** (USTOA; ✉ 342 Madison Ave., Suite 1522, New York, NY 10173, ☎ 212/ 599–6599 or 800/468–7862, FAX 212/ 599–6744, WEB www.ustoa.com).

TRAIN TRAVEL

India's two luxury trains—Rajasthan's *Palace on Wheels* and Gujarat's *Royal Orient,* which travels in parts of Rajasthan—are destinations in themselves, offering sumptuous meals and quarters as well as fine itineraries. The *Shatabdi* and *Rajdhani* expresses, are fast and have air-conditioned cars and reclining seats. The next-fastest trains are called "mail" trains. "Passenger" trains, which usually offer only second-class accommodations, make numerous stops, and are crowded. Even on the best trains in this group, lavatories are less than pleasant and seats can be well worn.

The *Shatabdi Express* and *Taj Express* travel between Delhi and Agra. Both leave early in the morning from Delhi; the *Shatabdi* takes about two hours, the *Taj* 2½. Each allows for a full day of sightseeing before returning to Delhi. The *Pink Express,* which links Delhi and Jaipur, takes six hours and allows for about five hours of sightseeing before returning to Delhi. Another convenient *Shatabdi Express* runs overnight between Bombay and Delhi; and the overnight *Rajdhani Express* connects Delhi and Calcutta.

For long train rides, **buy a yard-long chain with loops and a padlock to secure your luggage.** (You might find a vendor on the platform at a large train station.) After you've *locked* your bag and stowed it in its place,

loop the chain through its handle and attach it to a bar or post below the seat. Lock it once more and you won't have to mind your luggage. You can even step off the train to stretch your legs at interim stations, knowing your possessions are safe. Your journey will be more pleasant if you pack packaged snacks, sandwiches from a fast-food chain, juice, bottled water, plastic glasses, and a tea cup. Or ask the staff at your hotel to prepare sandwiches or a traditional Indian train meal.

CLASSES

Trains have numerous classes: first-class air-conditioned (private compartments with two or four sleeping berths); ordinary first-class (non–air-conditioned private compartments with two or four sleeping berths), second-class air-conditioned sleeper (only available on some trains), second-class two-tier sleeper (padded berths), and ordinary second-class (always crowded and never comfortable).

You'll find two kinds of lavatories, the Western-style commode lavatory and the Indian-style toilet (essentially a hole over which you squat). Although it can be hard to get used to Indian-style facilities, they're actually safer in the sense that there's no contact. (Toilet seats in trains are notorious conductors of urinary infections.)

DISCOUNT PASSES

A rail pass may cost more than individual tickets. If you plan to cover considerable ground **look into Indian Railways Indrail Pass,** which is available for everything from second-class trains to first-class air-conditioned trains. The costs are: 1-day pass, US$19–$95; 7-day pass, $80–$270; 15-day pass, $90–$370; 21-day pass, $100–$440; 30-day pass, $125–$550; 60-day pass, $185–$800; 90-day pass, $235–$1,060. Children between 5 and 11 pay half. Try to **buy rail passes at least two months before your trip.** Provide your agent with a complete itinerary to ensure seat confirmation. Every Government of India Tourist Office overseas has copies of the Tourist Railway Timetable, or you can consult Thomas Cook's International Railway Timetable. In India,

Travel Links, Trains at a Glance, and *Travel Hour* list plane and some train schedules.

To buy the Indrail Pass outside India, contact your travel agent, the Government of India Tourist Office, or one of the designated sales agents listed below. In India, you can buy the pass at railway offices in major cities; international airports; and government-recognized travel agents in Bombay, Calcutta, Delhi, and Madras. You must pay in U.S. dollars, U.S.-dollar traveler's checks, or pounds sterling.

➤ INDRAIL PASS AGENTS ABROAD: **Australia** (✉ Adventure World, Box 480, North Sydney, NSW NSW 2059, ☎ 02/9958–7766, FAX 02/9956–7707). **Canada** (✉ Hari World Travel Inc., 1 Financial Pl., 1 Adelaide St. E, Concourse Level, Toronto M5C 2V8, ☎ 416/366–2000, FAX 416/366–6020). **United Kingdom** (✉ SD Enterprise, 103 Wembley Park Dr., Middlesex, London, ☎ 0208/903–3411, FAX 0208/903–0392). **United States** (✉ Hari World Travel Inc., 30 Rockefeller Plaza, North Mezzanine, Shop 21, New York, NY 10112, ☎ 212/957–3000, FAX 212/997–3320).

➤ LUXURY TRAIN CONTACTS: *Palace on Wheels* (✉ Rajasthan Tourism Development Corporation, Palace on Wheels Division, Bikaner House, Pandara Rd., near India Gate, New Delhi 110011, ☎ 11/338–1884). *Royal Orient* (✉ Gujarat State Tourism Development Corporation, A/6 State Emporia, Baba Kharak Singh Marg, New Delhi 110008, ☎ 11/374–4015).

➤ TRAIN INFORMATION: **Indian Railways** (WEB www.indianrail.gov.in).

PAYING

In large cities, you can buy tickets with major credit cards. Elsewhere, expect to pay cash.

RESERVATIONS

You must **reserve seats and sleeping berths in advance,** even with a rail pass. If your plans are flexible, you can make reservations once you arrive in India. To save time, **use a local travel agent** (who may need to borrow your passport); otherwise, head to the train station and prepare for lines and long waits. Large urban stations have a special counter for foreigners, where you can buy "tourist quota" tickets. (Every train reserves a few seats for tourists who haven't made reservations.) If you arrive early in the morning—around 8—getting a ticket shouldn't take you more than half an hour; in peak season, however, tourist quotas fill quickly, and you may have to change your dates altogether. When it's time to travel, **arrive at the station at least half an hour before departure** so you have enough time to find your seat. Sleeper and seat numbers are displayed on the platform and on each carriage, along with a list of passengers' names and seat assignments.

TRAVEL AGENCIES

A good travel agent puts your needs first. Look for an agency that has been in business at least five years, emphasizes customer service, and has someone on staff who specializes in your destination. In addition, **make sure the agency belongs to a professional trade organization.** The American Society of Travel Agents (ASTA)—the largest and most influential in the field with more than 26,000 members in some 170 countries—maintains and enforces a strict code of ethics and will step in to help mediate any agent-client disputes if necessary. ASTA (whose motto is "Without a travel agent, you're on your own") also maintains a Web site that includes a directory of agents. (If a travel agency is also acting as your tour operator, *see* Buyer Beware *in* Tours & Packages.)

➤ LOCAL AGENT REFERRALS: **American Society of Travel Agents** (ASTA; ✉ 1101 King St., Suite 200, Alexandria, VA 22314 ☎ 800/965–2782 24-hr hot line, FAX 703/739–7642, WEB www.astanet.com). **Association of British Travel Agents** (✉ 68–71 Newman St., London W1T 3AH, U.K., ☎ 020/7637–2444, FAX 020/7637–0713, WEB www.abtanet.com). **Association of Canadian Travel Agents** (✉ 130 Albert St., Suite 1705, Ottawa, Ontario K1P 5G4, Canada, ☎ 613/237–3657, FAX 613/237–7052, WEB www.acta.net). **Australian Federation of Travel Agents** (✉ Level 3, 309 Pitt St., Sydney NSW 2000, Australia, ☎ 02/9264–3299, FAX 02/9264–1085,

WEB www.afta.com.au). **Travel Agents' Association of New Zealand** (⊠ Level 5, Paxus House, 79 Boulcott St., Box 1888, Wellington 10033, New Zealand, ☏ 04/499–0104, FAX 04/499–0827, WEB www.taanz.org.nz).

VISITOR INFORMATION

For general information and brochures on India before you leave home, contact the nearest tourist office.

➤ GOVERNMENT OF INDIA TOURIST OFFICES ABROAD: **Australia** (⊠ Level 2 Piccadilly, 210 Pitt St., Sydney NSW 2000, ☏ 02/9264–4855). **Canada** (⊠ 60 Bloor St. W, Suite 1003, Toronto, Ontario M4W 3B8, ☏ 416/962–3787). **United Kingdom** (⊠ 7 Cork St., London W1X 2AB, ☏ 020/7437–3677). **United States** (⊠ 30 Rockefeller Plaza, Room 15, North Mezzanine, New York, NY 10112, ☏ 800/953–9399; ⊠ 3550 Wilshire Blvd., Suite 204, Los Angeles, CA 90010, ☏ 213/380–8855).

➤ U.S. GOVERNMENT ADVISORIES: **U.S. Department of State** (⊠ Overseas Citizens Services Office, Room 4811 N.S., 2201 C St. NW, Washington, DC 20520, ☏ 202/647–5225 for interactive hot line, WEB http://travel.state.gov/travel/html); enclose a self-addressed, stamped, business-size envelope.

WEB SITES

India is extraordinarily well represented on the World Wide Web, so **use the Web to help plan your trip** if at all possible. You'll find everything from splendid photos of Heritage Hotels to close-ups of temple carvings to testimonials from former travelers.

For information specifically on India, visit the official Indian tourism ministry site www.tourindia.com or email the New York Indian tourist office at goitony@tourindia.com. Other good India travel sites like are www.rediff.com/travel/travhom1.htm, www.indiaserver.com/travel, www.indiamart.com/travel, and www.123india.com/travel_and_tourism. Both the Gujarat and the Rajasthan tourist boards have sites with details on Heritage Hotel: www.gujarattourism.com and www.rajasthantourismindia.com.

Be sure to **visit Fodors.com** (www.fodors.com), a complete travel-planning site. You can research prices and book plane tickets, hotel rooms, rental cars, vacation packages, and more. In addition, you can post your pressing questions in the Travel Talk section. Other planning tools include a currency converter and weather reports, and there are loads of links to travel resources.

WHEN TO GO

India's peak tourist season for the plains and the South (which encompass most of the major sights) is fall and winter: mid-September through March. **Make all reservations well in advance**—especially for trips to Rajasthan, Kerala, and Goa. By May and June, only the Himalayas are comfortable; the rest of India is unbearably hot. Himachal Pradesh and Ladakh, where the mountains usually hold back the monsoons, make great escapes from the torrential July and August rains that inundate most of North India; and summer is often the only time to visit these otherwise snowbound places. If you head for the hills in summer, reserve in advance.

India's monsoons disrupt plane schedules and phone and electrical systems; heavy rains also wash away roads or bury them in landslides. That said, the monsoons can be a pleasant time to see places that are hot the rest of the year: most of the South (except Kerala), central Gujarat, the Deccan Plateau (Madhya Pradesh and parts of Maharashtra). Rajasthan is also pretty and green in the rain, and Goa's resorts are nice and cheap then, too, if you don't mind having your swimming and sunbathing curtailed.

CLIMATE

India's climate is monsoon-tropical, with local variations. Temperate weather, which includes cool evenings, lasts from October to the end of February. Seriously hot and muggy weather hits South India from the beginning of April to the beginning of June, at which point the monsoon brings rain-laden clouds that then move north, watering nearly every part of India until September. The Himalayas can be extremely cold in winter, and deep snow renders many mountain passes and valleys impassable. Below are average daily maximum and minimum temperatures for key Indian cities.

➤ FORECASTS: **Weather Channel Connection** (☎ 900/932–8437), 95¢ per minute from a Touch-Tone phone.

BOMBAY

Jan.	88F	31C	May	92F	33C	Sept.	86F	30C
	61	16		79	26		76	24
Feb.	90F	32C	June	90F	32C	Oct.	90F	32C
	63	17		79	26		74	23
Mar.	92F	33C	July	86F	30C	Nov.	92F	33C
	68	20		77	25		68	20
Apr.	92F	33C	Aug.	85F	29C	Dec.	90F	32C
	76	24		76	24		65	18

CALCUTTA

Jan.	79F	26C	May	97F	36C	Sept.	90F	32C
	54	12		79	26		79	26
Feb.	85F	29C	June	94F	34C	Oct.	88F	31C
	59	15		79	26		75	24
Mar.	94F	34C	July	90F	32C	Nov.	85F	29C
	68	20		79	26		64	18
Apr.	97F	36C	Aug.	90F	32C	Dec.	81F	27C
	76	24		79	26		55	13

DELHI

Jan.	70F	21C	May	106F	41C	Sept.	93F	34C
	45	7		81	27		77	25
Feb.	93F	34C	June	104F	40C	Oct.	95F	35C
	50	10		84	29		66	19
Mar.	86F	30C	July	95F	35C	Nov.	84F	29C
	59	15		81	27		54	12
Apr.	97F	36C	Aug.	93F	34C	Dec.	73F	23C
	70	21		79	26		46	8

GANGTOK

Jan.	57F	14C	May	72F	22C	Sept.	73F	23C
	39	4		57	14		61	16
Feb.	59F	15C	June	73F	23C	Oct.	72F	22C
	41	5		61	16		54	12
Mar.	66F	19C	July	73F	23C	Nov.	66F	19C
	48	9		63	17		48	9
Apr.	72F	22C	Aug.	73F	23C	Dec.	59F	15C
	54	12		63	17		43	6

MADRAS

Jan.	84C	29C	May	100F	38C	Sept.	93F	34C
	68	20		82	28		77	25
Feb.	88F	31C	June	99F	37C	Oct.	90F	32C
	70	21		82	28		75	24
Mar.	91F	33C	July	95F	35C	Nov.	84F	29C
	73	23		79	26		73	23
Apr.	95F	35C	Aug.	95F	35C	Dec.	82F	28C
	79	26		79	26		70	21

SHIMLA

Jan.	48F	9C	May	73F	23C	Sept.	68F	20C
	36	2		59	15		57	14
Feb.	50F	10C	June	75F	24C	Oct.	64F	18C
	37	3		61	16		50	10
Mar.	57F	14C	July	70F	21C	Nov.	59F	15C
	45	7		61	16		45	7
Apr.	66F	19C	Aug.	68F	20C	Dec.	52F	11C
	52	11		59	15		39	4

TRIVANDRUM

Jan.	88F	31C	May	88F	31C	Sept.	86F	30C
	72	22		77	25		73	23
Feb.	90F	32C	June	84F	29C	Oct.	86F	30C
	73	23		75	24		73	23
Mar.	91F	33C	July	84F	29C	Nov.	86F	30C
	75	24		73	23		73	23
Apr.	90F	32C	Aug.	84F	29C	Dec.	88F	31C
	77	25		72	22		73	23

FESTIVALS AND SEASONAL EVENTS

India holds religious celebrations year-round, along with numerous fairs and cultural festivals. Dates of some celebrations are determined by the lunar calendar, so check with the Government of India Tourist Office for details.

➤ DEC.: For the five-day **Konark Dance Festival,** Odissi (classical Orissan dances) are performed at the Sun Temple and a craft fair is held. The **Shekhavati Festival** celebrates the frescoes on the local havelis (mansions), as well as other local arts, traditional music and dance, and cuisine from this Rajasthan region. At the **Shilp Darshan Mela** near Udaipur, master craftsmen show how they create award-winning handicrafts, and dancers and musicians perform.

➤ JAN.: **Republic Day,** the 26th, commemorates the adoption of India's constitution with a big parade in Delhi and celebrations elsewhere. Kerala's four-day **Great Elephant March** features caparisoned elephants, snake-boat races, and cultural events in various locales. The two-day **Camel Festival** in Bikaner (Rajasthan) celebrates the ship of the desert with parades, races, and dancing. **Makar Sankranti** has people engaging in kite duels from rooftops in Ahmedabad. In Tamil Nadu, **Pongal,** a colorful three-day festival at the close of the harvest season gives thanks to the rain god, the sun god, and the cow with bonfires, games, dancing, and cows bedecked with garlands.

➤ JAN.–FEB.: During **Gangasagar Mela,** the festival of the Ganges River, pilgrims from all over India celebrate the most important natural element in their mythology. Nagaur (Rajasthan) holds an enormous **cattle fair** complete with camel races and cultural programs. The five-day **Desert Fair,** Jaisalmer's gala, includes traditional Rajasthani music and dance, handicrafts, camel caravans, camel races, and turban-tying events.

➤ FEB.: For the three-day **Elephanta Festival of Music and Dance,** artists perform nightly on a platform near these Maharashtra caves. The **Surajkund Crafts Mela** draws crowds to a village near Delhi to watch traditional dances, puppeteers, magicians, and acrobats and to shop for crafts made by artisans from every state. On **Losar,** the Buddhist New Year, costumed *lamas* (monks) perform dances at monasteries in Sikkim.

➤ FEB.–MAR.: On the eve of **Holi,** the festival of spring, Hindus nationwide light a bonfire and send an effigy of a female demon up in flames, demonstrating the destruction of evil; the next day, children throw colored water on each other and you. On **Id-ul-Fitr,** the Muslim holiday that concludes the month-long Ramadan fast, the devout give alms to the poor, offer prayers, and feast and rejoice. The **Kumbh Mela,** a celebration of immortality, is India's largest religious festival and a stunning spectacle of bathers in the Ganges. Held every three years in Allahabad, Haridwar, Nasik, or Ujjain, it came to Allahabad in February 2001. The two-week **Taj Mahotsav** spotlights Agra's heritage through handicrafts and cultural events.

➤ MAR.: India's best performers entertain in the moonlight, with historic Kailasa Temple as a backdrop, for the three-day **Ellora Festival of Classical Music and Dance.** India's best dancers present classical works at the **Khajuraho Dance Festival,** held in part on an outdoor stage against the temples. Pachyderms have their day in Jaipur when the **Elephant Festival** sets off processions, races, and even elephant polo.

➤ MAR.–APR.: **Carnival**—the Mardi Gras held just before Lent—hits Goa as a big party with masked dancers, floats, and good eating. The **Gangaur Festival** of Jaipur and Udaipur honors the goddess Parvati with processions of young girls and images of the goddess and, in Udaipur, fireworks, dancing, and a procession of boats on Lake Pichola.

➤ APR.: Honoring Lord Jagannath, Bhubaneswar's 21-day **Chandan Yatra** features processions in which images of deities are carried to sacred tanks and rowed around in decorated boats.

➤ APR.–MAY: At **Puram,** a major temple festival in Trichur (Kerala), elephants sporting gold-plated mail carry Brahmins with ceremonial umbrellas and the temple deity, Vadakkunathan (Shiva), in a procession to the beat of temple drums. The spectacular 10-day **Chitra Festival** celebrates the marriage of goddess Meenakshi to Lord Shiva at Madurai's Meenakshi Temple.

➤ MAY: Buddhists celebrate **Buddha Jayanti**—the birthday, enlightenment, and death of Sakyamunni (Historic Buddha)—with rituals and chants at monasteries. Special celebrations are held in Sikkim and other major pilgrimage centers, such as Sarnath and Bodhgaya. On **Muharram,** Shiite Muslims commemorate the martyrdom of the Prophet Mohammed's grandson Hussain, who died in the battle of Karbala. Participants' intense self-flagellation may disturb the squeamish. On **Bakrid** or **Id-ul-Zuha,** celebrating the sacrifice of Harrat Ibrahim (Abraham), Muslims solemnly sacrifice one animal per family (or group of families) and conclude with a feast and joyous celebration.

➤ JUNE–JULY: Puri's seven-day **Rath Yatra,** honoring Lord Krishna, is Orissa's most sacred festival and draws big crowds. The two-day **Hemis Festival** at Ladakh's largest monastery commemorates the birthday of Guru Padmasambhava with masked lamas performing ritual *chaams* (dances) and haunting music.

➤ JULY–AUG.: In Jaipur, women and girls observe **Teej,** the arrival of the monsoon, dedicating their festivities to the goddess Parvati.

➤ AUG.: **Independence Day,** on the 15th, commemorates India's independence from British rule in 1947.

➤ AUG.–SEPT.: **Ganesha Chaturthi,** a 10-day festival celebrated in Bombay and Pune, marks the birthday of the Hindus' elephant-headed god; clay images of Ganesh are paraded through streets and installed on platforms. **Onam** celebrates Kerala's harvest season with dancing, singing, and exotic snake-boat races in Alleppey, Aranmula, and Kottayam. **Pang Lhabsol** offers thanks to Mt. Kanchenjunga, Sikkim's guardian deity, and honors Yabdu, the great warrior who protects the mountain.

➤ SEPT.–OCT.: Calcutta turns into one big party for **Durga Puja,** a five-day festival honoring the ten-armed Hindu goddess Durga. Farther south, Mysore hosts concerts and cultural events in Durbar Hall, and the the maharaja himself comes out in full regalia, complete with some palace treasures, for the traditional procession.

➤ OCT.: On **Gandhi Jayanti,** Mahatma Gandhi's birthday (the 2nd), pilgrims visit the Raj Ghat, where

Gandhi was cremated. Jaipur's **Marwar Festival** brings to life myth and folklore in Marwari culture, music, and dance.

➤ OCT.–NOV.: **Diwali,** the festival of lights, is India's most important Hindu festival, celebrating the day the Hindu God Rama (Vishnu) ended a 14-year exile, as well as the start of the New Year. Hindus worship Lakshmi, the goddess of prosperity; oil lamps flicker in most homes symbolizing the victory of truth (light) over ignorance (darkness); cities crackle with the explosion of fireworks; and Bengalis worship Kali, the black goddess of destruction.

➤ NOV.: Nomads assemble with their camels and gaily festooned cattle for Rajasthan's carnivalesque **Pushkar Festival.**

➤ NOV.–DEC.: The **International Seafood Festival** at Miramar Beach, near Panaji (Goa), offers three to five days of good food, music, and Indian, Western, and local folk dances.

1 DESTINATION: INDIA

Cosmic Chaos

New and Noteworthy

What's Where

Pleasures and Pastimes

Great Itineraries

Fodor's Choice

COSMIC CHAOS

STEP INTO INDIA and you are stepping into the most democratic and the most feudal country in the world. The marriage of feudalism to freedom is the grandest of India's many paradoxes, and part of its magic and charm. India's people are utterly free, yet the situations of many are fixed in time, at roughly 100 years ago. Contradictions in everyday Indian life may leave you nonplussed on your first trip here. No matter how quickly it charges onto the information superhighway, India remains an enigma, a perplexity, a puzzle you simply can't solve. And every time you think you know the place, something happens to jolt you out of your complacency.

The essence of contemporary Indian life is that people carry on with whatever activity pleases them, even if it's contrary to the law or the comfort of their neighbors—and neither the authorities mor the bemused neighbors bat an eye. Parades of disgruntled workers with blaring microphones obstruct a city thoroughfare for 12 hours, and life goes on around them. Villagers use a highway running through their hamlet as a place to dry that season's rice crop, and truck drivers simply drop to the shoulder of the road, navigating carefully for miles—even if it means landing in a ditch—to protect the grain. Your toddler irrigates the second-class train compartment you share with six other people, and your fellow passengers smile benignly and keep their feet up.

Any religious activity in India has society's full sanction. Half the populace occupies the main road in prayer; a whole town blushes orange with religious banners. Festivals turn communities upside-down with noise, color, and commotion, but a *tamasha* (spectacle, or happy confusion) is enjoyed by all.

Lunatics stand at crossroads directing imaginary traffic. Cows may even amble into your house. *Dacoits* (highway robbers) are welcomed home, forgiven for a string of crimes, and asked to go into politics. *Sadhus* (ascetic holy men) arrive at your door looking for money. Husbands vanish for years on religious pilgrimages. An employee takes two months off without leave for his uncle's wife's father's brother's funeral. Indians live as they please.

The flip side of this day-to-day liberty is that many Indian's fates are engraved in stone. The poor seldom become rich. The rich seldom become poor. Carpenters seldom become doctors. Widows seldom remarry. Wives seldom divorce alcoholic, do-nothing husbands. Untouchables never, technically at least, become touchable. Castes cannot be changed or ignored. Social mobility, while gaining momentum, is slow.

The people of India will warm your heart. Democratic or feudal, Indians can be touching in their respect, affection, and concern for you, a guest; their families; and their gods. Where else can you see thousands of people trudging barefoot through the night to pay their respects to a deity in a temple?

Indeed, religion in India is no one-day-a-week affair: It's a way of life, the force that moves the country. Faith governs the mind, defines most behavior, and sets much of the country's agenda and calendar. It becomes a personal lullaby or alarm clock for all, with Hindu temple bells tinkling intermittently and a muezzin calling the Muslim faithful to prayer five times a day. So many gods and goddesses are worshiped here that Mark Twain may have understated the case when he wrote in *Following the Equator* that "in religion all other countries are paupers, India is the only millionaire." Hinduism alone accounts for thousands of deities. Wherever you travel in this spiritual land, you'll find monuments with a sacred element: the Taj Mahal, with its carefully inlaid Koranic verses; Khajuraho's Hindu temples, with their astonishing erotic sculptures; the Ajanta Caves, with their serene murals of the Buddha; Catholic churches in Goa, with their Hindu-esque images of Jesus; Jain temples with their *tirthankaras* (perfect souls), whose poses and features resemble those of the Buddha; and even a handful of historic synagogues.

The earliest remnants of an Indian civilization date from at least 3200 BC, and since then the subcontinent's culture and heritage have endured repeated invasions. Some say India's ability to adapt is the very source of her strength and resilience. Persian-influenced Moghul tombs add delicacy to urban skylines. British bungalows anchor Himalayan hill stations and line major avenues. Cuisines, languages, dance and music styles, and artwork and handicrafts vary widely from state to state. There's no American-style homogeneity in India; each region is intensely proud of its own culture.

To be sure, many aspects of this country can be hard for the Westerner to understand. Why, for instance, do India's urban cows prefer to chew on newspaper rather than on rotting garbage (in plentiful supply) or on random patches of grass in a field? India can also be exasperating and exhausting—a difficult place for those accustomed to efficiency and a Western work ethic. To enjoy your stay in India, surrender, take it slow, and don't try to squeeze too much into a short trip. Prepare to give in to the laissez-faire attitude that seems a natural extension of India's fatalistic tendency. The favorite saying is, "Shall we adjust? We will adjust." In Hindi: "*Adjust karlenge.*" Accept that what happens is meant to be, or is the will of a supreme authority (frequent Indian explanations). If your flight is canceled, the phone doesn't work, or the fax won't go through, don't fly into a rage. When the slow-motion pace of workers in a government bank or post office is about to drive you crazy, remember that this lack of value for time will have an appealing effect when you venture into rural areas and start wondering why, exactly, you spend so much time in your office back home. You can sit for hours and watch the simplest routines: village women drawing water from a well, or a man tilling the soil with a crude wooden plow. Walking around a deserted ancient city such as Fatehpur Sikri, or watching orthodox Hindus in Varanasi go through their purification or cremation rituals, you'll begin to understand why the art of meditation evolved here. Arrive with the determination to experience India, and make every attempt to adapt; otherwise, this country—which travelers tend to love or hate—might rub you the wrong way.

It helps to be forgiving about some elements of India's inefficiency and overstretched infrastructure. When this country gained independence in 1947, the new democracy chose nonalignment, set up a large national government, and legislated protectionist policies that kept out most foreign products and led almost to economic isolation. The first prime minister, Jawaharlal Nehru, believed protectionism would make India self-reliant and ultimately improve the standard of living, especially for the impoverished. India did move toward self-reliance, but lack of competition stifled the country's own development, with its captive market forced to accept indigenous products that were often substandard or old-fashioned. Until half a decade ago, the dominant car on India's roads was the Ambassador, a British design from the early 1950s with a curvaceous yet bulky chassis: a nostalgic gas-guzzler.

Then, in 1991, a severe debt crisis and a shortage of foreign exchange forced the government to initiate economic reforms, the results of which have been nothing short of astonishing. Having studiously fended off foreign corporations for decades, India is suddenly encouraging them to invest. Coke and Pepsi are staging their old war on new turf, and software companies are helping turn Bangalore and Hyderabad into 21st-century boom towns. And everything from American toilet paper to Japanese karaoke systems to Johnny Walker scotch to Betty Crocker fruit roll-ups is now being imported and is available in the larger metros. India is now one of the world's most tantalizing consumer goods markets.

I**NDIA'S STIRRING** has profound implications, and has already affected her once-rigid lifestyle. Cable TV is changing India, as British, American, French, Pakistani, and Chinese commentators relay their own views of the news on satellite channels. Teenagers now dance to MTV India, a frenetic mixture of Indian and Western pop. American cartoons capture the attention of every Indian child with access to the Cartoon Network. Reruns of *The Bold and the Beautiful* show steamy scenes to a people whose own "Bollywood" movies (made in Bombay) were not allowed to include a kiss until a few years ago.

Friends is a hot favorite with the yuppies of Bombay and New Delhi. While most Indian women still wear saris or the casual, two-piece *salwar-kameez*, many now rush off to their corporate jobs in the latest Western fashions, and many men have become equally label-conscious about everything from the shirts they wear to the foreign liquor they drink. An increasing number of people working in the private sector complain of a new work-related problem: stress.

Yet India still teems with pavement dwellers who call the sidewalk their home. The poor are not shy about approaching strangers, and the Western traveler with a pocketful of rupees might find it hard to resist a plea, especially from a child. While it's not wrong to give money to beggars, you may want to visit a local school or medical clinic and make a contribution through a responsible adult.

If you get frustrated here, remember that everyone from villagers to wealthy urbanites is equally annoyed by lousy services, and impatient for the kind of infrastructure that most Westerners take for granted. And along with this impatience comes a sense of concern: many Indians lament the arrival of foreign competitors to solve their problems. They worry about the increasing disparity between the haves and have-nots as a result of reforms that have raised inflation. They wonder whether the benefits will really trickle down to the masses. Others wonder if India will succumb to a cultural imperialism that will rob them of their identity. And yet increased exposure to the Western world is unlikely to overturn Indian culture. Most imports will be examined, Indianized, and absorbed, the way Coca-Cola is drunk in western Uttaranchal: with salt, red pepper, and *chaat masala* (a tangy spice medley).

All of these issues add dimension to any trip to India, a country in profound transition. Today's India is more than its thousands of monuments; more than its hundreds of ethnic groups; more than its colorful fairs and festivals; more than the birthplace of Hinduism, Buddhism, Jainism, and Sikhism; more than the sum of its parts. India has taken its first steps toward becoming an economic giant. With a population of 1 billion as of 1999, it is a country that can't be ignored.

— Kathleen Cox and Vaihayasi Pande Daniel

NEW AND NOTEWORTHY

Microsoft has joined IBM, Oracle, Hewlett-Packard, Motorola, Sun Microsystems, and other technology firms in setting up development centers here, mostly in Bangalore and Hyderabad. **Software development** is one of India's fastest-growing industries; in fact, about 10% of Microsoft's employees worldwide are of Indian origin. With the recent worldwide slowdown the industry has taken a jolt but that does not stop the garages and workshops of Bangalore from being the bustling "back end" of some of the largest companies in the world.

There has been a flurry of activity in what is termed the FMCG sector, or the fast moving consumer goods market—appliances and frivolous gadgets of practically every international brand have moved in. As of 2001, the import barriers or quantitative restrictions on food and liquor products was removed, so pretty much any brand you like you can find on Indian shop shelves, albeit at a price.

As newly arrived multinationals and expanding domestic firms demand more electrical power, phone connections, and water, India's **infrastructure** will remain stretched beyond capacity for years to come. City traffic is hideous during work hours, and pollution is breathtakingly awful—most cars are not fitted with catalytic converters. And while India introduced unleaded gas in 1995 in Delhi, Bombay, Calcutta, and Madras, cars that required unleaded gas may have trouble finding it on long-distance trips through the countryside.

Economic liberalization has opened India's skies to **private domestic airlines,** which have proved that competition can lead to better service (including that of the national domestic carrier, Indian Airlines). Foreign partnerships, however, were blocked in 1997: the government decided not to open its domestic skies to investment by foreign carriers, who could bring in newer aircraft and higher standards of maintenance. This policy is still fiercely debated.

Finally, disturbances continue to beset the lovely but disputed state of **Jammu and Kashmir.** Ladakh is open to travelers, but if you want to see any part of Jammu and Kashmir consult your state department and the Government of India Tourist Office in your home country before making plans.

WHAT'S WHERE

India lies in the Northern Hemisphere, bisected laterally by the Tropic of Cancer (which also bisects Mexico). With a total land area of 3,287,000 square km (1,261,000 square mi) and a coastline 6,100 km (3,535 mi) long, it's the world's seventh-largest country. To the north, the Himalayas separate India from Nepal and China. To the east is Bhutan, still closely connected to India by a special treaty. More mountains separate India from Myanmar (formerly Burma) on the eastern border. Also to the east lies Bangladesh, wedged between the Indian states of Assam, Meghalaya, Tripura, and West Bengal. Pakistan borders India's northwest. Just off the subcontinent's southeastern tip lies the island nation of Sri Lanka, separated from the mainland by 50 km (31 mi) of water, the Palk Straits. Conversely, the Lakshadweep Islands in the Arabian Sea and the Andaman and Nicobar islands in the Bay of Bengal, much farther away, are part of the Indian Union.

The Himalayas (*hima* means snow; *laya,* abode), the wall of mountains sweeping 3,200 km (1,984 mi) across north India, are divided into distinct ranges. Among them are the Greater Himalayas, or Trans-Himalayas, a crescendo of peaks that includes some of the world's highest massifs—many above 20,000 ft. In Ladakh, the lunar Karakorams merge into the northwestern edge of the Greater Himalayas. In both ranges, massive glaciers cling to towering peaks; rivers rage through deep gorges, chilled with melting snow and ice; and wild blue sheep traverse craggy cliffs.

Stretching south of the Himalayas is the densely populated Indo-Gangetic Plain. Mountains and hills separate numerous plateaus, and the basins of the Ganga (Ganges) and Brahmaputra rivers make the land rich and productive. This is particularly true in the Punjab, India's breadbasket. The enormous plain also includes the Thar Desert, which extends across western Rajasthan. Except when the vegetation from irrigated fields grows lush after the monsoon, most of its terrain is marked by scrub, cactus, and low rocky hills. The unusual Rann of Kutch, a wide salt flat, is southwest of Rajasthan in the state of Gujarat. Just a few feet above sea level, this strange land mass, which floods during the monsoon, is home to former nomads dependent on camels and what meager income they receive from their exquisite handicrafts.

More mountains cut through India's peninsula and follow its contour. The Eastern Ghats mark off a broad coastal strip on the Bay of Bengal; the Western Ghats define a narrower coast on the Arabian Sea. These low ranges merge in the Nilgiri Hills, near India's southern tip. In the more remote areas of these mountains and plateaus, as in the states of Madhya Pradesh and Orissa, numerous tribes continue to share forested land with wild animals.

South India is tropical, with rice paddies, coffee plantations, and forests that shade spice crops. In the southwestern state of Kerala and part of neighboring Karnataka, exquisite waterways thread inland from the Arabian Sea through a natural network of canals connecting palm-fringed fishing villages.

The Himalayas

Inspiring awe like no other mountain range in the world, the snow-capped Himalayas cut a border between India, Nepal, and China, passing through the Indian states of Jammu and Kashmir, Himachal Pradesh, Uttaranchal, and Sikkim. A few hours north of Delhi you can indulge an adventure or spiritual retreat—river rafting, paragliding, yoga by the Ganges in the Garhwal foothills, or tiger spotting from elephant-back at Corbett National Park. Imagine hiking through the surreal landscapes of Ladakh or Spiti, or making a pilgrimage to some of India's most fascinating religious sites.

Delhi

India's capital is a sophisticated, world-class city. From the old bazaars and hectic, twisting streets of Old Delhi to the avenues lined with British-built bungalows, international hotels, museums, and restaurants in New Delhi, the city is unique among Indian cities. It's one of few places where the West strives alongside a more traditional India. Top sights include Jama Masjid, India's largest mosque, and Qutab Minar, the seventh wonder of Hindustan and the tallest stone tower in India. Other important monuments include the Imperial City, designed by the British architect Sir Edwin Lutyens, and Lal Qila, Emperor Shah Jahan's 17th-century capital.

North Central India

Anchored by Agra, Khajuraho, and Varanasi, this section of the traveler's trail heads southeast of Delhi into the state of Uttaranchal, detouring into Madhya Pradesh and Bihar. The history of these lands is ancient and vast, with a religious heritage spanning Hinduism, Islam, Buddhism, and even, in Lucknow, Christianity. The spectacular architecture includes Agra's incomparable Taj Mahal and Khajuraho's exciting Hindu temples. Varanasi is the holiest city in Hinduism, drawing a constant stream of pilgrims to bathe in the Ganges River.

Rajasthan

Literally the "Land of Kings," Rajasthan spans a wide, arid stretch of northwestern India. The region is best known for its martial history—the indomitable Rajput warriors who defended themselves against invaders and divided the region into princely states. The region is equally famous for its exuberant festivals and colorful folk art traditions. Travelers come from all over the world to visit the Pink City of Jaipur, the Jain temples in Ranakpur and Mount Abu, the enchanting lake-city of Udaipur, and Jaisalmer Fort, which rises dramatically out of the barren Thar desert.

Gujarat

The birthplace of Mahatma Gandhi, Gujarat (despite it's boundary with Pakistan) was and still is India's most politically stable state. It's a place where Hindus and Muslims live in harmony, reminiscent of a pre-colonial India. Major cities such as Ahmedabad and Vadodara, although modernized and culturally active, are preserved to the pace and progress of the local population, and are virtually unknown to tourists. The Kathiawar peninsula is best known for its territorial resort island of Diu, where Gujaratis and foreigners alike take refuge from the dry state. Folk life, crafts, and the traditions of Gujarat's nomadic culture are best preserved in the harsh and unfortunately earthquake-ravaged region of Kutch.

Bombay

Once Bombay was a string of seven islands belonging to fisherfolk. Today these precious seven islands, now united into an isthmus, are India's most important and prosperous urban center. Bombay, renamed Mumbai by the state government, embodies India's most modern and contradictory face—the city is home to the most glamorous, upwardly mobile, and wealthy of Indian citizens, as well as to millions who barely eke out a living. Bombay is famously the center of India's bustling film industry, dubbed Bollywood, and embraces both traditional *desi* (Indian) values and keenly hip Western styles.

Goa

Goa's remarkably beautiful beaches are India's most famous by far, and this former Portuguese colony is well-frequented by Indians and foreigners alike. A bright blue coastline stretches down sparkling, palm-lined beaches along the Arabian Sea. Wide inland rivers meander around small pastel houses and churches, revealing the Portuguese influence—Goa was once a trade center for spices, silk, and pearls. Goan cuisine, of pomfret, prawns, and other seafood preparations heavily doused with coconut meat and milk, is legendary. For some local culture, come at Christmas or in February for Carnival—and plan to take in some spectacular coastline views and to explore small villages and local markets.

Karnataka

Karnataka is known for two things: its high-tech, cosmopolitan capital of Bangalore, and the religious monuments scattered in nearby cities and villages. Most famous is Mysore, the City of Palaces, famous for its silks and sandalwood products. There are also Belur and Habelid villages, with meticulously wrought 12th-century temples, and the vast ruins of Hampi, the 14th-century center of the largest Hindu empire in South India. Then there's the picturesque coastline to the west, with palm-fringed beaches, and other delights, including watching wild elephants in Nagarhold National Park and visiting the monolithic statue of a Jain saint in Sravanabelagola.

Kerala

Natural splendor and a 5,000-year-old health-care system have combined to make Kerala India's hottest destination. The palm-strewn beach resorts of southern Kerala offer pampering Ayurvedic massage and wellness packages. The best way to see the central region is to float through backwater villages on a wooden houseboat, anchoring in the fabled port city of Cochin for a dose of colonial history and some spicy seafood. Lush forests swarm the cool hillsides of the inland districts, where tea, coffee, and spice plantations; elephants; and wildlife sanctuaries abound. The astonishing Theyyam dancers of unspoiled north Kerala offer a living glimpse into pre-Hindu society. Today, Kerala society boasts Hindu, Muslim, Christian, and Jewish communities, and is India's most densely populated, as well as its most literate (more than 90%) state.

Tamil Nadu

A state that takes great pride in its age-old religious and cultural traditions, lush, tropical Tamil Nadu stretches between the Eastern Ghats (mountains) and the Bay of Bengal, down to the southernmost tip of the subcontinent. Since the days of the Pallava dynasty, more than 13 centuries ago, the state has welcomed foreign trade and interaction, but has retained a personality distinct from other parts of Asia, and indeed from India itself. There is much of historical interest here: age-old temples endure on coastal sands and paddy fields, and colonial architectural splendor graces the towns and cities. Tamil Nadu is also a center for classical Indian dance, known as Bharatanatyam, and classical Carnatic music; in December, the Carnatic festival in Chennai, the capital, is a magnet for music-lovers.

Hyderabad

Known for its dynamic software and telecommunications industries, as well as for its textile, jewelry, and pearl trades, Hyderabad is a young city—only 400 years old. It has its roots in Buddhism and Islam, which are still reflected today, though the majority of people are Hindu. Hyderabadi cuisine is famously fiery—chilies, which grow on the plateaus, figure prominently in the cooking. Shopping is another draw: look for handicrafts; textiles; and, most importantly, pearls—Hyderabad is the center of India's pearl

trade, so you'll find a fantastic selection here, especially in the bustling Charminar Market.

Bhubaneswar

Better known as the city of temples (500) and the ancient kingdom of Kalinga, Bhubaneswar is the center for Odissi dance. This capital city is less like the other hectic and polluted cities of modern India and more like a slow-paced village. Besides the ancient temples of the city, the monumental horse-drawn chariot temple of Konark, the 12th-century Jagannath temple of Puri, the artisans of Ragurajpur and Pipli, and the tribal cultures of the state, Orissa is also known for its extensive coastline and pearly beaches.

Calcutta

Located 120 km (75 mi) from the Bay of Bengal and perched on the eastern bank of the river Hooghly, cosmopolitan Calcutta is the gateway to eastern India. It's also the artistic and literary soul of India, with an intellectual heritage that's famous worldwide—it's a city known for its writers, musicians, filmmakers, dancers, and philosophers. Home to more than 12 million people, Calcutta is a place of swank high rises and upscale residential blocks, as well as shanties and tenements. It's India's best city for walkers, with teeming bazaars and crowded narrow streets, colonial mansions, Victorian architecture, temples, mosques, and gardens and parks to get away from it all.

PLEASURES AND PASTIMES

Beaches

Between October and March you can spend a few days or an entire vacation at a deluxe resort, a beach cottage, or even a safari-style tent on a luscious Indian beach. Goa is perennially popular with Westerners; far less trafficked are the picture-perfect Lakshadweep islands, off Kerala, where you can snorkel around coral reefs. On Kerala's own coast, the sandy beaches at Kovalam are lined with palm-fringed lagoons and rocky coves. At Mamallapuram, south of Madras, the beaches are steps from some of India's finest temple ruins. Gujarat hides an incredibly pristine beach at Mandvi, in Kutch, with clear water and calm surf.

Dining

Indian cuisine varies widely from region to region. You'll find meat, seafood, vegetables, lentils, and grains in subtle and enticing combinations. The generic term "curry" doesn't really exist in India, but means, more or less, that a dish is cooked in a spicy sauce. Over the centuries, various invading forces brought new techniques, ingredients, and dishes to India. The Moghuls revolutionized Indian cooking, especially in the north, introducing *biriyanis* (rice dishes), *kormas* (braised meat or vegetable dishes), kebabs, *kofta* (meat or vegetable balls), *dum pukht* (aromatic, slow-cooked dishes), and tandoori cooking (which requires a tandoor, or clay oven). The British introduced simple puddings and custards. Tibetan immigrants brought *momos* (steamed dumplings), *kothay* (fried dumplings), and hearty noodle soups called *thukpa*. In the northeast, near the water, the Bengalis and Assamese learned to emphasize fish and seafood. Gujaratis, Rajasthanis, and South Indian Hindus, all of whom tend to avoid meat, developed India's vegetarian cuisine.

Tea, a staple in India, is brewed with milk and sugar. In Buddhist areas you'll find yak-butter tea, made with milk and salt; the butter keeps your lips from cracking in the dry Himalayan air. South Indian filter coffee has a caramel tang, something like café au lait; elsewhere you'll find little but instant coffee. India produces excellent beer, and its Riviera wine is reasonably good. Luxury hotels also import Western spirits, and sell them at luxury prices. Sikkim produces good rum, brandies, and *paan* liqueur. *Chang,* a local brew made from fermented barley, is available in many mountain areas. Goa makes tasty sweet wines and *feni,* a potent liquor made from cashew nuts.

Performing Arts

India's folk dances derive from various sources, but Indian **classical dance** originates in the temple. The four main dance forms are Bharatanatyam in the south, particularly in Tamil Nadu; Kathakali in Kerala; Manipur in the northeast; and Kathak in the north.

Bharatanatyam is a dynamic, precise style in which the dancer wears anklets of bells to emphasize the rhythm. Many figures in South Indian temple sculptures strike Bharatanatyam dance poses. **Kathakali,** developed over the 16th and 17th centuries, was inspired by the heroic myths and legends of Hindu Vedas (sacred writings) and involves phenomenal body control, right down to synchronized movements of the eyeballs. Boys between the ages of 12 and 20 study this dance form for six years. Kathakali makeup is a particularly elaborate process, with characters classified into distinct types according to the colors of their makeup and costumes. **Manipur** dances revolve around episodes in the life of Vishnu. They are vigorous when performed by men, lyrical when performed by young women. The women's costumes are richly embroidered. **Kathak** is exciting and entertaining—the most secular of the classical dances. The footwork is fast, clever, expressive, and accentuated by bands of bells around the dancers' ankles. The great masters of each of these dance forms command great respect in India. They have studied for years to perfect their artistry, and their age becomes a factor only when they decide to put away their costumes.

Buddhist dances are as stylized as classical Hindu dance forms, except that the movements of the masked and costumed monks are more ritualized, usually working from a slow pace up to a whirl in which flowing skirts become a blur of color. The accompanying music, usually dominated by long horns and cymbals, adds an eerie counterpoint to the monks' deliberate footwork. The dances are usually enactments of important Buddhist legends, or are performed to ward off demons.

As with classical dance, the beginnings of **classical Indian music** can be traced to the Hindu Vedas. Over time, this music—an adjunct to worship—developed definite laws of theory and practice. It also evolved into two broadly divided forms, Carnatic in South India and Hindustani in the north. North Indian music uses a wide range of beautiful instruments such as the sitar and the flute; in the south, musical forms are stricter, with less improvisation. In both schools, the fundamental form is a **raga,** a song based on a 12-tone system unusual, at first, to the Western ear. At a concert of ragas or **bhajans** (Hindu devotional songs with lyrics), the audience will participate with comments or gestures, expressing enthusiasm for the singer's technical skill and artistic power.

The arrival of the Moghuls in the 12th century led to a new form of northern music incorporating the Persian **ghazal,** an Urdu rhyming couplet expressing love. In the ghazal, however, the object of devotion can be a woman or the divine or even the singer's home state. Part of the joy in hearing ghazals, at least for those who understand Urdu, comes from deciphering oblique references that give layers of meanings to a single line and are attributed to the skill of the poet and even the singer. Audiences at ghazal performance show appreciation by mirroring a hand motion of the musician or singer, or by praising a turn of phrase.

As with dancers, years of concentrated study lead to revered status for musicians. India's finest singers and instrumentalists are well over the age of 30 and frequently in their 60s.

Shopping
Each part of India specializes in different products. There are still plenty of villages where the majority of residents are weavers, painters, or sculptors, and similar artisan districts are clustered in the old bazaars of large cities.

India has the world's largest **rug** industry. Exotic silk and wool carpets are crafted in Kashmir and Uttaranchal. Tibetan refugees and the Sikkimese make superb carpets with Buddhist themes. Dhurries, in wool or cotton, have charming folk or tribal motifs; some of the finest dhurries come from Rajasthan and Madhya Pradesh.

Delhi, Rajasthan, and Karnataka have wonderful **silver** work, including old ethnic and tribal jewelry. (Buyer beware: The silver is not always pure.) **Gold** jewelry is a smart purchase, and in many cities (Bombay, Calcutta, Delhi, Jaipur, and Madras in particular) you'll find jewelers who can quickly design to order. The price per gram is determined by the world rate, but the cost for the workmanship is a bargain. **Precious and semiprecious stones,** beautifully cut and highly polished, are another great buy here—Jaipur has wonderful gems that you can buy separately or have fashioned into exquisite jewelry. Jaipur also sells intricately worked

enamelware, as does Madhya Pradesh. In Hyderabad, the center of India's pearl trade, **pearls** of every shape and hue are polished and sold according to sheen, smoothness, and roundness.

Intricate Moghul- and Rajput-style **miniature paintings** and cloth **batik** wall hangings are specialties of Rajasthan. Orissa is known for **dhokra** (animal and human figures in twisted brass wires), **pata chitra** (finely wrought temple paintings), and **tala patra** (palm-leaf art). Weavers throughout India work **textile designs** into cotton or silk, the latter sometimes threaded with real gold or silver. Beautiful brocades and crepe silk come from Varanasi; the finest heavy silks, many in brilliant jewel tones, are made in Kanchipuram, near Madras. Bangalore and Mysore are also important weaving centers. *Himru* (cotton and silk brocade) is woven in Aurangabad. *Jamdani* weaving, a cotton brocade with *zari* (silver) thread, comes from West Bengal. Orissa is known for *ikat,* a weave that creates a brush-stroke effect to color borders on silk or cotton. Gujarat and Rajasthan create marvelous tie-dye and embroidered fabrics. To scan a good selection of all these products, stop into one of the fixed-price Central Cottage Industries Emporiums in Bangalore, Bombay, Calcutta, Delhi, Hyderabad, or Madras.

Beautiful **brass and copper** work are sold everywhere, but Tamil Nadu has especially fine sculptures and temple ornaments. Tribal areas in Orissa and Madhya Pradesh specialize in **metal figurines.** Hyderabad and Aurangabad produce jet and silver **bidriware,** especially boxes and bangles. Sculptors chisel delightful **stone statues** in Orissa, Tamil Nadu, and Rajasthan. Artisans in Agra create exquisite **marble inlay** work, carrying on a Moghul tradition: jewels are sliced petal-thin and embedded in marble with such precision that the joints are imperceptible even with a magnifying glass.

Wherever people live in wooden dwellings, you find hand-crafted **teak, ebony, cedar, sandalwood,** or **walnut.** Rajasthan is known for objects covered with enchanting thematic paintings, from small boxes to furniture and doors. Artisans in Orissa and Andhra Pradesh create charming painted toys. *Lac* turnery is an Indian art form in which layers of color are added to wood and then polished; the best lac products—bangles, toys, boxes—come from Jaipur and Gujarat. Kashmir specializes in carved walnut items: boxes, tables, and gorgeous screens. Kerala and Karnataka are known for finely wrought carvings in sandalwood.

Wildlife Sanctuaries

India has 59 national parks and more than 250 sanctuaries, home to more than 350 different mammals and 1,200 birds. Many of these creatures are unique to the subcontinent, such as the white tiger, royal Bengal tiger, Asian lion, lion-tailed macaque, Andaman teal, great Indian bustard, and monal pheasant.

Before 1947 India did not protect its wildlife. By 1952, 13 species had been declared endangered, and today the list has multiplied to 70 species of mammals, 16 species of reptiles, and 36 species of birds. Tigers, the symbolic mascot of India, were killed so frequently that by 1970, only 1,500 remained. In 1972, the Indian government finally passed the Wildlife Act, which designates natural parks and sanctuaries and provides for the protection of wild animals, particularly endangered species. Three years later, Corbett National Park became India's first tiger reserve, part of Project Tiger—a large-scale enterprise co-sponsored by India's Department of Wildlife and the World Wildlife Fund to ban killing and set up 10 reserves. The total number of tigers has risen to over 4,000, but poachers may yet finish off this rare animal.

India is also attempting to re-cover a third of its land with forests—a daunting task that requires more than saplings. The rural poor must find viable fuel sources to replace wood, and a humane initiative is needed to control the movement of foraging livestock, including the sacrosanct cow.

Still, many of India's parks and sanctuaries are enchanting. If you have a safari in mind, remember that many of India's animals are elusive, moving in small packs at daybreak and twilight or at night. Count yourself lucky if you spot a tiger, an Asian lion, or a leopard. Come with the proper expectations and you *will* see many animals: numerous species of deer, wild boar, langur of all descriptions, and spectacular birds. Keep your camera and binoculars ready. Shooting, of course, is prohibited, but the hunter's loss is the photographer's gain. Wear neutral clothes to better blend into the forest. If you want to stay overnight *inside* a sanctuary, arrange to arrive before it closes at sunset.

GREAT ITINERARIES

Classic India

This tour is a broader version of the well-trod Golden Triangle, which concentrates on **Delhi, Jaipur, and Agra.** For a more comprehensive and exciting experience, start in **Bombay** and include **Khajuraho** and **Varanasi.** You can fly any or all of these legs, but touring with a hired car and driver gives you a better look at the countryside and allows for impromptu stops along the way.

DURATION➤ 17 days

TRANSPORTATION➤ Fly to Delhi, drive from Delhi to Khajuraho, fly to Varanasi, and fly back to Delhi.

THE ROUTE➤ **Two days: Bombay.** Dive into this heady metropolis for a crash course in all things Indian. Explore the historic Fort district, navigate some bazaars, and stroll around lovely Malabar Hill, saving time to wander from Chowpatty Beach down Marine Drive along the Arabian Sea.

Three days: Delhi to Jaipur. Fly to Delhi. After touring Delhi, drive from Delhi to Rajasthan's Neemrana Fort Palace, just off the main highway between Delhi and Jaipur. Set high on a bluff, this restored fort has amazing views and invites complete relaxation or scenic afternoon walks. The next day, drive about three hours to Jaipur, where you can stay at a converted palace or Heritage Hotel while you explore Jaipur's unforgettable bazaars and monuments.

Three days: Fatehpur Sikri and Agra. En route from Jaipur to Agra, tour the splendid buildings of the ancient and deserted Moghul capital Fatehpur Sikri. In Agra you'll encounter the world-famous Taj

Mahal and the much less famous but almost equally beautiful tomb of Itmad-ud-Daulah.

Two days: Gwalior and Orchha. Drive from Agra to Gwalior to see its spectacular pre-Moghul Hindu fort and palace built into a high escarpment. An optional excursion brings you to Orchha, another seat of Hindu rajas that mixes palaces, temples, and monuments on a small, picturesque river.

Two days: Khajuraho. Drive on to Khajuraho and spend two days absorbing the exuberantly carved 10th- and 11th-century temples and the surrounding villages, which cling strongly to an agrarian lifestyle.

Two days: Varanasi. Fly from Khajuraho to Varanasi. Take a peaceful morning cruise on the Ganges River to witness Hindu rituals on the steps of the sacred waters. Wander among Varanasi's temples and silk or carpet emporiums and drive out to nearby Sarnath, imbued with Buddhist significance.

Three days: Delhi. Fly to Delhi to explore the old and new capitals. Old Delhi has Moghul remnants, such as the Red Fort, Jama Masjid, and Chandni Chowk, now a hodgepodge market; New Delhi has the Moghul Humayun's tomb and also the seat of the former British Raj and the lovely Lodi Gardens. Have a look at the Crafts Museum and save time for last-minute shopping.

Southern Idyll

Experience the tropical south beginning in **Tamil Nadu** with ancient towns and massive temples. Relax at seaside resorts and on small boats as you cruise through the lush backwaters of **Kerala.** Search for wildlife at Kerala's excellent **Lake Periyar Wildlife Sanctuary.** Add one more cultural dimension—say, a Kathakali dance performance—and, as a personal indulgence, a soothing Ayurvedic massage to chase away any lingering stress.

DURATION➤ 13–14 days

TRANSPORTATION➤ Hire a car and driver for excursions from Madras, then fly from Madras to Madurai. Hire another car and driver for the trip west to Lake Periyar in Thekkady; continue to Cochin and then pause for a slow cruise on the backwaters near Alleppey. Drive on to Ko-

valam and wind up at Trivandrum, where you can catch flights to other major cities.

THE ROUTE➤ **Four days: Madras and Mamallapuram.** Spend two days in Madras, originally developed by the Portuguese and British but now decidedly South Indian, with bazaars, bustling Hindu temples, and a thriving film industry. Take a leisurely two-day excursion to Mamallapuram via Kanchipuram, a silk-weaving center and the site of more than 200 temples. At Mamallapuram, on the Bay of Bengal, see the exquisite cave sculptures and shore temple left behind by the Pallava dynasty (4th–8th centuries). Catch some sun and surf at a relaxing resort, and return to Madras.

Two days: Madurai. Fly from Madras to Madurai and spend two days exploring the city and its astonishing Meenakshi Temple, whose marvelous architecture includes soaring *gopurams* (entrance towers) and prominent displays of ritual. Comb through the bazaars surrounding the temple complex.

Two days: Lake Periyar Wildlife Sanctuary. Drive west from Madurai across the Western Ghats to Kerala's Lake Periyar, where boat rides provide the leisurely means for a safari: wild elephants and other animals roam the banks of this lovely preserve.

Two days: Cochin. Proceed northwest by car to Cochin, and take two days to see this ancient port city, with its 16th-century synagogue, curio shops, and Portuguese fort. At night, try to attend a Kathakali dance performance, where you can see how the dancers apply their complicated makeup before they mesmerize you with their hard-honed talent.

One or two days: Backwater Cruise. Drive to Alleppey early in the morning and cruise through some of Kerala's backwaters, past palm trees, shaded villages, and bright-green paddy fields. If you get hooked, take an overnight houseboat cruise. Back in the car, repair to a special beach resort just south of Kovalam.

Two days: Kovalam. Spend two nights at the Surya Samudra Beach Garden, tucked away in a cove on the Arabian Sea. Swim, have an Ayurvedic massage, and loll about; you can even study yoga and meditation here. Fly out from nearby Trivandrum.

FODOR'S CHOICE

No two people agree on what makes a perfect vacation, but it's nice to know what others have experienced. For more details on each suggestion, see the appropriate regional chapter.

Ancient Wonders

Cave temples, Ajanta and Ellora. Dating back more than 2,000 years, these monolithic temples rank among the wonders of the ancient world. Monks and artisans carved them out of solid rock, decorating some with lavish frescoes and profusely carved statues.

Hampi, Karnataka. This ruined city was the center of the largest Hindu empire in South India prior to the 16th century. A jumble of vast stone temples, elephant stables, barracks, and palaces, it's an awesome spectacle.

Qutab Minar, Delhi. This 234-ft-high tower with 376 steps is known as the seventh wonder of Hindustan. At its foot is the Quwwat-ul-Islam Masjid, the first Muslim mosque in India. Most intriguing is the mosque's 24-ft-high, 5th-century iron pillar, inscribed with six lines of Sanskrit—legend has it if you stand with your back to the pillar and can reach around and touch your fingers, your wish will come true.

Sun Temple, Konark. The Sun Temple was built in the form of the sun god Surya's chariot, its 24 giant wheels pulled by seven horses. Every inch is carved with some of the most fantastic sculptures in India: mythical animals, erotic couplings, and whimsical scenes from daily life.

Taj Mahal, Agra. Resplendent in soft white marble and resonant with a bittersweet love story, the Taj lives up to its reputation. Both the photogenic exterior and the quiet, exquisitely decorated interior leave a lingering sense of peace and wonder.

Erotic Temples, Khajuraho. Hinduism under the Chandelas drew no strict boundary between sacred and profane. Khajuraho's 9th- to 12th-century temples have some of the best sculptures in India: sinuous, twisting forms of virile men and voluptuous women, throbbing with life, tension, and conflict.

Unforgettable Scenes

Backwaters, Kerala. To see life in Kerala at a Keralite pace, float slowly through its inland waterways. Gliding past graceful coconut palms and blindingly green paddy fields, you'll see tile-roof houses with canoes moored outside, tiny waterfront churches, and people washing themselves and their clothes in the river.

Chowpatty Beach and Marine Drive, Bombay. Bombay's setting is part of what makes it so intoxicating. Chowpatty Beach is a taste of the Bombay carnival, with vendors, food stalls, and rides. Walk east along perfectly curved Marine Drive for a lingering encounter with the incredible geography and with locals of every stripe.

Ganges River at dawn, Varanasi. The rising sun casts a dark-gold glow on the city devout Hindus hold most dear. Pilgrims and devotees perform ablutions on the riverbank, and temples begin to get crowded. Go down to the main Dashashvamedh Ghat at sunrise or climb to the roof of the Alamgir Mosque for a sweeping view of the city along the river's languid curve.

Mahabalipuram, Tamil Nadu. Between the beach and the sacred *rathas,* or monolithic rock temples, is the old port city of Mahabalipuram. Besides these exemplary designs of South Indian temple architecture, you'll see giant sculptures carved on boulders, temples on the beach, and cave temples cut into the hills.

Meenakshi Temple, Madurai. Both people and elephants crowd the sanctuaries of this temple complex, and the air is thick with incense and the sound of chanting. Glimpse the elaborate carvings in the Hall of the Thousand Pillars and take in the atmosphere of passionate worship.

North Calcutta. Wander the charming, European-tinged streets of Calcutta's oldest section for an immersion in the city's mixture of Western, Bengali, and Muslim elements, from mansions to bookstalls to pungent bazaars.

Pushkar, Rajasthan. With one of the few temples in the world dedicated to Lord Brahma, creator of the universe, Pushkar is one of Hinduism's holiest sites. Pushkar has more than 500 temples. During auspicious pilgrimage times, tens of thousands throng the holy ghats around Pushkar Lake to offer prayers. Pushkar is also uniquely famous for hosting an annual camel fair, during which the town becomes a virtual carnival—there are camel races, camels prancing around caparisoned in finery, and traders haggling over camel purchases.

Dining

San Gimignano, Delhi. Chef Eraldo Colazzo prepares sensuous, sculpted Northern Italian food in this tranquil, intimate restaurant in the Imperial Hotel. Choose from 18 varieties of cheese and a strong selection of Italian wines. The three-course menu includes veg or non-veg dishes, and changes several times weekly. $$$$

Fort Cochin, Cochin. Bamboo and traditional furnishings give this outdoor restaurant the feel of a Keralite cottage. The day's catch is wheeled before you in a wooden cart, and your choice is cooked specially for you—simply grilled or exquisitely curried. $$$

Vishalla, Ahmedabad. Snake charmers, folk musicians, and flickering lantern shadows cast an aura of magic at this outdoor restaurant, a re-created Gujarati village where you sit on straw mats and feast on superb local fare served on banana leaves. $$$

Raintree, Madras. The greenery and white verandahs across from the Raintree evoke an earlier era—of quiet colonial leisure that is increasingly hard to find in Madras. Add to that an expertly prepared meal of fiery, pepper-intense Chettinad food, and nightly dance or music, and you'll find yourself enthralled. $$$

Khyber, Bombay. A maze of rooms on three floors, Khyber is designed in a cozy Mughul style and decorated with murals by local artists. The kitchen serves pungent, delectable Muhglai and tandoori food that you won't forget in a hurry. $–$$

Flury's Tea Room, Calcutta. One of Calcutta's colonial legacies, Flury's is an institution, and the only tea room in Calcutta. Smack on Park Street, the geographical heart of Calcutta's culinary heritage, it has an old-world charm. Crack your crossword in peace here while you munch on sandwiches or delicious pastries. $

Park Baluchi, Delhi. North Indian barbecue inspires new superlatives at this wooded restaurant in the village of Hauz Khas. Incredibly delicate kebabs are followed by traditional and creative Baluchi dishes. $

Lodging

Amarvilas, Agra. Expect luxury treatment at this remarkable new Oberoi boutique resort that overlooks the Taj Mahal. Besides unbeatable views, expect plush treatment, lavish rooms with private terraces, and an Ayurvedic spa. The architecture reflects the classical Mughal style, with a stunning array of fountains and pavilions. $$$$

Ananda in the Himalayas, Rishikesh. A breathtaking ascent through a forest deposits you into this maharaja's palace turned spa resort. Indulge an Ayurvedic oil massage, a trek to nearby temples, or a river rafting trip. The lazy can opt for a spin in the jacuzzi or lounge in the 100-year-old library. $$$$

Lake Palace, Udaipur. This 250-year-old palace floats like a vision of white marble in the middle of Lake Pichola, oozing history and romance. The suites are colorfully opulent, and most rooms have lake views. $$$$

Surya Samudra Beach Garden, Kovalam, Kerala. This rambling, secluded resort overlooks the Arabian Sea and offers a full range of Ayurvedic treatments. Most rooms are in stunningly restored wooden homes, each with a carved facade and spacious open-air bathroom. $$$$

Taj Mahal, Bombay. India's most famous hotel, this Victorian Gothic extravaganza looks past the Gateway of India to the Arabian Sea. Built in 1903, its stunning brownstone exterior, with rows of jutting white balconies, has made it a Bombay landmark in its own right. $$$$

Ladakh Sarai, Ladakh. This green resort outside Leh offers stays in yurts and pretty views of the Indus River and the whitewashed Stok Palace. The rooms are charming but very simple, and the utter tranquillity of the Sarai is alluring. $$$–$$$$

Kabini River Lodge, Nagarhole National Park, Karnataka. A comfortable lodge located in the heart of one of India's cool, mysterious wildlife sanctuaries, Kabini was once a royal hunting lodge and the park was the Maharaja of Mysore's personal hunting grounds. $$$

Neemrana Fort Palace, near Shekhavati. Rooms in this 15th-century fort are furnished with antiques and decorated with Rajput handicrafts. Wooden latticework screens, cusped arches, niches, and gleaming pillars abound. Forget phones and TVs—relax and watch peacocks and parrots from the balconies and courtyards. *$$$*

Taj Hari Mahal, Jodhpur. The "Blue city of Jodhpur," famous for the color of its houses and crowned by a massive fort, rises out of the Thar Desert. In it resides the Taj Hari Mahal, a grand, soothing respite with an elegant, amber-color lobby, a gigantic pool, and landscaped gardens. Most unusual is the elaborate chess dance, in which women in traditional Rajasthani dress swirl across a life-size chess board. *$$$*

Houseboats in Kerala. Floating down Kerala's backwaters on one of its large houseboats is a sinful indulgence. These *ketuvellams*, boats fashioned out of cane and the wood of the jackfruit tree, are beautifully crafted and offer a completely unique form of accommodation. Between 200 and 250 houseboats operate in Kerala.

2 THE HIMALAYAS

Like the teeth of a giant ripsaw, the
snowcapped Himalayas cut a border
between India and China, passing through
four Indian states: Jammu and Kashmir,
Himachal Pradesh, Uttaranchal, and Sikkim.
They strike awe like no other mountain
range in the world. A few hours north of
Delhi you can escape the heat of the plains
in a Raj-era hill station, hike through terraced
fields and alpine passes on exhilarating
treks, or absorb religious teachings in a
Hindu temple or Buddhist monastery.

By Michael
Bollom, Andy
McCord,
Kathleen Cox,
Gaye Facer,
and David
Quegg

T HE REGIONS OF THE INDIAN HIMALAYAS are united only by their proximity to the same mountain range. Culturally, and even physically, they're quite different. The people of Sikkim look more East Asian and practice Tibetan Buddhism, while Kumaonis from Uttaranchal are Hindus with distinctly Aryan features and darker skin. The people of Leh speak Tibetan and eat *momos* (stuffed dumplings), while just several hundred miles away Kashmiris converse in Urdu over meals of kebabs. Geographically, the moonscapes of Ladakh stand in sharp contrast to the lush tea gardens of the Kangra Valley, and Manali's pine forests are a world apart from the rhododendron jungles around Gangtok. Because transportation between these regions is limited, few travelers have the time and energy to experience more than one or two, so choose your destination carefully.

If you're headed for the mountains of Himachal Pradesh, you may find Amritsar a worthwhile cultural detour. The largest city in the affluent, predominantly Sikh state of Punjab, Amritsar is the holiest city to the Sikh religion, its massive Golden Temple an inspiring destination in its own right. History buffs may also want to visit the site of the infamous Amritsar Massacre, a turning point in the fight for Indian Independence. Farther east—on the other side of Nepal—if you're Sikkim-bound, or just want a pastoral break from Calcutta, the historic hill station of Darjeeling invites exploration and easy alpine walks.

Whatever your interest, contact the recommended tour operators for details. Most will design a special trip just for you, whatever your budget or age. Try to make arrangements at least two months in advance. If you're planning a trek, contact a tour operator who is familiar with the specific area you have in mind. Play it safe: don't embark on any route without a guide. Travelers in high-altitude areas should heed all warnings about sun exposure and high-altitude sickness: even if you'll be ensconced in a jeep, bring powerful UVA/UVB sunblock, a widebrim hat, and sunglasses that block ultraviolet rays. Allow three days for full acclimatization. For travel to remote areas, bring a means of water purification, a quart-size canteen, and energy-producing snacks.

Foreigners must obtain an Inner Line Permit and travel with at least three other foreigners *and* a government-recognized tour operator to visit the Spiti Valley in Himachal Pradesh and the Khaltse (Drokhpa area), Nubra, and Nyoma subdivisions in Ladakh. Trekking in Sikkim requires a Restricted-Area Permit. Most tour operators can help you secure permits.

Numbers in the margin correspond to points of interest on the Northwest Indian Himalayas and Sikkim maps.

AMRITSAR

❶ Because of its proximity to the Pakistani border—Lahore is only 64 km (40 mi) away—Amritsar has not seen the development, and attendant sprawl, of other North Indian towns. The city is an important commercial hub: much of the aromatic Basmati rice that's now an international staple is exported by Amritsar dealers, and dried fruits and woolens from hill regions are handled by wholesalers here. The robust rural culture of Punjab's farmlands permeates Amritsar, with tractors plying the city roads and peasants making their way through the market centers and the famous Sikh temple.

The Golden Temple of the Sikhs is reason enough to come to Amritsar, and even if you think you've had enough of India's overwhelming religious pageantry you should not miss it. It resembles more a Moghul palace than a typical Indian temple, and its layout and ambience are a living lesson in the teachings of the Sikh religion, a syncretic movement combining Hinduism's *bhakti* (devotion to a personalized god) with Islam's monotheism and egalitarianism. Sikhism was founded by Guru Nanak around the turn of the 16th century, and developed under the gurus who succeeded him into a distinct new religion. Amritsar ("Pool of Nectar" in Punjabi and Sanskrit) takes its name from an ancient sacred pool that Nanak is said to have preferred for his meditation and teaching. The site was granted to the fourth guru, Ramdas, in 1577 by the great Moghul emperor Akbar, and gradually developed as a pilgrimage center. As the 1500s came to a close, songs by the Sikh gurus and selections from Hindu and Muslim poet-saints were canonized as the *Adi Granth* ("First Book") by the fifth guru, Arjan, at the same time as the great *gurdwara* (temple; "door to the guru") was being constructed here. In succeeding years, the temple and the sacred book together gained increasing importance in the Sikh faith. In 1699 the 10th guru, Gobind Singh, further consolidated the faith, establishing a distinctive physical appearance for his followers—most notably long hair kept in a turban for men, and braids for women. Singh marked this turning point by leading his followers to Amritsar from the Sikh gurdwara at Anandpur Sahib in the Punjab Hills. Upon his death in 1708, Singh's closest disciples announced his instruction that leadership of the Sikhs would henceforth be centered on the teachings of the sacred book (now called the *Guru Granth Sahib*) rather than a human guru. To this day, the life of the Golden Temple, as in all gurdwaras, revolves around the *Guru Granth Sahib,* beginning before dawn, when the book is taken out of a building called the Akal Takht and carried processionally across the huge, white marble compound—across a causeway on a square artificial pond—to Harmandir Sahib, the central temple whose gilded copper plating gives the complex its most commonly recognized name. The temple's day ends late in the evening, when the book is brought back to its resting place.

During the time of the gurus, the Sikhs' development as a separate community often brought them into conflict with other forces in Moghul India. In 1761, as the Moghul empire declined, the temple was sacked by the Afghan raider Ahmad Shah Durrani. (It was rebuilt three years later.) In 1802 the temple was covered in gilt copper by Maharaja Ranjit Singh (1780–1839), whose rule extended as far as Kabul and Kashmir and marked the height of Sikh power. In 1984, the Indian Army's "Operation Bluestar" brought tanks into the complex in a disastrous four-day firefight with heavily armed Sikh separatists who had virtually taken over the complex. India's Prime Minister Indira Gandhi was assassinated about five months later by two of her Sikh bodyguards, in what was widely believed to be retribution for the Army attack on the temple. Amazingly, the temple now shows few signs of this tragic event, or of the decade of separatist violence and state repression that plagued Punjab afterwards. The grievances of the Sikh community have perhaps not all been resolved, but the horrible tenor of the dispute is a thing of the past, and Amritsar and Punjab are generally safe places to travel. Harmandir Sahib was not badly damaged in 1984, and the outlying buildings that were harmed have been restored. All day long, while a select group of singers, or *ragis,* broadcast hymns from the *Guru Granth Sahib* throughout the complex, pilgrims from rustic Punjabi towns and villages—India's hugely productive breadbasket—make their way around it, some performing *seva* (voluntary service) by cleaning the marble or completing other tasks. These worshipers are very welcoming to strangers, proud to show off the most sacred place in the Sikh religion. The dignity that pilgrims invest in the site, and the grandeur of its design, transcend the turmoil of its past.

Most hotels and the train station are near the British-era cantonment, and the **Golden Temple** is about a 15-minute ride away. You approach the temple through the Hall Bazaar, which leads to the **clocktower** gate. To symbolize the religion's egalitarian welcome to all castes, all Sikh gurdwaras have four entrances, but this is the main one. To the left of the stairway leading into the complex is a counter where visitors leave their shoes (many of the attendants here are volunteers, and their handling of others' shoes is another illustration of the Sikh doctrine of caste equality). If you smoke, leave all tobacco products behind, as they're forbidden here. Pilgrims wash their feet at a spigot by the gate before entering the temple complex. Sikhs will already have their heads covered, with turbans for males and the *chunni* scarves worn by women; if you haven't brought a head covering, make use of the bin of colorful scarves by the stairs.

From the top of the gateway stairs, you look across a wide pool of water—known as the **sarovar,** or "sea"—at the golden roof of Harmandir Sahib. Go down the steps on the other side and you'll reach the white marble 24-ft wide walkway, known as the **parikrama** (circumambulatory path), that surrounds the pool. Each side of the pool is 510 ft long, and pilgrims normally make a complete circuit before they approach the Harmandir Sahib. Doing so gives a good sense of the scale of the place, as well as providing a series of angles from which to gaze at the Golden Temple. (You can take pictures from a distance, but put your camera away before you leave the causeway for the central sanctum.) Various points around the parikrama are considered auspicious places to bathe; the bathing steps along the east length of the walkway are said to mark a spot that equals the purifying power of Hinduism's 68 most holy *tirthas* (holy places). Just behind this is the entrance to a small garden that adjoins an assembly hall on the right and two large pilgrims' hostels to the rear. On the left, under two tall minarets that have yet to be fully restored from the damage they suffered in the 1980s, during the Operation Bluestar firefight, is the **Guru Ram Das Langar**—named after the fourth Sikh guru, this is the temple's communal dining hall. All gurdwaras have such a *langar* (the name of the place as well as the free meal served here), as eating together and serving a meal to others is perhaps the most fondly practiced of all Sikh rituals. Don't hesitate to join in; meals are served daily from 11 to 3 and 7 to 11, and the food (usually a few thick *chapatis* and some *dal*) is simple and robust. In another kitchen at the southwest corner of the parikrama, pilgrims make a donation in return for a packet of *halvah,* made from cream of wheat, which is then taken to Harmandir Sahib and presented as an offering, with a portion given back to worshipers as *prasad* (which some translate as the "edible form of God's grace").

Halfway across the east side of the parikrama, the causeway out to Harmandir Sahib is on your right, and to the left is the five-story **Akal Takht,** topped by a gilt dome. This building, whose name means "Timeless Throne," represents Sikh temporal authority—day-to-day administration—as opposed to the spiritual authority of Harmandir Sahib. It was here that much of the heavy fire that met the Indian Army during Operation Bluestar originated; the first building was largely destroyed during the fighting, but has now been fully restored.

To reach **Harmandir Sahib** you go under an archway known as the **Darshani Deorhi** ("Gateway of Vision") and cross a 204-ft long causeway, which has brass guide rails to separate arriving pilgrims from departing ones, as well as a central passageway for temple functionaries. Take the left passageway. (Note that sometimes, particularly at dusk, pilgrims arrive in great numbers for ceremonies. Access to the Harmandir Sahib is controlled at such times and pilgrims can back up the causeway, making a visit to the sanctum a lengthy undertaking.) Pilgrims typically bow down at the doorway after traversing the causeway, then circumambulate the central temple around a small exterior parikrama. Some stop to bathe on the east side. The exterior walls are decorated in beautiful *pietra dura* (marble inlaid with semiprecious stones) said to have been brought by Maharaja Ranjit Singh from Moghul monuments in Lahore.

On the temple's ground level, the *Guru Granth Sahib* sits on a special throne. Attendants wave whisks over it constantly to keep flies away, and a *granthi* (lay specialist in recitation) sits reciting the text with harmonium players and other musicians off to one side. Feel free to enter the temple and listen to the recitation of the holy book, or witness the continuous recitation (*akhand path*) of the second and third stories; just remember to keep your head covered and refrain from taking pictures. As you go back through the Darshani Deorhi (Gateway of Vision), a temple priest or volunteer will usually be stationed under a small tree handing out servings of the halvah that previous pilgrims have offered to the temple. The ritual of receiving prasad is one that Sikhs share with Hindus. Just around the northwest corner of the parikrama stands an old jujube tree that is said to have healing powers.

The **Central Sikh Museum,** upstairs in the clocktower entrance, contains graphic paintings depicting the tumultuous history of the Sikh gurus and their followers. Included are scenes from the British period and Operation Bluestar. ⊙ *Daily, usually 5 AM–10 PM.* ▧ *Free.*

Outside the temple's clock-tower entrance, about 500 yards north, a small plaque and narrow gateway mark the entrance to **Jallianwala Bagh.** Here, on April 13, 1919, occurred one of the defining moments in India's struggle for independence. The day was Baisakhi, celebrated by Sikhs as both the first day of the new year and the day that Guru Gobind Singh consolidated the faith under the leadership of the Khalsa ("God's own"; a fraternity of the pious) in 1699. The city was under curfew after reported attacks on some British residents, yet some 20,000 people had gathered here to protest the arrest of Indian nationalist leaders under the Rowlatt Act, a British legislation that allowed for detention without trial. Seeing this crowd, British Brigadier General Reginald E. H. Dyer positioned his troops just inside the narrow entrance to the small garden (which is surrounded on all sides by residential buildings) and ordered them to open fire. Some 1,200 people were wounded, and several hundred died. This massacre, which is chillingly reenacted in Richard Attenborough's film *Gandhi,* caused widespread outrage and contributed to the launch of Mahatma Gandhi's noncooperation movement. The British attempted to suppress news of the incident, and when an inquiry was finally held, such comments as "It was no longer a question of merely dispersing the crowd, but one of producing a sufficient moral effect" (Dyer) did nothing to assuage a worldwide response. Nobel Laureate poet Rabindranath Tagore renounced his English knighthood, and even Winston Churchill, himself no enemy of the empire, raised an uproar in Parliament (though a majority in the House of Lords approved of Dyer's actions). Jallianwala Bagh was subsequently purchased by Indian nationalists to prevent its being turned into a covered market, and it remains one of the most moving monuments to India's 20th-century history. Queen Elizabeth visited in 1997, after much negotiation over whether or not she should make a formal apology (she didn't, but she and Prince Philip removed their shoes before entering the grounds). Today the garden is planted with a few rosebushes, and the bullet holes from the British fusillade remain. The well, into which some dove in a vain attempt to save themselves, is on the north side. A modern memorial occupies the east end, and a small display to the left as you enter the garden features contemporary newspaper accounts of the incident. ☉ *Dawn to dusk.* ☜ *Free.*

Other sights in Amritsar include the 16th-century **Durgiana Temple** (opposite Gole Bagh, south of the train station), a Hindu shrine to the goddess Durga which in its design replicates its more famous Sikh neighbor. The **Ram Bagh** gardens, northeast of the train station (enter on Mall Rd.), date from the period of Maharaja Ranjit Singh (1780–1839). At the center of the garden, the **Punjab Government Museum** displays weapons and portraits from the maharaja's era in a period building; it's open Tuesday through Sunday 10–7.

Dining and Lodging

$$ ✕ **Bharawan Dhaba.** Amritsar is famous for its cheap *dhabas*, restaurants where the Punjabi love of good country cooking is emphasized over decor. Try this one or Surjit's Chicken House on Lawrence Road. River fish are a special attraction, as is chicken, cooked dry in a tandoor oven or with a spicy sauce. In winter, ask for *sarson ka saag*—mustard greens stewed in ginger with a dollop of *ghee* (clarified butter) and served on *makhai ki roti* (cornmeal chapatis). ⊠ *Opposite Town Hall on the way to the Golden Temple. No credit cards.*

$$–$$$ ☷ **Mohan International.** Though several new ones are going up in Amritsar, this remains the city's best-run modern hotel. The rooms are spacious, clean, and air-conditioned, and the restaurant is a popular place for Amritsar families to enjoy a fancy night out. ⊠ *Albert Rd., 143001 Punjab,* ☎ *183/227801–809,* ℻ *183/226520. 76 rooms. Restaurant, coffee shop, bar, pool, laundry service, travel services. AE, DC, MC, V.*

$–$$ ☷ **Bhandari's Guesthouse.** This sprawling set of bungalows in the
★   cantonment harkens back to an earlier era of travel in India. If you like "character" in your lodgings this is definitely the place to stay. The rooms, some of which have wall air-conditioners, are huge and well maintained, with high ceilings and an abundance of polished wood furnishings. Each room opens onto a well-maintained lawn. Mildly spiced Anglo-Indian meals are served in your room or in a mess area known as the "Commando Bridge" (Mrs. Bhandari, the aged proprietor, is an Indian Army widow). ⊠ *10 Cantonment Rd., 143001 Punjab,* ☎ *183/228509 or 183/225714,* ℻ *183/222390. 16 rooms. Restaurant, travel services. No credit cards.*

CHANDIGARH

❷ A starkly modernist contrast for an urban India largely constructed gradually, around its ancient monuments, Chandigarh was built in the 1950s from a plan designed by the French architect Le Corbusier. The capital of two bordering states, Haryana and Punjab, it's a refreshing stop-over on the long day's drive from Delhi to Shimla or other Himachal Pradesh destinations. It has spacious avenues and plenty of green space and bright bougainvillea, but its neglected areas, replete with barbed wire and garbage, make Corbusier's trademark concrete buildings seem less attractive.

It's easy to get around, as Chandigarh is organized on a grid; with a driver you can see the main sights in a day. Visit the innovative **Rock Garden,** built by Nek Chand, an Indian artist who, despite all his acclaim, still refers to himself as "an untutored former road inspector." This 6-acre fantasy is a maze of waterfalls and walkways through sculptures made from oddly shaped stones from the Shivalik foothills, industrial waste, and discarded materials collected by the artist on his bicycle. There's also an open-air pavilion and a theater with giant swings. The artist is often on-site and available to meet visitors—ask at the main reception area. The modernist **Art and Picture Gallery** in Sector 10 is worth a look—it has an outdoor sculpture gallery (open 10–4:30; closed Monday and holidays). Le Corbusier's **Capitol Complex** in Sector One (which includes **The High Court, Legislative Assembly, Secretariat,** and **Open-Hand Monument**) is the highlight of his stamp on the city, but its current-day use as the hub of two bureaucratic state administrations means that gaining entry— especially to the Secretariat— is not always straightforward. Tours are meant to run from the main reception every 30 minutes weekdays and sometimes on Saturday. Get your travel agent to arrange an entry permit in advance or get one from the Secretary of Tourism (☎ 172/704614) in Sector 17 near the bus station. Leave time to traverse extensive security checks by armed guards if you want to see the panoramic view from the Secretariat rooftop. The 2 km (1 mi) walk around the well-kept, man-made **Sukhna Lake** is pleasant in the early evening, when all of Chandigarh comes out to stroll; during the day you can rent paddle-boats.

In Pinjore, 20 km (12 mi) northeast of Chandigarh, the 17th-century Moghul-style **Yadvindra Gardens** are laid out on a gentle slope, with seven terraces of pools and fountains.

Lodging

$$$ 🏨 **Hotel Mount View.** This former Oberoi hotel transcends many of its newfound limitations as a government-run hotel, and is the solid favorite of business travelers to the area. Ask for a room in the newly renovated wing. Rooms overlooking the central area can get noisy until very late. The hotel is set against the backdrop of the Shivalik Hills, and encircles a manicured lawn. It's within easy walking distance to the Rose Garden park and Art Gallery. The hotel's delightful Chinese restaurant serves huge portions laced with fresh garlic and ginger. You can get an Indian breakfast—*sambar, idli,* and roti—and/or a Continental breakfast in the 24-hour coffee shop. Portions are generous. ✉ *Sector 10, 160011,* ☎ *172/74054,* 🖷 *172/742220. 156 rooms. Restaurant, bar, pool, business services. MC, V.*

$$ 🏨 **Shivalikview.** If you have stopped in Chandigarh because you are a modernist at heart, you'll like this place. The manager is friendly and helpful, but the hospitality is otherwise less than exemplary. Some of the (good-sized) rooms are slightly musty and err on the nylon-bedspread side of modernism—but the views of the mountains are the best in town, and the public areas are spacious, and have high ceilings, broad, open staircases, and big picture windows on every floor. The café serves a range of delicious South Indian snacks; the cocktail bar, Indian restaurant (specializing in Mughlai food) and rooftop Chinese restaurant are popular, lively, and good values. Rates include breakfast. ✉ *Sector 17E, 160017,* ☎ *172/703521,* 🖷 *172/701094. 104 rooms, 4 suites. 2 restaurants, laundry service, business services, travel services. AE, MC, V.*

Northwest Indian Himalayas

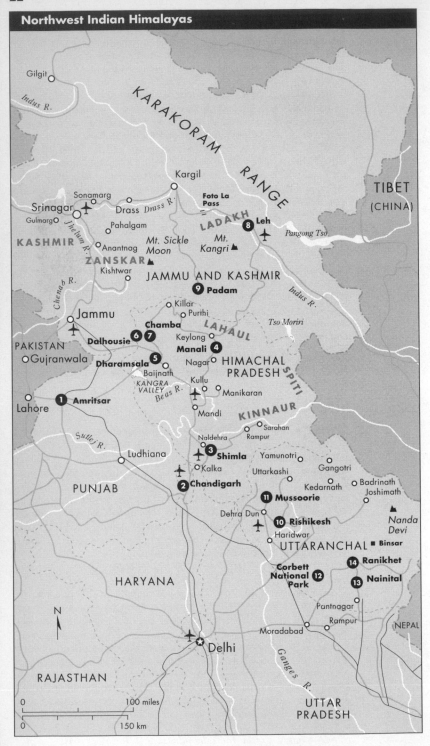

Gilgit

Indus R.

KARAKORAM RANGE

Kargil

TIBET (CHINA)

Srinagar

Sonamarg

Drass

Drass R.

Foto La Pass

LADAKH

8 Leh

Pangong Tso

Gulmarg

Jhelum R.

Pahalgam

KASHMIR

Anantnag

Mt. Sickle Moon

Mt. Kangri

Kishtwar

ZANSKAR

JAMMU AND KASHMIR

9 Padam

Chenab R.

Indus R.

Tso Moriri

Jammu

Killar

Purthi

6 **7** Chamba

Keylong

LAHAUL

PAKISTAN

Dalhousie

4 Manali

Gujranwala

5 Dharamsala

Nagar

HIMACHAL PRADESH

SPITI

Baijnath

KANGRA VALLEY

Kullu

Manikaran

Beas R.

Lahore

1 Amritsar

Mandi

KINNAUR

Sutlej R.

Naldehra

Sarahan

Rampur

Ludhiana

3 Shimla

Yamunotri

Kalka

Uttarkashi

Gangotri

PUNJAB

2 Chandigarh

Kedarnath

Badrinath

Joshimath

11 Mussoorie

Dehra Dun

Nanda Devi

10 Rishikesh

Haridwar

UTTARANCHAL

Binsar

14 Ranikhet

HARYANA

Corbett National Park

12

13 Nainital

Pantnagar

Rampur

NEPAL

N

Moradabad

Delhi

Ganges R.

RAJASTHAN

UTTAR PRADESH

0   100 miles

0   150 km

HIMACHAL PRADESH

The northwestern state of Himachal Pradesh spans five Himalayan mountain ranges (the Siwalik, Dhauladhar, Pir Panjal, Great Himalayas, and Zanskar) and is threaded with rivers and dotted with lakes. Except for the capital, Shimla, and the overpopulated destinations of Dharamsala in the district of Kangra, and Manali in the district of Kullu, Himachal is a state of villages. It's known as the Land of the Gods because it contains thousands of Hindu and Buddhist temples and monasteries.

Various cultures inhabit this alpine region, including two distinct semi-nomadic tribes, the Gaddi and Gujjar, who still follow many of their ancient traditions. The Gaddi, who travel with sheep, goats, and cattle, are Hindus; they believe in evil spirits that are appeased by animal sacrifices and animist rituals. Gaddi men wear a *chola* (a white thigh-length woolen coat) over *sutthan* (tight woolen trousers), held in place by a *dora* (a black rope of sheep's wool) coiled around the waist. Women wear a *luanchari* (a long, colorful dress) with a woven dora tied around the waist and lots of jewelry, both for good luck and to indicate wealth.

The Muslim Gujjar travel with buffalo and make their living by selling fresh milk and ghee. Normally bearded, the men wear turbans and long robes. Women wear the traditional Indian Muslim *salwar kameez,* a long tunic over loose pants tapered at the ankle. Often somber in color, this outfit is accentuated by paisley scarves and chunky silver necklaces, bracelets, and dangling earrings.

The peak tourist season in Himachal Pradesh runs from May though September. In April and November, the days can be sunny enough for short sleeves; "shoulder-season" hotel prices approximate winter rates, half of what they escalate to in summer. June and September are dry and warm; July and August have monsoon rains. In winter, temperatures hover above freezing. Some hotels close from December through February, but many stay open, and some even charge a premium during Christmas and New Year's. Only a few hotels have central heating.

If you hire a driver to tour Himachal Pradesh, consider combining the potentially hair-raising road trip with an Indian rail journey: send the driver ahead to **Chandigarh** and arrange for him to meet you as you arrive on the *Shatabdi Express* from Delhi, which departs at 7:30 AM and arrives at 10:30 AM. You'll arrive safe and rested.

Shimla

❸ *360 km (225 mi) north of Delhi, about 117 km (73 mi) northeast of Chandigarh*

Shimla is the capital of Himachal Pradesh, and is perhaps best perceived as a gateway to the newly opened district of Kinnaur. The charms of Rudyard Kipling's city have faded, however: paint peels on Victorian structures, and mortar is left to crumble. Plan to use Shimla only as a base if it's fresh mountain air and serenity you seek. Garish new developments now dot the surrounding hills, and traffic lines the road in high season and can cause delays for miles of switchbacks en route. Shimla is generally packed with Indian families on holiday, and also attracts many British travelers whose Raj ancestors once made the annual trip to the summer capital.

Take in the architectural and historical highlights with a walk through town and up to **Jakhoo Hill,** which at 8,054 ft is the highest peak around, crowned with a temple dedicated to Lord Hanuman. (It's 2 km/1 mi from the center of town.) The monkeys en route are notoriously mischievous (walking sticks are rented to tourists to fend them off)—so the usual cautions apply: don't carry food, don't look them in the eye (or wear sunglasses), and if they do approach you, don't shout. If you're nervous about encountering monkeys, take a local guide along—the clever creatures all recognize **Sanjay Sood** (☎ 177/205806; cell-phone 98170–16580), who visits the temple daily and lives at Rothney Castle near the base of the hill on Jakhoo Road. Sood can also take you on one of the many local heritage walks to **The Glen, Summer Hill** or **Chadwick Falls,** or ask him to arrange excursions further afield to nearby temples. The **Temple of Kamna Devi,** 5 km (3 mi) from Shimla on the way to Jutogh—and accessible partly on foot and partly by car— perches on the top of Prospect Hill, and offers glorious views of the surrounding hills and the Toy Train running from Taradevi to Jotogh. **Sankat Mochan Temple,** dedicated to Lord Hanuman, is about 7 km (4½ mi) outside town at an altitude of 6,073 ft. **Chail,** built on three hills in a forest setting, and an excellent spot for picnics, is 45 km (28 mi) southeast of Shimala, just over an hour by car. It's the former capital of the Maharaja of Patiala and is best known for having the highest cricket pitch in the world.

Crowds swarming in the main plaza, known as the **Mall,** sweep you along much at their pace, but afford a gracious break from traffic outside the pedestrianized areas. **Scandal Point,** where the Mall meets the Ridge, offers an endlessly fascinating view not just of the surrounding town but of families shopping, strolling, buying treats from vendors, and riding ponies. It's still a good place to gossip or to meet fellow travelers. **Christchurch,** the **Gaiety Theatre,** the **Town Hall,** and the **General Post Office** present a lively facade of architectural reminders of the Raj in Gothic, Arts and Crafts and timbered Tudor styles. Many of the less famous buildings are worn, and their facades obscured with modern shop fronts and advertising. The rebuilt **Oberoi Cecil Hotel** is a recommended stop for high tea. Beyond the Cecil Hotel is the **Viceregal Lodge,** which houses the Indian Institute of Advanced study and is worth a quick visit for its teak-paneled library or the view from its well-tended gardens.

Fast-food restaurants abound on the Mall but hygiene is clearly not a priority; you're better off eating at the hotels—notably the Oberoi Cecil hotel, Chapslee, and the Wildflower Hall—well worth the drive out of town for lunch. **Indian Coffee House** is a welcome option for vegetarians, with South Indian dosas, idli, *thalis* (sampler plates), and real filter coffee. The Oberoi Clarke's serves bountiful and reasonably priced lunch and supper buffets, and it has a good bar.

Shimla doesn't stand out as a shopping destination, but the lack of car traffic in the Mall area makes it easy to browse while you wander. There are bargains to be found on woolen goods (blankets, shawls, sweaters) and handwoven items from Kashmir and Tibet. **The Dewandchand Atmaram** (✉ 47 the Mall, ☎ 177/203000, closed Sunday) is rated as the best in town for woolen clothing and shawls. **Shezadi** (☎ 177/213333, the Mall) sells designer salwar kameez, shawls, and bathrobes. The small **Tibetan Handicrafts** shop here is friendly and packed with carpets, woven goods, and prayer bells. Fixed-price handicrafts are available at the state-run **Himachal Emporium** (☎ 177/201234, the Mall). **Lakkar Bazaar,** beyond the Ridge, sells a wide range of inexpensive wooden handicrafts that make interesting souvenirs. There are several **bookshops** on the Mall, stacked with the unexpected books and best-sellers: Asia Book House, Minerva Book House; and Maria Brothers is recommended for rare books, old prints, and lithographs.

HOW TO
USE THIS GUIDE

Great trips begin with great planning, and this guide
makes planning easy. It's packed with everything you
need—insider advice on hotels and restaurants, cool
tools, practical tips, essential maps, and much more.

COOL TOOLS

Fodor's Choice Top picks are marked throughout with a star.

Great Itineraries These tours, planned by Fodor's experts,
give you the skinny on what you can see and do in the time
you have.

Smart Travel Tips A to Z This special section is packed with
important contacts and advice on everything from how to get
around to what to pack.

Good Walks You won't miss a thing if you follow the numbered bullets on our maps.

Need a Break? Looking for a quick bite to eat or a spot to
rest? These sure bets are along the way.

Off the Beaten Path Some lesser-known sights are worth a
detour. We've marked those you should make time for.

POST-IT® FLAGS
Dog-ear no more!

"Post-it" is a registered trademark of 3M.

Favorite restaurants • Essential maps •
Frequently used numbers • Walking tours
• Can't-miss sights • Smart Travel
Tips • Web sites • Top shops • Hot
nightclubs • Addresses • Smart contacts
• Events • Off-the-beaten-path spots •
Favorite restaurants • Essential maps
Frequently used numbers • Walking
tours • Can't-miss sights • Smart
Travel Tips • Web sites • Top shops • Hot
nightclubs • Addresses • Smart contacts •
Events • Off-the-beaten-path spots • Favorite
restaurants • Essential maps • Frequently
used numbers • Walking tours •

ICONS AND SYMBOLS

Watch for these symbols throughout:

★	Our special recommendations
✕	Restaurant
🏠	Lodging establishment
✕🏠	Lodging establishment whose restaurant warrants a special trip
🐣	Good for kids
☞	Sends you to another section of the guide for more information
✉	Address
☎	Telephone number
FAX	Fax number
WEB	Web site
🎟	Admission price
☉	Opening hours
$-$$$$	Lodging and dining price categories, keyed to strategically sited price charts. Check the index for locations.
① ❶	Numbers in white and black circles on the maps, in the margins, and within tours correspond to one another.

ON THE WEB

Continue your planning with these useful tools found at **www.fodors.com**, the Web's best source for travel information.

"Rich with resources." —*New York Times*

"Navigation is a cinch." —*Forbes* "Best of the Web" list

"Put together by people bursting with know-how."
           —*Sunday Times* (London)

Create a Miniguide Pinpoint hotels, restaurants, and attractions that have what you want at the price you want to pay.

Rants and Raves Find out what readers say about Fodor's picks—or write your own reviews of hotels and restaurants you've just visited.

Travel Talk Post your questions and get answers from fellow travelers, or share your own experiences.

On-Line Booking Find the best prices on airline tickets, rental cars, cruises, or vacations, and book them on the spot.

About our Books Learn about other Fodor's guides to your destination and many others.

Expert Advice and Trip Ideas From what to tip to how to take great photos, from the national parks to Nepal, Fodors.com has suggestions that'll make your trip a breeze. Log on and get informed and inspired.

Smart Resources Check the weather in your destination or convert your currency. Learn the local language or link to the latest event listings. Or consult hundreds of detailed maps—all in one place.

Lodging

$$$$ 🏨 **Chapslee.** In this ivy-covered old manor house, now a Heritage Hotel, faded opulence surrounds you: Gobelin tapestries, European wallpaper, rare textiles and furnishings from the Doge's Palace in Venice, Persian carpets, and Indian pottery. Shelves and tables contain books from the owner's private collection. Each suite is uniquely decorated. The small formal dining room has exquisite imported wallpaper and furnishings. Expect a hot-water bottle slipped into your bed at night, an antique walking stick for your stroll, afternoon tea, and sumptuous fixed-menu Indian and Continental meals. Meals are included; nonguests may dine by reservation only. ⊠ *Lakkar Bazar, 171001,* ☎ *177/ 202542,* FAX *177/258663.* WEB *www.chapslee.com. 6 rooms. Restaurant, playground, travel services, parking. DC, MC, V.*

$$$$ 🏨 **Oberoi Cecil.** The towering Oberoi is on a ridge overlooking the valley, a good 25-minute walk from Shimla's town center. Rooms have hardwood floors, Victorian Raj-style furnishings, and elaborate tasseled draperies. This is the only hotel in Shimla with modern creature comforts and a high level of quality and efficiency. Business seminars are often held here, so the place can feel crowded and impersonal during the week. On weekends and off-season it's a luxurious retreat from the Mall. Relax in the pool or jacuzzi with a view of the hills, or book an ayurvedic massage in the spa to follow a day of walking. Afternoon tea (with excellent pastries) and evening cocktails are served in the atrium lounge. The children's activity center has computers and a VCR, games, toys, books, and a life-size doll's house. ⊠ *The Mall, 171004,* ☎ *177/204848,* FAX *177/211024,* WEB *www.oberoihotels.com. 71 rooms, 8 suites. Restaurant, bar, spa, pool, meeting room, business services, travel services. AE, DC, MC, V.*

$$$$ 🏨 **The Oberoi Clarke's.** The Cecil's sister hotel may not have the grandeur and polish of its counterpart, but its location—in the center of the action on the Mall—makes it a convenient base for shopping and short outings. Service is friendly and accomodating. Rooms and amenities are a good value for the region. The restaurant buffet includes high-quality and varied Indian and Continental food. Rates include all meals. ⊠ *The Mall, 170001,* ☎ *177/251010,* FAX *177/211321. 38 rooms. Restaurant, bar, laundry service, business services, travel services. AE, MC, V.*

$$$$ 🏨 **Wildflower Hall.** The former residence of Lord Kitchener, who famously demanded nothing but the best for himself, this majestic Oberoi "destination spa" is a 45-minute drive into the forested hills from Shimla. At an altitude of 8,250 ft above sea level, it's an ideal base for exploring the Himalayas. Facilities are state-of-the-art. The indoor pool is a greenhouse design: full of sunlight. Sitting in the spa jacuzzi you'll feel like you're floating in the snow-capped panorama. The spa staff are incredibly attentive—during a short walk to the look-out point you may be interrupted by a hotel limo bearing a picnic lunch. The Indian restaurant specializes in Northwestern cuisine but varies its regional thalis daily. The Brasserie offers delicious spa and Raj cuisine with international variations. ⊠ *Mashobra, Chharabra, 171012,* ☎ *177/ 480808,* FAX *177/480909; in Delhi* ☎ *11/436–3030,* FAX *11/436–0484.* WEB *www.oberoihotels.com. 87 rooms. Restaurant, bar, pool, spa, gym, horseback riding, mountain bikes, shop, business services, travel services. AE, MC, V.*

En Route North of Shimla, the highway north from Kullu town to Manali runs along the Beas River, and during the monsoon season (July–August), magnificent waterfalls drop from the peaks high above you. This road was built largely with the labor of Tibetan refugees after their exodus in 1959; they were employed by the Indian government to pave the way north for army convoys. Many died during construction from tuberculosis as well as accidents.

A lunch stop at the medieval **Hotel Castle** (☎ 01902/47816) in Nagar, on the eastern side of the Beas (5 km/3 mi, beyond Patlikuhl) will give you a spectacular view of the Kullu Valley. Built by Raja Sidh Singh in 1460, the castle is a fine example of authentic Himalayan architecture, complete with timbered mesh. In addition to a restaurant, the castle has a small museum and some rooms for overnight stays; nearby there's a gallery featuring the Russian artist Nicholas Roerich.

Manali

❹ *280 km (174 mi) north of Shimla*

Until about 10 years ago, Manali was a small, relaxed place near the top of the Kullu Valley. On one side of town was a settlement of Tibetan refugees, and on the other side, near the bus stop, backpackers smoked dope and swapped trekking stories. Then, in 1989, Kashmir descended into chaos following the kidnapping of the Indian Home Minister's daughter by militants. Most of the Indian and foreign travelers who would have otherwise headed to Kashmir detoured to the fast-growing village of Manali. The subsequent explosion of development has ruined Manali's tranquillity—concrete hotels have risen cheek-by-jowl along narrow alleys choked with garbage and motor vehicles.

Nonetheless, Manali's location is unbeatable: it's deep in the stunningly beautiful and culturally rich Kullu Valley. The friendly people are famous for their unique style of dress, including men's pill-box caps with colorful geometric embroidery. In fall, when the valley's many apple trees bear fruit, the famous Perahera Festival (a local variation on the Hindu festival Dussehra, celebrated all over North India in October) is held: 10 days after the new moon, villagers bring their local temple deities—more than 200—down to Kullu town, at the head of the valley. Dragged by hand on palanquins or wheeled carts known as *raths*, the idols are brought to pay respect to Raghunathji, Kullu's patron god. For three nights, people from all over the valley, including the descendants of local royalty, mill around a temporary market on the dusty fairgrounds next to the Beas River.

At the high end of the Kullu Valley, near Manali, and farther up toward the Rohtang Pass, 20,000-ft peaks loom on three sides. Day hikers will find endless exhilarating paths to hike, often alongside Gujjar shepherds with flocks of goats. Manali is also the origin and endpoint for more serious adventures into the Himalayan wilderness. From here you can launch trekking, driving, and rafting trips into the Lahaul, Spiti, and Kinnaur valleys. Heading west, more treks can take you toward the Kangra and Chamba valleys. Finally, the road through Manali and up over the Rohtang Pass is currently the only one on which travelers can drive to Ladakh. Manali now also has a short skiing season.

Dining and Lodging

$ ✕ **Mount View Restaurant.** Booths and tables are crammed into this narrow space, and the walls display photos of the Dalai Lama and Lhasa. The Tibetan chef creates Chinese, Tibetan, and Japanese dishes; try the momos, soups with homemade noodles, or spicy Szechuan fare. ⊠ *The Mall, opposite taxi stand,* ☎ *no phone. No credit cards.*

$$ ▥ **John Bannon's Guest House.** It isn't Manali's most beautiful lodge, but it has a garden and an orchard, and John Bannon is a delightful host. The upstairs rooms in this inn, built in 1934 and extended in the 1980s, have good orchard and mountain views. The old section has the advantage of sweeping verandas on both floors. All the rooms have

fireplaces; clean, simple furnishings; and showers. Meals are included. ⊠ *Manali Orchards, Manali 175131,* ☎ *1902/52335 or 1902/52388,* FAX *1901/2392. 10 rooms. Restaurant, travel services. No credit cards.*

$$ ☎ **Usha Sriram Snowcrest Manor.** High on a hill above Manali town, this large modern hotel has truly spectacular views of the Rohtang Pass and Kullu Valley. The deck is an especially nice place for a meal on a sunny day. In-season (summer and the fall festivals), you'll meet with lots of Indian honeymooners and vacationing families. Skiing, river rafting, and paragliding can be easily arranged. Traveler's checks are not accepted. ⊠ *Beyond Log Huts, 175131,* ☎ *1902/53351,* FAX *1902/ 53188; or reserve through Delhi,* ☎ *11/552/0914 or –0915,* FAX *11/551- 2501. 32 rooms. Restaurant, health club. AE, DC, MC, V.*

$ ☎ **Johnson's Lodge.** Set in an old family home, these apartments are spacious and clean, perfect for families or groups of four. Across the garden is a popular restaurant serving Continental and Indian dishes; fresh local trout is a specialty (people rave about this place). You can also stay in a lodge in the family's apple orchard 13 km (8 mi) south of Manali, in Raison, where the rooms are large but sparsely furnished. A new building with 14 rooms is being constructed near the restaurant. ⊠ *Circuit House Rd., The Mall, Manali (drive to top of Mall Rd., turn left at Nehru Park, and look for sign to Johnson's Restaurant),* ☎ *1902/53023,* FAX *1902/45123. 2 apartments. Restaurant. No credit cards.*

Kangra Valley

References to the Kangra Valley date back 3,500 years to the age of the Hindu *Vedas.* Densely populated, the valley climbs gently into Himachal Pradesh from the plains of Punjab; to the north is the pine-covered Dhauladhar Range, a Himalayan spur jutting out to the west. This upper part of the valley gave birth to the famous Kangra-style paintings: scenes from the life of Lord Krishna, often highly romantic, in a style heavily influenced by Moghul miniatures. A narrow-gauge train sometimes plies the tracks that wind slowly up the valley.

Today, with its tropical and alpine terrain backed by snow-topped mountains and intersected by rivers, the Kangra Valley is a popular destination for trekking, fishing, and horseback riding. Much of the land here is dedicated to agriculture. While local farmers grow mostly such "winter" crops as wheat and fruit, the plantations in Palampur contain the only tea gardens in this part of India. Take home a box of "Kangra Green Gold" to sip while remembering this gentle valley.

Up the road from Palampur is Baijnath, home of the **Vaidyanath Temple.** Dedicated to Lord Shiva, this 9th-century temple is really worth a visit—intricate stone carvings of Surya (the sun god) and the Garuda (a birdlike creature) adorn the interior and exterior walls. Aside from this, the valley has no sights per se; it's just a pleasant place to wander around. It's also home to two lovely Heritage Hotels. Given the valley's relatively low elevation and the lack of air-conditioning at any of its lodgings, try to come before mid-April or after mid-September.

Lodging

$$$ ☎ **Judges Court.** In an 8-acre orchard of mango, lychee, plum, persimmon, clove, and cardamom trees, this beautifully restored 300-year-old ancestral home of the Kuthiala Sood family includes three buildings, including the family's historic cottage and a country manor built in 1918. In spring and fall you can sit on a shady veranda and smell the trees in the garden; in winter, a fire can be arranged in the sitting room. When you're not gazing out over the distant Dhauladhar Range, stroll through the medieval Kangra hamlet of Pragpur, with its cobbled streets and

mud-plastered slate-roof houses—the entire village has been declared a "Heritage Zone" by the Himachal Pradesh state government. All meals are included in the room rate, and are served to guests only. ✉ *Jai Bhawan, Pragpur, 177107,* ☏ *1970/45035; or reserve through 3/44 Shanti Niketan, New Delhi, 110021,* ☏ *11/467–4135,* FAX *11/688–5970,* WEB *www.judgescourt.com. 10 rooms, 2 suites. Restaurant, pool. AE, MC, V.*

$$ ⌘ **Taragarh Palace Hotel and Jungle Camp.** This 1930s summer resort and its 15-acre forested estate are now a Heritage Hotel owned by a member of the Kashmir Hindu royalty. Take a dip in the pool, then relax in the art deco lounge. The teak-panel dining room has an exquisite fireplace and smoked-glass windows. The rooms are not opulent, but contain eclectic furnishings from the family's estate; rooms in the back are larger. You can also stay at the adjoining Jungle Camp in a fruit grove, between October and June (open as of autumn 2002). Here, safari-style tents have hand-blocked interior walls, mat floors, electricity, and attached bathrooms with hot water by the bucket. Treks, safaris, and general touring can be arranged. Note: the hotel is 60 km (20 mi) southeast of Dharamsala (between Palampur and Baijnath), but the drive takes just more than an hour. ✉ *P.O. Taragarh, Kangra Valley, 176081,* ☏ *1894/63034; or reserve through Delhi,* ☏ *11/464–3046,* FAX *11/469–2317* WEB *www.welcomeheritage.com. 12 rooms, 4 suites, 6 tents. Restaurant, pool, tennis court, horseback riding, travel services. No credit cards.*

Dharamsala

❺ *253 km (157 mi) west of Manali*

Perched high above the floor of the Kangra Valley, Dharamsala is an old British hill station, but its main attractions now are the Tibetan arts community; the Tibetan Government in Exile; and the home of the Dalai Lama, Tenzin Gyatso, who fled Tibet in 1959. Devastated by an earthquake in 1905, Dharamsala now suffers from an infusion of ugly hotels and too many travelers, who disturb the tranquillity that should surround the home of His Holiness.

Thousands of Buddhists live here and in the remote, high-altitude districts of Lahaul, Spiti, and Kinnaur. Most practice a Tibetan form of tantric Buddhism. The women twist their hair into numerous long pigtails held in place by a silver ornament; many men wear long maroon or brown overcoats. As with most Buddhist communities, men and women share all tasks, from raising a family to working in the fields, where they grow crops of barley, buckwheat, and potatoes.

The tourist office is in lower Dharamsala while many hotels and the Dalai Lama's residence are in the upper part of town, called McLeod Ganj, 10 km (6 mi) by road through the Indian Army cantonment (1,500 ft uphill as the crow flies). Just before you reach the bus and taxi stands, you'll see **St. John's Church in the Wilderness,** one of the few structures remaining from the British colonial days. The headstones in the churchyard are evidence of the difficulties and disease the British suffered; included is the grave of Lord Elgin, Viceroy of India, who died in 1862.

McLeod Ganj is at the center of Tibetan efforts to preserve and maintain their culture during their exile. Several sites devoted to this effort are worth visiting. The **Tibetan Institute of Performing Arts (TIPA)** is on the road to Dharamkot, and a query at your hotel about performance schedules might result in a wonderful evening of dance and music. TIPA also organizes the International Himalayan Festival every December.

The **Norbulingka Institute for Tibetan Culture,** 15 km (9 mi) below McLeod Ganj in Sidhpur, and registered as a trust under the Dalai Lama, is committed to preserving Tibetan art and craft skills. Master artists train young apprentices in *thangka* (Tibetan scroll painting depicting meditational deities), metalwork, appliqué, embroidery, and wood-carving. You can visit the artists in their studios, pick up a souvenir in the gift shop, and pop into the **Losel Doll Museum** to see a wonderful collection of traditional Tibetan costumes in authentic settings.

The **Dalai Lama's private residence** and **Thekchen Choling temple** complex are on the east end of Temple Road—the buildings are joined by a private footpath. The view across the valley from the temple balcony is magnificent, and the complex includes a bookstore and restaurant. The Dalai Lama gives public audiences several times a year, so inquire at your hotel and then apply for clearance at the security office on Bhangsu Road just beyond the Hotel India House (bring your passport). July 6, the Dalai Lama's birthday, is a festive occasion, especially for the performances by students at the Tibetan Children's Village school.

For educators and students, a trip to the **Tibetan Children's Village** (TCV), on the road north to Naddi, is a memorable experience, but it is best to arrange a visit in advance by e-mail(tcvho@vsnl.com). Established in 1960, the TCV's boarding school is home to 2,400 Tibetan orphans and refugees supported by individual and agency donors from all over the world, primarily the SOS Kinderdorf International in Vienna. In all, the organization has more than 11,000 children under its care in branches extending from Ladakh down to Bylakuppe, near Mysore. The pleasant 30-minute walk to the school takes you through deodar cedars (follow the water pipe). The **Handicraft Centre** (☎ 1892/21266) below the school has good crafts at reasonable prices.

Dining and Lodging

$ ✗ **Nick's Italian Kitchen.** If you need a break from tandoori chicken, try this restaurant in the Kunga Guest House. Quiches, pizza, and good pasta dishes are cooked by a Tibetan family whose kitchen skills were inspired by a benefit organized by a traveling Italian-American from New York. ⊠ *Bhagsunag Rd.,* ☎ *1892/21180. No credit cards.*

$ ✗ **Yak.** Stop in for a snack and watch the cook at work: here you'll get the best (cheesy) momos and (hearty) Tibetan noodle soups in town. Don't be put off by the dark doorway, the tiny seating area, or the grease-stained walls—this place is full of local Tibetans for a reason. ⊠ *Jogibara Rd. (opposite Aroma and Ashoka restaurants),* ☎ *no phone. No credit cards.*

$$ ✗🏨 **Hotel Tibet Restaurant.** McLeod Ganj's one fine-dining venue is attached to a good, low-end hotel. Run by the Tibetan Administration Welfare Society, the restaurant has a parquet floor and simple modern decor. Unfortunately its windows overlook garbage and slum dwellings; concentrate on the distant Himalayas, the old, black-and-white Tibetan photos on the walls, or the food: Japanese, Chinese, Continental (including grilled meats), and authentic Tibetan. The guest rooms are basic but carpeted. ⊠ *Bagsunagh Rd., McLeod Ganj,* ☎ *1892/21587. 20 rooms. Restaurant, bar. MC, V.*

$ ✗🏨 **India House.** Trying hard to raise the level of McLeod Ganj accommodations, this new hotel has an excellent restaurant with an ambitious menu. You'll know for certain you've arrived when you see the Astroturf in the entryway. The rooms have small balconies with pleasant views; furnishings are a bit heavy on velour, but the staff is attentive and the prices are reasonable. ⊠ *Bhagsunag Rd. (just beyond Tibet House),* ☎ *1892/21457,* 🆎 *1892/21144. Restaurant. MC, V.*

$$–$$$ 🏨 **Glenmoor Cottages.** The Indian owners of this secluded hideaway
★   live in a British bungalow that's been in their family since the 1940s.
       The cottages are a 20-minute walk from McLeod Ganj. A simple suite
       is available in the bungalow; separate cottages offer more privacy, and
       spectacular mountain and valley views. An absence of TVs (available
       upon request only) helps keep the atmosphere mellow. The cottages'
       modest concrete-and-wood exteriors conceal charming interiors: crisp
       white walls contrast with modern spruce and pine furnishings. All rooms
       have modern bathrooms with showers, and some have kitchenettes.
       Breakfast is included, and the (uninspired) prix fixe Indian and Con-
       tinental dinners are served to guests only. ⊠ *McLeod Ganj, 176219,*
       ☎ *1892/21010,* FAX *1892/21021,* WEB *www.glenmoorcottages.com. 1*
       suite, 5 cottages. Restaurant, travel services. MC, V.

$$ 🏨 **Chonor House.** Built and run by the Norbulingka Institute, this is
★   the best place to stay in McLeod Ganj. Each room is furnished with
       handmade furniture, carpets, and linens made by institute artists, and
       most have balconies. But the special touch is the murals, painted in
       each guest room on the Tibetan themes of myth, religion, and ecology.
       The Cyber-Yak Room has Internet connections, and the spacious read-
       ing room is available for meetings. The excellent restaurant serves tra-
       ditional Tibetan cuisine, which you can take outdoors on a large
       balcony in season. Rooms are heated in winter. The local Lhasa Apso
       dogs, which often set up a chain reaction of midnight yelping, are un-
       fortunately beyond the staff's control. ⊠ *Temple Rd.,* ☎ FAX *1892/21006.*
       11 rooms. Restaurant, meeting room. MC, V.

$ 🏨 **Norling Guest House.** Comfortable, carpeted rooms and a garden
       restaurant are set along a small stream with pleasant waterfalls. At the
       top of the central stairway is a temple with a 14-ft Shakyumani Bud-
       dha. ⊠ *From McLeod Ganj, go through Kotwali Bazaar and take the*
       road through Khanyara (14 km/9 mi); reserve through Norbulingka
       Institute, P.O. Sidhpur 176057, ☎ *1892/22664 or 1892/23522,* FAX
       18922/24982. 8 rooms, 3 suites. Restaurant.

Dalhousie

❻ *130 km (81 mi) northwest of Dharamsala*

Dalhousie was a hill station fashionable with British colonialists from
Lahore. It was established by the Marquess of Dalhousie, who, as India's
governor general in the 1850s, founded the Indian rail system. Today
Dalhousie is a crowded destination for Indian tourists during the sum-
mer months, so try to see it between March and May, or September
and November. The setting that drew the British is still spectacular, with
forested slopes, green valleys, and the Dhauladhar Range in the dis-
tance. Evidence of the British colonial days is mostly gone, barring the
two Christian churches at each *chowk* (crossroads or marketplace); **St.
Francis Church,** on Subhash Chowk, was built in 1894. The town has
vehicle-restricted walkways between Gandhi Chowk and Subhash
Chowk, and along Potryn Road. Dalhousie was for a short time the
assigned residence for Tibetan exiles, before they were directed to
Dharamsala; a visit to the **Tibetan Handicraft Center** in Upper Bakrota
is a must if you like hand-knotted Tibetan carpets.

Dining and Lodging

$$$ ✕ **Davat.** For a quick bite, try the restaurant Davat in the Hotel Mount
      View. The noise from the nearby bus stand detracts somewhat from
      the experience, but the food is reliable. ⊠ *Dalhousie St., Dalhousie.*
      ☎ *172/74054.*

$–$$ 🏨 **Guncha Siddhartha.** Each room in this new building has a terrace
      overlooking the owner's orchard and residence, with a scenic view of

the valley and mountains beyond. Rooms are tiered down the hillside, with a restaurant planned for the roof. Heating pads are provided in winter, and rates are discounted 50%. ⊠ *Church Baloon Rd.,* ☎ *1899/42709 or 1899/40620,* FAX *1899/40818. 9 rooms, 5 suites. refrigerators, laundry service, travel services. No credit cards.*

$ ⊡ **Aroma-n-Claire.** Virtually unchanged since 1959, this family-run hotel is a furnishings flashback with an eclectic twist. The charm of the hosts, the view from the balcony, and the home cooking offset the worn carpets and fading art in the public sitting room. Heating costs extra. ⊠ *Court Rd., 176304,* ☎ *1899/42199,* FAX *1899/42639. 13 rooms. Restaurant, refrigerators, laundry service. MC, V.*

$ ⊡ **Princess.** Rooms here are basic: clean, well-kept, and equipped with phones and, in the winter, with heat. The building has nice views across the valley. ⊠ *Thandi Sarak (Mall walkway),* ☎ *1899/42154,* FAX *1899/40057. 14 rooms. Restaurant. No credit cards.*

$ ⊡ **Silverton Estate Guest House.** Built in 1939, this small and gracious home has both charm and location. The host, Vickram Singh, runs the estate, which includes a terraced garden. Singh is incredibly hospitable—he attends to your personal needs in detail, tailoring your stay to your desires, and takes into account your taste in food and special interests. The cuisine is Indian vegetarian. ⊠ *Top of Moti Tibba, above Circuit House (off Mall Rd.),* ☎ FAX *1899/40674. 5 rooms. Restaurant, putting green, badminton, croquet. No credit cards.*

En Route The road from Dalhousie to Chamba has two delightful stops for nature lovers. The first is **Kalatope Wildlife Sanctuary,** a forest preserve with beautiful mountain views. Leave your car at the entrance (unless you have a permit from the Forest Officer in Chamba) and stroll to the end of the 3 km (2 mi) paved road, which continues through mature deodar cedars and yews. Halfway to Chamba is **Khajiar.** Ambitiously known as the mini-Switzerland of India, this is a spacious glade encircled by virgin forest and centered on a pond with a grassy island that seems to float. Some literature says there's a golf course here, but all that seems to remain are eight wire circles guarding the greens against grazing sheep and cattle.

Chamba

❼ *50 km (31 mi) east of Dalhousie*

The road into Chamba is not for the faint of heart. Isolated for centuries, Chamba offers a chance to see an India unaffected by tourism. Chamba Valley lies between the Pir Panjal and Dhauladhar ranges, and the town itself sits on a bluff overlooking the swift Ravi River. The business district surrounds a large green, the Chaugan, site of the midsummer Minjar Festival. The **Bhuri Singh Museum** (⊠ Museum Rd.), open Tuesday through Sunday from 10 to 5, has an interesting collection, including a variety of miniature paintings in the Basholi and Kangra styles. The distinctive spires of the **Lakshmi Narayan** temple complex, dedicated to Shiva and Vishnu, rises above the surrounding skyline. Up the hill is the **Himachal Emporium,** housed in an old palace. The Chamba Valley is well known for *rumals,* pictures sewn in a reversible stitch that shows no knots. Above the showroom is a workshop where fine shawls are woven on looms.

A few doors from the Lakshmi Narayan temple is the office of **Mani Mahesh Travels** (⊠ Lakshmi Narayan Temple La., 176310, ☎ 1899/ 22507 or 1899/22607, FAX 1899/25333), operators of the Himalayan Orchard Hut, a tented camp and farmhouse 12 km (7 mi) north of Chamba in Kut-Chadiara, near the River Saal. The staff lead well-organized tours and treks in the Chamba Valley and direct studies of flora, fauna, Gaddi-Gujjar mountain-village life, and spiritual meditation.

Dining and Lodging

$ ☏ **Aravati.** This government-owned hotel is clean and inexpensive. Its restaurant serves reliable South Indian food. ☒ *South end of village green, near tourist office,* ☏ *1899/22671,* FAX *1899/22565. 19 rooms. Restaurant. No credit cards.*

Lahaul, Spiti, and Kinnaur

About 200 to 250 km (125 to 155 mi) est of Chamba

Beginning 51 km (32 mi) north of Manali on the far side of the Rohtang Pass, **Lahaul** is a good place to take treks and jeep safaris. It's much smaller than Ladakh and has fewer and simpler *gompas* (monasteries), but the two share a general intermingling of religion and nature. Mountains bear in from all directions, and windswept passes overlook stunningly harsh, remote landscapes of stark mountains, boundless sky, and deserted spaces. Expect extremes of weather: mornings and evenings are freezing, afternoons are blazing. Glaciers look icy and somber, and an occasional lake sparkles under the hot sun. Prayer flags or a rare green valley pulse with color. But Lahaul is experiencing an influx of trekkers: work with your tour operator to choose a route that avoids crowds.

You can raft, day-hike, trek, and tool around by jeep in the **Spiti Valley,** a sensitive border area southeast of Lahaul, on the other side of the Kunzum Pass (15,055 ft). Spiti's landscape is more arid than Lahaul's; its mountains, split by the raging Spiti River, are steeper; and it's more thoroughly Buddhist. Here you'll find the 11th-century **Tabo Gompa,** one of the holiest monasteries for Tibetan Buddhists. Foreigners need an Inner Line Permit to visit Spiti, though formalities are getting looser over time.

Kinnaur, south of Spiti, is more fertile than the Spiti Valley. Newly opened to travelers, this district offers great day hikes, treks, and jeep excursions. The Sutlej River runs through Kinnaur, which is nestled in the towering Kinnaur Kailas Range. Like Spiti, Kinnaur hides wonderful old Buddhist monasteries.

Lodging

Facilities in Lahaul, Spiti, and Kinnaur are generally open to travelers between April and October.

$$$ ☏ **Banjara Camp.** The accommodations at Banjara Camp are Swiss-style deluxe tents with full-size beds and attached "loos" with running water. At 8,850 ft, the camp is on the Baspa River in the Sangla Valley, one of loveliest valleys in Kinnaur, and just 30 km (19 mi) from Tibet. The room price includes all meals. Banjara has other camps in Tabo (Spiti), well into the high, arid plateau of eastern Himachal Pradesh; and Chail, 45 km (28 mi) from Shimla, set in deodar cedars near the world's highest cricket pitch. ☒ *Reserve through 1A Hauz Khas Village, New Delhi 110016* ☏ *11/685–5153,* FAX *11/685–5152,* WEB *www.banjaracamp.com. 18 tents. Restaurant. AE, MC, V.*

$ ☏ **Kinner Villa.** Though their popular tented campsites have recently closed down, in addition to organizing treks and jeep safaris, the organizers of Timberline Camps still operate a good hotel in Kalpa (Kinnaur). Its splendid location overlooks Kinnaur Kailas—the winter abode of Lord Shiva. ☏ *1786/26006; reserve through the Travel Circuit, New Delhi 110062,* ☏ *11/608–4049 or 11/608–4037,* FAX *11/608–0746,* WEB *www.newber.com. 14 rooms. Restaurant.*

Adventures

Fishing

Fish for trout in the Pabar River near Rohru, a two-day trip from Shimla, or in the Larji River, at its confluence with the Tirthan River over the Jalori Pass. You can also catch trout in the Uhl River, near Barot, and in the Sangla. Try for *mahaseer* (a Himalayan river fish) in the Beas, near Dharamsala. The tour operator, Aquaterra Adventures, can help you get the appropriate license and take you to good fishing spots in each district. There is no bag limit for mahaseer, but conservation efforts dictate that you keep only as much trout as you can eat. The fishing season is March to October. You can rent poles here, but serious anglers should bring their own equipment.

TIRTHAN RIVER

The **Goshiani Guest House** (✉ Village and P.O. Goshiani, via Banjar, Kullu Hills, 175123, ☎ 1903/76808 or 76830), on the road past Larji, is a rare find, a cedar guest house set in a garden and orchard (which helps supply superb meals) on the Tirthan River. Owner Ranjiv Bharti is also a fishing guide who knows where those wily browns live. The house is a few miles past the trout hatchery on the opposite side of the river; you ride in a basket across the roaring stream—a sound that later fills your room as you fall asleep thinking of tomorrow's catch. Buy your fishing license in Larji before you head up the valley. Room and board should cost you less than Rs. 1000.

Jeep Safaris

MANALI–LEH

Many companies offer jeep trips from Manali to Leh, so the route can be crowded with vehicles. Take three days to enjoy the show-stopping vistas as you scale four passes, cross high-altitude plains, and wend your way through valleys.

SHIMLA–KULLU

This two- to three-day drive follows a newly opened road along the old colonial route from Shimla to Kullu over the Jalori Pass (11,230 ft). You'll get plenty of ups and downs as you drive through mountain forests, across alpine valleys, and through enchanting Gaddi villages. The route climbs past lakes bordered by modest wooden temples, and you cross the pass with views of Spiti and Kinnaur peaks. Camp near the pass by an old British Public Works Department bungalow—its garden is open mid-April to June and September to October. Contact Aquaterra Adventures for details.

Mountain Biking

MANALI–LEH HIGHWAY

This spectacular ride can be completed by avid bikers in eight days. There is plenty to see along the way, including spectacular scenery and views from 16,000-ft passes. The terminus, Leh, offers well-deserved rest and some monastery visits. A white-water rafting trip on the Indus River caps off this exciting tour, making it a kaleidoscope of activities. This is the only road to Leh, so the traffic can get intimidating; mountain drivers tend to be much more considerate than drivers on the plains. You must bring your own bike, but a support vehicle accompanies the group. The trip is only feasible from July through September; contact Aquaterra Adventures for details.

Pony Treks

KANGRA VALLEY

We highly recommend a Kangra Valley pony trek for experienced riders, who can enjoy lovely Himalayan views from high-spirited polo ponies owned by the family of the former Maharaja of Kashmir. Wandering through meadows and forests, you visit Kangra villages and a Tibetan monastery, and spend each night in a tent at various idyllic campsites. One five-day trip is usually scheduled in May, but customized trips can be arranged from April through June and mid-September through October. Contact the **Taragarh Palace Hotel** (⊠ P.O. Taragarh, Kangra Valley, 176081, ☎ 1894/63034; or reserve through Delhi, ☎ 11/464–3046, 𝖥𝖠𝖷 11/469–2317) for details.

KINNAUR TO SPITI

This five-day trek starts at Kafnoo, in Kinnaur (a little beyond Wangtu), and climbs over the 16,000-ft Babha Pass to reach the village of Muth in the Pin Valley, a land of ibexes and snow leopards. The trip combines the greens of Kinnaur with the stark desolation of Spiti. Return to Delhi via Manali or Shimla. The total round trip from Delhi is about a week and a half, but you can extend it to as long as three weeks to include visits to the various monasteries and high-altitude villages and even fossil-hunting, usually in Spiti. Contact Aquaterra Adventures for details.

Rafting

SPITI RIVER

Offered July through August only, this wonderful 12-day adventure from Manali to Shimla includes a three-day run on the scenic Spiti River, surrounded by mountains, and sightseeing drives and day hikes to historic monasteries and villages. This trip is not for hard-core rafters—its cultural aspects are emphasized over its physical adventure. No experience is required, but you must be fit for the high altitude. Contact Himalayan River Runners for details.

Skiing

MANALI

For those with a penchant for danger and a wallet full of cash, Manali now has a heli-skiing outfit. In the midst of 20,000-ft peaks, the skiing can begin as high as 16,000 ft. The powder is said to be exceptional and the snow-pack deep. Breathing can be difficult and avalanches are the rule, but Himachal Helicopter Skiing is a wholly professional operation, with Kiwi guides, a Canadian pilot, and a Swiss helicopter. All packages include 100,000 ft of vertical skiing; six days of guide service, skiing equipment, and the use of an avalanche transceiver; seven nights lodging at Manali and all meals; escorted transfers from Delhi to Manali and back; and local taxes. The season is short (mid-January to early April), and the local hotel is not up to jet-setter ski-bum standards. One week of skiing runs U.S. $5,000–$7,000. Contact Himachal Helicopter Skiing for details.

Trekking

DHAULADHAR

Starting at McLeod Ganj (Upper Dharamsala), in the Kangra Valley, at about 6,000 ft and passing over the mighty snowbound Dhauladhar Range, this trail ends at Machhetar, in the Ravi Valley. You follow the traditional migratory and grazing route of the Gaddis, who tend their flocks throughout the summer on the high alpine meadows adjoining the Dhauladhar and Pir Panjal ranges. Moving through forests of pine, oak, fir, and ash, the trail passes through open grazing areas and flowering meadows above the timberline. Wildlife such as black and brown bears, red foxes, and leopards, though hard to spot, inhabit these upper regions. An 18-day round trip from Delhi, this trek is best undertaken in early June or September–October. A shorter, six-day trek goes over the range from Dharamsala to Bharmaur.

LAHAUL-SPITI-KINNAUR

Many tour operators lead this popular moderate (but high-altitude) 17-day trip, with a 13-day trek that starts when you drive from Manali across the Rohtang Pass (13,048 ft) into Lahaul to Patseo village. From there you head over Baralacha Pass (16,016 ft), with its astonishing mountain panorama, cross Kunzum Pass (15,055 ft), and enter Spiti, where you follow the Spiti River to the villages of Losar and Hansa. You visit La-Darcha, the site of a popular trade fair attended by Tibetans and Ladakhis, and then head to Kibber village (13,546 ft), the highest Asian village accessible by road. Following a mountain ridge, you'll visit some Buddhist monasteries, then drive through the Pinn Valley and see some more key villages and monasteries, including Tabo, before continuing to Kinnaur and then Shimla. The trip is offered May through mid-October.

MANALI-BIR

This fantastic, moderate-to-strenuous two-week trek takes you from the Kullu into the Kangra Valley along a lesser-known high-altitude route. From Manali, you enter evergreen forests that lead to the Manaslu Valley, where you follow icy streams, cross alpine meadows, and catch great views of the Kullu Valley en route. Crossing the Kaliheyni Pass (15,500 ft), where the landscape changes to patches of snow and glacial moraines, you see distant views of Buddhist Lahaul. You traverse a glacier and enter the Sunni River valley, with its meadows and gorges. A snow bridge leads to forests and Barabangal village, an isolated valley home of some Gaddi shepherds. Your next stop is the base of Thamser Pass (15,750 ft); from here, you travel through meadows and by lakes and waterfalls until you enter the Kangra Valley and the Tibetan settlement in Bir. This trek can be done in June and September only.

MANALI-LEH

This strenuous, extremely popular 10- or 20-day trek starts after a drive across the Rohtang Pass and the descent into Lahaul. Expect to ford snow-fed streams, cross a high-altitude pass into Ladakh's Zanskar district, visit ancient monasteries and typical Buddhist villages, and experience a panoramic lunar landscape. You can take a jeep from Padam, the district headquarters in Zanskar, or continue trekking to Leh, the capital of Ladakh. The most rigorous route includes four more passes. Each version is rugged but stunning, with multi-hued mountains, jagged glaciers, and green village oases. You're likely to see traders leading horses laden with goods, and many, many foreign trekkers. The route is available mid-July to mid-September.

SANGLA

We recommend this moderate, 11-day Kinnaur trek, which starts after a drive from Shimla to Sarahan and gives you a chance to see the Kinnauri culture. Between May and October you can walk through forests, cross streams and old bridges, follow a mountain ridge with great views, and see ancient temples steeped in Kinnauri Buddhist mythology. Count on plenty of up- and downhill walking and a steep climb over the Shibaling Pass. You can also expect forest or meadow campsites near streams, and visits to typical villages such as Sangla and Chitkul (the highest village in the valley), where many residents create exquisite Kinnauri wool shawls on hand looms.

LADAKH

Tucked between the two highest mountain ranges in the world—the Karakoram in the north and the Greater Himalayas to the south—Ladakh offers an adventure in the world of Mahayana Buddhism.

Sometimes called Little Tibet, Ladakh is now more culturally pure than its namesake. Tourists in Leh, the capital, are diluting the Buddhist culture, but Ladakh's gompas are still splendid, with beautiful interior frescoes and statues as breathtaking as the landscape. With gray barren crags, an occasional green valley, jewel-like waterways, and mountains of different hues, this high-altitude desert is punctuated by colorful prayer flags and scattered *chortens*—memorial stupas or shrines for relics.

Outside the town of Leh, you can travel up and down Ladakh's windswept terrain and encounter few people. The 150,000 residents in this part of the disputed region of Kashmir occasionally appear near the reminders of Buddhist culture scattered around the countryside. On the most deserted stretch of road you'll find stones stacked into little chortenlike piles and *mani* (walls of beautifully engraved stones) that the inhabitants have erected to protect the land from demons and evil spirits. The walls are enticing, but don't touch the stones—they're sacred to the people who put them there.

The Government of India oversees a number of specified tour circuits in this region. Foreign tourists in groups of four, sponsored by recognized tour operators, are allowed to visit the Khaltse (Drokhpa area), Nubra, and Nyoma subdivisions after obtaining a permit from the District Directorate in Leh. If you're planning a trip here, take all precautions against high-altitude sickness and try to bring a flashlight for viewing poorly lit gompas. Ladakh gets crowded in July and August, but June and September are excellent months for touring this mountain state. The trekking season lasts from late May, after most of the snow has melted, until mid-October; rafting is best from early July to mid-September. Winter, when many accommodations are closed, will probably confine you to Leh and its vicinity.

Leh

8 *473 km (295 mi) north of Manali, 434 km (271 mi) east of Srinagar, 230 km (143 mi) east of Kargil*

The two-day overland route from Manali to Leh has reached mythical status as an automotive ordeal. This mode of arrival is incredibly scenic, and a good way to acclimatize yourself to the altitude, but the ride can be lengthy and uncomfortable. The army convoys on the road increase the danger *and* the time involved, as they have immediate right-of-way over all traffic. The prudent and the humble take Indian Airlines or Jet Airways: flights leave Delhi early in the morning, with the sun beginning to rise as you cross the great Indian plain and enter the Shivalik Hills. As the first snow-capped mountains appear, the plane seems to skim over the summits, and the ice fields stretch to the horizon before you reach the barren moonscape of the high Tibetan plateau. The flight attendant may instruct you to lower your window blind as you approach Leh, your first hint of the military security here—you are to take no photos from the plane. If you arrive before the plows have opened the Manali road (early to mid-June), you'll have your pick of lodgings.

Take strong sunblock, aspirin, and a thick novel to Ladakh: the altitude change and intense sunshine will require you to spend a few days just relaxing and taking slow walks. Drink water and avoid alcohol. A visit to Leh's **Ecology Centre** one afternoon will distract you while you acclimatize; in addition to various exhibits, its excellent video, *Ancient Futures,* illustrates how Ladakhi culture is threatened by a rapidly changing world. For as long as you're here, initiate greetings of "*Jule*" (ju-*lay*) and you'll be pleased with the smiles and kindness you receive in return.

Leh is built into the base of the snow-covered Karakoram Range at just over 11,500 ft. An important Buddhist center since the 3rd century BC, Leh has also been a major commercial hub on the Silk Road in central Asia. The 20th century has turned Leh into an important Indian military base and tourist boomtown. The **palace** and, above it, the **Temple of the Guardian Deities** are both in disrepair; still, Leh lends itself to exploration. The narrow lanes behind the main bazaar have tempting little shops, though everything here is overpriced. Find **Alisha,** the photo shop owned by Syed Ali Shah, beyond the Sunni mosque near the Sankar gompa. Shah sells a lifetime's worth of Ladakh photography, and his son will show you some treasures, especially the old black-and-white images. Taxi to the **Shanti Stupa,** in the village of Changspa, for a magnificent view of the valley—then walk down the 500-plus steps leading up to it. On your way south out of town, stop at the **Tibetan Refugee Handicraft Center** in the village of Choglamsar, open weekdays from 9 to 5. The beautiful crafts here include handwoven rugs and thick woolens.

Before you leave town, arrange trips to area monasteries and get a festival schedule from the tourist office (dates vary according to the Tibetan lunar calendar). Gompas are the center of Ladakhi religion and culture. Drive south to explore the Shey, Thiksay, Matho, and Hemis gompas; northwest are Spituk, Phyang, Likir, and **Alchi Choskor**—the jewel of Ladakh's religious sites. Plan an overnight stay in Alchi and travel onward and upward to the gompa at Lamayuru. The taxi union has reasonable fixed charges, but the roads are bumpy, so request a Tata Sumo to minimize bouncing. For a knowledgeable, English-speaking guide, contact Tondup Rahul at (☎ 1982/53476). Respect religious customs when visiting gompas: wear appropriate clothing, remove your shoes, don't smoke, circle all chortens or spin prayer wheels clockwise, leave a small donation, and never take a mani stone. Most monasteries do not allow flash photography.

Dining and Lodging

All of Leh's restaurants are small and informal. Try the standards: momos and *thukpa* (noodle soup). A *dzo* is a cross between a yak and a cow. Strange beast. You may also have a chance to try *chang* (a local brew made from fermented barley) or, more likely, some *gur-gur cha,* yak-butter tea mixed with milk and salt.

Hotels are divided into uniformly priced categories. The tourist office hands out a list of lodgings at the airport and in its main office. A handful of hotels now offer some form of heating; the most expensive cost around U.S. $80 a night including meals; the cheapest are the economy-class guest houses, which can be as low as U.S. $5 per night. During slow seasons, you may be able to negotiate. For extended stays, reserve a room for the first night or two, then spend a day checking out alternatives: you might end up in a lovely venue with a sun-filled room that has a terrace with a view, and a clean bathroom, which you'll most likely share. Begin your search in Changspa, near the Shanti Stupa, away from the traffic noise.

$ ✕ **Summer Harvest Restaurant.** This second-floor restaurant features good Kashmiri cuisine. A local crowd attests to the quality of the cooking. ⊠ *Down Fort Rd. from the taxi stand,* ☎ *1982/52336. No credit cards.*

$ ✕ **Tibetan Kitchen.** Locals agree that this joint serves the most authentic Tibetan food in Leh. ⊠ *Hotel Tsokar, Fort Rd.,* ☎ *no phone. No credit cards.*

$$$–$$$$ 　🏨 **Ladakh Sarai.** Here you stay in a yurt (large circular tent) in a wil-
★ 　low grove, with a view west across the valley to the Indus River and
　　the majestic Stok Kangi Range. Each yurt has twin beds and a sitting
　　area with a Western-style toilet attached to the tent, in the rear. You
　　dine in a hexagonal hall tastefully decorated with Ladakhi artifacts.
　　All meals are included. The camp is in the village of Sabu, 6 km (4 mi)
　　south of Leh. Jeep tours with both driver and guide can take you to
　　the monasteries; you can also opt for a five-day Stok-Martselang trek
　　and an eight-day Markha Valley trek. Rates include meals, airport trans-
　　fers and sightseeing. ⊠ *Reserve through Tiger Tops/Mountain Travel*
　　India, 33 Rani Jhansi Rd., New Delhi 110055, ☎ *11/777–1055 or 11/*
　　367–1035, ｆａｘ *11/367–7748,* ｗｅｂ *www.tigermountainindia.com. 14*
　　tents. Restaurant, travel services. AE, MC, V. Closed Nov.–Mar.

$$–$$$ 　🏨 **Lha-Ri-Mo.** A short walk from the markets, and nestled behind an
★ 　attractive garden, Lha-Ri-Mo is the loveliest hotel in Leh. The Ladakhi
　　look of the exterior is continued in the lobby and the restaurant, which
　　also has intricately hand-painted beams. Rooms are simple, with
　　Western toilets and hot and cold showers. Buffet-style Indian meals
　　are included in the price. ⊠ *Old Fort Rd., Leh, Ladakh 194101,* ☎
　　1982/52101, ｆａｘ *1982/53345; or reserve through 1542 Sector 29,*
　　Noida, Delhi, ☎ *91/445–1454. 30 rooms. Restaurant, travel services.*
　　AE. Closed Nov.–Apr.

$$–$$$ 　🏨 **Omasila.** Owned and operated by a Tibetan family since 1980, this
　　hotel below the Shanti Stupa is popular with European tour groups.
　　For its scenic views, cleanliness, privacy, and food, put it first on your
　　list. A spacious terrace looks south to a stunning view, the grounds are
　　planted with flowers, and a stream runs along the edge of the prop-
　　erty. Each room has a selection of Buddhist reading material. There
　　are no TVs or telephones, but the front desk has a cordless phone. Only
　　six rooms are heated in winter: ask for a room number in the 40s. The
　　evening meal is a buffet. ⊠ *Changspa, Leh, Ladakh, 194101* ☎ ｆａｘ
　　1982/52119 or 53735. 32 rooms. Restaurant. No credit cards.

$$ 　🏨 **Highland.** This two-story hotel has a Ladakhi-style exterior (white
　　with black-and-red trim), a lovely back lawn, and modern, comfort-
　　ably furnished rooms. Cultural performances are arranged on request.
　　Fixed-menu meals with some Ladakhi dishes, airport transfer, and
　　mountain bikes are included in the price. Highland is up the road from
　　the Ladakh Sarai hotel. ⊠ *Near the Stok Gompa, Stok;* ⊠ *Leh 194101,*
　　☎ *1982/42005. 12 rooms. Restaurant, bar, travel services, airport shut-*
　　tle. AE, DC, MC, V. Closed Dec.–May.

$$ 　🏨 **Khanghri.** Like all hotels in Leh, the Khangri has great views, but
　　it goes one step further in being one of the few places open year-round.
　　Rooms are heated in winter (for a small fee), though the plumbing is
　　not so luxurious. All meals are included in the room price. ⊠ *Near*
　　Nehru Park, Leh, Ladakh 194101, Jammu and Kashmir, ☎ *1982/52762*
　　or 11/646–1271, ｆａｘ *1982/52051. 40 rooms (15 in winter). Restaurant,*
　　laundry service, travel services. AE.

$$ 　🏨 **Shambha-La.** Built in 1978 by the Oberoi group, the Shambha-La
　　is now a family-owned, two-tier motel on a shaded courtyard. Com-
　　forts include a buffet restaurant with three cooks who will accomo-
　　date special needs, a rooftop deck, a VCR and video library, and—in
　　half the rooms—stove heaters in May and October. Acclimatize by re-
　　laxing in hammocks strung between poplar trees in the garden, or take
　　a walk through surrounding meadows or to the nearby village. The
　　manager will recommend local treks—his jeep drops you at one loca-
　　tion and picks you up in another in time to get back for the next meal.
　　The hotel is located between Leh and its airport; it offers a free shut-

tle from the airport into town. ✉ *Just south of Leh, off the road from the airport,* ☎ *1982/52607,* FAX *1982/51100; or reserve through K-40 Hauz Khas, 1st floor, New Delhi 110016,* ☎ FAX *11/686–7785. 27 rooms. Restaurant, laundry service, travel services. AE. Closed Nov.–Apr.*

Padam

❾ *270 km (169 mi) southwest of Leh*

The former capital of the Kingdom of Zanskar, Padam is in the vast, high-altitude Zanskar Valley, ringed by mountains, with the Karsha Gompa perched on a nearby cliff. The valley's sweeping panoramas are framed by mountains, and the bases of barren slopes are barricaded by sand and shaped by the wind and the water into oversize ramparts. Parts of the district consist of rocky desert punctuated by bits of green, and the Zanskar River races along a deep gorge. Here you'll see Zanskar men in robes galloping by on handsome ponies.

Within this sparsely populated district, the dominant sounds come from chattering birds or the wind, which grows intense by late afternoon, and rustles the wheat, barley, and countless prayer flags. The arrival of tourists, especially trekkers, has begun to alter Zanskar's lifestyle; the men, who traditionally worked alongside the women in the fields and helped with the household chores and child rearing, now look for jobs as porters. The women sell crafts. A growing attraction to money and Western goods is changing a society accustomed to bartering, and is threatening Buddhist traditions here.

Pangong and Moriri Lakes, Nubra Valley, and Drogpa Villages

Foreigners need an Inner Line Permit to visit any of these areas.

The brackish **Pangong Tso** and **Tso Moriri** (*tso* means "lake") in the eastern district of Changthang are astonishing alpine bodies of water. Pangong lake, at an elevation of 14,018 ft, is more than 150 km (90 mi) long—and two thirds of it lie in China. Tso Moriri, 240 km (150 mi) southeast of Leh at an elevation of 15,000 ft, is a pearl-shape lake rich in mineral deposits, giving it a mysterious range of colors against the barren mountains. Both lakes are accessible by road from Leh between late May and October.

North of Leh, Ladakh's "Valley of Flowers," the **Nubra Valley,** is sublime: a heady mixture of cultivated fields set in an arid desert surrounded by the Karakoram Range and sliced by rivers. (*Nubra* means "garden.") Getting to this richly vegetated area around the Shayok and Siachen rivers requires a journey over Khardungla Pass—the world's highest drivable road, at 18,383 ft. From here you descend through the towering peaks to the villages of Nubra, which were important stops for rations along the Silk Road to Central Asia. The trekking routes here go through virtually unexplored territory. Camel safaris and river rafting are available, and hot springs warm weary travelers at Panamik village.

In the **Drogpa villages** west of Leh, the Dard people still inhabit the shimmering Indus Valley. Isolated from the modern world, they remain Buddhist farmers, eking a living from the rugged mountainsides. You can arrange an overnight stay in Khaltsi, where the main road forks off toward Kargil, and in new tourist bungalows in the Dard village of Biama.

Adventures

Jeep and Camel Safari

NUBRA ADVENTURE

This special five-day adventure explores the Nubra Valley, a high-altitude area north of Leh that is home to Buddhists, Muslims, and double-humped Bactrian camels (once used for transport on the Silk Road). From Leh, a jeep takes you across the Khardungla Pass, with its exquisite valley and mountain vistas. Once you enter Nubra, you proceed to Disket village, your camping base, and visit its 500-year-old monastery followed by nearby Hunder village and its monastery. Then you begin a four-day safari through the ethereal valley on an intrepid Bactrian camel, with overnight stays at Panamik village (where you can take a dip in the hot springs) and Samtanling village, which has another old monastery. Finish back in Leh. Ibex Expeditions runs this tour mid-July–mid-October.

Jeep Safaris

MANALI-LEH

Many companies offer jeep trips from Manali to Leh, so the route can be crowded with vehicles. Take three days to enjoy the show-stopping vistas as you scale four passes, cross high-altitude plains, and wend your way through valleys.

LADAKH TOUR

Opened to tourists only in 1994, the Nubra Valley, Tso Moriri, and Dha Hanu remain largely mysterious to the outside world. This approximately 14-day trip—which can be bisected for those with less time—includes a visit to the Nubra Valley via the Khardungla Pass. Surrounded by snow-capped mountains, the valley also boasts some of the best monasteries in Ladakh and has preserved some of the finest Buddhist artifacts and ways of life. Across the More Plains are the remote Rupshu Plains and the Tso Moriri, surrounded by mountains towering over 20,000 ft. The nomadic Changpas, who camp here in yak-skin tents, graze their yaks and Pashmina goats (source of the coveted *shatoosh* wool) in the rich pastures adjoining the lake. For a short time in summer, these pastures are carpeted with wildflowers, giving the Nubra Valley its nickname. Finally, you visit the Dha Hanu region in the lower Indus Valley, home of the Drogpas, a group of Aryan Buddhists. Contact Aquaterra Adventures for details; the tour is available July–September.

PANGONG LAKE

Due to an expanding army presence on the banks of the lake, this four-day trip is less commendable than it used to be. The trek begins in Leh and heads across the Chang Pass (17,604 ft) to Pangong Lake, which, surrounded by mountains, straddles the border of Ladakh and Tibet. One of the world's largest glacier-fed lakes, Pangong dazzles the eye with its vibrant blue and green hues. The lake has long been a summer nesting place for migratory waterbirds and a summer home for shepherds (and their Pashmina goats), who cultivate barley and peas in fields near their lakeside villages. Ibex Expeditions leads this tour mid-July–mid-October.

Rafting

Only experienced rafters should attempt Ladakh's challenging rivers, which generally offer good runs in July and August. Make sure your outfitter has all the right equipment and expertise.

ZANSKAR–INDUS RIVER

A 15-day round-trip adventure from Leh can start with short hikes and drives to important monasteries and great vistas. On the eighth day, you raft from Padam to Saspul villages, beginning a six-day trip with five days of rafting and a spectacular day hike in the Markha Valley. For two days you're locked in a gorge—a rough, fantastic journey that rates classes II–IV. There are fixed departures between July and September, depending on the weather; book well in advance with Himalayan River Runners or Aquaterra Adventures.

Trekking

SPITI–TSO MORIRI

This remote trail forms a challenging 20-day trek in some of Ladakh's most spectacular areas. Following the traditional trade route between the people of Spiti, Changthang, and Tibet, it begins in the high-altitude meadows of Kibber, breeding ground of the famous Spiti horses and home to the endangered snow leopard. After descending into the Kibber gorge, the trail climbs over the Parangla Pass (18,480 ft). A Pare River crossing is followed by an incredible change of scenery as you walk toward the Rupshu plains of Changthang, known for an abundance of kiang (Tibetan wild ass). The last two nights you camp at spectacular sites, one on the southern edge of Tso Moriri; from there, walk along Tso Moriri until you reach Karzog, a settlement of the Changpas (Changthang nomads) on the shores of the Tso Moriri. Contact Aquaterra Adventures.

LAMAYURU–CHILLING

Starting at Lamayuru, an immense monastery built in the 11th century, this moderate-to-difficult trek covers rugged terrain on its way to a part of Ladakh famous for its copper work. Lamayuru hasn't lost its ancient aura, and the diligence of the monks here makes it one of Ladakh's most vibrant monasteries. From here, you walk down the valley and climb to the village of Sumdahchenmo, from which you can look toward the Zanskar River. Farther on, you can either follow the Zanskar route to Chilling (10 days) or head back toward the Indus River and Alchi Gompa (5 days), an exquisite, 11th-century Indus Valley gompa in one of Ladakh's pristine hidden villages. From Chilling you can trek up to Leh via Hemis.

MANALI–LEH

Starting your trek in Manali allows for safer acclimatization. This strenuous, extremely popular 10- or 20-day trek starts after a drive across the Rohtang Pass and the descent into Lahaul. Expect to ford snow-fed streams, cross a high-altitude pass into Ladakh's Zanskar district, visit ancient monasteries and typical Buddhist villages, and experience a panoramic lunar landscape. You can take a jeep from Padam, the district headquarters in Zanskar, or continue trekking to Leh, the capital of Ladakh. The most rigorous route includes four more passes. Each version is rugged but stunning, with jagged glaciers and green village oases. You're likely to see traders leading horses laden with goods, and lots of foreign trekkers. The route is available mid-July to mid-September.

NUBRA VALLEY

This easy but high-altitude seven-day trek starts after a drive from Leh to the Nubra Valley village of Sabu, with its apple and apricot orchards and unexpected fertile spots. You hike up to Polu Digar, a summer grazing pasture for yaks and sheep, then climb over the Digar La Pass, at 18,040 ft, and descend to Digar village. The next day you follow a river to the village of Khungru and from here you visit another typical Buddhist village before retracing the route back to Sabu. After visiting Sabu's monastery, wind things up by driving back to Leh. This trip is available July through September.

UTTARANCHAL

The Himalayan stretch of Uttar Pradesh, now officially called Uttaranchal, is locked in by Himachal Pradesh, Tibet, and Nepal. Figuring prominently in the Hindu epics, Uttarakhand is the mythological
abode of the Hindu pantheon. Every year thousands of pilgrims make
yatras (Hindu pilgrimages) to the Garhwal mountains and the sacred
Char Dhams (Four Temples)—Yamunotri, Gangotri, Kedarnath, and
Badrinath—the homes of the Hindu gods Vishnu and Shiva and source
of the holy Yamuna and Ganges rivers.

With more than 100 peaks towering above 20,000 ft, Uttaranchal's
Garhwal mountains (especially Mt. Nanda Devi, at 26,056 ft) inspire
climbers from all over the world. Trekkers are drawn to its natural sanctuaries, such as Nanda Devi (surrounding the peak of the same name)
and the Valley of Flowers, strewn with blossoms and surrounded by
glaciers and white-capped mountains. Few foreigners, however, are aware
of other good treks through equally sublime Himalayan vistas to
mountain villages and the revered Char Dhams and other hallowed
shrines. Rafters searching for serious white water will find that Uttaranchal's runs, ranked with Asia's best, are indeed swift, long, and
away from the mainstream.

In the Garhwal foothills, next to the Nepali border, is Uttaranchal's
second major region, the Kumaon. Like the Garhwal, this is a place
of temples and mountain walks, but on a smaller scale—the topogra-
phy is much gentler, the forests thicker. Far from the frenzy of Garhwal's
Hindu pilgrims and Mussoorie's honeymooners, the Kumaon has a more
relaxed atmosphere, and the animal-rich Corbett National Park makes
it a world-class destination.

Rishikesh

❿ *238 km (148 mi) northeast of Delhi*

Yoga, ayurvedic healing, spiritual retreats—the resurgence of western
interest in the mind-body-spirit connection that put this ancient holy
city on the map has revitalized its appeal for foreign tourists in a way
that hasn't been apparent since the Beatles visited in the 1960s. Its location on the Ganges is sacred, but the streets are anything but tranquil. You'll find the place crowded with sadhus (holy men), Hindu
pilgrims, con-men, monkeys, and hippies. Whether you come to check
in to an ashram or to check out the scene, to "find" yourself or just
to observe the spectacle of so many others doing so, you'll find Rishikesh
has a slightly bizarre, but irresistible, energy. It's worth a stop en route
to the nearby Ganges river rafting camps. Cross over the *Lakshman
Jhula* suspension bridge to find a relatively quiet spot along the bathing
ghats.

Lodging

$$$$ ▣ **Ananda in the Himalayas.** In the heart of the Tehri Garwhal region
★ of Narendra Nagar, a breathtaking ascent—14 km (8 mi) by car from
Rishikesh, through Sal trees—brings you to this magnificent spa resort, a converted maharaja's palace. First you're greeted with ginger-
lemon tea and escorted from the main palace to the guest wing—past
the marble yoga pavilion and the waterfall. Every room has a view,
best seen from the glass-pane bathroom that looks out into the forest.
Furnishings are understated, with ivory-color hand-sewn quilts. Rich
tandoori kebabs are artfully balanced with tasty but health-conscious
organic spa food. The spa offers numerous therapies, from ayurvedic
oil massages to colonic irrigation. You can also take a day trek to the

Kunjapuri Temple, go river rafting, bike, play billiards, use the 100-year-old library, or lounge in the pool or jacuzzi. Rates include breakfast and select spa treatments. ⊠ *The Palace Estate, Narendra Nagar, 249175,* ☎ *378/27500 or 378/27550; or reserve through New Delhi,* ☎ *11/689–9999,* FAX *11/820–8405,* WEB *anandaspa.com. 70 rooms, 5 suites. Restaurant, bar, pool, spa, steam room, gym, hiking, jogging, bicycles, shop, library, business services, travel services. AE, MC, V.*

$$ ⊞ **The Glass House.** The Ganges rapids flow auspiciously past the verandahs fronting this tranquil Neemrana Group Heritage Hotel, once a garden-retreat of the maharajas of Tehri Garhwal. Spiritual guru Ma Anandamayi, whose disciples came from all over the world, stayed here for the peaceful atmosphere; the hotel's private spring-fed water supply supposedly has rejuvenating qualites. Spend the day with one of the river rafting camps just up the road if you are want an adventure, go for a jungle walk, visit a nearby ashram, or just read in the tropical garden here and watch the Ganges flow by. In the evening, relax in front of the log fire and fill up on Indian and Continental buffet meals before retreating to your room in the main building or in one of the quiet cottages—simply but uniquely decorated with hand-dyed fabrics and paintings. ⊠ *23rd Milestone, Rishikesh-Badrinath Rd., Village Gular Dogi, 249303,* ☎ *01378/69224; or reserve through New Delhi,* ☎ *11/435–8962,* FAX *11/435–1112,* WEB *www.neemranahotels.com. 12. Restaurant, laundry service, travel services. AE, MC, V.*

Mussoorie

⑪ *278 km (172 mi) northeast of Delhi 110 km (68 mi) northwest of Rishikesh*

As you approach Mussoorie you'll see scads of cars with young, upper-middle-class Indian tourists and billboards advertising hotels. Both are tip-offs: Mussoorie is not a peaceful mountain getaway. At an altitude of about 6,500 ft, this former British hill station in the Himalayan foothills of Uttaranchal is, nonetheless, a good place to escape Delhi's dusty summer heat. The north side of the town's hill offers spectacular views of the Himalayas; the town itself looks out south over the plains.

Founded in 1823 by a British Army captain, Mussoorie has a few remnants of the Raj—an Anglican church, old British library, and a "Gun Hill" from which the noon cannon was fired—but they're less extensive than those in Shimla or Nainital. Besides strutting your stuff on Mussoorie's pedestrian-only thoroughfare, the Mall, you can take quiet walks around town, especially heading up through Landour Bazaar, with its imperial clocktower, toward Sister's Bazaar.

The most pleasant way to get to Mussoorie is to take the 5½-hour *Shatabdi Express* train from Delhi (departing 7:30 AM) to Dehra Dun, then take a one-hour taxi ride from that station to Mussoorie. You can also hire a car all the way from Delhi; the road trip takes about as long as the train journey, but the roads make for unpleasant travel. If you drive, expect to pay about Rs. 4,000–Rs. 5,000 (overnights increase the cost). Use a Delhi travel agency to make arrangements.

Lodging

$$$ ⊞ **The Claridges Nabha.** Once the property of the Mharaja of Nabha, this summer bungalow is the one place in Mussoorie that consciously maintains the ambience of an old-fashioned hill station. About a mile away from the crowded Mall, it lets you unwind in peaceful and natural surroundings. The 1845 main bungalow, with a typical red-tin roof, has an enormous foyer. Guest rooms were created in the 1940s. The best rooms open onto a veranda and face a courtyard; inside, rooms have an understated elegance. You can sit on the front lawn, under a gigantic cypress, and watch the escapades of langurs jumping through trees; take a stroll through terraced gardens with lilies and tuberoses; or a nature walk in the nearby woods. Breakfast and either lunch or dinner are included. ⊠ *Airfield, Barlowganj Rd., 248179,* ☎ *0135/ 631426,* FAX *0135/631425; or reserve through Claridges, New Delhi,* ☎ *11/301–0211,* FAX *11/379–2388,* WEB *www.claridges.hotel@gems. vsnl.net.in. 22 rooms. Restaurant, bar, lobby lounge, tennis court, billiards, business services, travel services. AE, DC, MC, V.*

The Kumaon Circuit

A relatively peaceful, underdeveloped corner of the country, the Kumaon (pronounced "koom-ah-oh") is a wonderful place to begin a love affair with India. Ceded by Nepal to British India in 1815, it remains a place of forests, farmland, temples, and tigers.

The Uttaranchal route outlined here and below will give you a colorful, but gentle, introduction to the region. The Kumaon has ancient culture, but it's not such an epicenter of Indian civilization as Varanasi, and its urban life is not the onslaught of Bombay's. It also has plenty of natural beauty that can be enjoyed without the physical intensity of a full-blown trek.

You must hire a car or jeep for this trip (make arrangements through a Delhi travel agency). All of the hotels listed have complimentary overnight facilities for drivers or can recommend an inexpensive place nearby. Start by driving northeast from Delhi to Ramnagar, site of Corbett National Park. (This is a six-hour drive *if* you leave Delhi at about 5 AM; after that, traffic around Delhi will extend the trip by several hours.) When you've had your fill of Corbett, drive east to Nainital for a taste of modern Indian culture with a Raj flavor. From Nainital go north to Ranikhet for golf or peaceful walks through the pine forests. From Ranikhet you can make side trips to several important Hindu temples, which lie just to the northeast. Finish by looping back at the north end of Corbett, perhaps by fishing on the Ramganga River. The entire circle takes anywhere from seven days to two weeks, depending on how much time you want to linger over such activities as searching for tigers.

The drive back to Delhi takes about seven hours—if you leave the Corbett National Park area before 2 AM. Depart after that and the rush-hour traffic outside Delhi will add an hour or four to this final leg of your trip. An alternative is to leave Corbett at a reasonable hour and, after a four-hour drive, spend the next night at the lovely Mud Fort in Kuchesar, 80 km (50 mi) west of Delhi. If you leave Kuchesar by 7 the next morning, you'll be back in central Delhi in 90 minutes.

The appeal of the Kumaon loop shifts during the year, but March and December are probably the best times to do it. Corbett National Park is closed from June 15 until November 15 for the monsoon; Nainital and Raniket get snow in January; and Indians throng to the hills during their school holidays, which begin April 15.

Lodging

$$–$$$ ⊡ **The Mud Fort.** Built in the mid-18th century with seven turrets and a moat as a defense against British cannon attacks, this white and saffron-color Jat fortress is now a bastion against the noise and crowds of urban India. Peace is broken only at dawn and dusk by peacocks

and parrots in the mansion ruins the hotel overlooks. Every room is distinctive, with different views, block-print quilts, original contemporary Indian art, and photographs from the maharaja/owner's private collection. Some peeling paint and faded curtains all seem part of the hotel's dusty romantic glamour. Service is inobtrusive, and there's no TV, telephones, or liquor license. Climb up to the rooftop terrace here for the view at sunset, or stroll in nearby traffic-free lanes, through sugarcane fields and mango orchards, and past ochre and indigo-painted houses, to get a rare glimpse of unspoilt villages. Meals are Indian/Continental buffets. ✉ *Village Kuchesar, Via BB Nagar, District Bulandshahr, 245402,* ☎ *9837/003084; or in Delhi,* ☎ *11/435–8962* FAX *11/435–1112,* WEB *www.neemranahotels.com. 10. Restaurant, pool, laundry. AE, MC, V.*

Corbett National Park

★ ⑫   *Ramnagar is 250 km (155 mi) northeast of Delhi.*

India's oldest wildlife sanctuary (founded 1936), Corbett National Park is named after Jim Corbett, the fearless hunter and author of *Man-Eaters of Kumaon* who later became a conservationist and photographer. Corbett grew up in these hills, and the local people—a number of whom he saved from tigers at the risk of his own life—revered him. Corbett hunted tigers, but later came to regret the sport as he saw the turn-of-the-20th-century population of up to 40,000 tigers drastically reduced. Upon his death in 1956, India honored Corbett by renaming Hailey National Park after this well-liked man.

The park, with elephant grass, forests, and the Ramganga River slicing through its entire length, covers 1,318 square km (527 square mi). You can explore the park on the back of an elephant as it sways quietly through the jungle brush; you can sit in an open jeep as it rolls along miles of tracks; or you can just peer into the vast vista from the top of a watchtower and listen to the sounds. This is a great park, worthy of Corbett's memory: here you'll see many deer, monkeys, and birds, and, if you're lucky, wild elephants, tigers, leopards, black bears, wild boars, snakes (including pythons), and crocodiles.

Only 100 day-trippers are allowed into the park each day, and the park is closed from June 15 to November 15. If you won't be staying overnight, you must get an entry permit from the tourist office at Ramnagar Reception to enter by the Amdanda Gate, which allows you to enter the Bijrani area for morning and evening safaris. If you stay at a private lodge, the staff there will make your daily excursion arrangements. A guide, available at the park, must accompany each vehicle. Before leaving Corbett, you may want to stop in at the small **museum** at Dhangarhi Gate, which houses some stuffed wildcats. ✉ *Ramnagar, Nainital district; for information contact Uttaranchal Tourist Office, 21 Barakhamba Rd., New Delhi 110001,* ☎ *11/335–0481 or 11/335–6620,* WEB *www.kmvn.com.* ✍ *Rs. 350; cameras Rs. 100, video cameras Rs. 500, cars Rs. 200, guides Rs. 200.*

Dining and Lodging

No trip to Corbett is complete without at least one overnight stay in the park itself. At the government-owned Forest Rest Houses, most of which were originally built as stopping points for British forest officers on their way to and from inspections deep inside the jungle, you can beat the convoys of jeeps entering the park in the morning to watch game until sunset, then fall to sleep amid a deep silence pierced only by the occasional cry of a wild animal. There are a total of 24 Forest Rest Houses in the park. Some, such as Dhikala, are quite large, with electricity and food service, but most are very basic and have four to six beds (in two to three rooms), no electricity, bucket baths, and only seasonal access. Take your own sleeping bags and sheets.

While you can make personal arrangements to stay in the rest houses, it's not advisable. Their management is highly bureaucratic and not attuned to customer service. Instead, stay at one of the lodges listed below, inform them of your wish in advance, and for a fee they'll make all the necessary arrangements, as well as provide conveyance and housekeeping provisions. These resorts are very close to Amdanda Gate, the park's main entrance, and offer package stays (called "Jungle Plans") that include full board and jeep and elephant safaris, both with knowledgeable naturalists. One guide recommended for "insider" tours is Manoj Mehta (☎ 05947/51878), who lives near the park. Contact his agent in New Delhi, Great Himalayan Adventures, to arrange travel and accomodation for the park (several weeks notice suggested).

$$$$ ✕🖬 **Infinity Resorts Corbett Lodge.** This popular resort, known by its former name "Tiger Tops," is magnificent. It's on a high bank of the Kosi River—so you can listen to rushing water while looking across the foothills. Each spacious room has a large picture window, a wall made of rough stone, a bamboo-and-tile ceiling, a modern bathroom with a shower, and a large private balcony overlooking the pool. Most impressive is the circular central lodge, with its vaulted timber dome, where you can eat, drink, and relax in front of a fire in winter. You can also take refreshments on the deck outside, which overhangs the river and lush jungle on the opposite bank—you may even spot a tiger. The room rate includes all meals (delicious homestyle Indian food, and some Continental food), and activities, such as jeep safaris and hiking. There's an elephant in residence for safaris and leisurely rides. ✉ *Dhikuli, Ramnagar, Nainital district, 244715,* ☎ *05947/51276 or 87957; in Delhi contact Khatau International, A-3 Geetanjali Enclave, New Delhi 110017,* ☎ *11/686–1189 or 11/686–1209,* FAX *11/ 686–1219,* WEB *www.infinityresorts.com. 24 rooms. Restaurant, bar, pool, Ping-Pong, playground, meeting room, travel services. AE, DC, MC, V.*

$$$–$$$$ ✕🖬 **The Claridges Corbett Hideaway.** This resort is on the banks of
   ★ the Kosi River, yet it lacks the dramatic views of its rival—Infinity Resorts. More than compensatory, however, are the professional management and the lush setting—in a mango orchard. Pebble walkways lead to the ochre cottages, which have *chaprel* (baked-tile) roofs, stone-tile floors, woven bamboo-mat ceilings, and fireplaces. Rattan and jute furniture give the place a rustic feel. Each cottage has a sitting area, a modern bathroom with a shower, and a veranda from which to enjoy the peaceful surroundings. Tea and snacks are served poolside. Fixed-menu meals are served in the new lodge on the riverbank; these are followed by bonfires on the lawn. The staff is happy to arrange hikes; mountain-biking excursions; and jeep, elephant, and (with advance notice) horseback safaris. ✉ *Zero Garjia, Dhikuli, Ramnagar, Nainital district, 224715,* ☎ *05947/87932 or 05947/87934,* FAX *05947/87933; in Delhi contact Claridges at* ☎ *11/301–0211. 28 rooms. Restaurant, bar, pool, archery, Ping-Pong, meeting room. AE, DC, MC, V.*

En Route Several miles north of the park's Dhangarhi Gate, driving along the river, you'll find the first of many small temples on this loop. The people of the Kumaon are predominately Shivites—worshipers of Shiva, the destroyer and re-creator of the Hindu pantheon. The **Garjia Temple** in Dhikuli is dedicated to Garjia Ma, a local incarnation of the goddess Parvati, Shiva's consort. Located in a small gorge, the temple is perched about 49 m (160 ft) up on a tall rock that becomes an island in the middle of the Kosi River during the monsoon. Drive down the access road through the wheat fields and banana trees, then walk from the parking area through the gauntlet of rickety shops selling Hindu paraphernalia. Several of these shops sell coconuts and flowers that can be used as offerings to the goddess. The temple is open from sunrise to sunset.

Nainital

⑬ *63 km (39 mi) east of Corbett National Park, 277 km (172 mi) northeast of Delhi*

The drive from Corbett to Nainital is less than two hours long, but is memorable for both its solitude and its scenery. East of Ramnagar the road leads you on a tour of unspoiled agrarian India. Mud dwellings with grass roofs stand guard next to fields of sugarcane, wheat, and lentils; interspersed with the fields are small stands of teak and *sal* (tall trees that resemble black oak), with an occasional banana plantation thrown in. In the distance are glimpses of the Himalayan foothills that await you. Just before you turn up into the hills at Kaladungi, you'll pass Jim Corbett's old winter home, a small colonial bungalow whose museum offers a short break from the journey. The road uphill begins in a sal forest, which occasionally gives way to terraced fields. As the trees thin out, the road gets steep and starts to wind. Toward the top you might be held up by troops of langurs sunning themselves on the road or children on their way home from school in the city. Suddenly the road turns downhill, and the congestion of Nainital begins.

Nainital is one of India's most popular hill stations. This one, "discovered" by the British in the 1840s, was later made the official summer capital of Uttaranchal (then known as the United Provinces). Nainital clutches the steep slopes that surround a lake of the same name. It's easy to see why the British fell in love with this idyllic spot, yet seemingly uncontrolled development is beginning to take its toll in the form of congestion, pollution, and noise. Indian tourists, especially honeymooners, come to Nainital in all seasons to enjoy the cool air and mountain views. The school holidays, April 15–June 15, bring the real crowds and should be avoided if possible.

As a former colonial capital, Nainital packs quite a bit of history. Those interested in colonial architecture are in for a particular treat. There's another British building, generally with a high-gable tin roof, around every corner; check out the Clocktower, the Boat Club, the Masonic Hall, the library, and the Church of St. John of the Wilderness. Most of these buildings are, however, slowly tumbling down. The north end of town is built up around the **Flats,** a large open field created by a landslide in the late 19th century. Facing the Municipal Office, this area is permeated by an air of perpetual carnival; magicians and acrobats perform as tourists munch away on snacks purchased from the many vendors. Sit and watch a cricket game, or take in a Hindi movie at the old Capital Cinema Hall on the Flats.

Elusive to the eye but unavoidable to the ear is the busy **Sri Ma Naini Temple** on the Flats. Open sunrise to sunset, this lakeside shrine is dedicated to many gods, including Shiva, but Naina Devi (an incarnation of Parvati, the wife of Shiva) is its focus. Take off your shoes, wander around, and watch the devout make offerings to the large black Shiva lingam by the lake. If you're interested in Indian religions, visit the **gurdwara** (Sikh temple) that faces the Flats. If Islam intrigues you, visit the **mosque** across from the Flats.

A fabulous place to take in Nainital's famous Himalayan views is **Cheena Peak.** It's the highest point near Nainital, at 2,611 m (8,566 ft), and was officially renamed Naini Peak after India's 1962 war with China. You can reach the peak on foot or on the back of one of the many horses for rent in town. The outlook called **Snow View** can be reached on foot or horseback, and there's a Tibetan monastery on the way. Tourists commonly take a gondola ride ("The Ropeway") to Snow View from town, which runs roughly, not reliably, 9:30–1 and 2–5 daily.

Lodging

$$$ ☎ **The Claridges Naini Retreat.** In this elegant retreat not far from Nainital, the new is connected almost seamlessly with the old. The old is Hari Bhavan, built as a summer maharaja's residence in 1926; the new is a hotel run by Claridges of Delhi. Set around a red-tile garden patio, the bluestone buildings have classic Kumaoni red-tin roofs with latticework windows and high gables. Rooms are simple, with hardwood furniture and floors; some look down past wrought-iron railings to Nainital and across the lake to the development creeping up the hillsides. The duplexes, though a bit dark, are great for families. Meals—which can include traditional Kumaoni dishes—are served in a high-ceiling dining room, with breakfast and either lunch or dinner included in your room rate. The hotel does not exchange currency. ✉ *Ayarpatta Slopes, Nainital, 263001,* ☎ *05942/35105,* FAX *05942/35103; in Delhi, contact Claridges at* ☎ *11/301–0625,* FAX *11/379–2388. 44 rooms. Restaurant, golf privileges, billiards, Ping-Pong. AE, DC, MC, V.*

$$$ ☎ **Mountain Quail Camp.** To avoid the congestion of Nainital, try this "camp" about half an hour's drive away. The deluxe tents have attached bathrooms and comfortable beds. At night you can sit around a communal fire and enjoy the peaceful, woodsy surroundings. The proprietor, "Sid" (Siddharth), is a true outdoorsman and naturalist, so make use of him. If you have time, stay a few days and let him arrange some outdoor activities for you. Sid regularly organizes day hikes and short treks farther up into the hills, or down to his mother's small resort near Kaladhungi. Fishing, pony-trekking, bird watching, mountain biking, and rock climbing are other distractions. All meals are included in the room rate. Bring cash: traveler's checks and most credit cards are not accepted. ✉ *Pangot 263001; in Kaladhungi,* ☎ *5942/4227 or 5942/ 35493; in Delhi,* ☎ *11/463–5797,* FAX *11/464–2063. Restaurant. AE.*

Ranikhet

⑭ *55 km (34 mi) north of Nainital*

As with Nainital, the drive here takes less than two hours but is an event in itself. After leaving the crowded confines of Nainital on a road that hugs the mountainside, you'll quickly enter the town of **Bhiwali**— this grubby little place, with small shops and tea stalls, is the center of the local fruit industry. In season the roadside is crowded with men selling crates of apples, peaches, and plums to travelers and commercial dealers, and for the next hour of your drive the bottom of the river valley is filled with small orchards. After crossing another small river, you'll head back up to Ranikhet, at which point the forests give way to some spectacular sections of terraced farmland.

Ranikhet itself is ensconced in evergreen confines on a Himalayan hilltop. Of all the British hill stations in India, only Ranikhet retains some of its original sylvan tranquillity. This may be because it's an army town, home of the Kumaon Regiment ever since the Raj, so development has been controlled. The spacious army cantonment stretches along the Mall, which winds along the top of hill, and many of the regiment's stone buildings, erected well before Independence, are still smartly maintained specimens of colonial architecture. Walk on the **Upper Mall Road** to see the Parade Ground or Regimental Headquarters.

Ranikhet has at least six old colonial churches that can be explored. While each is unique, all are made of stone and have the high tin roofs typical of this area. Two of these churches, facing each other across a small athletic field in the center of the cantonment, have been deconsecrated and converted into the **Ranikhet Tweed and Shawl Factory,** a hand-loom production center of woolens. This operation is run by the Kumaon Regiment for soldiers injured in the line of duty and for army widows. Let the clattering draw you inside for a look at how hand looms work, or visit the little store down by the field, housed in the regiment's old bank. The factory and store are open Monday through Saturday from 9 to 5.

Heading uphill (south) from the Westview Hotel, take the **Lower Mall Road,** almost completely abandoned now, for a peaceful stroll through a forest of pine and oak. About 2 km (1 mi) up the road, it merges once again with Upper Mall Road and you come upon the small, relatively new **Jhula Devi Temple,** open sunrise to sunset. The temple is bursting with brass bells; Hindu temple bells are traditionally rung to alert the god to the devotee's need. If you keep walking, in a few more miles you'll reach the **Chaubatia Orchards,** a 260-acre fruit orchard run by the state government. Feel free to stroll among the trees.

Dining and Lodging

$$ ✕⌧ **Westview.** Perched on a small hill, the Westview's yellow-flagstone main building was designed as a home in the mid-19th century. It has been designated a Heritage Hotel, but renovations have not altered the unique design of each room; the Westview Suite and suite 28 are large, bright, and quiet. In winter you can drift off in front of your own fireplace or wood-burning stove. The dining room, with its 25-ft ceiling, calico wallpaper, and linens, and high-back wooden chairs, is a treat, especially when a fire crackles in the hearth. Service is exceptional for such an unassuming place. The Continental food is superior to the Indian: try the roast leg of lamb with mint sauce or fish munière, followed by crème caramel. Order meals an hour in advance. ⌧ *Mahatma Gandhi Rd., 263645,* ☏ *05966/20261,* ℻ *05961/20396; or reserve through C-16 Greater Kailash 1, New Delhi 110048* ☏ *11/648–5981,* ℻ *11/331–7582. 20 rooms. Restaurant, coffee shop, badminton, horseback riding. No credit cards.*

Hindu Temples

If you have an extra few days, take a side trip from Ranikhet to see several important temples dedicated to Lord Shiva. Many are old, dating from the Katyuri (8th–14th centuries) and Chand (15th–18th centuries) dynasties. The most significant temples northeast of Ranikhet are at **Baijanth, Bhageshwar,** and **Jageshwar.** Unlike temples on the plains, these are built from rough-hewn stone, and their alpine locations—such as the cedar forest in Jageshwar—give Hinduism an entirely different feel. The hill at **Binsar** has both a nature sanctuary and some ruins of the Chand dynasty's former capital. The views from the top are fabulous.

Dining and Lodging

$$$ ⌧ **Binsar Valley Resort.** This small resort is both a pleasant rest stop after a temple tour and a base for Himalayan adventures. Ideally located at the edge of the Binsar Sanctuary (with exemplary bird-watching), it was built in 1934 as the summer home of Major B. P. Pande.

The original home is now a guest house. Rooms are in separate cottages; all have wood stoves and the public sitting room has an open fireplace, so winter stays are as enjoyable as summer visits. The staff can arrange adventures, including trekking, rafting, camping, and jeep safaris, but their crown offering is a stable full of trained Austrian mountain horses (Haflingers) for experienced riders and sturdy Tibetan mountain ponies for beginners and children. ⊠ *Village Basoli, P.O. Bhainsori, Almora district, 263684,* ☎ *5962/53028; or reserve through New Delhi,* ☎ *11/622–1698 or 622–4680,* ℻ *11/622–1699.* WEB *www.clubmahindra.com. 14 rooms. Dining room, horseback riding, travel services. AE, MC, V.*

Corbett National Park: North Side

The three-hour drive southwest from Ranikhet back down to Corbett National Park is breathtaking, both for its views of the Himalayas and for the sometimes frightening way the narrow road hugs the very steep mountainsides. If you're prone to motion sickness you might want to take medication before beginning this drive; but the winding road is almost deserted, so the drive is peaceful. After passing through a small town, it meanders through hillsides and farmlands, then sinks into sal forests. Just before arriving at Corbett, turn right at the Mohan Forest Rest House and climb over the heavily forested ridge that separates the Kosi from the Ramganga river valleys. This brings you to the seldom-visited north side of the park, which offers anglers a unique fishing experience and all travelers a rest stop en route back to Delhi.

Lodging

$$$–$$$$ 🏨 **Corbett Ramganga Resort.** While other resorts around Corbett allude to fishing facilities, this riverside resort specializes in helping the angler catch one, with a collection of well-maintained casting rods and a fishing guide whose successes are documented with photos in the reception room. Stay in a yellow-brick cottage (they're small, as are the beds, but are clean and freshly painted), a "safari tent" with attached brick bathroom, or one of the new family suites. The grounds are laced with flower beds, and the shallow pool sits in a spacious lawn next to the river. While Ramganga arranges park safaris, it's too far from Amdanda Gate (an hour's drive) to make this convenient; fishing, hiking and rafting (September to December) can occupy you here. Meals, served in a river-view dining lodge, are included in the room price. There is no foreign exchange. ⊠ *Reserve through Surbhi Adventures P. Ltd., New Delhi,* ☎ *11/652–2955,* ℻ *11/685–5428,* WEB *www.ramganga.com. 10 cottages, 10 tents. Restaurant, pool. AE, DC, MC, V.*

Adventures

Coming to Uttaranchal in the summer lets you avoid the crowd of foreigners that descends on Himachal Pradesh and Ladakh. Aside from a few routes frequented by Hindu and Sikh pilgrims (the road to Rishikesh can get very busy) you'll be alone with the villagers and shepherds. Given the great rafting on the headwaters of the Ganges and its tributaries, tour companies recommend combination trips, which include trekking and rafting in addition to, say, fishing and mountain biking. The downside of Uttaranchal is the poor travel infrastructure; the roads are not as well maintained as those in Himachal Pradesh. The lack of an airport deep in the mountains means more driving, but increased demand from the growing number of upmarket resorts in the area has encouraged Indian Airlines to offer three flights a week to the Jolly Grant Airport in Dehradun, with a view to improving this service in the near future.

Fishing

RAMGANGA RIVER

The Ramganga River bisects Corbett National Park. Prior to entering the park it flows past the Corbett Ramganga Resort, which has made a specialty of pursuing the mahaseer. If you plan to stay here, alert them in advance of your interest and they'll take care of your license (a one-day process) as well as provide high-quality poles and an expert guide. Leave everything to them; fish the day away; then relax in the garden or by the pool in the evening. The fishing season, which runs from October 1 to June 30, peaks between February and April.

Rafting

Whitewater rafting in Uttaranchal, especially on the Ganges River just upstream from Rishikesh, has become a major growth industry. At press time there were close to 15 separate rafting camps on the river in this area, set up by tour companies to provide Delhi's smart set with relaxing adventure vacations—people drive up for a weekend of rafting and horseplay on a sandy beach by the upper Ganges. This is a great time, highly recommended if you want to escape the city and do some rafting without committing to a long, strenuous adventure trip. The season runs from October to June; contact Aquaterra Adventures, Himalayan River Runners, Snow Leopard, or Outdoor Adventures India for information. The same companies can arrange the longer trips listed below. Outdoor Adventures India—run by a charming couple, Ajay Maira and Pavanne Mann—stands out. Their camp on the upper Ganges is a favorite with American expats and their families; the focus is on safety, ecology, and good food, and Ajay knows the river well. Aquaterra, led by Vaibhav Kala and his team of some of the most experienced, enthusiastic, and fun-loving guides on the river, is recommended for its hearty spirit—and heartier campfire barbeques.

ALAKANANDA RIVER

Five-day runs (November–mid-December and February–April) follow the Alakananda from Rudraprayag to Rishikesh. Expect good rapids, historic temples, good Himalayan vistas, campsites on secluded beaches, and Class III and IV rapids.

BHAGIRATHI RIVER

This six-day Himalayan run (November–mid-December and February–April) goes from Tehri to Rishikesh. You move through at least two gorges and river valleys, and even maneuver a small waterfall.

GANGES RIVER

Enjoy day-trips from the camps near Rishikesh or an easy three-day rafting trip on the Ganges (October–mid-December and February–June). Float from Deoprayag to Rishikesh, both in the lower Himalayas. You can even body-surf (only as your guide recommends and with life-jacket and helmet securely on) on quieter stretches of the river.

KALI RIVER

Flowing past densely forested hillsides, this trip is a wilderness experience in a league of its own. The Kali River forms the international border between India and Nepal, flowing past the terraced farms of Kumaoni and Nepali villages, sandy beaches, thick tropical jungles, cliff-sides of stalactite and stalagmite formations, riverside tea stops, and plantations. After the first few days of serene floating up to and past the confluence with the Saryu River at Pancheshwar (an ideal time to try landing a mahaseer), you hit some big rapids. The Kali makes its final descent to the plains on your last day on water, beginning with the mighty Chooka rapid. This 10-day round trip from Delhi is best undertaken between November and March. Aquaterra Adventures suggests that rafting be preceded by a jeep safari through the Kumaon, including Ranikhet, Binsar, and the temples of Mukteshwar and Bageshwar, indeed a most highly recommended trip that takes 12–15 days.

TONS RIVER

In the secluded pine forests of northern Uttaranchal (the river borders Himachal Pradesh 140 km/87 mi from Shimla). New camps run by both AquaTerra and Himalayan River Runners offer summer rafting May to July, together with fishing, rock climbing and hiking, in an area rich with flora and fauna.

Trekking

GANGOTRI–GAUMUKH

This moderate, but high-altitude, nine-day trek is probably the most popular in Uttaranchal with both foreign trekkers and Hindu pilgrims alike. Best from April to June and September to October, it heads to the source of the sacred Ganges River, with a trailhead at Gangotri Temple in northern Uttaranchal. You first pass through forests and a valley, following the pilgrim route that climbs above the tree line to Bhijbasa and its solitary ashram. You cross flowering meadows backed by towering peaks and camp on the wide, sandy beach of the Gaumukh, where the holy Ganges emerges from the Gangotri Glacier. The trail weaves through moraine, cuts across the glacier, and climbs steeply up grassy slopes to Tapovan Valley, with vast meadows that brush against the base of Shivling Peak. Camping at Tapovan, you take day hikes to Kirti Bamak Glacier, the base of Kedarnath Dome and Kirti, and Meru Glacier and the base of Mt. Meru (believed by Hindus to be the center of the universe). From Tapovan, you make an excursion across the moraine-covered Gangotri Glacier to Nandanvan, at the confluence of the Chaturangi and Gangotri glaciers. After camping in a meadow against the Bhagirathi Massif, which is home to *bharal* (blue sheep), you follow a grassy ridge that runs parallel to the Chaturangi Glacier toward Vaski Tal (Lake) before retracing the route back to Nandanvan and Gangotri.

SAHASRATAL–BHILANGANA VALLEY

The likelihood that you'll see another trekker on this challenging route is remote. The Sahasratal group of lakes lie at an average altitude of 15,000 ft in the Uttarkashi district of Uttaranchal. These lakes are considered holy by the local people who take an annual pilgrimage carrying the *doli* (deity) on their shoulders. The route climbs through only one village, Sila, passing through high pastures. Depending on the season, you might meet only goatherds and Gujjars here. The trail winds its way through massive open meadows littered with wild daffodils and climbs over the 13,200-ft Kyarki Khal pass, offering brilliant views of all the mountain ranges in the area from Bandarpunch and Kala Nag to Jaonli. Each of the Sahasratal lakes has a religious significance. Pilgrims from the Uttarkashi side return from the lake after making their offerings, but this route makes a steep descent through forested hillside to the Bhilangana Valley. The route now follows the river all the way to the roadhead at Ghuttu, starting point for the Khatling Glacier trek. The trip is accessible in June or September–October. Contact Aquaterra Adventure for details.

DARJEELING

⑮ Anyone with a yen for hill stations must see the "Queen of the Hills" in the far northwestern corner of West Bengal. Built during the British Raj as a center for the tea trade, Darjeeling quickly earned a reputation as a superb Himalayan spa resort. Most of the graceful old colonial buildings are a bit scruffy, but some still bear their regal stamp. Outside the pedestrianized town center, the traffic in high season can impede an exploratory stroll; yet the town's Old World charm enchants even jaded travelers. Long before you reach the town, as you ascend a winding road from the plains, you'll smell an invigorating blend of tea, verdant undergrowth, cedar, and wildflowers. The largely Nepali population of the region has made its imprint more subtly than the Raj— even the simplest homes are embellished with brightly painted trim, small gardens, or flower pots. With a few days here you can soak up the majestic alpine scenery—dominated, in good weather, by far-off Mt. Kanchenjunga (28,208 ft). You can also bargain in a local market or trek on a nearby hillside. Fog engulfs the town from below at unpredictable intervals, but when it clears and the sun sparkles on snowy Kanchenjunga, third-highest mountain in the world, the effect dazzles.

The pride of Daj, as it's affectionately called, is its main promenade, **the Mall.** Stroll around, or hop on a pony, and drink in the general air of well-being. If you're hungry after a long train journey, stop in a roadside café for a plate of steamed Tibetan momos or opt for roasted corn-on-the-cob (for yourself or the ponies) or popcorn masala. From the Mall you can wander off into some of the town's hilly cobble lanes.

Nature lovers have plenty to see right in town. Just be aware that many streets are one-way, so it can be confusing to get around. The **Bengal Natural History Museum** (✉ Meadowbank Rd.) houses an exhaustive collection of alpine fauna and a curiously eccentric display of big-game trophies and pickled snakes. Just north of the museum en route to the zoo, but not generally open to the public, is **Raj Bhavan,** former residence of the Maharaja of Burdwan, crowned by a shining blue dome. **Padmaja Naidu Zoo** (✉ off Jawahar Rd. W) is an ideal destination for a walk, and is justly famous for its rare snow leopards, as well as shy red pandas and other alpine animals. On the walk to or from the zoo, take a picnic or just a short detour up the hill—follow the sign "River Hill District Magistrate's Office" to **Shrubbery Park,** a quiet garden behind the Raj Bhavan, with great views. The **Himalayan Mountaineering Institute** (✉ beyond the zoo), a training center with some public exhibits, was long directed by none other than Sherpa Tenzing Norgay, who accompanied Sir Edmund Hillary up Mt. Everest in 1953. Farther down the Jawahar Road (signed at the zoo, which you pass on the way here) is the **Snow Leopard Breeding Center,** a pleasant walk through shady pines where you can often see newborn cubs with their mothers. The **WWF** (World Wide Fund for Nature) has a small office behind the Gym Khana Club exercise room with information on environmental programs; interested visitors are welcome to take part in tree-planting outings or "Project Serve Workshops"—they can also recommend eco-conscious tour and trekking guides.

Sacred sites also abound. South of the town center (below the train station), **Dhirdham Temple** was built along the lines of the Pashupatinath Temple in Kathmandu. Both Buddhists and Hindus revere **Observatory Hill** (above Windamere Hotel), topped by an unusual shrine. As the monkeys at the top can be quite aggressive, walk up with a group and don't carry food. There are several gompas, or Tibetan monasteries, nearby, including **Aloobari** (✉ Tenzing Norgay Rd.). The Tibetan monastery **Bhutia Busti** houses the original *Bhardo Thudol* (Tibetan *Book of The Dead*). Darjeeling's most celebrated house of worship is the **Yiga-Choling** (8 km/5 mi, south of Darjeeling) monastery in Ghoom, which houses the extremely sacred Maitreya Buddha ("Coming Buddha") image. It's a stop on the famous Toy Train that runs through the region. Ghoom is a regular stop on the return journey from the famed **Tiger Hill** look-out point, where views of Kanchenjunga, the Eastern Himalayas, and even Mount Everest make it worth getting up for well before sunrise. The fit and adventurous can walk the 8 km (5 mi) back to town on a quiet side road. If you're coming from the direction of Tiger Hill, ask your driver to stop at the **Japanese Peace Pagoda** for a lovely view of both the town and the mountains. The **Batasia Loop** is a new war memorial and a feat of railroad engineering; here you can see the Toy Train do a figure-eight turn amid a garden of daisies and wild poppies. Overlooking the Mall on Birch Hill, **St Andrew's Church** still takes pride of place—attending its Christmas carol service is a highlight of the Darjeeling's festive holiday season.

To see how Darjeeling tea is processed, visit the **Happy Valley Tea Estate,** 3 km (2 mi) outside town, an easy walk downhill through the tea bushes; it's fairly strenuous on the way back up. Tea is still made here in the orthodox way, and an obliging employee can be an impromptu but effective guide for the production process from Tuesday to Saturday. Stop en route for a steaming cup of tea, local gossip, and great opportunities to photograph the tea pickers (all women) heading out to work—at the tea stall Kusum has run in the same spot for more than 20 years.

The weather in Darjeeling is delightful year-round, barring only the monsoon season, when rain and fog can make driving treacherous. You'll get the best views of Kanchenjunga between November and March. The town sometimes gets snow in December; bring heavy woolens in winter, light woolens in summer.

Dining and Lodging

Most of Darjeeling's best restaurants are in the hotels, notably The Windamere and The New Elgin, but the town has a few independent classics, all within easy walking distance of the Mall. Take a flashlight if you plan to be walking back to your hotel after dark, as public electricity supplies are erratic.

$$$$ ✕ **Glenary's.** A popular meeting place for locals and travellers, and the town's best independent option, Glenary's has three floors, all with great views. The top floor is atmospheric in the evening (reserve a booth near the window) and serves Indian tandoori, Chinese, and Continental food with a range of Indian beer and wines. The new pub downstairs is multi-cuisine and has a range of cocktails. But most revered is the ground-floor café tea service and desserts. ⊠ *Nehru Rd.,* ☎ *0354/54122. AE, MC, V.*

$$–$$$$ ✕ **Embassy.** In the Hotel Valentino you can get hearty Chinese food with faintly Indian undertones in the "curried" spicing and textures of traditional Chinese favorites. In the cooler seasons (but best avoided in the monsoon), opt for the fish, which is brought up to Darjeeling from West Bengal. ⊠ *6 Rockville Rd.,* ☎ *0354/2228.*

$–$$ ✕ **Dekevas.** This small corner café has menus crumpled from much handling (an indication that the prices have long stayed the same), and a friendly, happy buzz of pleasant revelry. It's a hot destination for big American-style pizzas and Tibetan momos, stir-fried noodles, and big slurpy, garlicky soups. There are lots of vegetarian options, and a relaxed atmosphere where you can meet new people or hang out with a book. Dekevas is just east of the mall, under the Dekeling Hotel. ⊠ *51 Gandhi Rd.*

$ ✕ **Hot Stimulating Cafe.** Living up to its name (come in from the cold and try the Cosmic Veggie soup or a plate of hot greasy fries with a mug of hot tea) this tiny, unpretentious wooden shack serves Tibetan and Nepali snacks with much warmth and humor. It's the perfect rest-stop on a walk to or from the zoo area. The terrace out back is ringed with flower pots, and Kiran, the charming owner, is invigorated with the growing popularity of his café with tourists. He's full of suggestions for off-the-beaten-path walks; or if you have a flair for languages he welcomes new translations for his menu, currently available in English and Czech. ✉ *Jawahar Rd. W,* ☎ *0354/5682.*

$ ✕ **Keventer's.** Kev's, a snack bar as old as the town itself, serves breakfasts, cakes, sausage rolls, sandwiches, and ice cream. It shows signs of wear, and overlooks a busy intersection, but is worth a visit for a break from shopping. Try tea on the rooftop terrace, either in early morning or late afternoon when the traffic has abated. ✉ *Nehru Rd.*

$$$$ 🏨 **Cedar Inn.** This newly renovated resort has brilliant views and neo-Victorian Gothic architecture. Situated high above the town center, among majestic cedars, it's a serene retreat from the bustle of Darjeeling town (regular shuttle buses take you to and from The Mall). Wood, glass, and light predominate; rooms are bright, clean, and elegant, with bedspreads and curtains in soft, neutral colors. Expect hand-crafted woodwork, stripped wood floors, fireplaces, and cable TVs. Meals are included. ✉ *Jalapahar Rd., 734101,* ☎ *354/54446,* FAX *354/53916,* WEB *www.cedarinnindia.com. 22 rooms. Gym, billiards, business services, shop, babysitting. MC, V.*

$$$$ 🏨 **Mayfair Hill Resort.** Once a summer palace of the Maharaja of Nazargug, this smart new resort is downhill from the zoo road and has good views of the town. The manicured tea garden, polished marble-floor terraces with wrought iron furniture, grand "Tiffany" restaurant, and well-stocked bar are impressive, but in the busy season the general feel of the place can lack a certain warmth. A variety of room styles are available, so ask to see several; the cedar-panel attic rooms (with working fireplaces) are cozy and inviting. Prices include all meals. ✉ *The Mall, opposite Governor House, 734101,* ☎ *0354/56376,* FAX *0354/52674. 21 rooms, 5 attics, 10 cottages. Restaurant, bar, recreation room, laundry service, meeting room, business services, travel services. AE, MC, V.*

$$$$ 🏨 **Windamere.** This grande dame of the Raj is is an oasis that recalls its heritage as a spa retreat. High Tea here is an institution in itself— it's justly famous, and even people who can't afford to stay here come for the tea and cakes. The hotel, in the heart of Darjeeling, is comfortable and elegant. The drawing rooms have fireplaces, and the bar is lovely. From verandahs on both sides of the hotel you'll get magnificent views of the hills. "The Snuggery" is the club center for the Darjeeling Himalayas Railway Club—for train fanatics from the world over. Guest rooms, with Deco, Tibetan, and Raj furnishings, have fireplaces, heaters, hot-water bottles, and Victorian claw-foot bathtubs. Don't expect a TV unless you're in the Observatory House, which offers modern business facilities. Friendly staff skilled in serving royals and film stars will serve you under the exacting eye of owner Mrs. Tenduf-La ("Memsahib" to all). All meals are included in the room rate; the menu varies. Breakfasts are sumptuous, and meals are cooked on wood-burning stoves. ✉ *Observatory Hill,* ☎ *354/54041,* FAX *354/ 54041,* WEB *www.windamerehotel.com. 31 rooms, 6 suites. Restaurant, bar, laundry service, baby-sitting, playground, business services, travel services. AE, MC, V.*

$$$–$$$$ 🏨 **New Elgin.** Rooms are elegant and decorative in this classic, comfortable, and centrally located hotel. Antique furniture, Tibetan carpets on hardwood floors, thick drapes, working fireplaces (as well as room heaters), hot-water bottles, and 24-hour room service add to the general coziness. The restaurant and bar are both high-quality. Prices include all meals. ✉ *18 H. D. Lama Rd.,* ☎ *354/54114 or 354/54267,*

FAX *354/54267. 22 rooms, 3 suites. Restaurant, bar, laundry service. AE, DC, MC, V.*

$$$–$$$$ 🏨 **Sinclairs.** Spacious and full of light, with polished wooden floors and no clutter, this modern, centrally heated hotel is a short walk up-hill from the town center and commands excellent views (ask for a front room on the top floor). Some necessary upgrades to bedspreads, curtains, and carpets are under way. Breakfast and either lunch or dinner in are included in the room rate. ⊠ *18/1 Gandhi Rd.,* ☎ *354/56431,* FAX *354/54355,* WEB *www.sinclairshotels.com. 46 rooms, 2 suites. Restaurant, bar, recreation room, laundry service, meeting room, travel services. AE, DC, V.*

$$$ 🏨 **Dekeling Hotel.** Be prepared to feel welcomed as part of the family in this small, bustling, friendly Tibetan hotel. Expect very clean, simply furnished cedar-panel rooms with Tibetan wall hangings and stained-glass windows (ask for an attic room with a view)—it's an exceptionally good value, and the hospitality is informal and enthusiastic. This is a great place to stop and get your bearings if you're planning a trek out of town. Solo travelers looking to make friends will feel immediately at home in the communal sitting room; the "library" (a big bookcase relying on guest donations) has a superb selection of paperbacks. The hotel is two stories above Devekas restaurant, just off the Mall. ⊠ *51 Gandhi Rd., 734101,* ☎ *0354/54159,* WEB *www.dekeling. com. 18 rooms. Restaurant. MC, V.*

Shopping

For such a small town, Darjeeling is a serious shopping center, with top-quality orange-pekoe tea, Tibetan artifacts, jewelry, thangka scroll paintings, local woolen garments, hats, and carpets available in abundance. Most of the best shops are located within the pedestrianized area of town. Prices are generally better, and service friendlier and less pushy, than you'll find in cities. In the heart of the central area, Chowrasta, **The Oxford Book and Stationary Co.** (☎ 0354/54325) stocks hand-made stationery from Nepal and an exhaustive range of books on India and the Himalayas, including guides to textiles and artifacts, travel books, mind-body-spirit titles, classics, and new fiction.

Habeeb Mullick and Son (☎ 0354/54109) is a local landmark—established in 1890—for handicrafts and curios; jewelry; amber, turquoise, and moonstone gems; Kashmiri pashmina shawls; carpets; hand-carved wooden bowls from Nagaland; and exquisite silver Buddhas. The shop gets crowded after supper, so go early for personal attention; the proprietor has plenty on offer beyond the packed displays. Across the square from Habeeb Mullick and Son, **Jolly Arts** (☎ 0354/54059) has silk thankas (Buddhist prayer wall-hangings) and ritual silver, gold-painted, copper and bronze puja objects, and soft Tibetan shawls. At the corner of Chowrasta and Nehru Road, Latif Badami at **Eastern Arts** (☎ 0354/52917) is happy to let you take your time browsing over ornate silver jewelry and lapis lazuli. Clothing, bags, and other items crafted from Kashmiri leather and fur are the specialty of **Kashmir Arts** on Nehru Road.

For authentic hand-knotted traditional Tibetan carpets, try **Third Eye** (⊠ Ladenla Road, opposite State Bank of India, ☎ 0354/52920) is an "all women" enterprise accustomed to arranging export shipping. The **Tibetan Refugee Self-Help Centre** (⊠ 65 Gandhi Rd., ☎ 0354/52346) is worth the taxi-ride out of town to see the artisans (mostly elderly women) at work dyeing, weaving, and spinning wool on old bicycle wheels. Cuddly Lhaso Apso puppies (for sale if you are not going abroad) scamper around in the yard. In addition to items made from brightly colored handwoven textiles (shirts, jackets, wallets, back-packs), the store has beautiful carpet samples (but limited stocks). You can take your own design to be custom-made and shipped. The center is closed Sunday.

Nathmull's (✉ Laden La Rd.), famous for Darjeeling tea, has a vast selection, but is in a busy traffic area. To avoid the bustle, try **Chowrasta Tea Store** (✉ The Mall, ☎ 0354/54059) for a selection of high-quality teas. Two shops attest to the fact that Darjeeling retains its turn-of-the-20th-century demeanor. No picnic is complete without a visit to **Chowrasta Stores** (✉ the Mall), an old-fashioned general store where you'll find simply everything—wine, whiskey, chocolates, ice-cream, cheese, biscuits, and toiletries—but go at school closing time and you'll have to fight the children for penny candy. Next door to Chowrasta Stores, with the same glass-cabinet displays and friendly service, **S. Lekhrah and Co** (✉ the Mall, ☎ 0354/54275) has all manner of "suitings and hosiery"—from cotton T-shirts, socks, underwear, and towels to embroidery threads and fabrics for onsite tailoring.

SIKKIM

It's not surprising that Lepchas, or Rongkup (Children of Rong), the first known inhabitants of Sikkim, called their mountain home a paradise. The last *chogyal* (king), who ruled over Sikkim until it became India's 22nd state in 1975, was an avid conservationist who protected his Buddhist kingdom from development. Gangtok, the capital, is overbuilt and crowded, but once you escape its boundaries, you're surrounded by tropical forests rich with 600 species of orchids and 46 varieties of rhododendron. Waterfalls splash down mountains and power prayer wheels. Tidy hamlets with prayer flags flapping in the breeze and cultivated terraced fields occupy idyllic valleys. Sikkim's guardian deity, Mt. Kanchenjunga—the world's third-highest peak, at 28,208 ft; also spelled Khangchendzonga—is still revered by all who live in its shadow.

Three distinct ethnic groups live in Sikkim. The Lepchas originally lived in seclusion in north Sikkim, where they developed a harmonious relationship with the environment to ensure their survival. Although most Lepchas converted to Buddhism, many still worship aspects of their physical surroundings: rainbows, clouds, rivers, and trees. Village priests preside over elaborate rituals, including animal sacrifices, to appease their animist deities.

Bhutias from Tibet came into Sikkim with the first chogyal in the 17th century. Buddhism governs Bhutia life, with the monastery and the lama exerting tremendous influence over daily activities. Every village has its prayer flags and chortens, every home has an altar room, and most families have one relative in a monastery or convent. Buddhism even works its way into weavings, handwoven rugs, *thangka* (scroll) paintings, statues, and delicately carved *choktses* (tables). The Bhutias' culture, in turn, dominates Sikkim, right down to the women's national dress: the traditional *kho* or *bhoku*, the epitome of elegance, worn over a *wanju* (blouse), with the *pangden* (apron), the final colorful touch, restricted to married women and formal occasions.

Also sharing Sikkim are the Nepalese, who introduced terrace farming to the region. Although most Nepalese are Hindu, you'll see few Hindu temples in Sikkim, and their faith often incorporates Buddhist

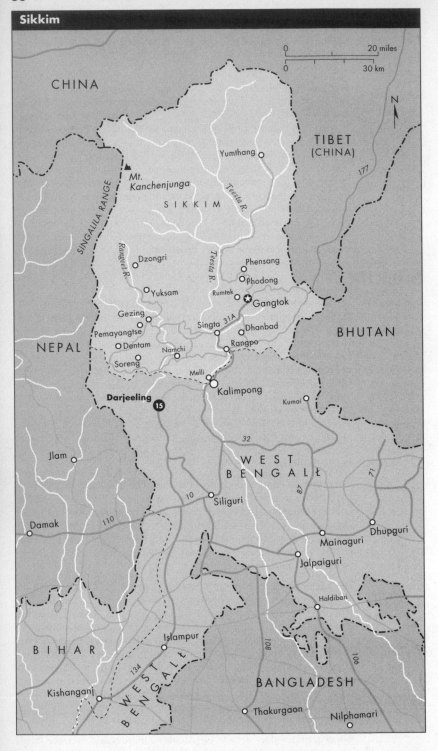

0   20 miles
0   30 km

N

CHINA

TIBET
(CHINA)

177

Yumthang

Mt.
Kanchenjunga

Teesta R.

SINGALILA RANGE

S I K K I M

Rangeet R.

Dzongri

Phensang

Phodong

Yuksam

Teesta R.

Rumtek

Gangtok

Gezing

Singta   31A

Dhanbad

BHUTAN

Pemayangtse

Dentam

Namchi

Rangpo

NEPAL

Soreng

Melli

Kalimpong

Kumai

Darjeeling

15

32

W E S T
B E N G A L

71

Jlam

87

Damak

110

10

Siliguri

Mainaguri

Dhupguri

Jalpaiguri

Haldibari

B I H A R

Islampur

108

106

134

W
E
S
T

B
E
N
G
A
L

BANGLADESH

Kishanganj

Thakurgaon

Nilphamari

beliefs and practices (as it does in Nepal). The Nepalese are dominant in business, and theirs is the language most often heard in Sikkim.

June, July, and August bring monsoon rains. December and January have cold snows, so the times to visit Sikkim are March–May and September–mid-November. The peak period, when tourist services are taxed to the limit, is late September–early October: during the Hindu festival Durga Puja.

Because of Sikkim's sensitive border location, foreigners need a Restricted-Area Permit (RAP) to visit.

Adventures

Yak safaris are available from Dzongri, and kayak trips on the Teesta or Rangeet rivers can be arranged for special groups.

Rafting

TEESTA AND RANGEET RIVERS

Rafting (October–November only) on the Teesta and Rangeet rivers offers everything from gentle rides through amazing mountain views and lush canyon vegetation to whitewater for the experienced rafter only. A trip on the Teesta will probably take you from Makha to Rongpo, while adventures down the Rangeet go from Sikip to Melli. Contact Tashila Tours and Travels for details.

Trekking

Trekking in Sikkim (March–May and October–December) means frigid nights and warm, tiring days. In the spring (April–May) you might face some nasty rain as well, but it's the best time for such flowers as orchids and rhododendrons. Winter is ideal for Himalayan vistas. Contact a tour operator for a customized trek.

KANCHENJUNGA

Because this moderate 7- to 10-day trek demands considerable up- and downhill walking, you should be physically fit. You hike from Yuksam, in western Sikkim, through forests of rhododendron, orchids, pine, and magnolia to Bakhim village. The next day's tough walk passes through a village populated by gentle yak-herding Tibetans to the outpost of Dzongri (13,218 ft), with views of Mt. Kanchenjunga. Here you can ride a yak, hike to Thangsing (12,890 ft), at the base of Jopino Peak, or climb to Zimathang (14,760 ft).

RHODODENDRON TREK

From the Soreng village in western Sikkim, you climb to Bershay (12,000 ft), in the forested Singalila Range, which is known as the rhododendron belt and has about 40 different varieties of flowering trees as well as numerous birds. From here you descend to Dentam village, inhabited mainly by Subba tribal people, and continue down to the historic and exquisite Pemayangtse Monastery. This easy, four- to five-day trek has views of Mt. Kanchenjung and is best in March, April, and May.

Dining and Lodging

Try Sikkimese sautéed ferns in season, sautéed bamboo shoots, nettle soup, and roast pork. If you like momos, order beef or vegetable—pork is risky if undercooked. Sikkim also makes good libations: cherry and musk brandy, wine, Teesta River white rum, juniper gin, *paan* liquor (made from a mixture of leaves and betel nuts), and *chang* (Tibetan barley beer) are all worth trying, especially the last two. Note that new-moon days and the first day of the full moon are dry. For traditional

Sikkimese meals, restaurants require advance notice and usually ask for parties of four or more. If you're solo, make some friends.

GANGTOK

$$ ✕ **Tibet Kitchen.** This upstairs eatery near the Hotel Tashi Delek is simple, clean, authentic, friendly, and cheap, and it's open for breakfast. Highlights are the *then-tuk* (flat-noodle soup) and delicious Tibetan bread with honey. You can sample home-brewed chang at the small bar. ⊠ *M. G. Marg,* ☎ *3592/21153. No credit cards.*

$ ✕ **House of Bamboo.** Popular with locals, this dark little upstairs
★ restaurant is very informal, very Tibetan, and very cheap. Good momos (pork or beef only) and filling *gyathak* (noodle soup) are the staples. You can also opt for Chinese food. Aim for one of the three window booths so you can watch the street activity below. ⊠ *M. G. Marg,* ☎ *no phone. No credit cards.*

$$$$ ✕🏨 **Nor-Khill.** Once a royal guest house, and now run by the Elgin group, Nor-Khill has lovely landscaped gardens and excellent views. Gangtok's oldest hotel sits on a quiet ridge below the city, just above the stadium. Traditional Sikkimese architecture is emphasized throughout with colorful masks, etchings, and local paintings. Rooms are simple, comfortable, and decorated with Buddhist and Sikkimese details, such as traditional carpets and religious artwork. Service is excellent, and meals are included in the price. Reserve in advance, and ask for a room with a view. The small, elegant Shangrila Restaurant serves very good Sikkimese, Indian, Chinese, and Continental food. ⊠ *Paljor Stadium Rd., 737101,* ☎ *3592/ 25637,* FAX *3592/25639,* WEB *www.elginhotels.com. 32 rooms. Restaurant, bar, travel services. AE, DC, MC, V.*

$$$ ✕🏨 **Hotel Tibet.** This popular hotel has a peaceful Tibetan atmo-
★ sphere, with thangka scroll paintings, colorful rugs, and other Buddhist artifacts. The hotel is centrally located and run by the Dalai Lama Charitable Trust. Rooms on the road side are the cheapest, and a little small; try for a mountain view. Not all bathrooms have tubs. A variety of meal plans are available, and the Snow Lion restaurant is one of the city's best. The menu mixes Tibetan, Japanese, Chinese, Continental, and Indian food; try the unusual *menyak polo* (slightly sweet, cheese-filled steamed dumplings). ⊠ *Paljor Stadium Rd., 737101,* ☎ *3592/22523,* FAX *3592/22707,* WEB *www.sikkiminfo.com. 40 rooms. Restaurant, bar, travel services. AE, DC, MC, V.*

$$$ ✕🏨 **Tashi Delek.** Don't be fooled by the drab facade: the public rooms
★ are wonderfully bright, and decorated in a sort of Baroque Sikkimese style. Guest rooms are simple in comparison, but they're pleasant and well maintained, and the suites have sitting rooms with Sikkimese decor. Ask for a mountain view. There are two excellent restaurants: the menu at Dragon Hall's includes exotic seasonal greens such as ferns and stinging nettles, and the Blue Poppy serves Sikkimese, Indian, Chinese, and Continental food. The rooftop garden is the nicest place in town (in season) to enjoy an afternoon meal or drink. ⊠ *M. G. Marg, 737101,* ☎ *3592/22991,* FAX *3592/22362,* WEB *www.hoteltashidelek.com. 40 rooms, 6 suites. Restaurant, bar, travel services. AE, DC, MC, V.*

PEMAYANGTSE

$ 🏨 **Mount Pandim.** This government-run hotel has an attractive garden and good views of Kanchenjunga from its fine hillside perch. Rooms are functional and reasonably sized, though some show signs of neglect. However, the hotel is in the process of upgrading the rooms. Ask for a room with a view. The restaurant serves a few local dishes, in addition to Indian and Chinese food. ⊠ *Pelling, 737113 West Sikkim,* ☎ *3595/50756,* WEB *www.sikkiminfo.com. 25 rooms. Restaurant. No credit cards.*

THE HIMALAYAS A TO Z

To research prices, get advice from other travelers, and book travel arrangements, visit www.fodors.com.

AIR TRAVEL

Indian Airlines flies Monday, Wednesday, and Friday from Delhi to Shimla's airstrip, Jubbarhatti Airport, a plateau created on top of a mountain 23 km (14 mi) south of Shimla. The flight costs US$115 one way; taxis into Shimla cost Rs. 500. For US$140 Indian Airlines will take you on to Kullu, whose airport is at Bhuntar, 9 km (5½ mi) from Kullu town and 50 km (30 mi) from Manali. Indian Airlines and Jet Airways also fly to Jammu daily (US$110–US$115 one way), from which it's a roughly four-hour drive to Dharamsala.

Jagson Airlines flies to the Kullu Valley twice daily and once on Sunday, at a cost of US$100. Jet Airways flies twice daily to Jammu for US$110.

Indian Airlines has daily flights from Delhi to Leh. Jet Airways now flies daily to Leh. Schedules change often, however, and flights are fewer in the winter. Summer flights are popular, so reserve tickets well ahead and confirm bookings 72 hours in advance. The fare is US$110–US$120 one way. Note that because of Leh's high altitude and capricious weather, flights are often canceled. Do observe the early check-in for your return journey, and carry a small travel pouch, as hand luggage is not allowed except for your passport, ticket, and wallet.

In Uttaranchal, Indian Airlines now flies three times a week (though cancellations are frequent) to Jolly Grant Airport in Dehra Dunn.

The airport at Bagdodra, West Bengal, is about 90 km (56 mi) southeast of Darjeeling and 124 km (77 mi) south of Gangtok. Jet Airways (U.S.$190) and Indian Airlines run daily flights from Calcutta and Delhi. For Darjeeling, hire a car to finish the trip with a three-hour drive, or taxi the 15 km (9 mi) to New Jalpaiguri to catch the Toy Train (☞ Train Travel). For Sikkim, hop on one of the shared jeeps that make the five-hour run to Gangtok.

CARRIERS
➤ CONTACTS: **Indian Airlines** (☎ 11/462–0566 in Darjeeling; ☎ 3592/23099 in Sikkim; WEB www.allianceair-india.com). **Jagson Airlines** (☎ 11/372–1593). **Jet Airways** (☎ 11/685–3700; WEB www.jetairways.com).

AIRPORTS
Local airports can be useful for travel information when airline offices have closed outside office hours or on holidays.
➤ AIRPORT INFORMATION: **Bagdogra** (☎ 353/551588); **Dehradun** (☎ 135/655111 and 135/656901); **Kullu** (☎ 1902/65037); **Jammu** (☎ 191/453888); **Leh** (☎ 9182/52255); **Shimla** (☎ 177/426675); **Srinigar** (☎ 194/433035).

BUS AND CAR TRAVEL
We don't recommend bus travel in the Himalayas. Breakdowns, 24-hour delays, and overturned buses are not uncommon in the region. Maniac bus-drivers have a reputation of being inexperienced, dangerous drivers.

In the winter, there is no land access to Ladakh. Two roads open up in summer, crossing passes over 15,000 ft high. These are supposedly open from early June (at best) through September.

It's safest and most comfortable to stick with hired cars over buses in the Himalayas—especially in Uttaranchal, where so-called "luxury" buses generally turn out to be rattle traps with taped TV entertainment blaring up front. Plan to leave Delhi early—before 6 AM. RBS Travels maintains a large fleet of cars and offers reasonable rates and—more importantly—experienced and safety-conscious mountain drivers. Night driving is extremely dangerous and is to be avoided, especially in the hills. Another option is to take a train to Dehradun or Kathgodam (☞ Train Travel) and hire a car there or send your car ahead from Delhi (to avoid the horrendous traffic around Delhi).

EMERGENCIES

In the remote areas of the Himalayas, your best emergency back-up is your own caution—and a knowledgeable and well-prepared touring agency, hotel manager, guide and/or driver, who can get you to the nearest and most appropriate emergency facility (not necessarily the closest government-run hospital) or doctor quickly. Carry a good first-aid kit, including sterile syringes and dental needles, pain-killers, and lots of bandages for blisters if you're trekking. Take altitude precautions seriously; the waiting list for flights out of Leh is often filled with those who do not. Medications are widely available from local chemists without a prescription. Another option is East-West Rescue, based in New Delhi. It operates India's first and largest air ambulance for medical emergencies that require evacuation from the remotest areas of India, Pakistan, Nepal, and Bhutan. East-West runs a 24-hour year-round alarm center with qualified, multilingual personnel who are experienced in dealing with Western clients. They have "cashless service" arrangements with a network of Indian medical centers/hospitals, and can arrange for diagnostic testing of patients anywhere in India.

➤ CONTACTS: **Casualty-District Hospital** (✉ Leh, ☎ 1982/52360). **East-West Rescue** (✉ 38 Golf Links, New Delhi, ☎ 11/462–3738, 11/469–9229, 11/469–8865, 11/469–0429, WEB www.eastwestrescue.com). **Police** (☎ 1982/52018).

MONEY MATTERS

ATMS

ATMS are popping up everywhere; your guide or hotel will be able to direct you to the nearest one—with a little luck it will be working that day. In Shimla, there is an ATM on the Mall at the State Bank of Patiala, near Scandal Point.

CURRENCY EXCHANGE

Many hotels will either handle currency exchange or direct you to the nearest bank that does. In Ladakh, the State Bank of India cashes traveler's checks.

➤ EXCHANGE SERVICES: **State Bank of India** (✉ Main Bazaar, Leh, ☎ 1982/52052).

TOURS

The Delhi-based firms Aquaterra Adventures India, Himalayan River Runners, Ibex Expeditions, and Outdoor Adventures India lead trips all over the Himalayas. Snow Leopard Adventures is newly recommended for Ganges river rafting. If you are planning your own itinerary, Outbound Travels are superb for arranging airline bookings. RBS Travels is a reliable agency for booking cars and drivers.

Modern Tours and Travels, run by the knowledgeable and enthusiastic Karma Tse Ten, offers treks to Western Sikkim. There's also a four-day tour to the Yumthang Valley: food and services are excellent. Yak Tours and Travels leads tours to the Yumthang Valley. Tashila Tours and Travels leads the way in river rafting on the beautiful Teesta and

Rangeet rivers. Tenzing Norgay Adventures is run by Dhamey and Jamling Tenzing—the sons of Norgay Tenzing, who climbed Mt. Everest with Sir Edmund Hillary. They offer treks in Western Sikkim, including flora treks; vehicular tours in the north; and cultural tours to monasteries, as well as overnight stays in villages.

HIMALAYAN TRIPS

➤ CONTACTS: **Adventure North Tours and Travels** (☎ 1982/53620). **Aquatera Adventures India** (✉ S-507, Ground Floor, Greater Kailash 2, New Delhi, 110048, ☎ 11/623–2641 or 629–2760, WEB treknraft.com). **Eddie Tamang** (✉ Darjeeling, West Bengal, ☎ 354/70347). **Great Himalayan Adventures** (✉ N-95 Sham Park, New Delhi, 110018, ☎ 11/546–5783, FAX 11/544-9682, WEB www.wildquestindia.com). **Himachal Helicopter Skiing** (G.P.O. Box 2489 V, Melbourne 3001, Australia, ☎ 61/3/9593–9853 or 61/3/9525–3405, WEB www.himachal.com). **Himalayan River Runners** (✉ F-5 Hauz Khas Enclave, New Delhi, 110016, ☎ 11/685–2602, WEB www.hrrindia.com). **Ibex Expeditions** (✉ G-66 east of Kailash, New Delhi, 110065, ☎ 11/691–2641, WEB www.IbexExpeditions.com). **Modern Tours and Travels** (✉ opposite Sikkim Tourist Information Centre, Traffic Point, M. G. Marg, Gangtok 737101, ☎ 3592/27319). **Outbound Travels** (✉ 216A/11 Gautam Nagar, 3rd floor, New Delhi, 110049, ☎ 11/6521308 or 11/6526316). **Outdoor Adventures India** (✉ S-234 Panchsheel Park, 2nd floor, New Delhi, 110017, ☎ 11/601–7485, WEB www.raftindia.com). **RBS Travels** (✉ Shop A1, Connaught Palace Hotel, 37 Shaheed Bhagat Singh Marg, New Delhi, 110001, ☎ 11/336–4603 or 11/336–3066). **Snow Leopard Adventures** (✉ Sector C-9, Vasant Kunj, New Delhi, 110070, ☎ 11/689–8654, WEB www.snowleopardadventures.com). **Tashila Tours and Travels** (✉ 31-A National Hwy., P.B. No. 70, Gangtok 737101, ☎ 3592/22979, FAX 3592/22155). **Tenzing Norgay Adventures** (✉ 1 D.B. Giri Rd., Darjeeling, West Bengal, ☎ 354/53718–56048, WEB www.tenzig-norgay.com). **Yak Tours and Travels** (✉ Yama House, M. G. Marg, Gangtok 737101, ☎ 3592/24643, FAX 3592/20878).

TRAIN TRAVEL

The convenient, comfortable, and all-air-conditioned *Shatabdi Express* departs New Delhi Railway Station at 7:30 AM for the five-hour trip to Amritsar.

The train is also the best way to get to Shimla. A 95-km (62-mi) narrow-gauge track built in 1903 climbs from Kalka (2,131 ft) to Shimla (7,170 ft). Tiny trains known as the Shimla Toy Trains travel at speeds of 9–15 mph, passing through 102 tunnels and over 845 bridges to make the journey in five hours. First class on the Toy Train is extremely comfortable, with upholstered chairs to sink into as you marvel at the scenery. Second class is crowded: people push and shove to sit on the wooden seats. The Toy Trains meet two trains from Delhi: the overnight train that departs Delhi at 10 PM and arrives in Kalka at 6 AM, and the *Himalayan Queen,* which departs Delhi at 6 AM and arrives at Kalka at 11:40 AM. The center of Shimla is pedestrian-only. From the train station it's a stiff uphill walk to the center, where most hotels are located. You may wish to hire a porter; he'll expect at least Rs. 50 (depending on the amount of luggage). Porters also double as hotel touts, so don't let them steer you away from your lodging of choice.

The trip to the Kangra Valley and Dharamsala is also more pleasant by train than by car. The *Pathankot Express,* which leaves Delhi at 8 PM and arrives at Pathankot in the morning, has first-class compartments; after a good night's sleep you can hop in a car and enjoy the remaining three hours to Dharamsala.

The best train to Chandigarh, from which buses go to Dharamsala, Kullu, and Manali, is the fast, all-air-conditioned *Shatabdi Express,* which leaves Delhi at 7:30 AM and arrives in Chandigarh at 10:30 AM. Spend the night in Chandigarh and travel by car or bus the next day for the 12-hour trip to Kullu or the 14-hour trip to Manali.

There is reasonably good train service to Mussoorie via Dehra Dun. If you're moving on to the Kumaon, the best train is to Kathgodam— the Delhi–Kathgodam–Ranikhet express leaves New Delhi at 11 PM and arrives in Kathgodam at 6 AM. From here, you must still drive 90 minutes to Ramnagar or an hour to Nainital. The night train from Delhi to Ramnagar (Corbett National Park) is only recommended for the adventurous, as it has no upper-class bogies.

Overnight trains from Calcutta's Sealdah Station go to New Jalpaiguri. Here you can grab a taxi for the three- to four-hour drive to Darjeeling or board the famous Toy Train for a stunning eight-hour journey up a landscape of terraced fields and hairpin turns. The ride is leisurely— you can actually hop on and off the train as it moves along. This is the long but justly celebrated way to reach the famous hill station.

Those coming from Delhi or Calcutta normally use the train station at Siliguri, in West Bengal. From here, shared jeeps and buses take you on to Gangtok, 114 km (71 mi) away, in four hours. In Gangtok, reserve your return trip at the Sikkim Nationalized Transport Petrol Pump on Paljor Namgyal Stadium Road. To make train bookings online, go to www.indianrailways.com.

VISITOR INFORMATION

Permits are required for the Spiti and Kullu Valleys. Groups of four foreigners can get permits from the Himachal Pradesh Tourism Development Corporation in New Delhi, which supposedly offers next-day service—but, given the Byzantine nature of Indian bureaucracy, we don't recommended this. Whether you're on your own or in a group, let your tour operator handle your permit in advance; just bring extra passport photos. (Note: the Himachal Pradesh Tourism Development Corporation is also in Shimla, Manali, and Dharamsala; all branches can advise you on transportation schedules and tour operators and hotels.)

The Sikkim Tourist Information Centre in New Delhi is helpful with trekking itineraries, tours, and accommodations. The Sikkim permit is good for 15 days, and is easy to get within 24 hours from all Indian missions abroad and the following places in India: the Foreigner's Registration Office in Delhi, Bombay, Calcutta, and Darjeeling, and the Sikkim Tourist Information Centre. When you apply, you must specify your date of entry into Sikkim. A 15-day extension is available in Gangtok from the Tashiling Secretariat (Home Department); one more 15-day extension brings you to the permitted total of 45 days. After that, you may not re-enter Sikkim within three months. No special permit is needed for Khecheopari Lake, Yuksom, Pelling (Pemayangtse), or Tashiling in Western Sikkim, but for points beyond these you need to travel with a government-recognized tour operator in a group of at least four people. The tour company will take care of the paperwork.

Your best bet for government-supplied information on Ladakh is the Jammu and Kashmir Tourism office in New Delhi. Mr. Sonom Dorjay, the tourist officer, comes from Leh and is extremely helpful. If you're in Ladakh, visit the tourist office just outside of Leh.

The new Uttaranchal Tourist Office in New Delhi has information about the Garhwal and Kumaon regions; but private agencies are more service-oriented for foreign visitors to India.

➤ TOURIST OFFICES: **Himachal Pradesh** (✉ Chandralok Bldg., 36 Janpath, New Delhi, ☎ 11/332–5320; ✉ Kotwali Bazaar, Dharamsala 176215, ☎ 1892/24928; ✉ the Mall, Manali 175131, ☎ 1902/53531; ✉ the Mall, Shimla, ☎ 177/252561). **Ladakh** (3 km/2 mi outside Leh, ☎ 1982/52297). **Jammu and Kashmir** (✉ 201–203 Kanishka Shopping Plaza, 19 Ashok Rd., New Delhi, ☎ 11/334–5373, WEB www.jktourism.org). **Sikkim** (✉ 14 Panchsheel Marg, Chanakyapuri, New Delhi, ☎ 11/611–5346; ✉ 4C Poonam, 5/2 Russell St., Calcutta 700017, ☎ 33/297516; ✉ SNT Bus Compound, Tenzing Norgay Rd., Siliguri, ☎ 353/432646; ✉ M.G. Marg, Gangtok, ☎ 3592/22064). **Uttaranchal** (✉ 102 Indra Prakash Bldg., 21 Barakhamba Rd., New Delhi, ☎ 11/335–0481 or 332–6620).

3 DELHI

Dynamic, cosmopolitan Delhi blends internationalism and tradition, from the top-notch cuisine and fine museums and art galleries of New Delhi to the bustling, twisting alleyways of Old Delhi's Chandni Chowk bazaar and Jama Masjid, India's largest mosque. Make sure when you shop to hit the streets: Delhi is one big emporium for all of India's handicrafts.

By Michael W.
Bollom

SOPHISTICATED, ENERGETIC DELHI became independent India's capital at midnight on August 14–15, 1947. It had been the capital since 1911, when the British shifted their center of power from Calcutta to Delhi. It was the ultimate prize, a place where the British could create the perfect imperial Western city. They did exactly this by building New Delhi, a carefully executed grid of roundabouts and well-organized streets—in wild contrast to Old Delhi's hectic alleyways. The British left behind a stubborn, strange legacy, a mishmash of East and West in which village life flourished among the fancy new bungalows and wide, tree-lined avenues. Delhi had always been prized by India's rulers—after all the city played a crucial role in the country's volatile history. What was originally a Hindu Rajput outpost (Rajput warriors governed the kingdoms of northwest India) became a Muslim capital when Muhammad Ghori from Central Asia invaded and defeated the ruler, Prithviraj Chauhan, in 1192. The "Slave Dynasty" that ensued was replaced by other Afghan and Uzbek dynasties many times over the next 300 years, during which time Delhi was both capital and outpost. During the reign of the Moghul Empire—founded in 1526 by Babur, also from Central Asia—the capital shifted between Delhi and nearby Agra until 1858. After the Delhi-based Sepoy Mutiny, a rebellion against the East India Company in 1857–58, the British overthrew the mutineers and Indian garrisons who had seized Delhi, and took the throne.

After Independence in 1947, when the subcontinent was partitioned into West Pakistan, India, and East Pakistan (now Bangladesh), there was a massive influx of refugees. As the long-standing seat of power, Delhi was ground zero for India's political transformation. The British were gone, and the princely kingdoms defunct, and India, finally coming into its own, was centralizing its power in Delhi.

When Rajiv Gandhi (grandson of Nehru) began to liberalize India's centralized economy in the mid-1980s, Delhi experienced tremendous change. With land scarce in Bombay, and Calcutta mired in leftist labor disputes, massive amounts of commercial growth took place in Delhi. Former Prime Minister Rao then launched economic reforms in 1991, and further liberalized India's economy. This attracted substantial foreign investment: over the years, as foreign companies arrived and set up shop, land prices skyrocketed. Residential enclaves cropped up everywhere, along with new commercial centers and industrial development areas. Villagers from rural areas descended on the capital to seek their fortunes—they moved into small open fields, narrow strips along the road, or unused neighborhood pockets, and built shanties that quickly became overcrowded slums. Since then, pollution and the suburban commute have become increasingly aggravating concerns.

Today, Delhi seems like it's in a perpetual state of flux. The harmonious lines of Delhi's historic structures and old buildings, in the midst of new European-style neighborhoods and even newer slums, give Delhi's urbanscape a hodgepodge quality that can overwhelm the first-time visitor.

Don't despair. Delhi rewards the determined sightseer with more than a thousand monuments and two old capital building complexes—including the present seat of the government, designed by the British architect Sir Edwin Lutyens (born 1869–1944). Cosmopolitan hotels, shopping, and fine restaurants abound. Delhi also offers a glimpse into the *real* India: the labyrinthine street bazaars of Old Delhi, and the temples and monuments of India's checkered colonial past. In the deepest sense, from Old Delhi's Red Fort and Jama Masjid mosque to New Delhi's chic art galleries and nightclubs, Delhi is a profoundly Indian city.

Turbaned shepherds still lead goats and sheep through ravines in Delhi's remaining open fields and near the airports. In Delhi's golf course, Muslim monuments share the fairways with peacocks. Eunuchs sashay past shops that sell Western products on Connaught Place. Rajasthani women in bright saris and men in *lungis* (skirtlike wraps) work with outdated tools on construction sites while executives work out on computerized equipment in health clubs. By day, temples are packed with the devout, and by night, hotel discos are packed with the affluent. You'll see *sadhus* (Hindu holy men) walking along the streets while young men zoom around on motorcycles.

Delhi is a city on the move—it's the gateway to the northern regions, and the seat of India's government. Don't be surprised if you see cavalcades of cars forcing traffic to the side of the road. These are the many VIP, VVIP, and VVVIP politicians of India's Parliament. It's no secret that movers and shakers predominate here—the decisions and behavior of Delhi's political big shots are the talk of the town. You can say a lot of things about Delhi, but you can't accuse it of being a humdrum town.

Pleasures and Pastimes

Dining
Delhi's dining scene is versatile. Top hotel restaurants bring in international chefs, and new independent restaurants are opening all over town. The selection of restaurants—Indian, East and Southeast Asian, and European cuisine—constantly grows. If you're feeling adventurous, stop in at one of the open-air roadside restaurants, called *dhabas*. The only downside to dining in Delhi is that you can't always get a drink with your meal. Government regulations make it difficult for most independent restaurants to obtain liquor licenses, and you can't BYOB.

Lodging
Except for such hotels as the Claridges and the Imperial, which cling to their Victorian heritage, many of Delhi's hotels are modernizing along Western standards. Modernization has its virtues: Western-style hotels have good facilities, such as health clubs and business services, which make them islands of refuge from the city's chronic power shortages, telephone disruptions, and crowds. But a chronic shortage of rooms has driven up room rates here, and upmarket hotels levy an additional 20% tax on your room rate and food-and-beverage bill. Note also that upscale hotels have separate dollar rates for foreign guests.

Cost-conscious travelers will be disappointed by the accommodations in Delhi. Hotels tend to be either five-star or flophouse, with the middle ground lacking. Fortunately, there are a number of "guest houses," such as the Jukaso Inn and Jor Bagh "27," in Delhi's various residential colonies; small hotels are often converted bungalows. Guest-house quality is uneven, and services are limited, but prices are about a fifth of those at the big hotels. The adventurous (or broke) traveler can always seek out backpacker hotels in Paharganj: some are adequate, and, importantly, inexpensive.

Performing Arts
From the intricate footwork of the Kathak dance to the emotive singing of Hindu *bhajans* or Muslim *qawwalis,* Delhi's arts scene offers a mix of folk, classical, and contemporary performances. Most evenings, there's a show somewhere in the city; the monthly *Around Town* car-

ries the most comprehensive and accurate event listings. Best, ticket prices are a bargain.

Shopping

Among Indians, Delhi is known for its shopping. In Old Delhi's Chandni Chowk, you can poke through shops that specialize in brassware, curios, and silver jewelry. New Delhi offers state emporiums that sell regional handicrafts, fabrics, and other items at reasonable prices. Head to Sunder Nagar, with its fancier shops to peruse gems, textiles, artwork, and curios. For a local experience, go to the INA wet market—bursting with spices, fresh produce, and squawking chickens. More "modern" shopping can also be done at South Delhi's upscale markets such as South Extension and GK I (M and N Block Markets), and there is now a mall at Ansal Plaza.

EXPLORING DELHI

Except for Chandni Chowk in Old Delhi, where lanes are too narrow for cars, Delhi is not a walker's city. But even in Chandni Chowk, watch out for fast-moving carts and overloaded humans who plow through whatever is in their way. The city has few sidewalks, and even these are subject to open manholes, dangling electric wires, and excrement. To make it easier on yourself, hire a car, taxi, or auto-rickshaw to get around.

The geographic center of Delhi is Connaught Place. South of Old Delhi, this was the commercial hub of the British Raj. Every attempt to spruce up this district seems to grind to a halt; the old buildings that ring the green traffic circle are getting a face-lift, but there's still plenty of trash and not a single trash basket. Connaught Place is also a haunt of beggars, unlicensed money changers, and others engaged in dubious pursuits.

About 2 km (1 mi) south of Connaught Place is the Imperial City. Designed by the British architect Sir Edwin Lutyens (1869–1944), it includes Rashtrapati Bhavan (the Presidential Palace), the North and South Secretariats, and the Sansad Bhavan (Parliament House). Just southwest of here is the Diplomatic Enclave; to the east is India Gate, a monument to British Indian Army soldiers killed in World War I and the Afghan wars. Southeast of India Gate and not far from the Oberoi hotel are the Purana Qila (Old Fort) and Humayun's Tomb; almost due south of India Gate is Lodi Gardens. The entire area surrounding these landmarks is filled with tree-lined boulevards, lovely old bungalows, and affluent residential neighborhoods.

Be prepared to remove your shoes when visiting religious institutions, including the Charity Birds Hospital. Women should bring a scarf to cover their heads. Shorts are not appropriate for adults of either gender.

Great Itineraries

Given Delhi's congestion and pollution, don't plan to do too much in any one day. Take your time or the city will overwhelm you.

Numbers in the text correspond to numbers in the margin and on the Delhi map.

IF YOU HAVE 3 DAYS

Spend your freshest, most energetic day in **Old Delhi.** See Lal Qila (Red Fort) early in the morning, then Jama Masjid across from it. Later in the afternoon, venture into Chandni Chowk. Explore **New Delhi** the next day. On day three, take a car south to the Qutab Minar or Hauz Khas, then head back to town and check out some museums and gal-

70

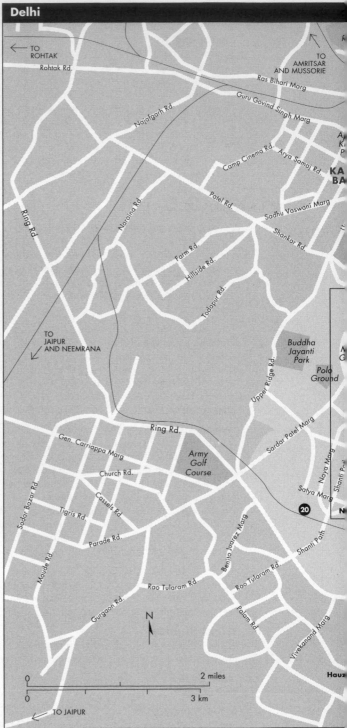

Delhi

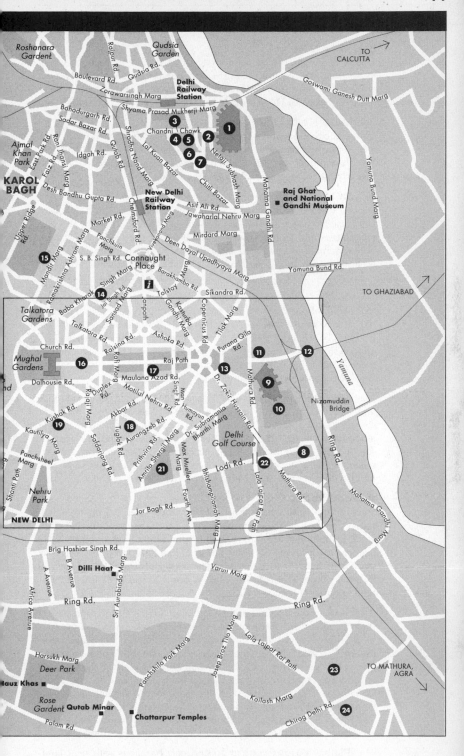

leries. That afternoon, shop at the state emporia or visit a local market.

Follow the three-day itinerary above, and on day four make an overnight excursion to the Neemrana Fort Palace outside the **Shekhavati** region of Rajasthan and unwind in Rajput splendor. On day five, make a leisurely return to Delhi and try to get to at least one museum.

Follow the five-day itinerary above. On day six, drive six hours northwest to **Corbett National Park** in Uttaranchal, one of India's most enjoyable wildlife sanctuaries, and devote day seven to a Jeep safari. Get an early-morning start back to Delhi on your last day.

When to Tour Delhi

It's best to visit Delhi between mid-October and late March. The heat is intense from April until the monsoon arrives in July; then rain and mosquitoes add to the misery. If you'll only be in Delhi a few days, note that most museums are closed Monday, the museum at Lal Qila is closed Friday, and Jama Masjid is closed to non-Muslims on Friday.

Old Delhi

Old Delhi, about 6 km (4 mi) north of the city center, is in a perpetual state of decay. The old *havelis* (mansions) that line the *galis* (alleyways) of Chandni Chowk, the main artery of this old district, are architecturally stunning—but cry out for repair. Old Delhi's monuments—Lal Qila and Jama Masjid—are magnificent, and Chandni Chowk is great fun to explore.

Watch out, though, because Old Delhi is crowded and hectic, and roads and footways are poorly maintained. Instead of walking, you might try a rickshaw tour. For about Rs. 200, you can get carted around in a rickshaw (which seats two slim people) for approximately two hours. The rickshaw wallahs who hang out in front of the Red Fort are serious bargainers, but they know the city well and many can show you places you probably won't discover on your own.

A Good Walk

Start in Old Delhi with a morning tour of **Lal Qila** ①, Emperor Shah Jahan's sprawling 17th-century capital. From here set your sights on a red, rectangular three-story building (look for a flock of pigeons flying overhead) on the opposite side of Nataji Subhash Marg, the busy street in front of the fort: this is the **Charity Birds Hospital** ②, a delightful hospital that is as much a respite for human visitors as for the non-human patients tended inside.

After leaving the hospital, return to Nataji Subhash Marg and walk a short distance north to the famous **Chandni Chowk** ③. Walk about four blocks down this crowded thoroughfare to the marble-face **Sisganj Gurdwara** ④, a Sikh shrine. Continue east on Chandni Chowk and cross three more galis; then turn left on **Gali Parante Wali** ⑤; the entrance is almost directly opposite the Central Bank of India. Continue down Gali Parante Wali until you see a signboard for the Vaishali Sahai Center at a fork in the road. Turn left onto Motiwali, which leads directly into Kinari Bazaar, a bridal-trimming market where Hindu families buy every item required in their symbol-rich wedding ceremony.

The Bombay Beads Centre at 2030 Kinari Bazaar is your next landmark; directly across from this shop is one of Chandni Chowk's most beautiful lanes, Naughara Gali, where beautiful old havelis, home to a community of Jains, are done up in art-deco colors—aquas, pinks, yellows. At the end of this peaceful lane is the exquisite Jain **Sweitana Temple** ⑥, with a white-marble elephant head on the railing and gleaming brass doors. Even if the temple is closed, Naughara Gali is an oasis, an ideal temporary escape from Chandni Chowk's bustle.

Return to Kinari Bazaar and turn right. If it suits your fancy, stop in a gimmicky but fun shop called **Shivam Zari Palace** (✉ 2178 Kinari Bazaar) and spend an hour or two dressing a tiny bronze statue of Gopal (baby Krishna) in an outfit of your choice, including a headpiece, necklace, bangles, and a throne. The cost for your finished memento is less than Rs. 350, depending on the size of the statue you choose.

Continue down Kinari Bazaar until it intersects with Dariba Kalan, the "Street of Silver." Visit the silver shops on your left or turn right and head down Dariba Kalan, which is lined with tiny stores selling gold and silver jewelry and artifacts. At the end of Dariba Kalan, turn right onto a broad street that leads through the brass and copper district. At a small corner shop, Prem Fireworks, turn right and walk about 20 ft, then turn left and walk under an arch that says ESTATE HANDICRAFTS. Head up Chah Rahat, a typical narrow lane with old wooden balconies and verandas.

When Chah Rahat opens into a small courtyard, take the hairpin turn to the left. Follow the arrow on a sign that reads SINGH COPPER AND BRASS PALACE and head down Chah Rahat. After about 30 ft, a second sign directs you down an alley on the right. Singh's emporium is filthy, but every floor is a great place to poke around.

From Singh's, return to the courtyard and Chah Rahat and walk left down a short, narrow lane. At the end of the lane you'll see the splendid **Jama Masjid** ⑦, preceded by an unexpected bazaar of small shops selling tools of every conceivable design.

At the end of this long tour, take a cycle-rickshaw to either Karim's or Chor Bizarre for a typical Muslim meal in Old Delhi.

TIMING

Allow a full day for this tour, and make sure you don't attempt it on a very hot day. Avoid Friday, when the fort museum is closed and entrance to the mosque is tricky for non-Muslims. Most shops in Chandni Chowk are closed on Sunday.

Sights to See

★ ❸ **Chandni Chowk.** Chandni Chowk is Delhi's former imperial avenue, where the Moghul emperor Shah Jahan rode at the head of his lavish cavalcade. Today, bullock carts, taxis, private cars, dogs, cows, autorickshaws, bicycles, horse-drawn tongas (two-wheeled equestrian taxis) and pedestrians plow indiscriminately through the congestion. As in the days of the Moghuls, astrologers set up their charts on the pavement; shoemakers squat and repair sandals and other leather articles; sidewalk photographers with old box cameras take pictures for a small fee; medicine booths conceal doctors attending to patients; and oversize teeth grin from the windows of dentists' offices. Peer through a portico and you might see men getting shaved, silver being weighed, or any other conceivable form of commerce, while outside a cow lies complacently on the street. ✉ *6 km (4 mi) north of Connaught Pl. Most shops closed Sun.*

❷ **Charity Birds Hospital.** Across from Lal Qila is a delightful and unusual attraction: a hospital not for humans, but primarily for birds. Founded by Jains in 1956, the hospital is modest, but it shows how tender loving care can stretch limited funds. Vegetarian birds (and rabbits) are treated inside, and carnivorous birds and other needy animals are treated in the courtyard. There's even an intensive-care ward and a re-search laboratory. Bathed, fed, and given vitamins, the healthy birds refuse to leave, and that's how you can spot the building—flocks of birds swirl around its roof. ⊠ *Nataji Subhash Marg, opposite Lal Qila.* ▦ *Free; donations welcome.* ☉ *Daily 8–8.*

❺ Gali Parante Wali. This congested, narrow lane is filled with shops sell-ing exquisite saris, including the well-known Ram Chandra Krishan Chandra's, where you can peruse some of the finest fabrics in India. The lane is named for the fabulous *parathas* (flat breads) also sold here, in simple, open-air eateries. Stuffed with a variety of fixings, such as radishes, cheese, and seasonal vegetables, they're a real treat. ⊠ *At the intersection of Chandni Chowk.*

★ ❼ Jama Masjid. An exquisite Islamic statement in red sandstone and mar-ble, India's largest mosque was completed in 1656 by 5,000 laborers after six years of work. It was the last monument commissioned by the Moghul emperor Shah Jahan. Three sets of broad steps lead to two-story gateways and a magnificent courtyard with a square ablution tank in the center. The entire space is enclosed by pillared corridors with domed pavilions in each corner. Thousands gather to pray in this courtyard, especially on Friday, which is why the Jama Masjid is also called the Friday Mosque.

The mosque is characteristically Moghul, with an onion-shape dome and tapering minarets. But Shah Jahan added an innovation: the novel stripes running up and down the well-proportioned marble domes. The whole structure exudes peace and tranquillity—climb the open minaret to see how finely the mosque contrasts with the commercial streets around and beneath it. Look inside the prayer hall (which you can only enter after a ritual purification at the ablution tank), for the pulpit carved from a single slab of marble. In one corner is a room where Shah Jahan installed the marble footprints of the Prophet Mohammed. ⊠ *6 km (4 mi) north of Connaught Pl., across from Lal Qila.* ▦ *Free, R. 1 to climb minaret (women must be escorted by a "responsible" man).* ☉ *Non-Muslims, Sat.–Thurs., 30 min after sunrise until 12:20 PM, 1:45 PM until 20 min before asar (afternoon prayer, roughly 3:30–4 PM), and 20 min after asar until 20 min before sunset; Fri., 30 min after sunrise until noon. Muslims, daily 7–5.*

★ ❶ Lal Qila. Known as the Red Fort because of its red sandstone walls, Lal Qila, near the Yamuna River in Old Delhi, is the greatest of Delhi's Moghul palace-cities, outdoing even Lutyens's Imperial City in majesty. Built by Shah Jahan in the 17th century, the Red Fort recalls the era of Moghul power and magnificence—imperial elephants swaying by with their *mahouts* (elephant drivers), a royal army of eunuchs, court ladies carried in palanquins, and other vestiges of Shah Jahan's pomp.

The view of the main entrance, called **Lahore Gate,** flanked with tow-ers and facing Chandni Chowk, is unfortunately blocked by a barbi-can (gatehouse), which the paranoid Aurangzeb added for his personal security—much to the grief of Shah Jahan, his father. From his prison, where he was held captive by his power-hungry son, Shah Jahan wrote, "You have made a bride of the palace and thrown a veil over her face."

Once you pass through the main gate, continue along the Chatta Chowk (Vaulted Arcade), originally the shopping district for the royal harem and now a bazaar selling significantly less regal goods. The ar-cade leads to the Naubat Khana (Imperial Bandstand), a red sandstone structure where music was played five times daily. This is the main gate-way to the fort; beyond this point, everyone but the emperor and princes had to proceed on foot, a rule that was observed until the Indian Sepoy Mutiny of 1857.

An expansive lawn, once a courtyard serving as the boundary at which all but the nobility had to stop, leads to the great **Diwan-i-Am** (Hall of Public Audience). You have now entered the Delhi of Shah Jahan. Raised on a platform and open on three sides, the hall evokes past glories—such as the moment described by François Bernier, a 17th-century French traveler overwhelmed by the hall's magnificence. According to Bernier, the emperor sat on a royal throne studded with decorative panels that sparkled with inlaid precious stones. (Stolen by British soldiers after the Indian Sepoy Mutiny, the panels were restored 50 years later by Lord Curzon.) Watched by throngs of people from the courtyard below, the emperor heard the pleas of his subjects; the rest of the hall was reserved for rajas and foreign envoys, all standing with "their eyes bent downwards and their hands crossed." High above them, under a pearl-fringed canopy resting on golden shafts in the royal recess, "glittered the dazzling figure of the Grand Moghul, a figure to strike terror, for a frown meant death."

Behind the Diwan-i-Am, a row of palaces overlooks the distant Yamuna River. To the extreme south is the **Mumtaz Mahal,** now the Red Fort Museum of Archaeology, with relics from the Moghul period and numerous paintings and drawings. Next is the **Rang Mahal** (Painted Palace), once richly decorated with a silver ceiling that was dismantled to pay the bills when the treasury ran low. The Rang Mahal, which may have been for the royal ladies, contains a cooling water channel—called the Canal of Paradise—that runs from the marble basin in the center of the floor to the rest of the palace and to many of the others.

The third palace is the **Khas Mahal,** the exclusive palace of the emperor, divided into three sections: the sitting room, the so-called dream chamber (for sleeping), and the prayer chamber, all with lavishly decorated walls and painted ceilings still intact. The lovely marble screen is carved with the Scale of Justice—two swords and a scale that symbolize punishment and justice. From the attached octagonal tower the emperor Muthamman Burj would appear before his subjects each morning or watch elephant fights in the nearby fields.

The next palace is the **Diwan-i-Khas** (Hall of Private Audience), the most exclusive pavilion. Here Shah Jahan would sit on his Peacock Throne, made of solid gold and inlaid with hundreds of precious and semi-precious stones. (When Nadir Shah sacked Delhi in 1739, he hauled the throne to Persia.) A Persian couplet written in gold above an arch sums up Shah Jahan's sentiments about his city: "If there be a paradise on earth—It is this! It is this! It is this!"

Finally, you reach the **Royal Hammams,** exquisite Moghul baths with inlaid marble floors. The fountain supposedly had rose-scented water. A state-of-the-art steam bath, the *hammam,* was a sort of 17th-century health club.

From here, a short path leads to the **Moti Masjid** (Pearl Mosque), designed by Aurangzeb for his personal use and that of his harem. The prayer hall is inlaid with *musalla* (prayer rugs) outlined in black marble. Though the mosque has the purity of white marble, some critics say its excessively ornate style reflects the decadence that set in before the end of Shah Jahan's reign. ⊠ *6 km (4 mi) north of Connaught Pl.,* ☎ *11/327–4580.* 🖼 *Rs. 470* ☉ *Sat.–Thurs., sunrise–sunset; museum Sat.–Thurs. 10–5. Sound-and-light show (weather permitting): Rs. 25. Purchase tickets 30 min in advance. Show times: Feb.–Apr. and Sept.–Oct., daily 8:30–9:30; May–Aug., daily 9–10; Nov.–Jan., 7:30–8:30.*

Raj Ghat and National Gandhi Museum. After Mohandas K. Gandhi was shot and killed by a Hindu fanatic on January 30, 1948 (the anniversary of which is now a national holiday), his body was cremated on the banks of the Yamuna River. This site is now a national shrine to the Mahatma. Indian tourists and pilgrims stream across the peaceful lawn to pay their respects to him. At the center of a courtyard is a slightly raised black-marble slab covered with flowers. At its head is an eternal flame and an inscription of Gandhi's final words, "Hai Ram!" ("Oh God!"). The sandstone walls enclosing the shrine are inscribed with various passages written by Gandhi, translated into 13 of India's 16 official languages, as well other languages. Raj Ghat was also the cremation site for two other assassinated heads of state, Indira Gandhi and her son Rajiv. Back across the busy street from which you entered is the National Gandhi Museum, run by a private foundation, which houses a collection of photographs and some of Gandhi's personal effects. ⊠ *Mahatma Gandhi Marg.* 🏛 *Free.* ☉ *Raj Ghat, daily sunrise–sunset; museum, Tues.–Sun. 9:30–5:30.*

❹ **Sisganj Gurdwara.** A Sikh shrine near the police station on Chandni Chowk, Sisganj Gurdwara is a restful place to take a break from the crowds. It marks the site where Aurangzeb beheaded Guru Teg Bahadur in 1675 when the guru refused to convert to Islam. Women must cover their heads. ⊠ *Chandni Chowk.* ☉ *Daily 24 hrs.*

❻ **Sweitana Temple.** The interior of this splendid Jain temple is majestic, with painted murals and sacred idols. Its paintings are what makes Sweitana Temple unique among other Jain temples in Delhi. ⊠ *End of Naughara Gali.* ☉ *Apr.–Sept., daily 5:30 AM–12:30 PM and 7 PM–8 PM; Oct.–Mar., daily 6 AM–1 PM and 6 PM–7 PM.*

New Delhi

New Delhi, which begins in Connaught Place and extends about 6 km (4 mi) south, is the city the British built when they moved their capital from Calcutta to Delhi in 1911. Colonial bungalows are slowly being replaced with office buildings, five-star hotels, and unsightly new residential quarters for government officials. New Delhi flows into South Delhi; the boundary is fluid. South Delhi also has its share of centuries-old monuments, such as the Qutab Minar, the village of Hauz Khas, and numerous Muslim tombs that lie abandoned in the center of a field or stand amid contemporary houses and apartments. Eastern South Delhi has the handsome new Bahai Temple.

A Good Tour

Hire a car or taxi and head to **Humayun's Tomb** ⑧ in the early morning. Created by the wife of the Moghul emperor, the 16th-century tomb is relatively peaceful at this time of day. Once the rush-hour traffic winds down, proceed north to check out **Purana Qila,** ⑨ the Old Fort—the site of India's sixth capital—and the white tigers at the adjacent **Zoological Park** ⑩. Depending on how much time you spend at the zoo, you may have to forego some of the other sights on this tour. After the zoo, go north another block to the **Crafts Museum** ⑪. From here, head southeast to Dilli Haat and the INA Market, two wonderful shopping-and-eating bazaars. If you want to see what locals do, head a block west instead, to **India Gate** ⑫ for a stroll around the park. If you're interested in Indian art, check out the **National Gallery of Modern Art** ⑬. In the early afternoon, drive northwest to the Sikh temple **Bangla Sahib Gurdwara** ⑭ to listen to hymns. Then drive a few streets west to check out the nearby colorful and ornate **Laxmi Naryan Temple** ⑮. Then drive south and then west—along Raj Path—to **Lutyens's Imperial City** ⑯. Choose only one or two of the following sights—all within a few kilometers of one another—to occupy the rest of your afternoon. If you're an ancient history buff, drive east, back down Raj Path, to see the Hindu sculptures and artifacts at the **National Museum** ⑰. If you're interested in the Independence movement, visit **Gandhi Smriti** ⑱ and the **Nehru Memorial Museum** ⑲. A good alternative, especially for railroad enthusiasts and children, is to continue south and visit the **National Rail Museum** ⑳, just southwest of Nehru Park. After visiting any of these museums, you may want to chill out for a bit in **Lodi Gardens** ㉑ with the locals or examine the ancient tombs of the 15th- and 16th-century Lodi rulers. Around 5 PM, drive to the Muslim bazaar in the old Nizamuddin neighborhood, about 3 km (2 mi) east of the Lodi Gardens. Taped qawwalis (Sufi songs of ecstasy) will set the mood as you walk down this village's winding lanes to **Hazrat Nizamuddin Darga** ㉒, the tomb of a Sufi saint. It's a lovely place to linger at dusk. If you're lucky, qawwali singers will perform as the sun sets.

For a different experience altogether, or if you have an extra afternoon, drive southwest a few kilometers to the village of **Hauz Khas** or to the **Qutab Minar** monument. Another option, especially in the early evening, is to head to the **ISKON (Hari Krishna) Temple** ㉓ or the lotus-shape **Bahai Temple** ㉔; both are a short drive southeast of the city.

TIMING

To see every sight on this tour in one day would be lunatic. You're better off dividing the itinerary into two or three days. Choose a monument and museum (or the zoo) for morning and midday, then punctuate it with a visit to a temple at sunset. Traffic and heat will slow you down considerably—especially between April and October, when the sun is intense. Lodi Gardens is a good place to take a break. Don't plan this tour for a Monday, as museums are closed. (Or choose non-museum sights for a Monday and visit museums on other days.)

Sights to See

★ ㉔ **Bahai Temple.** The Bahai Temple celebrates the lotus flower, symbol of purity throughout India, and the number nine, which represents the highest digit and, in the Bahai faith, unity. The nine pools on the elevated platform signify the green leaves of the lotus—and cool the stark, elegant interior. The sleek structure has two layers: nine white marble-covered petals that point to heaven, and nine petals that conceal the portals. From a short distance, it looks like a fantastic work of origami. The interior conforms to that of all Bahai temples: there are no religious icons, just copies of the Holy Scriptures and wooden pews. Completed in 1986, the temple was designed by Fariburz Sahba, an Iranian-born Canadian architect. ⊠ *Bahapur, Kalkaji (9 km/5 mi southeast of Connaught Pl., near Nehru Pl.), South Delhi.* ☒ *Free.* ☉ *Apr.–Sept., 9–7; Oct.–Mar., 9:30–5:30. Closed Mon.*

⑭ **Bangla Sahib Gurdwara.** Less than 2 km (1 mi) from Connaught Place, this *gurdwara* (Sikh temple) is always full of activity—no surprise given Delhi's huge Sikh population, most of whom came here as refugees from Pakistan in 1947. If you can't make it to Amritsar to see the Golden Temple, by all means come here to admire the distinctively ostentatious style of their temples. Like Sikhism itself, gurdwaras reflect both the symmetry of Moghul mosques and the chaos of Hindu temples. Bangla Sahib is built of white marble and topped with a shiny, gold onion dome.

The gurdwara stands on the site where Guru Hari Krishan, the 8th of 10 Sikh gurus who lived between 1469 and 1708, performed a small miracle. Before entering, remove your shoes and socks (check them at the counter on the left), get rid of cigarettes, and cover your head with a piece of cloth. As you walk up the stairs and enter the sanctum, you'll see people filling jugs of water from enclosed cisterns. Guru Hari Krishan used to distribute sanctified water to the sick, believing it had a miraculous healing effect on their mind, body, and soul, and people still treat the contents of these pools as holy water. Inside, devotees sit facing a small pavilion in the center that holds the *Granth Sahib* (Sikh scriptures). Hymns from the holy book are sung continuously from well before sunrise until approximately 9 PM, and you're welcome to sit and listen; if you fancy something cultural in the evening, come at about 9 to see the ceremony by which the book is stored away for the night. As you walk around inside, be careful to proceed in a clockwise direction, and exit on the right side in back. Out the door to the right a priest distributes *prasad*, a ritual resembling the Christian sacrament of communion: take a lump of this sugar, flour, and oil concoction with both hands, pop it into your mouth with your right hand, then rub the remaining oil into your hands. ⊠ *Baba Bangla Sahib Marg, across from Gole Post Office.* ▣ *Free.* ⊙ *4 AM–9 PM.*

OFF THE
BEATEN PATH

CHATTARPURR TEMPLES – If you're on your way south to Agra or Jaipur, drive a few miles beyond Qutab Minar, down Meharauli Road, and check out this massive Hindu temple complex. It's an untamed mishmash of architectural styles, but the unifying factor—from the huge dome over the Shiva lingam to the 92-ft statue of the monkey god Hanuman—is the ostentatious Punjabi Baroque architecture. Enter through the sanctum with the devotees, stop at the idols to pay respects, and take some prasad on the way out. Many gods and goddesses are represented, but the inner sanctum is dedicated to Adhya Ma Katyan, a mother goddess. Hymns are sung all night during full moons. *Chattarpur.* ▣ *Free.* ⊙ *Daily.*

⓫ **Crafts Museum.** Designed by the Indian architect Charles Correa, this charming complex near the Old Fort houses more than 20,000 artifacts and handicrafts. There are terra-cotta sculptures from Tamil Nadu on the spacious grounds. Inside, the annotations are sketchy, but the collection itself is fascinating. Items in the Folk and Tribal Art Gallery mix village life and tribal India. In the courtyard you'll see a wooden temple cart, built to carry deities in festive processions; one of the nearby buildings is a lavishly decorated Gujarati haveli (mansion). The Courtly Crafts section illustrates the luxurious lifestyle of India's erstwhile royalty. An upper-floor display showcases saris and textiles. In the village complex, which has replicas of rural homes, artisans demonstrate their skills and sell their creations. The museum shop sells high-quality art books and snacks. ⊠ *Pragati Bhavan, Mathura Rd.,* ☏ *11/337–1353.* ▣ *Rs. 5.* ⊙ *Tues.–Sun. 10–5:30.*

⓲ **Gandhi Smriti.** While Mahatma Gandhi lived a life of voluntary poverty, he did it in some attractive places. It was in this huge colonial bungalow, designed by a French architect for Indian industrialist G. D. R. Birla, that Gandhi was staying as a guest when he was assassinated. Gandhi's bedroom is just as he left it, with his "worldly remains" (only 11 items, including his glasses and a walking stick) mounted on the wall. Pictures and text tell the story of Gandhi's life and the Independence movement; there is also a collection of dioramas depicting events in Gandhi's life. In the theater, 10 different documentaries are available for viewing, upon request. Take off your shoes before entering the somber prayer ground in the back garden; an eternal flame marks the very spot where Gandhi expired. This, not the National Gandhi Museum at Raj Ghat, is the government's official museum dedicated to the Mahatma. ⊠ *5 Tees January Marg,* ☏ *11/301–2843.* ▣ *Free.* ⊙ *Daily 10–5.*

HAUZ KHAS – The road south to the urban village of Hauz Khas is lined on both sides by ancient stone monuments, and the entire village is dotted with domed structures—the tombs of minor Muslim royalty from the 14th to the 16th centuries. At the end of the road is the tomb of Firoz Shah Tughluq, who ruled Delhi in the 14th century. Hauz Khas means "Royal Tank," which refers to the now empty artificial lake visible from Firoz Shah's pillared tomb. The tank was actually built a century earlier by Allaudin Khiji as a water source for his nearby fort, then called Siri (the second city of Delhi). Walk around this area at your leisure, or, back in the village itself, wander through the narrow *galis* (alleyways) to experience a startling medley of old and new structures. In the 1980s, Hauz Khas was designated an upscale tourist destination, but (fortunately) the process of redevelopment was never fully completed, so some of the village character persists. Check out the latest art gallery or stop into a jewelry shop; just watch your step or you may trip over a buffalo chewing its cud as it lies on a bed of straw. After exploring, stop for a meal at one of the village's numerous restaurants, particularly Park Baluchi (a 5-minute walk to Deer Park) or Naivedyam. ✉ *7 km (4 mi) south of Connaught Pl.*

★ ㉒ **Hazrat Nizamuddin Darga.** Here you may have a chance to enjoy one of Delhi's greatest treats—hearing devout Sufis sing qawwalis (ecstatic religious songs). To get here, follow the twisting narrow lanes in Nizamuddin, an old neighborhood about 3 km (2 mi) east of the Lodi Gardens. You'll pass open-air stalls, small restaurants cooking simple Indian meals, and tiny shops selling cassettes—many by famous qawwali singers. When you see vendors selling flowers and garlands, you're getting close to the *darga* (shrine) of Hazrat Nizamuddin Aulia, who was born in Bukhara and later came to Delhi, where he became an important Sufi mystic and attracted a dedicated following. (He died in 1325.) Buy a few garlands (about Rs. 10 each) to present at the memorial.

In the small courtyard at the entrance—considered extremely sacred— are three small mausoleums. The saint's white mausoleum was built in 1562; it has a white, onion-shape dome with thin black stripes. The structure is modest, but it gets lovelier the longer you study its inlay work and the carved parapet above the verandas. His tomb is surrounded by a mosque and the graves of other important Muslims, including a daughter of the Moghul emperor Shah Jahan and another relative of the emperor Akbar, the 16th-century conqueror and reformer. Evenings from around 5 to 7, especially Thursday, the Sufi saint's male followers often sing in the courtyard. ✉ *Old Nizamuddin Bazaar, 5 km (3 mi) southeast of Connaught Pl.* ✉ *Free; make a charitable donation and request that it be used to feed the poor; give a small offering to musicians if you hear them perform.* ☉ *Daily 24 hrs.*

★ ❽ **Humayun's Tomb.** Erected in the middle of the 16th century by the wife of the Moghul emperor Humayun, this tomb launched a new architectural era that culminated in the Moghul masterpieces in Agra and Fatehpur Sikri. The Moghuls brought to India their love of gardens and fountains, and left a legacy of harmonious structures, such as this mausoleum, that fuse symmetry with decorative splendor.

Reminiscent of Persian architecture, this exquisite structure of red sandstone and white marble rests on a raised podium amid gardens intersected by water channels and enclosed by walls. The design represents India's first "tomb-in-a-garden" complex, and the marble dome covering the actual tomb is another first: a dome within a dome (the interior dome is set inside the soaring dome seen from the exterior), a style later used in the Taj Mahal.

Besides Humayun, seven other important Moghuls are buried here, along with Humayun's wife, Haji Begum—who lies in the octagonal shrine outside the gateway—and possibly his barber. As you enter or leave the gateway, stand a moment before the square, blue-domed structure to enjoy the view of the entire monument framed in the arch. The building's serenity belies the fact that many of the dead buried inside were murdered princes, victims of foul play. ⊠ *Off Mathura Rd., 5 km (3 mi) southeast of Connaught Pl.* ☒ *Rs. 470.* ☉ *Daily sunrise–sunset.*

⑫ **India Gate.** If you're curious to see what locals do during their free time, stop at this popular park for a stroll. Situated in a traffic circle that's almost a kilometer across, this tan and red sandstone arch was originally built to memorialize the 70,000 soldiers of the British Indian Army who fell in World War I and the 3rd Afghan War in the late 19th century. The Government of India has, since Independence, added a monument to India's unknown soldier (the *Amar Jawan Jyoti*). The monument is beneath the arch. There's a quick changing of the guard ceremony on Sunday morning at 10 AM. While traffic speeds around the outer circle, pedestrians and food vendors occupy the inner circle around India Gate. You'll find all sorts of activities going on, from men offering to make monkeys "dance" for a fee to cricket games on the grass. ⊠ *Just southwest of Connaught Pl.*

㉓ **ISKON (Hari Krishna) Temple.** Inaugurated by Prime Minister Vajpayee in 1998, the "Hari Krishna" temple offers a unique glimpse into the international character of Hinduism. Foreign devotees, heads shaved and wearing saffron robes, mingle with Indians, who come both to pray and as tourists. This massive temple, standing on a rock outcropping, is an amalgam of artistic styles: Moghul, Gupta, and "Punjabi Baroque." The sanctum contains three idols: Balram Krishna, Radha-Krishna, and Laksman (along with Ram and Sita). Each represents a different incarnation of Lord Krishna. Those interested in learning more about Krishna's life should also visit the on-sight "museum" (a collection of dioramas) and the Animatronics Show—a robotics display that enacts the Bhagavad Gita (the core religious text for Hari Krishnas and Hindus). Finish off with a meal at Govinda's, the on-site restaurant, with a cheerful dining area. The buffet of "Higher Taste Karma Free Food" includes North Indian vegetarian food for the low price of Rs. 150. *Hare Krishna Hill, Sant Nagar Main Rd., east of Kailash,* ☎ *11/623–5133.* ☒ *Free.* ☉ *4:30 AM–1 PM and 4 –9 PM.*

⑮ **Laxmi Narayan Temple.** This large, red-and-yellow temple (known as Birla Mandir) west of Connaught Place is an excellent example of a reformist Hindu temple—both architecturally and in terms of temple practices. It was built in 1938 by Indian industrialist G. D. R. Birla— the same man whose house is now the Gandhi Smriti—as a non-denominational temple. (The sign outside welcomes all "Hindus," including Jains and Sikhs.) The temple is colorful and ornate: note the lotus patterns at the top of each phallic steeple and the inlaid lotus pattern on the floor in front of the main *murti* (idol) of Laxmi Narayan. While the temple exhibits many of the gaudier elements of Hindu design, overall it's relatively subdued. This is a common feature of reformist, 20th-century Hindu architecture, which was influenced by European architecture. *Mandir Marg.*

㉑ **Lodi Gardens.** After Timur ransacked Delhi at the end of the 14th century, he ordered the massacre of the entire population—acceptable retribution, he thought, for the murder of some of his soldiers. As if in unconscious response to this horrific act, the subsequent Lodi and Sayyid dynasties built no city, only a few mosques and some mausoleums and tombs, the latter of which stand in what is now a lovely urban park.

Winding walks cut through landscaped lawns with trees and small flowers, past schoolboys playing cricket and groups of friends relaxing in the greenery. Near the southern entrance on Lodi Road is the dignified mausoleum of Mohammed Shah, third ruler of the Sayyid dynasty, and some members of his family. This octagon, with a central chamber surrounded by verandas carved with arches, is a good example of the architecture of this period. The smaller, equally lovely, octagonal tomb of Sikandar Lodi, surrounded by a garden in the park's northwestern corner, has an unusual double dome. ⊠ *Lodi Rd., 5 km (3 mi) south of Connaught Pl.* 🎫 *Free.* ⊙ *Daily sunrise–sunset.*

⑯ Lutyens's Imperial City. Raj Path—the broadest avenue in Delhi—leads to Delhi's eighth capital: Sir Edwin Lutyens's Imperial City, built between 1914 and 1931 in a symbolically imperialistic design. The Imperial City was built after the British moved their capital from Calcutta to Delhi in 1911. (While the British were building, they hit marshy land prone to floods, so they reversed direction and put the bulk of their capital, the Imperial City, a few miles to the south.) Starting from India Gate at the lowest and eastern end of Raj Path, nearby land was allocated to numerous princely states, which built small palaces, such as the **Bikaner House** (now the Rajasthan tourism office) and **Jaipur House** (now the National Gallery of Modern Art). It might be said that this placement mirrored the British sentiments toward the princes, who lost much of their former power and status during the British Raj. Moving up the slowly inclining hill at the western end of the avenue, you also move up the British ladder of power, a concept inherent in the original design. First you come to the enormous **North and South Secretariats,** facing each other on Raj Path and reflecting the importance of the bureaucracy, a fixture of Indian society since the time of British rule. Identical in design, the two buildings have 1,000 rooms and miles of corridors.

Directly behind the North Secretariat is the Indian parliament **Sansad Bhavan,** a circular building in red-and-gray sandstone, with an open colonnade that extends around its circumference. Architecturally, the Indian design is meant to mirror the spinning wheel that was the symbol of Mahatma Gandhi, but the building's secondary placement, off the main avenue, may suggest the attitude of the British toward the Indian legislative assembly.

At the top of the hill is the former Viceroy's House, now called **Rashtrapati Bhavan,** where the President of India (not the prime minister) resides. It was built in the 20th century, but the building's daunting proportions seem to reflect an earlier, more lavish time. Its scale was meant to express British supremacy. The Bhavan contains 340 rooms and its grounds cover 330 acres, including a Moghul-style garden that opens to the public for several weeks in February. The shape of the central brass dome, the palace's main architectural feature, reflects that of a Buddhist *stupa* (shrine).

The execution of Lutyens's design has a flaw: the entire palace was supposed to fill the vista as you approach the top of the hill, but the gradient is too steep, so only the dome dominates the horizon. And in a nicely ironic twist, a few years after the Imperial City was completed, the British packed up and went home, and this lavish architectural complex became the grand capital of newly independent India. Permission to enter Rashtrapati and Sansad Bhavan is almost impossible to obtain; unless you have contacts in high places, satisfy yourself with a glimpse from outside. ⊠ *2 km (1 mi) south of Connaught Pl.*

⑬ National Gallery of Modern Art. Facing India Gate, this neoclassical building was built by the British in the early 20th century as a palace for the Maharaja of Jaipur. With its small dome and large, open rooms, the structure makes a beautiful space for an art museum. The well-maintained museum was established in 1954 to preserve Indian art forms (mainly painting) that developed after 1850. The collection is broad, and well-displayed by local standards, but still somewhat uneven and oddly arranged. The highlights—Bengali Renaissance works by Rabindranath Tagore and Jamini Roy—are, regrettably, hidden in corner rooms upstairs, and the representative works by contemporary masters, such as M. F. Husain and Ganesh Pyne, are disappointing. Documentaries, shown daily at 11 AM and 3 PM, explain Indian art, but the museum's displayed works, unfortunately, lack written commentary. ⊠ *Jaipur House, India Gate,* ☎ *11/338–2835.* ▨ *Rs. 5.* ☉ *Tues.– Sun. 10–5.*

⓱ National Museum. The facade of this grand building imitates Lutyens's Presidential Palace in the Imperial City: a sandstone dome is supported by classical columns of brown sandstone on a red sandstone base. When you enter, you'll see a 13th-century idol—from the Konark Sun Temple in Bhubaneswar—of Surya, the sun god, standing beneath the dome. Such a statue is emblematic of the National Museum's strength— it showcases ancient, mainly Hindu, sculptures. An entire room is dedicated to artifacts from the Indus Valley Civilization, circa 2,700 BC, while others display works from the Gandharan, Chandela, and Chola periods. Besides sculpture, also on exhibit are jewelry, painting, musical instruments, coins, carpets, and weapons. However, the museum is not very well maintained, and there's no brochure to help you navigate the collections. ⊠ *Corner of Janpath and Rajpath,* ☎ *11/301– 5938.* ▨ *Rs. 150.* ☉ *Tues.–Sun. 10–5.*

⓴ National Rail Museum. This large, mostly outdoor, museum offers a glimpse into the largest railway system in the world. The 10-acre grounds are home to 75 authentic engines, bogies (railway cars), and even a working roundabout (a device that spins rail cars. Parked behind glass is the Fairy Queen; built in 1855, it's the oldest running steam engine in the world. It still takes nine trips a year to Sariska National Park and back for a weekend trip (contact the Director of the Museum if you are interested, but it's not worth the outrageous price). Inside the museum are displays that discuss the history of the India rail system. The museum will intrigue not only history buffs but also children, who love riding the tiny train that circumambulates the grounds. The museum is near Nehru Park. (From Ring Road, take a left onto Nyaya Marg, then another left.) *Chanakyapuri,* ☎ *11/688–1816 or 11/688– 0939.* ▨ *Rs. 5.* ☉ *Oct.–Mar. daily 9:30–5:30, Apr.–Sept. daily 9:30– 7:30, closed Mon.*

⓳ Nehru Memorial Museum. This colonial mansion, also known as Teen Murti Bhavan, was originally built for the commander of the British Indian Army. While the Viceregal residence (at the other end of South Avenue) became the home of India's president, India's first prime minister, Jawaharlal Nehru, took up residence here. Those interested in the Independence movement should not miss this landmark or the nearby Gandhi Smriti. Nehru's yellow mansion is fronted by a lawn where small groups of people often rest and chat. Out back, there's a beautiful, and tranquil, flower garden. Inside, several rooms are still decorated as Nehru left them, and extensive displays chronicle Nehru's life and the Independence movement. Move through the rooms in order: one by one, photographs, newspaper clippings, and personal letters tell the dramatic story of the birth of the world's largest democracy. On your way out, stop and see the 14th-century hunting lodge next to the Nehru Planetarium. (The latter, good for children, has shows in English at 11:30

AM and 3 PM.) ✉ *Teen Murti Marg,* ☎ *11/301–3765.* 🎫 *Free.* ⊙ *9–5:30. Closed Mon.*

❾ Purana Qila (Old Fort). India's sixth capital was the scene of a fierce power struggle between the Afghan Sher Shah and Humayun, son of the first Moghul emperor, Babur. Humayun, who believed deeply in astrology, probably considered himself star-crossed. When he started to build his own capital, Dinpanah, on these grounds in the 1530s, Sher Shah forced the emperor to flee for his life. Sher Shah destroyed what existed of Dinpanah to create his own capital, Shergarh. Fifteen years later, Humayun took revenge and seized control, but he died the following year, leaving Sher Shah's city for others to destroy.

Unfortunately, once you enter the massive **Bara Darwaza** (Western Gate), only two buildings are intact: the **Qila-i-Kunha Masjid,** Sher Shah's private mosque—an excellent example of Indo-Afghan architecture in red sandstone with decorative marble touches—and the two-story octagonal tower of red sandstone and white marble, the **Sher Mandal,** which ultimately became Humayun's library and his death trap: hearing the call to prayer, Humayun started down the steep steps, slipped, and fell to his death. ✉ *Off Mathura Rd., near Delhi Zoo.* 🎫 *Rs. 235.* ⊙ *Daily sunrise–sunset.*

OFF THE
BEATEN PATH
★

QUTAB MINAR – Don't miss this monument known as the seventh wonder of Hindustan. The 234-ft-high tower, with 376 steps, is the tallest stone tower in India. The Muslim campaigner Qutab-ud-din-Aibak began construction in 1193; his son-in-law and successor, Iltutmish, added the top four stories. The result is a handsome sandstone example of Indo-Islamic architecture, with terra-cotta frills and balconies. At its foot lies the **Quwwat-ul-Islam Masjid,** the first Muslim mosque in India. The Muslims erected the mosque in the 12th century after they defeated the Hindu Chauhan dynasty—they built it on the site of a Hindu temple and used materials from 27 demolished Hindu and Jain shrines. (Which explains why you see Hindu and Jain sculptures in the mosque.) The mosque is also famous for a 24-ft-high, 5th-century iron pillar, inscribed with six lines of Sanskrit. According to legend, if you stand with your back to the pillar and can reach around and touch your fingers, any wish you make will come true. (Unfortunately, it's currently fenced off.) ✉ *Aurobindo Marg, near Mehrauli, 14 km (9 mi) south of Connaught Pl.* 🎫 *Rs. 250* ⊙ *Daily sunrise–sunset.*

❿ Zoological Park. White tigers are the draw at the zoo, which was designed in the late 1950s by noted German designer Carl Hagenbeck. There are many noteworthy animals roaming about—such as wild monkeys and water birds. Animals in cages, including the famous white tigers and Asian lions, are part of the official collection. The zoo is spacious and leafy, a virtual botanical garden for peaceful walks. Also lovely is the central lake, where numerous species of Central Asian migratory aquatic birds (pelicans, storks, and cranes) pause on their way to Keoladeo National Park in Bharatpur Rajasthan for the winter. If you don't have time to make it to Bharatpur for bird watching or to a tiger reserve, this is a pretty good alternative. *Mathura Rd.* 🎫 *Foreigners Rs. 40.* ⊙ *9:30–4, closed Fri.*

DINING

Restaurants are generally open daily 12:30 to 3 for lunch and 7:30 to 11 for dinner. Dry days (on which you cannot buy alcohol) are strictly observed on the first and seventh day of each month and on national

Dining

Delhi Dining and Lodging

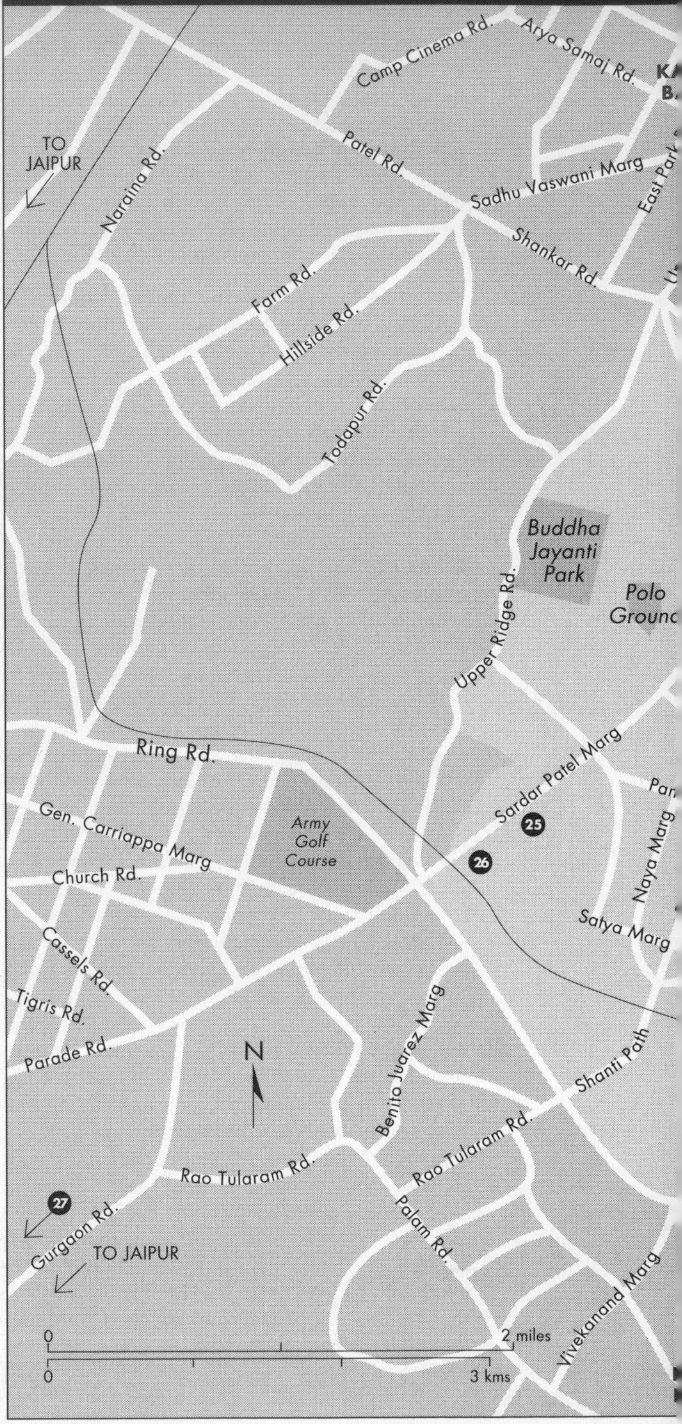

TO JAIPUR

Camp Cinema Rd.
Arya Samaj Rd.
Patel Rd.
Naraina Rd.
Sadhu Vaswani Marg
Shankar Rd.
Farm Rd.
Hillside Rd.
Todapur Rd.

Buddha Jayanti Park

Polo Ground

Upper Ridge Rd.

Ring Rd.

Sardar Patel Marg

Gen. Carriappa Marg

Army Golf Course

Church Rd.

Cassels Rd.

Tigris Rd.

Parade Rd.

N

Satya Marg

Naya Marg

Benito Juarez Marg

Shanti Path

Rao Tularam Rd.

Gurgaon Rd.

TO JAIPUR

Rao Tularam Rd.

Palam Rd.

Vivekanand Marg

27

25

26

0 ———————————— 2 miles
0 ———————————— 3 kms

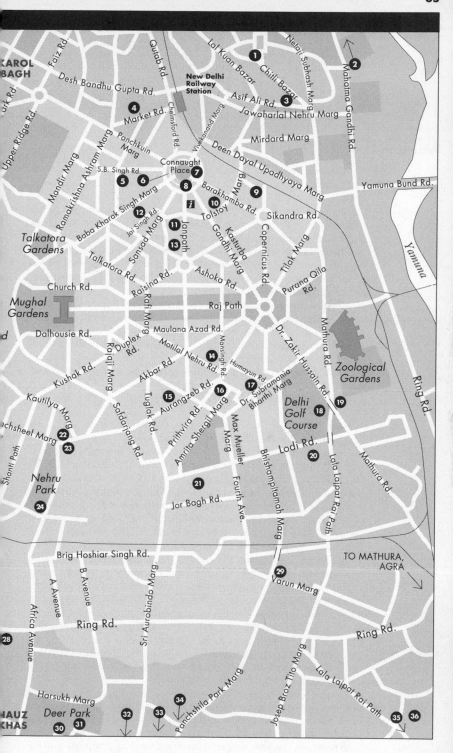

holidays. Expect a 20% tax on your food and beverage bill. Imported liquor is extremely expensive; inquire before you imbibe.

CATEGORY	COST*
$$$$	over Rs. 1,000
$$$	Rs. 600–Rs. 1,000
$$	Rs. 300–Rs. 600
$	under Rs. 300

per person for a main course at dinner

North Indian

$$ ✕ **Bukhara.** This small, local hotspot, with mounted Bukhara carpets
★ and hanging copper vessels, has a menu that by popular demand hasn't changed in years. Bukhara serves Northwest Frontier cuisine—mainly marinated meats. The delicately spiced, tender *sikandari raan* (lamb marinated in rum and cooked in the tandoor) is heavenly. Bukhara's *dal* (lentils) is so famous it's now sold in cans. Carnivores will be happier here, though vegetarians can opt for a tandoori salad of vegetables, pineapple, and paneer (cheese). ⊠ *Welcomgroup Maurya Sheraton Hotel, Diplomatic Enclave, New Delhi,* ☎ *11/611–2233. Reservations not accepted after 8:30. AE, DC, MC, V.*

$$ ✕ **Dilli ka Aangan.** The name means "courtyard," but the minimalist space resembles a five-star hotel coffee shop with an eclectic collection of indigenous artifacts in niches or on the walls. The Delhi cuisine is, on the other hand, inventive and on-target. The salmon *aali-shaan* (marinated Norwegian salmon) and *gosht chaamp taajdar* (rack of lamb) are both seared in the tandoor, infusing the food with a sweet, charcoal flavor. The restaurant doesn't start filling up until 9 PM. ⊠ *Hyatt Regency Bhikaiji Cama Pl., Ring Rd., New Delhi,* ☎ *11/679–1234. AE, DC, MC, V.*

$–$$ ✕ **Dum Pukht.** Like the *nawabi* (princely) culture from which it's drawn, the food at Dum Pukht is subtle and refined. The menu includes fusion dishes developed when East India Company officers were adapting to the nawabi way of life. The Lucknow- and Hyderabad-derived cuisine is delicately spiced but packed with flavor: *habibia* and *kakori* kabobs are a good choice, as are *baghare baigan* (baby eggplants) in a sharp peanut-sesame sauce, and marinated mutton chops in pomegranate sauce. The understated decor is spruced up with lovely embroidered ceiling fans. ⊠ *Welcomgroup Maurya Sheraton Hotel, Diplomatic Enclave, New Delhi,* ☎ *11/611–2233. AE, DC, MC, V.*

$ ✕ **The Amber Restaurant.** Connaught Place, once home to the city's trendiest restaurants and nightclubs, still has many restaurants, some dating back to the days when Nehru used to dine out after attending the cinema. Typical of the style of that time is Amber Restaurant, with a balcony seating area (sometimes reserved for "families and ladies") at the rear. Here you can find well-prepared Mughali food at modest prices; a bottle of beer costs Rs 80. Smartly dressed waiters efficiently manage the fast-moving crowd of mainly upper-class Indians who frequent the restaurant. ⊠ *N-19 Connaught Pl., New Delhi,* ☎ *11/331–2092, MC, V.*

$ ✕ **Bengali Sweet Home.** Order a drink and a snack and sit down to
★ people-watch by the open storefront. The large selection of Indian sweets are fabulous. The *gol gappa,* also called *pani puri,* is a favorite snack in India: the tiny, deep-fried bread is punctured at the top and filled with potatoes, chick peas, spices, tamarind sauce, and topped with coriander sauce. (A serving includes eight balls, and they fill your bowl twice.) ⊠ *27-37 Bengali Market, New Delhi,* ☎ *11/335–3310.*

$ ✕ **Chor Bizarre.** Expect a 1927 Fiat roadster for a salad bar, a spiral staircase that leads nowhere, and an eclectic mix of tables and chairs collected from *chor* (thieves) bazaars around India. You can also expect excellent North Indian cuisine—especially Kashmiri dishes. Try *ghazab ka tikka* (tandoori chicken coated with cheddar cheese), lightly cooked *haaq* (Kashmiri spinach), or *dum aloo* (Kashmiri spicy potatoes). Punctuate the meal with *kahwah*, fragrant Kashmiri tea. ✉ *Hotel Broadway, 4/15 A Asif Ali Rd., Old Delhi,* ☎ *11/327–3821. AE, DC, MC, V.*

$ ✕ **Daniell's Tavern.** Despite the low lighting and formal European-style decoration, this is primarily an Indian restaurant serving the "Cuisine of the Raj." Menu items are largely drawn from cuisines encountered by Thomas and William Daniell, two English painters who spent seven years exploring East India Company territories in the late 18th century. Dishes are from Bengal, Lucknow, Tamil Nadu, Kerala, and England: it's the Bengali and Kerala specialties that make this place unique. Try Hooglhly's Treasure, a Bengali river fish sautéed with mustard greens, or Major Witt's Order—pomfret (fish) in a sweet-and-tangy tamarind sauce. ✉ *Imperial Hotel, Janpath, New Delhi,* ☎ *11/334–1234. AE, D, MC, V.*

$ ✕ **Dhaba.** As the name indicates, this restaurant builds on the theme of a roadside eatery. Part of a truck sticks out of the wall behind the row of pots full of bubbling food, and the cane ceiling adds to the sense that you're indulging at a casual, roadside restaurant. The food is nothing special, but it does offer the relatively rare opportunity to sample the Punjabi fare served at truck stops in North India. ✉ *Claridges Hotel, 12 Aurangazeb Rd., New Delhi,* ☎ *11/301–0211. AE, DC, MC, V.*

$ ✕ **Farsaan.** You get only two options at Farsaan: Gujarati or Rajastani *thali* (a metal sampler plate with a selection of food). The northwestern Indian cuisine (from the desert) tends to exclude meats and root vegetables, such as onion and garlic. (In Gujarat especially, there are many adherents of Jainism, which prohibits all taking of life. When you pluck up onions, for example, you destroy the entire root, and so destroy its life.) *Sangri*, a hardy desert bean, is made to taste hot-and-sweet, or sweet-and-sour; these flavors are typical to the region. The food is light (no cream-based sauces), with a sharp kick. Farsaan is difficult to find: it's on a side street behind one of South Delhi's nuevo riche markets. It's a simple place with no decoration and good service. ✉ *M-27 Greater Kailash Part I, New Delhi,* ☎ *11/646–4318 or 11/641–3564.*

$ ✕ **The Great Kabab Factory.** It looks like a sci-fi movie set from the 1960s: waiters are decked out in industrial coveralls, and smokestack-like columns. The chefs prepare a new variety of kabobs nightly; these are served with two kinds of dal, a vegetable, a rice dish, yogurt, bread, and a dessert. Only the signature kabobs are available daily: the *galauti kabab* (minced mutton with raw papaya) and the *subz galauti* (mashed lentils and yam). Both are smoked, then fried. This place is extremely popular; reserve in advance. ✉ *Radisson Hotel, National Hwy. 8, New Delhi,* ☎ *11/612–9191. Reservations essential. AE, D, DC, MC. No lunch.*

$ ✕ **Haveli.** Every aspect of this restaurant's decor contributes to the look of an old haveli (mansion), including the earthy colors of Rajasthan. Antiqued walls showcase tiny replicas of *jharoka* (perforated stone) balconies, and yellow lights hang from gold-plated glass domes. Haveli's North Indian food is superb. Remarkably, some of chef Rajeev Janveja's creations are cooked with minimal or no oil. Start with the "street food," especially the marvelous *chaats* (a tangy dish made with lentils and potatoes). Also try the marvelous *rogini gosht* (lamb curry) or *machli ke tikka* (fish marinated in coconut and mint and cooked in the tandoor). Folk dancers, singers, and musicians provide entertainment. ✉ *Taj Mahal Hotel, 1 Mansingh Rd., New Delhi,* ☏ *11/302–6162. AE, DC, MC, V.*

$ ✗ **Karim Restaurant.** Karim's in Old Delhi is worth the effort to find,
★ because the mutton dishes are excellent. Try *mutton burra* (charred mutton chops) and *badam pasanda* ("almond delight"—mutton in a thick, slightly sweet gravy). To get here, walk down the street that runs out from Jama Masjid's Gate 1. About four shops down on the left, as you head away from the mosque, enter a doorway leading through a passageway, into a courtyard. All around you'll see smoking kabobs on spits and brightly lit seating areas. This is Karim's. It's clean and the service is excellent, but it's still a roadside place. For a more formal (but less delectable) meal, head to Karim's sister restaurant in Nizamuddin West, **Dastar Khwan-E-Karim** (✉ 168/2 Jha House Basti, Hazrat Nizamuddin West, Old Delhi, ☏ 11/469–8300). ✉ *Matiya Mahal, opposite Hotel Bombay Orient,* ☏ *11/326–9800. Alcohol is not served.* ⊙ *7 AM–12 PM daily (closed during daylight hrs of Ramadan). No credit cards.*

$ ✗ **Park Baluchi.** This sumptuous restaurant in Deer Park serves some
★ of the most distinctive barbecue dishes in Delhi. It's the perfect place to relax after roaming Hauz Khas. Cast-iron furniture and Oriental carpets create a lush environment inside. Sample the stupendous kabobs or the traditional Baluchi dishes, including *murg potli* (marinated chicken breast wrapped around minced mutton and served flambéed) and *mewa paneer tukra* (cheese stuffed with nuts, currants, and mushrooms, marinated in cream, then roasted). The house creations are also excellent. Note: kabobs are served all day; other dishes are not served from 3 to 6. ✉ *Deer Park, Hauz Khas Village, New Delhi,* ☏ *11/685–9369. AE, DC, MC, V.*

$ ✗ **Rampur Kitchen.** This funky little restaurant serves the cuisine from
★ the former nawabi capital of Rampur. You'll find much less cream in the dishes here than in most North Indian food. *Kichara* and *haleem* are two lentil-and-mutton Muslim dishes (served to break the Ramadan fast) that won't be found elsewhere in Delhi restaurants. Adorned with silver sheets (silver dust compressed into foil), the *gulatti*—rice, milk, and dried fruit—is a great dessert. This is a Muslim-owned establishment, so all the meat is *halal* (prepared according to Islamic dietary law) and no alcohol is served. ✉ *8A Khan Market, New Delhi,* ☏ *11/463–1222. AE, MC, V.*

South Indian

$$ ✗ **Coconut Grove.** This theme restaurant's original Malabar charm has worn away, but the food continues to be good. It's the only upscale restaurant in Delhi that serves the cuisine of coastal Kerala. Maliyali (Keralite) food takes many of its flavors from coconuts and curry leaves, and focuses on fish and other non-veg ingredients. The *konju thenga* curry includes prawns in a mild, turmeric-colored coconut sauce. Order this with *idi appam*, fried rice breads, and use the bread to scoop up the spicy morsels. Non-veg dishes from other parts of the south are available—try the pepper chicken *chettinad* (spicy hot), a specialty of Tamil Nadu. ✉ *Hotel Indraprstra (formerly Ashok Yatri Nivas), 19 Ashok Rd., New Delhi,* ☏ *11/336–8553. AE, DC, MC, V.*

$ ✗ **Naivedyam.** This charming, dimly lit restaurant designed by artisans from the Tamil temple city of Thanjavur has a polished stone Nandi (Shiva's faithful bull) facing its stained-glass entrance. The small dining room displays religious paintings, and Karnatic, or South Indian, classical music plays in the background. Waiters wear traditional *veshtis* (South Indian men's skirts). The restaurant specializes in Udupi food—from the temple town near Mangalore, in the south. All meals begin with a *rasam* (peppery soup) that must be the best in Delhi. For a snack try the *masala vadai* (fried lentil cakes). More filling is the *maharaja sajjasar masala dosa,* a lentil-flour crêpe filled with spicy potatoes and dried fruit. No alcohol is served. ⊠ *1 Hauz Khas Village, New Delhi,* ☎ *11/696–0426. AE, DC, MC, V.*

$ ✕ **Sagar.** A favorite among New Delhi's upper-middle-class, Sagar is
★ a three-story family restaurant that's bustling at mealtimes. Service is efficient, and the premises impeccably clean. The *upma* (steamed semolina with bits of cashew and peas) is especially good; so is the vegetable *uttapam* (rice-flour pancake). A separate North Indian vegetarian menu is also available. *Bhindi masala* (okra) is delicious. The meal is incredibly cheap: one person's bill is usually less than Rs. 100. The restaurant opens at 8 AM; thali are served from noon to 3 and 6 to 11. ⊠ *18 Defence Colony Market, New Delhi,* ☎ *11/461–7832. No credit cards.*

$ ✕ **Sagar Ratna.** Although it's more upmarket than its sister restaurant in Defense Colony (south of the Delhi Golf Course), Sagar Ratna's prices are still rock-bottom. A large idol of the elephant god Ganesh greets you as you enter this large, faintly lit dining hall. But be prepared to eat, because first and foremost, Sagar Ratna is a hard-core eating establishment. The food is very good, and the restaurant is well-frequented. The menu includes some delicious South Indian snacks. The fixed vegetarian platter, or thali, is excellent. Service is speedy. ⊠ *Lodhi Hotel, Lala Lajpat Rai Marg, New Delhi,* ☎ *11/436–4442.*

Chinese

$$$ ✕ **Taipan.** Taipan is the best Chinese restaurant in Delhi. The food is
★ authentic, luscious, and artfully presented, and the view from the top of the Oberoi—over the Delhi Golf Course toward the high-rise buildings of Connaught Circus—is grand. On the menu you'll find various Chinese cuisines, with a focus on Cantonese and Szechuan cooking. The highlight is the dim sum—21 varieties are prepared under the direction of a special dim-sum chef, chef Wong, from Singapore. Although dim sum is available weekdays à la carte, the real treat is the Rs. 695 fixed-price lunch on weekends, with unlimited dim sum. Reserve in advance for this feast. ⊠ *The Oberoi, Dr. Zakir Hussain Marg, New Delhi,* ☎ *11/436–3030. AE, DC, MC, V.*

$-$$ ✕ **House of Ming.** This popular Chinese restaurant gets raves for its food and hospitality. The decor is inspired by the Ming Dynasty, which introduced Cantonese cuisine to the West: pale teak latticework, a pagoda-style ceiling, and the dynasty's favorite colors—pale blues and greens. Taped Chinese music and soft lighting from brass lanterns add a nice touch. Chef Lam Kwai Tong, who hails from Hong Kong, concentrates on Szechuan and Cantonese cooking. The menu changes frequently, but ask about the exquisite yin-yang seafood soup; the steamed fish with *tausau* (black-bean) sauce; the unusual and delicious crispy Ming-style spinach; and the Peking-style lamb. ⊠ *Taj Mahal Hotel, 1 Mansingh Rd., New Delhi,* ☎ *11/302–6162. AE, DC, MC, V.*

$ ✕ **Fa Yian.** Don't let the dark, dingy location—the middle circle of Connaught Place—scare you away from this inexpensive little restaurant. Potted trees spruce up the exterior, where you may have to wait for one of the eight tables. Taped flute music and water spilling into a small fountain are soothing, but the decor takes second place to very good Chinese dishes, which are either steamed or stir-fried in minimal oil. Try the delicate steamed wonton, honey chicken, fish steamed with black beans and ginger, or shredded lamb with garlic sauce. Make sure you order the homemade date-coffee ice cream. ⊠ *A block, 25/2 Middle*

Circle (behind Marina Hotel), Connaught Pl., New Delhi, ☎ *11/332–4603. AE, MC, V.*

$ ✕ **Mandarin Court.** This place is a popular stop-off for East Asian tourists returning from the Qutab Minar. (The restaurant is opposite the Qutab Hotel.) Don't be put off by the dusty street out front. The interior is lovely: parchment walls painted with murals and an expansive dining room with wrought iron pagoda motifs on the backs of the booths. Except for the Chinese food at Taipan, the food at Mandarin Court is as good as that found in any of the big hotels—probably because Chef Kong used to work in the Maurya Sheraton. Even the fried dishes, such as Vegetable Sesame Gold Coins (vegetarian patties embedded with sesame seeds) contain little oil. The Fish Hunan (fried sole in a red sauce) is delicate. ✉ *F-126 Katwaria Sarai, Shaheed Jeet Singh Marg, New Delhi,* ☎ *11/652–4264. MC, V.*

$ ✕ **Tea House of the August Moon.** This restaurant is whimsically decorated with enormous carved dragons on the ceiling and red lacquer pagodas. The central dining area that recalls a traditional Chinese tea house—accessible by a bridge over a fish pond. Hong Kong chef Lo Ka Yan has created a menu that reflects his Cantonese and Szechuan roots. The food varies from average to excellent. The Peking onion cake has a flaky crust and a pungent cabbage-and-onion stuffing. Also fine are shredded barbecue duck and broccoli with shiitake mushrooms and soy sauce. Specialties of Southeast Asia, including the marvelous Thai steamed fish in coriander sauce, are also available. ✉ *Taj Palace Hotel, 2 Sardar Patel Marg, Diplomatic Enclave, New Delhi,* ☎ *11/611–0202. AE, DC, MC, V.*

Contemporary

$ ✕ **Basil and Thyme.** Head chef Bhicoo Manekshaw is 79 years old, but that doesn't stop her from changing her menu every 90 days and overseeing a daily special. The mainly vegetarian food she serves is artfully presented. There's no telling what she'll come up with, but you can bank on creative concoctions, such as tomato-orange soup, chicken-liver pâté, leek tarts, and mint soufflé. The decor is plain white, and the view overlooks the greenery of Santushti market. Alcohol is not served, but this little lunch spot is still popular with Delhi's upper classes and the embassy crowd. ✉ *Santushti Shopping Complex, New Wellingdon Camp, New Delhi,* ☎ *11/467–3322. Reservations essential. AE, DC, MC, V. Closed Sun., no dinner.*

$ ✕ **Fabcafe.** The Fabcafe's cheerful simplicity—ocean-blue herringbone floor tiles and seersucker curtains—mixes well with the refreshing California cuisine at this South Delhi restaurant. Fabcafe still has a coffeehouse sensibility—it's a great place to stop for an early meal or for a mid-afternoon espresso and lemon cake. The tossed green salad is a crunchy, colorful exception to Delhi's generally stewed repast. Don't be put off by the crowds; service moves quickly. ✉ *1 N Block Market, GK 1, New Delhi,* ☎ *11/647–8559. No credit cards.* ☯ *Mon.–Sat. 11–11, Sun. 11:30–4:30 only for brunch.*

French

$$$$ ✕ **La Rochelle.** Chef Bruno Cerdan is adept at incorporating local in-
★   gredients, such as *bekti* (the Indian equivalent of sea bass) into his Southern French cooking. His soups, such as crème of coco beans with truffle oil, are whipped until light and frothy. The delicate sweetness of the barbecued duck breast is balanced with a slightly bitter sauce of goose liver and port wine. Wines hail from seven countries, and vary in price from expensive to small-car down-payment. As is the case in most Oberoi establishments, service is impeccable. The slightly cav-

ernous dining room is nicest during lunch, when you can look out over the manicured rose garden below. Many of Delhi's upper crust know this, so reservations are recommended for lunch. ⊠ *The Oberoi, Dr. Zakir Hussain Rd., New Delhi,* ☎ *11/436–3030. AE, D, DC, MC, V.*

$$$$ ✕ **Orient Express.** This enchanting restaurant is inside a 19th-century
★ reproduction railcar, with handsome teak walls and brass fittings. Patrons at the 10 softly lit tables—separated by partitions of wood and beveled glass—will enjoy polished and grandiose service. The cuisine is French with influences from the *Orient Express* route (Paris to Istanbul). Try the Camembert soufflé with a tangy paprika sauce. The chef, inspired by another train that goes from Bangkok to Singapore, has added Asian flavors, too. The four-course meal is fixed-price; a three-course lunch is less indulgent, not to mention half the cost of dinner. Children under 17 are not allowed, and the dress code is smart-casual to semi-formal. ⊠ *Taj Palace Hotel, 2 Sardar Patel Marg, Diplomatic Enclave, New Delhi,* ☎ *11/611–0202.* ⊙ *12:30–2:30 and 7–11:30. AE, DC, MC, V.*

Italian

$$$$ ✕ **San Gimignano.** Chef Eraldo Colazzo combines the finest ingredi-
★ ents from Italy to create playful, absolutely sensuous dishes. The 18 varieties of cheese are imported, and the wines have been personally selected in Italy by the chef, but what's really remarkable is that even the vegetables are grown at the Imperial Hotel's farm—from seeds hand-carried from the chef's homeland. The three-course menu includes a choice of four vegetarian and four non-vegetarian entrées; the menu changes at least twice weekly, depending on the availability of ingredients. Expect regional dishes, such as Sardinian gnocchetti with spinach, pinenuts, and Gorgonzola, or chicken breasts prepared with artichoke hearts. The restaurant itself is tranquil and intimate, with authentic touches from the Tuscan town of San Gimignano. Service is attentive. ⊠ *Imperial Hotel, Janpath, New Delhi,* ☎ *11/332–5332. Reservations essential. AE, DC, MC, V.*

$$$ ✕ **La Piazza.** From the dark wooden beams to the wood-fired oven, this large, well-established Italian restaurant is informal and easygoing. Antipasto is the highlight—especially the lunch buffet's vast spread. The tomato mozzarella and the beef carpaccio are both long-time favorites. All of the dishes show the mark of Chef Gabriele Montevecchio, who likes to focus on simple preparations that bring out the freshness of the ingredients he uses. The dinner and drink menu is broad in terms of appeal—you can even get Italian food with an Indian flair, such as pizza with tandoori chicken. ⊠ *Hyatt Regency, Bhikaiji Cama Pl., Ring Rd., New Delhi,* ☎ *11/679–1234. AE, DC, MC, V.*

Japanese

$ ✕ **Tamura.** Hidden away in a corner of Nehru Park, this Japanese restaurant gets the nod from local Japanese expats as "authentic." Despite having no windows, the room is bright and airy—the restaurant has white granite walls and Japanese prints. The food is light, and artfully presented. Try the prawn-tempura noodle dish and the "Tamura-style" fillet steak (flown in from Bangkok). Fresh sushi is available, but only after a staff member has recently returned from Japan (call in advance to find out). You eat at upright tables or in one of three tatami rooms, floor-level dining alcoves enclosed by paper screens. The lunch "set" (soup, sizzler, salad, and rice) is a bargain at Rs. 350. ⊠ *Inside the NDMC Swimming Pool Complex (Nehru Park), Vinay Marg, New Delhi,* ☎ *11/611–0552. AE, D, MC, V.*

$$ ✕ **TK's.** The focus of this restaurant is the *teppanyaki* grill, used as both
★ a cooking tool and a performance space. Chef Huria has collected cooking ideas and specific dishes from all over Asia, though Japanese food is the focus. You dine facing an informative cook who guides you through the meal. The set meals are best, especially the lighter "Orchid" and the seafood-oriented "Shima," as they're designed to combine styles and dishes in unusual ways. Particularly good are jumbo prawns in yellow curry sauce, shredded chicken with black-bean sauce, and seasonal green vegetables with green curry. If you go at lunchtime, indulge in the Mongolian seafood barbecue. ✉ *Hyatt Regency, Bhikaiji Cama Pl., Ring Rd., New Delhi,* ☎ *11/679–1234. AE, DC, MC, V.*

Thai

$$ ✕ **Baan Thai.** This first Thai restaurant in Delhi remains the best. The corridor into this traditional Thai *baan* (house) is an Asian art gallery. More statues and exquisite embroidered hangings adorn the dining room, and Burmese teak latticework covers the windows, the partitions that create private alcoves, and parts of the ceiling. Sit at a regular table or on a traditional Thai *khantok* (floor cushion) on the raised platform. Chef Prakob Samranruen imports authentic ingredients from Thailand and fresh seafood twice a week from Cochin for his dishes. Baan Thai now has a Mongolian barbecue, served poolside (except in summer). The lunch buffet is popular. ✉ *The Oberoi, Dr. Zakir Hussain Rd., New Delhi,* ☎ *11/436–3030. AE, DC, MC, V.*

$ ✕ **Red Snapper.** With tropical fish tanks as windows, this Thai/Chinese restaurant trumpets its specialty from the get-go. Focusing on seafood could be a risky endeavor in Delhi, where conventional wisdom says you shouldn't eat fish during months with no "r" in them (May–August); but Red Snapper goes a long way toward addressing locals' legitimate concerns about freshness by using seafood whisked instantly north from Bombay and Orissa. (Only the lobster comes frozen.) Results are rewarding: the chili-crusted *koung land phrik sam rot* (three-flavor prawns) are fresh and tender. ✉ *A-3 Green Park, Aurobindo Marg, New Delhi,* ☎ *11/685–7815. AE, DC, MC, V.*

Pan-Asian

$$ ✕ **Spice Route.** The interior of this mock trading ship is decorated with
★ elements of Thai, Balinese, and Keralite temples, with antique teak columns and wall paintings reflecting the Indian epics. The menu includes cuisines from the lands of the ancient spice route—Kerala, Sri Lanka, Thailand, Malaysia, and Indonesia. Flavors rely heavily on lemongrass, curry leaves, and coriander. Dishes from Kerala outshine the others; try the sweet-and-spicy pineapple *rasam* (soup) and vegetable stew. The Thai *kaeng khew waan kai* (chicken in green curry) and *som tum chae* (papaya salad) are delicious. The menu changes seasonally, and special menus celebrate traditional festivals on the spice route. ✉ *Imperial Hotel, Janpath, New Delhi,* ☎ *11/334–1234. AE, DC, MC, V.*

LODGING

Unless we note otherwise, Delhi hotels have central air-conditioning, bathrooms with tubs, currency exchange, and room service. Many also have a house doctor. In addition, most luxury hotels have executive floors with special privileges or facilities designed for the business traveler.

CATEGORY	COST*
$$$$	over Rs. 11,500
$$$	Rs. 7,000–Rs. 11,500
$$	Rs. 2,300–Rs. 7,000
$	under Rs. 2,300

Prices are for a standard double room in high season, excluding 20% sales tax.

$$$$ 🖭 **Maurya Sheraton Hotel and Towers.** Entering the Maurya, you're greeted by a flower-petal *rangoli* (floor painting). The handsome sitting areas incorporate the colors of the gigantic folk painting set into the massive overhead dome, and fountains just outside the picture windows add a vibrant touch to the lobby. The Maurya has fabulous facilities, including four restaurants, multiple business centers, a lovely pool, and a health club that may just be the nicest in town. Rooms are decorated in both Western and Indian styles. The Sheraton Towers has a small private lobby, an exclusive dining room, swank bedrooms, and an executive wing—all of which make this (much more expensive) wing popular with corporate clients and dignitaries. ⊠ *Diplomatic Enclave, New Delhi 110021,* ☏ *11/611–2233,* FAX *11/611–3333. 444 rooms, 44 suites. 4 restaurants, bar, coffee shop, patisserie, pool, hair salon, tennis courts, health club, 2 nightclubs, baby-sitting, business services, travel services. AE, DC, MC, V.*

$$$$ 🖭 **The Oberoi.** Delhi's first luxury hotel (built in 1965) is perfect if you want elegance and quiet—an attribute that sets it apart from its counterparts. Even when the hotel is packed, the lobby is peaceful—it has a small, marble lotus fountain strewn with rose petals near the entrance, an illuminated carved Tree of Life set in the back wall, and Indian artifacts. Adorned with valuable aquatints and lithographs, the spacious guest rooms have Western decor and warm color schemes. All rooms have multiple-line phones and well-stocked minibars; deluxe rooms have more amenities, such as fax machines and DVD players with a large library. The best views take in the Delhi Golf Course, where you can usually spot a peacock; rooms on the other side face Humayun's Tomb. ⊠ *Dr. Zakir Hussain Rd., New Delhi 110003,* ☏ *11/436–3030,* FAX *11/436–0484. 290 rooms, 31 suites. 5 restaurants, bar, no-smoking floor, pool, barbershop, hair salon, health club, golf privileges, baby-sitting, business services, travel services. AE, DC, MC, V.*

$$$$ 🖭 **Taj Mahal.** The lobby of the Taj Mahal hotel has Awadhi tapestries and domes, and other nice touches, such as sections of stone exteriors from former havelis. Near Connaught Place, and in the center of New Delhi's exclusive neighborhood of ministerial bungalows, the Taj is popular among business execs—five floors are dedicated to business travelers, who enjoy a cozy private lounge and complimentary breakfast. The high-quality service will appeal to any visitor who likes being pampered. The rooms are average-size with simple furnishings. The best rooms are on the upper floors, overlooking the lovely pool and garden. Other rooms offer views of the grand (if decaying) government bungalows and high-rises. ⊠ *1 Mansingh Rd., New Delhi 110011,* ☏ *11/302–6162,* FAX *11/301–7299. 275 rooms, 15 suites. 2 restaurants, bar, coffee shop, pool, barbershop, hair salon, health club, baby-sitting, business services, meeting room, travel services. AE, DC, MC, V.*

$$$$ 🖭 **Taj Palace.** Facilities are top-notch in this giant, boomerang-shape hotel. The business center is paneled in teak; the health club is amply outfitted; the salon offers a range of treatments; and the outdoor pool overlooks manicured lawns. The sprawling lobby has smooth marble floors and big windows with a view of the garden. Room decor is Western, but some rooms have Indian prints and furniture. Deluxe rooms and suites face the pool and a swath of greenery; the rest have unremarkable city views. The top floors cater to business travelers, with private check-in, a lounge, and a business center. The 24-hour coffee shop, Kafe Fontana, serves fresh, authentic Mediterranean food. ⊠ 2 *Sardar Patel Marg, Diplomatic Enclave, New Delhi 110021,* ☎ 11/ 611–0202, FAX *11/301–1252. 388 rooms, 34 suites. 3 restaurants, coffee shop, bar, in-room data ports, pool, barbershop, hair salon, health club, hot tub, massage, steam room, 9 mini putting greens, baby-sitting, convention center, business services, travel services. AE, DC, MC, V.*

$$$–$$$$ ⊡ **Hyatt Regency.** One of the city's best deluxe hotels, the Hyatt fo-
★   cuses less on being Indian and more on being a first-rate international hotel. There are restaurants and a bakery with the best breads and pastries in town. The lobby has vaulted ceilings and white and green marble and brass-trim mirrors. A lovely pool, with a sculpture of a dancing goddess, connects to a waterfall that spills down to the lower lobby. Guest rooms, with contemporary furnishings, are bright and spacious. Beds are queen-size. Rooms in the Regency Club offer extra services (e.g., airport pickups, breakfast in a separate lounge). Rooms facing the pool and garden are slightly more expensive, but the rooms facing the road are still quiet. ⊠ *Bhikaiji Cama Pl., Ring Rd., New Delhi 110066,* ☎ *11/679–1234,* FAX *11/679–1212,* WEB *www.delhi.hyatt.com. 518 rooms, 27 suites. 4 restaurants, coffee shop, bar, pool, hair salon, health club, 2 tennis courts, baby-sitting, business services, travel services. AE, DC, MC, V.*

$$$ ⊡ **Ashok.** This enormous hotel across the street from beautiful Nehru Park has lovely gardens, some good restaurants, and a cheerful coffee shop. But alas, the service, housekeeping, and maintenance are lax at best. Nonetheless, if you need to stay within walking distance of the embassies in the Diplomatic Enclave or just want to experience Delhi's leafiest neighborhood, the Ashok might suit your needs. ⊠ *50 B Chanakyapuri, New Delhi 110021,* ☎ *11/611–0101,* FAX *11/687– 3216. 571 rooms, 112 suites. 4 restaurants, coffee shop, 2 bars, pool, hair salon, health club, putting green, tennis court, billiards, baby-sitting, business services, travel services. AE, DC, MC, V.*

$$$ ⊡ **Claridges.** In 1950, a Dutch hotel manager convinced an Indian fam-
★   ily to build a hotel with a British name and aesthetic. The family accepted this advice, and Claridges was the result. Claridges has a loyal following—many of them long-term visitors who appreciate the hotel's old-fashioned charm. The hotel is also near sights and the embassies but still in a quiet neighborhood where you can take a pleasant evening walk. The lobby is unique: one side is Victorian, the other resembles an Indian courtyard. Bedrooms are carpeted and filled with Victorian furnishings. Standard rooms are average in size; the large Regal rooms are worth the extra money. The most popular (and even more expensive) rooms, on the third floor, include balconies that overlook the pool. ⊠ *12 Aurangzeb Rd., New Delhi 110011,* ☎ *11/301–0211,* FAX *11/301–0625. 162 rooms, 11 suites. 3 restaurants, coffee shop, bar, pool, hair salon, health club, business services, travel services. AE, DC, MC, V.*

$$$ ⊡ **Imperial Hotel.** This landmark luxury hotel near Connaught Place
★   is known as the "first Maiden of the East." It was built in 1931, and has been gorgeously restored. The driveway is bordered by royal palm trees. Expect to be impressed with the elegant lobby, with inlaid marble floors, three-story atriums, Italian fountains, and British Raj lithographs. The Imperial was designed by Lutyens' assistant Bromfield, and was designated as the hotel for official guests of state. The "heritage" rooms and suites are the most spacious and sumptuous. Nonguests, too, should take a look, and try the fabulous restaurants (Spice Route, Daniell's Tavern, and San Gimignano). The 24-hour restaurant

"1911" (named for the year Delhi became the capital of British India) is the nicest place in town, especially for an al fresco breakfast in the flower garden. ✉ *Janpath, south of Tolstoy Marg, New Delhi 110001,* ☎ *11/334–1234,* 𝔽𝔸𝕏 *11/334–2255. 265 rooms, 33 suites. 3 restaurants, coffee shop, 2 bars, pool, hair salon, business services, travel services. AE, DC, MC, V.*

$$$ 🏨 **Parkroyal.** This new nine-floor hotel in South Delhi makes good use of its small property, with underground parking and a terrace over the main entrance. The lobby is sedate, and with its wood paneling and columns, fireplace, and tea lounge, it recalls the era of the British Raj. The spacious guest rooms have separate dressing rooms. Ordinary doubles have urban views; if you want a view of the Bahai Temple, splurge for one of the more expensive Lutyens Club rooms, which include complimentary breakfast and happy hour. ✉ *Nehru Pl., New Delhi 110019,* ☎ *11/622–3344,* 𝔽𝔸𝕏 *11/622–4288. 218 rooms, 15 suites. 2 restaurants, coffee shop, tea shop, bar, pub, pool, hair salon, health club, baby-sitting, business services, convention center, travel services. AE, DC, MC, V.*

$$$ 🏨 **Radisson.** While the brand-new Radisson is 22 km (13 mi) from the center of town (a taxi ride costs about 250 rupees), it suits short-term visitors, especially when considering that most sights and restaurants are in South Delhi. The rooms are large, each with a foyer, king-size bed, spacious sitting area, and desk. The pool, in back, is also substantial, and has a gazebo bar and pool chairs. Like many of Delhi's major hotels, the Radisson suffers from an unfortunate setting: it's inches from the Delhi-Jaipur Highway. The hotel has addressed this by installing double-paned windows, but these don't improve the view. An extra bonus: free in-house movies are broadcast in the evening. This is a good perk, especially since the noisy highway doesn't make the neighborhood conducive to evening strolls. ✉ *National Hwy. 8, New Delhi 110037,* ☎ *11/677–9191,* 𝔽𝔸𝕏 *11/612–9090. 256 rooms, 27 suites. 3 restaurants, 2 bars, coffee shop, tea shop, pool, hair salon, bowling, health club, squash, business services, travel services. AE, DC, MC, V.*

$$–$$$ 🏨 **Oberoi Maidens.** Overlooked by many travelers, this hotel has low rates, large rooms, and a good location. Opened in 1907, before New Delhi was even a gleam in the Viceroy's eye, the Oberoi Maidens is the oldest hotel in the city. It's a classic Raj building, with columns, high-arched windows, deep verandas, grand old trees, and pleasant green lawns. Named after its original owner, the Maidens is in North Delhi (near Old Delhi), so it's best suited for those doing business on that side of town. Thanks to the building's age, the rooms are huge (if a bit dark and viewless); the Superior rooms are really suites, and in the low season (summer), they're less than U.S. $100. The Curzon Room, the hotel's elegant Continental-Indian restaurant, is worth checking out if you're in the neighborhood. ✉ *7 Sham Nath Marg, Old Delhi 110054,* ☎ *11/39–5464,* 𝔽𝔸𝕏 *11/398–0771. 53 rooms, 1 suite. 1 restaurant, coffee shop, bar, pool, 2 tennis courts. AE, DC, MC, V.*

$$ 🏨 **Ambassador.** This highly recommended hotel is run by the Taj Group
★ but costs half the price of its glamorous Delhi siblings. Set in a small, late-Raj-era building in the Diplomatic Enclave, it's quiet and casual. Here you're just steps from Khan Market and Lodi Gardens. Service is exceptionally friendly and resourceful. The small marble lobby is outfitted with banquette seating; hallways are windowed and bright. Most of the guest rooms—which are large—have carpeting, basic teak furniture, and modern bathrooms. A few have tile floors, area rugs, and old-style bath fixtures. Try to get a room in front, with a balcony overlooking the garden—rooms in back are noisy. ✉ *Sujan Singh Park, Cornwallis Rd., New Delhi 110003,* ☎ *11/463–2600,* 𝔽𝔸𝕏 *11/463–2252. 80*

rooms, 8 suites. 3 restaurants, bar, in-room data ports, hair salon, baby-sitting, business services, travel services. AE, DC, MC, V.

$$ 🏨 **Connaught Palace.** This mid-size hotel offers a good value to the leisure traveler in need of a few conveniences and comforts. Located about 1 km (½ mi) from Connaught Place, it's close to the center of things but far enough away from the hubbub. The pink-and-cream marble lobby is bright, and belies the overall style of the hotel—of new Indian "new money" affluence (in a word, gaudy). The rooms, double or deluxe, are quite small, but they contain inlaid wood furniture and the price is right. Rooms on the east side overlook a hockey stadium. Note: Discounts of up to 50% on room rates can be easily negotiated between April and September. ✉ *37 Shaheed Bhagat Singh Marg, New Delhi 110001,* ☎ *11/336–4225,* 📠 *11/334–0757. 80 rooms. 3 restaurants, coffee shop, bar, room service, laundry, shopping, business services, travel services, car rental. AE, D, MC, V.*

$$ 🏨 **Hans Plaza.** Just off Connaught Place, this hotel looks like an office building—from the outside. It's too expensive to be "mid-price" and too simple to be considered luxurious. The lobby is clean and cozy, with pleasant sitting areas and Victorian-style furnishings. The quietest and most spacious rooms overlook Barakhamba Road. All rooms have Western furnishings, but the deluxe rooms have bathtubs and dhurries on gleaming granite floors. Lower-price (and less attractive) rooms have wall-to-wall carpeting and showers. The 21st-floor Club Cafe is inexpensive and has fabulous views; come for a buffet lunch or for an al fresco breakfast. ✉ *15 Barakhamba Rd., Connaught Pl., New Delhi 110001,* ☎ *11/331–6861,* 📠 *11/331–4830. 70 rooms, 3 suites. Restaurant, business services, travel services. AE, DC, MC, V.*

$$ 🏨 **Jukaso Inn.** This large guest house has a shiny, white marble lobby
★ and clean—albeit dark and drab—guest rooms. The bathrooms, smelling faintly of mothballs, have simple fixtures and no bathtubs. Meals are conveniently served in the ad hoc courtyard. ✉ *50 Sunder Nagar, New Delhi 110003,* ☎ *11/435–0308,* 📠 *11/469–4402. 50 rooms, 2 suites. Restaurant, laundry, business services, travel services, car rental. AE, DC, MC, V.*

$$ 🏨 **Nirula Hotel.** Nirula's lobby, Like the rest of the hotel, is compact. There's minimal natural light, and incongruous flourishes of style among otherwise functional decor. For those who don't need deluxe facilities but want more than a guesthouse out in Delhi's residential neighborhoods, the Nirula Hotel is a good choice. The mid-price restaurants downstairs—Chinese, Indian-Continental, Pub, Ice Cream Parlor, and Confectionery—are a major benefit of staying here. On the other hand, you'll have to forego views or natural lighting in the small rooms (some only have windows facing interior hallways). Several of the "single" rooms have double beds, while the doubles all have twin beds. ✉ *L Block Connaught Circus, New Delhi 110001,* ☎ *11/332–2419,* 📠 *11/335–3957. 28 rooms. 2 restaurants, patisserie, bar, travel services. AE, MC, V.*

$ 🏨 **Hotel Broadway.** Although the Delhi Stock Exchange and Delhi Gate are steps away, expect neither Wall Street nor an antique Moghul palace if you stay at this small hotel. It offers little in the way of style, but it has small, simple rooms at fabulous rates, and a central location. It has been in operation since 1956; the rooms, with central AC, have cable TVs and direct-dial phones. Valet parking (a must in this congested neighborhood) is available. Given its proximity to Old Delhi, it's not surprising that the hotel offers guided morning and afternoon walks. Hotel Broadway is not just for the budget-conscious; history buffs and culture vultures will also enjoy it. All rooms have twin beds. ✉ *4/15 A. Asaft Ali Rd.Old Delhi,* ☎ *11/327–3821,* 📠 *11/326–9966. 32 rooms. Restaurant, bar, room service. AE, MC, V.*

$ ⊞ **Jor Bagh "27."** Peace, proximity, and price—that's what this simple guesthouse has to offer. With Jor Bagh Market just five doors down and Lodi Garden also steps away, it's difficult to believe that such centrally located accommodations can seem so tranquil. Expect simple rooms that are a bit on the dark side. All 18 rooms are unique (the building is a converted house) so check what's available before you settle on a room. The standard doubles are fine, unless you need a fridge—then opt for a deluxe. Watch out, though: the "27"'s generator is not powerful enough to run all of the ACs, so this isn't the best bet for the hot season. Breakfast is prepared on-site, but other meals must be ordered in. ⊠ *27 Jor Bagh, New Delhi 110003,* ☎ *11/469–8647,* FAX *11/469–8475. 18 rooms. Dining room. MC, V.*

$ ⊞ **Metropolis Tourist Home.** If you are tired of spending your money in Delhi's overpriced hotels and want to stay in the midst of a bustling, crowded bazaar, consider the Metropolis. The hotel caters to Western backpackers (as does much of this neighborhood) so the rooms are Spartan and worn. Nonetheless, the rooms are clean, and have a surprising array of facilities: hot water, room phones (not direct-dial), AC (that runs when the civic power supply does; in other words, occasionally), and satellite color TVs. Some rooms have no windows; the best ones overlook the chaotic intersection below. The rooftop restaurant is a nice place to catch some sun or have some beer and barbecue. Like Jor Bagh "27," the generator at this hotel is only powerful enough to run fans. Stay away in the summer. ⊠ *1634 Main Bazaar, Pahar Ganj, New Delhi 110055,* ☎ *11/351–8074,* FAX *11/752–5600. 30 rooms. 2 restaurants, room service, laundry service, travel services. AE, D, MC, V.*

$ ⊞ **YMCA Tourist Hostel.** Just south of the Park Hotel, about a 10-minute walk from Connaught Place, the YMCA has some singles and twin-bed doubles with private bathrooms (showers only) and air-conditioning. (The Rs. 1,700 price gets you a double with AC.) The rooms are small, uncarpeted, and have modest furnishings that are so old and worn they seem to date from the hostel's construction in the late 1960s. But the linens are clean, hot water runs from the taps, and you can laze around on your own private balcony. Upper-floor rooms facing the back are the quietest. Other rooms in the hostel have shared bathrooms (also with showers) and overhead fans instead of air-conditioning. ⊠ *Jai Singh Rd., New Delhi 110001,* ☎ *11/336–1915,* FAX *11/374–6032. 123 rooms, 14 rooms with bath, 1 suite. Restaurant, pool, business services, travel services. AE, DC, MC, V.*

NIGHTLIFE AND THE ARTS

The Arts

Arts venues abound in Delhi. Well-known Indian dancers and musicians perform in the capital often, and Delhi's many theaters play both Indian and slightly dated Western films. It's also becoming quite popular for high-profile Western authors to give book readings in Delhi to launch the South Asian edition of their latest title. The only problem is figuring out what's going on—most events are publicized only a few days in advance. The most reliable sources are the monthly magazine *Around Town;* the weekly *Delhi Diary;* and the daily newspapers, especially *The Asian Age* and *The Hindustand Times.* Check out *First City,* too. Your hotel may also have the scoop.

Art Galleries

While many of Delhi's arts are subsidized by the government, the visual arts—especially painting—have a life of their own. Private galleries selling works by contemporary Indian painters have proliferated in the last decade. Some of the work blending traditional Indian with modern Western styles is excellent and affordable. Galleries come and go quickly. Most are in South Delhi neighborhoods: Sunder Nager, Defence Colony, New Friends Colony, and Greater Kailash. Since most of the galleries are quite small, it's easy to gallery-hop to get a taste for what's happening on the local art scene. Check for current listings.

Hauz Khas has three small galleries grouped together at 11, 12, and 14 Hauz Khas Village. All are open from 10:30 AM until 7 PM, and all take credit cards. **Art Konsult** (☎ 11/652–3382) features contemporary artists only, but has quite a large selection. The largest gallery in Hauz Khas, **Delhi Art Gallery** (☎ 11/696–7619), has works by old masters and contemporary artists. **The Village Gallery** (☎ 11/695–3860) has a fine collection of accomplished contemporary artists.

While not noted for its galleries, Connaught Place still has a number of places you can visit. **Art Heritage** (✉ Triveni Kal Sangam, 205 Tansen Marg, ☎ 11/371–9470) is a government-run institution in the Connaught Place area. **Art Today** (✉ A-1 Hamilton House, Connaught Pl., ☎ 11/332–0689) is an established gallery with thoughtful shows, and is open Monday through Saturday from 11 to 7. **Dhoomimal Art Center** (✉ A-8 Connaught Pl., ☎ 11/332–4492) has been around for a long time and often has good shows. It's open Monday through Saturday from 11 to 7, and, conveniently, is just a few doors down from the equally well-established Art Today gallery. **Habitat World** in the Indian Habitat Centre (✉ Lodi Rd., ☎ 11/468–2222), a government institution in the Connaught Place area, is a very dynamic gallery space. Stop in after seeing a music or dance performance at the Indian Habitat Centre. **Lalit Kala Akademi** (✉ Rabindra Bhavan, ☎ 11/338–7243) is a government institution that displays modern Indian art. It's in the Connaught Place area.

Music and Dance

Great musicians and dancers are always passing through Delhi, so tickets are readily available and are relatively cheap. **Dances of India** in Parsi Anjuman Hall (✉ *Bahadurshan Zafar Marg, opposite Ambedkar Football Stadium, Delhi Gate,* ☎ *11/331–7831; 11/332–0968 for reservations,* ✍ *Rs. 75.*) is a performance of six different folk, tribal, and classical dances. Shows are held daily at 6:45 PM.

India International Centre (✉ 40 Lodi Estate, ☎ 11/461–9431) is an established performance space near the Habitat Centre. The **Indian Habitat Centre** (✉ Lodi Rd., ☎ 11/469–1920) is the hot new venue for dance and music. **Kamani Auditorium** (✉ Copernicus Marg, ☎ 11/338–8040), near Connaught Place, is a well-known performance venue.

The Morning Ragas (✉ Nehru Park) have been a fabulous new addition to Delhi's classical music scene. Before a huge Kadama tree, in the midst of Nehru Park's expansive gardens, the two-hour concerts occur monthly, on a Sunday morning. (Check the paper for dates and times.) Since 1999, the New Delhi Municipal Corporation (NDMC) has been sponsoring these concerts, bringing many top performers in Indian classical music here. **Triveni Chamber Theatre** (✉ 205 Tansen Marg, ☎ 11/371–9470) is long-established; this performance space is near Connaught Place.

Theater

India has an ancient dramatic tradition. *Nautanki* plays, which feature drama, comedy, and song, are still held in the surrounding villages. Delhi itself has an active theater scene, and many shows are locally written, produced, and acted. Most run only for one weekend and don't travel afterward, so they can seem a bit unpolished even when they're fundamentally good. In addition to the following venues, check those listed under Music and Dance, and consult local listings. **Habitat World** (⊠ Lodi Rd., ☎ 11/468–2222) is the biggest and best venue for theater in Delhi. **LTG Auditorium** (⊠ Copernicus Marg, ☎ 11/338–9713) puts on plenty of shows. **Sri Fort Auditorium** (⊠ Asiad Village, ☎ 11/649–3370) stages plays. **Sri Ram Centre** (⊠ Mandi House, Safdar Hashmi Marg, ☎ 11/371–4307) is a venue for plays.

Nightlife

Delhi is not much of a party town. A traditional social evening involves having a drink at home with friends, enjoying a late dinner, and turning in. Note that women in Delhi, whether alone or in groups, do not go out unaccompanied at night.

Discos

Clubs have been dying a slow death in Delhi over the last several years, but there are still a few hip places to literally dance the night away. Wherever you go, know the facts of nightlife in Delhi. First, things don't get hopping until almost midnight, but liquor laws forbid the sale of alcohol after that time. Many solve this problem by getting blasted before they come. Second, solo males are not welcome at most discos.

CJ's (⊠ Le Meridien Hotel, Janpath, ☎ 11/371–0101) is not the hippest place in town, but it's reasonably convenient. If you have access to a car for the whole evening, head out to **The Fireball** (⊠ 32nd Mile Stone, National Hwy. 8, ☎ 91/325554 or 91/322528), 32 km (19 mi) outside Delhi. This place was built just a few feet across the Delhi-Haryana state border to take advantage of looser liquor laws. **Ghungroo** (⊠ Maurya Sheraton Hotel, Diplomatic Enclave, New Delhi, ☎ 11/611–2233) has regained some of its former glory, now that it is no longer restricted to hotel guests and members. **The Mirage** (⊠ Surya Hotel, New Friends Colony, in South Delhi, ☎ 11/683–5070) is a hike from the center of town, but it's currently Delhi's most popular nightclub.

Hotel Bars and Lounges

India does not traditionally have a bar culture. When Indian men drink (women generally don't), they do it discreetly, at home with their friends or at private parties. All the major hotels have bars, but most are better suited for a comfortable nap than a night of camaraderie. Richly decorated, often aiming for either a British Raj or a plush Continental look, these bars are generally open from 11 to 11 and closed on the 1st and 7th days of each month and on national holidays. If you're a serious drinker, bring a credit card—these are pricey places.

The **1911 Bar** (⊠ Imperial Hotel, Janpath, ☎ 11/334–1234) is a hopping place. Decked out the way it originally was during the Independence movement in the 1940s, this place is a classic nightspot, and the drinks are affordable by local standards. If you want to puff on a Cubano, try the austere **Club Bar** (⊠ The Oberoi, Dr. Zakir Hussain Rd., ☎ 11/436–3030). A pianist plays every night but Tuesday for those occupying discreetly positioned clusters of sofas and chairs in an elegant room. **The Patiala Peg** (⊠ Hotel Imperial, Janpath, ☎ 11/334–1234) is an up-and-coming place for the younger set.

By far the nicest hotel bar downtown is the **Pegasus Bar** (⊠ Nirula's Hotel, L-Block, Connaught Circus, ☎ 11/332–2419). It's a smart, but relaxed, little place. During the day it's filled with young Indian businessmen talking shop and tossing back a few beers. The crowd gets younger at night, but the drinks are still affordable. There's no foreign booze here. The **Polo Lounge** (✉ Hyatt Regency, Bhikaiji Cama Pl., Ring Rd., ☎ 11/679–1234), while very much a hotel bar, is very lively. The wood-paneled room has a curved bar, a leather sofa, a library with newspapers and an oddball collection of books. It even has sports channels on cable television. In the **Viceroy** (✉ Claridges, 12 Aurangzeb Rd.), a brass cannon, antique rifles, and Victorian antiques create a rugged, masculine mood. A pianist plays every night except Tuesday.

Pubs

Delhi's major hotels are slowly replacing their dance bars with what they call pubs—bizarre amalgams of English pubs and American sports bars, with a bit of food and dancing thrown in. These places tend toward softer music, they get going earlier, with happy-hour specials and menus featuring good snacks. The most publike nightspot is **Djinns** (✉ Hyatt Regency, Bhikaiji Cama Pl., Ring Rd., ☎ 11/679–1234). You enter what looks like the set for a *Cheers* episode, complete with hardwood floors and brass fittings. Waiters in French café aprons serve up tasty Middle Eastern food, and a good dance band generally gets going later in the evening. **Floats** (✉ Parkroyal Hotel, ☎ 11/622–3344) is a bit of a Djinn's rip off, but it's still a great place to hang out. **The Latin Bar** (✉ The Park, 15 Parliament St., ☎ 11/373–3737) opens at 6 PM for delicious tapas, reasonably priced Spanish wines, beer, and other international snacks. Subtle and sophisticated, **Rick's** (✉ Taj Mahal Hotel, 1 Mansingh Rd., ☎ 11/302–6162) is Delhi's latest nighttime sizzle, with warm lighting and a neon-green bar. Adding to the vibe is a jazzy female vocalist and baby grand piano. Rick's has an amazing selection of booze, and a delicious Southeast Asian snack menu. Go early to get a seat. **Someplace Else** (✉ The Park, 15 Parliament St., ☎ 11/373–3737) is both pub and disco, but lately hasn't been very popular. For a straightforward sports bar, complete with punching bags and bicycles hanging from the ceiling, head out to the **Sports Bar** (✉ Radisson Hotel, National Hwy. 8, ☎ 11/612–9191), near the airport. There's also a bowling alley in the hotel.

Outside the hotels, new bars tend to be much less expensive, and attract younger crowds. There are a bunch of drinking holes right around Connaught Place. **Blues** (✉ N-18 Outer Circle, Connaught Pl., ☎ 11/331–0957) is currently quite popular. **The Buck Stops Here** (✉ Ansal Plaza, Khel Gaom Road) is in the new Ansal Plaza mini-mall. If you want to bowl a few frames, have your drink at **Essex Farms** (✉ 4 Aurobindo Marg, ☎ 11/686–2145). **Geoffryes** (✉ Ansal Plaza, Khel Gaom Rd.), in the new Ansal Plaza mini-mall, is the place to pub-hop. **Good Times** (✉ Inner Circle, Connaught Pl.) is a well-frequented new bar. If you're hungry, it's convenient to get both some food and a drink at the **Pizza Express** (✉ Ansal Plaza, Khel Gaom Rd.), in the new Ansal Plaza mini-mall. **Rodeo** (✉ 12A Connaught Pl., ☎ 11/371–3780), a Mexican restaurant in the heart of town, is an old favorite. It has a guitarist in its bar nightly and karaoke on Tuesday. **Ruby Tuesday** (✉ M-48 Connaught Pl., ☎ 11/332–3627) is quite popular, and is conveniently located in Connaught Place. Two **TGIF** restaurants (✉ F-16 Inner Circle, Connaught Pl., ☎ 11/371–1991; ✉ 62 Basant Lok, ☎ 11/614–0964) have garish American decor and numerous TV sets. If you must go, take advantage of the drink specials, not the food. The new **Wheels** (✉ Inner Circle, Connaught Pl.) is already a popular bar.

SPORTS AND OUTDOOR ACTIVITIES

Participant Sports

Golf

The **Army Golf Club** (✉ Delhi Cantonment, ☎ 11/569–1972) is close to Delhi, but it's somewhat difficult to get a reservation. Delhi's newest golf destination, **Classics,** is an hour's drive away, in Haryana State (☎ 11/614–7507). This 27-hole, Jack Nicholas–designed course is great, even by international standards. You pay the price though—about US$70 for 18 holes. If you want to play golf against a backdrop of ancient monuments, try the 27-hole **Delhi Golf Club** (✉ Dr. Zakir Hussain Rd., ☎ 11/436–2768 or 11/436–2235). Contact the club for reservations and costs.

Swimming

City pools should be avoided, as there's no way to judge the water quality. The top hotels have excellent pools, some open to outsiders for a fee.

Tennis

If your hotel doesn't have a tennis court, reserve one at the **Delhi Lawn Tennis Association** (✉ Africa Ave., next to Safdarjung Enclave and near the Hyatt, ☎ 11/619–3955).

Yoga

The **Sivananda Yoga Vedanta Nataraja Center** (✉ 52 Community Center, east of Kailash, ☎ 11/648–0869) holds classes daily.

Spectator Sports

Check the newspaper or your hotel for **cricket** and **soccer** matches. Rivalries are intense, so these games are popular events; see if your hotel can get you tickets. Delhi's polo games (October–March) are another crowd-pleaser—contact the **Polo Club** (✉ 61 Cavalry Cariappa Marg, Delhi Cantonment, ☎ 11/569–9777).

SHOPPING

Delhi is the shopping center for all of India. Bargaining is often appropriate, but make sure to survey the situation at higher-end stores and "fixed price" shops before you start. Most shops are open six days a week; the day a shop is closed is determined by its location. In general, however, except for the Lal Qila bazaar, most businesses in Old Delhi shut down on Sunday. To be sure, ask around—every taxi driver knows which markets are closed on a given day.

Bazaars and Markets

On the sidewalks of **Chandni Chowk** (✉ 6 km/4 mi, north of Connaught Pl.) in Old Delhi, you'll find everything from astrologers to shoemakers to photographers. Every conceivable kind of commerce takes place here; it's a good area to hunt for bargains. Most shops are closed on Sunday.

The stalls on **Dariba Kalan** are filled with silver and gold jewelry.

Dilli Haat Market (✉ Aurobindo Marg, ☎ 11/611–9055) in South Delhi is a government-run food and crafts bazaar that's open daily. More than 60 stalls sell handmade products from all over India, and 25 serve regional food. Open-air music and dance occasionally accompany the proceedings in mid-afternoon or evening. Dilli Haat charges an admission fee of Rs. 5. It's across the street from the bustling INA food market.

INA Market (⊠ Aurobindo Marg) is a colorful stop in South Delhi. INA Market is the place to experience a Delhi food market: fruits and vegetables are sold in front, while the open-air butcher shops, with chicken, fish, and mutton, are on a slushy lane in the back. Wander around to see merchants selling spices, nuts, and dried fruits. The market is closed on Monday. If you get overwhelmed with the food market, cross the street and enter the government-run food and crafts bazaar, Dilli Haat.

On the streets behind the **Jama Masjid** in Old Delhi, many shops sell metalware curios and old utensils, and one street specializes in paper and stationery, some of it handmade and hand-printed.

Favored by Delhi's diplomatic community, the small **Khan Market** is full of surprises if you're looking for goods from abroad. Many of the specialty shops—from book stores and music shops to tailors and shoemakers—offer some of the best wares in Delhi, but at a premium price. The market is next to the Home Ministry, which is next to Sujan Singh Park.

Lajpat Nagar Market is a very lively market where middle-class locals shop. It's a good place just to stroll around and take in the chaos, as they have pedestrian-only zones—a rarity in India. Shopkeepers boisterously hawk their wares while men unload goods from auto- and cycle-rickshaws, shoppers scurry about, and diners pause over plates of greasy street food. This market has plenty of outlets for Western goods (such as an Oshkosh B'Gosh store). Lajpat also has lots of high-end Indian goods, especially expensive (very expensive) traditional cloths. It's open daily from about 10:30 to 7, and is closed Monday.

In Old Delhi, the bazaar inside **Lal Qila** is a good place to hunt for bargains.

The popular **Sarojini Nagar Market** is a favorite among middle-class locals, particularly because it's a small, clean, and quiet market. The vegetable market here is definitely worth seeing. The back streets of Sarojini are famous for selling rejected export apparel at bargain prices. The market is open daily from about 10:30 to 7, and is closed on Monday.

Sunder Nagar Market, a neighborhood shopping district near the Lodi Gardens, the Oberoi Hotel, and Delhi Zoo, specializes in jewelry, curios, artifacts, and artwork. It's closed on Sunday.

Shopping Centers

Connaught Place, with shops open every day but Sunday, is the former commercial district of the British Raj. Beneath the green park at the center of Connaught Place is **Palika Bazaar,** an air-conditioned underground emporium with the charm of a Times Square subway station. Avoid it: it's a favorite haunt of pickpockets and many shopkeepers are dishonest.

In South Delhi's **Hauz Khas Village** (⊠ near Deer Park, 7 km/4 mi, south of Connaught Pl.), boutiques and shops set in converted old homes among narrow alleys sell handicrafts, curios, old carpets, and kilims, and both Indian and Western designer clothing. Most stores are open Monday through Saturday from 10:30 to 7.

JJ Valaya (⊠ Main Temple Rd., Chattarpur, ☎ 11/680288) is a shopping complex clustered on a modern estate. Open daily, it sells designer clothing for men and women, furnishings, tapestries, and artwork. Ella, a café with a terrace, adjoins the complex.

The **Santushti Shopping Complex,** open every day but Monday, is a collection of upscale arty boutiques scattered around a small garden across the street from the Hotel Samrat (in the Diplomatic Enclave area). Prices are high, but this is a lovely place to stroll and browse. Other shops in the complex sell jewelry, leather, pottery, and home furnishings. For a break, stop into Basil and Thyme (⊠ Santushti Shopping Complex, New Wellingdon Camp) for lunch or a snack.

Specialty Stores

Books

Delhi has great book bargains, including lower-price Indian-language editions of new titles published abroad. Although better hotels have small bookshops, the best selections are on and around Connaught Place, and are open Monday through Saturday 10 to 7. **Oxford Book and Stationery** (⊠ Scindia House, Connaught Pl.) sells history, classics, and philosophy books. Khan Market—a few blocks west of the golf course, at the confluence of Nehru and Aurangzeb roads—has some excellent bookstores that are open Monday through Saturday 10 to 7. **The Bookshop** (⊠ 14A Khan Market) is the best of the bookstores in Khan Market—it has an excellent selection of fiction and non-fiction and a well-informed staff.

Carpets

India has one of the world's foremost Oriental-rug industries, and there are carpet vendors all over Delhi. Unfortunately, carpet sellers are a notoriously dishonest crowd. In addition to being obnoxiously pushy, they are likely to sell you inauthentic merchandise at colossally inflated prices and then deny it later. There are some exceptions to this rule, but none of the vendors has the sort of upscale showroom shops you'll find in the hotels.

The best exception to this rule is **Janson's Carpets** (⊠ A/375 Sarita Vihar, ☎ 11/694–2953 or 11/694–6325, cell phone 9811/129095), run by proprietor Jasim Jan. He delivers exactly what he describes—carpets old and new, silk and wool, Persian and tribal—and at fair (not cheap) prices. Jan hawks his wares at trade fairs all over Delhi, often to the rich and famous. The family that runs **Novel Exports** (⊠ D-23, Jangpura Extension, ☎ 11/431–2248) is from Kashmir, and they have absolutely stunning Kashmiri carpets, as well as shawls, jewelry, and papier mâché items.

Clothing

For funky block-printed cottons with a contemporary Indian flair, browse **Anokhi** (⊠ Santushti Shopping Complex, ☎ 11/688–3076) in the Diplomatic Enclave area. **Banaras House** (⊠ N-13 Connaught Pl., opposite Scindia House, ☎ 11/331–4751) sells sublime silks from all over India. In Old Delhi, **Ram Chandra Krishan Chandra's** (⊠ Gali Parante Wali, ☎ 11/327–7869), one of Delhi's oldest fabric shops, has three floors of fine silks and handloomed fabrics from all over India.

Tandon's (⊠ 4 Aurobindo Pl., opposite Green Park Church, Hauz Khas, ☎ 11/696–6552; closed Tues.) in South Delhi offers high-quality *chicken* (hand embroidery) on fine linen and traditional clothing. **Tulsi** (⊠ Santushti Shopping Complex, ☎ 11/687–0339) sells supple garments of handwoven silk, linen, and cotton. **Wild Orchid** (⊠ 12 Siri Fort Rd., ☎ 11/644–9347; ⊠ M-37, Main Market, Greater Kailash I, ☎ 11/643–2668) in South Delhi sells designer Indian clothing in exquisite hand-loomed cotton and silk, and a good selection of Western wear for women.

Crafts and Curios

Delhi's fixed-price government emporia are near Connaught Place and offer good values for travelers with limited time. There are more than 20 such emporia in Delhi; each state operates a store featuring its own native crafts and other products. The large, government-run **Central Cottage Industries Emporium** (✉ Jawahar Vyapar Bhavan, Janpath, opposite Imperial Hotel, ☎ 11/332–6790) has products from all over the country.

The **State Emporia** (✉ Baba Kharak Singh Marg) includes three blocks of about 15 state-run shops, with a wonderful selection of regional items. One of these, the Kashmir store, specializes in carpets.

Bharany's (✉ 14 Sunder Nagar, ☎ 11/461–8528) sells traditional Indian jewelry, exquisite old shawls, and textiles from all over India. **Kumar Gallery** (✉ 11 Sunder Nagar, ☎ 11/461–1113) stocks original tribal statues, old dhurries, Tibetan carpets and furniture, miniatures, temple art, and contemporary paintings by India's finest artists. Near Lodi Gardens, **Natesan's** (✉ 13 Sunder Nagar, ☎ 11/464–9320), with branches throughout India, sells magnificent art and antiques. At **Shivam Zari Palace** (✉ 2178 Kinari Bazaar, ☎ 11/327–1464) in ÇOld Delhi you'll find inexpensive Hindu wedding paraphernalia—turbans, fabric covered boxes, *torans* (auspicious door hangings), and tiny brass gods.

Food

The **Mittal Tea House** (✉ 12 Sunder Nagar, ☎ 11/461–0667) near Lodi Gardens sells Indian teas, herbs, and spices.

Jewelry

Old Delhi is packed with numerous delightful jewelry and curio shops. The small **Gems 'n' Jewels** (✉ No. 31, Lal Qila, ☎ 11/327–0524) has good miniature paintings and silver jewelry. **Multan Enamel Mart Jewellers** (✉ No. 246–247, Dariba Kalan, ☎ 11/325–5877) has fine old and new silver jewelry sold by weight with an add-on charge for labor. **Singh Copper & Brass Palace** (✉ 1167 Chah Rahat Gali, near Jama Masjid, ☎ 11/326–6717) has an entire building filled with old and new Indian brass, copper, and wood handicrafts. **Tula Ram** (✉ No. 36, Lal Qila, ☎ 11/326–9937) sells traditional Indian handicrafts, especially wooden objects, tribal work, and brass items.

In New Delhi, **Padma Gems** (✉ 9-A Sunder Nagar, ☎ 11/461–1513) has lovely contemporary and antique gold jewelry and a good variety of semi-precious and precious stones. Designs can be made to order in four to five days. **The Studio** (✉ 4 Sunder Nagar, ☎ 11/461–9360) has good contemporary silver jewelry, tribal jewelry, and some gold items.

DELHI A TO Z

To research prices, get advice from other travelers, and book travel arrangements, visit www.fodors.com.

AIR TRAVEL
CARRIERS
Several international airlines fly into Indira Gandhi International Airport (☞ Air Travel *in* Smart Travel Tips). Most flights from the West arrive close to midnight.

The Indian government's open-sky policy for private domestic airlines keeps changing, so routes and schedules for domestic flights are often unsettled. Indian Airlines is the national carrier; the top private carriers are Jet Airways and Sahara Airlines.

➤ DOMESTIC AIRLINES: **Indian Airlines** (☎ 11/462–0566 or 11/331–0517). **Jet Airways** (☎ 11/566–5405). **Sahara Airlines** (☎ 11/566–5357).

AIRPORTS AND TRANSFERS

Delhi's two airports are close together. International flights use Indira Gandhi International Airport, about 23 km (14 mi) southwest of Connaught Place. Domestic flights use Palam Airport, also called the "national" or "domestic" airport. Palam has two terminals, but most taxi drivers don't know which terminals apply to which flights, so when you buy or reconfirm a domestic ticket, find out which terminal to use. At Boeing Terminal, use the extreme right-hand entrance.

The trip between either airport and Delhi itself should take about 30 minutes if you arrive before 9 AM or after 8 PM. At other times, traffic can increase the time to an hour. All major hotels provide airport transfers for Rs. 500–Rs. 1,000, depending on their locations.

Taking a cab is the easiest way to reach your hotel. Because taxi drivers are famous for rigging their meters and overcharging, use the prepaid taxi service—at either airport, you can arrange a cab at designated counters outside the baggage-claim area and inside the arrival terminal. Unfortunately, hucksters have set up similar services, so ignore the others shouting at you and make sure the counter is operated by the Delhi Traffic Police (blue sign). Your destination and amount of luggage determine the rate, which you pay in advance at the counter. Take the receipt and note the number written on it. This is the licence number of your taxi. Walk out through the greeting hall and through the small doors on the right. When you get outside, you will be besieged by people trying to "help" you find your taxi or manage your luggage. Ignore them, and make sure they do not touch your things. Wheel your baggage down the ramp toward the cluster of taxis (black with yellow tops) below. The taxi drivers will help you find the correct vehicle. Tell your taxi driver where you are going. Do not hand him the receipt until you arrive at your destination. A taxi from the international airport to the city center should cost Rs. 250–Rs. 300; from the domestic airport, Rs. 200–Rs. 250.

Be aware that people at the airports, and even at hotel reservation counters, may try to trick you into booking another hotel room by claiming that your prior reservation is invalid. Ignore them. If you do need a room, go to the Government of India Tourist Office counter.

BUS TRAVEL WITHIN DELHI

Avoid public buses, which tend to be filthy, dangerous, and crammed with passengers. Women who take buses might also be subjected to pinches, flashing, or verbal abuse.

CARS AND DRIVERS

Only people with nerves of steel should drive in and around Delhi. Traffic rules exist, but few drivers observe them, and even fewer police officers enforce them. Every major thoroughfare is packed from 9 AM to 7 PM with bullock carts, auto-rickshaws, overcrowded buses and trucks, bicycles and motorcycles, cows, horses, goats, and dogs. Major highways (oversize two-lane roads) from Jaipur, Agra, and northern Uttaranchal are notorious for frequent accidents. Roads are unreliable—even new roads can develop craters overnight, and badly designed culverts can lead to flooding during the monsoon season.

If you're not on a tight budget, let an experienced driver chauffeur you around Delhi and outside town. Expect to pay about Rs. 800 for eight hours or 80 km (50 mi) for sightseeing in an Ambassador car with air-conditioning. (This is the least expensive vehicle.)

Expect prices to go up when you're going out of town on an extended journey. You'll pay no less than Rs. 2,000 per day for an Ambassador with air conditioning, driven by a English-speaking driver. Ask in advance about the cost for extra mileage or hours. If you're staying in an upscale hotel, a car hired on-site costs even more; you'll pay less if you can arrange one through an outside travel agent. Stick with a government-recognized tour operator. (☞ Travel Agencies) If you're determined to drive yourself around, contact one of the international car rental agencies, such as Avis. With many car rental agencies, rates are expensive (Rs. 2,600 per day, Rs. 25 per km after 150 km), but the vehicles are top-of-the-line Mitsubishi Lancers. An International Driver's License is required, as is 24-hour advance notice. The same agencies also supply drivers, but the rates then skyrocket to Rs. 400 per hour (two-hour minimum).

➤ CAR RENTAL AGENCIES: **Avis** (✉ Oberoi Hotel, ☎ 11/430–4187).

EMBASSIES

All of these embassies are in Chanakyapuri, New Delhi. They are generally open Monday to Thursday from 8:30 to 1 and 2 to 5, and Friday from 8:30 to 1.

➤ AUSTRALIA: **Australian High Commission** (✉ 1/50G Shanti Path, ☎ 11/688–8223).

➤ CANADA: **Canadian High Commission** (✉ 7/8 Shanti Path, ☎ 11/687–6500).

➤ NEW ZEALAND: **New Zealand High Commission** (✉ 50N Nyaya Marg, ☎ 11/688–3170).

➤ UNITED KINGDOM: **British High Commission** (✉ Shanti Path, ☎ 11/687–2161).

➤ UNITED STATES: **United States Embassy** (✉ Shanti Path, ☎ 11/419–8000).

EMERGENCIES

In any emergency, contact your embassy. There are emergency medical services in Delhi, but standards are low—and generally not acceptable to Westerners. (Wealthy Indians often leave the country for major health services.) For major, immediately life-threatening illnesses, (☞ Emergencies *in* Smart Travel Tips) go to Indraprasta Apollo Hospital, which is some distance out of town. This is Delhi's premier private hospital. From there, call Meera Rescue (mentioned in the Yellow Pages), which can arrange international evacuations.

While still unable to deal with trauma, Max Health Care—in conjunction with Harvard Medical International, one of India's major pharmaceutical companies—has opened up a first-rate clinic in South Delhi. It's the best thing to happen to Delhi medicine in a while. Many of the physicians are American-trained, and the equipment, including such high-tech items as CAT scans, are imported. There's a 24-hour pharmacy on-site. Whatever happens, *do not* go to a government hospital. For dental problems contact U.S.-trained Dr. Siddartha Mehta, who looks after many in Delhi's expatriate community. Most hotels also have house physicians and dentists on call.

Most hotels have chemists (pharmacies) open daily until about 9 PM. The chemist in Super Bazaar on Connaught Place is open 24 hours.

➤ MEDICAL CARE: **Indraprasta Apollo Hospital** (✉ Sarita Vihar, Delhi-Matur Rd., ☎ 11/692–5801, WEB www.apollohospdelhi.com). **Max Health Care** (✉ N 110 Panchsheel Park, ☎ 11/649–9870). **Meera Rescue** (✉ 112 Jor Bagh, ☎ 11/469–3508 or 11/465–3170).

➤ DENTISTS: **Siddhartha Mehta** (✉ 41 Khan Market, ☎ 11/461–5914).
➤ 24-HOUR PHARMACIES: **Max Health Care** (✉ N 110 Panchsheel
Park, ☎ 11/649–9870). **Pharmacy in Super Bazaar** (✉ Connaught Pl.,
☎ 11/331–0163).

MAIL AND SHIPPING

One centrally located post office is on the roundabout just southwest
of Connaught Place; another is the Eastern Court Post Office on Janpath. Hotels have mailing facilities, but if you really want your postcards to reach their destinations, go to a post office and have them
postmarked in front of you.
➤ POST OFFICES: **Main Post Office** (✉ Baba Kharak Singh, A Block,
Connaught Pl.). **Eastern Court Post Office** (✉ A Block, Connaught Pl.,
11/Eastern Court, Janpath, ☎ 11/332–1878).

MONEY

ATMS

While nonexistent in most of India, ATMs are starting to appear in
Delhi, but only in very limited numbers and in select locations. If you
need an ATM, head to Connaught Place, where the following are lo-
cated:
➤ CASH MACHINES: **American Express** (✉ A Block). **Standard Char-
tered and Grindlay's Bank** (✉ E Block). **CitiBank** (✉ Jeevan Bharati
Bldg., Outer Circle). **Bank of Tokyo** (✉ 13 Sansad Rd.). **Deutche
Bank** (✉ 15 Tolstoy Rd.). **Bank of America** (✉ 15 Barakhamba Rd.).

CURRENCY EXCHANGE

Most Western-style hotels have foreign-exchange facilities for their guests,
and will cash traveler's checks with twice the speed and half the hassle of banks. American Express cashes only its own traveler's checks,
as does Thomas Cook. The Thomas Cook branch in the Imperial
Hotel has the longest hours (Monday through Saturday, 9:30 to 8)).
The Central Bank of India is open 24 hours, except national holidays.
You can cash traveler's checks at the Bank of America, open weekdays
10 to 2 and Saturday 10 to noon. If you plan to change money at the
international airport, don't forget to do it at the counter on the left
before you go through Customs.
➤ EXCHANGE SERVICES: **American Express** (✉ Wenger House, A-Block,
Connaught Pl., ☎ 11/332–4149 or 11/332–4119). **Thomas Cook** (✉
Hotel Imperial, Janpath, ☎ 11/336–8060 and International Trade
Tower, 717–718 Nehru Pl., 7th floor, ☎ 11/646–7484).
➤ BANKS: **Central Bank of India** (✉ Ashok Hotel, Chanakyapuri, ☎
11/611–0101 ext. 2584). **Bank of America** (✉ 15 Hansaslaya, 4
Barakhamba Rd., ☎ 11/372–2332). **Citibank** (✉ Jeewan Bharati
Bldg., ☎ 11/371–4211).

TAXIS AND RICKSHAWS

Except in the Old Delhi's Chandni Chowk, 6 km (4 mi) north of Connaught Place, the best way to travel around Delhi is by taxi or hired
car with driver. To visit Chandni Chowk, take an auto- or cycle-rickshaw to Lal Qila, then walk or take a cycle-rickshaw through the market's maze of narrow lanes. (Cycle-rickshaws have all but disappeared
from Delhi streets, but if you get one, perhaps for a tour of Old Delhi,
ask a local merchant to help you negotiate the fare. Remember, when
you're negotiating or tipping, that these guys pedal hard for a living.)

While they're a novelty to ride in once or twice, three-wheeled auto-
rickshaws (known locally as "autos") are not a safe or speedy way to
get around. They are poorly maintained, and drivers tend to drive them
in a maniacal fashion. Most rickshaw-wallahs refuse to use the me-

ters, and quote fares 10 times higher than what's appropriate. Those who do use their meters rig them to run faster than the rickshaw. Opt for a taxi.

However, many cabbies also rig their meters or refuse to use them or revise the tariff. Drivers may carry a fare chart; ask to see it before you pay. If you don't have exact change, don't expect anything back. Taxis are available at every hotel and at taxi stands in every neighborhood and shopping area.

TOURS

Travel agencies offer varying rates for cars and drivers, tours, excursions, and even hotel rooms. Shop around, and use only government-recognized tour operators or travel agents—and ask to see a license. Ashok Travel and Tours has desks open during the evening at all Ashok hotels. The Great India Tour Company will help you not only with Delhi, but with South India as well. RBS Travels offers extremely competitive rates, has a huge fleet of cars, and is open daily 9 to 8:30. Thomas Cook is open Monday through Saturday 9:30 to 8.

➤ Travel Agencies: **American Express** (✉ Wenger House, A-Block, Connaught Pl., ☎ 11/332–4149 or 11/332–4119). **Ashok Travel and Tours** (✉ New Delhi House, 3rd floor, 27 Barakhamba Rd., ☎ 11/331–3233). **Cox and Kings** (✉ Indira Palace, H Block, Connaught Pl., ☎ 11/373–6031). **Great India Tour Company** (✉ G-44 Triveni Community Centre, Sheikh Sarai, Phase I, ☎ 11/628–6804). **RBS Travels** (✉ Shop G, Connaught Palace Hotel, 37 Shaheed Bhagat Singh Marg, ☎ 11/336–3036). **Sita Travels** (✉ F-12 Connaught Pl., ☎ 11/331–1122). **Thomas Cook** (✉ Hotel Imperial, Janpath, ☎ 11/336–8060).

TRAIN TRAVEL

The Delhi Railway Station, known as the Old Delhi Railway Station, is about 7 km (4 mi) north of Connaught Place. The New Delhi Railway Station is about 1 km (½ mi) north of Connaught Place. Most trains leave from New Delhi, but check before you set off. For tickets and information, you can save time and energy by using a travel agent (☞ Tours); otherwise, contact the International Tourist Bureau in the New Delhi station, open Monday through Saturday 8 to 5 for the use of foreigners with tourist visas only. You must purchase tickets in foreign currency, usually dollars or pounds sterling, unless you have a valid encashment slip. If you don't have an encashment slip, you can purchase a ticket in rupees at the general ticket counter, open daily 9:30 to 8 at the same location, but this can be a long and complicated process. Before you board any train, you must have a confirmed ticket and a reservation, including a reservation for your sleeping berth if you're traveling overnight (☞ Rail Travel *in* Smart Travel Tips). If hotel touts approach you at either rail station to offer you a room or claim that your room reservation is bogus, ignore them.

➤ Train Information: **International Tourist Bureau** (✉ New Delhi Railway Station, 1st floor, ☎ 11/373–4164).

VISITOR INFORMATION

The Government of India Tourist Office south of Connaught Place is open weekdays 9 to 6 and Saturday 9 to 2. Its airport counters are open for major flight arrivals, and its train-station counters are open 24 hours.

➤ New Delhi: **Government of India Tourist Office** (✉ 88 Janpath, ☎ 11/332–0005).

4 NORTH CENTRAL INDIA

Anchored by Agra, Khajuraho, and Varanasi, this section of the traveler's trail heads southeast of Delhi into the state of Uttar Pradesh, detouring into Madhya Pradesh and Bihar. The history of these lands is ancient and vast, their religions spanning Hinduism, Islam, Buddhism, and even—in Lucknow—Christianity. The spectacular architecture includes Agra's incomparable Taj Mahal and Khajuraho's erotic Hindu temples. Varanasi, the holiest city in Hinduism, draws a constant stream of pilgrims to bathe in the Ganges River.

By Andy
McCord,
Gaye Facer,
Smita Patel,
and Vikram
Singh

C ENTERED ON THE STATE OF UTTAR PRADESH, the Hindi heartland has long held the balance of power in North India, from the ancient Gupta kingdoms through the Moghuls and the British Raj to the present day. Together, Uttar Pradesh, Madhya Pradesh, and Bihar send far more representatives to Parliament than any other linguistic region in India. Sometimes disparaged as the Cow Belt, North Central India has often been slow to advance economically, but it remains a vital part of India's heritage and contemporary culture.

Agra was a seat of Moghul power. Dominated by Muslim influences in culture, art, architecture, and cuisine, the city testifies to the beauty and grandeur of Moghul aesthetics—most notably in the form of the Taj Mahal, but also in the forms of some exquisite smaller Muslim tombs and monuments. Today Agra is dusty and crowded, the spectacular Taj Mahal is being damaged by air pollution, and the nearby Moghul ghost town of Fatehpur Sikri is being choked by commercial encroachments. Still, the courts have stepped in with far-reaching orders that should go a long way toward cleaning up the urban environment.

Southeast of Agra, in the northern part of Madhya Pradesh, the sleepy village of Khajuraho predates the Moghuls. It was founded at the end of the classical age of Hindu civilization, and its stunning temples celebrate an eroticized Hinduism that flourished when Hindu kings adopted Tantric religion. Excavations have also uncovered a previously unknown complex of Buddhist temples here.

In many ways, Varanasi, in southwestern Uttar Pradesh, is the antithesis of Khajuraho. The holiest city in Hinduism and one of the oldest continuously inhabited cities in the world, Varanasi is crowded, filled with pilgrims, hospice patients, ascetics, priests, Hindu pundits, and worldly citizens of many religions. Unlike those in Khajuraho, Varanasi's temples are squeezed into the city itself, and the *ghats* (wide stone stairways leading down to the Ganges) are both key religious sites and secular promenades.

The popular Agra–Khajuraho–Varanasi route has plenty of worthwhile tentacles. The emperor Akbar's deserted city at Fatehpur Sikri lies just outside Agra, and a short drive from here across the Rajasthan border is the Keoladeo National Park in Bharatpur. A separate day trip takes you from Agra to the Moghul-influenced Hindu provincial capital at Gwalior. The magical town of Orchha, a two-hour drive from Gwalior toward Khajuraho, is riddled with 16th- and 17th-century ruins built by the Hindu Bundela rulers, including underground chambers and passageways. Buddha preached his first sermon in Sarnath, just outside Varanasi; the peaceful resonance of the stupas and abandoned monasteries at Sanchi draws Buddhists from all over Asia; and the international Buddhist center of Bodhgaya is east of Varanasi in the state of Bihar. The city of Lucknow, capital of Uttar Pradesh, was once the seat of an elegant Muslim province on a northern route between Varanasi and Delhi.

Pleasures and Pastimes

The Arts

This region provides ample opportunity to experience Indian classical music and dance. Both Agra and Khajuraho host annual festivals in attractive milieus; Khajuraho's Festival of Dance, normally held in March, stages some performances in front of the Western Group of temples. Varanasi also maintains a vibrant local tradition of music and dance, noted particularly for its *tabla* (drum) players.

The visual arts are strong here as well, beyond the splendid architecture. Khajuraho's archaeological museum displays sculptures that once graced the niches of the town's temples. The Bharat Kala Bhavan at Banaras Hindu University is one of the most attractively arranged museums in India and has superb collections of both miniature painting and locally discovered classical sculpture. The archaeological museum in Mathura, some 56 km (35 mi) northwest of Agra on the road from Delhi, has one of the best collections of classical sculpture (from the Hindu Golden Age, the Gupta dynasty) in the country.

Dining

Restaurants on this route serve kebabs, other grilled meats, *birianis* (rice casseroles), and the rich, almond- and saffron-scented concoctions of Mughlai cuisine, a culinary counterpart to the Moghuls' architecture. Hotels in Agra, not surprisingly, serve particularly good Mughlai dishes. Small restaurants in villages along the way, not always in hotels, have simpler, local vegetarian dishes that are often delicious and cheap. Most restaurants in this region are open from 7 to 10 for breakfast, noon to 3 for lunch, and 7:30 to 11 for dinner.

Varanasi, with its abundant food for the soul, is extremely light on restaurants; orthodox Hindus do not eat meat, and prefer to keep food preparation a family affair. The major hotels serve standard Indian and Continental dishes and have branched out competently into Chinese cuisine. There are some excellent cafés, however, and the city is known for its sweets, which are mostly based on distillations of milk and cream; one, called the *lavan lata,* tastes like a supercharged baklava. A few cafés in Varanasi and Khajuraho even serve such exoticisms as tacos and yak-cheese pizza. Khajuraho, with its laid-back atmosphere, is a good place to venture into a roadside tea stall, a cultural institution as important to India as Parliament. Concerns about hygiene may ward you off sampling street food, but when it's hot from the fire it's generally quite safe.

Festivals

Agra's cultural festival, Taj Mahotsav (February), and the Khajuraho Festival of Dance (March) are geared primarily toward travelers. The Lucknow Festival (November–December) highlights the refined Indo-Muslim background of this state capital. In Varanasi, the religious calendar takes precedence, creating a major festival practically every week. The Hindu calendar follows lunar months, so Hindu festival dates shift back every year, catching up to the solar calendar when a leap month is added every third year. Varanasi's great bathing days, when thousands stream down the ghats into the Ganges, include Makar Sankranti (January), the full moon of the Hindu month Kartik (October or November), and Ganga Dussehra (May or June). Durga Puja (September or October) ends with the city's large Bengali community marching to the river at sunset to immerse large mud-daubed images of the goddess Durga. The month leading up to Dussehra, also in September or October, features nightly reenactments of the epic of Rama in the Ram Nagar palace, across the river from Varanasi (some episodes also take place in the city itself). Buddhists from Tibet and all over Asia celebrate their festivals in Sarnath, Bodhgaya, and Sanchi. Muslim holidays are observed in Bhopal and by Varanasi's large Muslim minority as well as in the more predominantly Muslim cities of Agra and Lucknow.

Lodging

India's main hotel groups are represented in this region, providing increased amenities and efficiency at increasing prices. More and more good, air-conditioned hotels here cater to India's burgeoning upper middle class, but these are often quite generic. Outside the old British cantonment areas where most hotels are clustered, a few clean, well-run guest houses and small Heritage Hotels have sprung up; these are often more convenient to town centers and may be attractive to those who like to venture out on their own. Unless noted otherwise, all hotels listed have air-conditioning.

Shopping

Agra and Varanasi are craft centers. Marble work, jewelry, and leather are renowned in Agra, and the Varanasi area has long been known for its silk (particularly brocade) and rug weaving and for block-printing. There is a rigorous commission system, and prices are likely to be as high as (or even higher than) those for similar goods at a five-star hotel in New Delhi. Visits to artisans' workshops are always interesting; just prepare to feel overt pressure to buy at the end of a guided tour.

Exploring North Central India

Agra and Varanasi are at opposite ends of India's largest state, Uttar Pradesh. Both lie on the Gangetic plain, and the countryside around each is similar—a dry landscape planted with sugarcane, mustard, and wheat in winter and inhabited by poor peasants and wealthier landowners. The monsoon hits harder to the east, around Varanasi, so the terrain there is a little more lush. The Yamuna River, backdrop to the Taj Mahal, joins the Ganges at Allahabad, about a hundred miles west of Varanasi. Khajuraho, in contrast, has a more dramatic setting at the edge of the hills and ravines that separate the northern plains south of the Vindhya hills from the Deccan plateau. This area, called Bundelkhand, has been notorious since British times for harboring *dacoits* (highway robbers), including Phoolan Devi, the "Bandit Queen," who held a seat in Parliament until she was assassinated in 2001; yet the area is pacific from day to day.

Great Itineraries

Agra, Khajuraho, and Varanasi are well connected by air. The adventuresome can arrange to drive, but traffic is heavy between Agra and Delhi in particular. If you do choose to drive, avoid doing so at night to reduce the risk of accidents. Train service is reliable and comfortable between Delhi and Agra, Gwalior, or Bhopal, and Delhi and Varanasi. Between Agra and Khajuraho, a comfortable morning train runs as far as Jhansi, with Orchha just a few miles away and a pleasant overnight stop. The scenic drive on to Khajuraho takes about four hours. From Khajuraho to Varanasi the rail and road connection is more complicated; you may prefer the afternoon plane. Agra makes a convenient starting point for this region: from there you can hop to Khajuraho (a 35-minute flight) and then Varanasi (40 minutes by plane) and then back to Delhi. If you fly from point to point, aim for at least five days in this region; if you stick to land travel, allow at least a week.

IF YOU HAVE 4 DAYS

If time is limited and you're returning to Delhi, you may wish to drop either Khajuraho or Varanasi from this itinerary. Plane schedules make it necessary to stay overnight in each place. From Delhi, you can take a morning flight or a train to ⊞ **Agra** and proceed immediately to the Taj Mahal while the morning light lasts. Allow several hours to wander the grounds and inspect the fine marble work inside the tomb itself. After lunch you can visit Agra Fort *or* take a perhaps more rewarding road trip to **Fatehpur Sikri.** Also worth wedging in is Itmad-ud-Daulah's Tomb, a stunning but little visited gem of Moghul architecture. The next morning, fly to ⊞ **Khajuraho** and explore the Western Group of Temples; on your third day you can briefly visit some other temples or the museum before flying to ⊞ **Varanasi** for a late-after-

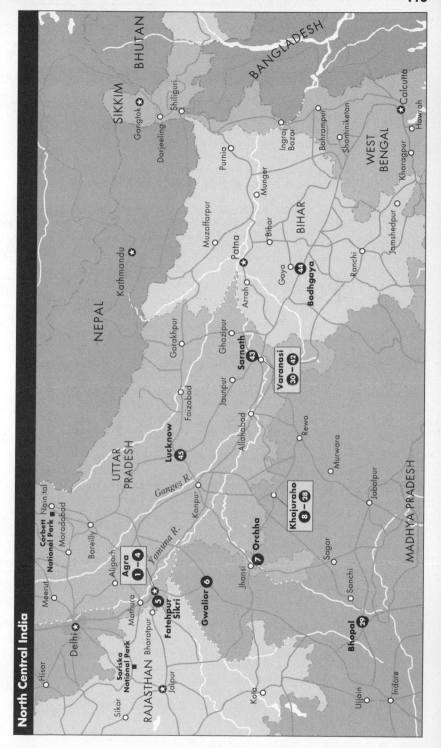

North Central India

BHUTAN

BANGLADESH

SIKKIM

Gangtok

Darjeeling

Shiliguri

Calcutta

Howrah

Kharagpur

Shantiniketan

Bahrampur

WEST BENGAL

Ingraj Bazar

Jamshedpur

Purnia

Munger

Bihar

BIHAR

Ranchi

Muzaffarpur

Patna

Goya

Bodhgaya 44

NEPAL

Kathmandu

Gorakhpur

Arrah

Ghazipur

Sarnath 43

Varanasi 30 – 42

Faizabad

Jaunpur

Allahabad

Rewa

Lucknow 45

UTTAR PRADESH

Murwara

Jabalpur

MADHYA PRADESH

Ganges R.

Kanpur

Khajuraho 8 – 28

Corbett National Park

Nainital

Moradabad

Bareilly

Yamuna R.

Aligarh

Agra 1 – 4

Orchha 7

Sagar

Sanchi

Meerut

Mathura

5

Fatehpur Sikri

Gwalior 6

Jhansi

Delhi

Bharatpur

Sariska National Park

RAJASTHAN

Jaipur

Kota

Bhopal 29

Hisar

Sikar

Ujjain

Indore

noon boat ride on the Ganges. Art lovers may want to spend an afternoon at the Bharat Kala Bhavan, on the campus of Banaras Hindu University; returning to town, you can stop at the Durga and Sankat Mochan temples. The Buddhist center of **Sarnath** makes for an easy side trip from Varanasi. The next morning, take a sunrise boat ride to see the ritual bathing and Varanasi's lovely skyline; then visit the main temple area around Kashi Vishvanath, the Golden Temple.

IF YOU HAVE 6 DAYS

Spend two days and two nights in ⚎ **Agra;** visit Agra Fort, **Fatehpur Sikri,** and Itmad-ud-Daulah's tomb or Akbar's tomb. If you've had enough urban bustle, head to the bucolic Keoladeo National Park at **Bharatpur,** just over the Rajasthan border, a hop, skip, and a jump from Fatehpur Sikri. Two days in ⚎ **Khajuraho** will allow leisurely exploration of the temples or a trip to the wildlife park at Panna. With two days in ⚎ **Varanasi** you can take at least one boat ride on the Ganges, visit the main temples, tour the palace at Ram Nagar, admire the artwork in the Bharat Kala Bhavan, and detour to **Sarnath.**

IF YOU HAVE 8–10 DAYS

If you're coming from Delhi, consider hiring a car for the potentially nerve-wracking three-hour trip to Agra, as driving will allow you to stop at Mathura, with its excellent archaeological museum; the tiny temple town of Vrindavan, where the god Krishna grew up as a cowherd; and Sikandra, site of Akbar's tomb. Spend two days in ⚎ **Agra.** Then, instead of the 40-minute plane ride to ⚎ **Khajuraho,** where you should also spend two days, take a two-day road trip, which involves a total of about 10 hours' driving and includes stops at ⚎ **Gwalior,** with its spectacular Hindu fort, and ⚎ **Orchha,** another seat of Hindu rajas on a picturesque river. To minimize your time on the road, you might arrange through a travel agent for a car to meet your train at Mathura, and perhaps travel from Agra to Gwalior or Orchha by train. Finally, fly from Khajuraho to ⚎ **Varanasi** and spend the better part of two days here. The morning of your eighth day, head west toward **Lucknow** or east to **Bodhgaya.** (The latter will lengthen your stay in the region to nine days—to fly out of Bodhgaya you'll need to stay the night and drive early the next morning to Patna.) Alternately, you can add two or three days in **Bhopal** and **Sanchi** by extending your train journey from Orchha (returning to Chansi and continuing on the Shatabdi Express to Bhopal, or flying direct from Delhi).

When to Tour North Central India

Nowhere in India is the common advice to come between October and March more apt. This region is hot, and the sights in Agra and Khajuraho involve hours in the sun. (It can be chilly in late December and January, however.) The weather from early February to mid-March is temperate and beautiful. Early October in Bhopal is warm but pleasant, and the reduced number of tourists will allow you to enjoy the natural peace of the rural surroundings. For adventurous travelers, the mid-monsoon period (late July and early August) is an attractive alternative: temperatures are usually in the 70s and 80s, downpours are intermittent and impressive, hotel rates are much lower, and Varanasi is probably in the midst of a festival. Orchha is at its best during the monsoons, when the river is in full flow and the surrounding scrubland is green.

AGRA AND ENVIRONS

The journey from Delhi to Agra follows the Grand Trunk Road, a royal route established by India's Moghul emperors in the 16th and 17th centuries, when their capital alternated between Delhi, Agra, and Lahore (now in Pakistan). If you get an early start, you can see Agra's sights in one day: turn off the Grand Trunk Road 10 km (6 mi) north of Agra to visit Akbar's Tomb, then move on to Itmad-ud-Daulah's Tomb, the Taj Mahal, and Agra Fort.

Several excursions from Agra make a trip here more interesting. Many find Akbar's deserted dream city at Fatehpur Sikri as rewarding as the Taj Mahal. A short drive on from Fatehpur Sikri (toward Jaipur) brings you over the Rajasthan border to the Keoladeo National Park in Bharatpur, winter home of the Siberian crane. A separate trip takes you to the Moghul-influenced Hindu provincial capital at Gwalior. If you drive on to Khajuraho, Orchha makes an excellent place to spend the night amid ruined temples and palaces.

Agra

200 km (124 mi) southeast of Delhi

Under the Moghul emperor Akbar (1542–1605) and his successors, Jahangir and Shah Jahan, Agra flourished. After the reign of Shah Jahan's son Aurangzeb (1618–1707), however, and the gradual disintegration of their empire, the city passed from one invader to another before the British took charge early in the 19th century. The British, particularly Governor General Lord Curzon (in office 1898–1905), did much to halt and repair the damage inflicted on Agra's forts and palaces by raiders and vandals.

Agra today is crowded and dirty, and some of the Moghul buildings are irrevocably scarred. Other monuments, however, are strewn like pearls in ashes, evoking that glorious period in Indian history when Agra was the center of the Moghul empire, and the empire itself was the focus of political, cultural, and artistic evolution.

Opening hours and admission fees—especially those of the Taj Mahal—change constantly; inquire in advance at your hotel or the Uttar Pradesh State Tourist Office. You can pick up day passes covering entrance to Agra's main monuments at any of the sights below; check to ensure that they cover all admission charges levied by both the Archaeological Survey of India and the Agra Development Authority.

Numbers in the text correspond to numbers in the margin and on the Agra map

A Good Tour

If you arrive in Agra late in the day, set out very early the next day. Hire a car and driver, and stop first to see the morning light on the **Taj Mahal** ①. Drive from there to **Itmad-ud-Daulah's Tomb** ② and then to **Akbar's Tomb** ③. Return to Agra for a tour of **Agra Fort** ④ *or* drive outside town to **Fatehpur Sikri.** Return to the Taj to see the marble at sunset.

Alternately, if you leave Delhi at 5 AM by car, you should reach Sikandra at 7:30, where you can see Akbar's Tomb in less than an hour. From there it's roughly 20 minutes' drive to Itmad-ud Daulah's Tomb, another short but delightful visit. A 30- to 45-minute drive will take you to the Taj Mahal. You can then visit Agra Fort or Fatehpur Sikri in the afternoon and relax by the Taj at twilight.

Sights to See

★ ④ **Agra Fort.** The architecture of this fort reflects the collective creative brilliance of Akbar, his son Jahangir, and his grandson Shah Jahan. The structure was built by Akbar on the site of an earlier fort. As with sim-

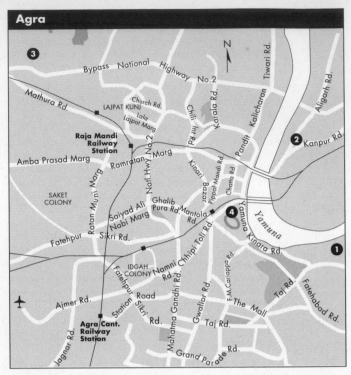

ilar Moghul facilities in Delhi and Lahore, the word "fort" is a little misleading. The complex contains royal apartments, mosques, and assembly halls as well as a dungeon—the whole cityscape of an imperial capital. A massive wall 2½ km (1½ mi) long and 69 ft high surrounds the fort's roughly triangular shape. With the Yamuna River running at its base, the fort was also protected by a moat and another wall, presenting a daunting barrier to anyone hoping to access the treasures within.

Today, entrance is easy through the Amar Singh Gate. North of this entrance sits the fort's largest private residence, the **Jahangiri Mahal**, built as a harem for Akbar's son Jahangir. (Akbar's own palace, closer to the entrance, is in ruins.) Measuring 250 ft by 300 ft, the Jahangiri Mahal juxtaposes *jarokhas* (balconies) and other elements of Hindu architecture with pointed arches and other Central Asian influences imported by the Moghuls—a mixture foreshadowing the stylistic synthesis that would follow at Fatehpur Sikri. The palace's central court is lined with two-story facades bearing remnants of the rich, gilded decoration that once covered much of the structure. Next to architecture and the arts, Jahangir's greatest loves were wine and his Persian-born wife Nur Jahan, who, failing to persuade him to pay some attention to managing his empire, did it for him, making short work of all rivals. This strong-willed woman was unable to consolidate her power after her husband died, however, and lived out her days in virtual seclusion in Lahore.

After Jahangir's death in 1628, Shah Jahan (whose mother was one of Jahangir's other wives) assumed the throne and started his own buildings inside the fort, often tearing down those built by his father and grandfather in the process. The **Anguri Bagh** (literally, Grape Arbor) shows the outlines of a geometric garden built around delicate water courses and chutes by Shah Jahan. The 1637 **Khas Mahal** (Private Palace) is an early masterpiece of Shah Jahan's craftsmen. The central pavilion, made of white marble, follows the classic Moghul pattern: three arches on each side, five in front, and two turrets rising out of the roof. Of the two flanking pavilions, one is of white marble and was supposedly decorated with gold leaf, while the other is made of red stone; these are said to have housed Shah Jahan's two daughters. The arched roofs of all three pavilions are stone translations of the bamboo architecture of Bengal. In one part of the Khas Mahal, a staircase leads down to the palace's "air-conditioned" quarters—cool underground rooms that were probably used in the summer.

The octagonal tower of the **Mussaman Burj** has fine inlay work and a splendid view down the river to the Taj Mahal. This is where Shah Jahan is sometimes said to have spent his last days, imprisoned but still able to see his greatest monument, the Taj Mahal. On the northeastern end of the Khas Mahal courtyard stands the **Sheesh Mahal** (Palace of Mirrors), built in 1637 as a bath for the private palace and dressing room for the harem. Each of the two chambers contained a bathing tank fed by marble channels.

The emperor received foreign ambassadors and other dignitaries in the **Diwan-i-Khas** (Hall of Private Audience), built by Shah Jahan in 1636–37. Outside, the marble throne terrace holds a pair of black and white thrones. The black throne, carved from a single block of marble, overlooks the Yamuna. The white throne was made of several marble blocks, and the inscription indicates it was used by Shah Jahan, while the black throne had been his father's seat of power. Both thrones face the **Machhi Bhavan,** an enclosure of fountains and shallow pools, and a number of imperial offices.

To the empire's citizens and to the European emissaries who came to see these powerful monarchs, the most impressive part of the fort was the **Diwan-i-Am** (Hall of Public Audience), set within a large quadrangle. This huge, low structure rests on a 4-ft platform, its nine cusped Moghul arches held aloft by rows of slender supporting pillars. Here the emperor sat and dispensed justice to his subjects.

Northeast of the Diwan-i-Khas is the **Nagina Masjid,** a private mosque raised by Shah Jahan for the women of his harem. Made of white marble and walled in on three sides, it has typical cusped arches, a marble courtyard, and three graceful domes. Nearby is the lovely **Moti Masjid,** a perfectly proportioned pearl mosque built in white marble by Shah Jahan. ⊠ *Yamuna Kinara Rd., near Nehru Park.* 🚇 *Foreigners Rs. 300.* ☯ *Daily 7–6.*

❸ **Akbar's Tomb.** Akbar's resting place was begun by the emperor himself in 1602, and completed after his death by his son Jahangir. Topped with smooth white marble and flanked by graceful minarets, this mausoleum of rough red sandstone sits in a typical Moghul garden comprised of four quadrants separated by waterways. The garden is not well tended now, and Jat raiders (who invaded Agra after the fall of the Moghul empire) destroyed much of the gold work that once adorned the tomb, though the British partially restored it. In a domed chamber three stories high, the crypt is inscribed with the 99 names of Allah, plus the phrases "Allah-o-Akbar" ("God is Great") at the head and "Jalla Jalalahu" ("Great is His Glory") at the foot. You can actually see the tomb's enormous gateway, topped with bright tilework, from the train from Delhi—look out the left window 10 or 15 minutes before the train is due to reach Agra. ⊠ *Sikandra, 10 km (6 mi) north of Agra on Grand Trunk Rd. to Delhi.* 🚇 *Foreigners Rs. 110.* ☯ *Daily 6–5:30.*

★ ❷ **Itmad-ud-Daulah's Tomb.** The empress Nur Jahan (Jahangir's favorite wife) built this small but gorgeous tomb for her father, a Persian nobleman who became Jahangir's chief minister. The monument, one of Agra's loveliest, was supposedly built by workers from Iran (then Persia). The tomb incorporates a great deal of brown and yellow Persian marble, and marks the first use of Persian-style marble inlay in India—both features that would later characterize the style of Shah Jahan. This building was a precursor to, and very likely an inspiration for, the Taj Mahal in its use of intricate marble inlay in particular. The roof is arched in the style of Bengali terra-cotta temples, and the minarets are octagonal, much broader than the slender cylinders of the Taj; yet in its fine proportions this mausoleum almost equals that masterpiece. Inside—where the elegant decoration continues—the central chamber holds the tombs of Itmad-ud-Daulah and his wife, with other relations buried in adjacent rooms. Most travelers to Agra never see this place, yet its beauty and tranquillity are extraordinary, and its well-maintained gardens make it a wonderful place to pause and reflect. ⊠ *5 km (3 mi) north of Taj Mahal on left bank of Yamuna River.* 🎟 *Foreigners Rs. 110.* ⊙ *Daily 6–6.*

★ ❶ **Taj Mahal.** The architecture alone has inspired reams of rapture over the years, but what really makes this marble monument so endearing is its haunting tale of love and loss. Arjuman Banu, the niece of Jahangir's wife Nur Jahan, supposedly captured the heart of the young Shah Jahan the minute he saw her. In 1612, at the age of 21, she married him and became his favorite wife, his Mumtaz Mahal (the Exalted of the Palace) and Mumtazul-Zamani (the Distinguished of the Age). Numerous stories recall this woman's generosity and wisdom, both as a household manager and as an adviser to her beloved husband. She bore 14 children, and it was in childbirth that she died in 1630 while accompanying her husband on a military campaign. On her deathbed, it is said, she begged the king to build a monument so beautiful that the world would never forget their love. Shattered by the death of his favorite, legend claims, Shah Jahan locked himself in his private chambers for a month; and when he finally emerged, his hair was white. Six months after Mumtaz Mahal's death, a huge procession brought her body to Agra, where Shah Jahan began the process of honoring her request.

Shah Jahan's chief architect, Ustad Ahmad Lahori, oversaw the construction, which began in 1632. Shah Jahan put an army of 20,000 laborers to work, even building a new village (Taj Ganj, which still stands) to house them as they spent 17 years creating a vast tomb of white marble on the banks of the Yamuna River, visible from Agra Fort. The Taj was completed on the exact anniversary of Mumtaz Mahal's death. The great emperor spent his last years locked in one of his own creations, gazing, according to the popular story, across the Yamuna at his wife's final resting place.

It's easy to cling to the legendary narrative behind this building—as well as the equally undocumented story of Shah Jahan's plan to build a black-marble tomb for himself across the Yamuna—yet the Taj Mahal, along with only a handful of world treasures, speaks for itself. It is both the culmination of and the best introduction to the elaborate aesthetic world that the Moghuls created in India, sometimes at the expense of their political power.

The Taj stands at the end of a large, four-quartered garden, or *charbagh,* symbolizing paradise, extending about a thousand feet in each direction from a small central pool. You enter the grounds through a huge sandstone gateway, with an arching Koranic inscription. Ahead, facing the long reflecting pool, the Taj stands on two bases, one of sandstone and, above it, a marble platform measuring 313 ft square and worked into a chessboard design. A slender marble minaret stands at each corner of the platform, blending so well into the general composition that it's hard to believe each one is 137 ft tall. The minarets are actually built at a slight tilt away from the tomb so that, in case of an earthquake, they'd fall away from the building. Facing the Taj from beneath its platform are two majestic sandstone buildings, a mosque on the left and its mirror image (built purely for symmetry) on the right. Behind the tomb, the Yamuna winds through its broad, sandy bed.

The tomb's central archway is deeply recessed, as are the smaller pairs of companion archways along the sides and the beveled corners of the 190-square-ft structure. The Taj's most extraordinary feature is its onion dome, crowned by a brass finial mounted in a scalloped ornament that inverts the Hindu motif of the lotus. The dome uses the Central Asian technique of placing a central inner dome, in this case 81 ft high, inside an outer shell to attain the extraordinary exterior height of 200 ft; between the two is an area nearly the size of the interior hall itself. Raising the dome above the minarets was the builders' great stroke of genius. Large *chattras* (umbrellas), another feature borrowed from Hindu design, balance the dome.

Inside the mausoleum, the changing light creeps softly in through marble screens that have been chiseled like silver filigree. Look closely at the tiny flowers drawn of inlaid semiprecious stones—at the detailed stonework on each petal and leaf. The work is so fine that not even a magnifying glass reveals the tiny breaks between stones; yet a single one-inch flower on the queen's tomb contains 60 separate pieces. Shine a flashlight to see the delicate stones' translucence. Directly under the marble dome lie the tombs of Mumtaz Mahal and Shah Jahan, surrounded by a screen carved from a single block of marble, with latticework as intricate as lace. In the center of the enclosure, diminishing rectangles lead up to what looks like a coffin; in fact, both Mumtaz Mahal and Shah Jahan are buried in a crypt below these tombs in deference to the Islamic tradition that no one should walk upon their graves. After his death, Shah Jahan was buried next to his wife by his son Aurangzeb, upsetting the perfect symmetry, most likely a cost-cutting measure that forms an ironic postscript to the munificence of Shah Jahan. But it may be fitting that the emperor lies in perpetuity next to his favorite wife, and the romantically inclined give Aurangzeb credit for bringing the two together. Mumtaz Mahal's tomb bears a Persian inscription: "The illustrious sepulcher of Arjuman Banu Begum, called Mumtaz Mahal. God is everlasting, God is sufficient. He knoweth what is concealed and what is manifest. He is merciful and compassionate. Nearer unto him are those who say: Our Lord is God." The emperor's epitaph reads: "The illustrious sepulcher of His Exalted Majesty Shah Jahan, the Valiant King, whose dwelling is in the starry Heaven. He traveled from this transient world to the World of Eternity on the 28th night of the month of Rajab in the year of 1076 of the Hegira [February 1, 1666]."

It's worth making more than one trip to see the Taj in varying lights. In early morning, the pale rays of the sun give the marble a soft pink luster, while at sunset the west side of the monument turns lemon-yellow, then pumpkin-orange. Once the sun goes down, the marble is pure white on a white sky.

The **Taj Mahal Museum** stands near the mosque to the left of the Taj. Though small, it holds interesting Moghul memorabilia and provides some historical background to the Taj, as well as paintings of the famous couple.⊠ *Taj Rd., Taj Ganj.* ▥ *Taj Mahal foreigners Rs. 750;*

museum foreigners Rs. 150. ☉ *Taj Mahal Mon.–Thurs. and weekends sunrise–7 PM; museum Tues.–Thurs. and weekends 8–5.*

Dining and Lodging

$$$$ ✕ **Esphahahan.** The chef here has mastered the subtlest of Indian dishes, *dum biriani,* which at Esphahahan means perfectly blended gold-, orange-, and wheat-color rice; caramelized onions; and aromatic lamb. Try this with *dal Esphahani,* a creamy black lentil dish. North Indian dishes dominate the pan-Indian menu, but the South Indian selections are equally delicious. Live instrumental music is performed nightly in the dining room, which makes use of functional art such as the *bidri* (gun metal inlaid with silver) table settings. ⊠ *Amarvilas Hotel, Taj East Gate Rd., Taj Nagri Scheme,* ☎ *562/231515. AE, DC, MC, V.*

$$$$ ✕ **Mahjong Room.** Dine on excellent Chinese dishes in this intimate, ★ dimly lit, wood-paneled restaurant with white and maroon linens and Chinese lanterns. Try the tangy hot-and-sour soup and the spicy chili chicken. The dining room overlooks the hotel courtyard and gardens. ⊠ *Welcomgroup Moghul Sheraton, 194 Fatehbad Rd., Taj Ganj,* ☎ *562/331701 through 562/331728. AE, DC, MC, V.*

$$$$ ✕ **Mughal Room.** A ceiling of faux twinkling stars overhangs this ★ dark, elegant top-floor restaurant decorated in pinks and reds. At night you might catch a live performance of *ghazals* (Urdu-language love songs). The menu mixes Indian, Chinese, and Continental cuisines, but the Indian dishes are particularly delicious. For dessert, see if the *shahi tukra* ("toast of kings"), a rich, bread-based pudding, is on offer. ⊠ *Clarks Shiraz, 54 Taj Rd.,* ☎ *562/226121 through 562/226127. AE, DC, MC, V.*

$$$$ ✕ **Nauratna.** Named for the "nine jewels" (ministers) of Akbar's court, this intimate restaurant has Moghul decor, with expanses of marble and lots of purple, the emperor's favorite color. The Mughlai cuisine is similar to what Akbar himself ate. Try a biriani, the quintessential Mughlai dish, or one of the excellent kebabs. Evening usually brings a live performance of ghazals. ⊠ *Welcomgroup Moghul Sheraton, 194 Fatehbad Rd., Taj Ganj,* ☎ *562/331701 through 562/331728. AE, DC, MC, V.*

$$$–$$$$ ✕ **Bellevue.** Chef Tawa from New Zealand modernizes old favorites, ★ both Indian and Continental, such as mulligatawny soup and wild-mushroom pasta. Translucent glass louvers, which are lit at night, separate dining areas while keeping the ambience light and airy. With your meal here you can also enjoy views of the garden, pool, and the top of the Taj Mahal. ⊠ *Amarvilas Hotel, Taj East Gate Rd., Taj Nagri Scheme,* ☎ *562/231515. AE, DC, MC, V.*

$$ ✕ **Dasaprakash.** A far cry from the traditional cuisine of Agra, the light ★ and spicy South Indian vegetarian dishes served here can be a nice change from rich Mughlai fare. With its Formica tables and fake Tiffany lamps, Dasaprakash resembles an American pizza joint, but the food is excellent, and service is fast. The *thali* (a sampler plate) may include the crisp *aplam* (fried wafers) and *rasam* (thin, spicy lentil soup), as well as fluffy *idlis* (steamed rice cakes) and crisp *dosas* (crisp rice crêpes). Also available are an unusual selection of fresh juices and a great dessert menu with ice creams and floats. ⊠ *1 Meher Cinema Complex (5 min from Taj Mahal, near Hotel Agra Ashok), Gwalior Rd., Agra Cantonment,* ☎ *562/363368. No credit cards.*

$$$$ 🏨 **Amarvilas.** Truly a monument in itself—not to love, like the Taj Mahal, ★ but to luxury tourism—the Amarvilas resort strives to reflect elements of Agra's culture and history with fine antiques, such as an 18th-century silk textile hanging on the lobby wall, and newly commissioned works of art, such as the gold leaf–covered dome over the reception area. The large rooms pick up on the turquoise and teak theme that pervades the hotel and incorporate original art, such as the *pietra dura* (marble inlaid with semiprecious stones) coffee tables. Every room faces the Taj, which is less than 1km (1/2 mi) away. If the cost is too high, consider at least eating in one of the hotel's two restaurants, Bellevue and Esphahahan. ⊠ *Taj East Gate Rd., Taj Nagri Scheme, 282001, Uttar Pradesh,* ☎ *562/231515,* FAX *562/231516,* WEB *www.oberoihotels.com. 106 room, 7 suites. 2 restaurants, bar, pool, spa, hot tub, gym, library, business services, travel services. AE, DC, MC, V.*

$$$ ▥ **Clarks Shiraz.** This Western-style high-rise, set on 8 acres with extensive gardens, evokes no era so much as the 1960s. The comfortable rooms have subdued contemporary decor. Odd-number rooms have distant views of the Taj; the newer rooms in the tower are more spacious and afford better views. Expect an evening barbecue on the beautifully lighted lawn. ⊠ *54 Taj Rd., 282001, Uttar Pradesh,* ☎ *562/226121 through 562/226129,* FAX *562/226128. 235 rooms, 2 suites. 4 restaurants, bar, pool, golf privileges, miniature golf, croquet, baby-sitting, business services, meeting room, travel services. AE, DC, MC, V.*

$$$ ▥ **Mansingh Palace.** This Western-style hotel has a spacious lobby with a fountain, and simply decorated modern rooms. ⊠ *Fatehbad Rd., 282001, Uttar Pradesh,* ☎ *562/331771 through 562/331775,* FAX *562/ 330202. 100 rooms, 3 suites. Restaurant, bar, coffee shop, pool, health club, meeting room, travel services. AE, DC, MC, V.*

$$$ ▥ **Taj View.** The Taj Mahal views from the upper stories of this Western-style hotel are some of the best in town, albeit still distant. This Taj-group hotel has a restful brown-tone lobby, good service, and spacious modern rooms. ⊠ *Taj Ganj, Fatehbad Rd., 282001, Uttar Pradesh,* ☎ *562/232400 through 562/232418,* FAX *562/232420,* WEB *www.tajhotels.com. 95 rooms, 5 suites. Restaurant, bar, coffee shop, pool, health club, badminton, baby-sitting, business services, meeting room, travel services. AE, DC, MC, V.*

$$$ ▥ **The Trident.** Oberoi staff from all over India train at this Oberoi hotel,
★ so service is correspondingly excellent. Built around a lovely garden courtyard with stone pathways, fountains, a sandstone pavilion, and a pool, it's simple, clean, and elegant—one of Agra's best values, if a little farther from the Taj Mahal than the hotels in Taj Ganj. The rooms have subdued modern decor and tile floors. ⊠ *Taj Nagri Scheme, Fatehbad Rd., 282001, Uttar Pradesh,* ☎ *562/331818,* FAX *562/331827,* WEB *www.oberoihotels.com. 139 rooms, 1 suite. Restaurant, bar, pool, barbershop, hair salon, badminton, tennis court, volleyball, travel services. AE, DC, MC, V.*

$$$ ▥ **Welcomgroup Moghul Sheraton.** This brick-and-marble edifice is one
★ of Agra's class acts, though its size is a little overwhelming. The huge, landscaped gardens even hold a miniature lake. Most of the spacious rooms have low-key modern decor, their soft white walls accented by handsome, dark-wood trim, but you can actually request an Indian-style room with local fabrics and furniture. Some rooms have views of the Taj. Forgetting nothing, the hotel retains its own astrologer and snake charmer. ⊠ *194 Fatehbad Rd., Taj Ganj, 282001, Uttar Pradesh,* ☎ *562/331701 through 562/331728,* FAX *562/331730,* WEB *www.welcomgroup.com. 300 rooms, 12 suites. 5 restaurants, bar, no-smoking rooms, pool, miniature golf, 2 tennis courts, croquet, health club, boating, dance club, business services, travel services. AE, DC, MC, V.*

$$ ▥ **Agra Ashok.** The architecture of this government-run Western-style hotel is Moghul-inspired, with lots of marble and red sandstone and an interior water fountain. Rooms are spacious and modern, and some have views of the Taj. ⊠ *6B The Mall, 282001, Uttar Pradesh,* ☎ *562/ 361231 or 562/361232,* FAX *562/361620. 53 rooms, 2 suites. 2 restaurants, bar, coffee shop, pool, baby-sitting, business services, travel services. AE, DC, MC, V.*

$ ⊡ New Bakshi House. If you'd like to stay in a middle-class Indian neighborhood, consider New Bakshi. All kinds of mementos, including the owner's collection of old maps, give the two-story house a homey feel. Each room is cozy and clean. Air-conditioned rooms cost more, but they're still inexpensive. For an additional fee, you can dine on home-cooked meals from an Indian or Continental menu. ⊠ *5 Laxman Nagar, 282001, Uttar Pradesh,* ☎ *562/302176 or 562/302616,* FAX *562/ 301448. 10 rooms. Restaurant, golf privileges, travel services. No credit cards.*

Shopping

Many shops sell hand-knotted carpets and dhurries, precious and semiprecious stones, inlaid marble work, and brass statues. Beware of drivers and touts who want to take you to places offering special "bargains"; they receive huge commissions from shopkeepers, which you pay in the price of the merchandise. Beware, too, of soapstone masquerading as marble: this softer, cheaper stone is a convincing substitute, but you can test it by scraping the item with your fingernail. Marble won't scrape. Finally, for what it's worth, local lore has it that miniature replicas of the Taj Mahal bring bad luck.

Cottage Industry (⊠ 18 Munro Rd., ☎ 562/226814) sells good dhurries and carpets. **Cottage Industries Exposition** (⊠ 39 Fatehbad Rd., ☎ 562/226813) carries a full selection of high-quality rugs, crafts, and gemstones at prices to match. **Ganesha** (⊠ 18 Munro Rd., ☎ 562/ 368856) has brass, copper, and bronze curios. **Ganeshi Lall and Son** (⊠ Welcomgroup Moghul Sheraton, 194 Fatehbad Rd., ☎ 562/ 330181) is Agra's old-time reliable jeweler, established 1843; the store also sells objets d'art. The **Handicrafts Gallery** (⊠ 18A/54 Jasoria Enclave, Eatchabad Rd., ☎ 562/330188) carries jewelry, silk-embroidered "paintings," handicrafts, and musical instruments, and hosts free live Indian musical performances daily. Call for details. **Kohinoor** (⊠ 41 Mahatma Gandhi Rd., ☎ 562/364156) has been selling jewelry for generations. **Oswal Emporium** (⊠ 30 Munro Rd., ☎ 562/360881 or 562/ 364567) has excellent inlaid marble items, though one customer, however, claimed to have been shipped a stone item instead of the marble piece that was paid for. **Subash Emporium** (⊠ 18/1 Gwalior Rd., ☎ 562/225828) was the first store to revive Agra marble work in the 1960s.

Fatehpur Sikri

★ ❺ *37 km (23 mi) southwest of Agra*

In the 16th century, the story goes, a mystic, Salim Chisti, blessed the Moghul emperor Akbar with a much-wanted male heir. In thanks, Akbar built a new capital in the saint's honor around 1571, adding "Fatehpur" to the name of the village where Salim Chisti had settled to form a name meaning "City of Victory." Standing on a rocky ridge overlooking the village, Fatehpur Sikri originally had a circumference of about 11 km (7 mi). Massive walls enclosed three sides, and a lake protected the fourth. What remains now is a beautiful cluster of royal dwellings on the top of the ridge. When some Elizabethans came to Fatehpur Sikri in 1583 to meet Akbar, they were amazed to see a city that exceeded London in both population and grandeur; they lost count of the rubies, diamonds, and plush silks. The remarkably preserved buildings, made mostly of red sandstone, incorporate architectural styles from Akbar's various Indian holdings, a reflection of the synthesizing impulse that characterized the third and greatest of the Moghul emperors. Akbar ruled here for only 15 years before moving his capital—perhaps in pursuit of water, perhaps for political reasons—to Lahore (now in Pakistan) and eventually back to Agra. Fatehpur Sikri's elegant blend of cultures and styles stands now as an intriguing ghost town in a picturesque setting, reflecting a high point in India's cultural history.

The usual starting point for a walk through Fatehpur Sikri is the Buland Darwaza (Great Gate) at the city's southwestern end. Unfortunately, the hawkers and guides who crowd the adjoining parking lot can be unrelenting in their efforts to assist you. If you arrive by car, you can avoid this minor annoyance by asking to be dropped at the subsidiary entrance at the northeastern end of the city: Coming from Agra, bear right just after passing through Agra Gate. The entrance—the main one in Akbar's day—is beside the imperial mint. Your driver can meet you outside the Buland Darwaza. The walk outlined below wends through the city from the subsidiary entrance on the Agra side.

Approaching the complex, you'll walk through the **Naubat Khana,** which was manned by drummers and musicians during imperial processions. Just ahead on the right is the **Mint,** faced by the smaller **Treasury** across the road. Fantasy and whimsy prevail in the Treasury's decorative stone *makaras,* or sea monsters, who were said to keep thieves from the crown jewels believed to have been kept in secret niches carved into the walls.

A few steps lead into the **Diwan-i-Am** (Hall of Public Audience), a large courtyard 366 ft long and 181 ft wide, with cloisters on three sides. Ahead is the balcony, where the emperor sat on his throne to meet subjects or observe celebrations and other spectacles. Chiseled marble screens on either side allowed the women of the court to watch the proceedings in privacy. Here, as the empire's chief justice, Akbar handed down his decisions: those condemned to die were reportedly impaled, hanged, or trampled under the feet of an elephant. In the courtyard behind the Diwan-i-Am, Akbar played pachisi (an early form of Parcheesi) using slave girls as life-size pieces.

The **Diwan-i-Khas** (Hall of Private Audience) is set back in the courtyard's far right corner. It looks like a two-story building with domed cupolas at each corner, but inside is one tall room where Akbar sat elevated on a platform connected by causeways to the balconies on four sides and supported by a stone column topped with an intricately carved lotus flower. The throne's position symbolized both the center of the world and the one god sought by several major religions, and removed the emperor from would-be assassins. Here Akbar is said to have held discussions with his ministers, the "nine jewels," each of whom occupied a window seat on the surrounding balcony.

Next to the Diwan-i-Khas at the northeast end of the complex is a small platform topped with a *chattri* (umbrella), constructed with brackets carved as elephant trunks, for Akbar's royal astrologer. Close by is the **Ankh Michauli** (Hide and Seek), named for Akbar's reported habit of playing the game with his harem inside the broad rooms and narrow passageways of this building. **Akbar's private chambers** abut the road on the south side of the courtyard; they're separated from the official buildings by a square fountain with a central platform where the famous court musician, Tansen, would sit and sing for the emperor. (The water softened the echo.) The small room near the fountain is thought to have been the **palace of Akbar's Turkish wife.** Covered with elaborate Persian carvings, many of them in angular zigzag patterns, this charming structure warrants close inspection. Silver supposedly plated the onetime sandalwood doors.

East of the Diwan-i-Khas, across a terrace designed as a life-size chessboard, rise the tiered colonnades of the five-story **Panch Mahal,** each floor smaller than the one below. This pavilion, the highest structure in Fatehpur Sikri, combines primarily Hindu and Buddhist architecture. The upper stories afford grand views of the city and the surrounding landscape. Behind the Panch Mahal, facing what was once a small garden, is the small **Nagina Mosque** used by the women of the court.

Farther along the terraces stands the **Hawa Mahal** (Palace of the Winds). Concealed by a red sandstone screen, this is a cool vantage point from which women could catch some breezes and peek out onto the trees or the court unseen. Beyond this, **Jodh Bai's Palace,** reputedly built for Akbar's Hindu wife, is the largest palace in the complex. The building incorporates elements of Gujarati design. The **House of Maryam** (on a diagonal between Jodh Bai's Palace and the Panch Mahal), supposedly the home of Akbar's Christian wife, is said to suggest the wooden architecture of the Punjab at that time. Look for the faded paintings of horses and elephants on the exterior walls. Though its actual purpose is not certain, **Birbal's Palace,** which sits northwest of Jodh Bai's Palace and the Hawa Mahal, is said to have housed the emperor's playfully irreverent Hindu prime minister. The palace's ornamentation makes use of Hindu motifs.

The city proper ends with Jodh Bai's Palace. As you emerge onto the road, the **Royal Stables** are on your left. Follow the left path down to the east gate of Akbar's **Jama Masjid** (Imperial Mosque); built around 1571 and designed to hold 10,000 worshipers, the mosque is still in active use. Note the deliberate incorporation of Hindu elements in the design—especially the decorations on the pillars.

In the courtyard of the Jama Masjid (opposite the Buland Darwaza) lies **Salim Chisti's tomb,** surrounded by walls of marble lace, each with a different design. Begun upon the saint's death in 1571 and finished nine years later, the tomb was originally faced with red sandstone but was refinished in marble by Jahangir, the heir Akbar received after the saint's blessing. Women of all faiths come here to cover the tomb with cloth and tie a string on the marble latticework in hopes of giving birth to a son. From here you can cross the courtyard and exit through the King's Gate (once reserved for Akbar alone).

Facing the mosque's southern gate is the exemplary **Buland Darwaza.** With its beveled walls and inset archways, the Great Gate rises 134 ft over a base of steps that raise it another 34 ft, dwarfing everything else in sight. Akbar built the gate after conquering Gujarat, in about 1576, and it set the style for later gateways, which the Moghuls built habitually as symbols of their power. An inscription quotes Jesus from the Koran: "The world is but a bridge. Pass over it, but build no houses on it"—an ironic reference to the ephemeral nature of even an emperor's monuments. Directly ahead is the parking lot, where you can prearrange to have you driver meet you.

To reach Fatehpur Sikri from Agra, hire a car and driver or join a tour. Plan to spend two or three hours wandering the grounds. Admission is Rs. 260 for foreigners. En route back to Agra, the small hotel in the **Gulistan Tourist Complex** (☎ 5613/882490) makes a convenient roadside lunch stop amid spacious gardens.

Gwalior

 120 km (75 mi) south of Agra

Now a bustling commercial city, Gwalior traces its history back to a legend: The hermit saint Gwalipa cured a chieftain named Suraj Sen of leprosy. On the hermit's advice, Suraj Sen founded his city here and named it for his benefactor. The city changed hands numerous times, and each dynasty left its mark. Gwalior was also the home of Tansen, whom many regard as the founder of North Indian classical music; and the annual Tansen Music Festival, in late November or early December, is one of the best in India.

The huge **Gwalior Fort** sits on a high, rocky plateau, and its 2-mi-long, 35-ft-high wall dominates the skyline. The first Moghul emperor, Babur, admired the structure, which may explain why it's the only pre-Moghul Hindu palace complex to survive in this region. The fort was often captured, achieving its greatest glory under the Tomar rulers of the 14th century. The main palace, **Man Mandir,** was once resplendent in gold and mosaic tiles. If you can, take a flashlight to explore the underground dungeons where the Moghuls kept their prisoners after finally capturing the fort in Akbar's time. Don't miss the beautifully carved 11th-century **Sas-Bahu** or the 9th-century **Teli ka Mandir** temples. The state museum in the **Gujari Mahal,** at the base of the fort, displays an excellent collection of sculptures and archaeological treasures dating as far back as the 2nd century BC. Ask to see the statue of the goddess Shalbhanjika, an exquisite miniature kept in the curator's custody. The English version of the sound-and-light show on the history of Gwalior fort starts at 7:30 and runs for 45 minutes. ✉ *Gwalior Rd.,* ☎ *751/480011.* 🎟 *Fort Rs. 250, museum Rs. 2, sound-and-light show Rs. 50.* ⊙ *Fort daily sunrise–sunset, museum Tues.–Sun. 10–5, sound-and-light show daily at 8.*

An opulent structure with Tuscan and Corinthian architecture, the **Jai Vilas Palace** belonged to the Scindias, Gwalior's rulers up through Indian Independence. Enormous chandeliers hang from the gilded ceiling of the massive **Durbar Hall.** In the dining room below, you can see the crystal train that carried liqueurs along the maharaja's banquet table. ✉ *Jayandra Gang, Lashkar,* ☎ *751/321101.* 🎟 *Rs. 75.* ⊙ *Thurs.–Tues. 10–5.*

Sarod Ghar is an elegantly designed museum with a collection of musical instruments from the family of India's best living sarod player, Amjad Ali Khan. ✉ *Jiwaji Ganj, Ustad Hafiz Ali Khan Marg, Lashkar,* ☎ *751/425607.* 🎟 *Rs. 10.* ⊙ *Tues.–Sun. 10–1 and 2–5.*

Lodging

$$$ 🏨 **Welcomgroup Usha Kiran Palace.** A Heritage Hotel, this white palace trimmed with filigreed sandstone has served as both a royal guest house and a royal residence. To see the view granted women of the royal family, stand in the passageway and look out through the stone screen over the beautifully landscaped lawns. The hotel exudes a gentle, old-world ambience, and while the Western-style rooms are not opulent, they are comfortable. ✉ *Jayendraganj, Lashkar, 474009, Madhya Pradesh,* ☎ *751/323993, 751/323994, 751/323213, or 751/323214,* FAX *751/321103,* WEB *www.welcomgroup.com or www.indianheritagehotels.com. 17 rooms, 10 suites. Restaurant, bar, indoor pool, badminton, croquet, horseback riding, billiards, meeting room. AE, DC, MC, V.*

$ 🏨 **MPSTDC Hotel Tansen.** Pleasant lawns surround this two-story white hotel. This place isn't luxurious, but it's clean and the staff is very friendly. Two-thirds of the rooms are air-conditioned and have TVs; the rest have fans only. ✉ *6 Gandhi Rd., 474009, Madhya Pradesh,* ☎ *751/340370 or 751/510555,* FAX *751/340371. 35 rooms, 1 suite. Restaurant, bar, meeting room. AE.*

Orchha

❼ *119 km (74 mi) southeast of Gwalior, 16 km (10 mi) east of Jhansi, 170 km (105 mi) northwest of Khajuraho*

In the 16th and 17th centuries the Hindu Bundela rulers, who were allies of the Moghuls, built up Orchha as a provincial capital on the banks of the winding Betwa River. In 1787 the Bundela capital was shifted from this isolated (but easy to defend) location, and today this sleepy town is little more than a village crowded with beautiful palaces, temples, and chattras—funerary monuments that resemble Muslim tombs but contain no remains of the Hindu rulers, who were cremated on the banks of the river. Orchha's isolation proved useful in the 1920s to Chandrashekhar Azad, a nationalist leader who hid from the British here, and even today you may feel you've entered a sort of benignly protected corner of the world.

Orchha has no real beaten path, so it's a great place to poke around in peace. Take a flashlight so you can explore the underground rooms and passageways that riddle the land beneath the town. Most of the sites are accessible around the clock, but some are open only from 10 to 5; inquire at the Sheesh Mahal Hotel, which also rents an audio tour. Unless otherwise indicated, all sites are free, though donations are always welcome at temples.

On the banks of the Betwa River next to Kanchana Ghat, a short walk upstream from the town proper, are 14 sandstone **cenotaphs** built in honor of the former rulers. The arches of these chattras—and their placement in a garden setting—suggest the architecture of the Moghuls and other Muslim rulers, yet spires, or *shikharas,* top the structures, recalling North Indian Hindu temples.

Towering over the center of Orchha opposite the fort, the **Chaturbhuj Temple** was built in the 16th century to house an image of the Hindu god Rama that would be brought to the capital by Kunwari, wife of Madhukar Shah (1554–92), the third and greatest of Orchha's kings. According to local lore, however, the temple was incomplete when Kunwari returned with the icon from Ayodhya, the mythic capital of Rama's kingdom. She installed it in her own palace, from which the image refused to move; that building is now the nearby Ram Raja Temple. A temple that never was, Chaturbhuj remains desolate.

Fronted by a pleasant plaza filled with people, trees, and vendors selling snacks and religious items, the **Ram Raja Temple** is the center of community life in Orchha. The structure, a large low-rise palace building in the shadow of the Chaturbhuj Temple, faces the bridge to the palace complex. The secular architecture and abandoned royal surroundings emphasize Rama's role as the ideal king in the Hindu pantheon. In late November, an annual reenactment of the epic hero's marriage takes place here. ☉ *Daily 8–12:30 and 7–9:30.*

Dinman Hardaul's Palace, below the fort, has some interesting underground rooms. The palace's **Phool Bagh** gardens have an ancient, intricate watering system.

★ The **Laxminarayan Temple,** less than 1 km (½ mi) west of town, is a 17th-century mix of temple and fort architecture. Vibrant well-preserved murals on the walls and ceilings depict both mythological and historical subjects. The upper terrace provides lovely views of the surrounding countryside. ➩ *Rs. 30.* ☉ *Daily 9–5.*

★ Perched on a small seasonal island where the river splits as it passes through town, the impressive **Sheesh Mahal** fort and palace is approached by a multiarch granite bridge. The first building you'll see is the 16th-century **Raj Mahal** (Royal Palace), which has beautiful murals and, from the upper stories, good views of the rest of the complex. Climbing further, the Sheesh Mahal Hotel is on your left; here you can pick up an excellent self-guided audio tour of the complex. Straight ahead stands the largest palace in the complex, the three-story, 17th-century **Jahangir Mahal.** Built for an expected, but never realized, visit from the Moghul emperor Jahangir (who had married, among others, the sister of an Orchha king), it elegantly blends Hindu and Moghul themes. Two stone elephants flank the main (east) entrance. North of these buildings is the **Rai Praveen Mahal,** a two-story brick palace named for the consort of the Bundela king Indramani. This one has accessible underground rooms, and an interesting system of watering its adjacent gardens from two wells. Scattered over the flood plain north of the royal residences are temples and ritual structures, including a compound containing three temples and several royal chattras. The images have been removed from the temples themselves, but the entrance to the sanctum of the largest one, **Panchmukhi Mahadeva** ("Shiva with Five Faces"), holds an appealing carving of the elephant-headed god Ganesh.

Lodging

$$$ ⊞ **Orchha Resort.** This air-conditioned hotel, on the river bank just opposite the cenotaphs, has a helpful and pleasant staff and comfortable modern rooms with unobtrusive decor in pale greens and burgundy. Its exterior design echoes the local sandstone, yet the hotel encroaches somewhat on its natural setting, near the river and some important monuments. The buffet restaurant serves a reasonable vegetarian version of the standard Mughlai-meets-Continental hotel menu. ⊠ *Kanchanaghat, Orchha, Tikamgarh district, 472246, Uttar Pradesh* ☎ *7680/52677 or 7680/52678,* FAX *7680/52677; or reserve through Oswal Motels and Resorts, 30 Munro Rd., Agra 282001,* ☎ *562/225710,* FAX *562/226520. 32 rooms. Restaurant, bar, pool, gym, sauna, laundry service, business services. AE, MC, V.*

$$ ⊞ **Sheesh Mahal.** Part of the fort-palace complex, this government-
★ run hotel was built in 1763 and has been renovated in a comfortable, if not luxurious, style. It's a great way to experience Orchha's past. The rooms are simply furnished, but they're clean; ask for the Royal Suite on the top floor, or the slightly less palatial Deluxe Room. Both afford wonderful views and are huge and regally decorated with wooden furniture that recalls the British Raj. A lack of phones and TVs in most rooms contributes to the peaceful environment. There's no air-conditioning, but you won't need it before March or April, and each room has a fan. ⊠ *Orchha, Tikamgarh district, 472246, Uttar Pradesh,* ☎ *7680/52624; 11/336–6528 in Delhi; or reserve through MPSTDC, Gangotri Bldg., 4th floor, T. T. Nagar, Bhopal 462003,* ☎ *755/778383,* FAX *755/774289. 8 rooms. Restaurant, bar. AE, MC, V.*

$ ⊞ **Betwa Cottages.** These charming modern cottages stand on the banks of the Betwa River. Each house has a little lawn outside, and the immaculate rooms have huge windows and are pleasantly furnished with comfortable beds and rugs. Some rooms are air-conditioned; the rest have fans. The chef prepares excellent kebabs and Chinese food. Even if you stay elsewhere, stop by for a cold *nimbu* soda (freshly squeezed lemon and soda) on your walk to the nearby monuments. ⊠ *Orchha, Tikamgarh district, 472246, Uttar Pradesh,* ☎ *7680/52618; 11/336–6528 in Delhi; or reserve through MPSTDC, Gangotri Bldg., 4th floor, T. T. Nagar, Bhopal 462003,* ☎ *755/778383,* FAX *755/774289. 10 cottages. Restaurant. MC, V.*

Shopping

An innovative development program, **Taragram** (⊠ 1077 Civil Lines, Jhansi, ☎ 7680/52821) focuses on the revival of traditional paper-making methods; here you can buy handmade notebooks and other items. It's just outside Orchha, where the road from town meets the main road between Jhansi and Khajuraho. The small local **market** has less hard-sell pressure than more touristy areas and sells an abundance of inexpensive mixed-metal objects, from votive *diyas* (prayer lamps) to *kumkum* boxes (with tiny compartments to separate color powders). For extraordinary value on beautifully crafted plaster sculptures of Hindu and Jain gods, head to the small, nameless **shop** run by the MP Archaeological Department, located just inside the main gate of the Palace Complex. Or ask at the Sheesh Mahal hotel, as there were plans at press time to relocate this outlet within the palace complex.

KHAJURAHO

The Vidhya hills in Madhya Pradesh's Chatarpur district form the backdrop to the small village of Khajuraho. Located 395 km (245 mi) southeast of Agra, this place is so rural that it's hard to imagine Khajuraho as the religious capital (10th–12th centuries) of the Chandela dynasty, one of the most powerful Rajput dynasties of Central India. The only significant river is some distance away, and the village seems far removed from any substantial economic activity. Yet this is where the Chandelas built 85 temples, 22 of which remain to give a glimpse of a time when Hindu art and devotion reached their apex.

During the Chandelas' rule, India was the Asian El Dorado. The temples' royal patrons were rich, the land was fertile, and everyone lived the 10th-century good life, trooping off to fairs, feasts, hunts, dramas, music, and dances. This abundance was the perfect climate for creativity, and temple-building was emerging as the major form of expression. There were no strict boundaries between the sacred and profane, no dictates on acceptable deities: Shiva, Vishnu, Brahma, and the Jains' saints were all lavishly honored, and excavations have even uncovered a complex of Buddhist temples as well. Despite the interest in heaven, the real focus was earth, and particularly the facts of human life. Here, immortalized in stone, virile men and voluptuous women cavort and copulate in the most intimate and erotic of postures. Khajuraho represents the best of Hindu temple sculpture: sinuous, twisting forms—human and divine—pulsing with life, tension, and conflict.

The Chandela dynasty reigned for five centuries, succumbing eventually to invaders. In 1100, Mahmud the Turk began a holy war against the "idolaters" of India, and by 1200 the sultans of Delhi ruled over the once-glorious Chandela domain. Khajuraho's temples lapsed into obscurity until their rediscovery by a British explorer in 1838.

The temples have more to offer than erotic sculpture. Their soaring shikharas are meant to resemble the peaks of the Himalayas, abode of Lord Shiva: starting with the smallest shikhara, over the entrance, each spire rises higher than the one before it, as in a range of mountains that seems to draw near the heavens. Designed to inspire the viewer toward the highest human potential, these were also the builders' attempts to reach upward, out of the material world, to *moksha*—the final release from the cycle of rebirth. One scholar has suggested that Khajuraho's temples were in effect chariots of the kings, carrying them off to a heavenly world resembling an idealized view of courtly life. Their combination of lofty structure and delicate sculpture gives them a unique sense of completeness and exuberance.

Of the 22 extant temples, all but two were made from sandstone mined from the banks of the River Ken, 30 km (19 mi) away. The stone blocks were carved separately, then assembled as interlocking pieces to form a temple. Though each structure is different, every temple observes precise architectural principles of shape, form, and orientation and contains certain essential elements: a high raised platform, an *ardh mandapam* (entrance porch), a mandapam (portico), an *antrala* (vestibule), and a *garbha griha* (inner sanctum). Some of the larger temples also have a walkway around the inner sanctum, a *mahamandapam* (hall), and subsidiary shrines on each corner of the platform, making a complete *panchayatana* (five-shrine complex).

A number of sculptural motifs run through the temples. The directional gods, for instance, have designated positions on each temple. Elephant-headed Ganesh faces north; Yama, the god of death, and his mount, a male buffalo, face south. The two goddesses guarding the entrance to the sanctum are the rivers Ganges and Yamuna. Other sculptures include the *apsaras* (heavenly maidens), found mainly inside the temples, and the Atlas-like *kichakas,* who support the temple ceilings on their shoulders. Many sculptures simply reflect everyday activities, such as a dance class. The sultry *nayikas* (human women) show various emotions, and the *mithunas* are amorous couples. The scorpion appears as an intriguing theme, running up and down the thighs of many female sculptures as a kind of erotic thermometer. It appears, too, on the breastbone of the terrible, emaciated goddess Chamundi on the corners of several temple platforms, suggesting a complex and imaginative view of sexuality on the part of the sculptors and their patrons.

No one knows for sure why erotic sculptures are so important here, though many explanations have been suggested. The female form is often used as an auspicious marker on Hindu gateways and doors, in the form of temple sculptures as well as domestic wall paintings. In the late classical and early medieval period, this symbol expanded into full-blown erotic art in many places, including the roughly contemporary sun temple at Modhera, in Gujarat, and the slightly later sun temple at Konark, in Orissa. Khajuraho legend has it that the founder of the Chandela dynasty, Chandravarman, was born of an illicit union between his mother and the moon god, which resulted in her ostracism. When he grew up to become a mighty king, his mother begged him to show the world the beauty and divinity of lovemaking. A common folk explanation is that the erotic sculptures protect the temples from lightning; and art historians have pointed out that many of the erotic panels are placed at junctures where some protection or strengthening agent might be structurally necessary. Others say the sculptures reflect the influence of a Tantric cult that believed in reversals of ordinary morality as a religious practice. Still others argue that sex has been used as a metaphor: the carnal and bestial sex generally shown near the bases of the temples represent uncontrolled human appetites, while the couples deeply engrossed in each other, oblivious to all else, represent a divine bliss, the closest humans can approach to God. The mystery lives on, but it's clear that the sculptors drew on a sophisticated and sensual worldly heritage, including the *Kama Sutra,* the classical Hindu love manual, some of whose specific instructions are illustrated here.

The best way to see Khajuraho is to hire a guide (especially for the Western Group of temples) and to visit the Western Group in the first rays of the morning sun, follow them with the Eastern Group, see the museum in the afternoon, and make it to the Chaturbhuj Temple in the Southern Group in time for sunset. The complex is open sunrise to sunset. Admission is $5/Rs. 250 to the temple grounds.

The popular 50-minute **sound-and-light show,** which runs in Hindi and English every evening, traces the story of the Chandela kings and the temples from the 10th century to the present. It takes place at 7 in the Western Group of Temples complex, and the cost is Rs. 200.

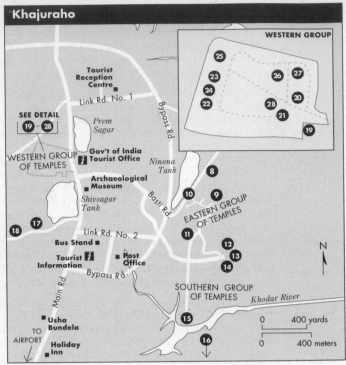

Khajuraho holds an annual **dance festival** set in part against the back-drop of the temples. If you'll be in India anytime around the beginning of March, don't miss this superb event. Contact Khajuraho's regional tourist office for details (☏ 7686/42347 or 7686/42348) or visit the Madhya Pradesh Tourism Web site (WEB www.mptourism.com).

For less than Rs. 50 you can rent a bicycle for the day from one of the many stands near the town center; it's a great way to get around this relatively traffic-free town and further afield. Entrepreneurial boys will gladly guide you around for another Rs. 50.

Eastern Group of Temples

Numbers in the text correspond to numbers in the margin and on the Khajuraho map.

Interspersed around the edges of Khajuraho village, the Eastern Group of temples includes four Hindu and four Jain temples, whose proximity attests to the religious tolerance of the times in general and the Chandela rulers in particular. Northernmost is the late-11th-century **Vamana Temple,** dedicated to Vishnu's dwarf incarnation (though the image in the sanctum looks more like a tall, sly child). The sanctum walls show unusual theological openness, depicting most of the major gods and goddesses; Vishnu appears in many of his forms, including the Buddha, his ninth incarnation. Outside, two tiers of sculpture are concerned mainly with the nymphs of paradise, who strike charming poses under their private awnings. The small, well-proportioned **Javari Temple,** just south of the Vamana Temple and roughly contemporary in origin, has a simplified three-shrine design. The two main exterior bands bear hosts of heavenly maidens.

The granite and sandstone **Brahma Temple,** one of the earliest temples here (circa 900), is probably misnamed. Brahma, a titular member of the triad of Hinduism's great gods, along with Shiva and Vishnu, rarely gets a temple to himself, and this one has a *linga*, the abstract, phallus-shape icon of Shiva. It differs in design from most of the other temples, particularly in the combination of materials and the shape of its shikhara.

⑪ All that's left of the the **Ghantai Temple** are its pillars, festooned with carvings of pearls and bells. Adorning the entrance of this little gem are an eight-armed Jain goddess riding the mythical bird Garuda and a relief illustrating the 16 dreams of the mother of Mahavira, the greatest religious figure in Jainism and a counterpart to the Buddha. The temple sits south of the Vamana, Javari, and Brahma temples, toward the Jain complex.

⑫ The late-11th-century **Adinath Temple,** a minor shrine, is set in a small walled compound southeast of Ghantai. Its porch and the statue of Tirthankara (literally, "Ford-Maker," a figure who leads others to liberation) Adinatha are modern additions. Built at the beginning of the Chandelas' decline, this temple is relatively small, but the shikhara and base are richly carved.

⑬ The **Parsvanath Temple,** built in the mid-10th century, is the largest and finest in the Eastern Group's Jain complex and holds some of the best sculpture in Khajuraho, including images of Vishnu. In contrast to the intricate calculations behind the layout of the Western Group, the plan for this temple is a simple rectangle, with a separate spire in the rear. Statues of flying angels and sloe-eyed beauties occupied with children, cosmetics, and flowers adorn the outer walls. The stone con-
⑭ veys even the texture of the women's thin garments. The **Shantinath** bears an inscription dating it to the early 11th century. It has been remodeled extensively and is still in active use, but it does contain some old Jain sculpture.

Southern Group of Temples

⑮ Though built in the customary five-shrine style, the 12th-century **Duladeo Temple** (about 900 yards south of the Eastern Group's Ghantai) looks flatter and more massive than most Khajuraho shrines. Probably the last temple built in Khajuraho, the Duladeo Temple lacks the usual ambulatory passage and crowning lotus-shape finials. Here, too, in this temple dedicated to Shiva, eroticism works its way in, though the amorous figures are discreetly placed.

⑯ The small, 12th-century **Chaturbhuj Temple,** nearly 3 km (2 mi) south of Duladeo, has an attractive colonnaded entrance and a feeling or verticality thanks to its single spire. It enshrines an impressive four-handed image of Vishnu that may be the single most striking piece of sculpture in Khajuraho. With a few exceptions, the temple's exterior sculpture falls short of the local mark (a sign of the declining fortunes of the empire), but this temple is definitely the best place in Khajuraho to watch the sun set.

A few hundred yards north of the Chaturbhuj Temple are ongoing excavations for a **Buddhist complex,** which archaeologists first announced in 1999. It will be years before reconstructions are complete, but you may find a recently unearthed piece of sculpture on view.

Western Group of Temples

Most of the Western Group is inside a formal enclosure with an entrance off Main Road, opposite the State Bank of India. The grounds are open daily from sunrise to sunset, and the admission fee (foreigners US $5 or Rs. equivalent) includes entrance to all the temples.

The first three temples, though considered part of the Western Group,
⑰ are actually at a slight distance from the enclosure. The **Chausath Yogini Temple,** on the west side of the Shivsagar Tank, a small artificial
lake, is the oldest temple at Khajuraho, possibly built as early as AD
820. It is dedicated to Kali, and its name refers to the 64 (*chausath*)
female ascetics (*yoginis*) who serve this fierce goddess in the Hindu pantheon. Unlike its counterparts of pale, warm-hued sandstone, this temple is made of granite and is the only one (so far excavated) in Khajuraho
that's oriented northeast-southwest instead of north-south. It was originally surrounded by 64 roofed cells for the figures of Kali's attendants;
only 35 cells remain. Scholarly supposition holds that this and a handful of other open-air temples, usually circular, in remote parts of India
were focal points for an esoteric cult.

⑱ Though **Lalguan Mahadeva** lies in ruins, and the original portico is missing, this Shiva temple is historically significant because it was built of
both granite and sandstone, marking the transition from Chausath Yogini to the later temples. Just outside the boundary of the Western
⑲ Group stands the **Matangesvara Temple,** the only one still in use here;
worship takes place in the morning and afternoon. The lack of ornamentation, square construction, and simple floor plan date this temple to the early 10th century. The building has oriel windows, a
projecting portico, and a ceiling of overlapping concentric circles. An
enormous linga, nearly 8½ ft tall, is enshrined in the sanctum.

Excavations at **Bija Mandal,** located 3 km (2 mi) southeast of the
Western Group, have uncovered the remains of several temples thought
to be even older than those already found. The temples date perhaps
to the 9th or 10th century.

Khajuraho's **Archaeological Museum,** across the street from Matangesvara, displays some exquisite carvings and sculptures from the temple
complexes recovered by archaeologists. The three galleries attempt to
put the various sculptures into context according to the deities they
represent. 🖼 *Rs. 10.* 🕐 *Sat.–Thurs. 10–5.*

⑳ **Varaha Temple** (circa 900–925) is dedicated to Vishnu's Varaha avatar,
or Boar Incarnation, which Vishnu assumed in order to rescue the earth
after a demon had hidden it in the slush at the bottom of the sea. In
the inner sanctum, all of creation is depicted on the massive and beautifully polished sides of a stone boar, who in turn stands on the serpent Shesha. The ceiling is carved with a lotus relief. As you enter the
Western Group complex, you'll see the temple to your left.

★ **㉑** Behind the Varaha Temple stands the **Lakshmana Temple,** dedicated
to Vishnu and the only complete temple remaining. Along with Kandariya Mahadeva and Vishvanath, this edifice represents the peak of
achievement in North Indian temple architecture. All three temples were
built in the early to mid-10th century, face east, and follow an elaborate plan resembling a double cross, with three tiers of exterior sculpture above the friezes on their high platforms. The ceiling of the
mandapam is charmingly carved with shell and floral motifs. The lintel over the entrance to the main shrine shows Lakshmi, goddess of
wealth and consort of Vishnu, with Brahma, Lord of Creation (on her
left) and Shiva, Lord of Destruction (on her right). A frieze above the
lintel depicts the planets. The relief on the doorway portrays the gods
and demons churning the ocean to obtain a pitcher of miraculous nectar from the bottom. The wall of the sanctum is carved with scenes
from the legend of Krishna (one of Vishnu's incarnations). An icon in
the sanctum with two pairs of arms and three heads represents Vishnu
as Vaikuntha, or the supreme god, and is surrounded by images of his

10 incarnations. Around the exterior base are some of Khajuraho's most famous sculptures, with gods and goddesses on the protruding corners, erotic couples or groups in the recesses, and apsaras and *sura-sundaris* (apsaras performing everyday activities) in-between. Along the sides of the tall platform beneath the temple, friezes depict social life, including battle scenes, festivals, and amorous sport.

★ ㉒ The **Kandariya Mahadev,** west of the Lakshmana Temple, is the largest and most evolved temple in Khajuraho in terms of the blending of architecture and sculpture, and one of the finest in India. Probably built around 1020, it follows the five-shrine design. Its central shikhara, which towers 102 ft above the platform, is actually made up of 84 subsidiary towers built up in increments. The feeling of ascent is repeated inside, where each succeeding mandapam rises a step above the previous one, and the garbha griha is higher still; dedicated to Shiva, this inner sanctum houses a marble linga with a 4-ft circumference. Even the figures on this temple are taller and slimmer than those elsewhere. The rich interior carving includes two beautiful *toranas* (arched doorways). Outside, three bands of sculpture around the sanctum and transept bring to life a whole galaxy of Hindu gods and goddesses, mithunas, celestial handmaidens, and lions.

㉓ The **Devi Jagdamba Temple** was originally dedicated to Vishnu, as indicated by a prominent sculpture over the sanctum's doorway. It now honors Parvati, Shiva's consort, but because her image is black—a color associated with Kali, goddess of wrath and an avatar of Parvati—it is also known as the Kali Temple. From the inside, its three-shrine design makes the temple appear to be shaped like a cross. The third band of sculpture has a series of erotic mithunas. The ceilings are similar to those in the Kandariya Mahadev, and the three-headed, eight-armed statue of Shiva is one of the best cult images in Khajuraho.

㉔ The small, mostly ruined **Mahadeva Temple** shares its platform with the Kandariya and the Devi Jagdamba. Now dedicated to Shiva, it may originally have been a subsidiary to the Kandariya Mahadev temple, probably dedicated to Shiva's consort. In the portico stands a remarkable statue of a man caressing a mythical horned lion.

㉕ The **Chitragupta Temple** lies slightly north of the Devi Jagdamba and resembles it in construction. In honor of the presiding deity, Surya—the sun god—the temple faces east, and its cell contains a 5-ft image of Surya complete with the chariot and seven horses that carry him across the sky. Surya also appears above the doorway. In the central niche south of the sanctum is an image of Vishnu with 11 heads; his own face is in the center, and the other heads represent his 10 (9 past and 1 future) incarnations. Sculptural scenes of animal combat, royal processions, masons at work, and joyous dances depict the lavish country life of the Chandelas.

㉖ Two staircases lead up to **Vishvanath Temple,** the northern flanked by a pair of lions and the southern by a pair of elephants. The Vishvanath probably preceded the Kandariya, but here only two of the original corner shrines remain. On the outer wall of the corridor surrounding the cells is an impressive image of Brahma, the three-headed Lord of Creation, and his consort, Saraswati. On every wall the form of woman dominates, portrayed in her daily 10th-century occupations: writing a letter, holding her baby, applying makeup, or playing music. The nymphs of paradise are voluptuous and provocative, and the erotic scenes, robust. An inscription states that the temple was built by Chandela King Dhanga in 1002. The temple sits on a terrace to the east of the Chitragupta and Devi Jagdamba temples. The simple **Nandi Tem-**

ple, which faces Vishvanath, houses a monolithic statue of Shiva's mount, the massive and richly harnessed sacred bull Nandi.

㉘ The small and heavily rebuilt **Parvati Temple,** near Vishvanath, was originally dedicated to Vishnu. The present icon is that of the goddess Ganga standing on her mount, the crocodile.

The collection at the **State Museum of Tribal and Folk Arts** includes more than 500 artifacts of terra-cotta, metal and wood crafts, paintings, jewelry, and masks from all over Madhya Pradesh. ⊠ *Chandella Cultural Complex, Rajnagar Rd.* 🎟 *Rs. 50.* ☉ *Tues.–Sun. noon–8.*

Dining and Lodging

$$$–$$$$ ✕ **Apsara.** This pleasant restaurant has lattice screens of teak and bird paintings on silk. The chef prepares good Indian and Continental dishes; try the tandoori kebabs or the vegetable *korma* (creamy tomato-and-onion curry). ⊠ *Jass Oberoi hotel,* ☎ *7686/72344. AE, DC, MC, V.*

$$ ✕ **Mediterraneo.** Eat on the rooftop or in a small dining room at this Italian restaurant near the Western Group. It has not a single frill, but the kitchen is spotless and the chef is from Italy. Go for pizza or one of the many pasta dishes. Payment is in rupees only. ⊠ *Jain Temple Rd., opposite Surya Hotel,* ☎ *7686/72340. No credit cards.*

$ ✕ **Raja Cafe.** This little open-air restaurant is a popular meeting place for local guides, so you can easily hire one here—or at the tourist office next door. Set under towering peepul trees, it's a great place for a cup of tea or a snack. The food is pretty basic, but the Continental dishes are popular, such as the chicken pancake béchamel (chicken in white sauce served in a crepe). Payment is in rupees only. ⊠ *Opposite Western Group entrance on main square,* ☎ *no phone. No credit cards.*

$$$ 🏨 **Chandela.** This elegant hotel run by the Taj group centers on a lovely pool and is surrounded by gardens. The Western-style rooms are perfectly comfortable, and each has a balcony or patio. ⊠ *Khajuraho 471606, Madhya Pradesh,* ☎ *7686/72355 through 7686/72365; 11/ 332–22333 in Delhi,* 🖷 *7686/72366,* 🌐 *www.tajhotels.com. 94 rooms, 4 suites. 2 restaurants, bar, coffee shop, pool, hair salon, miniature golf, tennis court, badminton, croquet, health club, baby-sitting, business services, meeting room, travel services. AE, DC, MC, V.*

$$$ 🏨 **Holiday Inn Khajuraho.** From the outside, the Holiday Inn looks more like an American condo complex than a hotel, but its interior, with plenty of marble, chandeliers, and curving staircases, is surprisingly elegant. The Western-style rooms are decorated in soft cream shades and have large bay windows, some with temple views. Suites incorporate cultural themes in the decor. ⊠ *Airport Rd., Khajuraho 471606, Madhya Pradesh,* ☎ *7686/72301 or 7686/72302; 11/621–9700 in Delhi;* 🖷 *7686/72304;* 🌐 *www.holidayinn.com. 56 rooms, 8 suites. 2 restaurants, bar, coffee shop, pool, hair salon, tennis court, health club, jogging, baby-sitting, meeting room, travel services. AE, DC, MC, V.*

$$$ 🏨 **Jass Trident Khajuraho.** The main motifs at this Oberoi just over
★   half a mile from the Western Group of temples are white marble and plants in brass pots. Rooms are modern and have balconies overlooking either the pool or the hills around town. ⊠ *Khajuraho 471606, Madhya Pradesh,* ☎ *7686/72344, 7686/72376, or 7686/72377,* 🖷 *7686/72345,* 🌐 *www.oberoihotels.com. 91 rooms, 3 suites. Restaurant, bar, pool, tennis court, health club, travel services, meeting room. AE, DC, MC, V.*

$$$ 🏨 **Usha Bundela.** This two-story, white colonial-style hotel is nicely illuminated and has abundant marble, which gives it a generally cool feel. The rooms are Western and very comfortable, with French doors and balconies overlooking pleasant gardens. ⊠ *Khajuraho 471606, Mad-*

hya Pradesh, ☎ *7686/72386 or 7686/72387; 11/552–0914 in Delhi,* FAX *7686/42385,* WEB *www.ushashriramhotels.com. 68 rooms, 2 suites. Restaurant, bar, pool, meeting room, travel services. AE, DC, MC, V.*

$$ 🛏 **Ken River Lodge.** Set near Panna National Park, about a half-hour's
★ drive from Khajuraho, this unique lodge has village-style mud huts and spacious tents, all with running hot water and private baths and showers. The restaurant is a platform built on tree limbs on the banks of the Ken River. The Rs. 3,500 fee includes all meals and two trips into the park. ✉ *Near Madla Village, Panna district 488001 Madhya Pradesh,* ☎ *7686/42291 or 7732/75235. 4 cottages, 4 tents. Restaurant, beach, boating, fishing. No credit cards.*

$ 🛏 **Jhankar.** This one-story government-owned hotel rents spacious, clean
★ rooms with modern decor. Rooms have either air-conditioning or fans.
✉ *Airport Rd., Khajuraho 471606 Madhya Pradesh,* ☎ *7686/74063 or 7686/74194; 11/334–1187 in New Delhi; or reserve through MP-STDC, Gangotri Bldg., 4th floor, T. T. Nagar, Bhopal 462003, Madhya Pradesh,* ☎ *755/778383,* FAX *755/774289. 19 rooms. Restaurant, bar. MC, V.*

Shopping

Numerous curio shops around the Western Group of temples sell sundry souvenirs, including humorous knockoffs of erotic sculptures and examples of tribal metalwork. **Shilpgram** (☎ 7686/72280), just off Airport Road, is a government project that hosts craftspeople from all over India for extended residences during the peak travel season; for Rs. 100 you can watch the artisans at work as you shop, and enjoy dance and drama performances in the evening. The campus is open daily from 11 to 9.

Side Trips

If you have time, take an extra day to explore and picnic in the beautiful country around Khajuraho. A bicycle, which can be rented from one of the many stands near the town center, is a good way to explore the area. Backed by the distant mountains, **Khajuraho Village** (west of the main square, near the Jain temples) is a typical Indian village, its small streets crammed with animals and bicycles. Drive or bike to the
★ **Gharial Sanctuary** on the Ken River, 28 km (17 mi) away; the park was set up to protect the slender-snouted crocodile and has some
★ lovely waterfalls. At **Panna National Park** you can see the elusive tiger and a host of other wildlife. Only 31 km (19 mi) from Khajuraho, it's still relatively undisturbed by visitors.

BHOPAL AND ENVIRONS

Bhopal, the capital city of Madhya Pradesh, blends natural beauty—it's known as the "City of Lakes"—ancient history, and modern comforts. Fine mosques, palaces, and markets take you back to the city's 18th- and 19th-century roots (little remains of the 11th-century settlement upon which Bhopal was built). Yet much of the city is new and modern, and it's easy to get around. And with superb accommodations, Bhopal makes for an ideal base for day trips nearby, such as Sanchi.

Bhopal

㉙ *744 km (461 mi) south of Delhi, 383 km (237 mi) southwest of Khajuraho*

Bhopal may best be known to outsiders for the toxic-gas leak at a Union Carbide chemical plant in 1984, which killed anywhere from 4,000 to tens of thousands of people and injured thousands more. Perhaps because Bhopal is known for this tragedy, the city has been slow to develop as a tourism destination, meaning its charms have thus far been preserved from the excesses of the tourism industry. Part of the city's appeal lies in its reputation as a nurturing ground for the study, writing, and performance of Urdu poetry. Poetry readings draw the kind of crowds you'd expect at a pop concert elsewhere. One urban legend even tells of a Bhopal taxi driver who kidnapped his favorite poet and forced him to recite.

Construction of the **Taj-ul-Masajid** mosque began during the reign of Bhopal's most famous queen, Shah Jehan Begum (1868–1901), but was completed only in 1971. The red-sandstone facade is striking; inside, a sense of tranquillity envelops you as you remove your shoes at the entrance and step onto smooth marble. Come just before dusk, when the sun sets over the nearby lake and small boys play cricket in the spacious courtyard. ⊠ *Taj-ul-Masajid.*

The only way into the 1837 **Jama Masjid** mosque, with its gold-crowned minarets, is on foot through the bustling narrow lanes of the central Chowk market. It's best to combine a visit to the mosque with a shopping excursion; after an hour of negotiating prices, you may appreciate the spiritual respite. Nearby the entrance to the market, look for the 1860 **Moti Masjid** mosque, similar in style to Delhi's Jama Masjid.

The small **Birla Museum,** attached to the Lakshmi Narayan Temple, houses a collection of ancient sculpture from the Raisen, Sehore, Mandsaur, and Shahdol districts of Madhya Pradesh. ⊠ *Lakshmi Narayan Temple,* ☎ *755/551388.* ☜ *Rs. 5.* ☉ *Tues.–Sun. 9–5.*

The **Government Archaeological Museum** displays sculpture from all over Madhya Pradesh and copies of paintings from the Bagh Caves near Mandu. ⊠ *2 Banganga Rd., opposite Ravindra Bhavan.* ☜ *Free.* ☉ *Tues.–Sun. 9–5.*

Indian architect Charles Correa designed Bhopal's center for visual and performing arts, **Bharat Bhavan,** to curve in harmony with its surroundings. Beneath the unobtrusive facade is a large gallery space with impressive collections of modern and tribal arts, a repertory theater, libraries of Indian poetry, and a café. An eclectic poetry display lists contributions from international poets, including a gem by Allen Ginsberg. Even if your visit doesn't coincide with a cultural event, this is a pleasant place to soak up some contemporary Indian culture and lounge away an afternoon. ⊠ *Shamla Hills,* ☎ *755/540353.* ☉ *Feb.– Oct., Tues.–Sun. 2–8; Nov.–Jan., Tues.–Sun. 1–7.*

Tribal Habitat (Museum of Man) consists of a museum of painting, sculpture, and costume as well as an open-air park exhibition of some 40 different tribal houses from all over India. A stroll around the quiet grounds transports you from one tribal culture to another. Avoid venturing off the path into the long grass, the authentic natural habitat of snakes. ⊠ *Shamla Hills,* ☎ *755/545458.* ☜ *Free.* ☉ *Tues.–Sun. 10–6.*

Van Vihar (Bhopal National Park), which runs along Upper Lake just beyond Tribal Habitat, is a glorified zoo really, but it makes for a pleasant walk. Park stations allow you to observe tigers, leopards, lions, bears, and crocodiles from the safe side of a fenced ravine. The best time to view wildlife is just before feeding times (usually 7 AM and 4:30 PM). If you bring a car, leave it at the entrance or have the driver drop you along the route so that you can walk back without disturbing the animals. ⊠ *Zoo rd.* ☜ *Foreigners Rs. 100, cars Rs. 30.* ☉ *Sat.–Thurs. 7–11 and 3–5:30.*

In Bhopal, the **Boat Club,** on the road to the zoo, rents sail, motor, and paddle boats for exploration on Upper Lake; fees range from Rs. 50–Rs. 150 a day, and you can also arrange for a guide.

Dining and Lodging

$$ ✕ **At Home in Bhopal.** Tour guide Mrs. Chopra serves delicious, healthful vegetarian cooking—generally dal, rice, roti, and vegetables—in her home. Bottled water and soft drinks are available. After eating, you're welcome to try your hand at rolling and making fresh roti. ✉ *Radiant Travels, 24 Ahmedabad Rd., ☎ 755/738540 or 755/738541. Reservations required. No credit cards.*

$$$ ✕⊡ **Jehan Numa Palace.** Expect to be treated by the seasoned staff
★ as an honored guest and not just a room number at this graceful hotel within walking distance of local sights. Most rooms open off a garden shaded by a sprawling mango tree and centered on a lotus fountain. Rooms are simple but well-appointed with solar-heated water, fresh flowers, and painted wicker chairs outside each door in the garden. A path winds through connecting gardens to a large palm-fringed pool, a spa, and stables. Shahnama ($$$–$$$$) serves Indian fare. ✉ *157 Shamla Hill, 462013, Madhya Pradesh, ☎ 755/661100 or 755/235100, ꜰᴀX 755/661720, ᵂᴱᴮ www.hoteljehanumapalace.com. 60 rooms. 2 restaurants, bar, pool, hair salon, tennis court, gym, horseback riding, jogging, shop, business services, travel services. AE, DC, MC, V.*

$$$ ⊡ **Noor-Us-Sabah Palace.** Built in the 1920s, the "Light of Dawn" palace, overlooking Bhopal Lake, is today a Heritage Hotel, resplendent with Italian white marble, blue and gold walls, and crystal chandeliers. Reception areas brim with antiquities, including a 200-year-old royal wedding palanquin and a model moti mosque (the size of a small room) carved from sandalwood. Rooms are contemporary, each with its own private terrace overlooking the lake. Rooms on the first floor afford the best views and have attractive decor in soft pinks and paisley. ✉ *VIP Rd., Kohe-Fiza, 462001, Madhya Pradesh, ☎ 755/749101, ꜰᴀX 755/749110, ᵂᴱᴮ www.welcomheritage.com. 70 rooms. 2 restaurants, bar, pool, hair salon, gym, shops, business services, travel services. AE, DC, MC, V.*

Shopping

At the **Chowk** market, in the heart of the old city, you can spend hours just wandering or bargaining for all manner of traditional Bhopali crafts and specialities, including silver jewelry, saris, ornate beadwork, and embroidered purses and pillows. The **MP Government Emporium** (✉ 23, Shopping Center, New Market, ☎ 755/554162), sometimes also called "Mrignayani," sells a wide range of textiles, ready-to-wear clothing, leather goods, jewelry, and metalwork crafts. **Mrignayanee** (✉ GTB Complex, New Market, ☎ 755/761656) specializes in saris rich with gold- and silver-thread embroidery. It also carries ready-to-wear blouses and brilliant textiles, as well as raw silks.

Side Trips from Bhopal

One of the most important Buddhist sites in India and a World Heritage Site, serene **Sanchi** consists of a group of stupas and abandoned monasteries situated on a remote hilltop. The famous first stupa, its gates elaborately carved with stories of the life of Buddha, is said to be one of India's oldest stone structures, dating to Mauryan emperor Ashoka's reign in the 3rd century BC. Nearby sit the remains of the 5th-century Gupta Temple, one of the earliest known examples of temple architecture in India. A museum near the entrance to Sanchi displays pieces from the excavation of the site. *46 km (29 mi) northeast of Bhopal on rural road.* ⊠ *Foreigners US$10 or Rs. equivalent.* ☉ *Sat.–Thurs. sunrise–sunset.*

A 15-km (9-mi) detour from Sanchi takes you to ruins at Vidisha, and the **Udaygiri Caves,** a group of cave sanctuaries carved into a sandstone hill, where some of the distinctive examples of Gupta art date to the 4th and 5th centuries AD. Don't miss Cave 3, where the face of Shiva appears on a linga with his third eye prominent upon his forehead, or Cave 12, where an image of Vishnu reclines on a snake bed. ▣ *Free.* ◐ *Dawn–dusk.*

★ More than 100 of the **Bhimbetka Caves,** with their well-preserved prehistoric art, are accessible to visitors along a 4-km (2½-mi) path. With little human habitation and minimal signs posted in the area, it's easy to pretend you've stepped back in time. Each cave serves as a window on the past, with fascinating depictions of animals and humans as well as religious symbols, instruments, and weapons. If you go with a guide, you can see a dramatic sample of about 10 caves in less than an hour, but this is a good place to bring a picnic, wander, and explore. The area is isolated, so if you go without a guide make sure you leave before dark. You can combine a visit here with a trip to Bhojeshwar Temple for a half-day or full-day excursion. *46 km (29 mi) south of Bhopal on rural road.* ▣ *Free.* ◐ *Daily, sunrise–sunset.*

The 12th-century **Bhojeshwar Temple,** dedicated to Shiva, includes a huge linga—7½ ft tall with an 18-ft circumference. An apparatus of ropes and pulleys "feeds" the linga with offerings of fresh milk. The temple was never completed, and the earthen ramp used to raise it still stands. In the tiny village of Bhojpur, the temple can be combined with a visit to the nearby Bhimbetka Caves. ✉ *Near Bhojpur village.* ▣ *Free.* ◐ *Daily, 24 hrs.*

VARANASI AND LUCKNOW

Spread out along the Ganges River, the interior lanes and river ghats of ancient Varanasi throb with religious and commercial energy like no other place in India. Sarnath, just north of Varanasi, is the historic center of the Buddhist world, and Bodhgaya, east of Varanasi in the state of Bihar, serves as a present-day international center of Buddhist worship. European-flavored Lucknow, the capital of Uttar Pradesh, is an easy diversion between Varanasi and Delhi.

Varanasi

676 kn (419 mi) northeast of Bhopal, 406 km (252 mi) east of Khajuraho, 765 km (474 mi) southeast of Delhi, 677 km (420 mi) northwest of Calcutta

Varanasi has been the religious capital of Hinduism through all recorded time. No one knows the date of the city's founding, but when Siddhartha Gautama, the historic Buddha, came here around 550 BC to deliver his first teaching, he found an ancient and developed settlement. Contemporary with Babylon, Nineveh, and Thebes, Varanasi has been called the oldest continuously inhabited city on earth.

Every devout Hindu wants to visit Varanasi to purify body and soul in the Ganges, to shed all sin, and, if possible, to die here in old age and achieve moksha, release from the cycle of rebirth. Descending from the Himalayas on its long course to the Bay of Bengal, the Ganges is believed by Hindus to hold the power of salvation in each drop. Pilgrims seek that salvation along the length of the river, but their holiest site is Varanasi. Every year, the city welcomes millions of pilgrims for whom these waters—fouled by the pollution of humans both living and dead—remain pristine enough to cleanse the soul.

Commonly called Banaras, and, by devout Hindus, Kashi ("Resplendent with Light"), Varanasi has about 1 million inhabitants. Its heart is a maze of streets and alleys, hiding a disorderly array of at least 2,000 temples and shrines. Domes, minarets, pinnacles, towers, and derelict 18th-century palaces dominate the river's sacred left bank. The streets are noisy and rife with color, and the air hangs heavy, as if in collaboration with the clang of temple gongs and bells. Some houses have simply decorated entrances; other buildings are ornate with Indian-style gingerbread on balconies and verandas. You're likely to encounter funeral processions; cows munching on garlands destined for the gods; and, especially near the Golden Temple (Kashi Vishvanath) and the centrally located Dashashvamedh Ghat, assertive hawkers and phony guides.

Its variety of shrines notwithstanding, Varanasi is essentially a temple city dedicated to Shiva, Lord of Destruction. Shiva is typically said to live in the Himalayas, but myths say he was unable to leave Kashi after manifesting himself here. Exiling the earthly maharaja to Ram Nagar, across the river, Shiva took up permanent residence here. (As a popular song has it, in Varanasi "every pebble is a Shiva linga.") The city itself is said to rest on a prong of Shiva's trident, above the cycles of creation, decay, and destruction that prevail in the rest of the world.

The maze of lanes may seem daunting, but you're never far from the river, where you can hire a boat for a quiet ride. Banarasis, as the locals call themselves, typically hire boats at sundown for twilight excursions, sometimes with tiny candlelit lamps made of leaves and flowers which they leave on the water as offerings. The Ganges turns sharply at Varanasi to flow south to north past the city, giving the riverbank a perfect alignment with the rising sun. In sacred geography the city is demarcated by the Ganges to the east and two small rivers—the Varana to the north, which winds by the cantonment area and joins the Ganges near Raj Ghat, and the Asi, a small stream in the south that has been diverted as a sanitation measure.

Traditionally, Varanasi is seen as a field divided into three sections named after important temples to Shiva. Omkareshvara is the namesake temple in the northern section, which is probably the oldest area but is now impoverished and seldom visited by pilgrims. The central section is named after Kashi Vishvanath, the famous "Golden Temple." Vishvanath itself means "Lord of the Universe," one of Shiva's names, and there are actually many Vishvanath temples. The southern area, the Kedar Khand, is named for Kedareshvara, a temple easily picked out from the river thanks to the vertical red and white stripes painted on its walls, a custom of the South Indian worshipers who are among the temple's devotees. The ghats stretch along the river from Raj Ghat in the north to Asi Ghat in the south; beyond Asi is the university, across the river from Ram Nagar Fort and Palace. The city itself spreads out behind the ghats, with the hotels in the cantonment area about 20 minutes from the river by auto-rickshaw.

A Good Walk

Numbers in the text correspond to numbers in the margin and on the Varanasi map.

To get a sense of the pilgrim's experience, walk from Dashashvamedh Road down the relatively broad, shop-lined lane to Vishvanath Temple. The lane turns sharply right at a large image of the elephant-headed god Ganesh, then passes the entrance to the temple of Vishvanath's consort, Annapurna, on the right, and **Kashi Vishvanath Temple** ㉚ itself. Just past the temple complex the Vishvanath lane intersects with

Kachauri Gali, a lane (*gali*) named for the small, deep-fried puris, or *kachauris,* cooked here for pilgrims.

Turning left, the entrance to the **Gyanvapi Mosque** ㉛ compound (closed to non-Muslims) is on the left. The short, stepped lane passes under a room in a house that spans both sides of the lane; the compound around the mosque is now cordoned off with steel bars, in response to an intermittent movement to restore the mosque as a Hindu temple. On the left are the Gyanvapi well and a cluster of tree-shaded Hindu shrines. Here many Hindus begin their pilgrimage to Kashi, declaring their purpose with the help of a Brahmin *panda* (temple priest) in a rite known as *sankalp,* or declaration of intention. Here a young tout will probably offer to escort you to a rooftop from which you can see into the Vishvanath Temple compound. The view is fascinating; just know that this process will also involve offers of tea and the display of various wares. Farther up Kachauri Gali, a lane on the right is marked by a sign pointing toward Lalita Ghat; take this lane to a junction beside a small temple dedicated to Neelkanth Mahadev. On the right, a lane marked Bishwanath Singh Lane leads to the main cremation ground, just upstream from **Manikarnika Ghat** ㉜. You can often find your way just by following the processions of funeral biers that pass with startling regularity toward Manikarnika, their bearers moving swiftly and chanting, "Ram nam satya hai" ("God's name is truth").

Walk north (upstream) past the broad, gradual steps of Scindia Ghat to the steps of Panchganga Ghat, the mythic confluence of five invisible rivers. The **Alamgir Mosque** ㉝ towers above Panchganga, and from its relatively short minaret you get a sweeping view of Varanasi and the Ganges. You can walk along the ghats back to **Dashashvamedh Ghat** ㉞, where a rickshaw-wallah can peddle you onward or you can take a boat.

Down the right fork of Dashashvamedh Road is Prayag Ghat. Here, at the top of the ghats on the right, is the white **Shitala Temple** ㉟. Continue south along the ghats fronting the somewhat quieter Kedar Khand section of town, which in ancient times was heavily forested and dotted with hermitages. After about 10 minutes you'll see steep steps leading up toward a house at the top of Chausath Yogini Ghat— a few yards up the lane on the right is the **Chausath Yogini Temple** ㊱. Farther south, you'll reach the **Dhobi Ghat** ㊲, where washermen and -women beat clothes against stone slabs on the water's edge. A little farther south is the **Kedareshvara Temple** ㊳, recognizable from the river by its South Indian–style red and white stripes. Anywhere along this section, you can climb up the ghats and enter the city, where you'll soon reach a broader gali that runs parallel to the river through Bengali Tola, home to a large community from Bengal as well as from South India. You can pick up transport a little farther south, where a broad road reaches the river by the small burning ground at Harish Chandra Ghat, preferred cremation site of the *panditas,* or learned Brahmins. If you'd like to break for lunch, head to the nearby restaurant Sindhi.

Another half hour's walk south brings you to Asi Ghat. Tulsi Ghat, just north of Asi, is where Tulsi Das, a medieval saint, is said to have composed his hugely popular Hindi version of the *Ramayana* epic (translated and revised from the Sanskrit). The ghat is now home to the offices of the Swachha Ganga Campaign, a movement to clean up the Ganges. From the top of Tulsi Ghat, the lane to the right leads to Lolark Kund, a deep step well surrounded by several small but important shrines. This is an extraordinary place to visit just after sunrise, when people from the neighborhood offer devotions. Asi Ghat itself

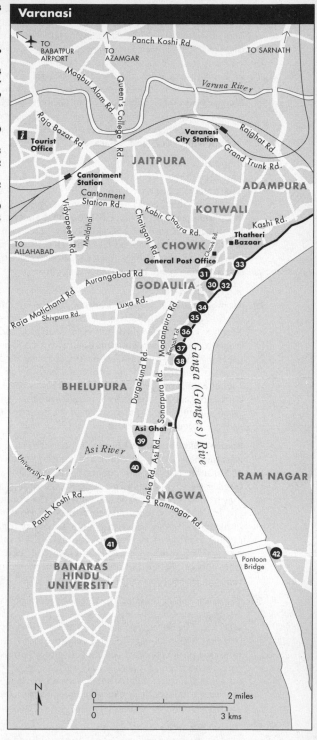

Varanasi

is an important bathing point and the only ghat in Varanasi where bathers access the river from a plain mud bank rather than stone steps. From here, walk or hire a cycle-rickshaw to take you to the **Durga Temple** ㉟, or Monkey Temple, a few hundred yards west of the river. From here you can walk or drive to **Sankat Mochan Temple** ㊵, whose *mahant,* or head priest, leads the Swachha Ganga Campaign. A 20-minute cycle-rickshaw ride or shorter cab ride takes you to the **Bharat Kala Bhavan Museum** ㊶ at Banaras Hindu University. Have your driver wait for you, and if you have time (and if, in the case of a cycle-rickshaw, your driver has the energy), proceed from the university across the Ganges to **Ram Nagar Fort and Palace** ㊷.

TIMING

The first part of this tour, starting and ending at Dashashvamedh Road, takes about two hours. The walk from Dashashvamedh to Kedareshvara takes 45 minutes if you stop to see the temples, plus 30 more minutes from Kedar Ghat to Asi Ghat. The last part of the tour, from Asi Ghat to Bharat Kala Bhavan, takes two more hours. A trip to Ram Nagar by car adds about two hours more. Varanasi is a labyrinth, however, so by all means allow some time to get lost. A boat ride will also stretch your sightseeing time.

Sights to See

㉝ **Alamgir Mosque.** From a dramatic high point, the Alamgir Mosque overlooks the Ganges River. Destroying the 17th-century temple Beni Madhav ka Darera, which had been dedicated to Vishnu, the Moghul emperor Aurangzeb built this mosque with an odd fusion of Hindu (lower portions and wall) and Muslim (upper portion) designs. Panchganga Ghat, down below, is an important bathing point, particularly on Makar Sankranti (January 14), when the sun crosses the tropic of Capricorn as the earth shifts on its axis following the winter solstice. ⊠ *From Dashashvamedh or Manikarnika ghats, head north along the river; the mosque towers above Panchganga Ghat.*

㊶ **Bharat Kala Bhavan Museum.** No one interested in Indian art should miss this museum on the campus of Banaras Hindu University, just south of Varanasi's traditional boundary. The permanent collection includes textiles, excellent Hindu and Buddhist sculptures, and miniature paintings from the courts of the Moghuls and the Hindu princes of the Punjab Hills. One sculpture with particular power is from Varanasi's immediate area—a 4th-century Gupta-dynasty frieze depicting Krishna (an incarnation of Vishnu) holding up Mt. Govardhan to protect his pastoral comrades from the rain. Have your car or rickshaw wait, as transport can be hard to find on the university's sprawling campus. ⊠ *Banaras Hindu University, Lanka.* 🕮 *Rs. 40.* ☉ *Mon.–Sat. 10:30–6.*

㊱ **Chausath Yogini Temple.** The interesting temples between Prayag and Asi ghats include this one, which is at the top of a particularly steep set of steps by the ghat of the same name. Originally devoted to a Tantric cult that is also associated with an important ruined temple at Khajuraho, it's now dedicated to Kali (the goddess most popular with Bengalis), who is known here simply as "Ma"—Mother. The worshipers now are mainly widows from Varanasi's Bengali quarter; in the early morning you'll see these women coming for the *darshan* (vision) of Kali after bathing in the Ganges. ⊠ *Just above Chausath Yogini Ghat.*

★ ㉞ **Dashashvamedh Ghat.** About 70 stepped ghats line a 4-mi stretch of the Ganges, effortlessly wedding the great Hindu metropolis to the river. Numerous lingas remind pilgrims that they're under Shiva's care here. If you decide to hire a boat, an essential Varanasi experience, come here, the unofficial "main" ghat for most purposes. The best time to see the ghats is at sunrise, when a solemn group of people and even animals—lit by the sun's darkly golden first rays—hover on the water's edge, bent on immersion in the holy stream. As you float on the river, you'll see young bodybuilders, members of the city's many wrestling clubs, exercising. Older men sit cross-legged in meditation or prayer, and pandas seated under huge umbrellas pray for their pilgrim clients. Some devotees drink from the polluted water. A carcass may even float by. ⊠ *Head east to the water from Godaulia Crossing, the central traffic circle in the Chowk district.*

㊲ Dhobi Ghat. At the Dhobi Ghat, south of Dashashvamedh, washermen and -women do early morning laundry by beating it against stones in the river while their donkeys bray disconsolately on the bank. This may be the sight that moved Mark Twain to declare that "a Hindu is someone who spends his life trying to break stones with wet clothes."

㊴ Durga Temple. This 18th-century shrine, dedicated to the goddess Durga, Shiva's consort, stands beside a large, square pool of water due west of Asi Ghat. The shikhara is formed on top of five lower spires, a convergence symbolizing the belief that all five elements of the world (earth, air, water, fire, and ether) merge with the supreme. This shrine is also called the Monkey Temple, for good reason: the pests are everywhere, and they'll steal anything. ⊠ *Durgakund Rd.*

NEED A
BREAK?

The **Vaatika Café** on the riverbank at Asi Ghat serves excellent pizza made with yak-milk cheese from Nepal, as well as pasta dishes, bona fide espresso, and other unlikely delicacies.

㉛ Gyanvapi Mosque. Moghul emperor Aurangzeb pulled down Vishveswara Temple to erect this mosque, and the building's foundation and rear still show parts of the original temple. The tallest of the mosque's minarets, which dominated the skyline of the holy city, collapsed during a flood in 1948. The surrounding area—just next to Kashi Vishvanath, the Golden Temple—has been the focus of Hindu revivalist attempts to reconsecrate the site of the former temple, and is currently staffed with police and fenced with barbed wire. It's normally very sedate, however, and is an important starting point for Hindu pilgrims.

㉚ Kashi Vishvanath Temple. Dedicated to Shiva, this temple in the old city is the most sacred shrine in Varanasi. Known as the Golden Temple for the gold plate on its spire—a gift from the Sikh maharaja Ranjit Singh in 1835—the temple is set back from the Ganges between the Dashashvamedh and Manikarnika ghats. Vishvanath is technically off-limits to non-Hindus, so your best bet is to glimpse it from the top floor of the house opposite (pay the owner a small fee). You'll see men and women making offerings to the linga in the inner shrine. The present temple was built by Rani Ahalyabai of Indore in 1776, near the site of the original shrine, which had been destroyed by Aurangzeb. ⊠ *Vishvanath Gali.*

NEED A
BREAK?

From the lane that leads from Kashi Vishvanath Temple to Dashashvamedh Road, turn right toward Godaulia Crossing. To the left, in the second-to-last cul-de-sac before the crossing (opposite a sign for the Union Bank of India), a short lane lined with cloth merchants leads to the friendly, slightly divey **Ayyar's Café** (⊠ Raman Katra, Dashashvamedh Rd.). Here milky, sweet South Indian filter coffee and South Indian desserts are served on worn marble tables at a slight remove from the city's tumult.

㊳ Kedareshvara Temple. You can recognize this temple, the most important Shiva temple in this part of town, by its candy-stripe red and white walls. Take off your shoes at the small rear door at the top of the ghats before entering. The linga here is an unsculpted stone and is said to have emerged spontaneously when a pure-hearted but feeble devotee of Shiva prayed for a chance to visit the famous Kedareshvara Shiva temple in the Himalayas. Shiva is the god of destruction and fierce in aspect, but, paradoxically, he is famously kind to his devotees, or *bhaktas*. In this myth, Shiva was touched by his bhakta's piety, so instead of bringing him to the mountain, Shiva brought his own image to the bhakta. The linga emerged out of a plate of rice and lentils, called *kicchari*, which believers see in the rough surface of the linga's natural stone. ⊠ *Bengali Tola.*

㉜ Manikarnika Ghat. Thin blue smoke twists up to the sky from fires at Varanasi's chief cremation center, adjacent to the ghat itself. Bodies wrapped in silk or linen—traditionally white for men and red or orange for women—are carried through the streets on bamboo stretchers to the smoking pyres. After a brief immersion in the Ganges and a short wait, the body is placed on the pyre for the ritual that precedes the cremation. Funeral parties dressed in white, the color of mourning, hover with their deceased. Photographing funeral ghats is strictly forbidden, but you are allowed to watch. Manikarnika itself has a small, deep pool, or *kund*, at the top of its flight of stone steps. The pool is said to have been dug by Vishnu at the dawn of creation, and thus to be the first *tirtha*—literally, "ford," and figuratively a place of sacred bathing. Shiva is said to have lost an earring (*manikarnika*) as he trembled in awe before this place, one of the holiest sites in Varanasi.

★ ㊷ Ram Nagar Fort and Palace. Across the Ganges from town is the residential palace of the former maharaja of Varanasi, who still lives here and performs important ceremonial and charitable functions. The **Durbar Hall** (Public Audience Chamber) and **Royal Museum** have collections of palanquins, furniture, arms, and costumes. The palace was built to resist the floods of the monsoon, which play havoc with the city side of the river. ⊠ *End of Pontoon Bridge.* ▦ *Rs. 7.* ☉ *Daily 9– noon and 2–5.*

㊵ Sankat Mochan Temple. Sankat Mochan, meaning "Deliverer from Troubles," is one of the native Banarasis' most beloved temples. While the city has now encroached all around it, the building still stands in a good-size, tree-shaded enclosure, like temples elsewhere in India. (Most temples in Varanasi are squeezed between other buildings.) While most of the city's major shrines are dedicated to Shiva or various aspects of the mother goddess, Sankat Mochan belongs to Hanuman, the monkey god revered for his dedicated service to Rama, an incarnation of Vishnu whose story is told in the *Ramayana* epic. The best time to see Sankat Mochan is in the early evening, when dozens of locals stop by for a brief visit at the end of the work day. ⊠ *Durgakund Rd.*

㉟ Shitala Temple. This unassuming but very popular white temple is dedicated to Shitala, the smallpox goddess. Despite the eradication of smallpox, Shitala is still an important folk goddess in North India. Here, as in many Shitala temples, a new shrine has been added in honor of Santoshi Mata, the "Mother of Contentment"—a goddess who gained popularity in the 1970s when a Hindi movie was made about her. ⊠ *Shitala Ghat.*

Dining and Lodging

$$ ✕ Anandaram Jaipuriya Bhavan. Most Hindu pilgrims in Varanasi dine in a sort of cafeteria called a *bhojanalaya*, where they can eat reliable, affordable meals cooked in the style of the region they come from. Housed in the third story of a building that is also a guest house for affluent Rajasthani pilgrims, this one is considered the best in the city.

Large meals of vegetables, dal, rice, chapatis, and yogurt are served on thali platters to patrons seated in rows on planks on the floor. The food is delicious, and mineral water is available. ⊠ *About 100 yards north of Godaulia Crossing, on west side of road to Chowk,* ☎ *542/ 352674. No credit cards.*

$$ ✕ **Bread of Life Bakery.** Specializing in "European breads and Amer-
★ ican cookies," this pristine café makes a great place for breakfast after a morning boat ride—it's about 10 minutes' walk from Asi Ghat. Lunch and dinner are also served. ⊠ *B 3/322 Shivala (on east side of main road to Godaulia Crossing),* ☎ *542/313912. No credit cards.*

$$ ✕ **Sindhi.** This unprepossessing, crowded restaurant is your best bet for a meal in central Varanasi. It serves delicious thalis (combination meals) as well as omelets and side dishes of fresh local vegetables. Try the creamy *malai kofta* (minced vegetables in a spicy cream sauce) or, for a lighter dish, *aloo methi* (potatoes and fenugreek greens). ⊠ *Opposite Lalita Cinema, near Bhelupura Police Station. No credit cards.*

$$$ ⌸ **Clarks Hotels.** The Clarks group, which manages three modern hotels in Varanasi, maintains a *haveli* (traditional Rajput mansion) on the Ganges at Raja Ghat for cultural programs in the evening and demonstrations of Hindu ritual in the morning. Trips are arranged for groups, but individual travelers can sign on if space is available. The Clarks Varanasi has attractive rooms with light and cheery decor; the best overlook the pool or the lawn. The salmon-pink and white exterior of the Clarks group's Best Western Kashika hides a spacious, white-marble lobby and large, simple rooms. And the newest addition, the Clarks Tower, is an imposing white block tower. Foreign tour groups favor the tower for its dependable modern standards, including garden barbecues, satellite TV, and a multicuisine restaurant. ⊠ *The Mall, 221002, Uttar Pradesh;* ☎ *542/348501 through 542/348512 for Clarks Varanasi; 542/348091 or 542/348092 for Best Western; 542/348250 or 542/ 348251 for Best Western and Clarks Tower;* ⅻ *542/348186 for Varanasi; 542/348685 for Best Western and Clarks Tower. 140 rooms in Clarks Varanasi; 40 rooms, 4 suites in Best Western; 58 rooms in Clarks Tower. 3 restaurants, bar, pool, travel services. AE, DC, MC, V.*

$$$ ⌸ **Taj Ganges.** Abutting the grounds of an old palace of Varanasi's ma-
★ haraja, this Western-style high-rise is the quietest hotel in town, particularly if you get an upper-story room facing the palace grounds. The lobby is large and pleasant, and rooms are spacious and modern. The restaurant's patio tables and the nicely landscaped pool area make lovely places to grab some tranquillity before plunging back into the city. ⊠ *Nadesar Palace, Raja Bazaar Rd., 221002, Uttar Pradesh,* ☎ *542/ 345100 through 542/345117,* ⅻ *542/348067. 120 rooms, 10 suites. 2 restaurants, bar, coffee shop, pool, hair salon, tennis court, meeting room, business services, travel services. AE, DC, MC, V.*

$ ⌸ **Ganges View.** This excellent guest house has small, immaculate rooms and a veranda with little tables overlooking the river and Asi Ghat. The owner is a repository of information on local culture, particularly Indian classical music. Delicious vegetarian meals are prepared with advance notice. This place is very popular; book months in advance to stay during peak season. ⊠ *Asi Ghat, 221006, Uttar Pradesh,* ☎ *542/313218,* ⅻ *542/369695. 8 rooms. Restaurant. No credit cards.*

$ ⌸ **Hotel de Paris.** Set on pretty grounds, this rambling old bungalow with a handsome cream-and-pink exterior is an elegant—if slightly shabby—relic of the British cantonment. Service is friendly and efficient. The rooms are spacious and simple, but lit with fluorescent lights; some have air-conditioning. ⊠ *15 The Mall, 221002, Uttar Pradesh,* ☎ *542/346601 through 542/346608,* ⅻ *542/348520. 50 rooms. 2 restaurants, travel services. AE, DC, MC, V.*

$ 🏨 **Pradeep.** This well-maintained small hotel is near Lahurabir, on the north side of the city. The multicuisine restaurant, Poonam, is popular with locals, and a rooftop barbecue serves up informal alfresco dining. Rooms have air-conditioners and are comfortably furnished; ask for one away from the road. ✉ C 27/153, Chetganj, 221002, Uttar Pradesh, ☎ 542/204963, ℻ 542/204898. 45 rooms. Restaurant, bar, travel services. MC, V.

Shopping

One of India's chief weaving centers, Varanasi is famous for its silk-brocade saris, many adorned with real gold and silver. Most hotels sell samples of this work in their shops, but the main bazaars for Banarasi saris are in the **Vishvanath Gali**—the lane leading from Dashashvamedh Road to the Kashi Vishvanath Temple, where the customers are mainly pilgrims and tourists. Among the brass vendors in **Thatheri Bazaar** (Brass Market), some shops sell silks and woolens to a local crowd. **Dharam Kumar Jain & Sons** (✉ K 37/12 Sona Kuan, ☎ 542/333354), operating out of their home near Thatheri Bazaar, have an extraordinary private collection of old brocade saris, pashmina shawls, and other textiles, and can help you find the best examples of contemporary weaving. **Mehta International** (✉ S 20/51 Varuna Bridge, ☎ 542/344489), near the major hotels, is a large showroom with a wide selection of saris and scarves.

Nightlife and the Arts

Nagari Natak Mandal (✉ Kabir Chowra) presents regular concerts of some of Varanasi's—indeed, India's—best musicians. There are also numerous seasonal music festivals; ask your hotel to check the local Hindi newspaper, *Aj.*

Sarnath

❸ *11 km (7 mi) north of Varanasi*

In 528 BC Siddhartha Gautama preached his first sermon in what is now Sarnath's Deer Park. Here he revealed his Eightfold Path leading to the end of sorrow and the attainment of enlightenment.

Three hundred years later, in the 3rd century BC, the Mauryan emperor Ashoka arrived. A zealous convert to Buddhism, he built in Sarnath several stupas (large, mound-shape reliquary shrines) and a pillar with a lion capital that was adopted by 20th-century India as the national emblem. The wheel motif under the lions' feet represents the *dharma chakra,* the wheel (*chakra*) of Buddhist teaching (*dharma*), which began in Sarnath. The chakra is replicated at the center of the national flag. Sarnath reached its zenith by the 4th century AD, under the Gupta dynasty, and was occupied into the 9th century, when Buddhist influence in India began to wane. By the 12th century, Sarnath had more or less fallen to Muslim invaders and begun a long decay. In 1836, Sir Alexander Cunningham started extensive excavations here, uncovering first a stone slab with an inscription of the Buddhist creed, then numerous other relics. It was only then that the Western world realized the Buddha had been an actual person, not just a mythical figure. Admission to the ruins is Rs. 100.

In the 16th century, the Moghul emperor Akbar built a brick tower on top of the 5th-century **Chaukhandi Stupa** to commemorate his father's visit some years earlier. It's on the west side of Ashoka Marg, just south of the archaeological museum.

★ The excellent **Sarnath Archaeological Museum** houses a copy of Ashoka's lion pillar and some other beautiful sculpture. Still more of

Sarnath's masterpieces are in the National Museum, Delhi, and the Indian Museum, Calcutta. ☒ *Ashoka Marg at Dharmapal Marg,* ☎ *542/ 585002.* ▣ *Museum Rs. 2.* ☉ *Sat.–Thurs. 10–5.*

The **Ashoka Pillar,** on Ashoka Marg north of the museum, is one of many inscribed monuments that Ashoka erected throughout his empire. This one stands in front of the main stupa where the emperor used to sit in meditation.

Dappled with geometric ornamentation, the **Dhamekh Stupa** (northeast of the museum) is, at 102 ft tall, the largest surviving monument in Sarnath. Built around AD 500, Dhamekh is thought to mark the place where the Buddha set the Wheel of Law in motion, though excavations have unearthed the remains of an even earlier stupa of Mauryan bricks of the Gupta period (200 BC).

Due east of the Dhamekh Stupa, and joining the old foundations of seven monasteries, is the **Mulagandha Kuti Vihari Temple,** built in 1931. The walls bear frescoes by a Japanese artist, Kosetsu Nosu, depicting scenes from the Buddha's life. On the anniversary of the temple's foundation—the first full moon in November—monks and devotees from all parts of Asia assemble here.

Before you leave Sarnath, walk north from the Dhamekh Stupa into **Deer Park** and buy some carrots for a few rupees to feed the deer. Legend has it that Buddha was once incarnated as King of the Deer here.

Bodhgaya

44 *266 km (165 mi) east of Varanasi*

Bodhgaya, a short drive from Varanasi (followed by a train connection from Gaya or an air connection from Patna), seems an oasis in central Bihar, one of the poorest states in India. In perhaps 530–520 BC (though the consensus on these dates is currently shifting), Gautama Buddha meditated under a peepul tree here until he achieved enlightenment. What's believed to be a descendant of a cutting of that tree still stands, and in recent decades Buddhists from around the world have built monasteries nearby. In the winter months Bodhgaya teems with the faithful and the curious, particularly when the Dalai Lama lectures, usually in December. Around town you'll encounter lay Buddhists from Maharasthra (center of a 20th-century Buddhist revival); Tibetan monks in maroon robes, some approaching the temple by prostrating themselves repeatedly; Sri Lankan and Thai *bhikkus* in yellow robes; and a growing number of Westerners. The contradictions between local poverty and the prosperity of these international monasteries have not been completely resolved; but most of Bodhgaya's Buddhist institutions do run a school, a dispensary, or another charitable project, and the global spirit in Bodhgaya today in some ways reenacts that of Buddhism during its early Indian history. Since many of India's other old Buddhist centers are primarily archaeological monuments, Bodhgaya gives you some idea of how Buddhism thrives as a contemporary faith.

The area around the temple compound is a mixture of shops for pilgrims, simple restaurants, and international monasteries, each built in the style of its home country. You can cover Bodhgaya on foot or in a cycle-rickshaw.

The **Mahabodhi Temple** is the physical as well as the symbolic center of town. Though it has been remodeled several times over the centuries, Mahabodhi may date from as early as the 2nd century AD and was certainly built before the 7th century, when the Chinese pilgrim Hsuan

Tsang visited. It's one of the earliest examples of the North Indian *nagara* style, which emphasizes the shikhara; rising some 160 ft, the spire can be seen far and wide from the surrounding flat country. The temple's four flat sides are tiered with niches for Buddha images offered by pilgrims, though only a few of these remain. At the top of the spire is a stone stupa, a representation of the reliquary mounds that the first Buddhists built all over the subcontinent, topped by a series of stone chattras, symbols of both the Buddha's princely lineage and the shelter provided by the faith he founded.

You enter the temple down a long flight of steps through its eastern gate, which faces an attractive pedestrian plaza. The temple itself is enclosed on three sides by a four-tier carved stone railing, which opens under a high torana (archway) on the eastern side. Much of the original railing has been carted away to museums and replaced by less elaborate reproductions, but you can see examples of the carving here and there, and more in Bodhgaya's archaeological museum. Pilgrims typically circumambulate the temple before entering the tall central chamber, which now houses a large gilt image of the Buddha in meditation. (According to Hsuan Tsang, in his day the image was made of a sandalwood paste.) The sanctum is strung with colored lights, and the surrounding space is enlivened by the obvious emotion of pilgrims. The **Bodhi tree,** standing outside the temple directly behind the inner sanctum, gives a more visceral feeling of sanctity. The railing around the tree forms a small courtyard, and pilgrims enter through a gate to place flowers on the stone slab representing the **vajrasan** ("diamond seat") where the Buddha meditated and to tie bits of colored cloth to the tree. Contemporary Buddhists often sit in emulation of the founder's practice along the railing under the tree. Dotted around the large temple compound, shaded by several trees, are small stone stupas sponsored by pilgrims over the centuries. The pathway of carved stone next to the north wall is said to mark the track of the Buddha's walking meditation, and he is thought to have bathed in the pretty lotus pond on the southeast side. 🖼 *Free, camera Rs. 5.* ⊙ *Apr.–Sept., daily 6–9; Oct.– Mar., daily 6–8.*

The main **Tibetan Monastery,** representing the Dalai Lama's *gelugpa* tradition (or Yellow Hat Tradition) is on the north side of town; the man himself teaches under a large tent in an adjacent field. The **Mahabodhi Society,** a Sri Lankan organization that played a key role in reviving the practice of pilgrimage to Buddhist centers in India, has its complex on the main road just across from the temple's northern wall. The attractive **Thai Monastery** is at the southern end of town. Bodhgaya's **Archaeological Museum** holds some of the Mahabodhi Temple's original carved-stone railing and some good classical sculpture. It's on the south side of town, off the short road leading up to the Hotel Bodhgaya Ashok. **Rajgir,** 85 km (53 mi) northeast of Bodhgaya, was capital of the ancient kingdom of Magadha and site of the first Buddhist Council in Buddha's time. If you can stay in Bodhgaya overnight, the ruins of the great Buddhist university at **Nalanda,** northeast of Bodhgaya, make a long but fascinating day trip.

Dining and Lodging

$$ ✕ **Cafe Om.** In winter, this seasonal restaurant serves soups and other Tibetan dishes to pilgrims and tourists alike. Try the *momos,* classic Tibetan dumplings. ⊠ *Opposite Tibetan Monastery,* ☎ *no phone. No credit cards.*

$$$ 🏨 **Bodhgaya Ashok.** The Indian government's Ashok chain is generally in decline, with frequent proposals to privatize, but this one retains some of the project's earlier strengths. Guest rooms are large and

comfortably furnished, with individual air-conditioners, and the restaurant is quite good. Service is friendly and efficient. ✉ *Bodhgaya, Gaya district 824231, Bihar,* ☎ *631/400789 through 631/400792,* 𝖥𝖠𝖷 *631/ 400788. 30 rooms, 2 suites. Restaurant, bar, laundry service, travel services. AE, DC, MC, V.*

$$ 🏨 **Sujata.** The Sujata has smallish, plain but comfortable rooms, some with air-conditioners. Its restaurant is the best in town for the typical hotelier's selection of North Indian, Chinese, and Continental dishes. ✉ *Bodhgaya, Gaya district 824231, Bihar,* ☎ *631/400761 or 631/ 400481,* 𝖥𝖠𝖷 *631/400515. 25 rooms, 2 suites. Restaurant, laundry service, travel services. MC, V.*

$ 🏨 **Bihar State Tourist Bungalow.** This building on the western outskirts of Bodhgaya provides clean, simple rooms, two of which are air-conditioned, and an attached restaurant. ✉ *Bodhgaya, Gaya district 824231, Bihar,* ☎ 𝖥𝖠𝖷 *631/400445. 13 rooms. Restaurant, laundry service, travel services. No credit cards.*

Lucknow

㊺ *300 km (186 mi) northwest of Varanasi, 516 km (320 mi) southeast of Delhi*

Lucknow is—in its lingering self-image, anyway—a city of almost ridiculously ornate manners, inherited from the last significant Muslim court to hold sway in North India. Though settled here on the banks of the Gomti River in the earliest period of Indian history, it came to its present prominence in 1775 (after Moghul power had declined in Delhi) as capital of the independent kingdom of Avadh. It is now capital of the state of Uttar Pradesh. Much of Lucknow's old lazy charm is being superseded, yet people still think of the city as one where passengers miss their train connections by getting caught up in elaborate exchanges of *"Phele aap"* ("You first") on the platform.

Lucknow's famous Nawabs of Avadh were members of the Shia sect of Islam, and the city remains an important center for that minority. Shia *imambaras*—gathering places used during Muharram, the month of mourning for Hussain, fifth Caliph of Islam—are Lucknow's most important monuments. Wajid Ali Shah, the last nawab and a legendarily impractical aesthete, was deposed by the British in 1856. Resentment over that act, combined with the decades of indirect control that preceded it, contributed to Lucknow's strong support for the rebels during the Mutiny of 1857, with members of Avadh's disbanded army manning the barricades against the British. British residents and troops, and an equal number of Indian troops and servants, were besieged for almost five months.

The city's plan was drastically altered after the Mutiny and is now crisscrossed with broad avenues. Driving along the Gomti at the eastern end of the city, you'll see the **Bara Imambara,** passing the Rumi Darwaza, or Turkish Gate, as you approach the complex. This is Lucknow's largest imambara, preceded by a wide plaza and set at an oblique angle to its accompanying mosque. Guides will pester you to avail yourself of their services, and you may need them when you climb up to the top floor: here a labyrinth of identical doorways, passages, and stairways, with hidden routes and many dead ends, makes up the *bhul bhulaiya* (roughly, "place of forgetting") leading back down to the ground level. You can go through the warren solo, but it takes time and patience. The imambara's raison d'être is the **tomb of Nawab Asaf-ud-Daulah,** who built his own resting place in 1784. The excellent views from the top floor take in a deep step well on the opposite side of the plaza from the mosque. 🎟 *Rs. 185.* ⊙ *Daily 6–5.*

The elegant **Hussainabad Imambara,** built in 1837 with a gilt dome, is west of the Bara Imambara. The city's **clock tower,** near the Hussainabad Imambara, is one of Lucknow's most remarkable Victorian Gothic structure.

Heading back toward the city center from the Bara Imambara, you'll come to the **Residency** compound, where the British garrison was besieged on June 30, 1857. A relief force entered (as you will) through the **Baillie Guard Gate** on September 25, only to end up besieged themselves. On the right is the **Treasury,** and behind that a large **Banquet Hall** that served as a hospital. (About 2,000 people died in the siege, more from disease than from gunfire.) Up a slight rise is a large open green, with an active shrine to a Muslim *pir* (holy man) under a tree to the left and an obelisk on the right commemorating Henry Lawrence, the Chief Commissioner who gathered his people here only to fall to gunfire on July 4. The Residency itself lies largely in ruins, but you can see how its stone walls mimic European plaster, and the first floor displays a model of the compound under siege as well as cannonballs and other artifacts. Below ground are the *tikhana* (cellar) chambers, where many of the women and children escaped intermittent fire from the rooftops of surrounding buildings. Down the slope on the far side of the Residency is a **cemetery** for the many who did not last until the siege was finally broken on November 17. Pre- and post-Independence markers and signs indicate graphically the differences in how events here have been viewed. (Until August 15, 1947, a Union Jack flew over the compound.) Other buildings are scattered throughout, and you'll want at least an hour and a half to absorb the Residency's melancholy significance. ☒ *Rs. 100.* ☉ *Daily 7–5:30.*

At the eastern edge of the city, on the banks of the Gomti, is **La Martinière College,** the most outlandish building in town. Now a high school, it was built as a palace by Major-General Claude Martin, an 18th-century French adventurer who profited handsomely from his military service to the nawabs and happily spread his epicurean tastes. The building's lower stories were designed to flood in the summer—an innovative, if malarial, cooling system. With its oddly angled wings, towering cupola, and assorted baroque gargoyles, the college suggests a fevered dream of Versailles. You can get a good sense of it from the outside, but can also arrange a tour in advance through the school administration (contact Uttar Pradesh Tourism, ☎ 522/228349).

Dining and Lodging

$$–$$$ ✕ **Tunday Kababi.** This is the downtown branch of a local institution
★ named after the kebab artist who founded it. You won't find much in the way of vegetables here, but the grilled meats are delicious, accompanied by naan and a range of other breads. The open-air cooking area fronts the street, facing a busy bazaar. ☒ *Near Ghari Wali Masjid, Nazirabad,* ☎ *522/216535. No credit cards.*

$ ✕ **Prakash Kulfi.** "Beware of imitations," warns a signboard, and
★ there are plenty all around this famous dessert joint on a rooftop overlooking the Akbari Gate. *Kulfi*—an ice cream with hints of almond and cardamom—is served with *faludi,* noodles floating in a sweet cream sauce. ☒ *12–13 Fruit La., Aminabad,* ☎ *522/226737. No credit cards.*

$$$$ ▥ **Clarks Avadh.** Thanks in part to its central location, Lucknow's original high-class hotel has managed to hold its own against new competition. Rooms are spacious, though somewhat dimly lit. You can dine in a rooftop restaurant. ☒ *8 Mahatma Gandhi Marg, 226001, Uttar Pradesh,* ☎ *522/216500 through 522/216509; 522/220131 through 522/220133,* ▥ *522/216507. 98 rooms, 3 suites. Restaurant, coffee*

*shop, hair salon, laundry service, business services, travel services.
AE, D, MC, V.*

$$$$ ⌂ **Taj Mahal.** This luxury hotel, a modern structure in the British colo-
★ nial style, is a bargain compared to its counterparts in more popular
destinations. Rooms are spacious and, like the public areas, appointed
with pleasing period detail. The Oudhayana restaurant serves near-per-
fect samples of Lakhnavi cooking. The remote location makes transport difficult to arrange on your own; reserve a car through the travel
desk. ✉ *Vipin Khand, Gomti Nagar, 226010, Uttar Pradesh,* ☎ *522/
393939,* FAX *522/392282. 106 rooms, 4 suites. 2 restaurants, bar, pool,
hair salon, golf privileges, health club, laundry service, business services, meeting room, travel services. AE, DC, MC, V.*

$ ⌂ **Arif Castles.** Guest rooms are comfortable, and service is pleasant
and efficient at this hotel near the Carlton. ✉ *4 Rana Pratap Marg,
Hazratganj, 226001, Uttar Pradesh,* ☎ *522/211313 through 522/
211317,* FAX *522/211360. 46 rooms, 6 suites. Restaurant, laundry service, travel services. AE, MC, V.*

$ ⌂ **Carlton.** If the remains of the Raj appeal, this may be the place for
you, though the furnishings seem nearly as moth-eaten as the stuffed
tiger in the lobby. The rooms are palatial, however, and some are air-
conditioned. The central location is key. ✉ *Rana Pratap Marg, Hazratganj, 226001, Uttar Pradesh,* ☎ *522/222439 or 522/222413,* FAX *522/
231886. 10 rooms, 18 suites. Restaurant, bar, laundry service, travel
services. AE, DC, MC, V.*

Shopping

Lucknow is famous for a style of straight-stitch embroidery on fine cotton cloth known as *chikan.* This is fashioned into *kurtas* (long tunics
for both men and women) as well as on larger pieces that can serve as
bedspreads or tablecloths. You'll see examples in hotel shops, but the
bazaar at **Aminabad** is the place to go for bargains and variety. Start
at **Chikan Paradise,** near Akbari Gate. Lucknow's other characteristic product is *attar,* the essential oils used in perfumes. **Ram Advani's
Bookshop** (✉ Mayfair Cinema Bldg., Mahatma Gandhi Rd., Hazratganj) stocks a good selection for general reading as well as works of
Lakhnavi history by scholars from around the world.

Nightlife and the Arts

The courtly cultivation of singing, dance, and poetry that characterized Lucknow in earlier eras has waned, but efforts are on to revive it.
The **Uttar Pradesh tourist office** (✉ 3 Nawal Kishore Rd., ☎ 522/
228349) stages occasional evenings of **ghazal singing,** once the specialty of the city's famous courtesans; and in February there's a music
and dance festival. **Bhat Khande Maha Vidhyalaya** (☎ 522/222926,
WEB www.swargram.org), a teaching institute of Indian classical music
near the Clarks Avadh hotel, hosts ghazal singing performances.

NORTH CENTRAL INDIA A TO Z

*To research prices, get advice from other travelers, and book travel ar-
rangements, visit www.fodors.com.*

AIR TRAVEL

In peak season, Indian Airlines and Jet Airways fly daily among Delhi,
Agra, Khajuraho, and Varanasi. Regular flights on Indian Airlines, Jet
Airways, and Sahara Airlines also connect Varanasi with Kathmandu,
Lucknow, and other major cities. Note that some Indian Airlines flights
from Varanasi to Delhi fly first to Bhubaneswar, a four-hour detour.
Indian Airlines and Jet Airways also offer regular flights from Varanasi
and Delhi to Bodhgaya.

Lucknow is well connected by air to Delhi, Varanasi, and Calcutta on Indian Airlines, Jet Airways, and Sahara Airlines.

Indian Airways flies daily from Delhi to Bhopal, with midday departure and arrival times. Expect some delays on this route; depending on how much time you have, you may prefer to get up early to take the train.

CARRIERS

➤ INDIAN AIRLINES: **Agra** (☎ 562/360982 or 562/226820; 562/302349 at airport). **Bhopal** (☎ 755/778434; 755/646123 at airport). **Delhi** (☎ 11/462–0566). **Khajuraho** (☎ 7686/74035; 7686/74036 at airport). **Lucknow** (☎ 522/220927; 522/436132 at airport). **Varanasi** (☎ 542/345959; 542/622090 at airport). **Web site** (WEB www.indian-airlines.nic.in).

➤ JET AIRWAYS: **Agra** (☎ 562/360303). **Delhi** (☎ 11/685–3700; 11/566–5404 at airport). **Khajuraho** (☎ 7686/44406). **Lucknow** (☎ 522/239612 through 522/239614; 522/434009 through 522/434010 at airport). **Varanasi** (☎ 542/511555 or 542/511444; 542/622577 at airport). **Web site** (WEB www.jetairways.com).

➤ SAHARA AIRLINES: **Lucknow** (☎ 522/372742; 522/437771 at airport). **Varanasi** (☎ 542/511489; 542/622334 at airport). **Web site** (WEB www.airsahara.net).

AIRPORTS

Agra's Kheria Airport is roughly 7 km (4 mi) from the Taj Mahal. Ask your hotel if it participates in the local airport shuttle; if not, you can generally have your hotel send an air-conditioned car to pick you up for about Rs. 250. You can also take a fixed-rate taxi or auto-rickshaw from the airport to the city center for less than Rs. 200.

The airport nearest Bodhgaya is in the city of Patna, from which it's a four-hour, 125-km (78-mi), Rs. 1,000 (Rs. 1,400 for an air-conditioned car) taxi ride to Bodhgaya.

Khajuraho's airport is 5 km (3 mi) from town; the taxi ride costs less than Rs. 100.

Lucknow's airport is about 30 minutes by car from most hotels; a taxi costs around Rs. 300.

Varanasi's airport is a 45-minute drive from most hotels. A taxi costs about Rs. 350 or Rs. 500 (air-conditioned) to the cantonment area, or from Rs. 400 to Rs. 600 into the city proper. Of the airport's two pre-paid-taxi counters, Airport Rent A Car Service, inside the terminal, is more reliable. The shuttle bus is only convenient if your hotel is in the cantonment; otherwise, you'll simply be dropped on the far side of the cantonment train station.

AUTO-RICKSHAWS

Be prepared to negotiate on auto-rickshaw rates, especially in Agra, as fares depend on several factors, including how far you want to go, how many times you want to stop, the time of day, and whether or not it is raining. You can generally expect to pay about Rs. 100 for a half day, Rs. 200 for a full day. If you're not comfortable with the price you're given, look for another auto-rickshaw, and if you don't want to haggle, take a metered taxi or book a car.

Auto-rickshaws are a fast way to scoot through Varanasi's crowded streets, but the fumes from other automobiles can be horrendous at busy times. When traffic is heavy, take an air-conditioned taxi with the windows closed, especially if you're coming from one of the hotels far from the ghats. Ask your hotel or the tourist office for the going rate and agree on a fare in advance. Note that these and other motor vehicles are not allowed into Godaulia Crossing, the traffic circle near the central bathing ghat, Dashashvamedh; they'll drop you off a short walk from the river if that's where you're headed.

BIKE AND CYCLE-RICKSHAW TRAVEL

You can get the latest rate estimates from the Government of India Tourist Office at your destination. Cycle-rickshaws should cost no more than Rs. 30 per hour in Agra or Khajuraho. They're a particularly pleasant way to get around Khajuraho, especially to the outlying temples. Distances are long in Varanasi, so a cycle-rickshaw is better for a leisurely roll through the old city (it frees you from fighting the crowds) than for cross-town transport. A trip from the cantonment to the ghats should cost about Rs. 50. If you hire a cycle-rickshaw for the day, agree on the price in advance and expect to pay at least Rs. 100.

Renting a bike in Khajuraho costs about Rs. 30 per day and is one of the most popular ways to get around this tranquil town. You can rent bikes across from the bus stand, behind the museum, and from some hotels.

BOAT TRAVEL

Boat rides on the Ganges in Varanasi should cost Rs. 50 for an hour for a small boat; the bigger, sturdier boats fit more people and cost Rs. 75–Rs. 100 per hour. At Dashashvamedh Ghat, however, touts will demand a lot more. If you just show up at sunrise, you'll have limited time to shop around; for a reasonable rate, chat with some boatmen the previous evening and arrange to meet one by the river the next morning. A boat from the main ghats to Ram Nagar should cost about Rs. 200 round-trip.

CAR RENTAL

Hire a car and driver only through your hotel, tour operator, or a recommended local travel agent.

For trips to Agra from Delhi, contact Dhanda Tours and Travels. An air-conditioned Ambassador with driver costs less than Rs. 3,500; a Tata Sumo jeep (for four–five people) is less than Rs. 4,000. Expect to pay about Rs. 500 extra for a worthwhile detour to Fatehpur Sikri.

Prices in Agra are generally Rs. 6–Rs. 8 per km (½ mi). A non-air-conditioned car for four hours or 40 km (25 mi) should cost about Rs. 400, the minimum charge. For overnight excursions, add a halt charge of Rs. 200. Budget Rent-a-Car has offices on Fatehbad Road and in the Mansingh Palace hotel; during peak season, reserve a car and driver in advance. You can also hire a taxi at the train station under a fixed-rate system. If you'd prefer not to be taken to the driver's choice of stores, restaurants, or hotels (where he gets a commission), say so firmly up front.

In Bhopal, a car is essential for side trips into the countryside. Depending on how much you want to see and the mileage involved, expect to pay Rs. 1,000–Rs. 1,500 for an air-conditioned car for the day.

In Khajuraho, a hired car can be convenient if you want to wander outside town or can't walk the 3 km (2 mi) to the most distant temples. A non-air-conditioned car should cost about Rs. 200 for two hours or 30 km (19 mi). You can hire a taxi for about Rs. 6 per km.

In Varanasi, a three- to four-hour car excursion should cost Rs. 400–Rs. 500. A taxi from Varanasi will drop you in Sarnath and wait about three hours for Rs. 300. Auto-rickshaws will make the round-trip for about Rs. 200. The Grand Trunk Road (NH 2) east of Varanasi passes south of Bodhgaya. The local connecting roads, for which you turn off just east of Auranagabad, are in poor condition and sometimes beset by robbers.

➤ LOCAL AGENCIES: **Budget Rent-a-Car** (✉ Fatehbad Rd., Agra, ☎ 562/ 331771). **Dhanda Tours and Travels** (✉ Dharam Marg, Malcha Marg Market, Chanakyapuri, New Delhi, ☎ 11/611–4969).

CAR TRAVEL

Madhya Pradesh is one of the most scenic Indian states to drive through. You can tailor a delightful trip covering Agra, Gwalior, Orchha, Khajuraho, Bhopal, and Sanchi over five or six days. Hire a car in Delhi or Agra from a tour operator or travel agency.

Agra is 200 km (124 mi) south of Delhi on roads built by the Moghul emperors to connect their two capitals. The roads are good, but heavily used—don't expect to travel much above 50 kph (30 mph). The trip should take 3½ to 4 hours. The best route is probably the Mathura Road (NH 2).

Lucknow is connected to Delhi by NH 2, the Grand Trunk Road, which runs through Agra and the industrial city of Kanpur before NH 25 turns north to Lucknow. This is one of the most heavily used truck routes in India, and is for the most part devoid of lanes. An alternate route is NH 24 through Bareilly and central Uttar Pradesh. NH 56 links Lucknow with the Grand Trunk Road at Varanasi, and allows a stop in little-visited Jaunpur, capital of an early Muslim sultanate.

To reach Varanasi by car, take National Highway (NH) 2 or NH 56 from the northwest, NH 29 from Gorakhpur (if you started in Kathmandu), NH 2 from Calcutta, or NH 30 and NH 2 from Patna.

MONEY

ATMS

ATMs that accept MasterCard, Visa, and Plus can be found in larger towns in the area; ask at your hotel or your taxi driver for one close to you. Note that some machines have a limit of Rs. 4,000.

CURRENCY EXCHANGE

Your hotel is the easiest place to change currency, but you can also change money at State Bank of India branches in Agra, Khajuraho, Bhopal, Varanasi, and Lucknow. Agra is also served by Canara Bank.

TOURS

The Uttar Pradesh State Road Transport Corporation conducts a daily guided bus tour of Fatehpur Sikri, Agra Fort, and Taj Mahal for Rs. 2,250 per person. For a personal guide, ask your hotel or contact the nearest Government of India Tourist Office.

Middle Ways Travels specializes in tours of Bodhgaya. Radiant Travels has one of the region's few female tour guides, who gives an insightful feminine perspective on Bhopal. Tornos House specializes in Lucknow's Avadhi culture, crafts, and cuisine as well as the history of the British in India.

➤ CONTACTS: **Middle Way Travels** (✉ 7/11 Main Rd., Bodhgaya, ☎ 631/400648). **Radiant Travels** (✉ 24 Ahmedabad Rd., PB No 24, Bhopal, ☎ 755/738540 or 755/738541). **Tornos House** (✉ C-2016, Indira Nagar, Lucknow, ☎ 522/380610, 🌐 www.tornosindia.com). **Uttar Pradesh State Road Transport Corporation** (✉ 96 Gwalior Rd., ☎ 562/72206; Platform No. 1, near inquiry window, Agra Cantonment Railway Station).

TRAIN TRAVEL

The Indian Railways Web site (www.indianrailways.com) provides comprehensive train information. Don't rely on telephone bookings; instead go to the station to collect your ticket in advance. Every main station has a Tourist Reservation Office. If you reserve at least two days before you travel, you should have priority.

Because fog often causes delays at Delhi's airport, especially in winter, trains can be more reliable for visiting Agra. Air-conditioned *Shatabdi Express* trains run daily on the Delhi–Agra–Gwalior–Jhansi–Bhopal route, offering frequent meals and snacks en route. The Agra to Gwalior link takes only an hour. The slightly slower *Taj Express* runs the same route. Orchha is 16 km (10 mi) from Jhansi, a major rail junction. To reserve tickets, head to the reservation office on the first floor of the New Delhi Railway Station, near the Paharganj entrance.

From Bhopal, the *Bhopal Express* overnight shuttle to Nizamuddin station in Delhi lets you save a night's hotel fare in Delhi.

The Madhya Pradesh State Tourism Corporation runs a daily air-conditioned deluxe train from Jhansi to Khajuraho.

India's premier train, the *Rajdhani Express,* has overnight service between Delhi and Varanasi twice a week. The *Kashi Vishvanath Express* also serves Lucknow. The best transport between Varanasi and Bodhgaya is the mid-morning *Poorva Express* train to Gaya, 16 km (10 mi) from Bodhgaya. Gaya is also served by the *Rajdhani Express* between Delhi and Calcutta five days a week. On days when the *Rajdhani* and *Poorva* express trains bypass Varanasi, they stop in Mughal Sarai, about an hour away by car.

VISITOR INFORMATION

You can pick up maps and information on approved guides at Government of India Tourist Offices in Agra, Khajuraho, and Varanasi's cantonment, and an information desk at Varanasi's airport. If you are planning your trip from New Delhi, the offices on Janpath, just across from the Imperial Hotel and south of Cottage Industries, are worth a visit.

The Madhya Pradesh State Tourism Development Corporation, one of India's better tourist offices, has friendly staff and information on Khajuraho, Gwalior, Orchha, Bhopal, and Sanchi.

Outbound Travel in Delhi can arrange flights and coordinate flights with train or car travel to help you make the most of limited travel time.

The Uttar Pradesh State Tourism Development Corporation arranges tours and cars in Agra and Lucknow. The New Delhi office (centrally located near across from The Imperial Hotel) has maps, brochures, and information on approved guides. The best information at Varanasi's Uttar Pradesh Government Tourist Office is in Hindi, but the staff can still help you, and there's a satellite desk at the train station.

For admission to sights, the rupees price fluctuates with the exchange rate daily, so don't be surprised if you're asked for a few rupees more than your guide has advised, or even more than the sign posted outside the monument. Prices have dropped in recent years, however, so beware of guides who may refer to old, higher prices. If you want to plan a budget, confirm the current prices with your travel agent or local Government of India Tourist Office. Note that foreigners are sometimes required to pay a higher fee than nationals.

➤ Tourist Information: **Government of India Tourist Office** (✉ 88 Janpath, New Delhi, ☎ 11/332–0109 or 11/332–0005; ✉ 191 The Mall, Agra, ☎ 562/363959 or 562/363377; ✉ Opposite Western Group of temples, Khajuraho, ☎ 7686/72347; ✉ 15B, The Mall, Varanasi, ☎ 542/343744). **Madhya Pradesh State Tourism Corporation** (✉ Kanishka Shopping Plaza, 2nd floor, 19 Ashoka Rd., New Delhi, ☎ 11/332–1187 or 11/336–6528; ✉ Chandella Cultural Center, Rajnagar Rd., near Powerhouse, Khajuraho, ☎ 7686/74051; ✉ Hotel Palash, T. T. Nagar, Bhopal, ☎ 755/553006; ✉ Hotel Tansen, 6 Gandhi Rd., Gwalior, ☎ 751/340370; ✉ Railway Station, Jhansi, ☎ 517/442622; WEB www.mptourism.com). **Outbound Travel** (✉ New Delhi, ☎ 11/652–6316 or 11/652–1306). **Uttar Pradesh State Tourist Office** (✉ 36 Chandralok Bldg., Janpath, New Delhi, ☎ 11/332–2251; ✉ 64 Taj Rd., Agra, ☎ 562/226431; ✉ Parade Kothi, opposite train station, Varanasi, ☎ 545/341162; ✉ 3 Nawal Kishore Rd., Lucknow, ☎ 522/228349).

5 RAJASTHAN

Steeped in tales of chivalry and romance, and famous for its striking desert landscape and colorful festivals, Rajasthan is one of India's best-loved regions. From its legendary cities of Jaipur, Jodhpur, Udaipur, and Jaisalmer, built by the mighty Rajput warriors, to its indigenous tribal and artisan communities, Rajasthan is a unique combination of royal and tribal India. The variety of its landscape is unparalleled: the region is packed with awe-inspiring forts, sparkling palaces, soothing lakes and gardens, and exquisite temples and shrines. The crafts and folk art produced here are world-renowned.

Updated by
Scott Carney

ONCE CALLED RAJPUTANA—"Abode of Kings"—this vast land consisted of more than 22 princely states before they were consolidated into modern Rajasthan in 1956. Each state was ruled by a Rajput, an upper-caste Hindu warrior-prince, and the Rajputs were divided into three main clans: the Suryavanshis, descended from the sun, the Chandravanshis, descended from the moon, and the *agnikuls,* who had been purified by ritual fire. When they were not fighting among themselves for power, wealth, and women, the Rajputs built the hundreds of forts, palaces, gardens, and temples that make this region so enchanting.

For centuries, many Hindu Rajputs valiantly resisted invasion, including attempts by the Muslim Moghuls. Their legendary codes of battle emphasized honor and pride, and they went to war prepared to die. When defeat on the battlefield was imminent, the strong Rajput women of Chittaur would perform the rite of *jauhar,* throwing themselves onto a flaming pyre en masse rather than live with the indignity of capture. With the prominent exception of the princes of Mewar, major Rajput states such as Jaipur, Bikaner, Bundi, and Kota, eventually stopped fighting and built strong ties with the Moghuls. The Moghul emperor Akbar was particularly skilled at forging alliances with the Rajputs; he offered them high posts in his *darbar,* or court, and sealed the deal with matrimonial ties. (He himself married two Rajput princesses.) Those kingdoms who sided with Akbar quickly rose in importance and prosperity.

Maharaja Man Singh of Jaipur was the first to marry his sister to Akbar. As the emperor's brother-in-law and trusted commander-in-chief, Man Singh led Moghul armies to many a victory. Both rulers benefited immensely, as a traditional saying indicates: *"Jeet Akbar ki, loot Man Singh ki"* ("The victory belongs to Akbar, the loot to Man Singh").

In addition to securing wealth, these marriages opened the gates of the royal Rajput households to the Moghuls' distinctive culture. Ironically, the same people who initially sacrificed their lives to resist the Moghuls quickly adapted themselves to Moghul domination and started borrowing heavily from Moghul aesthetics. Skilled craftsmen from the Moghul courts were enticed to Rajasthan to start craft schools, fomenting what would become a golden age of Indian art and architecture. The Moghuls' influence in Rajasthan is still visible in everything from food to palace architecture, from intricate miniature paintings to new musical styles, and from clothing to the tradition of *purdah* (the seclusion of women from males or strangers, or the act of covering the head and face with a veil).

The beginning of the 18th century marked the decline of the Moghul period, and with it came the decline of the Rajputs. The incoming British took advantage of the prevailing chaos. Not only did they introduce significant administrative, legal, and educational changes in Rajasthan, they also exposed the Rajputs to new levels of decadence. The British introduced polo and other equestrian sports, the latest rifles and guns, *shikar* (hunting) camps, Belgian glass, English crockery, French chiffons, Victorian furniture, European architecture, and—eventually—fancy limousines. The influence extended to Rajput children: sons were sent to English universities, and daughters to the best finishing schools in Switzerland.

While the rest of India launched their struggle for independence, many Rajput princes ended up defending the Raj. Unwilling to give up their world of luxury and power, they did their best to suppress rebellion outside their own kingdoms by sending their soldiers to help the British forces. When India won independence, the Rajput princes and kings were forced to merge their kingdoms into one state as part of the new nation, but they were allowed to keep the titles to their palaces, forts, lands, jewels, and other sumptuous possessions. Since then, however, the government has taken over much of their land and many of their palaces and forts. Stripped of feudal power, many of the maharajas became hotel owners, while others have turned their properties over to leading hotel chains. A few have become paupers or recluses.

Rajasthan's heritage goes well beyond the illustrious maharajas, however. The Marwari trading community is known far and wide for its dynamic entrepreneurial spirit and its ornate *havelis* (mansions with interior courtyards). Semi-nomadic indigenous tribes, such as the Bhils, Meenas, Garasias, and Sahrias, create a rich canvas of folk life and folklore, their art, dance, music, and drama contributing much to Rajasthan's vibrant, festive culture. The exquisite craft work of the state's rural artisan communities —leatherwork, textiles, puppetry, and miniature painting—is admired in India and around the world. The presence of saints and spiritual leaders from a variety of religious communities has also, over the years, made Rajasthan a trove of shrines, temple art, and religious architecture.

Cultures within Rajasthan vary in everything from the colors of their sandstone buildings to the languages they speak. Though five principal Rajasthani dialects are spoken here (Marwari, Mewari, Dhundari, Mewati, and Hadauti), a local saying has it that you hear a new language every 4 km. And despite the overwhelming spread of both English and Hindi, villagers continue to maintain the rich literary traditions, both oral and written, of their local tongues. Also regionally significant—and perhaps more noticeable to the traveler—are the brilliant colors of the women's *lehangas* (long skirts with separate veils), designed to stand out against the starkness of the desert. Women also wear elaborate jewelry, and Rajasthani men are famous for their turbans— called *saafas*—which vary in style from region to region and caste to caste; the style of wearing high turbans with a tail is preferred by Rajputs, for instance, while *pagris* (compact turbans, often orange) are worn by businessmen. Even facial hair is unique in these parts: Rajputs, in particular, sport long, Salvador Dali–like handlebar moustaches.

The region's natural variety is also compelling. The Aravalli Hills are a natural divider between northwest and southeast Rajasthan. Arid sand dunes characterize the northwest: The sizzling Thar Desert is referred to in the ancient Hindu epic *Mahabharata* as the Maru-Kantar, "the Region of Death." The landscape of the southeast, however, belies Rajasthan's image as a desert state: craggy hills, lush forests, and shimmering lakes are typical. A rich array of birds, animal life, and insect species makes its home in each environment.

With its stark colors and rich folk traditions, Rajasthan is one of India's most popular tourist destinations. The region is home to numerous cultural festivals, crafts fairs, and religious gatherings throughout the year. In the last decade, Rajasthan's poverty rate has plunged and the literacy rate skyrocketed to almost double what it was. Tensions with Pakistan have, in the past, made some people wary of coming here, but there is really nothing to fear. The cities and people remain lively and unaffected.

Pleasures and Pastimes

Dining

Rajasthan's culinary traditions are heavily influenced by its desert setting. Food tends to be highly spiced, for preservation. Instead of the rice and vegetables that are popular in regions with more rainfall, Rajasthani cuisine includes a lot of lentils and corn. Regardless, you'll find both North and South Indian food; many hotels also serve Chinese and/or Continental cuisine.

Make sure you try some local delicacies, such as *dal baati churma* (lentils with wheat-flour dumplings), *gatte ki subzi* (dumplings made out of chick pea flour, also known as gram flour), and *ker sangri* (green beans). Breads include *bajra ki roti* (maize bread), *makki ki roti* (corn bread), and *missi ki roti* (chick pea- and wheat-flour bread). *Mirchi badas* (spicy green pepper fritters) and *kachoris* (fried stuffed pastries) make hearty appetizers. Dessert is a highlight here—in some parts, sweets actually open the meal. Favorites include *ghevar* (funnel cake), *laddoo* (balls made of sugar, flour, clarified butter, and spices), *malpuas* (syrupy pancakes), and *diljani* (mini sugar balls). The traditional *thali* (a metal platter with various dishes and condiments) is a good way to sample everything.

Lodging

The most opulent hotels in India—and perhaps in the world—are in Rajasthan. You can literally live like a king in one of several converted palaces: stay in a pillared room surrounded by glittering mirrored walls, tiger skins, and stained-glass windows, dine in a vaulted, chandeliered ballroom, and still enjoy the best of the modern conveniences. The best-known of these lush lodgings are Udaipur's Lake Palace, Jodhpur's Umaid Bhawan Palace, and Jaipur's Taj Rambagh Palace. Unique to Rajasthan, too, are the Heritage Hotels, a group of castles, forts, and havelis that have been converted to charming accommodations. Samode Haveli (Jaipur), Castle Mandawa (Shekhavati), Rohet Garh (near Jodhpur), and Fateh Prakash Palace (Udaipur) are among the finest. All hotels are air-conditioned unless we note otherwise.

Shopping

JEWELRY

Rajasthani women adorn themselves with spectacular jewelry: bangles; tinkling anklets; armbands; and finger, nose-, toe-, and earrings. Men are also fond of wearing gold hoops in their ears and amulets around their arms. In Jaipur, look for gold settings of *kundan* (a glasslike white stone) and *mina* (enamel) work. Udaipur, Nathdwara, and Jaisalmer are all known for antique and contemporary silver jewelry. Decorated *lac* (lacquer) bangles are worn for good luck. Rajasthani artisans also specialize in cutting precious and semiprecious stones. Jaipur is a trade center for precious stones, and one of the emerald capitals of the world.

LEATHER

Men and women work together to produce Rajasthan's fantastic leather work. Men do the tanning, cutting, and stitching, and women add embroidery and ornamentation. Look for leather shoes, sandals, fans, pouches, saddles, and even musical instruments.

PAINTINGS

Rajasthan is famous for paintings in the *phad* and *pichwai* styles. The phad is a red, green, and yellow scroll depicting the life of a local hero; the dark and richly hued pichwais, hung in temples, are cloth paintings depicting Lord Krishna in different moods. Equally popular are reproductions of *mandana* art, designs traditionally drawn by women on the walls and floors of rural homes using a chalk solution on a crimson cow-dung background. These unique works are ritual decorations for festivals and ceremonial occasions. If you're looking for miniature paintings, you'll find the biggest and best selection in Udaipur—a center for this traditional art. Whether on paper, silk, marble, or bone, these astonishingly intricate works depict wildlife and courtly scenes, and illustrations of religious stories and mythological themes. Originally created by the *chittrekar* (artist) community, miniatures now usually blend both Rajput and Moghul styles. Building on the Rajputs' bright colors and courtly themes, the Moghuls added more detail to the faces and the landscapes.

PUPPETS

Puppetry (known as *kutputli*) has a proud history here. Most villages have a resident puppeteer, and many hotels and restaurants stage daily puppet shows. The wood-and-string creatures are sold throughout the state. Udaipur and Jaipur are the hubs: Udaipur's folk museum has a well-known puppetry program, and Jaipur's Kalbalia dancers also perform puppetry routines.

TEXTILES

Rajasthan is famous for its dyed and hand-blocked printed fabric, often further embellished by embroidery. Some hand-blocked patterns are familiar in the West, but the range of colors here is stunning. Of particular note are the *bandhani* (tie-dye), embroidered-mirror, and appliqué (patchwork) styles.

Exploring Rajasthan

You could easily spend a month in Rajasthan alone. The state's southwestern corner centers on Udaipur, a hilly town of palaces and artificial lakes. Central Rajasthan is anchored by Jodhpur, home to a glorious fort and the eye-catching blue houses of the Brahmin caste. Jaipur, the state capital, is in the east (toward Delhi). Western Rajasthan, largely given over to the Thar Desert, can best be explored via camel or jeep from the golden city of Jaisalmer. In the northeast, between Jaipur and Delhi, the Shekhavati region is home to lovely painted havelis, the mansions of prosperous merchants. The southern and eastern regions also have a number of first-rate wildlife parks.

Note that Rajasthan is a big state, with long stretches of territory between the most popular destinations. If you have limited time here, it's best to stay in one city and explore the surrounding area rather than try to rush through all the highlights.

Numbers in the text correspond to numbers in the margin and on the Rajasthan and Jaipur maps.

Great Itineraries

Distances here are long, and transportation is relatively slow. The best way to see Rajasthan is to fly to Jaipur, Jodhpur, and/or Udaipur and make excursions from each.

IF YOU HAVE 3 DAYS

Fly into ⊞ **Udaipur** and spend the day wandering the narrow, hilly lanes of the old city and visiting the vast City Palace. That evening, take a boat ride on Lake Pichola or a cab up to the Monsoon Palace at sunset. If you can, stay at the Lake Palace Hotel, smack in the middle of the lake—it's a sight in itself. The next day, fly to ⊞ **Jaipur** and explore the pink-hued Old City. Take a taxi out of town to the Amer Fort and Palace, then spend the night in one of Jaipur's havelis or palace

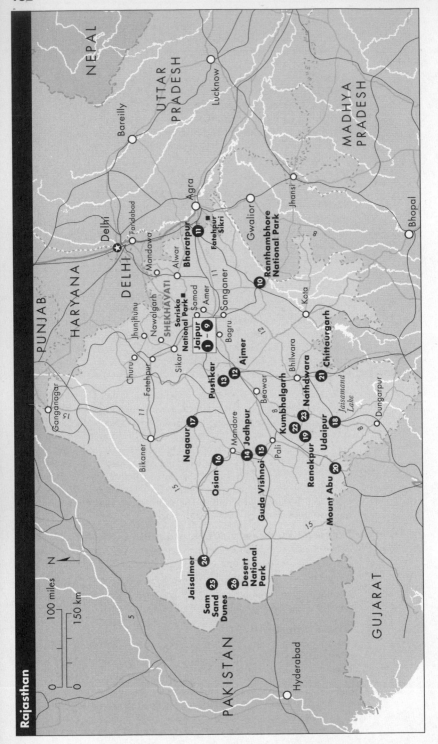

NEPAL

UTTAR PRADESH

MADHYA PRADESH

HARYANA

PUNJAB

DELHI

GUJARAT

PAKISTAN

Lucknow

Bareilly

Agra

Jhansi

Bhopal

Gwalior

Delhi

Faridabad

Mandawa

Alwar

Bharatpur **11**

Fatehpur Sikri

Ranthambhore National Park

10

Jhunjhunu

Nawalgarh

SHEKHAVATI

Sariska National Park

Samod

Amer

Jaipur **1 – 9**

Sanganer

Bagru

Kota

Churu

Fatehpur

Sikar

Mandore

Pushkar **13**

12 Ajmer

Beawar

Bhilwara

Chittaurgarh **21**

Kumbhalgarh **23** Nathdwara

Jaisamand Lake

Dungarpur

Gang_anagar

Bikaner

Nagaur **17**

Jodhpur **14** **15**

Pali

22 **19** Udaipur **18**

Osian **16**

Guda Vishnoi

Ranakpur

Mount Abu **20**

Jaisalmer **24**

Sam Sand Dunes **25** **26** Desert National Park

Hyderabad

N

100 miles

150 km

0

0

hotels. On your third day, hire a car and driver to explore **Shekhavati,** stopping in villages such as Jhunjhunu and Mandawa to see the lovely havelis, some with magnificent frescoes. Treat yourself to a meal at one of the Heritage Hotels. From here you can easily drive to Delhi.

IF YOU HAVE 6 DAYS

As on the three-day itinerary, fly into ⊞ **Udaipur** and spend a day and a night here. Try to pop outside the city to the crafts village of Shilpgram. The next day, drive northwest to the Jain temple at **Ranakpur,** and spend a few hours exploring the temple and the surrounding countryside. Continue on to ⊞ **Jodhpur** and spend the night in one of the city's splendid hotels. Head up to the fort the next morning, then spend the day exploring Jodhpur itself. Take the overnight train to ⊞ **Jaisalmer** and spend day four and the following night here. The morning of day five, embark on a half-day camel trek. Return to Jaisalmer in time for dinner and the overnight train back to **Jodhpur.** On your last day, fly to **Jaipur** to see the Amer Fort and Palace and the delightfully pink-colored Old City.

IF YOU HAVE 10 DAYS

Spend your first day exploring ⊞ **Jaipur.** After a night in one of Jaipur's luxurious hotels, hire a car, and leave early for a trip to one of Rajasthan's wildlife parks. ⊞ **Bharatpur,** on the eastern edge of the state, is one of the finest bird sanctuaries in India; if you prefer tigers, head to ⊞ **Ranthambhore National Park.** Spend the afternoon in the great outdoors and the night at a park lodge, then venture out early the following morning to watch the animals as they wake. Leave the park on day three for ⊞ **Shekhavati** (an easy hop from Bharatpur, a longer drive from Ranthambhore). Spend your third night at one of the Heritage Hotels in this region, and drive back to Jaipur on day four.

From Jaipur, fly to ⊞ **Jaisalmer** and consider devoting days five and six to a camel safari, which means you'll be sleeping in the desert those two nights. Fly or take the overnight train to ⊞ **Jodhpur** for day seven. Fly the next morning to ⊞ **Udaipur,** and splurge on one of the city's magical hotels for your last two nights here. If you like temple architecture, make a detour to the Jain temples at **Ranakpur** and **Mount Abu** or the Hindu temples at **Nathdwara.** Leave Rajasthan on day 10. This is a crowded schedule, but you'll get to see most of Rajasthan's highlights.

When to Tour Rajasthan

Rajasthan is best visited from October to March. Unfortunately, everyone knows this, so the sights can be crowded. If you want to get away from the hordes and can bear the heat of a desert summer, go in April. By May and June, it's brutally hot. The monsoon season (July–September) is fine unless you want to see the wildlife parks, which tend to flood. Alternatively, come for a festival: There's the Pushkar camel fair in November, the Shekhavati art festival in December, the Jaisalmer desert festival in January, Udaipur's Gangaur festival in April, and Mount Abu's summer festival in June.

JAIPUR AND ENVIRONS

You can take quite a few day trips around the countryside, from Rajasthan's capital. The craft villages of Sanganer and Bagru, just outside Jaipur, are populated almost entirely by artisans, and you're free to stop in and watch them make fine paper and block-print textiles by hand. If you're here in autumn, you may want to check out the town of Ajmer, a one-time Rajput stronghold that was later conquered by the Muslims—and which houses one of the most important shrines to a Muslim saint (Khwaja Mu'in-ud-din Chisti, 1142–1236) in India. The Hindu pilgrimage town of Pushkar is known for its annual camel festival in January. To escape civilization altogether, go animal-spotting at the Ranthambhore or Keoladeo National Parks.

Jaipur

261 km (163 mi) southwest of Delhi, 343 km (215 mi) east of Jodhpur, 405 km (251 mi) northeast of Udaipur

A Rajasthani proverb asks, *"Je na dekhyo Jaipario, To kal men akar kya kario?"* ("What have I accomplished in my life, if I have not seen Jaipur?")

Surrounded on three sides by the rugged Aravalli Hills, and celebrated for its striking pink buildings, Jaipur is the capital of Rajasthan, and a fine starting point for a trip through the region. Significantly, the city is also known for being one of the few planned cities in the world.

Jaipur takes its name from Maharaja Sawai Jai Singh II, an avid scientist, architect, and astronomer, and is said to epitomize the dreams of the ruler and the creative ideas of his talented designer and builder, Vidhydar. Jaipur was founded in 1727, when Sawai Jai Singh moved down from Amer (commonly misrendered as Amber), the ancient rockbound stronghold of his ancestors. Rectangular in shape, the city is divided into nine blocks based on the principles of the ancient architectural treatise *Shilp Shastra*. Every aspect of Jaipur—streets, sidewalks, building height, and number and division of blocks—was based on geometric harmony, sound environmental and climatic considerations, and the intended use of each zone. Originally colored yellow (a color you can still see on the backs of the buildings), it was painted pink when Prince Albert, consort of Queen Victoria, visited India in 1883. This explains why Jaipur is commonly referred to as "the Pink City." The tradition stuck: by law, buildings in the old city must still be painted saffron-pink.

A bustling metropolis-in-the-making, Jaipur has a population of almost 2 million. It has grown tremendously in the last two decades; some speculate that in 20 years it will be as large as Delhi. Part of the city is still enclosed in 20-ft-high fortified walls, surrounded by eight gates.

Timelessly appealing bazaars full of colorful textiles and trinkets—lac bangles, steel utensils, copper ornaments—and *mendhi* (henna) artists form an integral part of the city center and its outlying villages. Another cultural highlight of Jaipur is its mouth-watering cuisine, particularly desserts: ghevar, *pheeni* (strawlike sweets), *jalebis* (fried, pretzel-shape orange sweets), *churmas* (tasty wheat-flour dumplings), and *baati* (baked bread). The sensory whirl and jumble of colorful *ghagharas* (skirts) and turbans, towers of quilts, and sturdy *jutis* (pointed shoes), and streets packed with camel carts and cycle-rickshaws, make Jaipur a dazzling, spirited city like no other.

A Good Tour

Start outside the walled Old City, at the **Albert Hall Museum** ①, then walk north on Chaura Rasta into the Old City. Turn right on Tripolia Bazaar to reach the **Jantar Mantar** ② observatory. A left onto Sireh Deorhi Bazaar takes you to the **Hawa Mahal** ③ and **City Palace** ④. After a break for lunch, take a taxi north of town to the **Amer Fort and Palace** ⑤. Spend the afternoon here and at **Nahar Garh Fort** ⑥, and watch the sun set at the nearby **Kanak Vrindavan Gardens** ⑦.

The next day, visit **Sisodia Rani ka Bagh** ⑧ and, if you'd like to meet some local artists, **Jawahar Kala Kendra** ⑨.

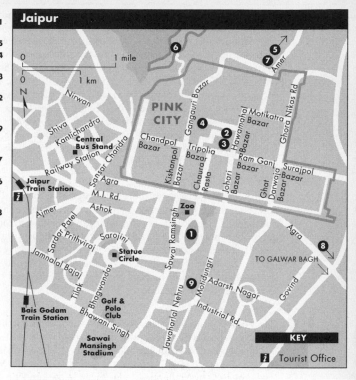

TIMING

Start early, as the Amer Fort closes at 4:30. If you're running late, save it for the next day.

Sights to See

❶ Albert Hall Museum. Worth a visit just for its architecture, this sandstone-and-marble building was built in the late 19th century in the Indo-Saracenic style. The collection, which unfortunately is not well-maintained or well-organized, includes folk arts, miniature paintings, traditional costumes, unexpected exhibits of yoga postures, and visual explanations of Indian culture and traditions. ⊠ *Ram Niwas Gardens.* 🎫 *Weekends and Tues.–Thurs. Rs. 3, free Mon.* ☉ *Sat.–Thurs. 10:30–4:30.*

★ ❺ Amer Fort and Palace. Surrounded by ramparts, this marvelous fortress is perched on a hill near Maota Lake. Built by Raja Man Singh, Mirza Raja Jai Singh, and Sewai Jai Singh over a period of 125 years, it was for centuries the capital of the Kachhawah Rajputs. When the capital shifted to Jaipur in the early 18th century, the site was abandoned, but, while the fort is in ruins, the interior palaces, gardens, and temples retain much of their pristine beauty. Both the art and the architecture combine Rajput and Moghul influences in felicitous ways.

You approach the palace complex by walking or riding an elephant up a sloping incline to the **Singh Pole** gate and **Jaleb Chowk,** the preliminary courtyard. Two flights of stairs lead up from the chowk; for now, skip the one leading to the Shila Mata temple and take the one leading to the palace itself. In the next courtyard, the pillared **Diwani-i-Am** (Hall of Public Audience) contains alabaster panels with fine inlay work—the kind of craftsmanship for which Jaipur is famous. Typical of the Moghul period, the rooms are small and intimate, whereas the palace's successive courtyards and narrow passages are characteristically Rajput.

From the latticed corridor over the elaborately carved and painted gate known as **Ganesh Pol,** after the elephant god Ganesh, the queen—always in purdah, or hiding—would await the King's return from battle and sprinkle scented water and flowers down upon him. Each room shows some vestige of its former glory, especially the **Sheesh Mahal** (Palace of Mirrors), with glittering mirror-work on the ceiling. Narrow flights of stairs lead up to the lavish royal apartments, and beyond the corridors and galleries here you'll find the small, elegant **Char Bagh** garden. Drink in the views of the valley, the palace courtyards, the formal gardens abutting the octagonal pool next to the lake, and the vast **Jaigarh Fort,** the ancient fortress on the crest of the hill above you. Also on the upper floor is **Jas Mandir,** a hall with filigreed marble *jalis* (screens) and delicate mirror and stucco work.

On your way out, peek into the 400-year-old **Shiladevi Temple** to the goddess Kali, with its silver doors and marble carvings. Raja Man Singh installed the image of the goddess after bringing it here from lower Bengal (now Bangladesh). Exit the palace by the gate near the temple, and just a few minutes down the road is the 450-year-old **Jagat Shiromani** temple. Dedicated to Krishna, this exquisitely carved marble and sandstone temple was built by Raja Man Singh I in memory of his son. ⊠ *Delhi Rd., 11 km (7 mi) north of Jaipur.* ⌨ *Rs. 4; with cameras Rs. 50.* ⊙ *Daily 9–4:30.*

★ ❹ **City Palace.** This complex of pavilions, courtyards, chambers, and palace was begun by Jai Singh II, with further additions from later maharajas. Once you're in the outer courtyard, the marble-and-sandstone building directly in front of you is the **Mubarak Mahal** (Guest Pavilion), built by Maharaja Madho Singh in the late 19th century. Now a museum, it's an ideal place to admire at close range some of the royals' finest brocades, silks, and hand-blocked garments and robes, many made in nearby Sanganer and some dating from as far back as the 17th century. The collection also includes musical instruments. The **armory** in the northwest corner of the courtyard has one of India's best collections of arms and weapons, including an 11-pound sword belonging to Akbar's Rajput general. Some of the paints on the beautiful, 250-year-old ceiling are said to be made of crushed semiprecious stones.

In the inner courtyard, through the gateway guarded by two stone elephants, is the art gallery housed in the cavernous **Diwan-i-Am** (Hall of Public Audience). Built in the late 18th century, the building has rows of gray marble columns, the second-largest chandelier in India, and a magnificent, vintage-1930s painted ceiling. The art includes scores of miniatures from the Moghul and various Rajput schools, rare manuscripts, and 17th-century carpets from the Amer Palace. From the inner courtyard, enter the Zenana courtyard on the left to see the seven-story **Chandra Mahal** (Moon Palace). Built by Jai Singh II, this attractive cream-hue building is still the official residence of the present maharaja, "Bubbles"—Lieutenant Colonel Sawai Bhawani Singh—who lives on the upper floors. The ground floor has sumptuous chandeliers, murals, and a painting of an old maharaja. ⊠ *Center of the Old City, enter the complex from the east, off the main road to Ajmeri Gate.* ⌨ *Rs. 70; cameras extra.* ⊙ *Daily 9:30–4:45.*

❸ **Hawa Mahal.** Jaipur's photogenic Palace of Winds was built by Maharaja Sawai Pratap Singh in 1799 so that the women of the court could discreetly take some air and watch the activity on the street below. Every story has semi-octagonal overhanging windows, and each has a perforated screen. This curious five-story structure—mainly a facade, named after the westerly winds that blow cool breezes through the windows—is just one room thick. The wind easily passes through the building and works like a cooler. (Traditionally, servants would also throw water on the lattice, so any breeze would be cooled by the water, and would lower the temperature.) The building facade's delicate honeycomb design, fashioned of pink sandstone, seems to glow. ⊠ *Sireh Deorhi Bazaar.* ⌷ *Rs. 2; cameras Rs. 30.* ⊘ *Sat.–Thurs. 10–5.*

★ ❷ **Jantar Mantar.** The Newton of the East, Jai Singh II was well aware of European developments in the field of astronomy, and wanted to create the world's finest observatories. He supervised the design and construction of five remarkable facilities in northern India, of which this is the largest and best preserved. Built in 1726 of masonry, marble, and brass, it's equipped with large solar instruments called *yantras,* which look like large, abstract sculptures, and are remarkably precise in measuring celestial data. If you don't have a guide with you, try to recruit one to explain how these devices work, as they're fascinating and, for nonscientists, somewhat complicated. ⊠ *Tripoliya Bazaar (near entrance to City Palace).* ⌷ *Rs. 4; cameras Rs. 50.* ⊘ *Daily 9–4:30.*

❾ **Jawahar Kala Kendra.** Jaipur's center for arts and crafts was founded by the state government with a specific vision: to create a space for understanding and experiencing culture and folk traditions amid the chaos and traffic of urban life. It's also becoming a venue for theatrical and musical performances. If you're an arts connoisseur, drop in to meet and talk with some of the locals who exhibit and perform here, or just to collect information on cultural events. ⊠ *Jawaharlal Nehru Marg (opposite Jhalana Institutional Area).* ⊘ *Daily 10–6; concerts some evenings.*

❼ **Kanak Vrindavan Gardens.** This picturesque set of gardens and temples is just below the majestic Amer and Nahar Garh forts. From here you can take a good look at the Jai Mahal palace in Man Sagar Lake. The gardens also make a great picnic spot, especially if you like to people-watch. If you're lucky you might even catch a glimpse of Bollywood's brightest filming a Hindi movie. ⊠ *Amer Rd.* ⌷ *Rs. 5.*

❻ **Nahar Garh Fort.** You can get a breathtaking view of Jaipur from Nahar Garh Fort's scenic hilltop location. Initially built by Sawai Jai Singh in 1734, it was enlarged to its sprawling, present-day glory in 1885 by Sawai Madho Singh, who commandeered it as a lookout point. Cannons placed behind the walls recall the days when artillery was positioned against potential attackers below. The Rajasthan tourist board runs a snack bar at the fort, and indeed it's a great place for a picnic. ⊠ *10 km (6 mi) north of Jaipur off Amer Rd.*

❽ **Sisodia Rani ka Bagh.** On the road to Bharatpur stands one of many palaces built for the *ranis,* or royal Sisodia Rajput queens, of Sawai Jai Singh II. Built in 1779, the palace still looks lovely against the backdrop of the hills. Its terraced garden is punctuated with fountains, and the palace itself is furnished with murals illustrating hunting scenes and the romantic legend of Krishna and Radha. From the terrace, you can see dancing peacocks and plenty of monkeys. Come during the day, as the site is often reserved for weddings and parties at night. ⊠ *8 km (5 mi) east of Jaipur on road to Bharatpur.* ⌷ *Rs. 5*

··

OFF THE
BEATEN PATH

★

Galwar Bagh Known by locals and rickshaw wallahs simply as Monkey Temple, Galwar Bagh is a popular pilgrimage site and temple complex on the outskirts of town. The temple itself is called **Gulta Ji Mandir**; it's a 30-minute walk from the ceremonial gate called Gulta Pol, located at the far eastern edge of the city, off Ajmer Road—about five minutes from the Muslim quarter. The walk leads you over a small mountain pass and past, inevitably, at least a few Hindu sadhus (holy men) and small temples. Jaipuri Hindus believe that at the site of the Gulta Ji Mandir, a local saint named Gala Rishi—nicknamed Gulta Ji—brought forth a spring of holy water from the Ganges and filled a water tank 18 ft deep. The waters here are said to be spiritually connected to the Ganges—if you bathe here, you get the same benefits as a pilgrimage to the Ganges. The temple, which venerates Lord Brahma, Creator of the Universe, is in violation of a curse by Brahma's wife Savatri; she confined his temples to Pushkar. ⊠ *Outside Gulta Pol, Near Agra Rd. on the east side of town.* 🎫 *Free.*

Dining and Lodging

$$$$ ✕ **Panghat.** Starting at 8, this dinner theater in a grove provides an
★ exquisite performance of traditional Rajasthani dance and music while you sip cocktails in a small open-air amphitheater that simulates village dining. After the performance (depending on the season) you can sit on cushions or chairs and watch a puppet show, or watch women prepare traditional breads over a wood fire. Thalis are served with freshly baked breads. The restaurant is seasonal from October to February. ⊠ *Taj Rambagh Palace,* ☎ *141/381919. Reservations essential. AE, DC, MC, V. No lunch.*

$$–$$$$ ✕ **Suvarna Mahal.** Once the maharaja's royal banquet hall, this room is so grand—with a soaring, painted ceiling, handsome drapes, and tapestry-covered walls—that it's hard to concentrate on the menu, which includes Indian, Chinese, and Continental dishes. Regional specialties include *murgh tikka zaffrani* (chicken marinated in yogurt and saffron and cooked in a tandoor) and *dahi ka mass* (lamb cooked in a yogurt-based curry). Go for the enormous thali, which mixes things up deliciously. ⊠ *Taj Rambagh Palace,* ☎ *141/381919. Reservations essential. AE, DC, MC, V.*

$$ ✕ **Apno Gaon.** If you won't have time to visit a small village, here's your chance to get a feel for Rajasthani folk culture. Like the state's half-dozen simulated villages, Apno Gaon offers camel rides, playground swings, traditional music, and puppet shows. The food is so good even locals feast here. You'll get farm-fresh, organically grown vegetables, and *bhajra* (maize) delicacies and milk products. Be prepared to sit on the ground and eat with your hands. Apno Gaon is open all day, but is better at night. The street signs are in Hindi, so ask your driver for directions. ⊠ *Sikar Rd. (past Vishwa Karma Industrial Area),* ☎ *141/ 331802. No credit cards.*

$$ ✕ **Chokhi Dhani.** Come hungry to this village complex, where you'll
★ sit on the floor in a lantern-lit hut and enjoy Rajasthani vegetarian dishes Indian-style (with your hands, no silverware). Around the compound, you'll see traditional dances, singing, puppet shows, and juggling. Entertainment is included in the cost of the meal, and tipping is discouraged. The temples here are real. If you're here at sunset, you'll see the traditional village *aarti* (prayer ceremony). Camel and boat rides cost Rs. 5; only rupees are accepted throughout. ⊠ *Tonk Rd. (19 km, or 12 mi, south of Jaipur via Vatika),* ☎ *141/583534, 141/580118, or 141/580850,* ℻ *141/580183. AE, MC, V.*

$$ ✕ **Laxmi Misthan Bhandar.** Known affectionately as LMB, this institution is famous all over Rajasthan for fresh and sumptuous sweets, including *ghevar* (funnel cake), *mave ki kachori* (a milk-based pastry), and other savory snacks and meals. The rest of the food is average, though the *shahi* thali has an impressive 15 items. This is a great place to pick up gifts for Indian families, or sweets to donate at an evening *aarti*. The store sells their sweets by the kilogram; prices range from Rs. 95 to Rs. 600 per kg, but you'll probably spend about Rs. 200 on sweets here. ⊠ *Johari Bazar,* ☎ *141/565844. No credit cards.*

$–$$ ✕ **The Copper Chimney.** Jaipur's jet set needs some place to go for a night on the town, and this restaurant often starts things off. It takes its name from a copper chimney that is displayed center stage. Diners sit behind beautiful etched glass and look out onto the street below. While the menu has Continental, Chinese, and Indian selections, it would probably be best to avoid some of the odd hybrids such as *paneer Manchurian,* but the *palak paneer*(peas with cheese) and the sweet-and-sour lassis are exceptional. ⊠ *Mirza Ismail Rd., near G.P.O.,* ☏ *141/ 360889. AE, MC, V.*

$–$$ ✕ **Handi Restaurant.** This no-frills restaurant with bamboo walls and a thatch roof has some of the best non-vegetarian Mughlai food in town. One bite of the *kathi* kebab (garlicky mutton wrapped in thinly rolled bread with onions and tomatoes) and you'll forget all about the plastic chairs. Other specialties include a tangy butter chicken (chicken marinated in yogurt and baked in a tandoor, then cooked in a tomato curry) and the specialty, *handi* meat (a spicy mutton dish cooked in a handi, or clay pot). Only rupees are accepted. ⊠ *M. I. Rd., opposite G.P.O.,* ☏ *141/364839. No credit cards.*

$–$$ ✕ **Niros.** This Jaipur institution is probably the most popular restaurant with the city's upper middle class. Amid mirrors and marble floors, it serves good Indian and Chinese food, as well as Continental dishes. Specialties include *reshmi* kebab (skewered boned chicken), paneer tikka (Indian cheese with skewered tomatoes, onions, and capsicum), and mutton *tikka masala* (tandoori lamb simmered in a spicy tomato-and-butter sauce). Niros also has the best cold coffee in town, topped with a scoop of ice cream. ⊠ *M. I. Rd.,* ☏ *141/374943. AE, DC, MC, V.*

$ ✕ **Lassiwalla.** No visit to Jaipur is complete without a stop at the most
★ famous lassi wallah in all of India. Located on the periphery of a long chain of imposters, the real thing can only be found under the sign "Kisan lal Govind Narayan Agrawal." Expect a long line. The lassi wallah himself wears a *tilak* and *moti mala* to demonstrate his devotion to God and good service, and sits elevated above a large bowl of yogurt and cream. Served in disposable red clay cups with a dash of hard cream on top, your only choices are medium or large. ⊠ *M.I. Rd., across from Natraj.,* ☏ *no phone. No credit cards.*

$ ✕ **Natraj.** Natraj is a terrific place for coffee and dessert, although the setting is a little rough around the edges. If you dine upstairs, over the main dining room, you can sit in a fiberglass shell made to look like a cave. The house specialty is *bundi ki laddu* (sweet graham balls), and the *rasgulla* (cheese balls in a sugary syrup) and *ras malai* (sweet cheese dumplings smothered in cream) melt in your mouth. The silver thali has a good assortment of vegetables and breads, and is one of the best on M.I. Road. ⊠ *M. I. Rd.,* ☏ *141/371863 or 141/402804. AE, MC, V.*

$ ✕ **Shivir.** This cozy rooftop restaurant has plush carpeting, a fine city view, and good Indian food. Live *ghazals* (Urdu-language love songs) set the mood during lunch and dinner. Shivir is known for its tandoori dishes, baked breads, and curries; try *aloo bhojpuri* (potato stuffed with paneer) and chicken *lajawaab* (boneless chicken served in a nicely spiced gravy). Top things off with a creamy dessert of ras malai. ⊠ *M. I. Rd., Govt. Hostel Junction,* ☏ *141/378771. AE, DC, MC, V.*

$$$$ 🏨 **Jai Mahal Palace Hotel.** This 250-year-old palace is not as grand as
★ the Maharaja's other ancestral homes, and is farther from the city center, but the elegant white structure is extremely romantic. The lavish, Moghul-style garden has a row of fountains and an enormous chessboard with virtually life-size pieces. The interior has been restored with Rajasthani handicrafts and heirlooms: the suites are sumptuous, with priceless antiques and artwork, and the other rooms are Western-style comfortable. Rooms look out over the lawns or the pool. On-site en-

tertainment includes puppet shows and folk dances. ✉ *Jacob Rd., Civil Lines, 302006,* ☎ *141/223636,* FAX *141/220707. 102 rooms, 6 suites. Restaurant, coffee shop, bar, pool, barbershop, hair salon, meeting room, travel services. AE, DC, MC, V.*

$$$$ ⊞ **Rajvilas.** Twenty minutes outside Jaipur, Rajvilas is a destination unto
★ itself. A complementary service escorts guests from the airport or train station and into the paradise of orchards and fountains. Rajvilas's standard double rooms have marble and glass bathtubs overlooking private gardens. The separate villas with private pools have been a favorite with Bill Clinton. The ayurvedic spa treatments here are gaining a worldwide reputation as some of the most comprehensive available. ✉ *Near Goner Rd., 303012,* ☎ *141/680101,* FAX *141/640202; reserve through Oberoi Group, New York,* ☎ *212/223–8800 or 800/562–3764,* FAX *212/223–8500. 54 rooms, 14 tents, 3 villas. Restaurant, bar, pool, health club, spa, 2 tennis courts, horseback riding, business services, meeting room, travel services, airport shuttle, helipad. AE, DC, MC, V.*

$$$$ ⊞ **Taj Rambagh Palace.** Once home to the Maharaja of Jaipur, this airy,
★ cream-color palace is relaxing and wistfully romantic, down to the peacocks strutting across the lawns and the arcaded back patios. Standard rooms are spacious and largely contemporary; Superior and Luxury rooms have traditional furnishings, and colorful Shekhavati-style frescoes on the walls. Most higher-end rooms have original furnishings. The suites are opulent: the exotic Maharani Suite has a ruby-red cushioned alcove—and the enormous Prince's Suite has its own fountain. The grandest suites are on ground-level; their floor-to-ceiling windows look out over lush foliage. Ask for Rajendra at the hair salon; she gives a wonderful scalp massage. The hotel is on the edge of Jaipur—not within walking distance of tourist sites. ✉ *Bhawani Singh Rd., 302005,* ☎ *141/381919,* FAX *141/381098. 106 rooms, 4 suites. 2 restaurants, coffee shop, bar, indoor pool, barbershop, hair salon, health club, golf privileges, 3 tennis courts, badminton, Ping-Pong, squash, baby-sitting, business services, meeting room, travel services. AE, DC, MC, V.*

$$$ ⊞ **Welcomgroup Rajputana Palace Sheraton.** This sprawling brick structure, designed as a haveli, has four courtyards and numerous fountains, but it's more chic than it is traditional. The Western-style rooms are plush and comfortable. The pool, set in the main courtyard along with an outdoor bar, is lovely, and the nightclub is one of the central meeting points for the city's upper-class youth. This is the place to be if you value comfort over nostalgia. ✉ *Palace Rd., 302006,* ☎ *141/401144; 800/325–3535 in the U.S.,* FAX *141/401122;* FAX *141/360017; 800/325–3535 in the U.S. 200 rooms, 16 suites. 3 restaurants, 2 bars, pool, barbershop, hair salon, health club, billiards, dance club, recreation room, business services, travel services. AE, DC, MC, V.*

$$ ⊞ **Alsisar Haveli.** This cheerful yellow haveli is close to the Pink City, but its large lawn distances you from urban noise. Built in 1892 as the city residence of Shekhavati Rajputs, the bungalow has elegant rooms with carved antique furniture, restored frescos, bedspreads with traditional Rajasthani prints, rug-covered tile floors, and brass-frame mirrors (in the bathrooms). In the public areas are crystal chandeliers, hunting trophies, and various weapons. Jeep and camel safaris—for hire at an extra charge—can take you to a nearby village and fort. ✉ *Sansar Chandra Rd., 302001,* ☎ *141/368290,* FAX *141/364652,* WEB *www.alsisarhaveli.com. 22 rooms. Restaurant, pool, billiard room, travel services. AE, MC, V.*

$$ ⊞ **Chokhi Dhani.** Separated by a wall from the restaurant of the same name, this little hotel south of Jaipur lets you stay in a village setting without giving up modern conveniences. Opt for a room in one of the mud huts, with wooden doors and carved furniture—unless you prefer to live like a landowner in the large painted haveli, with marble

floors and modern bathrooms. The complex mirrors a village right down to the swimming pool, designed to look like a village water tank. The vegetarian restaurant does, however, have Western-style tables and chairs. ⊠ *Tonk Rd., 19 km (12 mi), south of Jaipur via Vatika, 302015,* ☎ *141/583534 or 141/380118,* FAX *141/580183. 40 rooms, 8 suites. Restaurant, bar, pool, spa, massage, sauna, gym, tennis court, meeting room. AE, DC, MC, V.*

$$ 🏨 **Raj Mahal Palace.** Built in 1729 by Sawai Jai Singh II, this small palace has a world-weary air. It has a turbulent history: the palace was first used as a refuge by Queen Chandra Kanwar Ranawatji of Udaipur, who feared her son might be in danger from rivals to the throne. In 1921, the palace became the residence of a British political officer; in 1958, it was occupied by the Jaipur royal family. Now a Heritage Hotel, the palace offers spacious, if modest, rooms with high ceilings and few windows. The Maharaja suite was actually used by the Maharaja of Jaipur until the 1970s, and doesn't cost much more than the standard rooms, which are somewhat lackluster. The restaurant serves the same recipes it once served the king. ⊠ *Sardar Patel Marg, C-Scheme, 302001,* ☎ *141/383260-(2),* FAX *141/381887. 21 rooms, 5 suites. Restaurant, bar, pool, badminton, croquet. AE, MC, V.*

$$ 🏨 **Samode Haveli.** Tucked away in a corner of the Pink City, this lemon-
★ yellow haveli is now a Heritage Hotel. Built for a prime minister of the royal court in the mid-19th century, and arranged around two court-yards, the haveli still has an air of stately grace and some original frescoes. Rooms are spacious and simply furnished. For opulence, stay in one of the two Sheesh Mahals, the luxurious quarters of the local Rajput himself (still moderate in price), which have antique furniture, walls, and pillars inlaid with mirror work. Low arches and mazelike corridors add to its Rajasthani charm. The best views are of the elegant palace gardens. Camel and elephant rides are easily organized. The haveli also runs the **Samode Bagh** luxury-tent encampment in Fathepur village, Shekhavati. ⊠ *Gangapole 302002,* ☎ *141/632407 or 141/630943,* FAX *141/631397. 25 rooms, 2 suites. Restaurant, travel services. AE, MC, V.*

$$ 🏨 **Samode Palace.** Nestled in a narrow valley between red and green hills 45 km (28 mi) from Jaipur, this 18th-century palace, built in the shadow of a small fort, towers over its little village. The palace has splendidly painted and enameled public rooms. Guest rooms, which have their own pillars and arches, are furnished with traditional Rajasthani-style chairs and beds with mosquito-net canopies. They're not regal, but they're clean and comfortable. Royal Suites are spacious and even have their own fireplace, courtyard, and jacuzzis. The staff can arrange horse, camel, and jeep safaris. ⊠ *Samode, Jaipur district; reserve through Samode Haveli, Ganga Pol, 302002,* ☎ *1423/44114, 1423/44123,* FAX *141/632370. 43 rooms. Restaurant, bar, swimming pool, health club, horseback riding, travel services. AE, MC, V.*

$ 🏨 **Bissau Palace.** A sweeping courtyard and driveway leads to the ve-
★ randa of this two-story 1919 bungalow, now a Heritage Hotel, on the outskirts of the Old City. The lounge, library, and dining room are filled with paintings and artifacts. There's a small Royal Museum with weapons from the 17th century. The bar offers the finest selection in town. Guest rooms in the old wing have original furniture, cotton dhurries (rugs), and murals; those in the new wing are furnished with four-poster beds, divans, and pieces from the armory. Rooms aren't fancy (no phones or TVs), but they have Rajasthani touches, and are neat and clean. The family also has a beautiful retreat (visited by British royalty) 27 km (19 mi) outside town, where you can relax by the pool, sleep in a quaint two-room bungalow, and take a camel ride through surrounding villages. ⊠ *Outside Chand Pol (near Sarod Cinema),*

302016, ☎ 141/304371 or 304391, FAX 141/304628. 48 rooms, 13 suites. Restaurant, bar, pool, tennis court, baby-sitting, travel services. AE, MC, V.

$ 🖼 **Jasvilas.** If you stay at this upscale guest house, you'll forego the
★   facilities of a larger hotel for the comfort of a home away from home. Built during colonial times, the residence retains the traditional haveli shape of a mansion built around a courtyard. It also has a private pool in the courtyard. Western-style rooms have marble floors, two sinks, bathtubs, and Internet connections for laptops. Run by a Rajput family who returned to India from Chicago, they are happy to give tourist advice about Jaipur, and do their best to cater to the needs of foreigners. ✉ *C-9 Sawai Jai Sing Hwy., Bani Park, 302016,* ☎ *141/204638,* WEB *www.jasvilas.com. 5 rooms. Restaurant, swimming pool. AE, MC, V.*

$ 🖼 **Santha Bagh.** Once a lush garden commissioned by the Maharaja to stem local desertification, this Rajput family-run lodge offers personal service. The rooms contain beautifully carved antique and modern furniture. Most rooms lack TVs, but the hotel makes up for it with air-conditioning. The dining room gives you a glimpse into a martial past: elephant armor and photographs from the era of the Raj are on display. For a hotel that's just a few minutes from the center of town, the property is surprisingly peaceful and secluded. ✉ *Kalyan Path, near Police Memorial, 302004,* ☎ *141/566790,* FAX *141/560332. 14 rooms. Restaurant. MC, V.*

Nightlife and the Arts

Your best bet for a night out is one of the hotel bars, which are usually open from about 11 AM to 3 PM and 7 PM to 11:30 PM. Hotel discos kick in from about 7 to 11:30.

Many hotels stage cultural programs for their guests, such as the dance performances with dinner in Panghat, at the Rambagh Palace. In addition, such restaurants as **Apno Gaon** and the **Chokhi Dhani** village complex offer excellent performances of Rajasthani folk dance coupled with traditional regional meals. **Ravindra Rang Manch** (✉ Ram Niwas Garden, ☎ 141/619061) hosts occasional dinner-and-dance programs.

To experience a contemporary Indian institution, head to the movies. **Rajmandir Movie Theatre** (✉ 16 Bhagwandas Rd., near Panch Batti, ☎ 141/379372) plays song-and-dance Bollywood films only. It has a beautifully ornate interior and is known as the best movie hall in Asia. The theater disperses different blends of incense at occasional points in the film. Widely visited by Indian and foreign tourists, Rajmandir is still constantly flooded with locals, who sing, cheer, and whistle throughout each film.

Sports and Outdoor Activities

Polo is a passion in Jaipur. In season (late March and late October), matches are held at the **Rajasthan Polo Club.** Call the Taj Rambagh Palace (☎ 141/381919) or the **Rajasthan Polo Club** (☎ 141/383580) for information. The **Rajasthan Mounted Sports Association** (☎ 141/366276) gives polo lessons.

Golf lovers can phone the **Taj Rambagh Palace** (☎ 141/381919) to reserve access to a driving range.

Shopping

Rajasthan's craftspeople have been famous for centuries for their jewel settings, stonework, blue pottery, enamel, lacquer, filigree work, tie-dye, and block-printed silk and muslin. You'll find all this and more in Jaipur, but watch out: your drivers and/or guides are likely to insist that they know the best shops and bargains in the city. (They get a commission on whatever you purchase.) If you have a specific shop in mind, be firm. Don't rely on the phrase "government-approved." Easily painted over a shop door, it's essentially meaningless. The following shops are reliable, and you're bound to find others in your explorations. Note that many shops are closed on Sunday.

ARTS AND CRAFTS

If you have limited time and lots of gifts to buy or don't relish bargaining, head to an emporium. The enormous, government-run **Rajasthali** (⊠ Government Hostel, M. I. Rd., ☎ 141/367176 or 141/372974) is always flooded with interesting crafts. **Tharyamal Balchand** (⊠ M. I. Rd., ☎ 141/370376 or 141/361019) sells a variety of authentic, good-quality crafts ranging from jewelry and brass work to textiles, blue pottery, and wood work. Here you'll get a good sense of the diversity of crafts and textiles from the different parts of Rajasthan. **Manglam Arts** (⊠ Amer Rd., ☎ 141/37170) is filled with exquisite antique and contemporary fine art, including Hindu pichwais (cloth paintings depicting Lord Krishna in various moods), Jain temple art, tantric and folk art, terra-cotta sculptures, silver furniture, handwoven dhurries, wood carvings, and wonderful old fabrics. If you miss the store here, check out the branch in Udaipur.

For specialty shops, wander through the **Kazana Walon ka Rasta** lane in the Old City (accessible from Chand Pol) and watch stone-cutters create artworks in marble. For brass or other metalwork, visit **P. M. Allah Buksh and Son** (⊠ M. I. Rd.)—established in 1880, it still sells the finest hand-engraved, enameled, or embossed brassware, including oversize old trays and historic armour. The tiny, unpretentious shop **Bhorilal Hanuman Sahar** (⊠ Shop 131, Tripoliya Bazaar) has burlap bags full of old brass, copper, and bronze pieces that are sold by weight at bargain prices. The **Popular Art Palace** (⊠ B/6 Prithviraj Rd., C-Scheme, ☎ 141/360368) is great for both brass and wooden furniture, as well as miniature crafts and antiques.

For demonstrations of hand-block printing and other craftsmanship, visit **Rajasthan Cottage Industries** (⊠ Shilpgram Complex, Golimar Garden, Amer Rd., ☎ 141/630891). It offers a fine variety not only of textiles, but also of other handicrafts and gems. Purchases are guaranteed. **Rajasthan Small Scale Cottage Industries** (⊠ Jagat Shiromani Temple Rd., Amer, ☎ 141/530519) sells good selections of textiles, gems, and handicrafts, including hand-block printing. Purchases are guaranteed.

A special treat for lovers of miniature paintings is a trip to the home of award-winning artist **Tilak Gitai** (⊠ E-5 Gokhle Marg, C-Scheme, ☎ 141/372101), who creates exquisite miniatures in classic Moghul, Rajput, Pahari ("hilly"), and other styles. Using antique paper, Gitai applies colors made from semiprecious stones, then real gold and silver leaf, in designs so fine he'll give you a magnifying glass to admire them. This is not a quick visit—it's a lovely way to spend a few hours with a friendly Rajasthani family and learn about Indian art.

JEWELRY

Gem Palace (⊠ M. I. Rd., ☎ 141/374175) has Jaipur's best gems and jewelry, a small collection of museum-quality curios, and a royal clientele; prices range from US$2 to US$2 million. **Amrapalli Jewels** (⊠ Panchbatti, M. I. Rd., ☎ 141/377940 or 141/362768) has some great silver and ornamental trinkets, as well as semiprecious stone artifacts. For precious jewels, including gold ornaments, find the **Bhurmal-Rajmal Surana Showroom** (⊠ 368 J. L. N. Marg, ☎ 141/570429 or 141/570430) known worldwide for its kundan (a glasslike white stone) and mina (enamel) work. If you want something that's not so expensive and you're willing to bargain, you'll find your niche on **Chameli Valon**

ka Rasta (✉ off M. I. Rd.). Walk among the shops on this lane for silver and semiprecious jeweled ornaments, trinkets, and small toys.

POTTERY

Jaipur Blue Pottery Art Center (✉ Amer Rd., near Jain Mandir, ☎ no phone) sells a broad selection of Rajasthan's fetching blue pottery. Clay pots are "thrown," or made, on the premises. The blue pottery at **Neerja Internationals** (✉ S-19 Bhagwan Singh Rd., C-Scheme Extension, ☎ 141/380395 or 141/383511) is particularly funky—the designer/owner Lela Bordie has exhibited all over the world, and she runs this shop for a discriminating crowd.

TEXTILES

Channi Carpets and Textiles (✉ Mount Rd. opposite Ramgarh Rd., ☎ 141/672274) has an excellent selection of handwoven merino wool carpets, cotton dhurries, and hand-block cottons and silks. The staff can also tailor clothes on short notice.

Anokhi (✉ 2 Tilak Marg, opposite Udhyog Bhawan, C-Scheme, ☎ 141/381247) is a leading shop for designer and ethnic wear, mostly in cotton. The selection includes beautiful bedspreads, quilts, cloth bags, saris, and other clothing, both Indian and casual Western. You can also visit the on-site workshop. Run and managed by women, the cute **Cottons** boutique (✉ 4 Achrol Estate, Jacob Rd.) carries simple, attractive clothes for both men and women, as well as little bags, quilts, and other decorative household items. Catering to the aesthetically discriminating, **Soma** (✉ 5 Jacob Rd., Civil Lines, ☎ 141/222778) is a second-floor paradise of vibrant colors. Here you'll find everything from clothing to chutneys to decorative fabrics—including fabulous, hand-painted white cloth lamp shades. For fine hand-block fabrics, go to the nearby towns of Sanganer and Bagru.

Ranthambhore National Park

⑩ *161 km (100 mi) south of Jaipur*

Now incorporating several nearby sanctuaries in its borders, Ranthambhore National Park encompasses 1,334 square km (515 square mi). Its locale is spectacular: the rugged Aravalli and Vindhya hills, highland boulder plateaus, and lakes and rivers provide homes for hundreds of species of birds, mammals, and reptiles. Ranthambhore is noted for its tiger and leopard population, although you still have only a so-so chance of seeing a large cat on any given expedition. The best time to see tigers is right before the monsoon, in the summer, when the tigers emerge to drink from small water holes. (When it's dry and the water table is low, the tigers are forced out of hiding to quench their thirst.) What you will definitely see are numerous peacocks, deer (including large sauras), wild pigs, and often sloth bears.

The park is run by the Indian government, and the rules are somewhat inflexible: you can only enter the park in an official government jeep, and the jeeps keep strict hours, from 6:30 AM–9:30 AM and 3:30 PM–6:30 PM. In the off-hours, you can explore the surrounding region; **Ranthambhore Fort,** atop one of the nearby hills, is more than a thousand years old, and one of Rajasthan's more spectacular military strongholds.

Within the park itself are two government-run hotels, **Jhoomar Baori** and **Jogi Mahal.** Both are decent and, more importantly, offer the chance to spend a night near the animals. *For information call Sawai Madhopur Tourist Information Center,* ☎ *7462/20808.* 🎫 *Rs. 575 per jeep.* ⊙ *Oct.–June.*

Lodging

The neighboring town of Sawai Madhopur has numerous hotels, but most are extremely basic.

$$$ ⊞ **Sawai Madhopur Lodge.** The one luxurious accommodation near Ranthambhore National Park is this Taj-run property. Like most of Rajasthan's former hunting lodges, it has comfortable, atmospheric rooms, smooths out all the safari details with the forestry office, and has a good—and expensive—restaurant. Ask about packages that include meals in the room price. ⊠ *Ranthambhore Rd., Sawai Madhopur 322001,* ☎ *7462/20541,* FAX *7462/20718. 20 rooms, 6 tents, 2 suites. Restaurant, bar, tennis court, croquet, billiards, travel services. AE, DC, MC, V.*

Bharatpur

⓫ *150 km (93 mi) east of Jaipur, 55 km (34 mi) west of Agra, 18 km (11 mi) west of Fatehpur Sikri*

Founded by the Jat ruler Suraj Mal in 1733 and named for the brother of Lord Ram, the city of Bharatpur is famous for the **Keoladeo National Park** (also known as the Ghana Bird Sanctuary), once the duck-hunting forest of the local maharajas. The park is home to mammals and reptiles—blue bulls, spotted deer, otters, and Indian rock pythons—but birds are the main attraction. This famous waterbird haven is an ornithologist's dream—29 square km (10 square mi) of forests and wetlands with 400 species, more than 130 of which are resident year-round, such as the Saras crane, gray heron, snake bird, and spoonbill. In winter, birds arrive from the Himalayas, Siberia, and even Europe.

The best way to see the park is on foot, but there are plenty of other options. The park's main artery is a blacktop road that runs from the entrance gate to the center. Surrounded by marshlands but screened by bushes, this road is the most convenient viewpoint for bird-watching, and is also traveled by cycle-rickshaws (Rs. 30 per hour), a horse and buggy, and the park's electric bus. The rickshaw drivers, trained by the forest department, are fairly good at finding and pointing out birds. You can also rent a bicycle (about Rs. 20) and head into more remote areas; just remember that most roads are unpaved. There's a boating area at the beginning of the trail head, but it's quite small. The excellent guides at the gate (Rs. 35 per hour per person or Rs. 75 for a group) are familiar with the birds' haunts, and can help you spot and identify them.

Try to bring a bird guidebook: former royal-family member Salim Ali's *The Birds of India* is a good choice. The best time to see the birds is early in the morning or late in the evening, November–February; by the end of February, many birds start heading home. Stick around at sunset, when the water takes on a mirrorlike stillness and the air is filled with the calls of day birds settling down and night birds stirring. ⊠ *For information, contact the Tourist Reception Center, Hotel Saras, Agra Rd., Bharatpur 321001,* ☎ *5644/22542.* ۞ *Park daily 6 AM–6:30 PM.* 🎫 *Rs. 100; cameras Rs. 10; video cameras Rs. 250.*

Northwest Bharatpur holds the **Lohagarh Fort,** also known figuratively as the Iron Fort. Built of mud, the structure might seem fragile, but it was tested by a British siege in 1805: armed with 65 pieces of field artillery, 1,800 European soldiers and 6,000 Indian sepoys did manage to win the battle, but they failed to break the invincible fort.

The town of **Deeg,** 34 km (21 mi) north of Bharatpur, is known for its graceful palaces and gardens, complete with swings and ancient fountains. (The latter are now pressed into service as musical fountains, in which capacity their waters dance to the rhythm of taped classical music.) Also built in the 1730s, Deeg was the first capital of the Jat state.

Lodging

\$\$ ✕🏨 **Ashok Bharatpur Forest Lodge.** This ivy-covered bungalow inside the sanctuary has clean, comfortable rooms—some with decorative interior swings. All rooms have balconies, from which you may see spotted deer nibbling the grass outside. The Indian and Continental food in the restaurant is served buffet-style, and is excellent. ✉ *Bharatpur 321001,* ☎ *5644/22722 or 5644/22760,* ℻ *5644/22864. 17 rooms. Restaurant, bar. AE, DC, MC, V.*

\$\$ 🏨 **Laxmi Vilas Palace Hotel.** Still home to the former maharaja's uncle
★ and his family, this cozy Heritage Hotel is a two-story haveli built in 1899. The palace, on a 40-acre estate covered with mustard flowers, blends Moghul and Rajput styles. Each room is different, but many contain old brass beds and antique furniture. Pricier rooms have original tiles and painted walls and fireplaces; the others are smaller and have newer furniture, but they're still pleasant. A variety of cuisines are served in the dining room. The family is happy to organize jeep safaris or excursions to surrounding areas, such as Deeg, Agra, and Fatehpur Sikri. ✉ *Kakaji Ki Kothi, Bharatpur 321001,* ☎ *5644/25259 or 5644/23523,* ℻ *5644/25259. 7 rooms, 11 suites. Restaurant, travel services. AE, MC, V.*

Ajmer

⑫ *131 km (81 mi) southwest of Jaipur*

Situated in a green oasis roughly three hours' drive from Jaipur, Ajmer has an interesting past. Founded by Raja Ajay Pal Chauhan in the 7th century, the town was a center of Chauhan power until 1193, when Prithvi Raj Chauhan lost the kingdom to Mohammed Ghori. From then on, many dynasties contributed to making Ajmer what it is today—a fascinating blend of Hindu and Islamic culture—demographically, it's primarily a Muslim town, although its proximity to Pushkar gives it a Hindu feel. In the heart of the city is **Darga Sharif,** the tomb of Khwaja Moin-ud din Chisti. This site is comparable to Mecca in significance for South Asian Muslims, and is frequented by Muslims and non-Muslims alike, especially during Urs (a death anniversary celebration that takes place during six days in the Islamic month of Rajab—around September or October). If you visit, be sure to cover your head, and feel free to give *namaz* (prayers) and lay a *chaddhar* (sheet) on the saint's tomb.

Pushkar

★ **⑬** *11 km (7 mi) northwest of Ajmer*

With more than 500 temples, Pushkar is one of Hinduism's holiest sites. Its religious significance derives from the Vedic text *Padma Purana,* which describes how the town was created. Lord Brahma, Creator of the Universe, was looking for a place to perform the *yajna*—a holy ritual that involves placing offerings into a sacrificial fire for Agni, the fire god—that would signify the beginning of the human age. He dropped a lotus from his hand and it struck the earth in three places. The area in between became known as Pushkar. The most important temple, in the center of town, is **Brahma Temple,** supposedly the only temple dedicated to Brahma in the world. Pilgrims visiting the temple climb a long stairway into the walled area of the temple to take the blessings of the god—in the form of small sweets. There are varying versions of legend concerning the temple, but most have to do with Brahma's wife Savitri, who refused to attend the ceremony. Impatient, Brahma married the goddess Gayatri (some say she was a milkmaid), and when Savitri found out, she put a curse on Brahma: for the rest of eternity, Brahma could only be worshipped in Pushkar. Thanks to the legend, Pushkar has become one of Hinduism's most sacred places. During auspicious pilgrimage times, tens of thousands of people swarm the holy bathing ghats (flights of steps) on Pushkar Lake and get blessings from local Brahmins.

After you visit the Brahma Temple, check out the two temples that crown hills on opposite sides of Pushkar Lake—these are dedicated to both of Brahma's wives. It's a short walk: it only takes between a half-hour and an hour for either, and the view is worth it.

Make sure you spend some time at the holy ghats around Pushkar Lake. Many of the marble ghats at Pushkar were constructed for pilgrims by royal families who wanted to ensure power and prosperity in their kingdoms throughout Rajasthan by appeasing the gods. Even the British Raj built a ghat for Queen Elizabeth. When you pass an entrance to a ghat, be prepared for a priest to solicit you—he'll want you to receive a blessing, "The Pushkar Passport." He'll lead you to the water's edge, say a prayer, and will ask you to recite a blessing in Sanskrit (you'll repeat after him). Then he'll paste a *tilak* (rice and colored powder) on your forehead and tie a *raki* (a string bracelet, denoting a blessing) to your wrist. After the ceremony, you're expected to give a donation of about 100 rupees.

If you really want an experience, go to Pushkar during its famous annual **Camel Fair.** Every October or November—depending on the lunar calendar—people flock here to see the finest camels parade around the fairground in colorful costumes. People come to buy, sell, and trade camels, and to race one camel against another. A good male camel goes for about $250. The town gets packed during festival time, so make sure you reserve a room ahead of time.

While you're here, stroll around the streets of Pushkar's main bazaar, which teem with pilgrims, monkeys, cows, and merchants hawking their wares. It's one of the main attractions in Rajasthan—regional goods from all over the state are sold at the market. Restaurants abound on this 2-mi stretch, but don't come looking for meat or alcohol—they're forbidden in Pushkar because of religious ordinances.

For an oddball adventure in getting to Pushkar, schedule an overnight elephant safari from Jaipur; contact the Rajasthan Tourism Development Corporation (RTDC) or a local travel agency for more information.

Lodging

$$ ⊞ **Pushkar Palace.** Considered one of the best Heritage Hotels in Rajasthan, this majestic palace sits above its own ghat, with fabulous, panoramic views of Pushkar. Built by the Maharaja of Jaisalmer in the 15th century, the Pushkar Palace was later presented to the Maharaja of Kishangarh. In 1998, the hotel served as headquarters for the film *Holy Smoke,* starring Kate Winslet. All the rooms are outfitted with antique furniture from Rajputana's heyday. As a guest here you'll receive regal treatment. Horse, camel, and jeep safaris are available. ✉ *Hotel is right on the lake,* ☎ *145/772001,* FAX *145/772226. 30 rooms, 5 suites. Restaurant, bar, horseback riding, travel services. AE, MC, V.*

$$ ⊞ **Pushkar Resorts.** Pushkar Resorts blends the spirit of the maharajas with the comforts of resort living. Relax poolside under the shade
★ of a palm tree and escape from Pushkar's chaotic main bazaar, a 15-minute jeep ride from the hotel. European-style rooms have views of

the Savatri temple that crowns a mountain near the resort. Famous here are the hotel's regal camel cart rides—you journey through sand dunes on the grounds adjacent to the resort while watching the sun set. The staff is extremely attentive. The restaurant is open to guests but not the public; they serve superb chicken and spicy mutton dishes that are impossible to get in the city proper. The hotel is about 4 km (2½ mi) outside town. ⊠ *Village Ganhera, Motisar Rd.,* ☎ *145/772944,* FAX *145/772946,* WEB *www.pushkarresorts.com. Restaurant, bar, swimming pool, golf course, travel services. AE, MC, V.*

SHEKHAVATI

This large chunk of northeastern Rajasthan is renowned for its painted havelis and old forts. Shekhavati (literally "Garden of Shekha") takes its name from Rao Shekhaji, a Rajput king of this region, who was born in 1433. He was named after a *fakir* (Muslim holy man) named Sheikh Burhanby, who granted a boon to his parents that they would bear a son. In another unwitting contribution to history, the sheikh had come to India with the Mongol invader Tamerlane in 1398, dressed in a blue robe—hence the color of Shekhavati's flag. The region has had a turbulent history ever since, experiencing the conquests and defeats of Rajput princes, alliances with the Moghuls after Akbar, and finally suzerainty under the British Raj. The region is made up of smaller principalities, including Sikar, Lachhmangarh, Churi Ajitgarh, Mukundgarh, Jhunjhunu, Mandawa, Fatehpur, and Churu.

A regional center of trade between the 18th and 20th centuries, Shekhavati is now known as Rajasthan's open-air art gallery, thanks to the frescoes painted on the walls of ornate havelis throughout the region. Influenced by the Persian, Jaipur, and Moghul schools of painting, Shekhavati's frescoes illustrate subjects ranging from mythological stories and local legends to hunting safaris and scenes of everyday life. You'll even find illustrated experiences with the British and cars or planes. The introduction of photography in 1840 gave Shekhavati's painters still more to work with. The painters themselves were called *chiteras* and belonged to the caste of *kumhars* (potters). Initially, they colored their masterpieces with vegetable pigments; after mixing these with lime water and treating the wall with three layers of a very fine clay, the chiteras painstakingly drew their designs on a last layer of filtered lime dust. Time was short, as the design had to be completed before the plaster dried, but the highly refined technique insured that the images would not fade.

The havelis that contain these masterpieces are themselves spectacular. These havelis have courtyards, exquisitely latticed windows, intricate mirror work, vaulted ceilings, immense balconies, and ornate gateways and facades. They date from the British Raj, during which traditional overland trading routes to Central Asia, Europe, and China were slowly superseded by rail and sea routes. In the 19th century, Marwari traders (Hindus from the *vaisya,* or trading, caste) who had once profited from the overland trading system, then migrated to Calcutta, Bombay, and Madras to seek new fortunes. The wealthy Marwaris maintained connections with their ancestral homes, sending remittance from their new enterprises. Often this money was used to build lavish havelis, adorned with elaborate frescoes. Many of the havelis, as well as some old Rajput forts, are now open to the public. Some have been converted to Heritage Hotels (such as the Samode Palace in Jaipur). Stay in a few if you can, and take a day or two to explore the towns around them.

The golden age of fresco painting came to an end by the 1930s with the mass exodus of the Marwaris, who had left to resettle in the commercial centers. Since then, many of these beautiful mansions and their paintings have fallen into disrepair. Only a few handfuls have survived—some have been restored by their owners, and a few have been converted into hotels. In **Sikar,** formerly the wealthiest trading center, look for the Biyani, Murarka, and Somani havelis. **Lachhmangarh** features the grand Char Chowk Haveli, particularly evocative of the prosperous Marwari lifestyle. A planned city like Jaipur, Lachhmangarh is home to a popular ayurvedic center, **SPG Kaya Kalp and Research Center** (✉ Tara Kung, Salasar Rd., ☎ 1573/64230), which teaches yoga, meditation, and various therapies. In the village of **Churi Ajitgarh,** unusually erotic frescoes are painted behind doors and on bedroom ceilings in the Shiv Narain Nemani, Kothi Shiv Datt, and Rai Jagan Lal Tibrewal havelis. The frescoed temples of **Jhunjhunu** make for interesting comparisons: visit Laxmi Nath, Mertani Baori, Ajeet Sagar, and Qamrudin Shah Ki Dargah Fatehpur. **Mukandgarh** has an excellent craft market, known especially for textiles, brass ware, and iron scissors, in addition to the Kanoria, Ganeriwala, and Bheekraj Nangalia havelis. Warrior-statesman Thakur Nawal Singh founded **Nawalgarh** in 1737, and the town boasts some of the best frescoes in Shekhavati in its Aath, Anandilal Poddar, Jodhraj Patodia, and Chokhani havelis, as well as in the Roop Niwas Palace hotel.

Dining and Lodging

$$ ✕🏨 **Castle Mandawa.** Towering high above the town of Mandawa, this rugged, amber-color fort has been converted to a luxury Heritage Hotel. Sword-bearing guards welcome you at the gate; inside, the walls display 16th-century portraits of the Mandawa family. The spacious, airy rooms are furnished with period furniture. In the evening, you can sip tea on the main terrace and enjoy the view of the town and the Rajasthan desert below. Also check out the panoramic view from the canopied balconies and turreted battlements. Dinner is an enchanting candle-lit affair in an open-air courtyard. The evening's highlight is the spectacular Fire Dance: eight men in traditional attire follow an elderly retainer who dances with torches in his hands. Camel, horse, and jeep safaris are available. ✉ *Mandawa, Jhunjhunu district, 333704, 168 km (109 mi) northwest of Jaipur,* ☎ *1592/23124 or 1592/23480; reserve through 306 Anukampa Tower, Church Rd., Jaipur 302001,* ☎ *141/371194,* 🗏 *141/372084,* 🌐 *www.castlemandawa.com. 56 rooms, 14 suites. Restaurant, bar, horseback riding AE, MC, V.*

$$$ 🏨 **Neemrana Fort Palace.** This 15th-century fort, now a Heritage
★ Hotel, is one of the finest retreats in India. The fort is perched on a plateau in the Aravalli Hills. The rooms, which vary in size and price, are furnished with antiques and decorated with Rajput crafts. The architecture is characterized by wooden jalis (latticework screens), cusped arches, gleaming pillars, squinches, and niches. Forget about phones and TVs—just relax and watch preening peacocks and swooping parrots from the terraces, balconies, and courtyards. The restaurant serves fixed Rajasthani and French menus; breakfast and lunch or dinner are included in the room rate. Most bathrooms don't have tubs. The village nearby has an ancient step well—an enormous underground well with wraparound staircases and sitting areas on each level, where people once took refuge during the heat. ✉ *Village Neemrana, Alwar district, 301705, 100 km (60 mi) southwest of Delhi, off National Hwy. 8,* ☎ *1494/46007; reserve through A-58, Nizamuddin East, New Delhi 110013,* ☎ *11/4356145, 11/435896, or 11/4355214,* 🗏 *11/435112,*

WEB *www.neemranahotels.com. 42 rooms, 8 suites. Restaurant, bar, pool, spa, health club, massage, travel services. AE, DC, MC, V.*

$$ ⊡ **Desert Resort.** An eco-friendly resort, and the subject of many for-
★ eign travel features for its authentic village construction, Desert Re-
sort is an unusual, but worthwhile, place to stay. The interiors of its
clay-covered "village huts" on a large sand dune sparkle with the in-
laid glass embedded in the walls, and glow with the warmth of Ra-
jasthani fabrics and handicrafts. Even the main lounge is made of
mud, and the dining room gleams from the bits of glass and cowrie
shells in *its* walls. Sit by the pool or in the garden, and enjoy the strik-
ing desert panorama. ⊠ *Mandawa, Jhunjhunu district, 333704, 250
km (150 mi) southwest of Delhi,* ☏ *1592/23151; reserve through 309
Anukampa Tower, Church Rd., Jaipur 302001,* ☏ *141/371194,* FAX *141/
372084,* WEB *www.manvar.com. 18 rooms, 8 suites, 36 cottages. Restau-
rant, bar, pool, 9-hole golf course, tennis, croquet. AE, MC, V.*

$$ ⊡ **Hill Fort Kesroli.** This stone fort overlooking farmland and distant
hills has been turned into a Heritage Hotel by the same duo responsi-
ble for Neemrana. Kesroli doesn't have the same grandeur or scale as
Neemrana, but it's still an elegant place, and a good base from which
to explore the area. The origin of the seven-turret fort goes back six
centuries. Built by Yaduvanshi Rajputs, the building was later conquered
by the Moghuls and then the Jats before reverting to the Rajputs in
1775. The hotel is decorated with a tasteful mix of Indian antiques and
traditional crafts, and the price includes breakfast. The evening meal is
a sumptuous event. ⊠ *Kesroli village, Alwar district, 301030,* ☏ *01468/
89352; reserve through A-58, Nizamuddin East, New Delhi 110013,* ☏
11/4356145, 11/4358962, FAX *11/4351112,* WEB *www.neemranahotels.
com. 21 rooms. Restaurant. AE, DC, MC, V.*

$$ ⊡ **Mukandgarh Fort.** Founded in the mid-18th century by Raja Mukand
Singh, this picturesque fort in the town of Mukandgarh, famous for
its artisans, is now a Heritage Hotel. A bar overlooks the courtyard,
where an outdoor barbecue serves kebabs and curry in the evening.
Guest rooms have painted walls and ceilings, tie-dye curtains, and patch-
work bedspreads. Some of the rooms in the new wing don't have win-
dows, so check your room before you book it. The fort is just a
five-minute walk from the Babali Baba Mandir, the main temple in town.
⊠ *Mukandgarh, Jhunjhunu district, 333705, 250 km (150 mi) south-
west of Delhi,* ☏ *1594/52398 or 1594/52397,* FAX *1594/52395. 42
rooms, 4 suites. 2 restaurants, bar, travel services. AE, DC, MC, V.*

$$ ⊡ **Piramal Haveli.** Among the grandest of the traditional homes, this
one in the village of Bagar has three courtyards enclosed by colonial
pillared corridors. Originally built as the home of Seth Piramal
Chaturbhuj Makharia (1892–1958), who made his fortune trading
cotton, opium, and silver in Bombay, the frescoes here allude to
Makharia's wealth—they depict flying angels and gods in motorcars.
The Marwaris' traditional vegetarian cuisine is served; breakfast is in-
cluded in the room rate, and lunch and dinner are modestly priced.
⊠ *Bagar, Jhunjhunu district, 333023, 250 km (150 mi) southwest of
Delhi,* ☏ *01592/22220; reserve through A-58 Nizamuddin East, New
Delhi 110013,* ☏ *11/461–8962,* FAX *11/462–1112. 8 rooms. Restau-
rant. AE, DC, MC, V.*

$ ⊡ **Dera Dundlod Kila.** In the heart of the Shekhavati region, Dundlod
★ was built in 1750. Now a Heritage Hotel, the fort is still owned by the
descendants of the former *thakur* (landowner). Surrounded by a moat,
it has a mix of Moghul and Rajput architecture. Inside, the stunning
Diwan-i-Khas (Hall of Private Audience) has original wall frescoes, European-style portraits, Louis XIV furniture, and a well-stocked library.
The clean, simple bedrooms have painted walls. The family has 20 horses
and is mainly involved in promoting horse safaris (and camel and jeep

trips); they use the hotel as a base for these trips. In the rooftop restaurant, you can dine under the light of rustic oil lamps. ✉ *P.O. Dundlod, Jhunjhunu district, 333702, 250 km (150 mi) southwest of Delhi,* ☎ *15945/2519,* 𝔽𝔸𝕏 *15945/2519; reserve through Dundlod House, Civil Lines, Jaipur 302019,* ☎ 𝔽𝔸𝕏 *141/211276 or 141/211118. 20 rooms, 12 suites. Restaurant, bar, pool, horseback riding. AE, MC, V.*

$ ⌂ **Roop Niwas Palace.** This Heritage Hotel on the outskirts of Shekhavati combines Rajput and European architecture in its beautiful gardens and private cottages. It's far from grand, but the owners, descendants of the former thakur, aim to please. The rooms, with Victorian furniture, are modest but clean. The dining room is quaint and the grounds are lovely. The restaurant contains an eclectic assortment of antiques of both Rajput and British origin, and some firearms, including six-shooters and a blunderbuss. Jeep and camel safaris and bird-watching trips can be arranged. ✉ *Nawalgarh, Jhunjhunu district, Shekhavati 333042, 250 km (150 mi) southwest of Delhi,* ☎ *1594/22008,* 𝔽𝔸𝕏 *1594/ 23388. 30 rooms, 1 suite. Restaurant, bar, pool, horseback riding. AE.*

JODHPUR AND ENVIRONS

Jodhpur is rich in fort and palace treasures and a great place from which to take side trips—to Guda Vishnoi, home of the gentle Vishnoi community and a haven for wildlife, or the temple town of Osian in the Thar Desert. Nagaur Fort also entices—you can camp here splendidly, in fine tents, during the town's winter cattle fair.

Jodhpur

⑭ *343 km (215 mi) west of Jaipur, 266 km (165 mi) northwest of Udaipur*

Known as the Blue City because of the color of its houses, and guarded by one of the most imposing fortresses of Rajputana, Jodhpur looks like a sea on the fringe of the Thar Desert. Jodhpur is encircled by a wall 9 km (6 mi) around, which keeps out the desert sands. The city, at the base of a sandstone ridge, was the capital of the Marwar kingdom for five centuries. It was named after its 15th-century founder, Rao Jodha, chief of the Rathore clan of Marwar—which traces its lineage to Lord Rama, hero of the Hindu epic *The Ramayana*.

Getting around Jodhpur is relatively easy. Walk through a massive fort, palaces, and gardens as well as markets full of fruit, textile, and handicraft stalls. Take special note of Jodhpuri and *pathar* peach-color stone that makes Jodhpur's houses and buildings stand apart from others in Rajasthan. If you have extra time, take a desert safari on camelback.

Jodhpur is also famous for its food and hospitality, especially its *mithai* (sweets) and the *manuhar* ritual that accompanies its food. When you're offered a *mave ki kachori* (milk-based pastry) or *besan ki barfi* (a fudgelike sweet made of gram, or chick pea, flour), along with mirchi bada (fried, breaded green peppers) and *kofta* (deep-fried balls of potatoes or vegetables), don't resist: the offer will be repeated until you take some.

A Good Tour

With this plan you can tour Jodhpur in two days, covering the essentials first. Start your first day early, and spend a few hours at the majestic **Meherangarth Fort.** Take one of the waiting rickshaws down the mountain and north to the **Jaswant Thada** memorial. After a break for lunch, hire a car and driver for the short drive north of Jodhpur to the **Mandore Gardens.** From there, it's a hop, skip, and a jump to **Bal-**

samand Lake and Garden. If you have a little extra time, visit **Mahamandir.** End your day at the **Umaid Bhawan Palace Museum**—walk through the museum before it closes at 5, then stay for dinner and enjoy the fabulous sunset views.

If you have two days here, drive out of Jodhpur once again to see the wildlife-loving town of **Guda Vishnoi**, where deer and birds feed at water holes early in the morning. Return to Jodhpur for lunch and a bit of shopping. In the early evening, make a pilgrimage to the temple town of **Osian.**

Sights to See

★ **Balsamand Lake and Garden.** At this public park (really a wildlife sanctuary) you can enjoy a picturesque view of the park's 12th-century artificial lake and the royal family's beautiful 19th-century summer palace, now a hotel. The lake is surrounded by a thick jungle of fruit trees called *badis*. It's the perfect place for a tranquil stroll—just beware the mischievous monkeys, who are always on the watch for good pranks (and good vegetable *pakoras,* or fritters). Don't try to pluck the fruit from the trees, as the monkeys will catch you red-handed. ⊠ *5 km (3 mi) northeast of Jodhpur.*

Jaswant Thada. The royal marble crematorium was built in 1899 for Maharaja Jaswant Singh II. Capping the enormous white structure are marble canopies under which individual members of the royal family are buried. You may see people bowing before the image of the king, who is considered to have joined the ranks of the deities. ⊠ *Near Mehrangarh Fort.* 🎟 *Free.* ☉ *Daily 8–6.*

Mahamandir. Built in 1812 just outside Jodhpur, this old, walled monastery complex ("Mahamandir" means great temple) still contains a few hundred houses. The monastery belongs to the Nath community, warrior-priests who worked closely with the royal family to arrange support in times of war. Mahamandir is best known for the 84 beautifully carved pillars that surround it. ⊠ *9 km (6 mi) from Jodhpur.*

Mandore Gardens. Within the old Marwar capital at Mandore, these gardens house the exquisitely sculpted red-sandstone *davals* (memorials) to former rulers. The Hall of Heroes depicts 16 colorfully painted heroes and deities carved from a single piece of stone. The small **museum** on the grounds has sculptures from the 5th to the 9th centuries and ivory and lacquer work. There's even a **cactus nursery.** Unfortunately, due to the large number of picnics and dal baati churma (lentils with wheat-flour dumplings) feasts held here, the gardens have grown dirty and are not terribly well-maintained. ⊠ *Mandore, 8 km (5 mi) north of Jodhpur,* 🎟 *Free.* ☉ *Gardens daily sunrise–sunset, museum Sat.–Thurs. 10–4.*

★ **Mehrangarh Fort.** Perched on the top of a hill, this enormous fort was built by Rao Jodha in 1459, when he shifted his capital from Mandore to Jodhpur. Looking straight down a perpendicular cliff, the famously impregnable fort is an imposing landmark, especially at night, when it's bathed in yellow light. Approach the fort by climbing a steep walkway (the 40-minute hike is much more enjoyable than the rickshaw alternative), passing under no fewer than eight huge gates. The first, the Victory Gate, was built by Maharaja Ajit Singh to commemorate his military success against the Moghuls at the beginning of the 18th century; the other seven commemorate victories over other Rajput states. The last gate, as in many Rajput forts, displays the haunting handprints of women who immolated themselves after their husbands were defeated in battle.

Inside the rugged fort, delicate latticed windows and pierced sandstone screens are the surprising motifs. The palaces—**Moti Mahal** (Pearl Palace), **Phool Mahal** (Flower Palace), **Sheesh Mahal** (Glass Palace), and the other apartments—are exquisitely decorated; their ceilings, walls, and even floors are covered with murals, mirrorwork, and gilt. The palace museum has exquisite rooms filled with lavish royal palenquins, thrones, paintings, and even a giant tent. From the ramparts you can get an excellent city view. ⊠ *Fort Rd.* 🎫 *Rs. 50, camera Rs. 50.* ☉ *Daily 8:30–1 and 2:30–5.*

★ **Umaid Bhawan Palace Museum.** Built between 1929 and 1942 at the behest of Maharaja Umaid Singh during a long famine—the public-works project employed 3,000 workers—this palace is part museum, part royal residence, and part Heritage Hotel. Its Art Deco design makes it unique in the state. Amazingly, no cement was used in construction; the palace is made of interlocking blocks of sandstone, a fact to bear in mind when you stand under the imposing 183-ft-high central dome. The collection includes royal finery, local arts and crafts, miniature paintings, and a large number of clocks. You may catch a glimpse of the Maharaja of Jodhpur, who still lives in one large wing of the palace, but in any case you won't miss the magnificent peacocks that strut around the palace's marble *chattris* (canopies) and lush lawns.

One of Jodhpur's most exquisite places to watch the sun set is **Pillars,** the restaurant on the palace's elegant, colonnaded veranda. As you contemplate the immaculately manicured gardens, peacocks march up the steps and strains of sitar music fill the air. ⊠ *Umaid Bhawan Palace,* ☏ *291/510101.* 🎫 *Rs. 40.* ☉ *Daily 9–5.*

Dining and Lodging
Watch the hearty consumption of local grub at the local eating area **Rawat Mishtan Bhandar,** next to the train station. Your system might find the street food problematic, but the sight of crowds tucking into hot and spicy kachoris, koftas, and mave ki kachori can be enough of an appeal to indulge.

All the hotels listed below can arrange camel and jeep safaris, and usually other excursions as well, upon request.

$$–$$$ ✕ **Kabab Korner.** This open-air restaurant at Umaid Bhawan Palace has breathtaking views of Jodhpur at night. The tandoori food is excellent, as are the kebabs, skewered vegetables, and meats cooked over an open flame. When the sun is out this restaurant tends to heat up, so try going later in the day. ⊠ *Welcomgroup Umaid Bhawan Palace,* ☏ *291/510101. AE, DC, MC, V.*

$$–$$$ ✕ **Marwar.** Clearly one of the better attempts at upscale cuisine in Jodhpur, Marwar serves both Continental and Indian food. Every night, as live classical Indian music plays in the background, guests can choose from a buffet or order à la carte. The baby corn bezule (fish) and tandoori chicken are excellent, but the kitchen still has not perfected Continental cuisine. The restaurant is built in a neo-Moghul architectural style. ⊠ *Taj Hari Mahal, 5 Residency Rd., 342001,* ☏ *291/439700. Reservations recommended. AE, DC, MC, V*

$$–$$$ ✕ **Marwar Hall.** Huge chandeliers hang from the high vaulted ceilings of this gorgeous palace dining room, which was once the primary banquet hall of the Maharaja of Jodhpur. The chef prepares very good Continental and Indian food, including tasty Mughlai and regional Marwari dishes. Meals are served buffet-style. ⊠ *Welcomgroup Umaid Bhawan Palace,* ☏ *291/510101. AE, DC, MC, V.*

$–$$ ✕ **Khamaghani.** The walls of this classy restaurant are decorated with Rajasthani saris bunched up into circles. Half the tables, along with their red velvet chairs, are in a sunken enclave in the center of the room. Classical Indian music plays in the background. The menu includes local, Indian, Chinese, and Continental fare; the chicken tikka is particularly good, as are the Chinese dishes. ⊠ *Ratanada Polo Palace Hotel, Residency Rd.*, ☎ *291/43190. AE, DC, MC, V.*

$–$$ ✕ **Midtown Vegetarian Restaurant.** This unpretentious but spotlessly clean joint has Rajasthani wall hangings and specializes in Rajasthani and South Indian cuisine. Midtown specials include a *dosa* (Indian-style crêpe) filled with potato and cashews and *kabuli* (rice layered with vegetables, bread, and dried fruits and nuts). A salad bar rounds out the vegetarian menu. ⊠ *Hotel Shanti Bhawan, Station Rd.*, ☎ *291/621689,* ☏ *291/639211. No credit cards.*

$–$$ ✕ **On the Rocks.** This outdoor jungle-theme restaurant is aptly named, not because it has a well-stocked bar, but because the ground inside the restaurant (which is entirely outside) is primarily gravel. The recorded sounds of birds chirping might take it all a little too far over the top, but it is all done to match the style of Ajit Bhawan, the hotel it's housed in. The standard Indian fare is famous all around Jodhpur with the local upwardly mobile. After the meal try one of the milk shakes or relax with a drink by the fountain. ⊠ *Ajit Bhawan Hotel*, ☎ *291/ 510410. MC, V.*

$–$$ ✕ **Sukh Sagar.** Sukh Sagar specializes in South Indian food, but also serves North Indian and Chinese dishes. Try the *rava idli* (steamed semolina and rice cakes) and *vada sambar* (deep-fried lentil doughnuts served with spicy lentil stew), and take care to specify how hot you like your food. Down some South Indian filter coffee for an extra kick. ⊠ *Ratanada Bazaar*, ☎ *291/511450 or 291/621450. No credit cards.*

$ ✕ **Shri Misrilal Hotel.** In the highly competitive world of lassi wallahs,
★ only the strong survive. Standing in the shadow of Jodhpur's famous clocktower, this lassi shop—misleadingly called a hotel—is an age-old favorite among locals and foreigners. Look past the simple interior and neon lighting, and settle down on one of the long wooden benches. Then sit back and take in the rose water flavors; lassis here are consumed with a spoon. ⊠ *Near clocktower*, ☎ *no phone. No credit cards.*

$$$$ ▥ **Ratanada Polo Palace.** This hotel dedicated to the Rajasthani polo player Raorajahanut Singh is owned by his son. The marble entrance hall is lined with paintings and photos of Singh playing polo; horses' heads and profiles are a related motif. (One section was even a stable for polo players' steeds.) Bright, flowery bedspreads are the only traces of color in otherwise dark furnishings. The palace is in serious need of renovations, and seems to survive by reputation alone. The place is popular with business travelers and wedding parties; you'll find it easy to gate-crash, and join the fun of a traditional Indian wedding. ⊠ *Residency Rd., 342001*, ☎ *291/431910–(4)*, ☏ *291/433118. 80 rooms, 9 suites. Restaurant, bar, pool, tennis court, business services, meeting room, travel services. AE, DC, MC, V.*

$$$$ ▥ **Welcomgroup Umaid Bhawan Palace.** Built in the 1930s of pink sand-
★ stone—in the art deco style peculiar to colonial India—this magnificent fort palace is one of the grandest of Rajasthan's many such hotels. Still home to the Maharaja of Jodhpur, it has served as a backdrop for many Indian and foreign films. The public rooms are lavish, and filled with objects d'art; many of the rooms, though not opulent, are designed in period style. The newer rooms tend to be small and ordinary. Weary travelers can take a cool, refreshing dip in the beautiful, blue underground pool. ⊠ *Jodhpur 342006*, ☎ *291/510101*, ☏ *291/510100. 98 rooms, 4 suites. 3 restaurants, bar, indoor pool, sauna, health club, golf privileges, 2 tennis courts, horseback riding, squash, billiards, travel services. AE, DC, MC, V.*

$$$ ⊞ **Taj Hari Mahal.** The Taj's motif of running water is a cooling change
★ from the often harsh climate of Jodhpur. The rooms have original mod-
ern artwork from Rajasthan and other parts of the world, and the bath-
rooms are spacious and modern. This magnificent hotel is a respite from
the hustle-bustle of Jodhpur—it has a grand and elegant amber-color
lobby, and is, without a doubt, the place to stay if you're looking for
leisure. For special occasions, ask for a demonstration of the elabo-
rate chess dance, during which women in Rajasthani dress swirl across
a life-size chess board. ⊠ *5 Residency Rd., Jodhpur, 342001,* ☎ *291/
439700,* fAX *291/614451. 2 restaurants, bar, gym, shops, travel services,
conference rooms, pool, spa. AE, DC, MC, V.*

$$–$$$ ⊞ **Sardarsamand Lake Resort.** The hunting lodge of Jodhpur's former
Maharaja Umaid Singh is now a resort. Built in 1933, the verandas of
this pink sandstone-and-granite building have fabulous views of an ar-
tificial lake that attracts birds migrating between October to March.
Just beyond the lake are the expansive sands of the Thar Desert.
Rooms are decorated in their original fittings, though they also have
some art deco furnishings. ⊠ *Sardarsamand, nearby Jodhpur,* ☎ *2960/
952960. Reserve through Balsamand Lake Palace. 18 rooms. Restau-
rant, pool, tennis, horseback riding. MC, V.*

$$ ⊞ **Ajit Bhawan.** If you want an abundance of charm and few preten-
★ sions, stay in this small but enchanting palace and village complex, de-
signed and owned by the Maharaja of Jodhpur's uncle. The palace rooms
are now suites; each bungalow, which can sleep up to four, is uniquely
decorated in a Rajasthani motif and named after a month of the Hindu
calendar. The colorful, quaint rooms have painted tables and doors,
and traditional Rajasthani fabrics. Outside, paths wind through greenery and over little bridges. The garden areas are ample; with that and
the hotel's restaurant "On the Rocks," the complex effectively creates
its own lovely retreat. ⊠ *Near Circuit House, 342006,* ☎ *291/510410
or 511410,* fAX *291/510674. 40 rooms, 13 suites. Restaurant, bar,
pool, horseback riding. AE, MC, V.*

$$ ⊞ **Balsamand Lake Palace.** A fine example of Rajput architecture, this
★ red sandstone Heritage Hotel is surrounded by lush, expansive green
gardens on the outskirts of Jodhpur. Set on the banks of Balsamand
Lake, an artificial lake built in the 12th century, the palace has long
been a dreamy setting for royal R&R. The park around the lake con-
tains a small bird sanctuary; just watch out for aggressive monkeys.
Meals are prepared for guests only. ⊠ *Mandore Rd., 342006,* ☎ *291/
571991,* fAX *291/571240. 45 rooms. Restaurant, bar, pool, tennis court,
horseback riding. MC, V.*

$$ ⊞ **Fort Chanwa.** This century-old, somber red fort in the dusty village
of Luni is now a charming Heritage Hotel. It has spacious courtyards
and delightful rooms—with small arched windows called *jharokhas,*
Rajasthani-style furniture and fabrics, and old photographs. Many of
the small rooms have stairways leading to an alcove or to the bathroom. The water wheel—now a fountain in the bar—was originally
used to channel water around the fort. The restaurant has a fixed-price
Indian menu. ⊠ *Luni, south of Jodhpur 58 km (36 mi),* ☎ *291/84216;
reserve through Dilip Bhawan, House 1, P. W. D. Rd., 342001,* ☎
*291/432460. 20 rooms, 5 suites. Restaurant, bar, pool, horseback rid-
ing. V.*

$$ ⊞ **Jhalamand Garh.** Run and managed by the extremely hospitable
Jhalamand family, this small Heritage Hotel is an ideal setting for a
peaceful holiday. In addition to making sure you're comfortable, the
Jhalamands will help you plan your stay. By the end of your time here,
you'll feel like a member of the family. The terrace has stunning views
of Jodhpur. ⊠ *Village and Post Jhalamand, 342005, 10 km (6 mi) out-*

side town, ☎ *291/40481,* FAX *291/41125. 18 rooms, 6 suites. Restaurant, bar, horseback riding. AE, DC, MC, V.*

$$ 🏨 **Karni Bhavan.** This colonial-style bungalow, built of red sandstone in 1947, is now a Heritage Hotel. The hotel is famous for its personalized service. It also has great views of Mehrangarh Fort and Umaid Bhawan Palace. The rooftop restaurant serves Indian and Continental cuisine (the Rajasthani food is exquisite). This place is a kind of home away from home. Here you can also enjoy the hotel's beautiful pool and indulge a safari excursion around Jodhpur. ✉ *Palace Rd., 342006,* ☎ *291/512101–(4),* FAX *291/512105. 31 rooms, 5 suites. Restaurant, bar, pool. AE, DC, MC, V.*

$$ 🏨 **Rohet Garh.** This 17th-century desert fortress 40 km (25 mi) south
★ of Jodhpur is both a Heritage Hotel and the home of its Rajput family, whose members are your hosts. It's a great place to experience the lifestyle of Rajput nobility. The public rooms are decked out in original paintings and weapons; guest rooms, some of which have air-conditioning, are decorated in various ways with traditional carved furniture and colorful hand-blocked prints. Some even have swings, but none has a phone or TV. Horseback safaris are a specialty, as there are plenty of bird species and other animals nearby. ✉ *Rohet Garh Village, Pali district,* ☎ *2932/682321; reserve through Rohet House, P. W. D. Rd., 342001,* ☎ *291/431161,* FAX *291/649368,* WEB *www.rohetgarh.com. 26 rooms, 3 suites. Restaurant, pool, horseback riding, travel services. MC, V.*

$ **Haveli Guesthouse.** The old city has only one or two places to stay—despite the fact that it's clearly best to lodge in Jodhpur, with easy access to its important sites. The rooftop has excellent views of the city, and you'll be close enough to hear evening *arthi* (Hindu prayer service) at the temples near the clocktower. The rooms are basic and unpretentious, and lack A/C, phones, TVs and bathtubs—but what the hotel lacks in facilities it more than makes up for in convenience by being so close to the sights. ✉ *Makrana Mohalla, near clocktower,* ☎ *291/614615. Restaurant. No credit cards.*

Nightlife and the Arts

Your best bet for Jodhpur nightlife is one of the hotel bars, which are usually open from 11 AM to 2:30 PM and 6 PM to 11 PM. The **Trophy Bar** (✉ Umaid Bhawan Palace, ☎ 291/510101), with richly paneled walls and carpeted floors, is regal, but still feels intimate.

Mehrangarh Fort stages festivals and exhibits throughout the year; inquire at the **Tourist Information Center** (☎ 291/545083) or your hotel to see if anything is going on.

Sports and Outdoor Activities

Many hotels offer safaris to outlying villages. If yours doesn't, try one of the horse or camel trips offered by **Rohet Safaris** (☎ 291/431161).

Shopping

Jodhpur's vibrant bazaars are among the city's key sights, particularly **Sardar Bazaar** and the **Girdikot Bazaar,** near the clocktower. Wandering among the tiny shops dotting narrow lanes in the heart of town, you'll get a real feel for the life and color of Marwar. Everything from jewelry to underclothes, steel utensils to leather shoes, and trinkets to wedding clothes is sold here. Local spice merchants deal in saffron and other spices from all over India. Beware of tourist markups and young men guiding to their "uncle's store." **M.M. Spices** (✉ Shop 20613, clocktower, ☎ 291/624903) has a wide selection of spices clearly marked and packed in plastic for travelers with a passion for cooking Indian food. Polish your bargaining skills, because here, as with other shops, any foreigner is likely to get overcharged—packages are not marked with fixed prices.

There are plenty of stores to shop in, if you don't like haggling in bazaars. **Lalji Handicrafts Emporium** (⊠ opposite Umaid Bhawan Palace, ☎ 291/ 511378) has woodwork, antiques, leatherwork, and brass furniture. The collection includes unique painted boxes and *jharokhas* (carved doorways or windows) made of dark wood with brass decoration. This place is a joy if you love antiques. **Bhandari Handicrafts** (⊠ Old Police Line, Raika Bagh, ☎ 291/510621) sells wood items and antiques. For textiles, including cotton dress fabric, and other handicrafts, check out the four-story emporium **National Handloom** (⊠ Nayee Sadak, ☎ 291/638144). For high-end gifts, **Shenai** (⊠ Ratanada Polo Palace Hotel, ☎ 291/431910 or 291/431911) sells fine arts and crafts from all over Rajasthan, such as marble inlaid with gold and colored paints, silk scarves, and silver jewelry.

Guda Vishnoi

⑮ *25 km (16 mi) south of Jodhpur*

Guda Vishnoi is one of several immaculately kept villages of the Vishnoi community, a Hindu caste that takes its name from the 29 edicts its members agree to follow. In 1520, during a 20-year drought, the saint Jamboji came to the Vishnoi to ease their troubles by finding new water sources for them, and creating natural springs. Jamboji made a pact with the Vishnoi that if they accepted his commandments, they would never experience a water shortage again. The next year, the drought ended. The Vishnoi, who have faithfully kept to the teachings of Jamboji for almost 500 years, are one of Jodhpur's most distinct scheduled castes. Part of their pact was to respect the land and treat animals like their family—they are staunch believers in plant and animal life. The Vishnoi are very protective of their environment, and look harshly on anyone who appears to hurt their sacred deer and antelope populations, which they look on as members of their family. Notable are the rare migratory birds, such as the godavan and sara cranes, that pass through here. The Vishnoi are extremely outgoing and hospitable—they will invite you into their home for a cup of chai or *amala,* a mixture of opium and water traditionally reserved for special occasions and lazy days. Remember to bring your camera—unlike other Rajasthanis, the Vishnoi love having their picture taken. One word of advice: this area is difficult to navigate, as there are no real landmarks. Make sure you come with a tour guide.

Haveli Tours (⊠ *Makrana Mohalla,* ☎ *0291/614615*) offers a good tour of several local artisan communities and desert preserves. Contact Upendra Shirmali for details.

Shopping

Roopraj Dhurry Udyog. Local artisan Roopraj learned the art of weaving dhurries (carpets) from his father, who learned it from *his* father—the tradition goes back more than 200 years. His cotton carpets were originally reserved for the village thakur, or landowner, but once Indira Ghandi enacted the Industry for Rural Development Project (IRDP), his carpets were finally able to reach a wider market. The Roopraj Dhurry Udyog co-op cottage industry employs weavers from the village and keeps the tradition alive. It's as rewarding to watch the weaving process as it is to come with a purchase in mind, or just to shop for souvenirs. You'll definitely need a guide to help you get here. ⊠ *Salawas, 4 km (2½ mi) from the village, on the way to the*

town of Kakani; Salawas is near the railway crossing, ☎ *982/026658*
or 291/896658.

Dining

$ ✕ **Tulsi Ram ki Dhani.** Come for lunch in the home of Tulsi Ram, under
the sanctity of a thatch roof. It's the only restaurant in the area. For
the duration of the lunch, expect to feel as if you're part of his family.
This absolutely authentic meal is a must for anyone interested in Rajasthani cuisine and culture. As with all places in the area, this restaurant is very difficult to find unless you have a guide. ⊠ *Near the town
of Salwas.* ☎ *No phone.*

Osian

⑯ *58 km (36 mi) north of Jodhpur*

The ancestral home of the Oswal Jains, Osian is one of the birthplaces
of Jainism in India. Many invasions and several hundred years later, Osian
is now a popular Hindu pilgrimage site—though it has no significant
Jain community remaining. It's worthwhile coming here just to see the
temples, or to take a camel safari. Perched on a hill in the center of town
is the **Sachiya Mata Mandir** temple, where the (Jain) Naga Snake god
reliefs and etchings of Jain saints are readily apparent. Built around 1177
AD, some of the older statues were damaged during the reign of Aurangzeb
(1658–1707). An older, and arguably more important, 7th century
temple—said to be the first Jain temple in the world—is hidden in the
twisting alleys of the city. This temple, the **Mahavira Jain Temple,** is venerated from all over India. The feet of one particular statue of Bharu
on the outside of the temple are often covered with bright paper, oil,
coconuts, and even human hair. Hindus (not just Jains) believe that if
they make offerings here before they get married, their union will be
blessed and they'll be able to produce a child. To invoke the powers of
the god Bharu, devotees must make two pilgrimages to the temple. During the first pilgrimage they leave traditional offerings of coconuts and
oil to ask the god for fertility, they must also promise to return after
the child's birth to offer the newborn's hair to the god.

Sights to See

Just outside town is the home of Chuna Ram—he carves new statues
to help temple renovations, and encourages people to watch him work.
⊠ *Near Kushi Mundi, on the outskirts of Osian, toward Jodhpur,* ☎
2922/74577.

Lodging

$$$$ ⊞ **Camel Camp.** Perched on top of a sand dune is Camel Camp, a base
for operations for camel safaris in the Thar Desert. Every route takes
you through several different types of terrain and into the homes of local
craftsmen. Make sure you watch the sunset from the dunes—it's truly
a breathtaking experience. You can take two-, three- and four-day excursions; the accommodations throughout the trip will be luxurious (in
deluxe tents) the entire time. ⊠ *Near Railway Station. Reservations
through Jodhpur,* ☎ *0291/437023,* 🕸 *www.osiancamelcamp.com.*

Nagaur

⑰ *150 km (94 mi) northeast of Jodhpur*

Try to visit Nagaur during its colorful **cattle fair,** in late January or early
February, as only then can you can camp out royally at the historic
Nagaur Fort. Make sure you check out the remnants of beautiful fres-
coes on the fort's crumbling walls. Also note that the complex has an

amazing engineering system, which supplied enough water for the fountains and royal baths. The system also functions as a kind of air-conditioning in this otherwise arid land. Nagaur and its surrounding area are famous for making clay toys.

Lodging

$$$ 🏨 **Nagaur Fort.** Built between the 4th and 16th centuries, this enor-
★ mous fort serves as backdrop to a royal camp of spacious tents, dec-
orated inside with hand-blocked designs. Conveniently, the tents also
have electric lanterns, and attached bathrooms with flush toilets (hot
water is hand-carried in; it arrives via bucket). To signal for service,
you hang a little red flag outside the door of your tent. Meals are served
in a marble pavilion, in what was once a Moghul garden; in the
evening, you can sip cocktails and sit back on cushions, in front of a
bonfire, to watch a performance of traditional folk dances. Note: the
camp is open only during the cattle fair or by special arrangement. Re-
serve at least 60 days in advance. ✉ *Nagaur,* ☎ *1582/42082; reserve
through Umaid Bhawan Palace, Jodhpur 342006,* ☎ *291/510101,* FAX
291/635373. 35 tents. Restaurant. No credit cards. Closed Mar.–Dec.

UDAIPUR AND ENVIRONS

Expect to see marble palaces, elaborate gardens, serene temples, lush forests, and sparkling lakes as you explore Mewar, Rajasthan's southern region, in the marvelously green Aravalli Hills. Mewar also has several famous temples and religious sites attended yearly by thousands of pilgrims.

The region is perhaps most famous for having a rich military history—the chivalry and courage of its Rajput warriors are legendary. The Sisodia rulers of Mewar, who claim descent from the divine Lord Rama, are considered the most senior and respected members of all Rajput clans. The Mewar rulers were among the most determined foes of the Moghuls: long after other Rajput rulers conceded defeat, they alone resisted. The name Maharana Pratap still inspires pride in Mewar—Pratap resisted Emperor Akbar's reign through several guerilla wars. His struggle against Akbar is celebrated in murals and ballads all over Rajasthan, and it has been said that "As a great warrior of liberty, his name is, to millions of men even today, a cloud of hope by day and a pillar of fire by night."

Also famous for the vibrant festivals that take place in its cities and villages, Mewar's motto—"*Saat vaar, aur nau tyauhaar,*" which means "Seven days, nine festivals"—is apt. The biggest festival of the year is Gangaur, held in April in honor of the goddess Parvati, and observed primarily by girls of marriageable age. In the villages, the ancient tradition of *raati jagga*—all-night singing of mainly devotional songs by saint-poets, such as Kabir and Mirabai—takes place after weddings, childbirth, and sometimes even mourning, as a form of thanksgiving to a particular deity.

Mewar has two major indigenous tribal groups, the Bhils (also called *van putras,* or sons of the forest) and the Garasiyas. The lively songs, music, art exhibits, and dances of the tribes' festivals are a compelling reason to visit the region. Particularly memorable is the Ghoomer dance, in which hundreds of women dance in a giant circle. If you're here during a festival, try to see the *terahtal* dance, in which women dance—from a seated position—with *manjiras* (little brass discs) tied to their wrists, elbows, waists, arms, and hands. For added effect, the women may hold a sword between their teeth or balance pots or even lighted lamps on their heads.

To get a real feel for the spirit of the Mewar region, plan at least two or three days here, if not an entire week. Mewar is best seen at a somewhat leisurely pace: whether you see the area by taking quiet walks, long treks, or bike rides, you'll find lots of cultural variety, and you'll see some stunning sights. Udaipur, the major city here, warrants at least several days. From Udaipur, you can explore the ornately carved Jain temples of Ranakpur and Mount Abu, or see the medieval citadel of Chittaurgarh. West from Chittaurgarh, it's worth a stop to see the remarkable fort at Kumbalgarh. You can also take a wildlife safari or learn more about pichwai paintings at Nathdwara's Krishna temple.

Udaipur

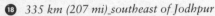 *335 km (207 mi) southeast of Jodhpur*

The jewel of Mewar is Udaipur, the City of Lakes. Some have dubbed it the Venice of the East. In his *Annals and Antiquities of Rajasthan*, Colonel James Tod described the valley of Udaipur as "the most diversified and most romantic spot on the sub-continent of India." The city of Udaipur was founded in 1567, when, having grown weary of repeated attacks on the old Mewar capital of Chittaur—Chittaur is the historic name of the area, and Chittaurgarh literally means "the fort of Chittaur"—Maharana Udai Singh asked a holy sage to suggest a safe place for his new capital. The man assured Udai Singh that his new base would never be conquered if he established it on the banks of Lake Pichola, and thus was born Singh's namesake, Udaipur.

Despite being one of Rajasthan's largest cities, with a population of about a half-million people, modern Udaipur retains a small-town atmosphere; its weather is balmy year-round, and the locals are friendly. Udaipur's city center is the old city, a labyrinth of winding streets, which borders Lake Pichola's eastern side. Five main gates lead into Udaipur's old city: Hathi Pol (Elephant Gate) to the north; Kishan Gate to the south; Delhi Gate to the northeast, Chand Pol (Moon Gate) to the west; and Suraj Pol (Sun Gate) to the east.

Anchoring Udaipur's old city are the famed City Palace and Lake Palace—right in the middle of Lake Pichola, and now a hotel. The old city itself is built on tiny hillocks and raised areas, so its lanes are full of twists and turns, leaving plenty of shady little niches to be discovered. Many lanes converge on the Jagdish Temple area, near the northeastern corner of Lake Pichola. The major landmarks in the new section are Chetak Circle, Sukhadia Circle, and Sahelion Ki Bari gardens.

The Mewar region is famous for its silver jewelry, wooden folk toys, miniature paintings, tribal arts, *molela* (terra-cotta work), appliqué, and embroidery. The landscape around Udaipur is dotted with crafts villages; the unique creations of the villages are sold in the city itself. Udaipur is also one of Rajasthan's great centers of contemporary art, as well as of miniature paintings. Mewar gastronomy features diljani (mini sugar balls) and *imarti* (pretzel-shape pastries dipped in sugary syrup) sweets, dal baati churma (lentils with balls of baked wheat dough), *chaach* (buttermilk with masala), various *makhi* (corn) products, and the guava. In or around Udaipur, make sure you travel with cash: most smaller shops and restaurants here accept rupees only.

Udaipur is also known for its spirit of voluntarism: it has one of the largest numbers of non-government organizations (NGOs) in India. Many of these groups are grappling with crucial environmental issues, such as drought and deforestation, and social issues, including the displacement of tribes and bride dowries.

A Good Tour

Start by wandering through the **Sahelion Ki Bari** gardens, north of the Old City. Then head south: walk or hire a car (it's a short walk) to **Bharatiya Lok Kala Mandal,** the folk museum. **MLV Tribal Research Institute** near the university (near the City Palace) also offers an in-depth look into rural Rajasthani culture. Continue to the **City Palace** and Jagdish Temple area, where you can have some lunch and explore; from here you can take a boat ride to see the two palaces on **Lake Pichola.** (Nonguests must pay a fee of Rs. 200.) Finish your day with dinner at the legendary Lake Palace Hotel (make reservations).

You can cram these activities into one very full day, but you should really spend at least two days in this glorious city, especially if you want to also fit in a trip to the arts-and-crafts village of Shilpgram, see some of Udaipur's art galleries, or check out the views from the **Sajjan Garh** fort or the **Neemach Mata** temple.

Sights to See

Bharatiya Lok Kala Mandal. This folk-art museum displays a collection of puppets, dolls, masks, folk dresses, ornaments, musical instruments, and paintings. The museum is known for its cultural performances—this is the reason to come here, because the museum itself is not well maintained. The nightly puppet shows, which run about 15 minutes, are cute. ⊠ *Near Chetak Circle.* ⚟ *Rs. 7 (evening program Rs. 20).* ⊙ *Daily 9–6; evening program, 6–7. Closed roughly Apr.–Aug.*

★ **City Palace.** The sprawling maharana's palace—the largest in Rajasthan—stands on a ridge overlooking the lake. Begun by Udai Singh and extended by subsequent maharanas, the sand-color City Palace has a harmonious design: it rises five stories, with a series of balconies. Cupolas crown its octagonal towers, which are connected by a maze of narrow passageways. The City Palace is one of a complex of palaces—two have been converted to hotels and one houses the current maharana, Arvind Singh of Mewar. Part of the palace is also a museum; the museum's entrance is near the Jagdish Mandir and the entrance to the City Palace Hotel is at the bottom of the hill, to the south. The rooms inside the City Palace Museum contain decorative art: beautiful paintings, colorful enamel, inlay glasswork, and antique furniture. This is one place to have a full-fledged site publication (buy one in the book shop) or a guide (hire one at the gate). ⊠ *City Palace Complex.* ⚟ *Rs. 20.* ⊙ *Daily 9:30–4:30.*

★ **Lake Pichola.** You can't leave Udaipur without seeing the stunningly romantic **Lake Palace** (Jag Niwas), which seems to float serenely on the waters of Lake Pichola. A vast, white-marble fantasy, the palace has been featured in many Indian and foreign films, including the James Bond film, *Octopussy.* Unfortunately, the palace's apartments, courts, fountains, and gardens are off-limits unless you're a guest at the Lake Palace Hotel or you have reservations at the restaurant (well-worth it). You can also pay a small fee and get a tour around the grounds. The equally lovely, three-story **Jag Mandir** palace occupies another island at the southern end of the lake. You can take a boat there during daylight hours. Built and embellished over a 50-year period beginning in the 17th century, Jag Mandir is made of yellow sandstone, lined with marble, and crowned by a dome. The interior is decorated with arabesques of colored stones. Shah Jahan, son of the Moghul emperor Jahangir, took refuge in Jag Mandir after leading an unsuccessful revolt against his father. Legend has it that Shah Jahan's inspiration for the Taj Mahal came from this marble masterpiece. ⊠ *Boats to both* *islands leave from the jetty at the base of City Palace. ⊠ Rs. 125 round trip to islands; Rs. 60 for ½-hr cruise. ☉ Boats run daily 2–6.*

MLV Tribal Research Institute. Stop in here if you have a serious interest in Mewar's tribal communities. The institute has a compact museum of tribal culture and a good library on tribal life and issues. ⊠ *University Rd., Ashok Nagar area,* ☎ *294/410958.*

Neemach Mata. This hilltop temple, dedicated to the goddess of the mountain, has a good view of Udaipur. Because no taxis or cars are allowed, you must make the climb up on your own, so have comfortable shoes ready. We recommend the less paved, more scenic path, but formal steps have been etched out for the more cautious. ⊠ *North of Fateh Sagar Lake.*

Sahelion Ki Bari. Don't miss Udaipur's famous "Garden of the Maidens," founded in the 18th century by Maharana Sangam Singh for the 48 young ladies-in-waiting who were sent to the royal house as dowry. Back then, men were forbidden entrance when the queens and their ladies-in-waiting came to relax (though the king and his buddies still found their way in). The garden is planted with exotic flowers and theme fountains—with carved pavilions and monolithic marble elephants. The fountains don't have pumps: designed to take advantage of gravity, the fountains run solely on water pressure from the lakes. If the fountains are not on, ask one of the attendants to turn them on. The pavilion opposite the entrance houses a small **children's science center.** For some touristy fun, you can dress up in traditional Rajasthani garb and have your picture snapped by a local photographer. ⊠ *Saheli Marg, in the north of the city, near Bharatiya Lok Kala Mandal.* ⊠ *Rs. 5.* ☉ *Daily 8–7.*

Sajjan Garh. High in the Aravalli Hills just outside Udaipur, this fort-palace glows: it looks golden-orange in the night sky, thanks to the lights that illuminate it. Once the maharana's Monsoon Palace, it's now a radio station for the Indian Army. The panoramic view is spectacular from the fort's lofty tower, and locals claim you can see distant Chittaurgarh on a clear day. The winding road to the top of Sajjan Garh, surrounded by green forests, is best covered by car; you can take an auto-rickshaw, but it's a long and bumpy ride. Last we heard, it's not open to the public.

....

OFF THE BEATEN PATH   **SHILPGRAM –** This rural arts-and-crafts village 3 km (2 mi) west of Udaipur includes a complex with 26 re-creations of furnished village huts (authentic right down to their toilets) from Rajasthan, Gujarat, Maharashtra, Goa, and Madhya Pradesh. The town comes alive in December with the **Shilpgram Utsav,** when artists and craftspeople from around India arrive to sell and display their works. Puppet shows, dances, folk music, and handicrafts sales take place year-round, however. You can see all of the compound on a slow camel ride. ⊠ *Rani Rd.,* ⊠ *Rs. 20 to enter compound.* ☉ *Daily 8–5.*

....

Dining and Lodging

$$$$ ✕ **Aravalli.** This restaurant has both Indian and Continental food. The *gatte ki subzi* (gram-flour dumplings), *lal maas* (spicy lamb curry), and *ker sangri* (sun-dried green beans) are local delicacies, and the *dal makhani* (lentils in a rich, buttery tomato sauce) is excellent. The pastas are good, as is the dark-chocolate mousse. Avoid the dinner buffet: it's overpriced and not too fresh. Be sure to specify how spicy you like your food. You can dine outside, on the Aravelli Terrace, which offers an array of regional thalis for dinner, and sponsors evening cul-

tural shows. ✉ *Trident Hotel, Haridasji Ki Magri, Mulla Tulai district,* ☎ *294/432200,* 𝔽𝔸𝕏 *294/432211. AE, DC, MC, V.*

$$$$ ✕ **Gallery.** Overlooking Lake Pichola from a gallery adjoining the
★ magnificent Durbar Hall in Fateh Prakash Palace, this restaurant offers one of the most lavish dining experiences in Udaipur. The menu
changes regularly, but the Continental food is consistently delicious,
and is accompanied by a selection of imported and local wines and beers.
You can also stop by in the afternoon for an English cream tea with
all the trimmings, and for U.S. $5 you can take a guided tour of the
crystal gallery above the restaurant—the palace's 200-year-old collection of Birmingham crystal includes everything from wine decanters
to beds. ✉ *Fateh Prakash Palace, City Palace Complex,* ☎ *294/
419023. Reservations essential. AE, DC, MC, V.*

$$$ ✕ **Neel Kamal.** Looking back on the City Palace from Lake Pichola,
the top Lake Palace restaurant serves Indian and Continental cuisines,
including Rajasthani specialties. Try the *sula chat* (spiced, marinated
mutton, grilled on skewers) or the vegetable *biriani* (rice). The buffet
is expensive and less tasty. The room is small, so non-guests should re-
serve in advance. ✉ *Lake Palace,* ☎ *294/528800. Reservations essential.
AE, DC, MC, V.*

$–$$ ✕ **Sunset Terrace.** Overlooking Lake Pichola from the mainland, this
lunch café benefits from a constant breeze and first-rate service—sit-
ting on the terrace, you'll feel as if you've joined the aristocracy and
have unlimited leisure. The menu includes both Indian and European
dishes, but most people just come for coffee or tea and to watch the
sunset. ✉ *Fateh Prakash Palace, City Palace Complex,* ☎ *294/528800.
No dinner. AE, DC, MC, V.*

$ ✕ **Ashiwarya Resorts.** A short ride northwest from the center of
town—toward the Monsoon Palace—Ashiwariya Resort's open-air
dining is best suited to large gatherings, but it's a good place to go on
nights when you want to relax or you need a break from Udaipur. It's
breezy and cool here, because it's a bit away from town and near Fateh
Sagar Lake. The Ashiwariya special incorporates five different masalas
(spiced sauces on rice) and the dal makhani is excellent. The restaurant, which draws a primarily Indian crowd, is becoming popular
with tourists, too. ✉ *Near Fateh Sagar Lake, Badi Rd.,* ☎ *294/523725.
No credit cards.*

$ ✕ **Jagat Niwas Palace.** A converted haveli, Jagat Niwas has retained
the mansion's lovely design and atmosphere, and its open-air restaurant has spectacular views of the Lake Palace. The premises and surroundings more than make up for the mediocre food and service. This
is a place to go for the romantic vistas alone. The palace is easy to find:
it shares a wall with the City Palace. ✉ *Lal Ghat, Jagdish Mandir,* ☎
294/420133. MC, V.

$ **Santosh Dal Bhati.** For the adventurous: Santosh Dal Bhati is Udaipur's
best bargain if you're looking for traditional Rajasthani food. The place
is a dive, and it's difficult to find, but the *dal baati churma* (lentils with
balls of baked wheat dough) is fantastic, and deservedly popular with
locals. Roll up your sleeves, wash your hands, and dig in. ✉ *Suraj Pole,*
☎ *no phone. No credit cards.*

$ ✕ **Shilpi.** Take a 15-minute cab ride from the city center to this casual
garden restaurant, which serves good Indian and Chinese food. You
can dine on the huge lawn or under the thatch roof of the dining
room. Try the *missi ki roti* and the butter chicken, baked in spices and
then cooked in rich tomato curry. Equipped with an outdoor swimming pool and bar as well as kitchen, Shilpi is a good place to relax
in the sun. ✉ *Rani Rd., near Shilpgram Village,* ☎ *294/432495. AE,
MC, V.*

$$$$ ⊡ **Fateh Prakash Palace.** This small but grand palace was built by Maharana Fateh Singh at the turn of the 20th century. The palace has suitably excellent views of Lake Pichola—it's right next to the City Palace. The suites are elegantly furnished with period furniture (some of it was once used by the royal family), heavy drapes, and brass fixtures, but they don't have TVs or air-conditioning. The standard rooms are also luxurious, but they lack the sense of history that the main palace has, and the glass doors might compromise your privacy. ⊠ *City Palace Complex; reserve through City Palace, 313001,* ☎ *294/419023,* FAX *294/419020. 9 rooms, 6 suites. Restaurant, bar, pool, health club, Ping-Pong, squash, boating, billiards. AE, DC, MC, V.*

$$$$ ⊡ **Lake Palace.** Now run by the Taj Group, this 250-year-old white-
★   marble palace—the main set for the James Bond film *Octopussy*—floats like a vision in the middle of Lake Pichola. You arrive, of course, by boat. The standard rooms are contemporary; if you want a room to match the stunning setting, opt for a suite. The fantastical Khush Mahal Suite takes in sunlight through stained-glass windows; the peach-tone Sarva Ritu Suite has a small interior porch with three arched windows and a window seat. Most rooms have lake views, though some look onto the lily pond or the courtyard. You might be able to take a meal on the hotel's wooden barge, *Gangaur.* ⊠ *Lake Pichola 313001,* ☎ *294/528800,* FAX *294/528700. 76 rooms, 8 suites. Restaurant, bar, coffee shop, pool, gym, boating, baby-sitting, laundry service, meeting room, travel services. AE, DC, MC, V.*

$$$$ ⊡ **Shiv Niwas Palace.** Laid out like a white crescent moon around a
★   large pool, Shiv Niwas Palace was once a royal guest house. Standard rooms, set apart from the main building, have contemporary furnishings. The regal suites are gorgeous, with molded ceilings, elaborate canopied beds, and original paintings and furniture. Some of the rooms have private terraces; all have excellent views of Lake Pichola. The Baneera Bar is styled with pleasant Victorian furnishings. Shiv Niwas Palace is adjacent to the City Palace. ⊠ *City Palace Complex; reserve through City Palace, 313001,* ☎ *294/528016,* FAX *294/528006. 13 rooms, 18 suites. Restaurant, bar, pool, boating, billiards, meeting room, travel services. AE, DC, MC, V.*

$$$$ ⊡ **Trident.** The Trident is down a long and solitary road, set among
★   acres of beautiful gardens—utterly removed from the bustle of downtown Udaipur. The hotel's architecture is striking, but the interior is somewhat lacking in aesthetic sensibility; rooms are well-equipped and modern, but nondescript. The pool is heated and pleasant day and night. The hotel sponsors boat rides around Lake Pichola. The smiling and attentive staff aim to please. ⊠ *Haridasji Ki Magri, Mulla Tulai,* ☎ *294/432200,* FAX *294/432211. 143 rooms. Restaurant, bar, pool, hair salon, gym, boating, meeting room, travel services, baby-sitting. AE, DC, MC, V.*

$$$–$$$$ ⊡ **Laxmi Vilas Palace.** You'll feel nostalgic for times past at this former royal guest house, built in 1933. The hotel is set on a hillside above the banks of Fateh Sagar Lake; from the hotel's verandas and gardens, you can get a lovely view of the lake and the nearby Sajjan Garh fort. The maharana's hunting trophies line the entranceway. Rooms in the new wing are modern; the old wing, though not lavish, has original architecture and Rajput relics. The restaurant has good Indian food. ⊠ *Sagar Rd., 313001,* ☎ *294/529711,* FAX *294/526573. 54 rooms, 10 suites. Restaurant, bar, pool, travel services. AE, DC, MC, V.*

$$$ ⊡ **Jaisamand Island Resort.** This large, white hotel leans against a brown and green slope on an island in Jaisamand Lake, one of the largest artificial lakes in the world. The hotel's spacious lobby and its bar have granite floors and Rajasthani furniture. The rooms are Western-style and comfortable. Catch the hotel boat on the lake's boardwalk. ⊠ *51 km (32 mi) southeast of Udaipur, on Jaisamand Lake,* ☎ *2906/30355, for reservations call 294/431400,* FAX *294/431406. 35 rooms. Restaurant, bar, boating, fishing, meeting room, airport shuttle. AE, MC, V.*

$$ ⊡ **Hilltop Hotel Palace.** Perched on a hill overlooking Fateh Sagar Lake, the Hilltop Hotel Palace has splendid views of Udaipur. It's a modern hotel, with a spacious marble lobby, a glass elevator, an elegant garden, and a number of rooftop terraces. The hotel may not take you back in time, but it's an excellent value. The Western-style rooms are simple but clean, and each has a balcony. ⊠ *5 Ambavgarh, Fateh Sagar 313001,* ☎ *294/432245,* FAX *294/432136. 62 rooms. 2 restaurants, bar, pool, shops, meeting room. AE, DC, MC, V.*

$$ ⊡ **Paras Mahal.** This hotel is clean and modern. It's not fancy, but it's conveniently only ½ km (¼ mi) from Udaipur's train station, and it's also close to a Hindi-movie theater. The main feature is a glass elevator that shoots up through the hotel's central atrium. Rooms have low-lying beds, with lavish, colorful bedspreads; the walls are hung with Rajasthani paintings. All rooms have TVs, phones, sofas, and desks. ⊠ *Near Paras Cinema, Hiran Magri, Sector 11, 313001,* ☎ *294/ 483391–(4),* FAX *294/584103. 60 rooms. Restaurant, bar, pool, shops, laundry service, business services, travel services. MC, V.*

$$ ⊡ **Shikarbadi.** Just outside the city, this former hunting lodge of the local
★   royal family—now a Heritage Hotel—is a lovely, rustic retreat, complete with a private lake. The rooms are attractive, with tile ceilings and stone walls. Deer and monkeys venture close, almost to the door. The hotel's open-air restaurant serves traditional Mewari food. You might want to try one of the horseback-riding excursions or safaris that the hotel offers. The Shikarbadi hotel is only a few kilometers outside the city. ⊠ *Goverdhan Vilas, which is a side street from Ahmedabad Rd.,* ☎ *294/583201,* FAX *294/584841; reserve through City Palace, 313001,* ☎ *294/528016,* FAX *294/528006. 21 rooms, 4 suites. Restaurant, bar, pool, horseback riding, travel services. AE, DC, MC, V.*

$ ⊡ **Lake Pichola Hotel.** Run by a Rajput family, the hotel benefits both from an excellent location and friendly service. Each suite has a jacuzzi and a terrace with beautiful city views. The rooms are full of artifacts and colored glass panes. You can request a boat ride on the lake or cultural performances with a little advance notice. ⊠ *Outside Chandpol,* ☎ *294/431197,* FAX *294/430575,* WEB *www.lakepicholahotel.com. Restaurant, travel services. AE, MC, V.*

$ ⊡ **Udai Kothi.** Udai Kothi offers regal accommodations at cut-rate
★   prices. It's probably the best hotel for the money in all of Rajasthan. From the rooftop pool you can swim and enjoy spectacular views of the Udaipur skyline—the hotel is across Lake Pichola from the City Palace. Every room has a theme that's related to a specific region and group of people in Mewar history. The rooms are decorated with antique furniture and art. A new spa and jacuzzi is slated for completion in 2002. ⊠ *Outside Chandpol on Hannuman Ghat,* ☎ *294/ 432801–(12),* FAX *294/430412. 24 rooms. Restaurant, pool, massage, sauna, laundry. MC, V.*

Shopping

Udaipur's main shopping area spans the area around the **Jagdish Temple.** You'll discover interesting nooks and crannies around here, but watch out for would-be guides. There's plenty of stores to explore and items to buy: along with wooden toys, silver, and Udaipuri and Gujarati embroidery, you'll find miniature paintings in the Moghul and Rajput styles. Most of these paintings are machine-made prints, a fact reflected in the wide disparity in prices. If you want to buy original art, ask the proprietor to show you what's in the back room—and plan to bargain. From Jagdish Temple, stroll down to **Ganta Ghar** (Clocktower), ground zero for silver jewelry. Browse freely, but take care not to purchase items that are merely coated with silver-tone paint. **Gehrilal Goverdhan Singh Choudhary** (✉ 72 Jagdish Marg, Clocktower, ☎ 294/410806) has a good selection of fixed-price, antique jewelry, and contemporary designs with stonework. Choudhary has been in the business more than 22 years, and has exhibited several times abroad. Right next door is a sweet stall, Lala Mishtan Bhandar, where you can satisfy your sweet tooth and refuel with the best *gulab jamun* (fried milk balls in syrup) and imarti (fried sweets made with lentils) in town. While you're in the Jagdish Temple area, make sure you check out the collection of more than 500 hand-made wooden puppets at the **University of Arts** (✉ 166 Jagdish Marg, City Palace Rd., ☎ 294/422591). Ask the proprietor, Rajesh Gurjarjour, for a private demonstration.

If your time is limited, you'll find everything under the sun under a few key emporiums (and you won't have to bargain). The **Manglam Arts** (✉ Sukhadia Circle, ☎ 294/560259) emporium deals in Rajasthani handicrafts, including rugs, block-printed textiles, knickknacks, and furniture. Government-run **Rajasthali** (✉ Chetak Circle, ☎ 294/528768) sells high-quality Rajasthani arts and handicrafts.

Serious art collectors should know that Udaipur has many galleries that exhibit original work by internationally renowned and burgeoning artists. The **B. G. Sharma Art Gallery** (✉ 3 Saheli Marg, ☎ 294/560063) has 45 years of work by B. G. Sharma himself, one of the most eminent painters in India. Unlike most artists of miniature paintings, Sharma doesn't copy traditional pictures, but makes his own—and has made huge contributions to advancing the Moghul, Kishangarh, and Kangra painting styles. **Ganesh Art Emporium** (✉ 152 Jagdish Chowk, ☎ 294/422864) is a trendy little shop focusing on a gifted young artist, Madhu Kant Mundra, whose oeuvre includes more than 125 funky representations of Lord Ganesh. Don't miss the artistic refrigerator magnets, sculptures, and antique photographs. **Pristine Gallery** (✉ 6 Kalapi House, Bhatiyani Chohatta, Palace Rd., ☎ 294/415291) specializes in both contemporary and folk art, with many small pieces by Shail Choyal, a guru of contemporary Indian painting. Other highlights include the stylized work of Shahid Parvez, a very fine up-and-coming local artist. At the **Sharma Art Gallery** (✉ 15-A New Colony, Kalaji - Goraji, ☎ 294/421107), Kamal Sharma paints mainly birds and animals on paper, marble, silk, and canvas—all are for sale. Apart from being the chief resident artist at Udaipur Medical College, **S. N. Bhandraj** has been creating sculpture out of sea foam for over 20 years; he demonstrates this unique craft in his home studio (✉ Studio 70, Moti Magri Colony, ☎ 294/561396). At the **Traditional Art Gallery** (✉ 13 Bhatiyani Chohetta, Jagdish Mandir, ☎ 294/529095), you can see the watercolor tribal portraits and village scenes of the talented young artist Anil Sharma.

Sadhana (✉ Seva Mandir Rd., Fatehpura, ☎ 294/560951) open weekdays 11–6, is run by Seva Mandir—one of the oldest non-government organizations in India, working for the advancement of the village poor. Among Seva Mandir's activities is a rural women's income-generation program that encourages women to produce traditional appliqué work on cushion covers and bedspreads. The lovely results are sold in the organization's office building, and the full proceeds are returned to the women (rather than pocketed by middlemen, as they would be if the work was sold in stores).

Ranakpur

★ ⑲ *96 km (60 mi) northwest of Udaipur*

Nestled in a glen northwest of Udaipur is one of the five holy places for India's Jain community. Legend has it that this 15th-century **Jain temple,** dedicated to Lord Rishabadeva, was built after it appeared in a dream to a minister of the Mewar king. The three-story temple is surrounded by a three-story wall that contains 27 halls supported by 1,444 elaborately carved pillars—no two carvings are alike. Below the temple are underground chambers where statues of Jain saints were hidden to protect them from the Moghuls. The way the white marble complex rises up from the fertile plain will easily inspire your awe— the relief work on the columns are some of the best in all of India. As you enter, look to the left for the pillar where the minister and the architect provided themselves with front-row seats for worship. Another pillar is intentionally warped, to separate human works from divine ones—the builders believed only gods could be perfect, so they intentionally added imperfections to some of the columns to avoid insulting the gods. Outside are two smaller Jain temples and a shrine adorned with erotic sculptures and dedicated to the sun god. 🎫 *Free; camera charge.* ☉ *Non-Jains, daily 11–sunset.*

Dining and Lodging

$$ ✕🏨 **Maharani Bagh Orchard Retreat.** You'll find it's easy to relax at this 19th-century pied-à-terre for the Maharani of Jodhpur. Scattered among huge mango trees, the little brick cottages have traditional decor: painted wooden beds and tile floors. The kitchen serves Indian and Rajasthani specialties under small thatch shelters; in the background you hear the sound of water rushing through a canal in the middle of the property. The rooms do not have phones or air-conditioning. ✉ *Sadri, Ranakpur,* ☎ *2934/85151,* ℻ *2934/85105; reserve through Welcomgroup Umaid Bhawan Palace, Jodhpur 342006,* ☎ *291/ 510101,* ℻ *291/510101. 19 rooms. Restaurant, pool. MC, V.*

Mount Abu

⑳ *185 km (115 mi) west of Udaipur*

High in the Aravalli Hills, Mount Abu has long been the site of one of Hinduism's most sacred rites, the *yagya* (fire ritual). Legend has it that the clan of the mighty *agnikula* Rajput warriors rose from this mystical fire. Today, Mount Abu is Rajasthan's only hill station, and a pilgrimage center for Jains, who come here to see the famous Dilwara Temples. Mount Abu is also a great place to stop if you like taking long walks. **Nakki Lake,** resting between green hills, is believed to have been carved out by the gods' fingernails. The far side of the lake is quieter and cleaner. At **Sunset Point** you can imbibe a romantic Mount Abu sunset, but you can't avoid the crowds here.

Mount Abu's newest landmark is the **Brahma Kumaris Spiritual University,** which attracts thousands of followers from all over the world. Members of the sect don white robes or saris, and study spiritual knowledge or Raja Yoga meditation. (Potential devotees beware: their services don't come cheap.) The Brahma Kumaris have also designed the **Peace Park,** which includes a series of beautiful gardens. Beyond the park, on Guru Shikhar Road, is **Guru Shikhar,** the highest point between South India's Nilgiri Hills and the Himalayas, in the north. From Guru Shikar you can enjoy excellent views of the countryside. The stunningly carved, unforgettably beautiful **Dilwara Temples,** dedicated to Jain saints, were built entirely of marble between the 11th and 13th centuries.

Lodging

$$ ✕▥ **Cama Rajputana Club Resort.** Cradled in the hills, this 100-year-old club combines modern amenities with country style. Its peaceful atmosphere gives the weary walker a chance to rest and recharge. ✉ *Mount Abu,* ☎ *2974/38205,* ℻ *2974/38412; or reserve through Cama Hotel Ltd., Khanpur Rd., Ahmedabad 380001, Gujarat,* ☎ *79/550–5281,* ℻ *79/550–5285. 40 rooms, 2 suites. Restaurant, pool, tennis court, squash. AE, MC, V.*

$$ ▥ **Palace Hotel (Bikaner House).** Formerly the summer residence of the Maharaja of Bikaner, the Palace Hotel was the center of Mount Abu's aristocratic social life for decades. Now a Heritage Hotel, it still feels something like a hunting lodge, and is a good place to retreat and relax for a few days. Service is excellent. The gardens are nice, but the tennis court is a bit dilapidated. ✉ *Delwara Rd.,* ☎ *2974/38673,* ℻ *2974/38674. 24 rooms, 13 suites. Restaurant, tennis court, billiards. AE, DC, MC, V.*

Chittaurgarh

㉑ *112 km (69 mi) northeast of Udaipur*

If any one of Rajasthan's myriad forts had to be singled out for its glorious history and chivalric lore, it would be Chittaurgarh. This was the capital of the Mewar princely state from the 8th to the 16th centuries, before Maharana Udai Singh moved the capital to Udaipur. The sprawling hilltop **fort** occupies about 700 acres on a hill about 92 m (300 ft) high. It was besieged and sacked three times: after the first two conquests, the Rajputs recovered it, but the third attack clinched it for the Moghuls for several decades.

The first attack took place because of a woman: the beauty of Rani Padmini, wife of the then-current ruler, so enamored the Sultan of Delhi Allauddin Khilji that he set out to attack the fort and win her in battle. Thirty-four thousand warriors lost their lives in this struggle, but the Sultan did not get Padmini: she and all the women in the fort committed *jauhar*—mass self-immolation in anticipation of widowhood and perversions by invading armies—and burned themselves to death. Frustrated, Khilji entered the city in a rage, looting and destroying much of what he saw. Chittaurgarh was also the home of the saint-poet Mirabai, a 16th century Rajput princess and devotee of Lord Krishna who gave up her royal life to sing *bhajans* (hymns) in his praise.

The massive fort encompasses the **palaces** of Maharana Kumbha and Maharani Padmini, victory towers such as **Vijay Stambh** and **Kirti Stambh,** and a huge variety of temples, including **Kunbha Shyam** and **Kalika Mata.** The **Fateh Prakash Mahal** displays some fine sculptures.

Kumbhalgarh

㉒ *84 km (52 mi) north of Udaipur*

Isolated and serene, this formidable **fort** was a refuge for Mewari rulers in times of strife. Built by Maharana Kumbha in the 15th century, the fort ramparts run 4 km (2½ mi) and the outer wall encloses an area of 32 square mi. At one time, its ramparts nearly encircled an entire township, self-contained to withstand a long siege. The fort fell only once, to the army of Akbar—whose forces had contaminated the water supply. The fort was also the birthplace of Maharana Pratap. The **Badal Mahal** (Cloud Palace), at the top, has an awesome view of the surrounding countryside. Surrounding the fort, the modern-day **Kumbalgarh Sanctuary** is home to wolves, leopards, jackals, nilgai deer, sambar deer, and various species of birds, and makes for delightful treks. Have a leisurely lunch at the open-air restaurant of the Aodhi Hotel.

Dining and Lodging

$$ ⊡ **Deogarh Mahal.** Built in the 17th century, this Heritage Hotel is run by its resident once-royal family. Set in the rugged countryside of the Aravalli Hills, this saffron-color mansion—rife with battlements, domes, and turrets—towers over the town below. The hotel offers jeep and camel safaris and excellent views of the region's migratory birds. Don't miss the family's exquisite collection of miniature paintings. ⊠ *Deogarh, Madarja, Rajsamand,* ☎ *2904/52777,* ℻ *2904/52555. 34 rooms, 2 suites. Restaurant, travel services. MC, V.*

Nathdwara

②③ *48 km (30 mi) north of Udaipur*

The town of Nathdwara is totally built around the **Shrinathji Temple,** visited by thousands of pilgrims each year. Built in the 18th century, this simple temple is one of the most celebrated shrines to Lord Krishna: it houses a unique image of the deity sculpted from a single piece of black marble. Nathdwara is known for its pichwais, large cloth paintings depicting legends from Krishna's life, and for its special style of devotional music.

A few minutes outside Nathdwara is **Rajsamand Lake,** which attracts a large number of migratory birds. Maharana Raj Singh ordered the construction of the lake in 1662 as a famine-relief work project, so a workforce of 60,000 people brought it into being over the course of 10 years. The architecture of its main dam, **Nauchowki** (Nine Pavilions), combines Rajput and Moghul styles; interestingly, the Rajaprashasthi (Rajput Royal Eulogy) is engraved on 25 of the dam's niched slabs. Locals come here early in the morning to learn to swim, in the pool behind the dam.

Also near Nathdwara is the village of **Molela,** where artisans craft and paint fine terra-cotta images of gods, goddesses, and animals, as well as more functional pots and utensils.

JAISALMER AND ENVIRONS

The stark, compelling beauty of the Thar Desert draws travelers to far-western Rajasthan—for good reason. Jaisalmer, resplendent with golden buildings and a towering citadel, is a good base for camel safaris into the desert, and photogenic Sam Sand Dunes and Desert National Park are a short distance from this striking medieval city.

Jaisalmer

★ **②④** *663 km (412 mi) northwest of Udaipur, 285 km (160 mi) northwest of Jodhpur, 570 (353 mi) west of Jaipur*

Jaisalmer seems like a mirage: its array of sandstone buildings are surrounded by the stark Thai Desert and illuminated in a gold hue by the penetrating sun. The ancient medieval city is defined by its carved spires and palaces, and the massive sandcastlelike fort that towers over the imposing wall that encircles the town. Jaisalmer is a remote and unusual city; it's out of the way, but it's worth it if you want to see a different side of India, and definitely if you want to take a camel safari.

Founded in 1156 by Rawal Jaisal, a descendent of the Yadav clan and a Bhatti Rajput, Jaisalmer lies near the extreme western edge of Rajasthan, about 100 mi east of the Pakistan border. It began as a trade center: from the 12th through the 18th centuries, rulers amassed their wealth from taxes levied on caravans passing through from Africa, Persia, Arabia, and other parts of Central Asia. Smugglers were also known to frequent Jaisalmer to work the profitable opium trade. The rise of Bombay as a major trading port in the 19th century, however, eclipsed Jaisalmer's role as a staging post.

Today Jaisalmer attracts travelers attracted by the mystery and harsh, remote charm of the desert. A welcome change from crowded, polluted cities, the city is an architectural masterpiece that never fails to amaze. At night the fort is bathed in golden light, which illuminates the seemingly impregnable walls; most of the buildings inside are made out of yellow sandstone. Jaisalmer is also known for its ornate 19th century havelis—mansions with facades so intricately carved the stonework looks like lace. It's also worth wandering through the mazelike alleys and bazaars, though the markets have a bad reputation among tourists. Expect some harassment, especially if you're a woman traveling solo.

Unfortunately, following the nuclear tests in nearby Pokharan in May 1998, and given ongoing border tensions with Pakistan, travelers are sometimes wary of going this far west. Don't be deterred—to skip Jaisalmer is to skip the real jewel of Rajasthan. When you get here you'll see that life in Jaisalmer remains unaffected.

With clean lanes, no traffic, and few crowds, Jaisalmer is easily covered on foot. Camel safaris are a good way to see the desert. These are great fun, but choose one carefully—don't skimp and choose a cheap outfitter. Take a light scarf to protect your face in case of a sandstorm.

Spend at least two nights in Jaisalmer. Nothing is more romantic than a Thar Desert sunset, and the city's cultural festivities—the heart and soul of its people—begin at night. For the traveler, these can reach intoxicating levels of passion: around blazing bonfires, dancers and musicians gather together and recreate the ancient traditions of Rajasthan. To get an even bigger dose of it, visit during the Desert Festival, in late January and early February. You'll see music, dance, camel races, turban-tying contests, and craft bazaars with regional traders.

A Good Tour

Jaisalmer is like Venice in that it's next to impossible to follow a straight path: it's a maze of streets and passageways. Trust your instincts and don't be afraid to ask the locals for directions. You may have fun getting a little lost—especially because Jaisalmer isn't big enough to get hopelessly turned around. The major landmark is the **fort,** which is every bit as labyrinthine as the rest of the city; allow several hours to explore the attractions within. From here, walk north to the **havelis.** Finally, hop a camel—you must arrange this with a local travel agent a day in advance—and head southeast toward **Gadsisar Lake** and the nearby Folklore Museum.

If you spend a second day in town, visit the lovely **Bada Bagh** garden and then drive northwest from there to the **Ludarva Temples.**

Sights to See

Bada Bagh. Much of the city's vegetables and fruits are grown at Bada Bagh, which is more like a giant orchard than a garden. On the banks of an artificial lake, and with so much lush greenery, the garden resembles a beautiful oasis (presuming there's no drought). In the gardens, you'll also see royal cenotaphs, with canopies under which members of the royal family are buried. Notice the beautifully carved ceilings and equestrian statues of the former rulers. Bada Bagh is 6 km (4 mi) northwest of the city.

★ **Fort.** What's extraordinary about this fort is that 5,000 people live here, just as they did centuries ago. Some 250 ft above the town, the fort is protected by a 30-ft-high wall and contains 99 bastions. Several great *pols* (gateways) approach and jut outward from the battlements of this 12th-century citadel. Built of sandstone and extremely brittle, the fort is rumored to be an architectural time bomb, destined to collapse in the face of a particularly aggressive sandstorm. Yet so lovely is this structure in the meantime that the poet Rabindranath Tagore composed *Sonar Kila (The Golden Fort)* after seeing it, and inspired another creative Bengali in turn: Satyajit Ray made his famous film *Sonar Kila* after reading Tagore's work.

Inside the web of tiny lanes are Jain and Hindu temples, palaces, and charming havelis. The seven-story **Juna Mahal** (Old Palace), built around 1500, towers over the other buildings. The **Satiyon ka Pagthiya** (Steps of the Satis), just before the palace entrance, is where the royal ladies committed *sati,* self-immolation, when their husbands were slain.

Within the fort are eight **Jain temples** built from the 12th to 16th centuries: these house thousands of carved deities and dancing figures in mythological settings. No photography is allowed here, and you'll have to leave your leather items at the gate. (Jains worship life in all forms, so leather is sacrilegious.) The **Gyan Bhandar** (Jain Library) inside the Jain temple complex contains more than 1,000 old manuscripts—some from the 12th century, written on palm leaf, with painted wooden covers—and a collection of Jain, pre-Moghul, and Rajput paintings.

The historic **Tazia Tower** is a delicate pagoda rising five tiers from the **Badal Mahal** (Cloud Palace), each tier designed to include an intricately carved balcony. Muslim craftsmen built the tower in the shape of a *tazia*—a replica of a bier carried in procession during Mohurram, a Muslim period of mourning. ⊠ *Juna Mahal* 🎫 *Rs. 5.* ⊙ *Daily 8–5. Jain temples* 🎫 *free.* ⊙ *Daily 7–noon. Library* 🎫 *free.* ⊙ *Daily 10 AM–11 AM.*

Gadsisar Lake. Just south of Jaisalmer is a freshwater lake (otherwise known as Gadsisar Sagar, or Tank) built in the 12th century. Surrounded by numerous golden-hued shrines, it's also frequented by a spectacular and diverse avian community. Plan for a camel ride, a picnic, and perhaps a short paddle-boat excursion. Near the shrines is a charming little **Folklore Museum,** built in the style of a traditional home. Filled with memorabilia, it's the perfect place to ground yourself in local history and culture. ⊠ *Museum behind main bus stand.* 🎫 *Rs. 2.* ⊙ *Daily 9–noon and 3–6.*

Havelis. Outside the fort, about 3 km (2 mi) from the main gate, is a string of five connected havelis built by the Patwa brothers in the 1800s. The Patwas were highly influential Jain merchants back when Jaisalmer was an independent principality. The Patwa brothers forbade the repetition of any motifs or designs between their mansions, so each is distinctive.

Two of the five havelis are now owned by the government and open to the public, and you can explore the interiors of the others by offering a small fee (not more than Rs. 50) to the residents. Three havelis are noteworthy in this area: **Patwon Ki Haveli** is arguably the most elaborate and magnificent of all Jaisalmer's havelis. In addition to exquisitely carved pillars and expansive corridors, one of the apartments in this five-story mansion is painted with beautiful murals. The 19th-century **Nathamalji Ki Haveli** was carved by two brothers, each working independently on his own half; the design is remarkably harmonious, though you can spot small differences. The interior of the **Salim Singh Ki Haveli,** built in about 1815, is in sad disrepair, but the mansion's exterior is still lovely—it has an overhanging gallery on its top floor. Note the havelis' ventilation systems: the projecting windows and stone screens keep them cool even in the searing summer months.

Ludarva Temples. The founder of Jaisalmer, Rawal Jaisal, lived here before shifting to his new capital. Here you can still see the ruins of his former city. The Jain temple complex is known for its *nag devta* (snake god), a live snake that appears on auspicious days and nights. The snake is worshiped because, as legend goes, it has been protecting this temple for thousands of years. The temples are famous for their graceful architecture and detailed carving. ✉ *16 km (10 mi) northwest of Jaisalmer.*

Dining and Lodging

There are very few decent restaurants in Jaisalmer. The good hotels are your best bet for a savory meal.

$ ✕ **8 July Restaurant.** Run by an eccentric Indo-Australian, this restaurant serves simple snacks, pizzas, vegetable dishes, and wonderful coffee milk shakes throughout the day. The restaurant is just inside the fort, up a staircase. It has a breathtaking view of Jaisalmer. *Across from the Badal Maha,* ☎ *no phone. No credit cards. Closed summer months.*

$$$ ▥ **Fort Rajwada.** The most luxurious hotel in all of Jaisalmer, Fort Ra-
★   jwada blends French interior design with historic Marwari touches. The entranceway once belonged to a 500-year-old haveli from the fort, and the marble elephants come from the famous Jaipuri *mortiwallas* (statue makers). Standard rooms are Western, with contemporary furnishings; these rooms often have views of the fort. The suites are far more extravagant, with frescoes on the walls and antique beds with pure silver bedposts. The restaurant is outrageously upscale, and by far the best in Jaisalmer. The full bar incorporates French design techniques with sleek, minimalist furnishings. It closes, however, at 11. ✉ *No. 1 Hotel Complex, 345001,* ☎ *2292/53233,* FAX *2992/53733. Restaurant, bar, pool, massage, billiards, business services, travel services.*

$$$ ▥ **Himmatgarh Palace.** Just opposite the royal cenotaphs, this hotel is about 1 km (½ mi) from the city, but it offers one of the best views in town, especially at sunset. It also sponsors performances of folk dance and music. The standard rooms are modern and comfortable, but the small, circular *burj* (tower) rooms are the most charming, with marble beds and lights concealed in the nooks of the stone walls. ✉ *1 Ramgarh Rd., 345001,* ☎ *2992/52002–(4),* FAX *2992/52005. 40 rooms. Restaurant, bar, pool, travel services. AE, MC, V.*

$$$ ▥ **Rang Mahal.** This mid-level sandstone complex has an austere, non-descript interior. Frescoes occasionally decorate the walls, which are for the most part vast and white-washed. Standard rooms are spacious and furnished with Western amenities, but include Rajasthani bed frames. Definitely get a room with a balcony and take a dip in the pool when you get overwhelmed with the heat. ✉ *5 Hotel Complex, Sam Rd., 345001,* ☎ *2992/50907,* FAX *2992/5130. Restaurant, bar, pool. AE, MC, V.*

$$ ▥ **Gorbandh Palace.** Built of golden sandstone, this fairly new hotel is spacious and elegant. Rooms are arranged in haveli-style blocks around a series of small interior courtyards with skylights and fountains. Interiors are Western-style, with some Rajasthani touches and large,

lovely windows. This expansive retreat us frequented by foreign tour groups in search of a respite from the city center. The palace's pool is the deepest in Jaisalmer. ⊠ *1 Tourist Complex, Sam Rd., 345001,* ☎ *2992/53801–(8),* FAX *2992/53811. 64 rooms, 3 suites. Restaurant, bar, pool, travel services. AE, DC, MC, V.*

$$ 🏨 **Heritage Inn.** Not to be confused with a Heritage Hotel, this inn was constructed in 1990. This hotel has a functional, subdued interior. Accommodations are in bungalows dotted around the garden. Beds are set into depressions in the floor, walls are of rustic stone, and the bathrooms lack tubs. Ask for a suite: they're much plusher and are not much more expensive than standard rooms. There's a tandoori barbecue in the garden, where you can eat outdoors and Rajasthani folk dance in the evenings. The hotel is about 3 km (2 mi) from the town center. ⊠ *PB-43 Sam Rd., 345001,* ☎ *2992/52769 or 50901,* FAX *2992/51638. 55 rooms, 6 suites. Restaurant, bar, coffee shop, meeting room, travel services. AE, DC, MC, V.*

$$ 🏨 **Narayan Niwas Palace.** This carved stone palace was once a caravansary, and its interior courtyard still feels like an oasis for caravans traveling through the area. Now a Heritage Hotel, it has plain modern rooms, a lovely pool, expansive lawns, a well-stocked bar, and a friendly staff who can arrange camel and jeep safaris. Rooms are furnished with carved wooden furniture from the craft village of Barmer, and sandstone beds—stone frames filled with sand and covered with a sheet to give you the feel of sleeping in the desert. Some rooms are air-conditioned. ⊠ *Near Malka Prol, 345001,* ☎ *2992/6562047–(48),* FAX *2992/52101; or reserve through Q6/7 DLF, Phase 2 Gurgaon, New Delhi 110048,* ☎ *11/648–6807,* FAX *11/648–6806,* WEB *www.narayanniwas.com. 38 rooms, 5 suites. Restaurant, bar, pool. AE, DC, MC, V.*

Camel Safaris

Royal Safaris (⊠ Gandhi Chowk, ☎ 2992/52538) is the recommended agent, tailoring trips to nearby villages or overnight sojourns in the desert. You can also contact the Rajasthan Tourism Development Corporation in the Hotel Moomal, or the Indian Tourism Development Corporation at the Dhola Maru hotel, for reservations. Note that safari prices vary dramatically depending on the itinerary and the level of tourist crush.

Shopping

Jaislamer is famous for its mirrorwork, embroidery, and woolen shawls. Local artisans also make attractive, good-quality wooden boxes, silver jewelry, and curios. The main shopping areas are **Sadar Bazaar, Sonaron Ka Bas, Manak Chowk,** and **Pansari Bazaar,** all within the walled city, near the fort and temple areas. Sonaron Ka Bas, in particular, has exquisite silver jewelry. Avoid solicitors dispensing advice, take time to browse carefully, and bargain.

Damoder Handicraft Emporium (⊠ Fort, near Rang Prol) has an excellent selection of local handicrafts, especially old textiles.

Khadi Graamudyog, in the walled city, has an array of *khadi* (handspun cotton) shawls, Nehru jackets, scarves, and rugs. The government emporium **Rajasthali** (⊠ Gandhi Chowk) has fair prices, so it's a good way to gauge the prices of other stores.

Sam Sand Dunes

㉕ *42 km (26 mi) west of Jaisalmer*

No trip to Jaisalmer is complete without a visit to Sam Sand Dunes, a photographer's feast. The ripples of these wind-shaped dunes create fantastic mirages. Take a camel safari to the dunes, if you can cope with the heat and the time it takes to get here. Stay for the sunset and enjoy an evening with artists and melodious folk singers—who reinforce the beauty and romance of the setting.

Desert National Park

26 *45 km (28 mi) southwest of Jaisalmer*

Wildlife-lovers will delight in this place. The desert birds include everything from birds of prey, such as vultures and desert hawks, to sandgrouses, doves, shrikes, bee eaters, and warblers. The rarest, most remarkable bird is the great Indian bustard, a large, majestic crane said to be found only in the Thar Desert.

RAJASTHAN A TO Z

To research prices, get advice from other travelers, and book travel arrangements, visit www.fodors.com.

AIR TRAVEL

There are domestic airports in Jaipur, Jodhpur, Udaipur, and Jaisalmer. Indian Airlines flies between the four and connects Rajasthan with Delhi, Bombay, and Aurangabad. Ask your travel agent about service on private airlines and remember that flights to Rajasthan fill up—reserve in advance.

Flights to Jaisalmer are less frequent than those to the other major cities, but during peak season, several airlines fly from Jodhpur to Jaisalmer three times a week.

New private carriers, such as Jet Airways and Sahara, offer extensive connections all over Rajasthan, including daily flights from Delhi to Jaipur, Udaipur and Jodhpur.

Air India has an office in Jaipur.

CARRIERS

➤ CONTACTS: **Air India** (✉ On Tonk Rd., Jaipur, ☎ 141/68569). **Indian Airlines** (☎ 141 in Delhi or 11/329–5121 elsewhere; ✉ Nehru Pl., Tonk Rd., Jaipur, ☎ 141/514500 or 141/514407; Jodhpur, ☎ 291/636757 or 291/636758; ✉ Outside Delhi Gate, Udaipur, ☎ 294/527711).**Jet Airways** (✉ 13 Community Center, Yusuf Sarai, Delhi, ☎ 11/685–3700).**Sahara India Airlines** (✉ 4g-31-32 Ansal Chamber, Camal Place Delhi, ☎ 11/573–7744).

AIRPORTS

Jaipur's Sanganer Airport is about 13 km (8 mi) south of town; a taxi into town costs about Rs. 150. Jodphur's airport is 5 km (3 mi) from the city center; a taxi into town costs about Rs. 150. Udaipur's Dabok Airport is 25 km (16 mi) from the city center; the ride costs about Rs. 200. Jaisalmer's airport is about 10 km (6 mi) from the city; a taxi into town runs about Rs. 100.
➤ AIRPORT INFORMATION: **Jaipur** (☎ 141/551729). **Jaisalmer** (☎ 2992/51952). **Jodhpur** (☎ 291/430617). **Udaipur** (☎ 294/655433).

BIKE TRAVEL

Some hotels offer bikes for hire; so do shops around Jagdish Temple in Udaipur. Rates are typically Rs. 15–Rs. 20 per hour. Biking in Jaipur can be dangerous, but elsewhere it's a nice way to get around.

The cycle-rickshaw is dying out in Rajasthan, but if you do find one, say in Jaipur, it should cost about Rs. 30 per hour. Make sure you agree on a rate in advance.

BUS TRAVEL

If convenience and a cheap price are more important to you than a comfortable journey, travel by bus—but know in advance that the quality of buses in India varies widely. Some "tourist" buses end up picking up hitchhikers, so by the time you reach your destination, there will be people sitting in the aisles and on the roof. If you don't mind an adventure, or if you have no other choice, by all means take a bus. Otherwise take a train or rent a car.

The best way to get a bus ticket is not from the bus stations, but from any one of the private vendors who amass in major tourist areas. Ask your hotel or local travel agent for details.

CARS AND DRIVERS

It's not cheap, but having a car and driver to yourself is highly efficient if you're short on time. It's also a great help if you're exploring forts and small towns just outside the major cities. Hire a car through your hotel or a recognized travel agent, the latter of which will be cheaper. It should cost about Rs. 10–Rs. 12 per km. Expect to spend about Rs. 3,200 from Delhi to Jaipur in an air-conditioned car, or about Rs. 2,500 in a non-A/C alternative. Know that because the driver has to return to his port of origin, you pay the round-trip fare even if you're going one-way.

Rajasthan's roads are not in good shape, and local truck and bus drivers can be reckless, particularly at night. In any case, the going is slow—when calculating driving time, plan to cover 40 kph–50 kph (25 mph–31 mph) at best. That said, driving is an excellent way to see the Indian countryside and glimpse village life.

Jaipur is a 5½-hour drive from Delhi on National Highway (NH) 8. This is a congested industrial road with a high accident rate, so prepare for a trying experience.

The Shekhavati region is usually a three- to four-hour drive from Delhi, and in this case driving is much quicker and smoother than train travel. Hire a car and driver through a Delhi travel agency and plan to pay about Rs. 10 per km, with a halt charge (for stopping overnight) of Rs. 200–Rs. 250 per night. A thorough tour of the region should cost about Rs. 1,800.

Roads are rough in and out of Jodhpur, and the going is slow. Don't expect to average more than 40 km (25 mi) per hour. Udaipur is on NH 8, which links Bombay and Delhi. Again, expect your road speed to top out at 40 km (25 mi) per hour.

If you have time, you can design a delightful road trip to Jaisalmer by traveling from Delhi through Shekhavati, spending each night in a Heritage Hotel. You can also fly into Jodhpur and continue to Jaisalmer by road.

EMERGENCIES

In India, always be prepared with basic first-aid supplies. For more serious problems, the best hospitals in Rajasthan are in Jaipur and Udaipur, where the country's best and brightest doctors are available for anyone willing to pay for their services. Many hospitals have free ambulance services for the severely ill.

It's best not to deal with the Indian police force, which is often corrupt and ineffectual. You can certainly report a crime to them, but don't expect results unless you have connections. The best way to deal with the police, or with a crime, is through your embassy. However, if you opt to contact the police, dial 100 on any phone to get in touch with the central police switchboard.

At the Maharana Bopal Government Hospital in Udaipur, Dr. H.C. Sharma is the English-speaking superintendent. In Jaipur, Soni Hospital has a 24-hour emergency room and state-of-the-art facilities.
➤ CONTACTS: **Maharana Bopal Government Hospital** (✉ near Chetak Circle, ☎ 294/528811–(19). **Soni Hospital** (✉ 38 J. L. Nehru Marg, near Police Memorial, ☎ 141/562028).

MAIL AND SHIPPING
The cost per-kg for registered sea mail is Rs. 300. Air rates are significantly higher. All packages must be sewn closed and sealed with wax; there is usually a shop within 100 meters of every post office, which specializes in just that.
➤ POST OFFICES: **Jaipur** (✉ G.P.O on M.I. Rd., near Government Hostel, ☎ 141/204263). **Jaisalmer** (✉ G.P.O, Fort Wali Rd., ☎ 2992/53233). **Jodhpur** (✉ Head Post Office, Railway Station Rd., ☎ 0291/636695). **Udaipur** (✉ G.P.O at Chetak Circle, under the radio tower, ☎ 294/528622).

MONEY
ATMS
ATMs are beginning to emerge in Rajasthan. In major cities it's possible to at least get a credit card advance from a bank (which works for Master Card and Visa), if not actually withdraw money from a machine. The Bank of Baroda in Jaisalmer offers credit card advances weekdays 10–2 and Saturday 10:30–11:30. Most Bank of Baroda's are open 9–1 and 2–3:45.
➤ CASH MACHINES: **Citibank** (✉ M.I. Rd., near G.P.O., Jaipur, ☎ 141/204263). **Bank of Baroda** (✉ at Amarsagar Gate, Jaisalmer, ☎ 2992/52402). **Bank of Baroda** (✉ Sojati Gate, Jodhpur, ☎ 291/636613 or 291/636539). **HDFC Bank** (✉ Chetak Circle, behind Chetak Cinema, Udaipur, ☎ 294/426022).

CREDIT CARDS
Most major businesses accept Visa or Master Card, but cash is preferred.

CURRENCY EXCHANGE
Most upscale hotels will change currency for their guests. You can also change money at the State Bank of India. Banks and businesses associated with Western Union are your best bet.
➤ EXCHANGE SERVICES: **State Bank of India** (✉ Tilak Marg, C-Scheme, Jaipur, ☎ 141/380421; ✉ High Court Rd., Jodhpur, ☎ 291/45090 or 291/44169; ✉ Hospital Rd., Udaipur, ☎ 294/528857).

TAXIS AND AUTO-RICKSHAWS
Taxis are unmetered in Jaipur, Jodhpur, and Udaipur, so ask your hotel for the going rate and negotiate with the driver before you set off. For sightseeing within Jaipur and Jodphur, hire a cab through your hotel or the RTDC's Tourist Information Center (☞ Visitor Information). Depending on the distance to be covered, a taxi for half a day will cost about Rs. 600, and for a full day about Rs. 1,200.

Auto-rickshaws in Jaipur are metered, but the meters are often ignored. Insist on adhering to the meter *or* set the price in advance. The rate should be no more than Rs. 4.50 per km, with a minimum total of Rs. 10. Auto-rickshaws in Jodphur and Udaipur are unmetered, so you *must* agree on a price before departing. You can also hire an auto-rickshaw by the hour, for about Rs. 30 per hour. Note that all of these rates go up by about 50% after 11 PM.

TOURS

Alternative Travels organizes terrific stays in artisan villages; trips focusing on music and dance; treks; and bike, jeep, horse, and camel safaris. Historic Resort Hotels leads horse safaris around the Udaipur area, with overnight accommodations in tented camps or in hotels. The Rajasthan Mounted Sports Association gives riding and polo lessons in Jaipur; runs elephant, horse, and camel day trips in Shekhavati; and leads horse and jeep safaris that may include stays at palaces and forts. Rajasthan Safaris and Treks offers less luxurious but more authentic camel, camel-cart, and jeep safaris out of Bikaner. Food (traditional desert food) and water are provided, but you're on your own when it comes to toilet facilities.

Roop Nivas Safaris leads a Shekhavati Brigade Horse Safari around the colorful painted towns of this region, and offer longer safaris from Nawalgarh to Pushkar or Bikaner. You'll be sleeping in tents with bathroom facilities or at palace and fort hotels. Royal Safari administers treks, camel safaris, and nights in the desert around Bikaner, Jodhpur, and Jaisalmer, as well as visits to traditional villages, craftspeople's homes, little-known fairs, and ashrams.

Karwan Tours in Jaipur and TGS Tours and Travels (an American Express representative) in Jaipur and Udaipur can also help with general travel arrangements, including a hired car with driver to any location in Rajasthan Tourism Development Corporation also leads tours.

➤ CONTACTS: **Alternative Travels** (✉ Nawalgarh, Shekhavati, ☎ 1594/22129). **Historic Resort Hotels** (✉ Shikarbadi, Udaipur, ☎ 294/83200). **Karwan Tours** (✉ Bissau Palace Hotel, outside Chand Pol, Jaipur, ☎ 141/308103, WEB www.karwantours.com). **Meera Tour and Travels** (✉ 14 Badu Ji, Udaipur, ☎ 294/415249). **Rajasthan Mounted Sports Association** (✉ c/o Dundlod House, Hawa Sarak, Civil Lines, Jaipur, ☎ 141/366276). **Rajasthan Safaris and Treks** (✉ Birendra Singh Tanwar, Bassai House, Purani Ginani, Bikaner, ☎ 151/28557). **Rajasthan Tours** (✉ Garden Hotel, Udaipur, ☎ 294/525777; ✉ Airport Rd., Jodhpur, ☎ 291/36942 or 291/628265.) **Roop Nivas Safaris** (✉ c/o Roop Nivas Palace, Nawalgarh, Jhunjhunu district, Shekhavati, ☎ 15941/22008; 141/46949 or 141/351511 in Jaipur). **Royal Safari** (✉ Royal Safari, Box 23, Nachna Haveli, Gandhi Chowk, Jaisalmer, ☎ 2992/52538 or 2992/53202). **TGS Tours and Travels** (✉ Tholia Circle, Mirza Ismail Rd., Jaipur, ☎ 141/367735; ✉ Chetak Circle, Udaipur, ☎ 294/29661).

TRAIN TRAVEL

Rajasthan is still in the process of converting all its lines to broad gauge, a change that is improving train service but which is also altering routes and schedules. If you want to travel overnight, it's safer and more comfortable to take a train than a bus or car. Trains offer classes of service for all budgets (seats and sleepers, air-conditioning and non-air-conditioned, reserved and unreserved).

The *Shatabdi Express*, an air-conditioned chair-car train, travels every day but Sunday from New Delhi to Jaipur, a roughly five-hour trip. The *Pink City Express* covers the same ground in about six hours. The *Shekhavati Express* runs daily from Delhi to Jaipur, stopping at Jhunjhunu, Mukungarh, and Sikar. The Shekavati Express runs overnight and arrives in Jaipur around 7 AM.

The daily *Bikaner Express* from Delhi passes through Shekhavati en route to Bikaner. The overnight *Superfast Express* leaves New Delhi at 8 PM and reaches Jodhpur at 5:30 AM. A separate *Superfast Express* connects Jodhpur with Jaipur in four hours; contact the Tourist Information Center in either city for more information.

Daily trains connect Udaipur with Jaipur, Ajmer, Chittaurgarh, Jodhpur, Ahmedabad, and Delhi; for more information, call the Tourist Reception Center. Trains also run out to Jaisalmer from Jodhpur and Udaipur, but they're significantly slower than the road routes.
➤ TRAIN INFORMATION: **Shatabdi Express** (☎ 131 for inquiries, 135 for reservations anywhere in Rajasthan). **Superfast Express** (☎ 291/131 or 291/132 in Jodhpur). **Tourist Information Center** (Jodhpur ☎ 291/44010). **Tourist Reception Center** (Udaipur ☎ 294/41535; general train information, 294/131).

VISITOR INFORMATION
Many hotels provide regional information and travel services. In Jaipur, Jodhpur, Udaipur, and Jaisalmer, the Tourist Information Centers of the Rajasthan Tourism Development Corporation provide information, travel assistance, and guides. *Jaipur Vision* and the *Jaipur City Guide,* available in most hotels, are periodicals with visitor information and up-to-date phone numbers.
➤ TOURIST OFFICES:: **Government of India Tourist Office** (✉ Hotel Khasa Kothi, Jaipur, ☎ 141/372200). **Rajasthan Tourism Development Corporation** (✉ Paryatan Bhawan, Government Hostel Campus, Jaipur, ☎ 141/376362; Jaipur main train station, ☎ 141/69714; ✉ Hotel Ghoomar, High Court Rd., Jodhpur, ☎ 291/44010; ✉ Shastri Circle, Udaipur, ☎ 294/411535; ✉ Hotel Moomal, Station Rd., Jaisalmer, ☎ 2992/52392). **Tourist Information Bureau** (✉ Hotel Shiv Shekhawati, Jhunjhunu, Shekhavati, ☎ 15945/32909).

6 GUJARAT

Art, ancient civilizations, and wildlife thrive in this northwestern coastal state. Le Corbusier built more buildings in Ahmedabad than he did in all of the United States; lions roam about the Gir Wildlife Sanctuary; and traditional crafts are nurtured by modern institutions and sold in time-honored bazaars throughout the region.

By Andy
McCord and
Julie Tomasz

Updated by
Ami Trivedi

G UJARAT IS ONE OF INDIA'S RICHEST STATES, both economically and culturally. The arts flourish in its cities, and artisanship thrives in its villages. At the Gir Wildlife Sanctuary,
the last prides of Asiatic lions are growing in number. The Hindu
Solanki dynasty produced a flowering of architecture late in the classical period, and some of India's earliest Muslim kingdoms were
founded here a few centuries later.

Ahmedabad, the state's capital, is a repository of architectural styles:
from the early Indo-Saracenic forms of the 15th-century Muslim sultans to the modern forms of Le Corbusier, the contemporary Indian
architect Charles Correa, and the American Louis Kahn. The city is
congested and hectic, but it has a wealth of museums, performing-arts
centers, and galleries. In Ahmedabad and elsewhere in Northern India,
you'll find curious and ornately decorated step-wells, or *baolis,* that
plunge fathoms down into the earth's water table.

Southwest of Ahmedabad, the Saurashtra region has remarkable
wildlife preserves, and the palaces of the dozens of princes who ruled
here before Independence. Southeast of the capital, the pretty college
town Vadodara (a Sanskrit name commonly anglicized as Baroda) is
the former headquarters of an important princely state; today it has a
vibrant cultural life, with good art museums and bookstores. Scattered
about the state are pilgrimage centers of the Jains, members of an ancient religion that practices strict nonviolence.

Previous neglect of tourism in Gujurat means that the hard-sell approach
is rare among guides, touts, and taxi drivers. And yet, Gujaratis are
relatively unfazed by visitors from overseas: they themselves are India's
greatest travelers, composing about a quarter of Indian immigrants
around the world. Even their most famous son, Mahatma Gandhi, began
his adult life as a lawyer in South Africa. Welcoming, but not overly
touristy, Gujurat offers a glimpse into workaday Indians' India.

At this writing the Kutch region, on the state's northwestern edge bordering Pakistan, was still inaccessible because of a devastating earthquake that hit Gujarat on January 27, 2001. The tremors, which
ravaged the remote town of Bhuj and the surrounding district, measured between 6.9 and 7.9 on the Richter scale and were felt from Pakistan to Rajasthan. The Indian Defense Minister estimated a loss of
100,000 lives.

Pleasures and Pastimes

Dining

The rich sauces and meats of North India are foreign here, though many
hotels have restaurants featuring classic Mughlai cuisine. Gujaratis prefer a delicious variety of vegetable dishes stir-fried in light vegetable
oils, served with unleavened breads—fritters made from bean flours
and rice—and washed down with *lassi,* a cold drink made with yogurt. You can try all of the above by ordering a *thali,* the traditional
sampler platter. Note that Gujarat is a dry state: alcohol is available
only in a few hotel shops, and then only for consumption in your room.
Ask your hotel how to obtain a permit from the Excise Department
to purchase from these stores. Also, restaurants tend to close for a few
hours in the late afternoon.

Festivals

Makar Sankranti—the point when the sun reaches the Tropic of Capricorn after the winter solstice—is celebrated on January 14 with a

tremendous kite festival in Ahmedabad. A dance festival is organized immediately afterward at Modhera's sun temple, about 100 km (62 mi) north of Ahmedabad.

Navaratri, the goddess festival in late September or early October, is celebrated throughout the state with performances of Ras Garba, Gujarat's folk dance, nowadays often embellished with disco moves and amplified music. Tarnetar, northeast of Rajkot in the center of the Kathiawar Peninsula, is the site of a large folk fair in October or November. Diwali—the November or December festival of lights marking the return of the epic hero Rama from exile with his wife, Sita—is celebrated distinctively here by the Jains, as is the birthday of their founder, Mahavira, in April.

Lodging

Ahmedabad and some other cities have some good business hotels, and in the countryside some formerly state-run tourist facilities have been refurbished under private ownership. Several of the modest palaces of former princes are being converted to Heritage Hotels in charming rural locations. Still, accommodations in Gujarat are largely works in progress.

Shopping

Gujarat's traditional crafts are nurtured by such modern institutions as Ahmedabad's National Institute of Design. In Ahmedabad, emporia and street markets deliver a wide selection. It's now very difficult to buy pieces made with the mind-boggling detail you see in museums, but contemporary crafts are vibrant with color and charming vernacular.

Visual Arts and Architecture

If you visit only one museum, make it Ahmedabad's Calico Museum of Textiles. The displays will convince you that weaving and embroidery are fine arts. The art school in Vadodara is India's best, so Ahmedabad and Vadodara both have good collections of sculpture and painting from various periods as well as galleries of contemporary art. Architecture enthusiasts can see three buildings by Le Corbusier in Ahmedabad, and the city's Indian Institute of Management Studies was designed by Louis Kahn. Ahmedabad's pre-Moghul Muslim buildings have a lightness and exuberance equal to that of the better-known architecture that followed.

Wildlife

Even if you don't see lions in the Gir Wildlife Sanctuary, you won't leave disappointed. Gujarat's hilly landscape teems with deer and other animals, giving a sense of the natural landscape celebrated in Indian art and literature. At Velavadar Wildlife Sanctuary, you're likely to glimpse great herds of blackbuck on a large, grassy plain.

Exploring Gujarat

Great Itineraries

Numbers in the margin correspond to points of interest on the Gujarat map.

IF YOU HAVE 2 DAYS

Spend one day sampling the sights and culture of 🔲 **Ahmedabad.** The next day, venture out to the ruined capital of the Solanki dynasty at **Patan** and the ornately carved sun temple at nearby **Modhera,** a structure that predates the more famous sun temple at Konark, Orissa, and rivals it in beauty if not in scale. *Alternately,* take a fast train to **Vadodara** and visit the palace and museums of the maharaja as well as the ghost town of Champaner.

Gujarat

IF YOU HAVE 4 DAYS

Visit ☑ **Ahmedabad,** then venture south onto the Kathiawar Peninsula. Leave Ahmedabad early to arrive at ☑ **Gir Wildlife Sanctuary** in time for a late-afternoon game drive. The next morning, take another game drive just after dawn and end the day on the beach at ☑ **Diu.** Alternately, if you leave ☑ **Ahmedabad** in the late afternoon, spend the night at the Palace Utelia, near ☑ **Lothal,** and arrange for transport to **Velavadar Wildlife Sanctuary** the next morning before visiting **Palitana** in the afternoon. Spend the night at ☑ **Bhavnagar** before flying out to Bombay.

When to Tour Gujarat

As in much of India, the months between October and March are the best times to come here.

AHMEDABAD AND ENVIRONS

Gujarat's richness and variety are apparent in the immediate region of its capital. The ruins at Patan and Modhera bear testament to the classical Hindu period, and Ahmedabad itself shows how a sense of style persisted through eras of Muslim rule and the modern period.

Ahmedabad

❶ *545 km (338 mi) north of Bombay*

Founded in AD 1411 by the Muslim Sultan Ahmed Shah, Ahmedabad flourished under the Gujarat dynasty and became the seat of the Moghul governors of Gujarat—Jahangir, Shah Jahan, and Aurangzeb—all of whom later became emperors. It was said that Ahmedabad hung on three threads: gold, silk, and cotton. The city's present prominence is due largely to one family of textile magnates, the Sarabhais, who were patrons of the arts (they invited Le Corbusier to build here) and supporters of Mahatma Gandhi. Family members are still active in the city's cultural life. Although textiles remain a principal industry in Ahmedabad, the city is also a booming national and international center for the mineral, power, agribusiness, petro-chemical, scientific-development, computer-software, and pharmaceuticals industries.

Ahmedabad is divided into old and new by the Sabarmati River, a now mostly dry riverbed; much of the new development is on the river's west side. The pace and scope of the development are amazing: towering office complexes, designed by well-known Indian architects, are going up everywhere, particularly along C. G. Road, the up-and-coming business and shopping strip where real-estate prices challenge those of Bombay.

In some ways, Ahmedabad doesn't quite look the part of a major international business hub. Ashram and C. G. roads, the main streets, lined with shopping complexes and office buildings, are perpetually under construction, with deep, dusty shoulders instead of sidewalks and a constant crowd of camels, cows, and monkeys. Although Ahmedabad wasn't the hardest hit by the January 2001 earthquake that shook Gujarat, there are subtle signs of the disaster: you can spot cracks on inside walls of the Sabarmati Ashram (Gandhi's home between 1915 and 1930) and occasionally, in the midst of standing buildings, you'll spot the skeletons of those collapsed. Amid this turmoil is a self-confident city full of cultural attractions and intellectual life, accessible and welcoming.

A Good Tour

Traffic in Ahmedabad is chaotic: lanes exist, but largely in theory. Getting around on foot in busy areas is tricky because there are no sidewalks to speak of, just dirt, and traffic hurtles toward you from every direction. To see the main sights in a day, arrange for a car and have the driver pick you up well before the traffic kicks in at 9 AM. Head first to the **Jama Masjid,** then to **Ahmed Shah's Tomb** and the **Sidi Saiyad Mosque,** all in the central, walled part of town. Then proceed north to the **Hatheesing Jain Temple.** After lunch, trek a few kilometers farther north to the **Calico Museum of Textiles**—take the tour, which starts at 2:45 PM. If you prefer, skip the second (religious) part of the Calico tour and go directly on to **Sabarmati Ashram,** just across the river to the west. If there's time afterward, get on the highway to Ghandhinagar to **Adalaj step-well** and then a few minutes farther on the highway for a quick look at the **Vaishnavadevi Temple.** These two stops should take you less than an hour. If time permits, end your day by heading north on the highway to **Akshardham** where you can relax in the peaceful gardens, participate in the evening prayers, and have a Gujarati thali dinner in the Premvati Restaurant. To fully tour Akshardham, you'll need a few hours to view all the exhibitions and temples.

TIMING

This tour runs from sun-up to sun-down, and can be divided into two days for a more leisurely pace. You'll probably spend the biggest chunks of time in the Hatheesing Jain Temple, the Calico Museum, and the Sabarmati Ashram.

Sights to See

OFF THE
BEATEN PATH

ADALAJ STEP-WELL (WAV) – Step-wells *(wavs* or *baolis)* are unique to Northern India. The intricate structures around the wells are all below-ground and were used as cool resting places for nomads and traveling merchants. Richly carved pillars and friezes lead down to this 16th-century octagonal well 17 km (10½ mi) north of Ahmedabad. The surrounding gardens are a lovely respite from the dry environs. ⊠ *Ghandhinagar Hwy., Chharodi.* ☎ *Free.* ☺ *Daily.*

Ahmed Shah's Tomb. The grave of Ahmedabad's founder is venerated with incense, flowers, and colorful cloths called *chadars*, in the manner of a Muslim saint. ⊠ *Gandhi Rd.* ☎ *Free.*

Akshardham. This 23-acre cultural and religious complex dedicated to the Lord Swaminarayan took thousands of devoted volunteers interested in preserving Indian heritage and the religious legacy of the Swaminaryan Sanstha 13 years to build. The whole complex at Akshardham is made of intricately carved pink sandstone (6,000 tons of it). It includes three temples, four exhibition halls, gardens, a game area, a restaurant, and a bookstore. The largest of the three temples, Hari Mandapam, houses a 7-ft gold-leaf covered statue of Lord Swaminarayan. Behind the Hari Mandapam is the Vibhuti Mandapam, a temple dedicated to the revelations of Swaminarayan that are etched in brass and glass structures and the Hari Smruti where the *arti* (prayer or mass) takes place at 7 PM daily. *J Rd., Sector 20 (on National Hwy. 8c), Gandhinagar,* ☎ *2712/60001 or 2712/60002,* ⓦⒺⒷ *www.akshardham.com.* ☎ *Free; exhibitions Rs. 20.* ☺ *Daily 9:30–7:30; exhibitions daily 10:00–6:30. Closed Mon.*

★ **Calico Museum of Textiles.** Visiting this vast collection is a rich way to experience the lavish colors and textures of Ahmedabad's age-old primary industry. Housed in a composite *haveli* (traditional Gujarati carved mansion), the museum buildings are connected by paths through gardens. The museum is filled with beautiful examples of embroidery, dyeing, weaving, and other textile traditions from all over India—heavy royal costumes with gold brocade, battle scenes embroidered on silk, silver gilt, 12-ft-long Banarasi silk cummerbunds, 17th-century painted prayer cloths, and so on. For reasons of security and preservation, you must go on a guided tour. The tour of the first section, the larger historical exhibit, begins at 10:30 and ends at 11:30, when part two, comprising religious textiles, begins (it, too, lasts one hour). The same two-part sequence begins again at 2:45. If you miss the first tour, you can't enter until the next one begins. ⊠ *Retreat Bungalow, near Shahibag overpass,* ☎ *79/786–8172.* ☎ *Free.* ☺ *Mon.—Tues. and Thurs.–Sun. 10:30–12:30 and 2:45–5.*

Hatheesing Jain Temple. The finest of Ahmedabad's beautiful Jain temples is an elaborate white-marble structure. Dedicated to Dharmanath, the 15th Jain apostle, it took 25 years to complete in the mid-19th century. Every surface of every pillar and arch is intricately carved with figures and ornaments; just pick a spot and allow yourself to get lost in the details. The main structure is surrounded by 52 miniature temples. The magnificent stone lattice screens of the second-floor windows look as if they're woven of stone threads. A few restrictions: photography of gods or goddesses is prohibited, and menstruating women are theoretically banned from entry. ⊠ *Balvantrai Mehta Rd., by Delhi Gate.* ☎ *Free.* ☺ *Daily 5:30–1 and 3:30–7:30.*

Jama Masjid. The city's largest mosque is best seen before business hours congest the surrounding streets. The mosque was built in 1424 by Ahmed Shah. The prayer hall, with its niche facing Mecca, is covered by five domes held up with 260 pillars, carved in a style reminiscent of Hindu and Jain temple architecture. ⊠ *Gandhi Rd.* ☎ *Free.*

Sabarmati Ashram. Born in Gujarat, Mahatma Gandhi established his simple retreat, the Satyagraha (literally, "seizing truth"), here when he returned from South Africa in 1915. Eventually the nerve center of the

Indian independence movement, this ashram occupies a tranquil spot on the bank of the nearly dry Sabarmati River just outside the city center. It was from here, in 1930, that Gandhi and 79 followers began the 241-mi march to the seacoast at Dandi to protest the British salt tax, galvanizing the movement that brought India independence after World War II. The main, open-air building houses exhibits, including a photo display documenting Gandhi's life and work; and the grounds give a deep, if less tangible, impression of Gandhi's legacy. Under shade trees on the green lawns, students and others come to talk quietly or reflect on the history of this place and on modern India. When you sign the register in the humble cottage where Gandhi lived, your name will share the pages with those of Nelson Mandela and other dignitaries and peace workers who come to pay homage to the father of modern India. ⊠ *Ashram Rd. and Sabarmati River, 7 km (3 mi) north of city center.* 📼 *Free; sound-and-light show Rs. 5.* ⊙ *Daily 8:30–6:30; sound-and-light show in English Wed., Sat., and Fri. 8:30 PM; tickets on sale at box office after 2.*

Sidi Saiyad Mosque. Named for a slave in Ahmed Shah's court, this intimate mosque stands at a busy intersection in the heart of Ahmedabad, but the chiseled stone friezes on its western wall, depicting the tree of life, will transport you out of the hubbub. Built in the late 1500s, the mosque is a masterpiece: its stonework has the delicacy of filigree (though the full effect is reduced, as the central screen is now in Delhi's National Museum). Women are not allowed under the dome, but you can see the friezes from a small garden outside it. ⊠ *Relief Rd.* 📼 *Free.*

OFF THE BEATEN PATH

VAISHNAVADEVI TEMPLE – This temple, dedicated to the goddess Vaishnadevi (whose incarnations include Laxmi, Sarasvati, Kali, and Durga), was recently built as a replica of a larger, original Vaishnavadevi temple set in a mountain cave in Kashmir. Five thousand years ago Vaishnadevi herself is said to have meditated in the Kashmir cave, waiting for Krishna to incarnate on earth. The temple here resembles a chunk of limestone rock and is crowded with Hindu devotees who can no longer make the pilgrimage to Kashmir because of the armed conflict there. Walk up the winding path to the top and crawl through the narrow, cavelike passage to the main chamber to pay homage to Laxmi, the goddess of wealth and prosperity. The three *avatars* you see are, from left to right, Sarasvati, Vaishnavadevi, and Kali. Encircling the room are nine idols of Durga (a fierce version of the mother goddess) representing her nine different incarnations on earth. Ring the bell and accept the coin from the priest as a blessing of good fortune. ⊠ *Ghandhinagar Hwy., Chharodi.* 📼 *Free.* ⊙ *Daily.*

Dining and Lodging

$$$$ ✕ **The Waterfall.** Named for the simulated waterfalls cascading behind a glass window in the dining room, the Holiday Inn's restaurant is intimate and elegant, with candlelit tables. The menu offers Indian, Chinese, and Continental items. Specialties include Kerala kebab (a moist, spicy chicken leg stuffed with dried fruits, nuts, and cheese and baked in a tandoor oven) and *kadai* chicken (boneless chunks in a tangy brown sauce named for, cooked, and served in, an Indian woklike pot). ⊠ *Holiday Inn Ahmedabad, Chand Suraj Estate, Khanpur,* ☎ *79/550–5505. Reservations essential. AE, DC, MC, V.*

$$$ ✕ **Vishalla.** Try to make time for this famous restaurant, a re-created
★ Gujarati village outside Ahmedabad. You're welcomed with a flower garland, and a *bindi* (colored dot) is placed on your forehead. Place your order at the entrance, and then try a sugarcane aperitif from the thatch-roof hut where a young boy cranks a giant cog-and-wheel con-

traption that squeezes juice out of the cane. Stroll on dirt paths lit by candles and lanterns and discover a Rajasthani puppet show performed under a palm tree, or wander into a clearing where musicians sing folk songs. When your order is ready—they run around calling your name until they find you—you sit on straw mats at low, rough wood tables while turbaned waiters serve authentic thali on banana leaves. Come hungry, be prepared to eat with your hands, and bring insect repellent. ⊠ *Vasana Tol Naka,* ☎ *79/643–0357. Reservations essential. No credit cards.*

$$ ✕ **Mirch Masala.** Done up in imitation of a roadside truck stop, with
★ painted murals of rural scenes, this basement restaurant on Ahmedabad's main shopping strip draws a congenial affluent crowd of young people and families. Specialties include a variety of Jain-inspired vegetarian dishes made without onions or garlic. You can also sample traditional street snacks, prepared in a cleaner environment than the street. Expect to wait for a table. ⊠ *Chandan Complex, C. G. Rd., near Swastik Char Rasta, Navrangpura,* ☎ *79/640–3340. AE, MC, V.*

$$ ✕ **Rajwadu.** Like the better-known Vishalla, this outdoor restaurant in a residential suburb serves Gujarati meals in a faux-rural ambience. Relatively new in town, it already has a loyal local following. The menus are only in Gujarati, so you're best off asking for help. ⊠ *Jivaraj Tolanaka, near Ambaji Temple, Malar Talav,* ☎ *79/664–3845. No credit cards. No lunch.*

$$ ✕ **"10."** As its numerical name implies, this classy restaurant strives for perfection. Heated plates, free bottled water, and linen napkins embroidered with the names of restaurant regulars reflect the management's mission of personalized service. The chef prepares top-notch Punjabi, Continental, and Chinese fare. Try the *paneer khada masala* (cheese chunks in a spicy clove and nutmeg gravy) with some floppy garlic *naan* (bread). ⊠ *Urja House, Swastik Char Rasta,* ☎ *79/642– 5703. AE, MC, V.*

$$ ✕ **Tomato's.** This trendy downstairs eatery resembles a 1950s-style American diner and it's crammed with American pop paraphernalia. The menu mixes Mexican, Chinese, Punjabi Indian, and Continental food, and tacks on coleslaw and apple pie. The decor outdoes most of the food, which is fresh but far from the real thing; stick with the Indian offerings. ⊠ *Mardia Plaza, off C. G. Rd.,* ☎ *79/642–5975. No credit cards.*

$ ✕ **Gopi Dining Hall.** This popular sit-down lunchroom in the center of town is a good place to restore yourself after a morning's sightseeing. Serving hundreds of hungry office workers at once, it specializes in large Gujarati thalis. The setting is hectic, with service to match, but you'll have a tasty and filling vegetarian meal. ⊠ *Opposite Town Hall, Ashram Rd., Ellisbridge,* ☎ *79/657–6388. V.*

$ ✕ **South-Indian Restaurant.** Tucked into the hotel pocket on the east side of the Sabarmati River, this tiny, simple restaurant fills up at lunchtime with businesspeople and hotel staff enjoying large portions of tasty, inexpensive vegetarian fare. Choose from nearly 30 different *dosas* (stuffed crepes), or try the fixed thali menu. Service is efficient. ⊠ *Opposite Ministry Chambers, near Cama Hotel, Khanpur,* ☎ *79/ 550–1343. No credit cards.*

$ ✕ **Toran Dining Hall.** Barefoot waiters dressed in plain gray uniforms
★ swarm around the dining room of this Ahmedabad institution tossing handfuls of *chapati* and *puri* bread and spooning refills of the various vegetarian concoctions, chutneys, and condiments into your stainless-steel thali bowls. Each waiter carries just one garnish or type of food and will hover over you throughout the meal, replenishing your tray before you can eat the last bite. The large, simple room is air-conditioned and dark, with pale-gray walls and mirrors set into pillars.

✉ *Opposite Sales India, Ashram Rd.,* ☎ *79/754–2197. No credit cards. No dinner Mon.*

$$$$
★
🏨 **Cama.** The upscale, 40-year-old Cama has more competition than it once did, but it still has the city's loveliest gardens. The lawns, palm trees, chirping birds, and small swimming pool in the back garden grant respite after a hectic day. The reception area has an elegant art deco motif and mixes post-colonial elegance and old Indian splendor. The lobby is decorated with Gujarati handicrafts, antiques, and has large white-marble *jalis* (intricately carved window frames). Rooms are large, modern, and luxurious, with pale walls, dark bedspreads, and huge tubs. Request a room facing the river—the Cama's views of the dry Sabarmati are the best in town. The hotel has a liquor store. ✉ *Khanpur Rd., Khanpur, Ahmedabad 380001,* ☎ *79/550–5281 or 79/550–5289,* FAX *79/550–5285. 46 rooms, 5 suites. Restaurant, coffee shop, pool, dry cleaning, laundry service, business services, meeting room, travel services. AE, DC, MC, V.*

$$$$
🏨 **Fortune Hotel Landmark.** This new business hotel is challenging its more established competitors. Guest rooms are comfortably furnished and spacious, and service is excellent. The location—near the central business district—is more convenient than that of Ahmedabad's other upscale hotels, which are out in Khanpur. ✉ *Ashram Rd., Osmanpura, Ahmedabad 380013,* ☎ *79/755–2929,* FAX *79/755–2912,* WEB *www. fortunehotellandmark.com. 96 rooms, 2 suites. 2 restaurants, coffee shop, pool, dry cleaning, laundry service, business services, meeting room, travel services. AE, DC, MC, V.*

$$$$
🏨 **Holiday Inn Ahmedabad.** Glass elevators glide up and down in the soaring atrium of Ahmedabad's classiest hotel. Gleaming with glass and polished marble, the lobby is a hushed bustle of businesspeople. Rooms are contemporary and elegant, with occasional clashes among the fabric colors and furniture styles. On the east bank of the Sabarmati River, the hotel is slightly removed from the city center, a short trip across the Nehru Bridge. Rooms facing west have river views with a tragic twist on the modern Indian paradox: just below the towering white hotel, a dense stretch of slum housing lines the shore. ✉ *Chand Suraj Estate,, Khanpur, Ahmedabad 380001,* ☎ *79/550–5505,* FAX *79/550–5501,* WEB *www.sixcontinentshotels.com. 61 rooms, 2 suites. 2 restaurants, coffee shop, patisserie, pool, health club, baby-sitting, dry cleaning, laundry service, business services, meeting room, travel services, free parking. AE, DC, MC, V.*

$$$
Comfort Inn Sunset. This comfortable business hotel is convenient to the airport. Rooms are spacious, bright, and well-appointed; they include work areas. Complimentary Continental breakfast is included in the room rate. 🏨 *Airport Circle, Hansol Ahmedabad 382 475,* ☎ *79/286–2591,* FAX *79/286–1627,* WEB *www.comfortinn.com. 33 rooms. Restaurant, laundry service, shop, baby-sitting, business services, meeting room, travel services, airport shuttle. AE, MC, DC, V.*

$$
Hotel Klassic Gold. Because this quality, four-story business hotel sits across the Ellis Bridge, away from the Khanpur hotel district, it's able to offer exceptional room rates. The sleek, modern building has a trim front courtyard. The large rooms have white marble tile floors and low beds with dark bedspreads. As a convenience for business travelers, the hotel has a reception counter at Ahmedabad's airport. *42 Sardar Patel Nagar, behind Navrangpura, Ahmedabad 380006,* ☎ *79/644–5508 or 79/644–5525,* FAX *79/656–9195. 35 rooms. Restaurant, laundry service, shop, business services, meeting room, airport shuttle. AE, DC, MC, V.*

$$
🏨 **Shalin.** Each of the Shalin's suites has a tiny sitting and work area separated from a small bedroom by a sliding glass door. Although guest quarters show signs of wear, the modern, functional furnishings are

uniform throughout, and the lobby's marble and teakwood sparkles. Rooms facing the pool and street have the best views; for less street noise, request a room at the back or on an upper floor. The location, near the stock exchange and busy M. G. Road, is convenient for business travelers, and there's a liquor store on the premises. ☒ *Gujarat College Cross Rds., Ellisbridge, Ahmedabad 380006,* ☎ *79/642–6967 through 79/642–6976,* FAX *79/656–5334 or 79/656–0022. 70 suites. 2 restaurants, pool, dry cleaning, laundry service, business services, meeting room, travel services. AE, DC, MC, V.*

$ ⊞ **Inter Residency.** This promising new hotel has a choice central location between Ashram and C. G. roads. The lobby has low ceilings, white pillars, and a kitschy, rainbow-color water sculpture on the back wall. With clean white walls, modern blond-wood furniture, aqua carpeting, and coordinated geometric-pattern soft furnishings, the guest rooms are cool and bright. All rooms face the pool or the front terrace. ☒ *Opposite Gujarat College, Ellisbridge, Ahmedabad 380006,* ☎ *79/656–5222 through 79/656–5231,* FAX *79/656–0407. 74 rooms, 5 suites. Restaurant, coffee shop, patisserie, pool, dry cleaning, laundry service, business services, meeting room. AE, DC, MC, V.*

$ ⊞ **King Palace.** This addition to the main strip of hotels in Khanpur is a clean and attractive option for travelers on a budget. The rooms are carpeted, and furnished with basic upholstered chairs. ☒ *Khanpur, Ahmedabad 380001,* ☎ *79/550–0276 through 79/550–0282,* FAX *79/550–0275. 37 rooms, 2 suites. Restaurant, laundry service, meeting room, travel services. AE, DC, MC, V.*

$ ⊞ **Rock Regency.** A giant, red neon sign blazes above this white, four-
★ story hotel, just off C. G. Road. The lobby is stylish and contemporary, with polished granite floors and twisting white pillars; in the rooms, pea-green floral upholstered chairs and headboards with white wooden frames create a garden look. ☒ *Law Garden Rd., Navrangpura, Ahmedabad 380006,* ☎ *79/656–2101 through 79/656–2105,* FAX *79/ 642–3694. 37 rooms, 2 suites. Restaurant, coffee shop, dry cleaning, laundry service, meeting room, travel services. AE, DC, MC, V.*

Nightlife and the Arts

You won't find discos in this dry city, but you may well discover a new master of the sitar or the next great Indian painter. The **Darpana Academy of the Performing Arts** (☎ 79/755–1389, FAX 79/755–0955) in Usmanpura, a neighborhood just north of the Khanpur hotel district, has regular performances ranging from classical dance to folk puppet shows. The complex also has an arts bookstore.

Other performances are held in the **Tagore Auditorium** (☒ Sanskar Kendra municipal complex, Bhagtacharya Rd.), designed by Le Corbusier. The Sanskar Kendra complex also houses an intriguing kite museum.

The **Amdavad-ni-Gufa** (☒ Gujarat University) is an eccentric collaboration between the painter M. F. Husain and the prominent local architect Balkrishna Doshi, who collaborated with Le Corbusier. It displays contemporary arts and crafts in a cavelike space.

The **L. D. Institute of Indology Museum** (☒ L. D. Institute of Indology, opposite Gujarat University, Navrangpura) specializes in classical miniature painting. It's open Tuesday to Sunday from 11 to 6.

The **N. C. Mehta Gallery** has an excellent collection of medieval sculpture. It's housed in the L. D. Institute of Indology as well. The **National Institute of Design** (☒ Paldi, ☎ 79/663–9692, FAX 79/663–8465) holds regular exhibitions. The **Archer Art Gallery** (☒ Archer House, Gurukul Rd., Paldi, ☎ 79/741–3594) is a leading gallery for modern and contemporary art.

Shopping

Ahmedabad is a great place to buy authentic Gujarati handicrafts, famous throughout India. Textiles are outstanding, from finely woven silk *patola* fabrics and *bhandej* (tie-dyed) materials to embroidered vests, purses, wall hangings, slippers, and bedspreads from the Kutch desert and Saurashtra. Look also for *moti-kaam* (beadwork) textiles and figures, and for copper, brass, and bronze metalwork. Mobiles and chains of small stuffed parrots, horses, and other figures of various sizes make inexpensive decorative accents. Most shops are open Monday through Saturday, 10 to 6 or 7. Some stores accept credit cards.

Banascraft (⊠ 8 Chandan Complex, near Mirch Masala Restaurant, C. G. Rd., Swastik Char Rasta, Navrangpura, ☎ 79/640–5784) is a boutique featuring embroidery and other high-quality craftwork by members of the Self-Employed Women's Association (SEWA), a highly successful women's cooperative. The organization works with slum dwellers in Ahmedabad.

Gurjari (⊠ opposite La-Gajjar Chamber, Ashram Rd., ☎ 79/658–9505), also known as the Gujarat State Handicrafts Emporium, is a fixed-price government shop with low prices, no taxes, and guaranteed quality. It sells an impressive variety of brightly embroidered dresses, handwoven wall hangings, beaded tribal jewelry, brass figures, traditional silver and brass *pataris* (jewelry boxes), and other examples of Gujarati craftwork.

Kapasi Handicrafts Emporium (⊠ 105 B. K. House, C. G. Rd., near Stadium Circle, ☎ 79/754–1092) has a good selection of handicrafts, particularly brass and other metalwork.

Law Garden Market (⊠ Netaji Rd.) gets going only at around 7 or 8 each night, when the road is transformed into a vibrant, chaotic scene. Vendors drape their stalls with exquisitely embroidered wall hangings, shirts, vests, bedspreads, and more, studded with tiny mirrors. Bargain like mad.

Manek Chowk (⊠ off Ramanlal Jani and Desai Rds.) is a colorful bazaar in the old city where crowded, narrow streets are packed with stalls and shops selling excellent fabrics and ready-made clothes.

Patan and Modhera

②–③ *Modhera is 100 km (62 mi) northwest of Ahmedabad. Patan is 30 km (20 mi) northeast of Modhera.*

Northwest of Ahmedabad, these two groups of ruins can be combined in a day trip or worked into a longer road trip to or from Rajastan. **Patan** was capital of the Hindu Solanki dynasty from the 8th to 12th centuries. The ornate **Rani-ka-Vav,** built in 1050, is Gujarat's most stunning baoli. A great flight of steps leads down into the well, halting at a covered colonnade just above the waterline; the walls are covered in fine sculptures of Vishnu, Ganesh, and other Hindu gods. The nearby **Sahasra Linga Tank** once housed a thousand *lingas* (abstract stone icons of the great god Shiva, sometimes characterized as phallic symbols). Little remains of the shrines today, but the outlines of the extensive water tanks are impressive.

On the way into town from the Sahasra Linga Tank, you can see the last makers of patola saris, who use a weaving technique called ikat—threads used for both warp and weft are tie-dyed before they're woven into saris. It can take up to seven months for two weavers to produce a single 6-yard-long sari; the slightly blurred but intricate pattern recalls an impressionist painting. The process is fascinating to watch—ask for directions to the Salvi family's shop, **Patolawala** (⊠ Salviwado, Patolawala St., ☎ 2766/32274). In the center of the sleepy contemporary town of Patan there is an attractive Jain temple complex, and next to the temple a "Jnan Mandir," or temple of knowledge, with an important collection of illuminated manuscripts. Mornings from 8 to 10 and afternoons from 2 to 4, young monks come to study the manuscripts. The caretaker has a photo album of the collection, and upon request he'll bring out a few of the original works, which are masterpieces of miniature painting. Make a small donation in return for his help.

The 11th-century sun-temple complex at **Modhera** is the Solanki dynasty's most striking architectural achievement. The main temple sits on a moderately high plinth, which is now missing its spire, or *shikara*. Fronting this is the *ranga mandapa*, or hall for dance and other entertainments, and a large stone bathing tank, which contains some 108 small shrines. The temple, mandapa, and tank were lined up so that on the fall and spring equinoxes, the sun rose to shine directly on the temple's main image of Surya, the sun god. All three structures are embellished with high-quality sculpture reminiscent of the better-known temples at Khajuraho, which date from the same period. A guide can point out scenes of the Hindu epics *Mahabharata* and *Ramayana*, as well as images of the sun god and numerous erotic scenes. On the east side of the bathing tank, a shrine houses a fine relief of Vishnu reclining on the serpent Anant Nag, preparing for the sleep that follows the cosmic dissolution and precedes the rejuvenation of the universe.

NEED A BREAK? **Hotel New Janapath** (☎ 2762/52441), on the highway near Radhanpur Char Rasta, Mahesana, 80 km (48 mi) north of Ahmedabad, has an excellent air-conditioned vegetarian restaurant where you can break your journey between Ahmedabad and Patan or Modhera.

Lodging

$$$ 🏨 **Balaram Palace Resorts.** If you plan to enter or leave Gujarat via Rajasthan, this Heritage Hotel at the edge of the Aravalli Hills makes an ideal base. Patan and Modhera are 73 km and 112 km (50 mi and 67 mi) away, respectively, and Mount Abu, in Rajasthan, is even closer. Once a princely mansion, it's well restored and professionally run. Palanpur, a stop on the main rail line between Ahmedabad and Delhi, is 15 km (10 mi) away. ⊠ *Chitrasani Village, off Abu-Palanpur Hwy. No. 14,* ☎ *2742/84278 through 2742/84280,* FAX *2742/84336. 17 rooms. Restaurant, pool, health club, laundry service, travel services. AE, D, MC, V.*

KATHIAWAR PENINSULA

Gujarat's Kathiawar Peninsula, fanning out west of Ahmedabad and bounded by the Gulf of Kutch to the north and the Gulf of Khambat to the south, was once made up of dozens of small princely states, lending the region the name Saurashtra, or the "Hundred Kingdoms." Mahatma Gandhi's father was an official in Porbandar, on the coast, and the grandfather of former Pakistani prime minister Benazir Bhutto was a minister in Junagadh, near the center of the region. The landscape is dry and flat, but dotted with hills, many of which hold temples on their summits.

Krishna, the incarnation of Vishnu whose story is told in the epic *Mahabharata*, is believed to have lived his last years in the legendary kingdom of Dwarka, at the peninsula's northwest tip. Somnath, site of one of India's most famous Shiva temples, is also on the Saurashtra coast, and just off it is Diu, an island settled by the Portuguese in

the 16th century. Though cities such as Rajkot and Surat are booming industrial centers, Saurashtra is entirely rustic. Men and women
both wear traditional costumes: an all-white ensemble of turban, jodh-
purs, and a pleated shirt for men, backless embroidered blouses, called
cholis, for women. The land supports limited agriculture, which has
inadvertently led to the preservation of two excellent wildlife preserves. Good hotels, including Heritage Hotels, are gradually being established here. The easiest way to get around is by hired car and driver;
trains are slow, and air connections are few.

Gir National Park and Wildlife Sanctuary

❹ *60 km (37 mi) southeast of Junagadh via Visavadar, 400 km (240 mi)
southwest of Ahmedabad*

The Gir National Park and Wildlife Sanctuary (informally known as
Sasan Gir for its entrance town) is a remarkable success story. Established in 1965 to protect a dwindling population of lions, it's now preparing to export prides to other areas. The sanctuary and the national park
it surrounds encompass about 1,400 square km (540 square mi) of hill
country covered in teak forest southeast of Junagadh, an important religious center since at least the time of Ashoka in the 3rd century BC.
About 300 lions live here, along with leopards, spotted deer, *sambhal*
(another deer), king cobras, langur monkeys, and hundreds of peacocks
and other birds. A project to stock the reservoir with *makara,* the Indian crocodile, is also underway.

The male lions are smaller and have sparser manes than their African
relations, and they're used to the presence of humans. A cattle-herd-
ing people known as the Maldhari lives inside the sanctuary. In dry
weather the lions are more easily encountered, as they tend to take the
Jeep roads to water points in the park. The park is most beautiful, however, from October to March, when the forest is green and teeming with
life. The Kamaleshwar Reservoir is a fine place for a picnic under the
watchful eyes of crocodiles in the water and eagles in the air. To tour
the park, hire a Jeep from your hotel or the orientation center and a
tracker from the orientation center. ✉ *Gir Wildlife Sanctuary and National Park, Sasan Gir district, Junagadh 362135, ☎ 2877/85540.* ☞
*Rs. 15 for 3 days, plus small additional charges for vehicles and cam-
eras. Tracker Rs. 10 for three hours, Rs. 4 for each additional hour;
tipping encouraged.* ☼ *Oct. 15 (or Nov. 15, depending on rainfall)–
June 15, sunrise–sunset.*

Lodging

$$$ 🛏 **Gir Lodge.** Run by the Taj Group, this modern cement structure at
★ the sanctuary's edge has comfortable, air-conditioned rooms. The staff
is knowledgeable and can take you on dawn or dusk game-viewing
rides—these are expensive, but the hotel's open Jeeps are quieter and
less likely to disturb the animals than the other available vehicles. The
staff can also book cars for excursions *from* Sasan Gir. A fixed menu
of simple Indian buffet meals is included in the room rate. A swim-
ming pool is in the works. ✉ *Sasan Gir district, Junagadh 362135.* ☎
2877/85521; 2877/85501 through 2877/85504, ☏ *2877/85528. 27
rooms, 2 suites. Dining room, laundry service, travel services. AE, DC,
MC, V.*

$ 🛏 **Maneland Jungle Lodge.** This small lodge is a slight distance from
the road, giving an impression of remoteness. The stone rooms are sim-
ple, well appointed, and quite inexpensive. Jeeps are available for trips
to the park. ✉ *Sasan Gir district, Junagadh 36215,* ☎ *2877/85555;*

or reserve through North West Safaris ☎ *79/661–0609,* 🖷 *79/656–0962. 10 rooms. Dining room. No credit cards.*

$ 🏠 **Sinh Sadan Guest House.** This forest-department guest house has large rooms, some with air-conditioning, surrounding a British-style flower garden next to the park orientation center. Breakfast and thali lunch and dinner are served for an additional charge. Reserve in advance, as the guest house can fill up with officials. ✉ *Deputy Central Forest Service Superintendent, Wildlife Division, Sasan Gir district, Junagadh 362135,* ☎ *2877/85540. 20 rooms plus a dormitory. Restaurant, laundry service. No credit cards.*

Somnath

⑤ *45 km (25 mi) southwest of Sasan Gir*

The Gujarati coastline has attracted traders and invaders for centuries. The **Shiva temple** at Somnath, which is believed to hold a naturally occurring Shiva linga, was a landmark to mariners from time immemorial until it was destroyed in the 11th century by Mahmud of Ghazni, an iconoclastic invader from Afghanistan. Since then the temple has been rebuilt several times, most recently in 1950 under the patronage of Sadar Patel, a Gujarati minister in Jawaharlal Nehru's government.

The modern structure is not architecturally spectacular, but its beach setting is. Devotees stream in—through metal detectors, due to ongoing Muslim anger at the reconstruction—and pay homage to one of the country's most sacred Shiva shrines. At dawn, noon, and sunset, kettle drums are beaten and conch shells blown while a large oil lamp is circled around the icon. This ceremony, known as *arati*, is meant to summon the god's presence in the temple. A small museum holds remnants of the temple's earlier incarnations. ☉ *Thurs.–Tues., 9–noon and 3–6.* 🎟 *50 paise. Closed 2nd and 4th Sat. of each month.*

Diu

⑥ *90 km (48 mi) southeast of Somnath*

Diu, a narrow island measuring 11 by 3 km (7 by 2 mi), is an early Portuguese enclave that was taken over by the Indian government in 1961 and is now administered as a federal Union Territory, separate from Gujarat. The Portuguese first sought the island—then held by the Ottoman empire—in 1520 but didn't gain possession until a representative of the Moghul emperor Humayun granted it to them in 1535. Today it's popular with budget travelers as well as Gujaratis taking advantage of its free-flowing liquor laws. Once you cross the short causeway that separates Diu from the mainland, you'll feel as though you've entered a sleepy Mediterranean market town. The streets are lined with two- and three-story buildings bearing the names of similar towns in Portuguese Africa. Note that although there are many small beer halls, the island's restaurant fare is disappointing.

An enormous **fort,** which is open daily 7–6, dominates the island's seaward end. When you walk along its ramparts you'll understand just how tenuous the colonists felt their hold on India was. Toppled gravestones alongside the fort's chapel date from as early as 1608. The churches of St. Paul, St. Thomas, and St. Francis of Assisi, all with whitewashed, baroque facades, hold faded paintings from the Portuguese era. St. Thomas's, at the market square's north end, is now a **museum** with some interesting artifacts and a small café.

Lodging

$$ **★** 🏨 **Hotel Kohinoor.** Designed to resemble a Portuguese villa, this plush hotel has the best (and technically the only) disco in the Gujarat region. Spacious rooms, accented by Italian marble floors, look out onto the trim flower garden with fountains or the large pool and open-air hot tub. The resort is close to the city center and overlooks the Arabian Sea. Try a Manchow soup, a spicy thick vegetable noodle soup, and the Hyderabadi *biryani* at the restaurant. ✉ *Fofrara-Fudam, 362 520,* ☎ *2875/52209; 2875/53575 through 2875/53577,* 𝔽𝔸𝕏 *2875/ 52613. 50 rooms. Restaurant, bar, pool, health club, dance club, recreation room, laundry service. No credit cards.*

$$ **★** 🏨 **Magico do Mar Beach Holiday Resort.** The town of Diu has a variety of fairly new hotels and, for budget travelers, older Portuguese-style lodgings. None are as attractive as this complex of rooms and cottages just across the border in Gujarat, within striking distance of the town of Diu. The plain reception room was constructed in 1937 by the Maharaja of Junagadh. Rooms are rather ordinary, though some are air-conditioned. The cottages, however, are luxurious versions of typical, Gujarati two-room village homes, complete with large wooden swings on the front porches. The resort looks out over the wide, clean, and private Ahmedpur Mandavi beach where meals—included in the room rate—are served under a thatch canopy. ✉ *Diu Checkpost, Ahmedpur Mandvi, Una district, Junagadh 362510,* ☎ *2875/52567,* 𝔽𝔸𝕏 *2875/ 52568. 32 rooms, 15 cottages. Restaurant, laundry service, airport shuttle. No credit cards.*

$$ 🏨 **Radhika Beach Resort.** Right on Diu's most popular beach, Radhika's two-story white villas with red shingle roofs encircle a courtyard and pool area. The rooms are attractive, with light floral Indian bedspreads and matching curtains; white-marble tiles; and large, albeit old, bathrooms. Private cottages are available for honeymooners and others seeking seclusion and romance. ✉ *Nagoa Beach 362520,* ☎ *2875/52553 through 2875/52555,* 𝔽𝔸𝕏 *2875/52552,* 𝕎𝔼𝔹 *www.radhikaresort.com. 30 rooms and 4 cottages. Restaurant, bar, pool, health club, travel services. No credit cards.*

$ 🏨 **Hotel Samrat.** A few blocks from the tourist office and town square, this is the best and most hospitable budget hotel in town. The rooms, some with balconies, offer beautiful views of the city and are clean and comfortable. *Near vegetable market, 362520,* ☎ *2875/52354, 54554, or 52514,* 𝔽𝔸𝕏 *2875/52754. 18 rooms. Restaurant, bar, laundry service. No credit cards.*

Palitana

❼ *150 km (90 mi) northeast of Diu, 277 km (166 mi) southwest of Ahmedabad.*

Hilltop pilgrimage sites are a common feature in Saurashtra, but none is quite so expansive as **Shatrunjaya,** a city of some 900 temples built by followers of the Jain religion near modern-day Palitana. A prosperous but small merchant community, the Jains have maintained and refurbished the temples over the centuries; so while many of the temples here date from the 1600s, the attraction is not that of an ancient ruin but that of a living faith. High above the surrounding flood plain, the place has an eerie calm about it. The temples are only open to the public during the day; at night, the gates are closed, and the temples' only inhabitants are their figures: white marble sculptures that each represent a Jina, one of the extremely few human souls in myth and history who, the Jains believe, have been able to liberate themselves from the cycle of rebirth. This hill marks the spot where, according to myth, such a Jina was liberated; he's worshiped in Shatrunjaya's largest temple as Adinath, the original master.

You reach the temples by climbing the mountain—a mile-long stretch of 4,000 steps rising some 2,000 ft to the summit. Accompanying you will be lay pilgrims, white-garbed monks and *sadhvis* (female sadhus). The central tenet of Jain philosophy is nonviolence, or *ahimsa*, and the Jains' practice thereof is believed to have influenced Mahatma Gandhi. Some of the ascetics here wear gauze filters over their mouths so as not to harm micro-organisms with their breathing; and before they prostrate themselves at the shrines, they take care to sweep the ground of any tiny creatures beneath them. There is a small fee for both still and video cameras within the temple complex, and photography is not allowed inside the individual temples.

Lodging

$ 🏨 **Nilambag Palace.** The former palace of Bhavnagar's local raja is now a Heritage Hotel and the most upscale lodging in the area. It makes the most comfortable base for excursions to Palitana (50 km/31 mi southwest of here) and Velavadar. ✉ *Bhavnagar 364002,* ☎ *278/429323, 278/424241, or 278/432295,* FAX *278/428072. 25 rooms, 2 suites. Restaurant, pool, laundry service, travel services. AE, D, MC, V.*

$ 🏨 **Sumeru.** Run by the Tourism Corporation of Gujarat, this hotel is the best place to stay in Palitana itself and its dining room is the only restaurant in town. Still, the rooms are no more than basic (though some are air-conditioned), and the dining room keeps an erratic schedule. ✉ *Station Rd., Palitana,* ☎ *2848/2327; or reserve through the Tourism Corporation of Gujarat, Ltd., H. K. House, Ashram Rd.,* ☎ *79/449683 or 79/449172,* FAX *79/656–8183. 13 rooms plus a dormitory. Restaurant. No credit cards.*

Velavadar Wildlife Sanctuary

⑧ *65 km (40 mi) north of Bhavnagar, 85 km (53 mi) north of Palitana, 140 km (84 mi) south of Ahmedabad*

Once a hunting reserve, this small grassland sanctuary is home to large herds of the Indian blackbuck. Often depicted in miniature paintings, this elegant and fast-running antelope has been hunted almost to extinction elsewhere, but here its only predator is the Indian wolf, also an endangered species. The park is only 36 km (22 mi) square, but it's home to about a thousand blackbuck, with more coming in from surrounding areas when foraging is plentiful. Chances of seeing both are best in October–November and February–March, the blackbuck's mating and foaling seasons, respectively. ✉ *10 km (6 mi) off main Bhavnagar-Ahmedabad hwy.; turnoff is between the towns of Vallabhipur and Barvala.* 🎟 *Rs. 15 for foreigners, camera Rs. 15, car Rs. 5.*

Lothal

⑨ *105 km (63 mi) north of Bhavnagar, 70 km (42 mi) southwest of Ahmedabad*

Gujarat's most accessible Indus Valley Civilization site is the prehistoric port center at Lothal. Now some 10 km (6 mi) inland from the Gulf of Khambat, the excavated area reveals a large dry dock as well as kilns and other work areas for a once-renowned manufacturing center. Archaeologists have also discovered signs of communication in sites on the Persian Gulf. The adjacent **Archeological Museum,** however, displays a good selection of seals, tools, and artifacts from the site. ▨ *Free.* ◷ *Sat.–Thurs. 9–5.*

Lodging

$ ☒ **Palace Utelia.** This family-run Heritage Hotel is on the edge of a
★ small, picturesque village very close to Lothal and within day-tripping
distance of the Velavadar Wildlife Sanctuary and Nalsarovar Bird
Sanctuary. Besides the excursions possible from here, the village itself
is an attraction, and the family's cordial relations with the villagers make
it possible to receive an intimate welcome. The rooms, some with
small balconies and some air-conditioned, are furnished with attrac-
tive old bedsteads, tables, and wardrobes. Meals, which include both
local and Rajasthani specialties, are served buffet-style. ✉ *Village
Utelia, Via Lothal Burkhi,, Ahmedabad district, 382230,* ☎ *2714/62222;
or reserve through Utelia House, 9 Gandhi Bagh, Ahmedabad, 380006,*
☎ *79/656–9937,* ⨳ *79/644–5770. 20 rooms. Restaurant. No credit
cards.*

Vadodara

⑩ *112 km (68 mi) south of Ahmedabad, 419 km (260 mi) north of Bom-
bay*

Vadodara—commonly called Baroda—was until recently a laid-back
garden city and college town on the banks of the Vishwamitri River.
It's now an urban hub with a population of just over a million peo-
ple. The city dates back to the days of legend, and before Independence
it was the capital of one of the largest and (with Mysore) best-admin-
istered princely states of the British period. Its ruler, called a Gaekwad,
helped his people prosper and accumulated for himself a great many
artistic treasures from all over India and the world. The city retains a
pleasant and civic atmosphere, though much of its greenery has been
overwhelmed by urban sprawl.

The **College of Fine Arts** at Maharaja Sayajirao University is known as
the best in India, and its graduates include India's best-known con-
temporary painter, M. F. Husain. Many graduates stay in town, exhibiting
their work at the **Nazar Arts Gallery** (☎ 265/322945). The university's
Archaeology Faculty has a small display area with an excellent rendi-
tion of life and crafts in the ancient Indus Valley Civilization. The large
park known as Sayaji Bagh, on University Road, contains the **Vado-
dara Museum and Art Gallery,** open daily 9:30–4:45, which has an ex-
cellent collection of Hindu and Jain sculpture as well as miniature
paintings.

The former royal collection is housed in the **Maharaja Fateh Singh Mu-
seum** on the run-down grounds of the maharaja's palace. It includes
a fine collection of works by the important 19th-century painter Raja
Ravi Verma, as well as pictures attributed to Titian, Poussin, and
Raphael. ✉ *Nehru Rd.,* ☎ *265/56372.* ◷ *Tues.–Sun. 9–noon and 3–
6.* ▨ *Rs. 2.*

Better-maintained examples of the maharaja's architectural taste are
the **Naya Mandir,** or Law Courts, and the **Kothi Building,** or Secretariat,
both in the center of town. Both structures display the mixture of Moghul
and Gothic elements common to the public works of British India. The
Kirti Mandir, a memorial to the Gaekwad family, is decorated with mu-
rals painted by Nandalal Bose, a leader in the Bengal school of paint-
ing that launched contemporary art in India early in the 20th century.

The **Makarpura Palace,** designed in an Indo-Italianate style, now houses a training school for the Indian Air Force; take an auto-rickshaw through the campus to get a glimpse of the grounds.

If you stay in Vadodara, you can make side trips to some truly out-of-the-way medieval sights. **Champaner,** 47 km (28 mi) northwest of Vadodara in the Girnar Hills, was an old Rajput and later Muslim capital; it's now an intriguing ghost town full of wonderful architecture. Preservation groups are working to spruce it up, but the place is not yet on many travelers' itineraries. Most of the buildings date from the 15th century and blend Muslim and Jain influences; a few Hindu temples date from as early as the 11th century. On the way back to Vadodara you can stop at **Pawagadh Fort,** just a few km outside Champaner, for an impressive view. The fort is mostly in ruins, but the Hindu and Jain temples here remain active pilgrimage centers. Overshooting Vadodara brings you to **Dabhoi Fort** (30 km, or 18 mi, southeast of town), built by the Raja of Patan in the 13th century. The fort's four ornate gates are early masterpieces of the Solank Rajput style. Nearby, the town's **Kali temple** also has beautiful carvings. Dabhoi is also home to the world's largest collection of steam locomotives. To make travel arrangements or change money in Vadodara, ask your hotel or contact **Narmada Travels** (✉ 19–21 Panorama, 2nd floor, R. C. Dutt Rd., ☎ 265/333941).

Lodging

$$$$ ⊞ **Welcomgroup Vadodara.** This luxury hotel is an excellent place to relax after the rigors of traveling. The restaurant Ruchika serves good North Indian Mughlai food; the Cascade features Western and Chinese dishes. There's also a 24-hour coffee shop. ✉ *R. C. Dutt Rd., Vadodara 390005,* ☎ *265/330033,* FAX *265/330050. 102 rooms. 3 restaurants, coffee shop, pool, massage, meeting room. AE, DC, MC, V.*

$ ⊞ **Aditi.** Well run and centrally air-conditioned, the Aditi is within walking distance of the university and a short auto-rickshaw ride from the train station and most of Vadodara's sights. The restaurant serves a range of North Indian and Gujarati dishes. ✉ *Opposite Sadar Patel Statue, Sayajigunj, Vadodara 390005,* ☎ *265/361188,* FAX *265/362257 through 265/362259. 64 rooms. Restaurant. AE, DC, MC, V.*

GUJARAT A TO Z

To research prices, get advice from other travelers, and book travel arrangements, visit www.fodors.com.

AIR TRAVEL

Indian Airlines flies to Ahmedabad from Bombay, Delhi, Bangalore, and Madras. You can also fly to Vadodara from Bombay or Delhi. Four flights a week connect Bombay with Bhavnagar, and regular flights leave Bombay for Diu and Keshod (the nearest airport to Sasan Gir). Jet Airways connects Ahmedabad with Delhi and Bombay, and Vadodara with Bombay. Contact your travel agent or the Government of India Tourist Office for the latest on other domestic carriers.

CARRIERS
➤ CONTACTS: **Indian Airlines** (☎ 79/550–3061 through 79/550–3063 in Ahmedabad or 278/426503 on Kathiawar Peninsula, WEB indian-airlines.nic.in). **Jet Airways** (✉ First floor, Ratnanabh Complex, Opposite Gujarat Vidyapith Income Tax, Ashram Rd., Ahmedabad, ☎ 79/754–3304 through 79/754–3310, 79/286–8308, 79/286–6540, or 286–6240).

AIRPORTS

Ahmedabad Airport is 15 km (9 mi) from the city center. You'll find plenty of taxis plus a booth selling pre-paid fixed-price rides. The trip should cost roughly Rs. 150–Rs. 200.

➤ AIRPORT INFORMATION: **Ahmedabad Airport** (☎ 79/286–6240 or 79/286–6540).

CARS AND DRIVERS

With a car and driver, you can move around without having to spar over fares. Rates for cars without air-conditioning start at Rs. 4–8 per km, usually with a minimum of 250 km per day. Additional charges apply to overnight stays and the driver's return trip. Arrange for a car and driver through a travel agency or tourist office—your hotel can do it for you, but you'll pay more.

EMERGENCIES

➤ HOSPITALS: **Civil Hospital** (✉ Shahibaug, ☎ 79/212–1379 or 79/212–3712). **Rajasthan Hospital** (☎ 79/286–6311 or 79/286–6313). **Sushrusha Hospital** (✉ Navrangpura, Ahmedabad, ☎ 79/640–3784). **V.S. Hospital** (✉ Ellis Bridge, Ahmedabad, ☎ 79/657–7621 through 79/657–7624).

➤ 24-HR MEDICAL SERVICES: **Amrit Medico** (✉ Navrangpura, Ahmedabad, ☎ 79/748–9613). **Chetan Medical Store (pharmacy;** ✉ Ellis Bridge, Ahmedabad, ☎ 79/657–8092). **Sarvoday Medical Store (pharmacy;** ✉ Navrangpura, Ahmedabad).

MONEY

ATMS

Ahmedabad is probably the best place to find an ATM. C. G. Road is the city's major financial center, home to Citibank, HSBC, and other banks. The State Bank of India at Lal Darwaja (the bus stand) and the Bank of Baroda on Relief Road on the eastern bank of the Sabramati River also have ATMs.

CREDIT CARDS

Credit cards are accepted at major chain stores and hotels, but rarely at restaurants and never at smaller establishments or markets that cater to locals.

CURRENCY EXCHANGE

Nearly all hotels exchange foreign currency for their guests. You might get better rates at state banks, but the hassle of waiting in line may defeat the purpose. Try the Bank of Baroda. Green Channel Travel Services can also change currency.

➤ EXCHANGE SERVICES: **Bank of Baroda** (✉ Ashram Rd., Ahmedabad, ☎ 79/656–1835). **Green Channel Travel Services** (✉ 576 Sun Complex, Navrangpura, Ahmedabad, ☎ 79/656–8457).

TAXIS AND AUTO-RICKSHAWS

A savvy auto-rickshaw driver can reach your destination faster than a cabbie or chauffeur. At this writing, fares in Ahmedabad were about Rs. 1 per km, with a starting charge of about Rs. 4; but rates change as fuel prices increase, and fares are theoretically calculated by matching the meter amount to the adjusted rate on the driver's tariff card. If the driver refuses to show you the card, get another rickshaw or agree on a fare in advance (ask a hotel staffer or a passerby what the fare should be). You can catch a taxi at the Ahmedabad airport or call one through your hotel. They're not plentiful, however, so you may have to hire a car and driver for the day.

TOURS

Twice daily, at 9 AM and 1:30 PM, the Ahmedabad Municipal Transport Service offers tours of the city in English. The tour departs from the local bus stand at Lal Darwaja and lasts four hours.

➤ CONTACTS:: **Ahmedabad Municipal Transport Service (AMTS;** ✉ 0 Number Bus Platform, Opposite State Bank of India, Lal Darwaja, Ahmedabad, ☎ 79/550–7739, 🖷 Rs. 75).

TRAIN TRAVEL

Ahmedabad and Vadodara are connected to Bombay, Delhi, and Rajasthan by good, fast trains, including the *Rajdhani Express*. The air-conditioned *Shatabdi Express* connects Ahmedabad with Vadodara in 1½ hours every day except Friday, and Vadodara with Bombay's Central Station in 5½ hours.

Because Gujarat was ruled separately from British India (by various local princes), its rail network has yet to be fully integrated into the Indian grid—many lines are on slow, meter-gauge tracks. Tickets are more easily obtained in Ahmedabad than in other Gujarati towns, as there's a separate line for tourists at the Ahmedabad Junction reservation counter. A comfortable but expensive way to see Ahmedabad, Sasan Gir, Diu, and Palitana is the *Royal Orient* luxury train. It makes a seven-night round trip from Delhi, stopping for sightseeing in both Rajasthan and Gujarat. Rates in season are U.S.$200 per person per night for a double-occupancy berth, $175 for triple occupancy.

Two express trains run daily between Bhavnagar and Ahmedabad, and there is slower service on the meter-gauge line between Palitana and Ahmedabad. The station nearest Diu is at Veraval, near Somnath, on the Gujarati mainland 90 km (50 mi) to the northwest. Overnight trains connect Ahmedabad with Veraval and Junagadh, and taxis outside the Junagadh station can take you the final 60 km (37 mi) to Sasan Gir for about Rs. 500 if you haven't arranged to be picked up by your hotel.

➤ TRAIN INFORMATION: **Royal Orient Train** (Tourism Corporation of Gujarat, Ltd.; ✉ Ashram Rd., Ahmedabada, ☎ 131/132 for train information, 131/135 for ticket information, 🌐 www.gujarattourism.com).

TRAVEL AGENTS

Travel agents can help with general arrangements and with guided tours and car-and-driver hire.

➤ CONTACTS: **Alka Travel Service** (✉ Ashish Complex, C. G. Rd., near Swastik Cross Rd., Ahmedabad, ☎ 79/642–1197). **Green Channel Travel Services** (✉ 576 Sun Complex, Navrangpura, Ahmedabad, ☎ 79/656–8457). **Travel Corporation of India** (✉ Ashram Rd., behind Handloom House, Ahmedabada, ☎ 79/658–7601 through 79/658–7603).

VISITOR INFORMATION

Based in Ahmedabad, the Tourism Corporation of Gujarat provides information, organizes tours, and arranges cars and drivers.

➤ TOURIST OFFICES: **Tourism Corporation of Gujarat, Ltd.** (✉ H. K. House, Ashram Rd., Ahmedabad, ☎ 79/658–9683, 79/658–9172, or 79/658–7217, 🌐 www.gujarattourism.com; www.infoindia.com/tcgl; www.allindia.com/gujtourism). **Union Territory's Office of Tourism, Information, and Publicity** (✉ Marine House, Bunder Rd., near market square, Diu, ☎ 28758/52653, www.diuindia.com; www.gujuland.com; www.daman-diu.org).

7 BOMBAY AND MAHARASHTRA

Urbane, stylish Bombay, which curves dramatically around the Arabian Sea, simmers with international commerce, hip youth culture, and a glamourous film industry. Yet the city remains exuberantly Indian, its streets packed with traffic of every kind: cows, fancy cars, and motor scooters. While street vendors sell sugar cane juice and fresh coconuts, wealthy Indians and foreigners luxuriate in sleek hotels and visit art galleries and nightclubs. Nearby, the stunning 2,000-year-old cave temples of Ajanta and Ellora and the lovely hill station of Pune offer welcome retreats from Bombay's bustle.

By Julie Tomasz
and Vaihayasi
Pande Daniel

RAZZLE-DAZZLE INDIAN-STYLE—that's Bombay, the country's seaside financial capital and trendsetting East-West nexus. India's greatest port and the capital of Maharashtra, Bombay perches on the Arabian Sea, covering an island separated from the rest of India by a winding creek. A world unto itself, Bombay hits you with an intensity all its own. It's distinctly tropical, with pockets of palm trees and warm, salty breezes—and its culture is contemporary, vibrant, and often aggressive, reflecting both the affluence and poverty of more than 12 million people crowded onto this island. Behind all this, weathered Victorian mansions, some still privately owned, and grand public buildings, many beautifully lit at night, stand as lingering reminders of the British Raj.

Bombay's name was officially changed in 1995 to Mumbai, after Mumba Devi, the patron Hindu goddess of the island's original residents, the Koli fishermen. However, many residents continue to call their city Bombay. It's all rather confusing, but in many ways this is but another chapter in the city's labyrinthine history.

Bombay initially consisted of seven marshy islands—Colaba, Old Woman's Island, Bombay, Mazgaon, Worli, Mahim, and Parel—belonging to the Muslim kings of the Gujarat sultanate. The Muslims passed the parcel to the Portuguese (who occupied much of western India in the 16th and 17th centuries), who in turn passed it in 1661 to England's King Charles II as part of a dowry in his marriage to the Portuguese Princess Catherine de Braganza. The British established a fort and trading post that grew quickly in size and strength.

Soon enough, land reclamation joined the seven small islands into one, grafting a prototype for today's multifarious metropolis. The pride of the British in Bombay, and in their power over western India, is memorialized in the city's most celebrated landmark, near a statue of the young 17th-century Marathi leader Shivaji: the Gateway of India, built to welcome King George V to India in 1911.

The Bombay you see today is a city of mind-boggling contrasts: sometimes exciting, sometimes deeply disturbing. As your plane descends toward the runway, usually late at night, your first view of Bombay takes in vast stretches of slums, stacked and piled onto each other like cardboard boxes—only a fleeting glimpse of the staggering poverty that coexists with the dazzling wealth flashed in trendy boutiques and deluxe hotels. In the neighborhoods of Churchgate or Nariman Point, Bombay's slick hotel and business centers, a fleet of dark-suited executives may breeze by on its way to a meeting while a naked little girl with matted hair scavenges in the gutter beneath them. Bombay is a city, a journalist once pointed out, where the servant walking the pedigreed, handsomely groomed dog has no formal education but his charge has been to an expensive training school.

It is important to view Bombay in perspective. Like New York City, Bombay can be considered so different from the rest of India that it could be another country. Bombay operates according to its rules, and its pulse beats far more quickly than the rest of the country, which views Bombay as the city of opportunity. Bombay tantalizes millions with prospects of wealth and success. Every day, migrants arrive here—be they software engineers or laborers—to see if they too can make a life here. Apart from the city's original Maharasthrian population, every Bombayite, from the eunuch (*hijra*) to the taxi driver to the white collar worker, is living out his or her dream—in a hovel or a palace. It's true that more often than not, Bombay is a place to build a better life.

For the traveler, Bombay is both disturbingly eye-opening and incredibly exciting. Here in the heady sun and breeze of the Arabian Sea you can feast in fabulous restaurants, bargain in street bazaars, browse in exclusive boutiques, take a horse-drawn ride past stately old Victorian buildings, get lost in the stone carvings of the 7th-century Elephanta Caves, watch the sun rise over the Gateway of India, and stroll at sunset along Marine Drive's endless waterfront promenade.

Pleasures and Pastimes

Dining

Known for its chic restaurants and Western-style pubs, Bombay is a city where you can get not only great meals, but can taste a wide choice of cuisines—Continental, Chinese, Italian, Thai, Lebanese, and Mexican.

You'll find, among Indian food, a wide range of kebabs and tandoori food—meat, bread, and vegetables cooked inside a charcoal oven. This, often served with Mughlai (a variety of Muslim cuisine) and Punjabi cuisine, is by far the most popular food in town. Authentic South Indian vegetarian food—dosas, idlis, wadas, and simple, light thalis—are a city staple. Gujarati vegetarian thalis—a little oilier—are also popular. You may also encounter some Jain food—not only is the cuisine vegetarian, but it's cooked without root vegetables, such as onions and garlic, because destroying the root of a plant destroys life, and Jainism bans all destruction of life. Seafood from the Konkan coast—from Maharashtra south through Goa all the way to Mangalore, in Karnataka—is the current rage in Bombay. Many Bombay restaurants are pricey by Indian standards, but there are plenty of tasty bargains that will leave your taste buds and your wallet equally satisfied. Many hotels have good restaurants and all-night coffee shops that serve full meals.

CATEGORY	COST*
$$$$	over Rs. 1,000
$$$	Rs. 600–Rs. 1,000
$$	Rs. 300–Rs. 600
$	under Rs. 300

*for one main course at dinner (a main course includes dal, rice, and a vegetarian and non-veg dish)

Lodging

Hotels in Bombay, Pune, and Aurangabad (your base for visits to the Ajanta and Ellora caves) range from the skid-row to the palatial. In Bombay, unlike elsewhere in India, even mid-range hotels can cost a pretty rupee. The Taj and Oberoi chains run several massive lodgings, most of them deluxe; these cater to leisure and business travelers, and movie stars with money to burn. If you reserve with a hotel directly, rather than through a travel agent, ask for a discount.

Bombay's cheaper hotels are often decent. You'll get good value for the money. During the monsoon season, from mid-June through late September, these hotels are overrun by large groups of vacationers from various Arab nations, during which time noise levels can be very high, and solo women travelers should probably stay elsewhere.

Unless otherwise indicated, hotels have room service, doctors on call, and currency exchange, and rooms have cable TVs and private bathrooms. Many luxury hotels also have exclusive floors with special privileges or facilities for the business traveler.

CATEGORY	COST*
$$$$	over Rs. 8,000
$$$	Rs. 5,000–Rs. 8,00
$$	Rs. 2,300–Rs. 5,000
$	under Rs. 2,300

for a standard double room in high season, excluding 20% sales tax

EXPLORING BOMBAY

There's plenty to see in Bombay, but not generally in the form of stationary monuments like those in London, Paris, or even Delhi. The art of experiencing Bombay lies in eating, shopping, and wandering through strikingly different neighborhoods and markets. The best way to see Bombay is to immerse yourself in the city's pulsing life and soak up the aspects that blend and clash to make the city utterly unique. Bombay is essentially a 30-mi-long open-air bazaar.

Churchgate and Nariman Point are the business and hotel centers. Major bank and airline headquarters are clustered in skyscrapers on Nariman Point. The district referred to as Fort—which includes Bombay's hub, Flora Fountain, in a square now called Hutatma Chowk—is the city's commercial heart, its narrow, bustling streets lined with small shops and office buildings, as well as a number of colleges and other educational facilities. Farther north, Kemps Corner is a trendy area with expensive boutiques, exclusive restaurants, and high-priced homes. Another upscale residential neighborhood, Malabar Hill, is older—leafy, breezy, and lovely, with fine, old stone mansions housing wealthy industrialists and government ministers.

Shopping and people-watching are most colorfully combined in Bombay's chaotic bazaar areas, such as Chor Bazaar, Zaveri (Jewelry) Bazaar, and Mahatma Jyotiba Phule (Crawford) Market. More recently, Bombay's suburbs have seen explosive business and residential development, as more and more people move out of Bombay center to escape its soaring real-estate prices and simple lack of space. Many of the city's newest and trendiest shops and restaurants are out here. A number of travelers opt to stay in Juhu Beach, a popular coastal suburb between Bombay and the airports (about 20 km/12 mi north of the city center). Alas, Juhu's beaches are polluted and unsafe for swimming, and the general look of the place is scruffy and honky-tonk, but staying out here is a nice way to observe everyday Indian life outside the shadow of Bombay's skyline. Sunday nights bring families down to the beach for an old-fashioned carnival, complete with small, hand-powered Ferris wheels, and lantern-lit snack stalls hawking sugar cane.

Great Itineraries

India's most cosmopolitan city gives way to Maharashtra's rugged interior, which hides the spectacular Ajanta and Ellora caves, 370 km (229 mi) northeast of Bombay, as well as the lovely hill station of Pune to the southeast. Maharashtra's landscape fuses stark, semi-arid mountains and rock formations with lush, green countryside and virgin beaches. To see this state well, you should really spend the better part of a week here.

IF YOU HAVE 2 DAYS

On your first day, wander around Bombay's **Fort** district, home to the city's museums and such trappings of the British Raj as the stone Gateway of India. Spend the next morning at the **Elephanta Caves,** an hour's ferry ride away: although not as spectacular as those at Ajanta and Ellora, these 7th-century cave temples are much more accessible for those with little time in the region. That afternoon, take a taxi to **Malabar Hill** and spend some time exploring Kamala Nehru Park, the Jain Temple, Banganga, Babulnath Temple, and Gandhi's former home, Mani Bhavan.

IF YOU HAVE 4 DAYS

Follow the two-day itinerary. On your third day, visit the **Haji Ali Shrine,** a mosque set on a rocky jetty in the Arabian Sea; then drive outside the city center to the South Indian enclave of **Matunga,** where (every day but Monday) an array of temples, bazaars, and casual restaurants will more than eat up the lunch hour. Devote this afternoon to a walk around the fishing dock and handicraft stalls in **Colaba.** On your fourth day, go shopping—hit the bazaars, craft emporiums, shops, and boutiques in earnest—and/or take a tour of Bombay's old **synagogues.**

IF YOU HAVE 7 DAYS

Follow the four-day itinerary, then hire a car or join a bus tour down the coast to the **Maharashtra beaches.** These are remote and beautiful, as they're not very developed. Spend two nights at one of the area's comfortable resorts before returning to Bombay. Another option would be to go to **Pune** for a few days, or head to the **Ajanta and Ellora caves.**

When to Tour Bombay

Maharashtra is best explored between November and February, when the weather is warm but not unbearable and the monsoons are absent. Ajanta and Ellora explode with life during and after the monsoon season, if the rains have been good; at Ajanta, a river springs into being at the bottom of the gorge into which the caves are cut. If the rains haven't been good, it can be quite hot.

Fort District and Environs

The most manageable, and probably the most colorful, walks in Bombay center on the Fort district. If Bombay is the first stop on your first trip to India, remember that sightseeing here is nothing like touring, say, Europe—the streets are packed, some lack sidewalks, traffic takes many forms, crosswalks are a rarity, and people may stare or call out to you with sales pitches as you pass. Stopping to take a picture can make you feel terribly conspicuous. You'll get used to it soon enough, however, and will quickly learn to revel in the whole *masala* whirlwind.

A Good Walk

Numbers in the text correspond to numbers in the margin and on the Bombay, Ajanta Caves, Ellora Caves, and Maharashtra Beaches maps.

Start your walk by exploring the **Mahatma Jyotiba Phule Market** ①, commonly known as Crawford Market, and the surrounding lanes. Abdul Rehman Street will take you north into **Zaveri Bazaar** ②. At all bazaars, be sure to keep your eyes and hands on your wallet. From Crawford or Zaveri you can either head south to the main Fort district or, if you're up for more narrow-lane navigation, detour to **Chor Bazaar,** ③ a bustling old antiques market.

To find Chor Bazaar, walk or cab it (15 minutes by taxi) north from Crawford Market on Mohamed Ali Road, which joins Rahimtulla Road to bring you into South Bombay's main Muslim quarter. After passing the Beg Muhammed School, Mandavi Telephone Exchange, and Mandavi post office on the left, you'll hit Sardar Vallabhbhai Patel Road: turn left and you can enter Chor Bazaar on Mutton Street. When you're almost bazaared out, retrace the route back down to Crawford Market, either on foot or by taxi.

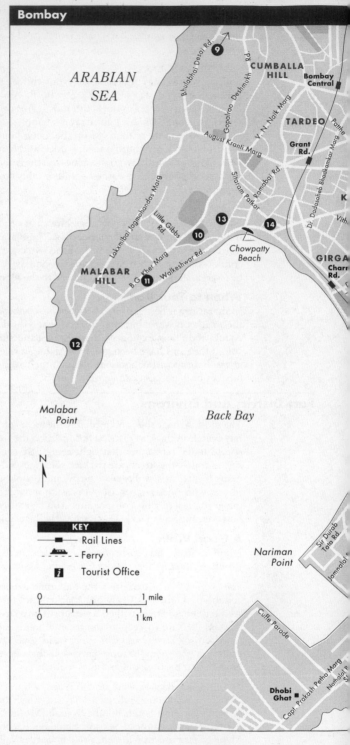

Bombay

Byculla
Sant Savta Marg
Reay Rd.
Boatyard Rd.

Dr. Anandrao Nair Rd.
Mohd. Shahid Marg
Maulana Azad Rd.
Dr. Motishah Rd.
Mascarenhas Marg

BOMBAY CENTRAL
MAZAGAON

Jehangir Boman Behram Marg
Mirza Galib Marg
Sir Jamshedji Jijibhoy Rd.
Marg
Dockyard Rd.

R. S. Nimbkar Rd.
Dimtimkar Rd.
Dockyard Rd.

KAMATIPURA
Maulana Azad Rd.
Wadi Bunder Rd.

Bapurao Marg
Maulana Shaukatali Rd.
Ramchandra Bhatt Marg

KHARA TALAO
Jail Rd.
Jar. R.P. (East)
Sandhurst Rd.

KHETWADI
Ibrahim Rahimtulla Rd.
Mohamed Ali Rd.
Keshavji Naik Rd.
Malet Rd.

Vithalbhai Patel Rd.
Cawasji Patel Tank Rd.
MANDVI
UMERKHADI

GAUM
arni
BHULESHWAR
A. Rehman St.
Yusuf Meherali Rd.
Manson Rd.

Dr. Babasaheb Jaykar
Bhuleshwar Rd.
KALBADEVI
Masjid

Dr. Babasaheb Jaykar Rd.
Jagannath Shankarsheth Rd.
Kalbadevi Rd.
S. Gandhi Marg
N. Naha St.

Maharshi Karve Rd.
K. Sharma St.
Lokmanya Tilak Rd.
PYDHUNI
P.D'Mello Rd.

Marine Lines
A. Poddar Marg
Pallan Rd.
Dr. D. Naoroji Rd.
Police

Netaji Subhash Rd.
Mahatma Gandhi Rd.
Municipal Corporation Building
Chhatrapati Shivaji Terminus

Marine Drive
General Post Office

Churchgate Station
Dr. D. Naoroji Rd.

Veer Nariman Rd.
Shahid Bhagat Singh Marg
Shoorji Vallabhdas Marg

High Court
FORT
Custom Basin

Jamshelji Tata Rd.
Madam Cama Rd.
Rajabhai Clocktower
Oval Maidan
Cross Island

Free Press Journal Rd.
Maharshi Karve Rd.
Cooperage Maidan
Bhaurao

Gen. Jaganathrao Bhonsale Marg
Nathalal Parekh Marg
K. Dubash Marg
C. Shivaji Maharaj Marg

al Pareth Marg
Shahid Bhagat Singh Marg (Colaba Causeway)
Merewether Rd.
Komstandom Marg

COLABA
A. Bunder Rd.
Taj Mahal Hotel

Sassoon Dock

TO ELEPHANTA CAVES

Middle Ground

To move south toward the center of the Fort district, follow A. Rehman Street until it becomes Dr. D. Naoroji Road: You are now in the heart of downtown, an area of broader streets and crowded sidewalks. On your right is the imposing, V-shaped, early Gothic–style Municipal Corporation Building, vintage 1893, with Indian motifs and a large dome; on your left is Bombay's chief train station, the huge **Chhatrapati Shivaji Terminus,** also called by its old name, Victoria Terminus. Push your way through the crowds of people and cars to cross the chaotic roundabout; rejoin Dr. D. Naoroji Road on the other side, and continue heading south. After about 15 minutes you'll arrive at the **Flora Fountain** ④, the true center of Bombay.

Take a right here onto Veer Nariman Road, pass the Central Telegraph office and its open-air book bazaars, and in a few minutes you'll hit K. B. Patil Marg. Turn left, keep heading south, and on your left you'll see the High Court, built in the early Gothic style in 1878. Farther south on the same street you'll see Bombay University's 260-ft Rajabhai Clocktower, also Victorian Gothic. Turn left onto Mahatma Gandhi Road (also known as M. G. Rd.) and you'll soon reach a cluster of three major museums. The **Jehangir Art Gallery** ⑤ will be on your left. Across the street from Jehangir, in the lane heading behind the music store Rhythm House, is the Keneseth Eliyahoo Synagogue. From Mahatma Gandhi Road, hang a left down K. Dubash Marg to the **Prince of Wales Museum** ⑥. The **National Gallery of Modern Art** ⑦ is across the street. From here, take C. Shivaji Maharaj Marg to the **Gateway of India** ⑧, where you can relax among locals at the water's edge.

Right across the square from the Gateway of India is the historic Taj Mahal hotel. Even if you can't afford to stay here, it's a treat just to walk around the lobby and shopping areas (they don't mind) and perhaps have an Indian meal at the Tanjore restaurant or Sea Lounge coffee shop.

TIMING

This walk takes a full day: the going is slow and the bazaars eat up time in a stealthy manner. You'll probably want to spend close to an hour at both the Prince of Wales Museum and the Jehangir Art Gallery. Note that Crawford Market is closed Sunday, the Prince of Wales Museum is closed Monday, and Chor Bazaar shuts down on Friday. Early morning tends to be less humid, so you may want to set off then.

Sights to See

Chhatrapati Shivaji Terminus. Built by the British in 1888 at an supposed cost of @300,000, this is one of Bombay's busiest train stations, overflowing at rush hour with enormous, surging, scurrying crowds. Formerly called Victoria Terminus, and bearing a hefty statue of Queen Victoria on its imposing dome, the haughty structure combines Indian and Victorian Gothic architecture for an Eastern version of London's St. Pancras station. ⊠ *D. Naoroji Rd.*

❸ **Chor Bazaar.** With a colorful name meaning "Thieves' Bazaar," this narrow thoroughfare is lined with stores crammed with both antiques and general bric-a-brac—clocks, old phonographs, brassware, glassware, and statues. Over the years the value of much of this stock has dwindled, but there's still a chance that you'll find some unusual, memorable piece. Haggle. In the same lane a number of shops are engaged in the profitable business of constructing new furniture that looks old; many will openly tell you as much. Some shops do stock genuine antique furniture from old Parsi homes. ⊠ *Mutton St., off Sardar Vallabhbhai Patel Rd.* ⊙ *Daily except Fri. 11–7.*

❹ **Flora Fountain.** Standing tall in the middle of a major five-way intersection, this fountain marks the heart of Bombay's Fort district. The ornately sculpted stone fountain was created as a memorial to one of Bombay's early governors, Sir Bartle Frere, who was responsible for urban planning in the 1860s. The square in which it stands is called Hutatma Chowk (Martyr's Square) in honor of those who died in the violence surrounding the establishment of Maharashtra in the 1960s (the Bombay Presidency was split into the states of Maharashtra and Gujarat). It's a hot spot for rallies, political and otherwise. ⊠ *M. G. Rd., at Veer Nariman Rd.*

★ ⑧ **Gateway of India.** Bombay's signature landmark, this elegant 26 m (85 ft) stone archway was hastily erected as a symbol of welcome to Queen Mary and King George V of England when they paid a visit to India in 1911. In the years following, artisans added decorative carvings and lovely *jharoka* work (window carvings), finishing in 1923. Less than 25 years later, the last British troops departed India through the same ceremonial arch. The monument serves as a launching point for boats going to Elephanta Island; this is also where the *Queen Elizabeth 2* and other luxury liners dock on their cruises. The majestic Taj Mahal hotel, built before the Gateway of India, in 1903, now stands just behind it. ⊠ *Peninsula at end of C. Shivaji Maharaj Marg.*

OFF THE BEATEN PATH	**COLABA** – Bombay's budget-tourist district is often packed with vacationing Arabs in the rainy season and Western backpackers in the winter. Cheap boarding houses, handicraft stalls, and eating places stand cheek-by-jowl on the tip of Bombay's peninsula.

One of Colaba's most interesting sights is its fishing dock, built back in 1875. Extraordinarily smelly, mucky, and noisy, **Sassoon Dock** must be seen at dawn, when most of Bombay's seafood catch is unloaded. Piles of pink prawns are sorted, and grisly-looking fish are topped and tailed. The odor is severe, but you won't see this kind of chaos and five-sensory color anywhere else in the world. Out toward the ocean, Bombay duck, a fish unique to this coastline, dries on rack after rack, in the sun.

Walk north toward Navy Nagar (the naval cantonment area) on Shahid Bhagat Singh Marg for about 10 minutes. Just beyond Colaba Post Office is the old **Afghan Memorial Church of St. John the Baptist.** Rather out of place in the heart of Colaba, this somewhat imposing structure honors British soldiers lost in the Afghan wars of the late 19th century. The plaques inside say things like, "In the memory of Captain Conville Warneford of the Bombay Political Dept and the Gurkha Rifles who was born 13th October 1871 and was treacherously murdered by an Arab at Amrija in the Aden hinterland. . . ."

From the church, retrace your steps on Shahid Bhagat Singh as far as the fork outside Colaba Post Office; take Wodehouse Road to Panday Road, then turn left and you'll see Capt. Prakash Petha Marg. Turn left again, walk for five minutes (past the Taj President hotel), and just beyond the Colaba Woods park on your right is a **Dhobi Ghat,** behind a facade of huts. (If you get lost, just ask a local for help.) Another fascinating open-air sight, the *ghat* consists of a square half-kilometer of cement stalls where *dhobis,* or washermen, pound their garments to what seems like pulp to get them threadbare-clean. Rows of racks flutter with drying laundry, and in little huts nearby the incorrigibly dirty stuff is boiled with caustic soda. ⊠ *Sassoon Dock: Shahid Bhagat Singh Marg, near Colaba Bus Station; Dhobi Ghat: Cuffe Parade, Colaba.*

⑤ **Jehangir Art Gallery.** Bombay's chief contemporary-art gallery hosts changing exhibits of well-known Indian artists. Some of the work is lovely, and all of it is interesting for its cultural perspective. There's plenty of art outside as well—the plaza in front of the building is full of artists selling their works and their talents for commission assignments. ✉ *M. G. Rd., Fort,* ☎ *22/284–3989.* 🎫 *Free.* ☉ *Daily 11–7.*

NEED A
BREAK? **Cafe Samovar** (✉ M. G. Rd., Fort, ☎ 22/284–8000), next to a bit of courtyard greenery in the Jehangir Art Gallery, is a popular, arty place for a quick snack or a glass of lime juice. It's open daily 11–7.

★ ❶ **Mahatma Jyotiba Phule Market.** Also known by its former name, Crawford Market, this building was designed in the 1860s by John Lockwood Kipling, father of Rudyard—who was born in this very neighborhood. Check out the stone relief depicting workers on the outside; the market's stone flooring supposedly came from Caithness. Come here early one morning for the most colorful walk through Bombay's fresh-produce emporium, and if it's late spring or early summer, treat yourself to a delicious Alphonso mango, a food fit for the gods. The meat section can be a bit hair-raising. Across the street from the market's main entrance, spread across a trio of lanes, is the popular bazaar area Lohar Chawl, where the selection ranges from plastic flowers to refrigerators. Farther up the middle lane, Sheikh Memon Street, is the chaotic **Mangaldas Market** (closed Sunday), a covered, wholesale cloth market with a tremendous variety of fabrics at hundreds of indoor stalls. ✉ *D. Naoroji Rd., at L. Tilak Rd.* ☉ *Mon.–Sat. 11:30–8.*

NEED A
BREAK? **Rajdhani** (✉ Sheikh Memon St., ☎ 22/342–6919) serves up hot Gujarati and Rajasthani *thalis* (combination platters; Rs. 125) from 11 to 3:30 in spartan but clean surroundings near Crawford Market. Eat sparingly so you don't live to regret the meal; the restaurant uses a lot of ghee, or clarified butter, in its preparations.

❼ **National Gallery of Modern Art.** This museum is housed in a circular building resembling New York's Guggenheim Museum. Modern Indian art is displayed in an uncrowded, easy manner on four floors. It's not as spectacular as the Prince of Wales Museum across the street, but it's worth a visit, especially if you're an art lover. ✉ *M. G. Rd.,* ☎ *22/285–2457, 22/204–4285, or 22/288–1790.* 🎫 *Rs. 5.* ☉ *Tues.–Sun. 11–6.*

❻ **Prince of Wales Museum.** Topped with Moorish domes, Bombay's finest Victorian building and principal museum was completed in 1911 and named for King George V, who laid the cornerstone in 1905. It's divided into three sections: art, archaeology, and natural history. The picture gallery contains scores of Mogul and Rajput miniature paintings, works by European and contemporary Indian artists, and copies of magnificent cave temple paintings from Ajanta. ✉ *M. G. Rd.,* ☎ *22/284–4519, 22/284–4484.* 🎫 *Rs. 5.* ☉ *Tues.–Sun. 10:15–6.*

❷ **Zaveri Bazaar.** Zaveri and Dagina bazaars, a little beyond Fort in Kalbadevi, are Bombay's crowded, century-old jewelry markets, where the shops are filled with fabulous gold and silver in every conceivable design. At the end of Zaveri Bazaar is the **Mumbadevi Temple,** a noisy, busy structure that houses the mouthless but powerful patron goddess for which Mumbai is named. In front of the temple is the *khara kuan,* or saltwater well, actually an age-old water station funded by the jewelry bazaar. Free water is doled out to the thirsty from giant copper drums. One of the lanes leading off Zaveri Bazaar is called Khao Galli (literally "Eat Lane"), as its endless food stalls feed most of the bazaar workers daily. ✉ *Sheikh Memon St.* ☉ *Mon.–Sat. 11–7.*

OFF THE
BEATEN PATH **SYNAGOGUES** – Jews were a prominent stream in Bombay's population until many of them migrated to Israel in the 1950s. Left behind is an assortment of synagogues, some in what seem like strange locales. None

is striking by itself, but a tour of four gives you a peek into one of India's oldest and rarest communities. Hire a car or hail a taxi for this two- to three-hour excursion.

The most attractive structure is the old Baghdadi synagogue at the southern edge of Fort: the ornate, sky-blue **Keneseth Eliyahoo Synagogue** (✉ Forbes St., Kala Ghoda, Fort), across from Jehangir Art Gallery, has some interesting stained glass windows and balconies. You can visit daily between 10 and 6:30, and visitors are welcome for Sabbath prayers between 6:30 and 7:30 on Fridays.

A few miles north (beyond Crawford Market via P. D'Mello Road, past Carnac Bunder and near the Masjid train station), in the heart of the wholesale district, is the hard-to-find **Shaare Rahamim** (Gate of Mercy; ✉ 254 Samuel St., Masjid). This sleepy, mildly dilapidated synagogue seems totally out of place in its surroundings, which bustle with trucks, handcarts, and workers unloading sacks, boxes, and crates into scruffy warehouses. Tiny and relatively plain, the building is set apart from its drab neighbors by its traditional blue and cream colors. The synagogue is still in use, and you're free to peek inside.

At Jacob Circle, a 20-minute taxi ride north of Shaare Rahamim (✉ Khare Rd., past Chinchpokli station, near Shirin Talkies) is **Tiphaereth Israel Synagogue,** home of the Bene Israel Jews—a still-thriving but tiny Maharashtrian Jewish community. Tiny and shiny, this synagogue is charming; unlike Shaare Rahamin, it seems well loved and maintained. Have a chat with the slightly woozy caretaker, if he's around to take you inside.

The same caretaker can guide you to the **Magen Hassidim Synagogue,** a few streets away (✉ Morland Rd./Maulana Azad Rd., near Fancy Market and Jula Maidan, Agripada). Another Bene Israel shrine, this one is in the strongly Muslim area of Madanpura. The congregation and caretakers at this prosperous, well-attended shrine can lend insight into the future of this community: Magen Hassidim is the face of India's modern Jews, the ones who generally don't plan to migrate to Israel and who are now part of the nation's mainstream. There is a vigor to the Magen Hassidim synagogue that seems absent at other synagogues.

Malabar Hill and Environs

Several of the attractions in this upscale residential area have stunning views of the city across Back Bay.

A Good Tour

After checking the tides, take a taxi to the **Haji Ali Shrine** ⑨, passing **Chowpatty Beach and Marine Drive** en route. At Haji Ali, have your taxi wait for you while you walk out on the jetty; then drive to **Kamala Nehru Park** ⑩, take some air, enjoy the views, and walk to the **Jain Temple** ⑪. From here you can either walk or take a taxi along Walkeshwar Road to the **Banganga** ⑫ area. Finally, have your taxi take you to **Babulnath Temple** ⑬ and Gandhi's former home, **Mani Bhavan** ⑭. If you're interested in South Indian culture and have some extra time, drive out to **Matunga.**

TIMING

This tour takes about two hours. The journey by taxi from Mani Bhavan to Matunga, a little way out of south Bombay, will take you half an hour—be sure to avoid rush hour. Spend half an hour seeing Matunga, or longer if you pop in for a dosa break (crispy lentil pancakes) at any of the restuarants we have suggested in Matunga.

Sights to See

⓭ **Babulnath Temple.** To get the flavor of a large, traditional Indian temple, a visit to the Babulnath Temple is a must. After climbing a few hundred steps to reach the temple, you'll be rewarded with a panoramic view of south Bombay. The first Babulnath Temple was apparently built by Raja Bhimdev in the 13th century and named after the *babul* trees that forested this area. The architecture of this imposing shrine, one of Bombay's most important, is not remarkable, but it's interesting to watch the melée of worshipers coming, going, and milling about. Outside are rows of flower sellers hawking a temple-visitation kit—coconut plus flowers plus rock sugar—and a cluster of vendors concocting sweetmeats in *karhais* (large woks) in the open air. Temple authorities are sometimes prickly about allowing foreigners into its innermost areas, but it's worth a try. ⊠ *Babulnath Rd.*

★ ⓬ **Banganga.** This undervisited temple complex in the Malabar Hill area is considered one of the city's holiest sites. It is also the oldest surviving structure in Bombay. The small, sometimes dilapidated temples are built around a holy pool of water and surrounded by the ever-encroaching houses of Bombay's newer residents. Cows and people mingle freely here, as do bathers who come to sample the "healing powers" of the water. ⊠ *Walkeshwar Rd.* ▨ *Free.*

★ **Chowpatty Beach and Marine Drive.** Chowpatty is not much of a beach in the resort sense, but this and the rest of Bombay's long, spectacular, perfectly curved Marine Drive capture at once the mammoth, cheeky, beautiful seaside beast that is Bombay. Chowpatty is a taste of the Bombay bazaar and *mela* (festival; hullabaloo) rolled into one. A hundred species of salesmen throng the beach in the evening, especially Sunday, selling everything from glow-in-the-dark yo-yos and animal-shaped balloons to rat poison. Men stand by with bathroom scales, offering complacent strollers a chance to check their heft. Hand-operated Ferris wheels and carousels are packed with children. A few stalls nearby distribute Bombay's own fast food—crunchy *bhelpuris* (puffed-rice snacks), *ragda pattices* (spicy potato cakes), and *paav bhaji* (fried vegetable mash eaten with bread). From the beach, walk east down Marine Drive toward Nariman Point and you'll bump into flotillas of evening exercisers, cooing couples wandering past the waves in a daze, and dogs and kids being walked by their respective nannies.

⑨ **Haji Ali Shrine.** Set far out on a thin, rocky jetty in the Arabian Sea, this striking white shrine was built in honor of the Muslim saint Haji Ali, who drowned here some 500 years ago on a pilgrimage to Mecca. When a coffin containing his mortal remains floated to rest on a rocky bed in the sea, devotees constructed the tomb and mosque to mark the spot. The shrine is reached by a long walkway just above the water, lined with destitute families and beggars ravaged by leprosy, some writhing, chanting, and (calling on the Muslim tradition of giving alms) perhaps beseeching you as you make your way down—a deeply discomfiting experience, but one that is unfortunately quintessentially Bombay. Inside, the shrine is full of colored-mirror mosaics and crowded with worshipers praying over the casket, which is covered with wilted flower garlands. Men and women must enter through separate doorways. ⊠ *Off Lala Lajpatrai Marg, near Mahalaxmi Race Course, Breach Candy. Approachable only at low tide.*

⑪ **Jain Temple.** This may be the most impressive temple in Bombay. This Jain Temple belongs to the prosperous, strictly vegetarian Jain community—the largely Gujarati followers of Lord Mahavira. The temple's colorful, peaceful interior has an understated elegance. Check out the intricate work on the walls and ceilings. Worship at this shrine takes a somewhat different form than the *hungama,* or chaos, at Hindu temples. It's more introspective and humble in aspect. Around 8 AM, freshly bathed Jains in swaths of unstitched off-white cloth walk here barefoot from their nearby homes to pay homage to the splendid idol of Adinath, an important Jain prophet. (Jains show respect by arriving clean and without shoes—originally Jains used to wear only a silk cloth, the best and hence most respectful material, but plenty now also wear cotton, and many others simply make do with ordinary clothes.) ⊠ *B. G. Kher Marg, Teen Batti, near Walkeshwar.*

⑩ **Kamala Nehru Park.** On the eastern side of the top of lovely Malabar Hill, this small, unpretentious park is primarily a children's playground (kids look especially cute popping out of the "Old Woman Who Lived in a Shoe" boot), but it offers gorgeous panoramic views of the city below. From the special viewpoint clearing, you can see all of Marine Drive and the Bombay skyline, from Chowpatty Beach to Colaba Point. Try to come up after dark to see why Marine Drive, sparkling with lights, is known as the Queen's Necklace. Just across the road, another park, the **Hanging Gardens,** also has pleasant views. A few minutes north of here are the **Towers of Silence,** where Bombay's Parsi community—followers of the Zoroastrian faith—dispose of their dead. Pallbearers carry the corpse to the top of one of the towering cylindrical bastions, where it is left to be devoured by vultures and crows (a roughly two-hr process) and decomposed by the elements. None of this is visible to would-be onlookers, even relatives, and high walls prevent any furtive peeping. ⊠ *B. G. Kher Marg.* ۞ *Daily 6 AM–9 PM.*

★ ⑭ **Mani Bhavan.** This charming, three-story Gujarati house, painted brown and yellow and ensconced in a quiet, tree-shaded Parsi neighborhood on Malabar Hill, was the home of Mahatma Gandhi from 1917 to 1934. Now overseen and maintained by the Gandhi Institute, it houses a library and a small museum on Gandhi's life and work. Gandhi's simple belongings are displayed in his room, including his original copies of the Bible, the Koran, and the *Bhagavad Gita;* other displays include colorful dioramas and some important and moving letters from the fight for Indian independence. ⊠ *19 Laburnam Rd.,* ☎ *22/380–5864.* ⊡ *Rs. 3.* ۞ *Daily 10–5:30.*

Matunga. About 30 minutes west of Bombay's business district, this suburb is home to a sizable chunk of the city's South Indian population. It's a little bit of Madras up north—it even has a few South Indian temples complete with distinctive *gopurams,* or towers (the **Asthika Samaj Temple** on Bhandarkar Road is a good example). Bazaars and shops sell banana leaves, Kanchipuram saris, and typical South Indian vegetables, flowers, and pickles (bottled relishes); nearby eating houses serve clean, simple South Indian thali lunches on banana leaves or hot crispy *dosas* (lentil pancakes). **Shree Sunders** (☎ 22/ 416–9216) is known for having a large variety of dosas. The legendary banana-leaf-lunch provider **A Ramanayak Udipi Shri Krishna Boarding** (☎ 22/414–2422; ۞ Lunch served 10:30–2:30 and Dinner 7–10) is near the train station. Matunga's shops and restaurants are closed on Monday. ⊠ *Telang Rd. near Matunga Central Railway Station.*

Elephanta Caves

★ *9 nautical mi from Gateway of India*

Exactly who carved these 7th-century cave temples on Elephanta Island is not known. We do know that the island was originally called Gharapuri; the Portuguese renamed it Elephanta after they found a large stone elephant near their landing place. (The figure collapsed in 1814 and was subsequently moved to the far-off Victoria Gardens and re-assembled.) Shortly before these temples were created, Bombay had experienced the golden age of the late Guptas, under whom the talents of artists had free range. Sanskrit had been finely polished, and under the court's liberal patronage, Kalidasa and other writers had helped incite a revival of Hindu beliefs. It was Shivaism, or the worship of Shiva, that inspired the building of these temples.

The outside of the main cave consists of a columned veranda 30 ft wide and 6 ft deep, which you approach on steps flanked by sculptured elephants. The entire temple, carved out of the basalt hillside, is 130 ft square. The principle sculptures are on the southern wall at the back. The central recess in the hall contains the most outstanding sculpture, the unusual Mahesamurti, the Great Lord Shiva—an 18-ft triple image. Its three faces represent three aspects of Shiva: the creator (on the right), the preserver (in the center), and the destroyer (on the left).

Other sculptures near the doorways and on side panels show Shiva's usefulness. Shiva brought the Ganges River down to Earth, the story says, letting it trickle through his matted hair. He is also depicted as Yogisvara, lord of Yogis, seated on a lotus, and as Nataraja, the many-armed cosmic dancer. The beauty of this stonework lies in the grace, balance, and sense of peace conveyed in spite of the subject's multiple actions.

In winter the Maharashtra Tourism Development Corporation (MTDC) organizes a top-notch dance festival in this memorable setting. The island itself is quiet and picturesque, with light-green foliage and monkeys scampering about. The MTDC leads an excellent daily tour and runs a tiny restaurant on the island for refreshments and beer. ⊠ *Motor launches (1 hr each way) depart daily every half hour, 9–2:30 from Gateway of India and 10–4:30 from Elephanta Island, unless sea is very choppy.* ☎ *Round-trip fare Rs. 85; 85 caves $10.*

DINING

Café

$ ✕ **Café Mondegar.** Next door to Regal Cinema, this Western joint is one of Bombay's popular hangouts. The jukebox plays at full volume, and has a wide selection of jazz and pop anthems. The walls are adorned with cartoons and glib quotes from the likes of George Bernard Shaw. The café is open all day, and it's usually jam-packed. The onion rings and french fries are good and greasy, and the coffee float is delicious. ⊠ *Colaba Causeway,* ☎ *22/202–0591. MC, V.*

Chinese

$–$$ ✕ **China Garden.** This restaurant is the second avatar of the erstwhile China Garden at Kemps Corner. Like the original, which didn't have an unreserved table since it opened in 1984, this incarnation bustles with Bombay's trendiest young VIPs and film stars. Owner and Chinese master chef Nelson Wang takes great personal interest in the management of his restaurant and his diners. The restaurant is spacious and has expanses of black marble and a prominent bar. Mr. Wang's unusual Chinese artifacts decorate the room, and the windows are framed with white lace Chinese curtains. The original menu remains, plus a few additions. Hot favourites include prawns wrapped in bacon, crispy Peking chicken, crispy beans, Shantung prawns, gin chicken, and hakka fish. ⊠ *Crossroads, Pt Madan Mohan Malviya Rd., near Haji Ali,* ☎ *22/495–5588, 22/495–5589, or 22/495–5590. AE, DC, MC, V.*

$–$$ ✕ **Oriental Blossom.** Honey-glazed spare ribs, deep-fried corn curd, co-conut pancakes, dim sum—the Chinese food at the Marine Plaza hotel's showcase restaurant is lightly spiced, a mixture of Cantonese and Szechuan. The decor is simple and elegant, the service unobtrusive. If you want seclusion, book a table in one of the almost-private dining alcoves. ✉ *Hotel Marine Plaza, 29 Marine Dr.,* ☎ 22/285–1212. *Reservations essential. AE, DC, MC, V.*

$ ✕ **Legacy of China.** One of the best Chinese restaurants in the suburbs, and close to Bollywood, Legacy of China attracts starry, as well as starry-eyed, customers. Thai and Schezwan (the Bombay favourite), Hunan, Cantonese, and Peking food are available. Folks love to dig into the Yin Yang fried chicken, crispy fried spinach, Kwandhong soup (lettuce, bean curd, mushroom, prawns, and chicken), Thai green curries, Thai barbecue chicken, sizzled *chilly* prawns, and Malaysian fish curry (pomfret curry). The restaurant is large and decorated with swords, Chinese landscapes, and mirrors. Note that Jay Prakash Road is better known as JP Road. ✉ *5-6, Tirupati, Jay Prakash Rd., Seven Bungalows, Versova, Andheri West,* ☎ *22/636–8223, 22/631–1332. Reservations essential. AE, DC, MC, V.*

$ ✕ **Leopold Café.** Founded in 1871, this is one of the city's oldest
★ restaurants and a popular tourist haunt. With a highly international, eclectic, sometimes outlandish clientele, it's a great place to people-watch. The tables are well spaced, and the paintings and posters recall a French café; at the back is a fruit bar lined with mangos, papayas, and pineapples. The selection of tandoori and Chinese food is broad, and the milkshakes are delicious. Portions are very large. ✉ *Colaba Causeway,* ☎ *22/287–3362, 22/202–0131. AE, MC, V.*

$ ✕ **Ling's Pavilion.** Baba Ling and his family have been providing Bom-
★ bay with excellent Chinese food for two generations, formerly in tiny Nanking, a favorite with film stars and yuppies alike, and now in the much bigger and fancier Ling's Pavilion. Enter through the moon-shaped door and you find yourself on a bridge overlooking a gurgling stream, complete with fish. Some tables look down from a balcony. A testimony to Ling's popularity and authenticity is the number of Chinese tourists and consular corps digging into their meals with gusto. Don't miss the barbecue platter, baby lobsters, or steamed fish. The Chinese bread is soft and succulent—terrific with the ginger-garlic crab. ✉ *19/ 21 Mahakavi Bhushan Marg, behind Regal Cinema,* ☎ *22/285–0023, 22/282–4533. Reservations essential. AE, DC, MC, V.*

Continental

$$$$ ✕ **Zodiac Grill.** This Continental restaurant in the legendary Taj Mahal hotel is Western in style, with subdued lighting, handsome chandeliers, captains in black jackets, and waiters wearing white gloves. Specialties include Camembert *dariole* (soufflé) and a creamy Kahlua mousse for dessert. Entrées favor meat and seafood, such as New Zealand steak, Cajun lobster, and grilled lobster. ✉ *Taj Mahal hotel, Apollo Bunder,* ☎ *22/202–3366. Reservations essential. Jacket and tie. AE, DC, MC, V.*

$$ ✕ **Society.** If you're in the mood for Continental cuisine—or a good steak—pay a visit to this elegant Victorian restaurant, decorated with mirrors and handsome maroon velvet. The best steak, "à la Fernandes"—named after a former maître d'—is richly seasoned with cinnamon, spices, and cream; it's cooked and flambéed at your table. The crêpes suzette are delectable. Excellent Indian dishes are also served. ✉ *Ambassador hotel, Veer Nariman Rd., Churchgate,* ☎ *22/204–1131. Reservations essential. AE, DC, MC, V.*

244

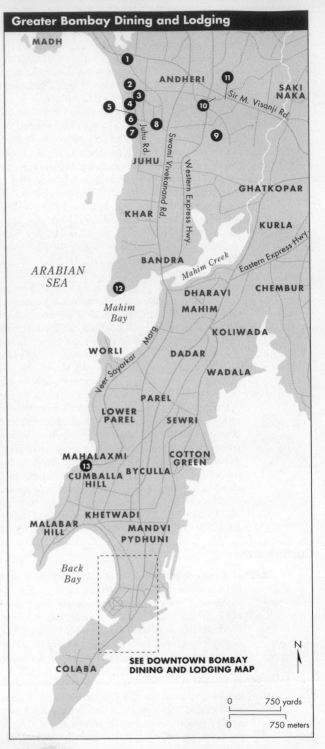

Greater Bombay Dining and Lodging

Downtown Bombay Dining and Lodging

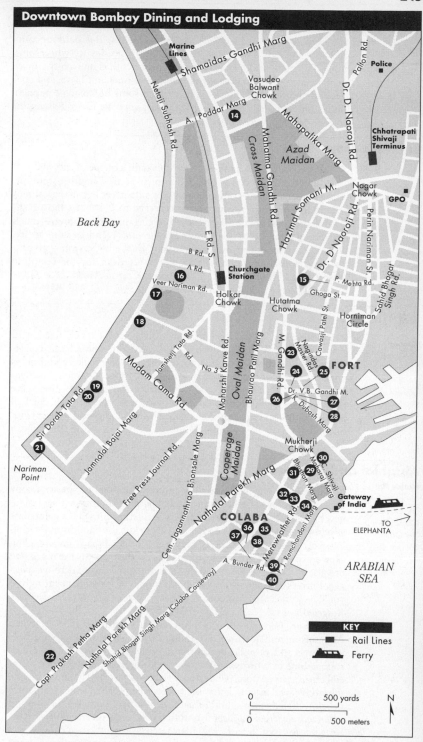

Marine Lines

Shamaidas Gandhi Marg

Vasudeo Balwant Chowk

A. Poddar Marg

14

Mahapalika Marg

Police

Dr. D. Naoroji Rd.

Pation Rd.

Chhatrapati Shivaji Terminus

Azad Maidan

Mahatma Gandhi Rd.

Cross Maidan

Hazimal Somani M.

Nagar Chowk

GPO

Back Bay

Netaji Subhash Rd.

E Rd. S.

B Rd. S.

A Rd.

16

Veer Nariman Rd.

17

18

Churchgate Station

Holkar Chowk

Perin Nariman St.

Sahid Bhagat Singh Rd.

Dr. D Naoroji Rd.

15

P. Mehta Rd.

Ghoga St.

Hutatma Chowk

Horniman Circle

Madam Cama Rd.

Jamshedji Tata Rd.

Maharshi Karve Rd.

No 3 Rd.

Oval Maidan

Bhaurao Patil Marg

M. Gandhi Rd.

Nagindas Master Rd.

Cawasji Patel St.

23

24

25

FORT

Dr. V.B. Gandhi M.

26

27

28

Dubash Marg

19

20

Sir Dorab Tata Rd.

Jamnalal Bajaj Marg

21

Nariman Point

Free Press Journal Rd.

Gen. Jagannathrao Bhonsale Marg

Cooperage Maidan

Nathalal Parekh Marg

Mukherji Chowk

30

29

31

C. Shivaji Maharaj Marg

Bhaurao Marg

32 **33**

34

Gateway of India

TO ELEPHANTA

COLABA

36 **35**

37

38

Nereweather Rd.

J. Ramchandani Marg

39

40

A. Bunder Rd.

ARABIAN SEA

Capt. Prakash Petha Marg

Nathalal Parekh Marg

Shahid Bhagat Singh Marg (Colaba Causeway)

22

KEY	
■—	Rail Lines
⛴	Ferry

0   500 yards

0   500 meters

N

$ ✕ **Café Churchill.** This tiny six-table eatery serves fresh, delicious pasta, pizza, and other Continental dishes. It's a simple place, with a television perpetually tuned to MTV. At lunchtime, the line outdoors outnumbers the café's entire seating capacity. Besides its wholesome home-like meals and first-rate desserts, Churchill is unusually convenient: it opens early in the morning and stays open until late, and provides any kind of takeout. It's also close to some of Colaba's popular budget hotels. ⊠ *103-B Colaba Causeway, opposite Cusrow Baug,* ☎ *22/284–4689. No credit cards.*

Contemporary

$–$$ ✕ **Indigo.** The narrow lane out front fills with a queue of cars at lunch and dinnertime. Reservations are a must at this small restaurant, housed in an attractive old mansion on a side street in Colaba. A nouvelle Indian-Western fusion cuisine is served to Bombay's most fashionable denizens in simple, woodsy but elegant surroundings—much like dining in an old Goan home. Try the *rawas* (Indian salmon) fry, filet mignon, tandoori rosemary chicken, or the big *raviolo*—all pastas here, actually, are commendable. Save room for the tempting desserts. ⊠ *4, Mandalik Rd., Colaba, near Cotton World,* ☎ *22/285–6316, 22/202–3592. Reservations essential. AE, DC, MC, V.*

Eclectic

$ ✕ **Wayside Inn.** This sleepy, unpretentious place hasn't changed in 50 years: plants are perched in open windows, red-and-white checked tablecloths cover the tables, fans whir overhead, and crockery and mugs populate the walls and sideboards. All of this gives Wayside Inn a casual, inviting look. On Tuesday, Wednesday, and Thursday, they serve Parsi cuisine, including *dhansak* (brown rice, served with chicken cooked with lentils) and chicken pilau. The rest of the week expect Continental food or the popular pomfret and chips. ⊠ *38 K. Dubash Marg, Kala Ghoda,* ☎ *22/284–4324. No credit cards.*

Mughlai and Tandoori

$$ ✕ **Peshawari.** The Welcomgroup of hotels decided to spawn a copy of their much-loved Delhi restaurant, Bukhara, in Bombay, at their brand-new hotel in the city. Peshawari sports beaded curtains and a giant glass window with a view of the kitchen, where kebabs hang from the ceiling; you may also see cooks preparing Indian breads and juggling skewers loaded with succulent kebabs. Also heavenly is the black *dal*; breads, too, are excellent, and desserts are authentic, and above-average. Entrées are expensive, but the portions are large. Eat sparingly— you'll be stuffed after one course. ⊠ *Sahar Airport Rd.,* ☎ *22/830-3030. Reservations essential. AE, DC, MC, V.*

$–$$ ✕ **Khyber.** Named for the Himalayan mountain pass between
★ Afghanistan and northwestern India, Khyber is one of Bombay's most attractive and popular restaurants, with three floors of delightful rooms done in Northwest Frontier style—white marble floors, terracotta urns, carved stone pillars, low wooden rafters, and handsome fresco murals by local artists. The waiters, dressed in Pathan tribal garb, serve delicious kebabs, rotis, and other North Indian food. Try the pomfret green *masala* (fried pomfret fish stuffed with tangy green chutney), Khyber *raan* for two (leg of lamb marinated overnight, then roasted in a clay oven), or *paneer shaslik* (cottage cheese marinated with spices and roasted). ⊠ *145 M. G. Rd., Fort,* ☎ *22/267–3228. Reservations essential. AE, DC, MC, V.*

$–$$ ✗ **Palkhi.** Much-ballyhooed when the restaurant opened some years ago, Palkhi's decor was designed by leading socialite Parmeshwar Godrej. Giant electric candles drip faux plastic wax, and little caverns in the wall hide tableaux by the well-known Indian artist Subhash Awchat. It's startling and rather Halloween-like, yet the effect is not unappealing. The menu includes some relatively unusual tandoori and North Indian dishes, thoughtfully seasoned. The mixed Palkhi platter of kebabs is a good bet, as are the ring kebab, vegetable kebabs, *murg kali mirchi* (chicken with black pepper), seafood in "Delite" sauce (spicy), and the *paneer* Amritsari (cottage cheese cooked in a white sauce). Save room for the special dessert, "Hot Romance"—gulab jamuns flambéed with Cointreau. ✉ *Walton Rd., near Electric House, Colaba,* ☎ *22/284–0053. Reservations essential. AE, DC, MC, V.*

North Indian

$ ✗ **Chetana.** Rajasthani decor—hand-blocked fabrics on the ceiling
★ and traditional *toranas* (ornamental carvings above temple entrances) on the walls—provides a cozy warmth for tasty vegetarian Rajasthani and Gujarati thalis. Chetana also does a low-cal Gujarati thali. Sample Rajasthani *dal bati* (lentils with wheat cakes), *kadhi* (curd curry), and mint *raita* (a spiced yogurt dish). Service is excellent, and the owners' adjacent philosophy bookshop–cum–craft store is worth a visit after your meal. Note that the restaurant is closed between 3 and 7. ✉ *34 K. Dubash Marg, Kala Ghoda,* ☎ *22/284–4968, 22/282–4983. AE, DC, MC, V.*

$ ✗ **Govinda's.** This Hare Krishna restaurant offers sumptuous 40-item vegetarian *thalis*. Expect Lord Krishna's food—that is, Vedic meals, which are cooked without garlic and onions. The management, in fact advertises its "transcendental dining experience"—the food served has already been offered to the gods, and the *bhajans*—the joyful devotional music playing, livens up your meal. On weekends and Hindu holidays the restaurant often organizes food fests. ✉ *ISKCON, Hare Krishna Mandir, Juhu Tara Rd.,* ☎ *22/620–0337, 620–6860. MC, V.*

Pan-Asian

$$ ✗ **Sidewok.** Expect Pan-Asian food and cheerful music at this happening restaurant run by the Taj Group, at the National Centre for the Performing Arts. When they're not handing out courses, waiters hit the dance floor to their own special numbers. Best bets include lemongrass pomfret, tandoori salmon, house chicken, Asian wok (grilled vegetables), and orange soufflé. ✉ *Nariman Point,* ☎ *22/281–8132. Reservations essential. AE, DC, MC, V.*

Seafood

$–$$ ✗ **Trishna.** Once just another neighborhood lunch place, this small restaurant near busy M. G. Road has been very much discovered. Now yuppies and film stars crowd into the rows of benches and tables alongside Trishna's old-time regulars, all devouring fresh seafood or Indian and Chinese cuisine, both vegetarian and nonvegetarian. Favorites include squid or oyster chili and salt-and-pepper butter crab (Rs. 450). Ask to see the crab before it's cooked: the creature's giant, snapping claws will dispel any doubts about freshness. Call in advance to inquire about the daily catch. ✉ *7 Rope Walk La. (next to Commerce House), Fort,* ☎ *22/270–3213, 22/261–4991, or 22/261–4991. Reservations essential. AE, DC, MC, V.*

$ ✕ **Ankur.** If you're a seafood fanatic and you want to try Konkan cui-
★ sine, Bombay's ragingly hot trend, don't miss Ankur, named for the
spicy seafood of the Konkan coast. In Konkan cuisine, the seafood is
typically garnished with coconut and *kokum* (a tangy tamarind-like
sauce). Once a down-market fish house but now sporting wood and
glass accents, Ankur does the popular Manglorean and Konkan dishes
rather well. Dine on semolina-fried jumbo prawns, fried *kane* (lady-
fish), tandoori crab, or *teesri* (clams) in pepper sauce—served with *sana*
(fluffy rice cakes tempered with toddy) or *neer dosa* (lacy rice pancakes)—
and you're sure to attain nirvana. Vegetarians can choose from among
Mughlai dishes and *sana* with chutney. ⊠ *Meadows House, Tamarind
La. (behind Kendeel bar), Fort,* ☎ *22/265–4194, 22/263–0393. Reservations essential on weekends. AE, DC, MC, V.*

$ ✕ **Mahesh Lunch Home.** One of the first Bombay restaurants to pop-
★ ularize the seafoods of the Konkan coast, the formerly humble Mahesh, a two-level eatery tucked away on a narrow street, has gone
upmarket with marble, brass, plastic floral arrangements, and smartly
clad waiters. (The diners have gone upmarket too; no more leaving fish
bones on the side of the table.) You'll get what may be Bombay's
freshest and best seafood, personally selected at the nearby Fort fish
market every morning for the past 20 years by the owner Mr. Kark-
era. Local office workers, bankers, five-star hoteliers, suburban families, and cricket and film stars in the know come here for giant portions
of exquisite crab, *rawas* (Indian salmon), and pomfret dishes, all suc-
culently tender and light—essentially oil-free—and seasoned with tangy
tandoori or Mangalorean spices. The seafood dishes prepared with butter, garlic, and pepper are also popular. ⊠ *8-B Cawasji Patel St., Fort,*
☎ *22/287–0938. AE, DC, MC, V.*

South Indian

$ ✕ **Dosa Diner.** At this spacious Apollo Bundar branch of the hot new
chain, Dosa Diner, you can have hot dosas of every stripe in a cheerful, comfortable setting. Traditionally, the best dosas in Bombay have
been available only in grimy or uncomfortable places—roadside carts
or small vegetarian dosa (or Udipi as they are called) joints that cater
to armies of office workers. The dosas here aren't as tasty as those served
at your corner *annah* (literally "brother"; meaning dosa joint), but they're
fresh, crisp, and served up fast. Eat your dosas with fish curry or a spicy
mutton stew—and wash them down with a beer. Dosa Diner also
serves kids' meals and other South Indian food. ⊠ *above Central Cottage Emporium, Apollo Bunder,* ☎ *22/282–9934, 22/282–9935. AE,
DC, MC, V.*

$ ✕ **Woodlands Garden Cafe.** The queue at this vegetarian restaurant
on weekends is an unequivocal testimony of the quality of the food.
This is the place for authentic South Indian food. Excellent dosas and
South Indian thalis in no-fuss but comfortable surroundings. Wood-
lands' tasty *bisi beli hule,* a spicy lentil and rice mixture, hard to find
elsewhere, deserves a special mention. ⊠ *Vaikuntlal Mehta Rd., Juhu-
Vile Parle Scheme,* ☎ *22/617–2727, 22/611–9119. Reservations recommended. No credit cards.*

Thai

$-$$ ✕ **Sanuk Thai.** Thailand is thousands of miles away, but walk into Sanuk
Thai and you'll feel like you're there. Sanuk Thai poses as a magical
Thai kingdom—with twinkling stars, sparkling orchids, and Buddhist
artifacts and pagoda-style furnishings that designed to create a special
appeal. The Thai curries are excellent, as are the pepper-and-garlic prawns

When you pack your MCI Calling Card, it's like packing your loved ones along too.

Your MCI Calling Card is the easy way to stay in touch when you travel. Use it to call to and from over 125 countries. Plus, every time you call, you can earn frequent flier miles. So wherever your travels take you, call home with your MCI Calling Card. It's even easy to get one. Just visit **www.mci.com/worldphone.**

EASY TO CALL WORLDWIDE

1. Just enter the WorldPhone® access number of the country you're calling from.
2. Enter or give the operator your MCI Calling Card number.
3. Enter or give the number you're calling.

Australia ◆	1-800-881-100
China	108-12
Hong Kong	800-96-1121
India	000-127
Japan ◆	00539-121▶
Kenya	080011
Morocco	00-211-0012
South Africa	0800-99-0011

◆ Public phones may require deposit of coin or phone card for dial tone.
▶ Regulation does not permit intra-Japan calls.

EARN FREQUENT FLIER MILES

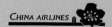
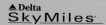

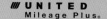
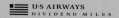

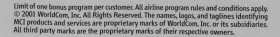

SEE THE WORLD
IN FULL COLOR

Fodor's Exploring Guides bring all the great sights vividly to life with hundreds of photographs, fascinating historical background, and colorful anecdotes. Detailed maps and practical information keep you headed in the right direction.

Pair a **Fodor's** Exploring Guide with your trusted Gold Guide for a complete planning package.

Fodor's EXPLORING GUIDES

At bookstores everywhere.

and the crispy bean sprouts. Start with corn cakes if you're really hungry, and wind up your meal with banana fritters. ⊠ *30 K. Dubash Marg, Kala Ghoda, Fort,* ☎ *22/204–4233, 22/204–4239. Reservations essential. AE, DC, MC, V.*

$–$$ ✕ **Thai Pavilion.** Thai Pavilion's small dining room is tastefully deco-
★ rated with inlaid teak surfaces, candles, and orchids. The food is exceptional, and portions are unusually generous. Start with a clay crock of *tom yum koong,* a spicy prawn soup aromatic with lemongrass and fiery with chilis (not for the faint of palate). Try this fabulous entrée: *kai haw bai toey,* sweet marinated chicken chunks wrapped in pandanus, or screw-pine, leaves (don't eat them), then steamed and deep-fried. Knowledgeable, attentive waiters provide fantastic service. ⊠ *Taj President Hotel, 90 Cuffe Parade, Colaba,* ☎ *22/215–0808 Ext. 5621. Reservations essential. AE, DC, MC, V.*

LODGING

$$$$ 🏨 **Ambassador.** Once an apartment house, this nine-story 1940s hotel in the heart of Bombay is less sleek in service and appearance than its South Bombay counterparts, but offers a bit more old-fashioned personality, and good value. Rooms are furnished in a functional modern style, each with the Ambassador chain's signature brass knocker on its door. The bathrooms are little tacky-looking, but they're fully functional and very clean. India's first revolving restaurant crowns the hotel—it offers gorgeous views over the city and the Arabian Sea, and great Far Eastern food. ⊠ *Veer Nariman Rd., Churchgate, 400020,* ☎ *22/204–1131,* FAX *22/204–0004. 120 rooms, 3 suites. 3 restaurants, bar, coffee shop, dry cleaning, laundry service, travel services. AE, DC, MC, V.*

$$$$ 🏨 **Holiday Inn.** Built in the 1970s, this Western-style high-rise on Juhu Beach has a spacious lobby, executive floors for business travelers, and rooms that are uniformly decorated with standard contemporary furniture and pastel wall-to-wall carpeting and fabrics with an accent on green. The best standard rooms have limited views of the beach; only deluxe rooms face the sea directly. Each room comes equipped with an electric kettle, a safe, and a hairdryer. The tariff covers complimentary breakfast and airport pick up. ⊠ *Balraj Sahani Marg, Juhu Beach, 400049,* ☎ *22/693–4444,* FAX *22/693–4455. 182 rooms, 13 suites. 2 restaurants, bar, coffee shop, pool, health club, dry cleaning, laundry service, business services, meeting room, travel services. AE, DC, MC, V.*

$$$$ 🏨 **The Leela.** Close to both airports, 25 km (16 mi) outside the city, this stylish, posh hotel is the stopover hub for high-powered businesspeople and airline employees; its airport location is not convenient if you'll be sightseeing or doing business for a few days in Bombay proper. Although the consistently high occupancy rate detracts somewhat from the personalized service, all else is superior five-star deluxe. Rooms are spacious and immaculate, with plush carpeting, armchairs in white and ivory, exquisitely comfortable beds, but perhaps not as sumptuous as the new competition that has come up next door. Outside, 11 acres of beautifully maintained gardens include lotus pools and a small waterfall. No other luxury hotel in Bombay can boast of similarly verdant surroundings. A popular Italian restaurant and an excellent Chinese restaurant, "The Great Wall," are located in the hotel. ⊠ *Sahar, 400059,* ☎ *22/691–1234,* FAX *22/691–1212. 425 rooms, 32 suites. 4 restaurants, 2 bars, pool, steam room, 2 tennis courts, health club, business services, meeting room, travel services, airport shuttle. AE, DC, MC, V.*

$$$$ ⊞ **Le Royal Meridien.** Although this neat, small, luxury hotel doesn't have a high-falutin' entrance (from the outside), its shining marble lobby and inviting pool out back add plenty of grandeur. Conveniently, it's five minutes from Bombay's international airport, in the thick of the city's growing neighborhood of airport hotels. Rooms are no less swanky for being comfy—they are decorated with lots of wood and crisp whites. Bathrooms are done in chrome and glass, and have both shower cubicles and tubs. The hotel's restaurant La Brasserie serves a variety of meals around the clock; another restaurant on-site, Captain Trumpet, offers a variety of Asian cuisines. Airport pick up is complimentary. ⊠ *Sahar Airport Rd.,* ☎ *22/838–0000,* ℻ *22/838–0101. 171 rooms, 6 suites. 4 restaurants, 2 bars, pool, hair salon, health club, sauna, dry cleaning, laundry service, business services, meeting room, travel services. AE, DC, MC, V.*

$$$$ ⊞ **Marine Plaza.** The polished, smoky-glass exterior of this Marine Drive
★   hotel promises elegance. The Marine Plaza—which calls itself a "fashionable small hotel"—delivers with a modern, black-marble interior and a clean, uncluttered sleekness. Glass elevators whiz you up to rooms that are small but very comfortable, and fairly luxurious. Rooms have sea views and dressing rooms. Breakfast is included in the room rate. The glass-bottom pool, located outside on the roof of the hotel offers enchanting vistas of Bombay. ⊠ *29 Marine Dr., 400020,* ☎ *22/285–1212,* ℻ *22/282–8585. 68 rooms, 46 suites. Restaurant, bar, coffee shop, in-room data ports, in-room safes, refrigerators, health club, dry cleaning, laundry service, business services, meeting room, travel services. AE, DC, MC, V.*

$$$$ ⊞ **The Oberoi.** This elegant high-rise in the heart of the business dis-
★   trict caters to business travelers. From service to decor, everything is sleek and efficient, yet the fabulous, high-ceilinged lobby and various public spaces are punctuated with traditional pieces for warmth. The Oberoi is easily one of the classiest hotels in the country. Each floor is staffed with a butler for personal assistance, and each room has small, separate dressing and luggage areas to allow for clutter-free in-room meetings. The rooms are decorated in subtle pastel colors. A superior business center and complimentary personalized stationery are extra touches. If at all possible, arrange for a room with a view of the Arabian Sea. The Oberoi's Indian restaurant, Kandahar, serves unusual, healthy meals—prepared with little or no oil—and the Brasserie coffee shop serves 80 dishes from around the world. ⊠ *Nariman Point, 400021,* ☎ *22/232–5757,* ℻ *22/204–1505. 337 rooms, 22 suites. 3 restaurants, bar, pool, barbershop, hair salon, sauna, Turkish baths, health club, dry cleaning, laundry service, business services, meeting room, travel services. AE, DC, MC, V.*

$$$$ ⊞ **Oberoi Towers.** Adjoining The Oberoi, this enormous, 35-story high-rise is geared toward the business traveler but hosts a mixed international crowd of both executives and tourists. True to the Oberoi chain's characteristic efficiency, it runs like a well-tuned instrument. Public spaces are many and varied, some overlooking the vast, gleaming, glass-wall lobby from smart mezzanines. Guest rooms are modern and classy. Rooms are furnished with patterned bedspreads and drapes, brass-framed prints of Indian monuments, and smooth, contemporary wood furniture. Sea-facing rooms on high floors have stunning views of the Arabian Sea and Marine Drive, which turns into the "Queen's Necklace" at night. The Frangipani restaurant has an international menu, as does the laid-back coffee shop, The Palms. ⊠ *Nariman Point, 400021,* ☎ *22/232–5757,* ℻ *22/204–3282. 537 rooms, 44 suites. 3 restaurants, 2 bars, pool, sauna, health club, laundry service, business services, meeting room, travel services. AE, DC, MC, V.*

$$$$ ⊡ **The Orchid.** This small eco-hotel has low-key but attractive rooms
★ that are brightly lit, decently sized, and very comfortable. The hotel is
right next to Bombay's domestic airport, and a few minutes' drive from
the international airport. Boasting proudly of "eco-friendly waste
management and recycling policies," the hotel built its "green" rooms
with a minimal amount of wood, plastic, and paper. A bedside button
allows you to turn up your air-conditioning thermostat by a degree or
so to save energy. The waterfall, which runs on recycled water, looks
like falling glass—it lights up the lobby and provides humidity for the
lustrous orchids that populate the hotel's interior. ⊠ *Nehru Rd., Vile
Parle East, 400050,* ☎ *22/616–4040,* ℻ *22/616–4141. 201 rooms,
55 suites. Restaurant, bar, pool, health club, baby-sitting, dry cleaning, laundry service, business services, meeting room, travel services,
airport shuttle. AE, DC, MC, V.*

$$$$ ⊡ **The Regent.** In a city where space is extremely tight and real-estate
★ prices are some of the highest in the world, the opening of a brand-
new five-star hotel—and a very plush one at that—in the heart of Bombay is an event. The Regent opened in 1999 after almost 15 years, and
it does seem worth the wait. It's opulent: the lobby seems like an acre
of marble, with huge, sparkling chandeliers, fountains, and automatic
revolving doors opening into the lobby. Facing the ocean from the suburb of Bandra, the Regent has some remarkably luxurious modern rooms,
complete with bedside controls for the lights, curtains, and air-conditioning. Bathrooms have both showers and tubs. ⊠ *Lands End, Bandstand, Bandra West, 400050,* ☎ *22/655–1234,* ℻ *22/651–2471. 508
rooms, 7 suites. 3 restaurants, bar, coffee shop, patisserie, in-room data
ports, in-room safes, minibars, pool, barbershop, hair salon, health club,
dance club, baby-sitting, dry cleaning, laundry service, business services, meeting room, travel services. AE, DC, MC, V.*

$$$$ ⊡ **Taj Mahal.** Looking past the Gateway of India to the Arabian Sea,
★ the Taj's stunning brown stone exterior sports rows of jutting white balconies and Gothic windows. Onion domes on the corner turrets echo
the high, central Italianate dome. The first hotel in what is now a pan-
India luxury chain, this Victorian extravaganza was built in 1903. Foreigners and wealthy Indians choose this hotel over other fancy hotels
in town because it's a beautiful and regal landmark. A less expensive
19-story modern wing called the Intercontinental, which throws in
some Moorish elements, towers just inland from its older sister. Every
corner of the older building is exquisitely decorated, often with antiques
(for which the hotel's decorator scours India) and always with warm,
tasteful colors. Rooms and suites in this turn-of-the-century building,
some of which surround small, quiet interior verandas, retain their Victorian character with high ceilings, pastel colors, antiques, and cane furniture. Rooms facing the harbor are extremely attractive. Rooms in the
Intercontinental, slightly less expensive, are spacious and modern, and
offer a tiny sitting area and a desk. ⊠ *Apollo Bunder, Colaba, 400039,*
☎ *22/202–3366,* ℻ *22/287–2711. 582 rooms, 49 suites. 5 restaurants, 3 bars, coffee shop, patisserie, pool, barbershop, hair salon,
health club, dance club, baby-sitting, dry cleaning, laundry service,
business services, meeting room, travel services. AE, DC, MC, V.*

$$$$ ⊡ **Taj President.** In a residential neighborhood near the World Trade
Center shopping emporium, this luxury hotel (and its buffet breakfast)
is very popular with business travelers. The comfortable rooms have
high ceilings and modern furnishings. The Taj President is not as extravagant as some others in its price range, the service here is outstanding.
Ask for a slightly more expensive "superior room" on one of the upper
floors. Some of the floors, the coffee shop and the lobby have been refurbished to sport a cozy "living room" look. The Trattoria, a coffee
shop and Italian eatery, has been refurbished, and its kitchen opens out

into the restaurant; tours are welcome. ✉ *90 Cuffe Parade, Colaba, 400005,* ☎ *22/215–0808,* ℻ *22/215–1201. 300 rooms, 20 suites. 3 restaurants, café, bar, pool, hair salon, health club, laundry service, business services, travel services. AE, DC, MC, V.*

$$$ 🏨 **Fariyas.** The shiny, small marble lobby is filled with glass chandeliers and brass ornaments. With contemporary furnishings and wall-to-wall carpets, the rooms are inviting. That and the hotel's facilities and location—half a block from the eastern shore in trendy Colaba, near the Gateway of India—combine to give Fariyas certain advantages that suburban hotels lack because of their distance from the city proper. Select a room for its sea-facing view. However the rooms are overpriced for their size and decor, and the clientele occasionally below par. Only two suites have tubs; the rest of the rooms have showers. A swinging pub–tavern is located in the basement and plays a lot of "classic" rock and oldie-goldie numbers. ✉ *25 Devshankar V Vyas Marg (at Shahid Bhagt Singh Marg), off Arthur Bunder Rd., Colaba, 400005,* ☎ *22/ 204–2911 or 22/285–5431,* ℻ *22/283–4992. 87 rooms, 6 suites. Restaurant, bar, pool, health club, meeting room, travel services. AE, DC, MC, V.*

$$$ 🏨 **Grand Maratha Sheraton.** Bombay's newest hotel, the Maratha is indeed grand. Rooms overlook a pleasant shrubbery-lined atrium where meals are served. The hotel is very spacious and has a luxurious atmosphere—it has endless expanses of granite and marble. The view, however, is the hitch—the slow construction of another five-star hotel is taking place across the road. (Opt for pool-facing rooms.) Rooms are very elegant: posh with colorful but attractive accents and exotic bathrooms (with tubs and glass shower cubicles). The hotel staff is very attentive and efficient, and each room has a television. Here you'll get a lot of luxury for a lot less cost. ✉ *Sahar Airport Rd.,* ☎ *22/830– 3030,* ℻ *22/830–3131. 386 rooms, 48 suites. 4 restaurants, café, bar, pool, hair salon, health club, sauna, hot tub, laundry service, business services, travel services, meeting rooms. AE, DC, MC, V.*

$$$ 🏨 **Juhu Centaur.** The Centaur is one of the more expensive, and certainly the largest, of the hotels on Juhu Beach. Built in the 1980s, this sprawling, five-story cement building has an immense lobby and a quiet public sitting area on each floor. The lobby is a touch seedy and antiseptic, but the rooms are contemporary and large, with plush carpeting; each room has two sofas or armchairs, and all rooms have balconies. Ask for a room overlooking the beach, and watch the Juhu locals take their seaside constitutionals early in the morning. A number of the rooms have been renovated; non-renovated rooms, which are in perfectly good shape, cost less. Bathrooms could use updating. Rates, which include a complimentary breakfast and an airport pickup, are a bargain. ✉ *Juhu Tara Rd., Juhu Beach, 400049,* ☎ *22/611–3040,* ℻ *22/611–6343. 357 rooms, 16 suites. 3 restaurants, bar, coffee shop, pool, health club, laundry service, business services, travel services. AE, DC, MC, V.*

$$$ 🏨 **Mercure Guestline.** This small, compact, business hotel about 500
★ ft from the ocean in Juhu has attractive, plush rooms with all the standard amenities, such as fridges and minibars. The Ivy Club serves healthful breakfasts, salad lunches, and a cake buffet to executives and their clients in a quiet lounge area. But since the hotel isn't perched right on the sea and its rooms are small, the hotel is slightly overpriced despite the fact that it's very efficient. Ask for a discount if you are booking directly. ✉ *462 A. B. Nair Rd., Juhu Beach, 400049,* ☎ *22/ 670–5555 or 22/690–5555,* ℻ *22/620–2821. 91 rooms, 2 suites. Restaurant, bar, coffee shop, pool, health club, dry cleaning, laundry service, business services, meeting room. AE, DC, MC, V.*

$$$ 🏨 **Ramada Palm Grove.** When you view the hotel from the front—with its small entrance, squeezed driveway, and parking lot—you initially get the impression that this is a small place, but in fact the Ramada is fairly spacious. The long lobby of this Juhu Beach high-rise is lined with marble and etched glass. Rooms are quite large, with subdued contemporary furnishings in shades of cool green. Each room has a small sitting area. Only deluxe suites and executive salons face the water; the rest of the rooms have limited views. The modest pool is a pleasant, if slightly cramped, place to unwind. Breakfasts and airport pickup are complimentary. The Oriental Bowl, with its excellent black marble and green setting and its Thai and Chinese food, is an exciting place to dine. ✉ *Juhu Tara Rd., Juhu Beach, 400049, ☎ 22/611–2323, ℻ 22/611–3682. 114 rooms, 3 suites. 3 restaurants, bar, pool, hair salon, health club, windsurfing, business services, meeting room, travel services. AE, DC, MC, V.*

$$$ 🏨 **Sun 'n' Sand.** There's a tangibly friendly atmosphere at this 1963 Juhu Beach hotel, approached via a small circular driveway that curves up to a colorful exterior. The intimate lobby leads out to a lovely garden terrace and pool overlooking the sand. In spite of the hotel's upscale facilities, there is something slightly seedy about the place—a sort of B-grade Hindi-movie air—which can perhaps be attributed to its age. The renovated lobby dispels some of the seediness, and the rooms are comfortable and modern. About 60 rooms face the sea. Rooms are equipped with an electric kettle, a safe, and a hairdryer; bathrooms could use a facelift. Breakfast and airport pickup is complimentary. Despite its mildy eccentric nature, Sun 'n' Sand offers the best value for money among the hotels that line Juhu beach. ✉ *39 Juhu Beach, 400049, ☎ 22/620–1811 or 22/620–4821, ℻ 22/620–2170. 120 rooms, 9 suites. 2 restaurants, bar, pool, hair salon, health club, business services, meeting room, travel services, airport shuttle. AE, DC, MC, V.*

$$–$$$ 🏨 **Gordon House.** One of the city's newest hotels, Gordon House is a boutique hotel that claims to be small but "big on style." The rooms, lobby, and restaraunt are simply but fashionably decorated; the lobby is on the second floor. Rooms are on the Mediterranean, Country, and Scandinavian floors. The decor of the rooms matches the floor theme and is spartan, no-fuss but chic—earth-colored buffed tiles, bright white bedspreads, and blond-wood furniture. Tariffs are cheap now and include breakfast. Gordon offers meals at its trendy Asian restaurant, All Stir Fry, where diners can cook their own meals—you ladle raw materials for an all-you-can-eat meal onto your plate, then take the plate to a chef who cooks it for you with a sauce you choose. ✉ *5 Battery St, Apollo Bunder, ☎ 22/287–1122, ℻ 22/287–2026. 🌐 www.ghhotel.com. 28 rooms, 1 suite. Restaurant, bar, coffee shop, dry cleaning, laundry service, travel services. AE, DC, MC, V.*

$$ 🏨 **Godwin.** The nine-story Godwin is a good, low-frills bargain. Accommodations vary widely, however—opt *only* for one of the 10 renovated deluxe rooms. These have clean marble floors and in-room amenities; non-deluxe rooms are rather shabby. Most deluxe rooms have window air-conditioning units, but several are centrally air-conditioned. The bathrooms attached to the deluxe rooms could be cleaner, but are passable. Request an eighth-floor room with a distant view of the Taj Mahal Hotel and Gateway of India—many rooms have no view or outright depressing views. The hotel's highpoint is the glass restaurant Cloud 9, which commands a beautiful view from the ninth floor. The downstairs restaurant serves Indian and Chinese food. Also ask about rooms at Godwin's sister hotel Garden, next door. ✉ *41 Garden Rd., Colaba, off Colaba Causeway, near Electric House, 400039, ☎ 22/287–2050 or 22/284–1226, ℻ 22/287–1592. 56 rooms, 8 suites. Restaurant, bar, refrigerators, laundry service. AE, MC, V.*

$$ ⚏ **West End.** More than half a century old, the West End has a simple charm. The spacious rooms have private balconies, bathtubs, and out-dated furniture (that is, modern items that are not modern anymore). The restaurant, the lobby, and even the bellboys still have a 1940s look. Indian, Chinese, and Continental food are served on-site at Gourmet Restaurant, and the popular Gujarati-thali restaurant Panchvati Gaurav is two minutes away. The building is centrally located near the humming Bombay Hospital, where doctors and relatives swarm in and out until late at night. Corridors and rooms have a slightly musty smell, but the rooms are clean. Some rooms are more spacious than others, so check out your room before booking it and opt for a front-facing room. West End, however, with its spacious, atmospheric rooms at a good price, offers fairly good value. ⊠ *45 New Marine Lines, 400020,* ☎ *22/203–9121 or 22/205–7484,* 𝗙𝗔𝗫 *22/205–7506. 80 rooms, 25 suites. Restaurant, bar, meeting room. AE, DC, MC, V.*

$ ⚏ **Cowie's.** Minutes from the Gateway of India promenade, Cowie's has a few rooms in an old, roughly turn-of-the-20th-century building. The rooms are very simple, but they're clean and come equipped with refrigerators. Three or four rooms have balconies, and these are the most charming overall—and are the main reason for staying in this hotel, rather than at its neighbor, Godwin (*see above*). Splurge on dinner at popular Palkhi, next door, run by the same management: a Mughlai meal here costs about what your room does. ⊠ *15 Walton Rd. (off Colaba Causeway, near Electric House), Colaba, 400039,* ☎ *22/284–0232 or 22/284-0437,* 𝗙𝗔𝗫 *22/283–4203. 19 rooms. Restaurant, laundry service. AE, MC, V.*

$ ⚏ **Sea Green.** The green trimmings on this five-story building have been weathered by the Arabian Sea (and pollution) over its more than 50 years of hosting guests. Beyond its friendly service, the Sea Green's only virtue is that it's a remarkable bargain for its price and location, if you don't mind the lack of facilities and worn, government-office look. Narrow halls open onto surprisingly large rooms with window air-conditioners and clean but institutional (think 1960s-asylum) furnishings, such as metal wardrobes and turquoise vinyl couches. All rooms but one have small balconies; a few look across Marine Drive to the sea and offer a splendid view of Bombay's famous sea promenade. The bathrooms have only open showers, no stalls or tubs. Room service offers beverages and simple breakfasts only. Don't mistake this place for the hotel's twin, next door—the Sea Green South Hotel, where rooms are a lot less nice. ⊠ *145 Marine Dr., 400020,* ☎ *22/282–2294,* 𝗙𝗔𝗫 *22/283–6158. 34 rooms, 4 suites. Room service, refrigerators AE, DC, MC, V.*

$ ⚏ **Shelley's.** This attractive, old-fashioned hotel has plenty of char-
★ acter and sits right on the waterfront in the shadow of the Gateway of India. Despite the lack of facilities, Shelley's quaintness makes it a memorable place to stay, and the rooms—and especially the bathrooms—are clean. The sea-facing rooms, priced Rs. 300 more (and called suites/apartments) are reserved for extended stays only, but they have grand views of the waterfront, so try to stay in one if you can. The negative point of this otherwise fine hotel is the surly front desk-staff. ⊠ *30 P. J. Ramchandani Marg, Apollo Bunder,* ☎ *22/284–0229,* 𝗙𝗔𝗫 *22/288–1436. 20 rooms 4 suites. Breakfast room, refrigerators. AE.*

NIGHTLIFE AND THE ARTS

The Arts

The best source of arts information is the fortnightly culture calendar "Programme of Dance, Music and Drama," free at the Government of India Tourist Office. The daily *Times of India* newspaper usually lists that day's films, concerts, and other events on the last two or three pages; on Friday, the afternoon paper *Midday* publishes "The List" to highlight the coming week's events. Program information and details usually appear on the MTDC's city-guide programs, shown regularly on hotels' in-house TV stations. The **National Center for the Performing Arts** (NCPA; ✉ Nariman Point, ☎ 22/283–3737, 22/283–3838, or 22/283–4678) posts its performance schedule on the bulletin board at the main entrance and at the entrances to its Tata and Experimental theaters. Note that many NCPA performances are open to members only; a year's membership is Rs. 1,200. Other performance tickets in Bombay are usually very inexpensive (from entirely free to Rs. 360) and can be purchased from box offices or from the ticket counter at **Rhythm House Private Ltd.** (✉ 40 K. Dubash Marg, Rampart Row, ☎ 22/285–3963), near the Jehangir Art Gallery, one of Bombay's main music stores and another source of information on what's happening.

Dance

The **National Center for the Performing Arts** complex (✉ Nariman Point, ☎ 22/283–3737, 22/283–3838, or 22/283–4678) houses the **Godrej Dance Academy Theater**, a main venue for classical Indian dance performances, as well as workshops and master classes, and the **Drama Opera Arts Complex**, a 1,000-seat auditorium is Bombay's ballet and opera theater. The restaurant **Tanjore** (✉ Taj Mahal hotel, ☎ 22/202–3366) doubles as a dance venue, where local performers present a classical Indian dance demonstration (explanations are provided on enquiry) every evening from 8:15 to 8:30, 9 to 9:15, and 9:45 to 10. Confirm exact times with the Taj Mahal concierge.

Film

Bombay, a.k.a. "Bollywood," is the center of the Indian film industry—the largest film producer in the world. Most of the epic Indian musicals shown in movie theaters are in Hindi. Every tourist should take in a Hindi film—full of song, tears, gun battles, and around-the-trees love dances, Indian films provide plenty of tamasha, or spectacle. To catch a Hindi film, your best option is **Metro Cinema** (✉ Metro House, M.G. Rd., ☎ 22/203–0303). **Nehru Centre Auditorium** (✉ Dr. Annie Besant Rd., Worli, ☎ 22/496–4676) in the Worli area sometimes shows interesting art films, some in English. If you're looking around for films, make sure you check listings for the **National Center for the Performing Arts** (✉ Nariman Point, ☎ 22/283–3737, 22/283–3838, or 22/283–4678). The **Regal Cinema** (✉ Shaheed Bhagat Singh Rd., Colaba, opposite Prince of Wales Museum, ☎ 22/202–1017) usually shows current English-language movies. The **Sterling Cinema** (✉ Tata Palace, Murzban Rd., off D. Naoroji Rd., near Victoria Terminus, ☎ 22/207–5187 or 22/207–5189) shows current English-language films.

Music and Theater

The **National Center for the Performing Arts** (NCPA) complex includes the **Tata Theatre**, a grand 1,000-seat auditorium that regularly hosts plays, often in English, and classical concerts by major Indian and international musicians. The **Little Theatre** is the NCPA's smallest, hosting small-scale plays and Western chamber music. The **Experimental Theatre**, with 300 seats, is usually used for avant-garde drama and occasionally for concerts and small-scale dance performances. The **Nehru Centre Auditorium** (✉ Dr. Annie Besant Rd., Worli, ☎ 22/496–4676) is Bombay's second major venue, where theater, music, and dance performances are regularly held. The **Prithvi Theatre** (Janaki Kutir, Church Rd., Juhu, ☎ 22/614–9546), run by the famous Kapoor acting family, stages a variety of plays each week, some in English, with reasonably priced tickets.

Nightlife

Between couples strolling on the breezy promenade around the Gateway of India and fashion-forward twentysomethings dancing at Beyond 1900s, Bombay has what may be the most vibrant nightlife in India. Because of astronomical real-estate prices and bullying by racketeers, however, only a few private groups have opened their own bars or clubs. Quite a few of the nightspots in Bombay proper are in established hotels and restaurants; many of the rest are in wealthy suburbs like Juhu and Bandra, where the after-dark scene thrives on suburbia's young nouveau riche as well as city folk willing to travel for a good night out.

Note that many clubs and bars have "couples" policies, whereby a lone man is not permitted to enter without a woman—a circuitous attempt to prevent brawls, pick-up scenes, and prostitution. To avoid an unpleasant encounter at the door, check with your hotel staff if you are a man traveling alone or in a group of men. Dress nicely (jackets or a tie for men) and you'll probably get in; an advance call from your hotel concierge might also make your entry smoother. Most nightspots, even pubs that would otherwise be conducive to cozy talks over beers, tend to have extremely loud music and are very smoky. If you'd like to converse beyond a few shouts over blaring rock music, opt for the more reserved bars and lounges in hotels.

Revelry peaks from Thursday to Sunday nights, with primarily a late-20s-to-mid-30s crowd—on Sunday. Pubs open at around 7 or 8 (except a few that open in the afternoon) and close by midnight or a little later. Only few remain open longer, depending on current police rules in the area. Some places collect a nominal cover charge at the door. As in any metropolis, the reign of a nightspot can be ephemeral; ask a young hotel employee to brief you on the current scene.

Bars and Lounges

The **Athena** (⊠ 41/44 Minoo Desai Marg, Colaba, near the Fariyas, ☎ 22/202–8699) faces the waterfront. Very austere and sleek, this "champagne cigar lounge" has a postmodern look. The **Bay View Bar** (⊠ The Oberoi, Nariman Point, ☎ 22/232–4343) facing the Arabian Sea, is elegant and more reserved than many of its peers, encouraging a rather expensive cover charge. It has live music and a dance floor. The **Copa Cabana** (⊠ 39D Chowpatty Beach, ☎ 22/368–0274) is a small, Spanish-style tapas bar with an open loft upstairs and a trendy crowd. **Geoffrey's** (⊠ Hotel Marine Plaza, 29 Marine Dr., ☎ 22/285–1212) draws a relatively staid yuppie crowd with golden oldies and a clubby setting. **The Ghetto** (⊠ 30 Bhulabhai Desai Rd., ☎ 22/492–4725) is a psychedelic/rave bar with a fairly grungy clientele, a strange combination of '60s and techno music, and convincingly graffitied walls. It can be fun late in the evening. **The Tavern** (⊠ Fariyas Hotel, Colaba, ☎ 22/204–2911), a friendly, small, dark room with wooden rafters, is open noon to midnight, and has very loud pop and rock music.

Clubs and Discos

Beyond 1900s (⊠ Taj Mahal hotel, Apollo Bunder, ☎ 22/202–3366), intended primarily for Taj Mahal guests, is an upmarket club with a high-tech, Gotham City theme—full of metal girders and waiters dressed like the Joker's henchmen. It's open 8:30 PM–2 AM. **Cyclone** (⊠ The Leela, Sahar, ☎ 22/691–1234), which admits only hotel guests, members, and invitees, nearly outdoes every disco in town with its flashing electronic gadgetry, sophisticated sound system, and posh decor. Ask your concierge for help getting in. **Fire and Ice** (⊠ Phoenix Mills Compound, 462 Senapati Bapat Marg, Lower Parel ☎ 22/498–0444) is Bombay's newest and biggest club, with room for 100 dancers. **J-49** (✉ Juhu Residency, Juhu Tara Rd., ☎ 22/618–4546) is the hottest disco in the 'burbs. One wonders why, as it's small and has little in the way of decor, but it packs in rockers of all ages, even on weekdays. **Not Just Jazz By The Bay** (✉ 143 Marine Dr., ☎ 22/285–1876 or 22/282–0957) is one of Bombay's few jazz venues, with live music several nights a week. Its location by the sea is beautiful. It serves a buffet lunch, and it stays open until 12:30 AM. At **Razzberry Rhinoceros** (✉ Juhu Hotel, Juhu Tara Rd., Juhu Beach, ☎ 22/618–4012) the feel is young and casual, the look rustic, and the music loud rock, pop, or jazz.

SPORTS AND OUTDOOR ACTIVITIES

Billiards and Bowling

Bowling and pool have captured the imagination of Bombay folks in a big way. Hundreds of pool parlors have sprung up in the last few years, and the city's few bowling alleys are doing a brisk business. **The Bowling Company** (✉ Phoenix Mills Compound, 462 Senapati Bapat Marg, Lower Parel, ☎ 22/491–5677, 22/491–4000) is the fanciest alley in town, with 20 lanes. It's open daily, noon to midnight. Fees are Rs. 80–Rs. 150 per game depending on the day of the week. The Bowling Company also has six pool tables, for which it charges Rs. 60 per frame. Its café serves drinks, coffees, and exotic desserts to live jazz. **Buddy's** (✉ Jyoti Studio, next to Kennedy Bridge, near Nana Chowk, ☎ 22/387–5495) has four lanes, for which it charges Rs. 130 per game, and eight pool tables, for which it charges Rs. 50 per frame. There's a Rs. 50 cover charge on weekends and holidays. Buddy's is open daily, noon to midnight. **Superdrome** (✉ Film Centre Building, Tardeo, ☎ 22/491–2313) has four lanes and charges Rs. 80–Rs. 150 per game, depending on the day of the week. For use of one of the eight pool tables, you'll pay Rs. 80 per frame. Superdrome also has a video arcade and a snack bar; they serve Pan-Asian food. It's open daily, noon to midnight.

Cricket

Wankhede Stadium (✉ D. Rd., Churchgate) hosts Bombay's major domestic and international cricket matches. In season—October through March—there are usually several matches a week. You can buy tickets, which range in price from Rs. 150 to Rs. 5,000, through the **Bombay Cricket Association** (✉ D. Rd., Churchgate, ☎ 22/281–9910, 22/281–2714).

Golf

The **Willingdon Sports Club** (✉ K. Khadye Marg, ☎ 22/494–5754) has an 18-hole golf course. Nonmembers can usually play as "guests" of the secretary for $77 per week. Call ahead to make arrangements.

Horse-and-Buggy Rides

For a quick tour of Bombay's illuminated sights by night, hop in one of the horse-drawn buggies parked at Nariman Point, next to the Oberoi Towers, at the northern end of Marine Drive, or at the Gateway of India. Neither the carriages nor the horses are in particularly good shape, let alone elegant, but if you don't require luxury this can be an enjoyable jaunt. A spin from the Gateway of India to Churchgate and back, taking in key sights on the way, takes about an hour and should cost less than Rs. 150 (settle the price ahead of time).

Horse Racing

Bombay's **Mahalaxmi Race Course** (✉ Mahalaxmi, near Nehru Planetarium, ☎ 22/307–1401) is one of the finest courses in the East. A visit here in season is a social experience: for a few months each year, this green patch in central Bombay becomes Ascot in the 1950s, with faux British accents and outfits to kill. The season usually runs from November through April, with races on Thursdays and Sundays.

Sailing

Members of any yachting association affiliated with the **Royal Bombay Yacht Club** (⊠ Apollo Bunder, Bombay 400039, ☎ 22/202–1880) can charter a boat for local sailing, October to June. The club also offers visiting memberships for a reasonable Rs. 450.

SHOPPING

From crowded street bazaars to exclusive air-conditioned boutiques, Bombay can keep the enthusiastic shopper riveted for days. Colaba Causeway, Flora Fountain, Kemps Corner, and Breach Candy are all trendy shopping areas; the latter two are chic and pricey. The air-conditioned World Trade Center on Cuffe Parade, at the southern tip of Bombay, looks discouraging from the outside but houses a useful cluster of government-run emporiums with fixed-price crafts from all over India. Crossroads is Bombay's newest mall, and a swanky one at that: it's unusually spacious and attractive, and is open daily. India's most fashionable clothing labels have stores here, and the rest of the 130 shops sell everything from napkins to videos. The arcades in top hotels—those at the Oberoi, Oberoi Towers, and Taj Mahal are particularly good—offer a little bit of everything for a lot more money than anywhere else, but the merchandise is beautiful and the atmosphere unhurried and climate-controlled. For lower prices and a more vibrant atmosphere, throw yourself into the middle of one of Bombay's famous bazaars.

Once you've exhausted Bombay proper, you can venture out to the suburbs, where prices can be lower. Linking Road in Bandra is a trendy place to shop, and Juhu's main strip, Juhu Tara Road, is lined with trendy new boutiques, shops, art galleries, and restaurants. Note that each neighborhood has a different closing day for shops. In Colaba, up to Worli, shops are closed Sunday; in Worli, up to Bandra, they're closed Monday; and in Bandra, up to the suburbs, they're closed Thursday. Throughout Bombay, many shops are closed on Sunday.

Bazaars and Markets

Chor Bazaar (⊠ Mutton St. near Kutbi Masjid) is a bustling flea market where you can find exactly what you don't need but have to have—old phonographs, broken nautical instruments, dusty chandeliers, furniture, and brass objects ranging from junky knickknacks to valuable antiques and curios. Keep an eye on your purse or wallet and come relaxed—it can be chaotic. **Fashion Street** (⊠ M. G. Rd. opposite Bombay Gymkhana) is a cotton bargain trove set in a row of open-air stalls, with mounds of colorful, cheap, mainly Western clothing for all ages. Come around 11 AM, when the crowds are thinner and the sun has not yet peaked—and bargain. **Zaveri Bazaar** (⊠ Near V. Vallabh Chowk) is the place to go for diamond, gold, and silver *zevar* (jewelry). The tumultuous streets are lined with tiny, decades-old family jewelry businesses. Duck into one and sip a customary cup of tea or coffee while a salesperson shows you the merchandise. Most shops are authentic, but beware of false silver and gold; it's difficult to spot.

Art and Antiques

The **Jehangir Art Gallery** (⊠ Kala Ghoda, Fort, ☎ 22/284–3989) has at least three art shows every week, either on the main floor or at the **Gallery Chemould** (☎ 22/283–3640) or even on the pavement racks outside in fair weather. Prices vary vastly. **Natesans Antiquarts Ltd.**

(✉ Basement of Jehangir Art Gallery, Fort, ☎ 22/285–2700; Taj Mahal hotel, ☎ 22/202–4165), which has branches in many Indian cities, sells magnificent but expensive curios, subcontinental antiquities, wood carvings, sculptures, and paintings. **Phillips Antiques** (✉ Madam Cama Rd., opposite Regal Cinema, ☎ 22/202–0564) has the best choice of old prints, engravings, and maps in Bombay. Phillips also sells many possessions left behind by the British—Staffordshire and East India Company china, old jewelry, crystal, lacquerware, and sterling silver. **The Raj Company** (✉ Volga House, opposite the turf club, near Mahalaxmi suburban railway station, ☎ 22/494–1971) sells colonial furniture and faithful reproductions.

Books

Most large hotels have small bookshops, but Bombay's best selection is at **Crossword** (✉ Mahalaxmi Chambers, Bhulabhai Desai Rd., Breach Candy, near Mahalakshmi temple, ☎ 22/498–5801, 22/498–5802 or 22/498–5803), probably the largest bookstore in Bombay and a comfortable place to browse. **Danai** (✉ Khar Danda Rd., Khar, ☎ 22/648–7123) is the largest suburban bookstore and also sells CDs and cassettes. **Nalanda** (✉ Taj Mahal hotel, ☎ 22/202–2514), open until midnight, has plenty of books on India, including travel guides and fiction, and the latest foreign papers. The **Strand Book Stall** (✉ Dhannur Sir P. M. Rd., Fort, ☎ 22/266–1994, 22/266–1719, or 22/261–4613) offers good discounts. The sidewalk book market on **Veer Nariman Road,** opposite Flora Fountain (near the Central Telegraph office) and toward Victoria Terminus, is a great source for secondhand books. You can score some rare finds here—bargain.

Carpets

The **Central Cottage Industries Emporium** (✉ Apollo Bunder, Colaba, ☎ 22/202–6564, 22/202–7537) stocks an excellent selection of traditional Kashmiri carpets at reliable prices. **CIE** (✉ Electric House, Colaba, ☎ 22/281–8802) has a very large variety of Indian crafts from carpets to bronze art pieces and what not. Prices are very steep. **Coir Board** (✉ 5 Stadium House, Veer Nariman Rd., Churchgate, ☎ 22/282–1575) has cheap jute and coir matting. There are several Kashmiri-run carpet shops in **The Oberoi** (✉ Nariman Point, ☎ 22/232–5757). On **Colaba Causeway** (between Regal Cinema and Cusrow Baug, and on lanes leading off the causeway), you'll find lots of carpet stores. You may find a genuine, well-priced carpet in any of these shops, but you're on your own vis-a-vis unscrupulous shopkeepers. A carpet's mix of silk, wool, and cotton has a lot to do with its price; visit several shops, including the government emporiums, to get a sense of the market before cutting a deal in an independent shop. A small, fixed-price outlet for the well-known brand **Shyam Ahuja** (✉ Crossroads, 3rd floor, 28 Pandit M. M. Malviya Rd., opposite Haji Ali, ☎ 22/460–3075, 22/460–3077; ✉ C Wing, Gazdar Apartments, Juhu Tara Rd., Juhu, ☎ 22/615–2140, 22/615–1749) has cotton dhurries and wool carpets.

Children's Clothing and Toys

Bombay Store (✉ Sir Pherozeshah Mehta Rd., Fort, ☎ 22/288–5048, 22/287–3443) has a range of cottons for children. The **Central Cottage Industries Emporium** (✉ Apollo Bunder, Colaba, ☎ 22/202–7537, 22/202–6564) has a small but imaginative assortment of Indian costumes for kids and traditional Indian toys. Mirror-work elephants, Indian dolls, wood and cane doll furniture, tiny brass tea sets, stuffed leather animals, and puppets can all be found on the second floor, as can *kurtas* (collarless or band-collar shirts) and long skirt ensembles in cotton and silk. **Colaba Causeway** is lined with pavement stalls selling various children's trinkets—leather animals, small drums, beads, peacock-feather fans. A number of shops here also sell Indian clothing for kids. **Fab India** (⊠ Navroze Apartments, Pali Hill, near HDFC bank, Bandra, ☎ 22/605–7780) sells cotton clothing for children. **Piramyd** (⊠ Crossroads, 28, Pt M M Malviya road, Haji Ali., ☎ 22/494–5890, 494–5891) has some of India's best cottons for kids.

Several shops in the **Oberoi Towers** sell Indian children's clothes, cool cotton dresses, and wooden dolls.

Clothing

Anokhi (⊠ opposite Cumballa Hill Hospital, Kemps Corner, ☎ 22/383–0639, 22/382–0636) has colourful clothes with block printing designs from Rajasthan. The large, attractive, and friendly **Bombay Store** (⊠ Sir Pherozeshah Mehta Rd., Fort, ☎ 22/288–5048, 22/287–3443) has a good-size selection of men's shirts, kurtas, ties, women's *salwar kameez* (a loose-fitting tunic over loose pants tapered at the ankle), blouses, skirts, shawls, saris, silk by the meter, and cotton clothes for children. **Charagh Din** (⊠ 64 and 81 Wodehouse Rd., Colaba, ☎ 22/218–1375) is one of the best-known Indian names for top-quality, pure silk shirts for men in a tremendous variety of styles and patterns. **Christina** (⊠ The Oberoi, ☎ 22/282–5069) is a tiny, classy boutique with exquisite silk blouses and shirts, scarves, ties, *dupattas* (long, thin scarves for draping), and silk-edged purses and wallets. **Cotton World** (⊠ Ram Nimi, Mandlik Rd., Colaba, ☎ 22/285–0060, 22/283–3294; ⊠ Vipul Apartments, near Podar High School, Tagore Rd., Santa Cruz, ☎ 22/605–1602) is small but has some excellent Western cotton items at reasonable prices.

Ensemble (⊠ Great Western Building, 130/132 Shahid Bhagat Singh Marg, ☎ 22/284–3227, 22/287–2882; ⊠ 2nd floor, Crossroads, ☎ 22/495–5064, 22/495–5164), a pricey boutique not far from the Taj Mahal hotel, has exclusive men's and women's Indian and Western fashions, and lovely costume jewelry, all by high-profile Indian designers. Ask to see the rare Banarasi silk saris, in rich colors woven with real gold and silver thread. The second outlet at Crossroads stocks more casuals. **Fab India** (⊠ Navroze Apartments, Pali Hill, near HDFC bank, Bandra, ☎ 22/605–7780) is good for cotton clothing tailored from vegetable-dye prints—skirts, blouses and kurtas for men and women. The Bombay branch of the famous Madras store **Nalli** (⊠ Trimurti Apartments, Bhulabhai Desai Rd., Breach Candy, ☎ 22/496–5577, 22/496–5599), one of the largest sari stores in India, has a fair selection of classic silk saris. Have a look at the authentic *zari* Kanchipuram saris (gold-embroidered borders), the Bangalore saris, and the uncut silk, sold by the meter.

Go to **Piramyd** (⊠ Crossroads, 28, Pt Madan Mohan Malviya road, Haji Ali., ☎ 22/494–5890, 494–5891) for a wide selection of Indian and Western clothes for men and women, some of it quite reasonable, as well as designer labels. **Ravissant** (⊠ Kemps Corner, ☎ 22/368–4934) was India's first haute-couture salon; it sells its own women's and men's clothing in exquisite patterns and fabrics, from rich silks to feather-light moiré. The branch in the Taj Mahal hotel (☎ 22/281–5227) also sells unique silver housewares and furnishings. A few shops in the **Taj Mahal** sell quality silks; try Burlington or the Indian Textiles Company. **Vama** (⊠ 72 Peddar Rd., ☎ 22/387–1450) looks like just another Benetton or Lacoste outlet, but it also has gorgeous, high-fashion Indian women's and men's wear, and the nearly sacred Paithani saris—handwoven silk with real gold and silver thread.

Handicrafts

Anokhi (⊠ opposite Cumballa Hill Hospital, Kemps Corner, ☎ 22/383–0639, 22/3820636) has colorful tablecloths, cushion covers, and more, decorated with atttractive block printing designs from Rajasthan. **Aurocraft** (⌧ Swami Vivekanand Rd., Bandra) sells crafts made at the Auroville commune in Pondicherry, including crocheted shoes, earrings, pottery, and toys. **The Bombay Store** (⌧ Sir Pherozeshah Mehta Rd., Fort, ☎ 22/288–5048, 22/287–3443) has a classy collection of popular Indian handicrafts—metal work, sandalwood, china, marble, carpets, linens, and lamps. Prices are a tad higher here than at the government emporiums, but the store is enticingly laid out and service is competent. The **Central Cottage Industries Emporium** (⌧ Apollo Bunder, Colaba, ☎ 22/202–7537, 22/202–6564) is packed with textiles, carvings, and myriad other traditional Indian handicrafts from all over the country. It's a wonderful place to buy souvenirs, despite less-than-brilliant service. **Contemporary Arts and Crafts** (⌧ 19 Nepean Sea Rd., opposite Baskin-Robbins, ☎ 22/363–1979; ⌧ Juhu Vile Parle Shopping Centre, Gul Mohar Rd., Juhu, ☎ 22/620–4668) has a small but nicely representative selection of Indian handicrafts at reasonable prices. Go to **Fab India** (⌧ Noble House, junction of Khar Danda and 18th Rd., Khar, ☎ 22/605–7780) for vegetable-dye print tablecloths and linen. **Mrignaynee** (⌧ World Trade Center, Cuffe Parade, Colaba, ☎ 22/218–9191) sells statues and clothing from the state of Madhya Pradesh. If you won't be traveling farther south, peruse regal Mysore silks at **Mysore Sales International** (☎ 22/218–4952). Browse Maharashtra's own crafts and an outstanding collection of statues, sculptures, and idols at **Trimourti** (☎ 22/218–9191 Ext. 278). The **World Trade Center** (⌧ Cuffe Parade, Colaba, ☎ 22/218–9191) gathers government-run handicrafts emporiums and boutiques from most of India's states under one air-conditioned roof. Fixed prices offer respite from bazaar-style haggling. **OMO** (⌧ Kaypee Mansions, 84, 29th Rd., Bandra West, ☎ 22/642–9110) has attractive home furnishings. **Tresorie** (⌧ 60A Linking Rd., Santa Cruz West., ☎ 22/661–2041, 22/661–2042) sells expensive but tasteful knick knacks for the home. **Yamini** (⌧ President House, Wodehouse Rd., Colaba., ☎ 22/218–4143, 22/218–4145) sells a wide variety of home furnishings, and fabrics for the home—sold by the metre.

Incense and Perfumes

Ajmal (⌧ 4/13 Kamal Mansion, Arthur Bunder Rd., Fort, ☎ 22/285–6976) has a wonderful selection of rare Indian and French perfumes stored in huge decanters. It also stocks *agar* wood, a rare incense base, 1000 grams of which costs as much as a night at the Taj Mahal hotel.

Jewelry

In business since 1865, the venerable **Tribhovandas Bhimji Zaveri** (⌧ 241–43 Zaveri Bazaar, ☎ 22/342–5001) is said to be the largest jewelry showroom in India, with five floors of gorgeous 18-, 22-, and 24-karat gold, diamond, and silver jewelry. It's *much* more cost-effective, however, to buy from a smaller outfit, such as Narandas and Sons, Zaveri Naran Das, or Ram Kewalram Popley, all on Sheikh Memon Street. Insist on knowing how many karats you're buying and whether or not the store will stand by the piece's purity. For silver jewelry, try **The Bombay Store** (⌧ Sir Pherozeshah Mehta Rd., Fort, ☎ 22/288–5048, 22/287–3443). Bargain hunters looking for silver jewelery should head for the heart of **Colaba Bazaar,** a little south of the Taj Mahal hotel, where a series of tiny jewelry shops sells rings, earrings, necklaces, and more. Haggling is a must here. If you prefer calm, air-conditioned excursions, look for silver jewelry in the arcade at **The Oberoi.**

Leather and Shoes

Brave bargain-hunters should take an adventurous trip to **Daboo Street** (off Mohammed Ali Rd., a five-minute walk from Chor Bazaar, near Shalimar Hotel) for leather goods and shoes. The posh shopping arcade at **The Oberoi** includes a variety of leather and shoe shops whose stylish goods are still priced lower than they would be in the West.

Tailoring

A number of Bombay tailors can turn splendid fabric into custom-made clothing—Indian or Western—in a matter of hours. **Kala Pushp** (✉ Oberoi Towers shopping arcade, 2nd floor, ☏ 22/232–5757, ask the Oberoi operator to connect you) has a tailoring department for both ladies and gents, ready to make suits, trousers, shirts, and even complicated women's ensembles in a very short time. Armed with the latest catalogs from Europe, these tailors will faithfully copy a design from a picture. Bring fabric from elsewhere or choose from the store's own assortment. **Narisons Khubsons** (✉ 49 Colaba Causeway, opposite the police station, ☏ 22/202–0614) carries fine cotton and silk and can make excellent shirts, trousers, or women's outfits in one day if need be. They also sell ready-made women's clothing. There are two shops named Khubsons, back to back; make sure you have the right one. **Raymond** (✉ Bhulabhai Desai Rd., Breach Candy, opposite Breach Candy Hospital and Research Centre, ☏ 22/368–2644) is an outlet for Raymond Mills, which makes some of India's finest men's suits. They can tailor a first-rate suit for about Rs. 3,500 in two days to a week. Call ahead to ask about delivery time; during the wedding season (winter) they can get very busy.

PUNE

This hill station in the Sahyadris at 1,973 ft and just three hours southeast of Bombay, is a delightful town. Pune is also Maharashtra's second-largest city—with 2.8 million people—and its proximity to Bombay has made Pune quite a cosmopolitan and happening place. There are new restaurants, stores, pubs, and hotels opening all the time. The hottest fast-food chains and stores have their outlets in Pune. And Bombay wannabes keep the pubs rocking.

Despite its modernity, Pune remains a cantonment town with turn of the century Raj touches—languid grace, fancy bungalows, wide boulevards, and some interesting architecture. At 1 PM much of the city halts for a lunch break and a siesta. Markets and shops down their shutters until 4 in deference to Lord Somnus. The Indian army still has a major presence in Pune.

Also a conservative Maharashtrian town, Pune is steeped in Marathi culture. The older parts of the city—the *peths* (bazaars), *wadas* (homes) and Ganesh temples—are deeply Maharashtrian. You'll find in Pune and nearby areas Peshwa palaces and Maratha forts. This was the fierce, medieval Maratha warrior Shivaji's backyard, and his legendary battles with Mughal conquerors took place in this neighborhood. Lip-smacking Maharashtrian delicacies—like *puran poli* (sweet lentil-stuffed pancakes), *shrikhand* (sweet yogurt), *batata wada* (potato savory), *zunkhar bakri* (millet bread with spicy lentils)—are widely available. Nowhere is Ganesh Chaturthi, the biggest festival of the state—a 10-day event in August and September that honors the elephant god Ganpati—celebrated with more joy and *dhoom dham* (pomp) than in Pune.

In the past two decades, Pune has become more international. Bhagwan Rajneesh, a.k.a. "Osho, the captivating godman", who some call a sex guru, fled his commune in Oregon to set up shop here in 1985. His charisma was such that with him came a giant band of Western followers, who settled in Pune. Osho died 12 years ago, but in spite of a host of *masala*, or salacious, controversies that dog the commune, it continues to thrive—and draws hordes of let-it-all-hang-out Westerners. As a result, an entire upscale neighbourhood of Pune is inhabited by maroon-clad spacey foreigners seeking a new twist to their life. This has spawned an entire Osho tourist district where everything from German bread to New Age meditation tunes to Kathmandu trinkets is available.

Exploring Pune

Most of the sights in Pune are far flung, so you'd be wise to hire the services of an autorickshaw (the local three-wheeler) or a car to explore the town. To experience the staunchly Maharashtrian quarters of the city, head to **Shaniwarwada Palace** in the heart of the old city. The palace, actually, no longer exists. Tall ramparts and imposing, two-story-high teak gates, lined with enough spikes to ward off an army of elephants, front an empty courtyard, once home to the once beyond-your-wildest-imagination Shaniwarwada Palace. Built in the 18th century by the Maratha king Baji Rao I, the palace was decimated less than a hundred years later, in 1827. The premises aren't well-maintained, but the atmosphere helps conjure images of the extravagant kingdom the Peshwas once ruled. The view from the ramparts of the palace gates is intriguing. Rocky outcrops (once foundation stones) set in endless lawns are the only remnants of this seven-story royal residence that once was famous, near and far, for its Shish Mahal (glass house), *hamam* (palace bathroom), and Mastani Mahal (dancers' wing). The Palace of Music, known as the Nagarakhana, still survives. The Maharashtra Tourism board holds a sound and light show (daily except Tuesdays) at the palace, on the history of the Peshwas and Shivaji. The show takes place between 8:30 and 9:30; tickets are available on the premises for Rs. 25 per head. ✉ *Shaniwarwada, Bajirao Rd., Kasba Peth,* ▦ *Rs. 5.* ☾ *Daily 8:30 to 6.*

The little lanes leading away from the palace are narrow and populated with small temples, old homes, and vendors hawking their goods. Make sure you dive into some of these side lanes to sample typical *peth* life. (The older, non-cantonment sections of Pune were divided into *peths*, or areas, and named after the days of the week.) On your exit from the palace if you take a sharp right you'll arrive at a *chowk* or cross roads. If you continue walking and pass two more crossroads you will be at **Shrimant Dagdu Sheth Halwai Ganpati Mandir.** This temple is a simple construction—essentially an idol under a roof, in an open-air shed—and worship proceedings are visible right from the road. The idol is cherished not just by locals but by all Maharashtrians. Dagdu Sheth was a *halwai*, or sweetmeat maker. He was also a good friend of Lokmanya Bal Gangadhar Tilak, a key figure in India's indpendence movement in the late 1800s. When Tilak gave the call for public or community celebrations of Ganesh Chaturthi (the state's biggest festival, held in late summer in honor of the elephant god) to disconcert the British rulers, this *halwai* was the first to institute a kind of "block" celebration of the festival in 1893. Unlike other idols of the elephant god, which are immersed in the river/ocean after Ganesh Chaturthi festivities are over, the Dagu Sheth Halwai Ganpati (Ganesh) stays on, and over the years has been lavished with affection and prayers. Much of the idol has been embellished with gold by grateful devotees—solid-gold ears (a gift from a film star), as well as 8 kilos of gold decorate his garments. Visit this temple in the evening, around 8:30, if you want to be around when locals worship.

About 10 minutes away, on foot from Dagdu Sheth Halwai Ganpati, is the **Raja Dinkar Kelkar Museum.** This celebrated museum in the old city houses some 2,000 carefully catalogued daily utensils and objets d'art of metal, wood, stone, and earthenware from the remotest corners of India (18,000 items are still in storage). The range of items, accumulated over 60 years, is bewildering. The artifacts are illustrative of everyday life: coconut meat scrapers, *hookahs* (a steam-operated smoking pipe), pots, and water containers to musical instruments, toys, lamps, locks, and ornate implements. None are heirlooms or possessions of the wealthy, but they nevertheless adequately reflect Indian culture and history.

The household tools have been chosen on the basis of their utility and for their unusual form or design. The Chitrakathi paintings from Paithan, Maharashtra, are intriguing, as is the large Vanita Kaksha, or lady's parlor, devoted to personal and domestic objects women used. Equally fascinating is the miniature replica of the Mastani Mahal, at the Shaniwarwada Palace, where Mastani, Baji Rao I's kept woman, lived. Do check out the poison testing lamp, a design that dates back to the Peshwa era, that was used to check for poisoned food. This collection was put together by a well-traveled Maharashtrian and award-winning poet, Adnyatwasi, a.k.a. Dr. Dinkar Gangadhar Kelkar, who was a devoted collector of art, and his wife Kamlabai. Late in life, Kelkar donated his collection of artifacts to the government for a museum in memory of his son Raja. The museum is housed in one of those atmospheric rambling *peth wadas* or bungalow-courtyard complexes—Kelkar's own home—near Shaniwarwada Palace. If you have time, chat with Surendra Ranade, the grandson who runs the museum. He'll tell you all about the amazing poet, who was once offered a blank check for his collection by another collector, but refused. ⊠ *1377–78, Natu Baug, off Bajirao Rd., Shukawar Peth,* ☎ *20/448–2101.* ☎ *$2.50.* ☉ *8:30 to 5:30 daily except Jan 26, Aug 1, and Aug 15.*

An air of secrecy and silence shrouds the **Osho Commune International** (OCI). The exterior of the ashram's buildings is well-concealed by bamboo copses and tall walls. Started by the Osho godman/sex guru, OCI was once described by a *Washington Post* correspondent as a cross between a college campus, Disney Land, and a resort. Lavishly constructed from white and black marble, and spread across 40 acres, the commune has wonderful greenery, as well as cafés, shops, a pool, and zennis (Zen tennis) courts. Ashram members say it has the largest meditation hall in the world.

The ashram, or "Multiversity," offers meditation and self-knowledge courses of all varieties (variety being the operational word here). The Osho had no use for organized religion. He believed personal religion should be relatively painless—happy, not ascetic. The commune, run by more than 500 disciples, attracts rootless folks from all over—mainly Germans, Americans, and the Japanese. For a fee, these disciples chill out, spring clean their souls, and improve their morale.

You can take a very limited guided tour to see OCI's grounds. A day-long meditation workshop, after you complete the compulsory HIV test, will set you back $50. Another reason to come is to visit the nearby neighborhood, full of interesting shops and watering holes. You'll find hawkers selling Tibetan artifacts, Kashmiri crafts, jewelery, and cotton clothing nearby. The tea houses and restaurants are packed out with Osho-ites. Do visit the German Bakery for a flavor of this strange world. The ashram, in Koregaon Park, is across town, 4 km (2½ mi) east and slightly north of the Shaniwarwada area. For the general public, the ashram is only open during tour hours. ⊠ *17 Koregaon Park,* ☎ *20/401–9999.* ☎ *Morning tour: 10:30 to 11. Afternoon tour: 2:30 to 3:30. Tickets need to be purchased one day before for Rs. 10 per head. Ticket window open 9:30–1 and 2–4. Children under 15 not permitted. No smoking, drugs, or photographs.*

NEED A
BREAK?

Park yourself at one of the wooden benches at the **German Bakery,** suck down a banana *lassi* (yogurt drink), and eavesdrop on the maroon robes (commune members) talking about the arcane. You can also get tasty and fresh breads, herbal tea, pizza, salads, lasagne, and lemon cake. ⊠ *291 Vaswani Nagar, Koregaon Park,* ☎ *20/613–6532.*

After visiting OCI in Koregaon Park, head to the charming, tiny shrine **Shinde Chhatri** (also called Shindechi Chhatri; a *chhatri* is a cenotaph or a monument to someone dead and revered). From Koregaon Park, go past the civil lines (non-army areas) and the British landmarks, and right through the old-style cantonment or Camp area. That journey will give you a feel of the old British cantonment Pune. The *chhatri*, with its striking gold embossed roof, is the Hindu "chapel" of the Scindias, a famous royal family who once ruled Gwalior in Central India and who today are a political dynasty. The *chhatri* is a monument to one of the more famous Shindes (from whom the Scindias descended)— Mahadji Shinde, the commander of the Peshwa army. Give the gate-keeper a small something and he may allow you in to see the intriguing inner sanctum. Incidentally, one of their lesser palaces is located across the street. ⊠ *off Prince of Wales Dr., Wanowrie, near Clover Apartments, 2 km from the race course,* ☉ *Daylight.*

Dining and Lodging

Pune offers a wide variety of reasonably priced restaurants. Here you can get Mughlai, Chinese, Thai, and Italian food. Dining options range from posh restaurants serving elaborate meals to fast-food chains— Dosa Diner at Jungli Maharaj Road (20/553–2443), McDonald's, Domino's, and Baskin-Robbins all have branches here. If you're brave, head to Jungli Maharaj Road, where all types of Indian snack and junk food—*pav bhajee, sev uri, batata wada, idlis*—are available hot and fresh off the griddle. Nearby Vaishali (20/553–1244), a modest dosa, or Udipi, joint at Fergussen College, draws crowds for its *dosas.*

Pune, which is slowly becoming the destination for the business traveller, has its fair share of hotels. The city now has three luxury hotels and a number of business hotels. Luxury hotel prices are steep, but not as high as the prices in the larger cities. If you are making your booking directly, ask for a discount. A variety of accommodation geared to tourists has always been available in the Koregaon Park area. Quite a few more-than-adequate rooms, marginally cheaper than those listed below, can be found in this neighbourhood. Such deals and tariffs are available for long-term stays, and can be made on the spot. Try contacting **Escape Getaways** (☎ FAX 20/605–2577), a Koregaon-based travel agent, for long-term stays.

$$ ✕ **Spice Island.** This restaurant at Pune's top five-star hotel is Pune's fanciest restaurant. Dining here is an extravagant affair—the restaurant is decorated with East Asian paintings and touches of gold. Tasty and innovative Thai and Chinese food are served. Try the corn cakes, stir-fried tiger prawns, prawn cakes, and the warm five-spice chicken salad. ⊠ *Raja Bahadur Mill (RBM) Rd., near the main railway station,* ☎ *20/605–0505. Reservations essential. Jacket and tie.* AE, DC, MC, V.

$ ✕ **Arthur's Theme.** A cozy, small restaurant with wood highlights and a casual, simple setting, Arthur's Theme serves some of the best Continental food in Pune. The lightly cooked, mildly spiced entrées have oddball names. Alexander the Great, Marquis de Sade, and Marie Curie may be a trio of Europeans but it also indicates a meal of, respectively, French onion soup, baked fish, and chicken in mushroom sauce. There are plenty of pastas, fine desserts (try the tiramisu or lemon soufflé), and other dishes, including cheese croquettes, stuffed chicken roulade, and grilled kingfish. ⊠ *Vrindavan Apartments, North Main Rd., Koregoan Park,* ☎ *20/613–2710. DC, MC, V.*

$ ✕ Blue Nile. Decoration in this popular Pune non-vegetarian restaurant is zilch. But the ambience is of a 40-year-old Muslim eating house with high ceilings and faded charm. In any case, the ambience or decor is not what brings the clientele. The excellent *biryani* does. Blue Nile offers both chicken and mutton *biryani*—spicy meat simmered with rice for many hours. A plate of *biryani* will set you back by just Rs 70. No need to try the veg food, this is a carnivore's paradise. No liquor is served. ⊠ *4 Bund Rd.,* ☎ *20/612–5238. No credit cards.*

$ ✕ The Chinese Room. Owned by the old and popular Kwality chain, the posh, granite-and-glass Chinese Room is the place to go for Indian Chinese, the particular type of Chinese food in currency in India—food that leans heavily on cilantro, spices, and hot peppers. Try the sesame chicken, house specialty chicken *saiwoo* (chicken slices in a spicy sauce), sesame prawns, three treasure vegetable *hunani*, or the coconut pancakes. ⊠ *2434 East St.,* ☎ *20/613–1336. AE, DC, MC, V.*

$ ✕ Coffee House. This established vegetarian restaurant has gone upscale. Wood accents, plants (plastic), and busy upholstery have contributed to its swanky new atmosphere. The total effect is pleasing to the eye. This multi-cuisine restaurant serves Chinese, Mughlai, and South Indian food for lunch or dinner, but a South Indian breakfast with coffee is your best bet. Recommended: crispy dosas, *uttapams* (spiced pancakes), and vegetable biryani are good choices. ⊠ *2 Moledina Rd., Pune Camp,* ☎ *20/613–8275. AE, DC, MC, V.*

$ ✕ Hot Breads Bakers and Confectioners. Indian pastries and baked items here are often startlingly good, because they are fresh and made from scratch. Satisfy your sweet tooth on luscious strawberry tarts, rich mousses, and mousse cakes. Equally good are the salty foods—quiche, chicken rolls, pizza slices, and stuffed croissants. Soups and salads are served for lunch from 12:30 to 4. The café, which remains open till 11 pm, has a cozy atmosphere, a young clientele, and a picture window that overlooks the leafy Koregaon Park neighborhood. ⊠ *Gera Sterling, North Main Rd., Koregaon Park,* ☎ *20/613–3757, 20/605–4307. MC, V.*

$ ✕ Malaka Spice. This simple but cheerful restaurant has orange walls and black tables, and the focus is the art (for sale) that hangs on the wall. Several tables have also been set up on the porch outside. The menu includes entrées and starters from places all over Asia—Vietnam, Indonesia, China, Thailand, Japan, Malaysia, and Korea. The place is managed by a husband-wife duo, Cheeru and Praful Chandawarkar. The *pad thai* is crunchy and tasty. Try chicken in *pandan* leaves or Singaporean *laksa* soup (noodles, prawns, chicken, bean sprouts. Finish up with the "half moons with ice cream"—the half moons resemble fortune cookies and are stuffed with honey and bananas. The restaurant serves beer. *Vrindavan Apartments, North Main Rd., Koregoan Park,* ☎ *20/613–6293, 20/614–1088. DC, MC, V.*

$ ✕ Nandu's. Leave your bow ties and high heels at home, roll up your sleeves, and prepare for some typical *desi* dining. Nandu's is not your conventional restaurant. This small vegetarian eatery's USP (unique selling point) is the fat, sizzling, vegetable-stuffed *parathas* (stuffed and griddle-fried whole wheat pancakes) they serve with yogurt and a dollop of butter. Stuffings range from peas, cauliflower, potatoes, onion, and fenugreek to cottage cheese. The corn and *bajra rotis* are also worth a try. Nandu's offers a variety of other Punjabi dishes, but you should definitely opt for the *parathas*. The shady outside seating offers a pleasant enough atmosphere to chomp down the divine food. Come either for lunch or for an early dinner—hungry locals pack the place by 9. No liquor is served. ⊠ *Damodar Narain Dhole Patil Market, Dhole Patil Rd.,* ☎ *20/634–728. No credit cards.*

$ ✕ **Sanskruti.** Head out to this "cultural garden restaurant," 15 km (9 mi) away—at Loni Kalbhor on the Sholapur highway. The restaurant spans 4 acres of green lawns dotted with stalls serving up to 22 North Indian snack foods per day and typical Indian *mela* (fairground) attractions—astrologers, a pottery wheel, magicians, Hindi film singing, bangle makers, *ghazal* singers, swings, and Rajasthani dancers. When the starters and thrills are done, indulge a sumptuous Rajasthani and Gujarati 16-item *thali* (unlimited servings). Sanskruti is a distance from Pune proper, so call in advance. ⊠ *Sholapur Highway,* ☎ *22/757–6557 or 22/757–4556 in Bombay (the restaurant has no phone) or 982/106–1742 mobile. No credit cards. No. lunch Fri. and Mon.–Wed.*

$$$ ☷ **Holiday Inn.** Glass elevators take you up and away from the shiny black granite-finished lobby. Of the luxury hotels in Pune, however, this is probably the least appealing. The rooms are overpriced, mildly musty and small compared to what the chain offers the world over. Nevertheless, rooms are equipped with a variety of amenities, including an electric kettle for your morning tea or coffee. Bathrooms are clean and adequate. Buffet breakfast and airport pick-up are complimentary. The hotel runs a coffee shop, an attractive Chinese restaurant, and an Indian restaurant. ⊠ *262 Bund Garden Rd.,* ☎ *20/613–7777,* FAX *20/613–4747. 115 rooms, 2 suites. 2 restaurants, bar, coffee shop, in-room data ports, in-room safes, refrigerators, health club, dry cleaning, laundry service, business services, meeting room, travel services. AE, DC, MC, V.*

$$$ ☷ **Le Meridien.** The very large Meridien is the first Bombay-class hotel in Pune. Glowing expanses of marble, shiny fittings, elegant furnishings, and no fewer than seven restaurants make Le Meridien a rather luxurious option. The rooms are plush, with soft carpeting and classic wood and white furnishings. Breakfast and airport pickup are complimentary. Unfortunately, rooms have exciting views of the railway station across the street. ⊠ *Raja Bahadur Mill (RBM), near the main railway station,* ☎ *20/605–0505,* FAX *20/605–0506. 176 rooms, 12 suites. 4 restaurants, 2 bars, coffee shop, in-room data ports, refrigerators, health club, dry cleaning, laundry service, business services, meeting room, travel services. AE, DC, MC, V.*

$$$ ☷ **Taj Blue Diamond.** The oldest five-star hotel in Pune, Blue Diamond is the only luxury hotel here that has rooms with pleasant views of the green Koregaon Park. The rooms are large, modern, and luxurious. Bathrooms are tidy and shiny. The hotel, however, is renovating its rooms, so make sure your room is far enough away from the work. The already renovated rooms are stylish, more cheerful and US$35 more expensive than the older rooms. The hotel's 24-hour coffee shop serves excellent biryani; there's also an Indian restaurant and a popular Chinese restaurant. Breakfast is complimentary. ⊠ *11, Koregaon Rd., ,* ☎ *20/612–5555,* FAX *20/612–7755. 110 rooms, 9 suites. 3 restaurants, bar, coffee shop, in-room data ports, in-room safes, pool, refrigerators, health club, dry cleaning, laundry service, business services, meeting room, travel services. AE, DC, MC, V.*

$$ ☷ **The Central Park Hotel.** As you enter this hotel, two features immediately strike you: the hotel's light, airy, modern look, and the gracious staff. This new hotel is small, but rooms are comfortable and neat, and it's a good deal. Choose your room according to the view: the roadside view is more pleasant than the views of a construction area (in front and on the side of the hotel). Breakfast and airport pickup are complimentary. ⊠ *Bund Garden Rd., near the Council Hall,* ☎ *20/605–4000,* FAX *20/605–0211. 74 rooms, 5 suites. Restaurant, bar, shop,* *in-room data ports, in-room safes (some), refrigerators, health club, dry cleaning, laundry service, business services, meeting room, travel services. AE, DC, MC, V.*

$ ⌂ **Ritz.** The Ritz is a century-old bungalow that has been converted into a hotel. The rooms are reasonably clean though slightly musty. Each room has a balcony that overlooks a busy thoroughfare. The attached bathrooms are simple and fairly tidy and offer showers only, no tubs. Deluxe rooms have tubs. The hotel serves only vegetarian food and presents a very competent Gujarati *thali* meal to its guests. Stay here for the good value. There is a computer station with Internet access that you can use here (for a fee). ⌂ *6 Sadhu Vaswani Path, opposite the main post office (G.P.O.),* ☎ *22/285–0500 or 22/282–0141,* FAX *20/613–6191. 74 rooms, 10 suites. 2 restaurants, room service, laundry service, meeting room, travel services. DC, MC, V.*

$ ⌂ **Shrimaan.** This medium-budget hotel offers comfortable, brightly furnished, and clean rooms at a decent price. All rooms are equipped with telephones and a TV and are reasonably sized. Rooms don't have carpets, and the bathrooms are clean but lack tubs. Air-conditioned rooms are slightly more expensive. The attached restaurant, La Pizzeria, serves competent Italian food, as well as Mexican food. Shrimaan is located in a quiet area of town, a hop, skip, and jump from Koregoan Park. ⌂ *361/5 Bund Garden Rd., opposite Bund Garden,* ☎ *20/613–3535 or 20/613–6565,* FAX *20/612–3636. 30 rooms, 8 suites. Restaurant, room service, laundry service, meeting room, travel services. AE, DC, MC, V.*

$ ⌂ **Sunderban.** Once the home of the royalty family of Nepal, this bungalow-hotel has character and old-style class. It's owned by the Talera Group, which operates several hotels in Pune. Popular with Osho commune members and located in a quiet street of the Koregaon Park area, it has air-conditioned rooms each with its own mini-patio that faces the green lawns. The 20-odd deluxe rooms are spacious, tidy, and cushy; some have kitchenettes, including microwaves. "Regular" rooms are more basic, small with a no-frills bathroom (shower only) but very clean. The hotel offers very generous off-season discounts from April to September. Sunderban doesn't have its own restaurant but offers room service for beverages and breakfast, and will organize meals from their sister hotels. Alcohol and meat are not permitted in the hotel. ⌂ *19 Koregaon Park,* ☎ *20/612–4949,* FAX *20/612–3131. 43 rooms. Refrigerators, dry cleaning, laundry service, travel services. AE, DC, MC, V.*

Nightlife and the Arts

During Ganesh Chaturthi, which is celebrated in late August or September, MTDC organizes a special cultural festival for this occasion, during which top classical Indian dancers and musicians perform here. Pune has plenty of pubs where you can sample Pune nightlife. Visit **10 Downing Street** (⌂ Gera Plaza, Boat Club Rd., ☎ 20/612–8343); it's a popular pub in Pune.

Shopping

Shopping in Pune can be a thrill, given the immense variety and the good prices. And unlike other Indian cities, the shopping avenues are pretty much adjacent to each other. Comb Mahatma Gandhi Road, Moledina Road, and East Street for the best bargains. The **Bombay Store** (⌂ 302 Mahatma Gandhi Rd., ☎ 20/631–1891), closed for lunch from 1:30 to 4, has some of the best buys for handicrafts, clothing and artifacts. Westside, next to Dorabjees on Moledina Road, offers a variety of casual wear. Along Mahatma Gandhi Road you'll find plenty of shops, one after the next, selling cottons and salwar-kurta ensembles (a two-piece tunic and pants outfit). You'll even find road-side hawkers offering tops and skirts. Off Mahatma Gandhi Road is a lane lined with open-air stalls; vendors here sell garments of all varieties. At Centre Street you may find a good selection of jewelry. On the shops and stalls at Koregaon Park you'll find Kashmiri handicrafts, silver jewelry, cotton garments, and Tibetan knick-knacks. Remember that Pune snoozes from 1 to 4.

Pune A to Z

AIR TRAVEL

Pune and Bombay are only 35 minutes apart by air. A one-way ticket costs about $90. Jet Airways flies the route three times a day. Pune is also connected to New Delhi and Bangalore by daily flights on Jet Airways and Indian Airlines

➤ AIRLINES AND CONTACTS: **Jet Airways** (243/244 Century Arcade, B/2 Narangi Baug Rd., off Boat Club Rd., ☎ 20/613–7181, 20/612–4056; airport office 20/668–5591, 20/668–5592; tele-check-in 20/668–5591). **Indian Airlines** (Ambedkar Rd. opposite the R.T.O., near Sangam Bridge, ☎ 20/426–0932, 20/426–0938, 20/140, or 20/141; ☎ airport office, 20/668–9433).

BUS AND CAR TRAVEL

Reaching Pune by road is a reasonably comfortable option. Several competing companies run luxury buses to Pune from Bombay; it's a four- or five-hour journey. You can arrange such a ride through your Bombay hotel or travel agent. Driving to Pune by car is the best option, however. With the opening of the Bombay-Pune expressway, one of India's first world-class highways, the trip takes under three hours if you avoid the Bombay rush hour.

MONEY MATTERS
CURRENCY EXCHANGE

Most hotels will change money for guests. You can also change money at Thomas Cook between 10 and 6 daily from Monday to Saturday. Or you could try the American Express, operated by TTK Forex, between 9 and 5 daily from Monday to Saturday. If you want to advance cash against your Master Card or Visa you will have to head for the Citibank ATMs.

➤ EXCHANGE SERVICES: **American Express** (✉ 4 Hermes Kunj, next to Air-India, Mangaldas Rd., ☎ 20/613–3706). **Thomas Cook** (✉ 13, Thacker House, 2418 G Thimmaya Rd., off Mahatma Gandhi Rd., ☎ 20/634–8188).

TOURS

Pune Muncipal Transport (PMT) offers a daily eight-hour Pune city tour that departs at 9 for Rs. 100 per head. The buses depart from the Deccan stand and tickets may be purchased there as well. You can arrange to hire a car through your hotel travel desk or from one of the agencies below. To hire a non–air-conditioned car for eight hours/80 km (50 mi) (whichever comes first) will set you back Rs. 500 to Rs. 800, depending on the type of car you opt for and apart from the tips and "lunch money" to the driver.

➤ CONTACTS: **Deccan Luxury** (✉ Fergusson College Rd. near Deccan Gymkhana and Champion Sports, ☎ 20/553–2305). **Europcar** (✉ City Point, Boat Club Rd., ☎ 20/611–3085).

TRAIN TRAVEL

Several excellent fast trains run to Pune from Bombay and vice versa. Try the Shatabdi Express, Deccan Queen, Pragati Express, or Sahyadri Express. The Shatabdi is the fastest: the journey takes 3½ hours. Call Train information: there are daily connections between Pune and Madras, Hyderabad, Bangalore, Trivandrum, and several other destinations. Ask a travel agent for details.

➤ TRAIN INFORMATION: **Train Information** (☎ 20/612–6575).

VISITOR INFORMATION

The Maharashtra Tourism (MTDC) office in Pune, near the main railway station, is open from 10 to 5:30. There's an MTDC counter at the railway station and at the airport. In addition to these bureaus, most hotels have travel desks to help you plan your day—for a price.

➤ TOURIST OFFICES: **MTDC Tourist Office** (✉ Block I, Central Building, Pune, ☎ 20/612–6867).

AJANTA AND ELLORA CAVES

★ Dating back more than 2,000 years, the cave temples of Ajanta and Ellora rank among the wonders of the ancient world. Here, over a period of 700 years—between the 2nd century BC and the 5th century AD— great armies of monks and artisans carved cathedrals, monasteries, and entire cities of frescoed, sculptured halls into the solid rock. Working with simple chisels and hammers and an ingenious system of reflecting mirrors to provide light, they cut away hundreds of thousands of tons of rock to create the cave temples. These craftsmen inspire perpetual awe with the precision of their planning, their knowledge of rock formations, and the delicacy and profusion of their artwork. Together, the cave temples span three great religions—Buddhism, Hinduism, and Jainism. For optimum absorption of the vast and phenomenal caves, allow one full day for each site, remembering that both are closed on Monday. To get to Ajanta and Ellora, take a train, bus, or plane to Aurangabad, the nearest major city. From Aurangabad you can hop on a tour bus or hire a car and driver for about Rs. 1,300 to the Ajanta caves (a two- to three-hour trip), Rs. 550 to the Ellora caves (30 minutes).

Aurangabad

388 km (241 mi) east of Bombay, 30 km (18 mi) southeast of Ellora, 100 km (62 mi) southwest of Ajanta

With several excellent hotels and a growing number of good restaurants, Aurangabad is a good base from which to explore the cave temples at Ajanta and Ellora. The city has an intriguing old bazaar, and is known for its *himru* (cotton and silk brocade) shawls and saris, and its gorgeously decorated Paithani saris. If you're interested, pop into the Aurangabad Standard Silk Showroom or Aurangabad Silk, both near the train station; Ajanta Handicrafts in Harsul, on the highway to Ajanta; or Himroo Saris, on the highway to Ellora.

More than a mere gateway, Aurangabad has a number of ancient sites of its own, such as the imposing **Daulatabad Fort** (✉ 13 km/8 mi, west of Old Town on the highway to the Ellora Caves; ☉ sunrise–6; ✆ foreigners US$5), built in 1187 by the Hindu king and surrounded by seven giant walls more than 5 km (3 mi) long, Daulatabad was once called Deogiri, "hill of the gods," but was changed to "city of fortune" when the sultan of Delhi overtook it in 1308. Devote at least half a day to this fascinating and impregnable fort, considered one of India's most impressive. As you enter the fort you enter a labyrinth—note the moats, spikes, cannons, and dark maze of tunnels designed to make the fort as impregnable from enemies as possible. Equally interesting is the Jami Masjid inside; it was conceived from horizontal lintels and pillars of Jain and Hindu temples.

The 17th-century **Bibi-ka-Maqbara,** (☉ sunrise–10 PM; ⌧ foreigners US$5) is also known as the mini–Taj Mahal; located 550 yards north of the old town, beyond Mecca Gate, you can usually see it from the plane when you're flying into Aurangabad. A pale but noble imitation of the original Taj Mahal, the tomb is dedicated to the wife of the last of the six great Mogul emperors, Aurangzeb (founder of Aurangabad and son of the Taj Mahal's creator, Shah Jahan). It was supposed to be a shining, white-marble edifice but money ran out, so only the bottom two ft of the monument were built with marble; the rest is stone with a facade of plaster. Somewhat awkwardly proportioned, the structure can be said to illustrate the decline of Mogul architecture.

About 160 km (99 mi) east of Aurangabad, beyond Jalna, is the **Lonar Crater.** If you have a day free, or you have an extra day because the caves are closed, visit this serene 50,000-year-old meteoric crater. Off the beaten path and away from postcard sellers, bead hawkers, and soft-drink-stall owners, the 1,800-meter-long crater lake—probably formed from a meteor—is one of India's more phenomenal sites. Exceedingly beautiful, Lonar is an extremely peaceful spot, full of wildlife and greenery.

Dining and Lodging

Most hotels in Aurangabad will discount their rates upon request. Especially if you've booked directly, push for 15% off—or more. Unless otherwise noted, all hotels listed are fully air-conditioned.

Aurangabad has few great restaurants. Most of them offer multiple cuisine options, including Indian (Mughlai and tandoori, or South Indian), Chinese, and the local variant of what passes off for Continental food. It's best to stick with Indian cuisine—it's generally well-prepared and tasty. Know that Aurangabadi restaurants aren't big on decoration: a few plastic plants, jazzy upholstery, and darkened light bulbs pass off as restaurant style. But they are comfortable and the meals well presented. Most restaurants here don't serve meals outside typical meal hours.

$ ✕ **Angeethi.** One of Aurangabad's most popular restaurants, Angeethi is packed on weekends with locals enjoying their time off. Named after a traditional Indian cooking vessel, this dark, cozy restaurant serves reasonably priced Punjabi, Continental, and Chinese food, a knack for cooking tandoori items. Other specialties include Afghani kebab *masala* (boneless chicken in sweet cashew sauce) and the two-person *sikandari raan* (goat marinated in rum and spices, and seared in a tandoor oven). There are plenty of tasty vegetarian choices. Service is friendly but not terribly efficient. The restaurant serves only Indian food between 3 and 7. ⌧ *6 Mehar Chambers, Vidya Nagar, Jalna Rd.,* ☎ *240/ 441988. MC, V.*

$ ✕ **Tandoor.** The hospitality of manager Syed Liakhat Hussain is one very good reason to visit this brightly lit, cheerful restaurant. The kebabs are another—especially the *kasturi* (chicken) kebab. People come here for authentic and well-made tandoori food. Try the *paneer tikka, biryani,* black *dal* (lentils), and fried local fish—which is very fresh. Shoot for lunch instead of dinner if you're coming by autorickshaw, because later in the evening it's difficult to find transportation. ⌧ *Shyam Chambers, Station Rd.,* ☎ *240/328481. MC, V.*

$ ✕ **Bhoj.** Both branches of this *thali* restaurant serve quick-and-tasty, light vegetarian Gujarati or Rajasthani platters for lunch and dinner, which makes a welcome change from the overdose of Mughlai and tandoori food available elswhere. The choice of preparations is wide, and the price is right. Decor is purely functional, however, and the din deafening; this is not a place for leisurely dining. Alcohol is not served. The restaurant is closed between 3 and 7. ⊠ *Kamdar Bhavan, CBS Rd., no phone;* ⊠ *Hotel Sai, Jalna Rd.,* ☎ *240/329915. No credit cards.*

$$ 🏨 **Taj Residency.** Inside and out, this gleaming Mogul palace is done in bright white marble and stone, with gold accents. The windows and doors arch to regal Moghul points, and the grand dome over the lobby is hand-painted in traditional Jaipuri patterns. The Taj easily looks like the city's top hotel, but service can sometimes be a bit slow. The Ajanta-esque rooms have teak furniture with matching headboards and mirror frames, and a small sitting area. All rooms open onto the garden and have balconies or patios, most with a teak swing. Stone paths wind through 5 acres of beautifully landscaped lawns. The Taj is no longer the most expensive hotel in Aurangabad and therefore is now a much better bang for the buck. ⊠ *8-N-12 CIDCO,* ☎ *240/381–1106 through 240/381–1110,* FAX *240/381053. 40 rooms, 2 suites. Restaurant, pool, exercise room, dry cleaning, laundry service, business services, meeting room, travel services. AE, DC, MC, V.*

$$ 🏨 **Welcomgroup Rama International.** A long driveway takes you away
★ from the main road and through spacious grounds to this attractive hotel, with red bands of elephants chiseled on its bleach-white facade. The efficient and friendly staff provide personalized service of the highest order, and create the kind of warm, intimate atmosphere you'd normally associate with a smaller hotel. Standard rooms are spacious and comfortably elegant, with views onto the verdant garden of palms and bright flower beds. Corner suites are like vast living rooms. Rooms in the old wing are substandard but are slated for renovation. ⊠ *R-3 Chikalthana, 431210,* ☎ *240/485441, 240/485444, or 240/485454,* FAX *240/484768. 90 rooms, 2 suites. Restaurant, bar, coffee shop, pool, hair salon, exercise room, massage, sauna, steam room, miniature golf, 2 tennis courts, croquet, Ping-Pong, dry cleaning, laundry service, business services, meeting room, travel services. AE, DC, MC, V.*

$$ 🏨 **Ambassador Ajanta.** Next door to its rival, the Rama, this five-story marble hotel sits amid sweeping lawns, well-kept flower beds, and towering trees alive with singing birds. Filled with brass goddesses, marble elephants, wood carvings, and myriad other Indian antiques, the lovely garden is typical of that cluttered Indian elegance look. The rooms have an Indian feel—they have local furnishings and garden-view windows—but are, nonetheless, slightly dreary. Don't miss a dip in the pool, where you can imbibe mid-swim at the bar at the shallow end. The restaurant offers live *ghazal* music on weekends. ⊠ *Jalna Rd., CIDCO,* ☎ *240/485211 or 240/485214,* FAX *240/484367. 100 rooms with bath, 16 suites. Restaurant, bar, pool, tennis court, badminton, dry cleaning, laundry service, business services, meeting room, travel services. AE, DC, MC, V.*

$$ 🏨 **The Meadows.** The Meadows offers the services of a tropical resort. Accommodations are in simple (carpet-free) ultramodern cottages, each with a private lawn. The hotel prides itself on its architectural awards and environmental record—it uses a biotechnological system of plant roots to purify its air and waste water. The grounds, planted with trees and flowers, house rare birds. It's intensely quiet here, as the hotel is 5 km (3 mi) from the city center. The hotel is ideal for kids—there are rabbits, parrots, and ducks, and ample space to run around. But rusticity costs: prices are higher than at comparable hotels in the city, and the facilities are a bit spartan. The restaurant serves excellent food, including tasty Continental meals. Service is above average. A courtesy coach runs into Aurangabad twice daily. ⊠ *Village Mitmita,*

Padegaon, Bombay-Nasik Hwy., 431002, ☎ 240/677412, 240/677415, 240/677417, or 240/677421, ℻ 240/677416. 50 rooms. Restaurant, bar, pool, health club, hair salon, laundry, business services, meeting room, travel services. AE, DC, MC, V.

$ ⊞ **Hotel Amarpreet.** Rooms in this centrally located hotel are above-average—in Indian terms, neat enough. The rooms are cheerful—not over-decorated enough to be overbearing—and are equipped with telephones and televisions. The bathrooms are passably clean. The simple, airy lobby opens out onto a small patch of lawn. The hotel has two in-house restaurants offering Indian, Chinese and Continental food. Opt for a room with a view of the Bibi ka Maqbara. ⊠ *Jalna Rd., ☎ 240/351346 or 240/351361, ℻ 240/351/347. 30 rooms, 2 suites. 2 restaurants, bar, hair salon, laundry, business services, meeting room, travel services. AE, MC, V.*

$ ⊞ **Hotel President Park.** In this attractive contemporary building, designed around a central garden, every room has a pool view. Ground-floor rooms are the most attractive; they open directly onto the garden—you can walk out of your room and dive into the pool. The rooms have balconies or patios and are cheerful inside, with teak-trimmed furniture, dark-toned fabrics, and brass fixtures. Bathrooms are on the small side. Executive rooms have been renovated and are slightly more expensive (by US$12). Overall, this hotel is a great choice—it seems like a luxury hotel but has far better prices. The restaurant serves vegetarian food only. ⊠ *R 7/2 Chikalthana, Airport Rd., 431210, ☎ 240/486201, ℻ 240/484823. 60 rooms, 4 suites. Restaurant, bar, coffee shop, pool, sauna, steam room, tennis court, gym, dry cleaning, laundry service, meeting room, business services, travel services. AE, DC, MC, V.*

$ ⊞ **MTDC Holiday Resort.** If you don't mind sleepy service and a starchless atmosphere, this centrally located hotel offers excellent value. The staff are amiable, and the no-frills rooms are clean. Each room has a telephone. Only 22 rooms have air-conditioning; don't try the others. There is a restaurant serving basic Indian food. ⊠ *Station Rd., 431001, ☎ 240/331513, ℻ 240/331198. 48 rooms, 22 with air-conditioning. Restaurant. No credit cards.*

Ajanta Caves

It is thought that a band of wandering Buddhist monks first came here in the 2nd century BC searching for a place to meditate during the monsoons. Ajanta was ideal—peaceful and remote, with a spectacular setting. It's a steep, wide, horseshoe-shaped gorge above a wild mountain stream flowing through a jungle below. The monks began carving caves into the rock face of the gorge, and a new temple form was born.

Over the course of seven centuries, the cave temples of Ajanta evolved into works of incredible art. Structural engineers continue to be awestruck by the sheer brilliance of the ancient builders, who, undaunted by the limitations of their implements, materials, and skills, created a marvel of artistic and architectural splendor. In all, 29 caves were carved, 15 of which were left unfinished; some of them were *viharas* (monasteries)—complete with stone pillows carved onto the monks' stone beds—others were *chaityas* (Buddhist cathedrals). All of the caves were profusely decorated with intricate sculptures and murals depicting the many incarnations of Buddha.

As the influence of Buddhism declined, monk-artists were fewer, and the temples were swallowed up by the jungle. A thousand years later, in 1819, Englishman John Smith was tiger-hunting on a bluff nearby in the dry season and noticed the soaring arch of what is now dubbed Cave 10 peeking out from the thinned greenery; it was he who subse-

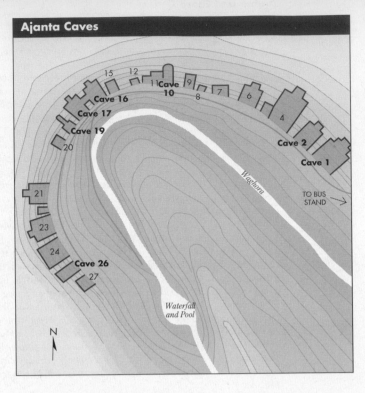

Ajanta Caves

quently unveiled the caves to the modern world. Incidentally tigers are not too far from this area (the thick forests from Ajanta to Kannad are the Gautala wildlife sanctuary).

At both Ajanta and Ellora, monumental facades and statues were chipped out of solid rock, but at Ajanta, an added dimension has survived the centuries—India's most remarkable cave paintings. Monks spread a carefully prepared plaster of clay, cow dung, chopped rice husks, and lime onto the rough rock walls, and painted pictures on the walls with natural local pigments: red ocher, burnt brick, copper oxide, lampblack, and dust from crushed green rocks. The caves are now like chapters of a splendid epic in visual form, recalling the life of the Buddha, and illustrating tales from Buddhist *jatakas* (fables). As the artists lovingly told the story of the Buddha, they portrayed the life and civilization they knew—a drama of ancient nobles, wise men, and commoners.

Opinions vary on which of the Ajanta caves is most exquisite. Caves 1, 2, 16, 17, and 19 are generally considered to have the best paintings; caves 1, 10, 17, 19, and 26 (with its statue of the reclining Buddha) the best sculptures. (The caves are numbered from west to east, not in chronological order.) Try and see all 7 of these caves. If you're not sightseeing with a guide, ask one of the attendants at each cave for help.

Most popular at Ajanta are the paintings in **Cave 1.** These depict the Bodhisattva Avalokitesvara and Bodhisattva Padmapani. Padmapani, or the "one with the lotus in his hand," is considered to be the alter ego of the Lord Buddha; Padmapani assumed the duties of the Buddha when he disappeared. Padmapani is depicted with his voluptuous wife, one of Ajanta's most widely reproduced figures. When seen from different angles, the magnificent Buddha statue in this cave seems to wear different facial expressions.

Cave 2 is remarkable for its ceiling decorations and its murals relating the birth of the Buddha. For its sheer exuberance, the painting of women on a swing is considered the finest.

The oldest cave is **Cave 10,** a chaitya dating from 200 BC, filled with Buddhas and dominated by an enormous stupa (a dome, or monument, to Buddha). It's only in AD 100, however, that the exquisite brush-and-line work begins. In breathtaking detail, the Shadanta Jataka, a legend about the Buddha, is depicted on the wall in a continuous panel. There are no idols of Buddha in this cave, indicating that idol worship was not in vogue at the time—but the fact that Cave 19, hardly nine caves later, contains idols of Buddha shows the progression of thought and the development of new methods of worship as the centuries wore on.

The mystical heights attained by the monk-artists seem to have reached their zenith in **Cave 16.** Here a continuous narrative spreads both horizontally and vertically, evolving into a panoramic whole—at once logical and stunning. One painting here is riveting: known as *The Dying Princess,* it is believed to represent Sundari, the wife of the Buddha's half-brother Nanda, who left her to become a monk. Cave 16 has an excellent view of the river and may have been the entrance to the entire series of caves.

Cave 17 holds the greatest number of pictures undamaged by time. Luscious heavenly damsels fly effortlessly overhead, a prince makes love to a princess, and the Buddha tames a raging elephant. (Resisting temptation is a theme.) Other favorite paintings include the scene of a woman applying lipstick and one of a princess performing *sringar* (her toilette).

A number of unfinished caves were abandoned mysteriously, but even these are worth a visit if you can haul yourself up a steep 100 steps. You can also walk up the bridle path, a gentler ascent in the form of a crescent pathway alongside the caves; from here you have a magnificent view of the ravine descending into the Waghura River. There is a much easier way to reach this point. On your return by car to Aurangabad, 20 km (12 mi) from the caves, take a right at Balapur and head 8 km (5 mi) towards Viewpoint, as it's called by the locals.

A trip to the Ajanta caves needs to be well-planned. You can see the caves at a fairly leisurely pace in two hours, but the drive to and from the caves takes anywhere from two to three hours. Come prepared with water, lunch or snacks (from a shop in Aurangabad, because you won't get much here), comfortable walking shoes (that can be slipped on and off easily, because shoes are not allowed inside the caves), a flashlight, and patience. Aurangabad can be hot year-round, and touring 29 caves can be tiring. The paintings are dimly lit to protect the artwork, and a number are badly damaged, so deciphering the work takes some effort. The caves are connected by a fair number of steps, both up and down; it's advisable to start at the far end and work your way back, to avoid a hot trek back at the end. Flash photography and video cameras are prohibited inside the caves; the admission fee includes having the lights turned on as you enter a cave. Right outside the caves, a shoddy MTDC-run restaurant, predictably called the Ajanta, offers simple refreshments. ⊠ *100 km (62 mi) northeast of Aurangabad.* ☞ *Foreigners US$10 per head, video cameras Rs. 25.* ☉ *Tues.–Sun. 9–5:30 (arrive by 4).*

Ellora Caves

In the 7th century, for some inexplicable reason, the focus of activity shifted from Ajanta to a site 123 km (76 mi) to the southwest—a place

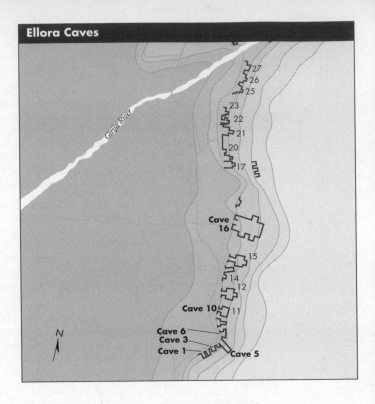

Ellora Caves

known today as Ellora. Unlike the cave temples at Ajanta, those of Ellora are not solely Buddhist. Instead, they follow the development of religious thought in India—through the decline of Buddhism in the latter half of the 8th century, the Hindu renaissance that followed the return of the Gupta dynasty, and the Jain resurgence between the 9th and 11th centuries. Of the 34 caves, the 12 to the south are Buddhist, the 17 in the center are Hindu, and the five to the north are Jain.

At Ellora the focus is on sculpture, which covers the walls in exquisitely ornate masses. The carvings in the Buddhist caves are a serene reflection of the Buddhist philosophy, but in the Hindu caves they take on a certain exuberance and vitality—gods and demons do fearful battle, Lord Shiva angrily flails his eight arms, elephants rampage, eagles swoop, and lovers intertwine.

Unlike Ajanta, where the temples were chopped out of a steep cliff, the caves at Ellora were dug into the slope of a hill along a north–south line, presumably so that they faced west and could thus receive the light of the setting sun.

Cave 1 (which is two stories high) and **Cave 3** (three stories high) are remarkable for having more than one floor. The two caves form a monastery behind an open courtyard. The deceptively simple facade looms nearly 15 m (50 ft) high; a lavish interior lies beyond. Gouged into this block of rock are a ground-floor hall, a second-story shrine, and a hall on the top story—with a gallery of Buddhas seated under trees and parasols.

The largest of the Buddhist caves is **Cave 5**. It was probably as a classroom for young monks. The roof appears to be supported by 24 pillars; working their way down, sculptors first "built" the roof before they "erected" the pillars.

Cave 6 contains a statue of Saraswati, the Hindu goddess of learning—also identified as Mahamayuri, the Buddhist goddess of learning—in the company of Buddhist figures. **Cave 10** is the "Carpenter's Cave," where Hinduism and Buddhism meet again. Here the stonecutters reproduced the timbered roofs of their day over a richly decorated facade that resembles masonry work. Inside this chaitya—the only actual Buddhist chapel at Ellora—the main work of art is a huge sculpture of Buddha.

The immediate successors to the Buddhist caves are the Hindu caves, and a step inside these is enough to stop you in your tracks. It's another world—another universe—in which the calm contemplation of the seated Buddhas gives way to the dynamic cosmology of Hinduism. Thought to have been created around the 7th and 8th centuries, these kinetic sculptures depict goddesses at battle; Shiva waving his eight arms; life-size elephants groaning under their burdens; lovers striking poses; and boars, eagles, peacocks, and monkeys prancing around.

Ellora is dominated by the mammoth Kailasa temple complex, or **Cave 16.** Dedicated to Shiva, the complex is a replica of his legendary abode at Mount Kailasa in the Tibetan Himalayas. The largest monolithic structure in the world, the Kailasa reveals the genius, daring, and raw skill of its artisans.

To create the Kailasa complex, an army of stonecutters started at the top of the cliff, where they removed 3 million cubic ft of rock to create a vast pit with a freestanding rock left in the center. Out of this single slab, 276 ft long and 154 ft wide, the workers created Shiva's abode, which includes the main temple, a series of smaller shrines, and galleries built into a wall that encloses the entire complex. Nearly every surface is exquisitely sculpted with epic themes.

Around the courtyard, numerous friezes illustrate the legends of Shiva and stories from the great Hindu epics, the *Mahabharata* and the *Ramayana*. One interesting panel on the eastern wall relates the origin of Shiva's symbol, the linga, or phallus. Another frieze, on the outer wall of the main sanctuary on the southern side of the courtyard, shows the demon Ravana shaking Mount Kailasa, from a story from the *Ramayana* epic. The Jain caves are at the far end. If you have a car, consider driving there once you've seen the Hindu group of caves. The Jain caves are attractive in their own right and should not be missed on account of geography. **Ellora Caves,** for one, is as complex as a rabbit burrow; it's marvelous to climb through the numerous well-carved chambers and study the towering figures of Gomateshvara and Mahavira.

Ellora is said to be the busiest tourist site in the state of Maharashtra. The Ajanta caves are a bit off the beaten track, but Ellora, a mere half an hour from Aurangabad, gets packed with crowds. Try to avoid coming here during school holidays. ✉ *Foreigners US$10, video cameras Rs. 25.* ☉ *Tues.–Sun. 9–5:30.*

NEED A BREAK?	**Ellora Restaurant** (✉ parking lot, Ellora Caves) is a convenient place to stop for a cold drink and a hot samosa (deep-fried meat or vegetable turnover). The outdoor patio has fruit trees (home to many monkeys) and pink bougainvillea flowers.

Nightlife and the Arts

The annual **Ellora Dance Festival,** held in December, draws top classical Indian dancers and musicians from around the country to perform outdoors against the magical backdrop of the Ellora Caves.

Ajanta and Ellora Caves A to Z

AIR TRAVEL

Aurangabad and Bombay are only about 45 minutes apart by air. A one-way ticket costs about $80. Indian Airlines flies the route daily. Ask your travel agent about the current status and schedules of other domestic airlines.

➤ AIRLINES AND CONTACTS: **Indian Airlines** (☏ 240/485421 or 240/483392).

➤ AIRPORT INFORMATION: **Aurangabad Airport** (☏ 240/482111 or 240/485780).

BUS TRAVEL

It's not the most comfortable option, but several competing companies run "luxury" overnight buses to Aurangabad from Bombay, a 12-hour journey. You can arrange such a ride through ITDC or MTDC, or your Bombay hotel or travel agent.

MONEY MATTERS

ATMS

There are no cash machines in Aurangabad.

CURRENCY EXCHANGE

Hotels generally change money for their guests. Aurangabad's State Bank of India is open weekdays 10:30–1:30 and Saturday 10–12:30. Trade Wings is open Monday–Saturday from 9:30 to 6:30 or 7.

➤ EXCHANGE SERVICES: **State Bank of India** (✉ Kranti Chowk, Aurangabad, ☏ 240/331386, 240/331872, or 240/334778). **Trade Wings** (✉ Near Bawa Petrol Pump, Jalna Rd., Aurangabad, ☏ 240/357480, 240/332952, 240/322677, or 240/34748).

TOURS

The Government of India Tourist Office in Aurangabad oversees about 50 expert, polite, multilingual tour guides. You can hire one through the tourist office itself; the MTDC office, also in Aurangabad; and most travel agents. For parties of one to four, the fees are Rs. 255 per half day (four hours) and Rs. 380 for a full day (up to eight hours). An extra Rs. 250 is charged for trips of more than 100 km (60 mi); a guided day trip to the Ajanta caves, for example, would run around Rs. 630. It's best to book ahead. But the tourist office has a legitimate and qualified guide posted at the Ajanta caves as well. Ask at the ticket office there—request Mr. Mohammed Chaus, who offers an informative tour.

Once you have a guide, you'll probably want to hire a car and driver. Rates are unusually high in Aurangabad, but moving around by autorickshaw is a slow business. A full-day trip in an air-conditioned Ambassador with a driver may cost around Rs. 2,750 to Ajanta, Rs. 1,050 to Ellora. A full-day trip in a non–air-conditioned Ambassador with driver may cost around Rs. 1,400 to Ajanta and Rs. 700 to Ellora. You can arrange car hire through your hotel travel desk, one of the travel agencies below, or the Government of India Tourist Office.

➤ CONTACTS: **Classic Travel Related Services** (✉ MTDC Holiday Resort, Station Rd., Aurangabad, ☏ 240/335598 or 240/337788). **Aurangabad Tours and Travels** (a.k.a. Aurangabad Transport Syndicate, ✉ Welcomgroup Rama Hotel, Airport Rd., Aurangabad, ☏ 240/482423 or 240/485441 [Welcomgroup Rama number]).

TRAIN TRAVEL

Slow trains run to Aurangabad from Bombay, Hyderabad, Delhi, and other major cities. Ask a travel agent for details.

VISITOR INFORMATION

The Government of India Tourist Office, across from the train station, provides a warm and informative welcome to Aurangabad during weekdays from 9 to 6, or Saturdays and holidays from 9 to 1:30. Ask for the helpful Mr. D.M. Yadav or Mr. I.R.V. Rao. The equally helpful MTDC stays open 24 hours, with an additional airport counter that opens when flights arrive.

In addition to these bureaus, most hotels have travel desks and concierges who can help you plot your moves.

➤ TOURIST OFFICES:: **Government of India Tourist Office** (✉ Krishna Vilas, Station Rd., Aurangabad, ☎ 240/331217). **MTDC** (✉ MTDC Holiday Resort, Station Rd., Aurangabad, ☎ 240/331513).

MAHARASHTRA'S BEACHES

The Maharashtra coastline north of Goa may yet become the most beautiful resort area in India. Some of this region's many 17th-century forts are actually built on tiny offshore islands that are dwarfed by the ramparts. The coastline creates wide panoramas without any encroachment of the modern world, and you pass traditional villages that are usually the home of Kolis, one of the original fishing tribes. Koli women walk with a fine stride, their saris worn in the Marathi fashion, skintight between their legs; the men master the waves and bring back the fish, which is then cooked in the zesty Konkan style.

In the early 1990s, the state of Maharashtra enacted a plan to control the growth of resorts, protect valuable marshlands, and restore at least one coastal fort. There are no upscale accommodations here, but you can still spend a few nights under rustling palm fronds in idyllic coves and harbors at simple yet enjoyable tented beach resorts set up by the MTDC.

Because these areas are still only minimally developed, the beaches at or near the tented resorts are your best bets for comfortable sun and sand. (The resorts and beaches are grouped together below.) Each resort has walk-in two- and four-bed tents with windows, front and back entrances, and plenty of interior space. All provide comfortable cots, clean linens, electricity, fans, filtered drinking water, and separate bathrooms and shower facilities in clean, if unappealing, concrete buildings. The restaurants are often open-air affairs under thatched roofs, and usually offer Indian (sometimes Konkan) and limited Continental menus that may include the catch of the day. All of these resorts, except Ganapatipule and Bordi, which offer cottages in addition to tents, close for the monsoon season—usually between June 15 and November 1, but naturally these dates vary, depending on the monsoon. Each tent costs between Rs. 300 and Rs. 500 per day, double occupancy or for four persons depending on the season, and occupation is restricted to couples and families. For the latest details about tented beach resorts, contact the helpful Mr. U.V. Dingankar at the MTDC office (☎ 22/202–1843). To reach the beaches, you'll need to hire a car and driver from Bombay.

⑮ MTDC Bordi Beach Tented Resort. The town of Bordi, north of Bombay, is a favorite holiday spot for urban escapees. Dormitories, cottages, and tents populate an otherwise isolated beach backed by casuarina trees. ✉ *Thane district, 130 km (81 mi) north of Bombay,* ☎ *2528/41243,* FAX *2528/41243. 12 2-bed tents with shared bath, 4 rooms, 1 dormitory.*

⑯ MTDC Harihareshwar Beach Tented Resort. Set on an inlet backed by hills, this delightful complex stands near two beaches, of which the more

Maharashtra Beaches

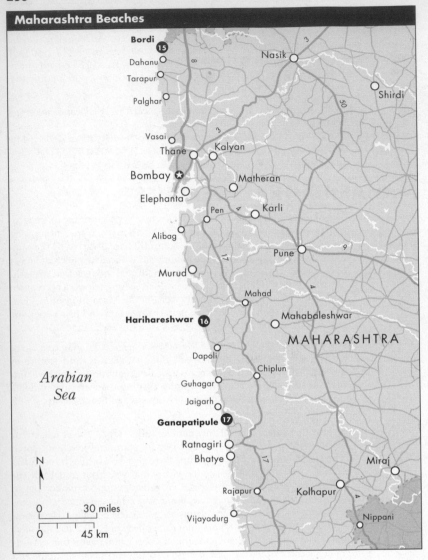

secluded one is preferable. Authentic Konkan fare is served in a rustic restaurant, often followed by a crackling campfire. ⊠ *Raigad district, 230 km (143 mi) south of Bombay,* ☎ *2147/26036,* 𝔽𝔸𝕏 *2147/26036. 60 2-bed and 10 4-bed tents.*

⑰ MTDC Ganapatipule Beach Tented Resort. Nestled in a coconut grove, with a backdrop of the stiff and straight *sura* trees, the cottages and tents in this complex have views onto the white-sand beach, and plenty of privacy. Because Ganapatipule is an important Hindu pilgrimage site, liquor is not available, but the restaurant serves good food. There is now also an MTDC hotel, the Konkani House, here, with some air-conditioned rooms. You can reserve through the number below or the MTDC in Bombay. ⊠ *Ratnagiri district, 375 km (233 mi) south of Bombay,* ☎ *2357/35248, 2357/35061,* 𝔽𝔸𝕏 *2357/35328. 104 beds in 2-bed and 4-bed tents with shared bath, 1 tent with private bath, and cottages and rooms.*

BOMBAY A TO Z

To research prices, get advice from other travelers, and book travel arrangements, visit www.fodors.com.

AIR TRAVEL TO AND FROM BOMBAY

Bombay's international airport—located in Sahar, 30 km (18 mi) north of the city center—is India's most active for international flights. The domestic airport is at Santa Cruz, 26 km (15½ mi) north of the city center. *Reconfirm your international flight* at least 72 hours before departure and arrive at the airport at least 60 minutes before takeoff for domestic flights, two hours before international flights (some airlines require three hours). Both airports have 24-hour business centers available to holders of major credit cards.

CARRIERS

Bombay is served daily or frequently by Air France, Alitalia, Swissair, Lufthansa, Cathay Pacific, Emirates, Singapore Airlines, Air-India, British Airways, Delta, and KLM/Northwest. Domestic carriers include Indian Airlines, Sahara, and Jet Airways; check with your travel agent for current domestic airlines and schedules.

➤ AIRLINES AND CONTACTS: **Air France/Continental** (☎ 22/202–5021). **Air-India** (☎ 22/202–4142, 22/836–6767). **Alitalia** (☎ 22/204–5023). **British Airways** (☎ 22/282–0888). **Cathay Pacific** (☎ 22/202–9112). **Delta** (☎ 22/288–5659). **Emirates** (☎ 22/283–7000). **Gulf Air** (☎ 22/202–1777). **Indian Airlines** (☎ 22/202–3131, 20/287–6161,or 20/615–6850). **Jet Airways** (☎ 22/288–1184, 20/285–5691, 20/285–5693, or 22/615–6666). **KLM/Northwest** (☎ 22/838–0838). **Lufthansa** (☎ 22/202–3430). **Singapore Airlines** (☎ 22/202–2747). **Swissair** (☎ 22/287–0122). **Sahara Airlines** (☎ 22/ 283-5671, 22/283–5672, 22/283–5673, or 22/615–6363).

AIRPORTS AND TRANSFERS

The trip from Sahar International Airport to south Bombay should take about 45 minutes if you arrive before 7:30 AM or after 11 PM (many international flights arrive around midnight). At other times, traffic near the city center can increase transfer time as much as 90 minutes. Most hotels provide airport transfers starting at Rs. 900 and going up to Rs. 1,800, and some offer complimentary transfers to those staying in a suite or on an exclusive floor.

The international airport has a prepaid-taxi service. Head to the prepaid-taxi counter outside the baggage-and-customs area to hire a regular cab, either air-conditioned or non–air-conditioned. Your rate is determined by your destination and amount of luggage and is payable up front; Rs. 500 should get you to the center of town. If you wish to travel by an air-conditioned taxi and do not spot one then call 22/822–7006 or 22/824–6216 (these are general numbers for taxi drivers, not for a taxi company).

At the domestic airport, metered taxis are available outside; a policeman notes the taxi's license plates before dispatching you on your way. A metered (not prepaid) taxi from the domestic airport to the city center should cost about Rs. 300 and from the international airport about Rs. 350.

➤ AIRPORT INFORMATION: **Sahar International Airport** (☎ 22/836–6700). **Santa Cruz Domestic Airport** (☎ 22/615–6500).

PHARMACIES

Most hotels have pharmacies that are open daily until about 9 PM. Royal Chemists is open 24 hours.

➤ CONTACTS: **Nanavati Hospital 24 Hour Chemist** (✉ Swami Vivekanand [S.V.] Rd., Vile Parle, near Juhu, ☎ 22/618–2255). **Royal Chemists** (✉ Acharya Dhonde Marg, opposite Wadia Hospital, Vishwas Niwas Bldg. 8, Shop 3, Parel, ☎ 22/411–5028).

BUS TRAVEL

The transport department of the India Tourism Development Corporation and the MTDC can organize, quite painlessly, bus tickets on reliable coaches to a variety of destinations, including Nasik, Aurangabad, and Pune (☞ Tours; also Visitor Information). But the Asiad and Metrolink buses, which depart from the Asiad bus stand at the circle outside Dadar TT, offer the best service between Bombay and Pune. These buses depart every 15 minutes; tickets can be purchased on the spot and one can hop right on.

➤ BUS INFORMATION: **Asiad** (✉ Opposite Dadar post office, near Sharda Talkie, Dadar East, ☎ 22/413–6835). **Metrolink** (✉ Next to Pritam Hotel, Dadar East, ☎ 22/418–1273).

CARS AND DRIVERS

In certain areas, such as bazaars, you really have to walk for the full experience. Aside from these, having a car at your disposal is the most convenient way to sightsee, as you can zip around town without the repeated hassle of hailing taxis and haggling over fares. To arrange a hired car, inquire at your hotel's travel desk or contact one of the travel agencies listed below. (You'll probably pay more if you book through your hotel.) You'll get lower rates from the India Tourism Development Corporation (☞ Travel Agencies): Rs. 850 for a full day (8 hours, or 80 km/50 mi) in a non–air-conditioned Ambassador or Maruti van; Rs. 1,250 for a car (Ambassador or a Maruti van) with air-conditioning. Rates go up for Toyotas, Mercedes, and other "luxury" cars.

CAR TRAVEL

Fairly good roads connect Bombay to most major cities and tourist areas. Hiring a car and driver gives you a chance to watch the often beautiful surroundings whiz by, but it can also be loud, hair-raising, and less than time-efficient. If you have the time and the nerves for a road trip, you'll experience what many people miss when they fly. Some distances from Bombay: Pune, 172 km (107 mi); Panaji (Goa), 597 km (371 mi); Ahmedabad, 545 km (339 mi); Hyderabad, 711 km (442 mi). Bombay is 1,033 km (642 mi) northwest of Bangalore, 432 km (268 mi) northwest of Madras, and 1,408 km (875 mi) southwest of Delhi.

CONSULATES

The U.S. Consulate is open weekdays 8:30–1 and from 2–4:30, and the staff is on duty 24 hours in case of emergencies. The Canadian Consulate is open Monday–Thursday 9–1 and 1:30–5, Friday 1:30–3:30. The British Consulate is open weekdays 8:30–1 and 2–3. The Irish Consulate is open weekdays noon–1. The South African Consulate is open weekdays 9–noon. The Australian Consulate is open weekdays 9–5.

➤ AUSTRALIA: **Australian Consulate** (✉ Maker Towers E, Cuffe Parade, ☎ 22/218–1071).

➤ CANADA: **Canadian Consulate** (✉ 41–42 Makers Chambers VI, 4th floor, Nariman Point, ☎ 22/287–6027, 22/287–6028, 22/287–6029, or 22/287–6030. 011/687–6500 in an emergency).

➤ IRELAND: **Irish Consulate** (✉ Royal Bombay Yacht Club., ☎ 22/202–4607).

➤ SOUTH AFRICA: **South African Consulate** (✉ Gandhi Mansion, Altamount Rd., ☎ 22/389–3725).

➤ UNITED KINGDOM: **British Consulate** (✉ Makers Chambers IV, 1st floor, 222 J. Bajaj Marg, Nariman Point, ☎ 22/283–2330 or 22/283–0517; 22/283–4040 in an emergency).

➤ UNITED STATES: **U.S. Consulate** (✉ Lincoln House, 78 Bhulabhai Desai Rd., Warden, ☎ 22/363–3611).

EMERGENCIES

Most hotels have house physicians and dentists on call. Your consulate can also give you the name of a reputable doctor or dentist. Otherwise, try the emergency room at Breach Candy Hospital and Research Center or the Jaslok Hospital. Bombay emergency services do not respond to an emergency as quickly as these services do in more modern parts of the world.

➤ EMERGENCY SERVICES: **Fire:** ☎ 101. **Ambulance:** ☎ 102, 105 (only for those with a sudden heart attack). **Police:** ☎ 100.

➤ HOSPITALS: **Breach Candy Hospital and Research Center** (✉ Bhulabhai Desai Rd., Breach Candy, ☎ 22/367–1888, 22/367–2888, or 22/368–0368). **Jaslok Hospital** (✉ Dr. G. Deshmukh Marg, near Haji Ali, ☎ 22/493–3333). **Lilavati Hospital** (✉ Bandra Reclamation, Bandra West, ☎ 22/645–5927).

MAIL AND SHIPPING

➤ POST OFFICES: **General Post Office** (✉ near Victoria Terminus, ☎ 22/262–4343).

MONEY MATTERS

ATMS

➤ ATM MACHINES: **ANZ Grindlays Standard Chartered** (✉ 65 F.V. Patel Rd., Santa Cruz West). **Citibank** (✉ Kohinoor Bhavan, Nariman Point; ✉ C-61 Bandra Kurla Complex, G Block, Bandra East).

CURRENCY EXCHANGE

Most luxury hotels will change money for their guests. American Express is open Monday–Saturday 9:30–6:30. Thomas Cook is open weekdays 9:30–6.30 and Saturdays to 6. The State Bank of India is open weekdays 10:30–4:30, as are most other banks. L.K.P Forex is open weekdays 10–4.30, Nucleus Forex is open weekdays 9:30–5.

➤ EXCHANGE SERVICES: **American Express Travel Services** (✉ Regal Cinema bldg., Chhatrapati Shivaji Maharaj Rd., Colaba ☎ 22/204–8291). **L.K.P. Forex** (✉ 22/B Cusrow Baug, Colaba, ☎ 22/282–0574). **Nucleus Forex** (✉ Nucleus House, Saki Vihar Rd., Andheri East, ☎ 22/857–4484). **State Bank of India** (✉ Madame Cama Rd., Fort, ☎ 22/202–2426). **Thomas Cook India, Ltd.** (✉ Thomas Cook Bldg., D. Naoroji Rd., Fort ☎ 22/204–8556).

TAXIS

Auto-rickshaws are permitted only in Bombay's suburbs, where you can flag them down on the street. As with regular taxis, insist on paying by the meter and ask to see the tariff card.

Yellow-top black taxis or silver-and-blue air-conditioned taxis can be flagged down anywhere in the city. Insist that the driver turn on the meter, a rusty mechanical contraption on the hood of the car, before setting off. Because the development of taxi meters cannot keep up with the rising costs of fuel, it takes some arithmetic to compute the latest (higher) fares, based on the meter reading. Drivers are required to show you their revised tariff cards for easy reference, but they sometimes conveniently misplace them, or whip out a chart for air-conditioned cabs, or show you fares chargeable after midnight; examine the card carefully, and look for a policeman if you have doubts. At press time the legal fare was 14 times the total amount shown on the meter, based on roughly Rs. 13 for the first kilometer and roughly Rs. 1.5 for each additional kilometer. Air-conditioned taxi fares are 25% higher—the starting rate is Rs 16.50. Ask your hotel what the going rates are. You may call for a cool cab at 22/822–006, 22/824–6216, 22/490–5151, or 22/490–5152.

TOURS

The Government of India Tourist Office (open 9:30–5:30) trains and oversees knowledgeable, multilingual tour guides, available directly from the office or through the MTDC (☞ Visitor Information) or just about any travel agency. Rates are approximately Rs. 255 per half day for groups of one to four, Rs. 380 for a full eight-hour day with no lunch break (Rs. 510 with lunch break). Additional fees of Rs. 330 apply for trips beyond 100 km (62 mi) and for those involving overnight stays.
➤ CONTACTS: **Government of India Tourist Office** (☎ 22/207–4333 or 22/207-4334). **India Tourism Development Corporation** (ITDC; ✉ 11th floor, Nirmal Bldg., Nariman Point, ☎ 22/288–0992 or 22/202–6679).

TRAIN TRAVEL

Bombay has two train stations. Chhatrapati Shivaji Terminus, formerly Victoria Terminus, is the hub of India's Central Railway line. Bombay Central Station is the hub of India's Western Railway line. Be sure to go to the right train station—check before you set out. To avoid the pandemonium at the stations, have a travel agent book your ticket; this costs a bit more but saves time and stress. If you do it yourself, head for the tourist counter established specially for foreign travelers. Eliciting information about trains on the telephone is rather difficult because the lines are busy more often than not and the interactive voice response numbers are in Hindi. Instead, check out the Indian Railways site at www.indianrailways.com. For information on confirming a ticket or the arrivals and departures ask a local to make the phone call. For more information and recommended trains, *see* Train Travel *in* Smart Travel Tips A to Z.
➤ TRAIN INFORMATION: **Bombay Central Station** (✉ Bombay Central, adjacent to Tardeo, ☎ 22/135 for general information, including delays in arrivals or departures, in English; 22/132 for recorded information on arrivals and departures, in English; 22/263–5959 for recorded information on reservation status, in English). **Chhatrapati Shivaji Terminus** (✉ D. Naoroji Rd., ☎ 22/134 for general information, including delays in arrival or departure of a train. Call 22/265–6565 for recorded information on arrivals and departures in Hindi; 22/263–5959 for recorded information on reservation status in English).

TRAVEL AGENCIES

American Express and Ashoka Travels can help with general travel assistance and car hire; the former is open Monday–Saturday 9:30–6:30. The transport department of the India Tourism Development Corporation is also helpful with travel arrangements. For a complete list of travel agencies, pick up a copy of the ITDC's "Mumbai" brochure.
➤ CONTACTS: **American Express Travel Services** (✉ Regal Cinema bldg., Chhatrapati Shivaji Maharaj Rd., Colaba ☎ 22/204–8291). **Ashoka Travels** (✉ Kothari Mansion, 9 Parekh St., opposite Girgaon Court, ☎ 22/385–7622 or 22/387–8639). **Europcar** (✉ Vins Overseas India, 25A Nutan Nagar Turner Rd., Bandra West, ☎ 22/645–2796).

VISITOR INFORMATION

Don't count on hotels to stock general tourist information. The Government of India Tourist Office, near the Churchgate train station, has useful material; it's open weekdays 8:30 to 6, Saturday and holidays 8:30 to 2. The Tours Division of the Maharastra Tourism Development Corporation (MTDC) is open daily from 8:30 to 7. Both bureaus have counters at the airports; the MTDC also has counters at Chhatrapati Shivaji Terminus and the Gateway of India.

➤ TOURIST OFFICES: **Government of India Tourist Office** (✉ 123 Maharishi Karve Rd., Churchgate, ☎ 22/207–4333 or 22/207-4334; for recorded tourist background on Pune, Goa, Bombay, Ahmedabad, Aurangabad, and more, call 22/203–3144 or 22/203–3145). **MTDC** (✉ Madame Cama Rd. opposite L.I.C. Bldg., ☎ 22/202–6713 or 22/202–7762).

8 GOA

The former Portuguese colony of Goa is India's most famous beach destination. Silvery strips of sand are never more than a short walk from charming villages here, and the towns—among the cleanest in India— are a pleasing blend of Portuguese and Indian culture and architecture, including a number of historic churches.

IT'S HARD TO TELL where the coast ends and the towns begin in Goa. With more than 36 gorgeous beaches strung along the west side of its 5,945 square km (2,295 square mi), this tiny state—a Portuguese colony until 1961—is India's most famous resort destination. With the exception of the monsoon season (June to September), the temperature stays warm and the air stays dry. Wide, palm-bordered rivers move lazily down to the Arabian Sea, and in small towns the houses gleam with a light wash of color set off by brightly painted front porches.

By Julie Tomasz

Updated by Jayanth Kodkani and R. Edwin Sudhir

Goa was already a flourishing trade center before the arrival of the Portuguese in the 16th century—a marketplace for spices, silk, Persian corals, porcelain, and pearls. Yet ever since Alfonso de Albuquerque defeated Adil Shahi and established what turned out to be a 450-year dominance, the Latin influence has defined Goan culture. The quintessential Goan is fun-loving and extroverted—Goans love a good drink and a hearty meal—yet always has time for an afternoon nap. Even today, most shopkeepers lower their shutters for a long siesta. Beer is cheap, and *feni*—cashew or coconut-palm hooch—is a favorite local drink at the state's 6,000 watering holes.

But the sweep of development and modernity is gradually undermining Goa's vestigial Portuguese culture in favor of Indian culture at large. Fewer houses and lodges begin their names with "Casa" or "Loja"; barbers are no longer known as *barbarias,* nor tailors as *alfaitarias.* A few signs remain: HOSPICIO on the hospital in Margao, CINE NACIONAL on the movie theater in Panaji, and some shop signs with a Portuguese twist on common Hindu names, like POY for Pai, QUEXOVA for Keshava, and NAIQUE for Naik.

Although most travelers come to Goa for its beaches, both Margao, in the south, and the state capital of Panaji, farther north, are worth visiting for their sights alone. Panaji has whitewashed churches, palm-lined plazas, and clean streets and is a short taxi ride from the exquisitely beautiful Portuguese church town of Old Goa, the final resting place of St. Francis Xavier. Margao's Sunday food market is a chaotic spectacle, highlighted by garrulous fisherwomen selling their fish out of baskets.

Pleasures and Pastimes

Architecture

Goa is best known for its grandiose churches, exquisitely sculpted temples, and mosques, all three to four centuries old. The most illustriuos structures are Old Goa's *sé* (cathedral) and Basilica of Bom Jesus, where the remains of St. Francis Xavier lie in a silver casket entombed in a Florentine-style marble mausoleum.

Carnival

If you visit in February just before Lent, you'll see the Goans' zest for life in its finest form. Carnival time remains the official season for nonstop revelry, directed by King Momo ("King of Misrule"), a Goan appointed by his peers as the life of the party. Festivities include fanciful pageants (with some 50 floats depicting elements of Goa's folk culture, or more contemporary messages like preservation of the environment), hordes of musicians strumming the guitar or playing the banjo, and dancers breaking into the *mando* (a folk fusion of the Portuguese *fado* and the waltz)—all in streets spangled with confetti. This is prime time to have a beer or a feni and savor Goa's legendary warmth.

Dining

The Goans' legendary passion for seafood is borne out in the lines of the state's Poet Laureate, B. B. Borkar: "O, God of Death! Don't make it my turn today, because there's fish curry for dinner!" Portuguese dishes are generally adapted to Goan tastes with a healthy pinch of red chili, tempered with coconut milk. Typical local dishes include zesty-sweet prawn-curry rice, *chouris pao* (sausage bread), chicken *cafreal* (amply seasoned with ginger, garlic, green chilis, and lime), and ultrahot vindaloo dishes. Goa's seafood is superb, especially fresh crabs, pomfret, squid, lobster, and prawns. Try pomfret in a red or green sauce, or tiger prawns *baffad* (in spicy Goan style). For dessert, *bebinka* is a wonderfully rich layered pastry dense with butter, egg yolk, and coconut. And no Goan experience is truly complete without at least a taste of feni, the potent local brew made of either palm sap or cashew fruit.

Goa's best upscale restaurants are in the Bardez district, north of Panaji, but most travelers enjoy exploring the clusters of shack restaurants that line every major beach, serving up whatever the local fishermen happened to catch that day.

Lodging

Most of Goa's ritziest hotels are in the Bardez district, north of Panaji, but you might want to try one of the little lodging houses that have sprung up along the coast in recent years. If you want to explore Old Goa, consider staying in one of Panaji's grand hotels; the most notable of them, the Hotel Fidalgo, has a shopping arcade that sells everything from postcards to pearls. From December to February, traveling hordes often fill the hotels, so be sure to reserve in advance. During the monsoon season, prices fall by up to half. Unless mentioned otherwise, hotels have central air-conditioning, room service, doctors on call, and currency-exchange facilities, and rooms have cable TV and bathrooms with tubs.

Nightlife and the Arts

Head straight to the beaches for Goan nightlife. On Sunday night, all of southern Goa seems to descend on Colva for a night of drinking, eating, dancing, and playing *hausi,* a local version of bingo. Dancing and partying also happen at Baga, Anjuna, and any of the more remote beaches. The arts scene in Panaji and Margao is generally limited to Konkani-language theater and music.

Outdoor Activities and Sports

There's plenty to do in the Arabian Sea—in addition to swimming, you can waterski, jet ski, windsurf, and so on. You can rent sports equipment from any of the major resorts or from **Watersports Goa,** which operates out of a shack on Bogmalo Beach. The **Aqua Sports Association** (☎ 832/433192), based in Panaji, can refer you to other local outfitters.

Shopping

Most of the arts and crafts sold in Goa come from elsewhere in India, and the state has few flashy shopping areas. Between September and May, head to Anjuna's Wednesday flea market to browse through Rajasthani bags and clothing or Kashmiri blankets. Margao has a food market on Sunday, and Mapusa has a big, multifarious market on Friday. In March, Panaji hosts the spring festival of Shigmo, which fills the streets with stalls selling blankets, furniture, and sweets.

Exploring Goa

Closest to the capital of Panaji (also called Panjim) are Miramar and Dona Paula beaches, both city beaches written up in tourist brochures.

Avoid them. At Miramar, a strong undertow mars the swimming, broken glass and garbage litter the sand, and some of the buildings are architectural eyesores. Dona Paula is a glorified cement dock crowded with vendors.

For the most seclusion, head north toward Arambol Beach, cloistered in cliffs (and popular with European hippies), or, farther south, to Palolem Beach or another less developed beach below Colva. For pure beauty coupled with the comforts of a beach resort, opt for either Colva or Baga beach. If you want to windsurf or waterski, go to Sinquerim or Bogmalo beach, both an easy drive from Panaji. Surfers find that Goa's waves and wind generally only rise high enough during monsoon season.

Integral to the Goan beach experience are the vendors. You'll be approached constantly by men and women offering "Pineapples?" "Cheese?" "Cold drink?" "Drums?" Their persistence can drive you into the water. Nomadic Lambani women dressed in vibrant colors and silver jewelry set up blankets cluttered with handicrafts, jewelry, embroideries, and quilts.

Goa's inland sights are somewhat scattered, but taxis and hired cars connect them easily. Panaji and Margao are about a 40-minute drive apart.

For a slice of native Goan life, visit a weekly market. On Wednesday between September and May, vendors sell mostly Indian and Tibetan crafts and artifacts on Anjuna Beach, where a strong smell of fish fills the air. Friday is the big market day in Mapusa, the main town in the Bardez district; people from adjoining villages and even transplanted hippies convene to sell everything from vegetables to blue jeans to handicrafts. It's an ideal place to buy souvenirs.

Great Itineraries

Goa is a small state, so everywhere is within a few hours of everywhere else and taxis are affordable, even between Panaji and Margao. It's a leisurely, pleasure-oriented place, best seen in a state of relaxation.

IF YOU HAVE 3 DAYS

If you have only a few days in Goa, you might well spend them all swimming in the warm waters of the Arabian Sea and eating delicious fresh fish. Base yourself in the Bardez district and spend your first day on **Baga Beach.** Drive the next day to **Old Goa** for a few hours of sightseeing *or* take a longer, tourist-office bus tour of either south or north Goa. Stretch out on **Calangute Beach** on day three.

IF YOU HAVE 5 DAYS

Start your trip in the north. Spend a day and night at ⊡ **Baga Beach** or the isolated, ruggedly beautiful ⊡ **Arambol Beach** even farther north. The next day, explore ⊡ **Panaji** and **Old Goa,** and in the evening take a boat ride from Panaji. On your third day, hit ⊡ **Colva Beach** or ⊡ **Sinquerim Beach** and linger to watch the sun set. The next day, if you're up for more traveling, take a taxi down the coast to ⊡ **Palolem Beach,** another isolated and beautiful stretch of sand. Spend your valuable time on all of these beaches both swimming and exploring: walks away from the designated swimming areas are both enchanting and—a rare blessing in India—sometimes solitary. Taxi back to Panaji or ⊡ **Margao** to leave Goa.

When to Tour Goa

It's best to come to Goa in winter or early spring. During the rainy season, which stretches from the end of May to September, most beach-shack restaurants close due to heavy winds and violent surf. April and

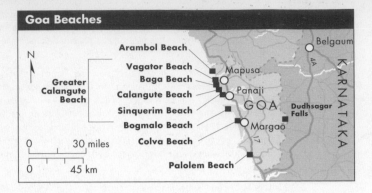

May are the best months for lolling around on the beach. If you come in early February, you'll experience the added excitement of Carnival.

PANAJI AND THE NORTH

Lovely old churches in Old Goa and a stretch of developed beach head the list of reasons to visit North Goa. Laid-back Panaji serves as a good base for exploring the area.

Panaji

600 km (372 mi) south of Bombay

The state capital of Panaji has whitewashed churches, palm-lined plazas, and clean streets, and there's none of the hustle and bustle you might expect from other capitals. The unhurried attitude of the residents adds to Panaji's charms and reminds you to take it slowly here.

Church of Our Lady of Immaculate Conception. This grand shrine was a mere chapel before 1541. Soon after it became a parish in 1600, its structure was rebuilt entirely, and the church now almost presides over one of Panaji's lovely squares. The building's most distinguishing stamp may be its beautiful zigzag staircase. The church's annual December festival draws huge crowds. ⊠ *Near Municipal Garden.* ⊠ *Free.* ☉ *Mon.–Sat. 9–6, Sun. 10–6.*

Dining and Lodging

$ ✕ **Cybercafe 2000.** Goa's first cybercafé is in the heart of Panaji. The approach to Cybercafe 2000 snakes through narrow alleys, but once you get here you can relax. Surf the Web for Rs. 30 an hour or just treat yourself to a coffee, snack, or ice cream. ⊠ *Shop No. 1, Sapana Center,* ☎ *832/231892. No credit cards.*

$$$ ⌂ **Cidade de Goa.** Built into a hillside near Panaji and modeled after a Portuguese hill town, this stylish resort works well if you prefer an urbane beach scene to a rustic retreat. Open, multilevel corridors run through the building, and the public areas have flat matte surfaces painted with contrasting oranges, tile floors in geometric patterns, and murals depicting the travels of Portugeuse navigator Vasco da Gama. The rooms offer two distinct decors: "Damao" rooms have a Gujarati ambience with terra-cotta, mirror work, and a sleeping platform; "casa" rooms are faintly Iberian, with white walls, blue tiles, and wicker furniture. Request a terrace and a sea view. ⊠ *Vainguinim Beach, Dona Paula, Tiswadi 403004,* ☎ *832/454545,* FAX *832/454541,* WEB *www. cidadedegoa.com. 205 rooms, 5 suites. 5 restaurants, 2 bars, pool, hair salon, massage, sauna, 2 tennis courts, exercise room, volleyball, beach, windsurfing, boating, jet skiing, parasailing, waterskiing, baby-*

sitting, dry cleaning, laundry service, meeting room, travel services, airport shuttle. AE, DC, MC, V.

$$ ⊞ **Hotel Nova Goa.** If you prefer amenities and comfort to stylish decor, check into this modern hotel in the center of Panaji. The rooms are large, though fairly crowded with furniture; bathrooms are also spacious. Some of the deluxe suites have bars and refrigerators. Ask for a room overlooking the Mandovi River. A doctor is on call here, and postal and laundry services are available. ⊠ *Dr. Atmaram Borkar Rd., Panaji 403001,* ☎ *832/226231 or 832/226237,* FAX *832/224958. 85 rooms, 6 suites. Restaurant, bar, pool, business services, travel services. AE, DC, MC, V.*

$ ⊞ **Hotel Fidalgo.** This majestic, neo-Victorian red and white hotel is Panaji's best-known lodging. The rooms are spacious, with wooden bedsteads and velvet drapes; bathrooms are merely adequate. A shopping arcade dominates the ground floor, and the vegetarian restaurant (A Machila) and coffee shop (Piri Piri) are popular with locals. ⊠ *18th June Rd., Panaji 403001,* ☎ *832/226291 or 832/226299,* FAX *832/ 225061. 123 rooms. Restaurant, pool, travel services. DC, MC, V.*

Outdoor Activities and Sports

The **Aqua Sports Association** (☎ 832/433192) can help you arrange water sports. Contact the **Yachting Association** (☎ 832/421901) for the scoop on local sailing.

River cruises, complete with live music and folk dance, leave Panaji's Nehru Bridge hourly to ply the Mandovi River. The short, hourly cruise costs Rs. 90; the full-moon special cruise costs Rs. 130. You can hire the piloted *Santa Monica* launch (☎ 832/230496) for Rs. 6,000 (lower deck) or Rs. 7,000 (upper deck) per hour.

Shopping

The **Silk House** (⊠ Dr. Atmaram Rd., ☎ 832/434691) sells saris and colorful *salwar-kameez*; credit cards are accepted. **The Khadi Shop** (⊠ Dr. Atmaram Rd., across from the Silk House), purveyor of handwoven cotton clothing, was established as part of the Gandhian tradition of economic self-sufficiency.

The shopping arcade at the **Hotel Fidalgo** is worth a short visit for jewelry, hand-woven textiles, and general knickknacks.

Old Goa

10 km (6 mi) east of Panaji

The beautiful church town of Old Goa served as the capital of the Portuguese colony until repeated outbreaks of cholera forced the government to move to Panaji in the mid-19th century. Though the town—once said to have rivaled Rome in splendor and Lisbon in population—has shrunk in size and importance, its glorious churches, fragrant gardens, and stately mansions still remain.

Dedicated to the worship of the infant Jesus, the **Basilica of Bom Jesus** is also known throughout the Christian world as the tomb of St. Francis Xavier, patron saint of Goa. The saint's incorruptible body has "survived" almost 500 years now without ever having been embalmed, and now lies in a silver casket. Built under the guarantee of the Duke of Tuscany, the basilica itself took the Florentine sculptor Giovanni Batista Foggini 10 years to complete around the turn of the 17th century. The basilica is the huge building on your right as you drive into town from Panaji. 🎫 *Free.* ☉ *Mon.–Sat. 9–6:30, Sun. 10–6:30.*

The imposing white **Sé (St. Catherine's Cathedral),** the largest church in Old Goa, was built between 1562 and 1652 by order of the King of Portugal. Fine carvings depict scenes from the life of Christ and the Blessed Virgin over the main altar, which commemorates St. Catherine of Alexandria. Several splendidly decorated chapels are dedicated to St. Joseph, St. George, St. Anthony, St. Bernard, and the Holy Cross. Only one of the cathedral's two original majestic towers remains; the other collapsed in 1776. The huge belfry contains the "Golden Bell," the largest bell in Goa. ⊠ *Across the road from Basilica of Bom Jesus.* 🎫 *Free.* ⊙ *Mon.–Sat. 9–6:30, Sun. 10–6:30.*

If your driver knows the local back roads, make a trip north to **Anjuna.** Even when it isn't market day (Wednesday), this town is spectacular, with windswept palm trees and a splendid coastline of sand and rock. It's a wonderful place to watch the sun set.

Mapusa

24 km (15 mi) northwest of Old Goa

Friday is the big market day in Mapusa, the main town in the Bardez district. People from adjoining villages and even transplanted hippies convene to sell everything from vegetables to blue jeans to handicrafts. It's an ideal place to buy souvenirs.

Dining

$$$$ ✕ **Cajueiro.** This local favorite serves up tasty Goan cuisine. You dine
★ outdoors, on a raised platform under a large straw-thatched roof supported by long betel-nut tree trunks. Candles and wood lanterns provide soft lighting at night. Specialties include pomfret fillets stuffed with prawns, and hearty mutton dishes. ⊠ *Mapusa Hwy., Alto Betim, Bardez district,* ☎ *832/417375.* V.

$$$$ ✕ **O Coqueiro.** Here the extensive, well-worn menu features fresh
★ prawn curries, hearty Goan sausages, and other local dishes. You dine outdoors, at rustic wood tables under a large thatched roof. If you have your own ideas, the chef is happy to cook up Goan dishes that don't appear on the menu. ⊠ *Alto Porvorim, Bardez district,* ☎ *832/217271. AE, MC, V.*

Arambol Beach

★ *36 km (22 mi) northwest of Mapusa*

Goa's northernmost beach, also known as Harmal, is ruggedly lovely. You enter through a lively but slow-paced hippie colony where young foreigners live in small huts. The best beach is a 20-minute walk to the right, beyond the ragged food and drink shacks. Here, the scenery is spectacular: a freshwater pond nestles at the base of the hillside just 50 yards from the crashing surf below, and the ocean foams around dark rocks rising just offshore. The sea is rougher here than at other beaches—still good for swimming but a bit more fun for surf-seekers. It can be crowded in season, but if you walk beyond the pond you'll find quieter tide-dependent inlets and rock ledges. ⊠ *Pernem district.*

Vagator Beach

12 Km (7 mi) west of Mapusa

At the north end of Calangute Beach (entrance beyond Mahalaxmi Bar and Restaurant), this tiny, semicircular getaway is backed by high palms. To the right and behind, Fort Chapora's dark-red walls rise above a low hill; to the left, a striking white cross tops a rock jetty. The picturesque setting makes Vagator a popular lunch spot on organized sightseeing tours. The gentle surf is good for swimming. Some shacks sell food just beyond the dirty, rocky rise on the right. ⊠ *Bardez district.*

Lodging

$$$ ⊞ **Sterling Holiday Resort.** This secluded, Goan-sty
white tile-roofed cottages sits in a palm grove just 43
high-tide line on pretty Vagator Beach. The rooms have
floors, geometric-print upholstery, and painted wood furniture. ⊠ *Vagator, Bardez 403515,* ☎ *832/273313 or 832/274337,* FAX *832/273314. 70 rooms. 2 restaurants, 2 bars, pool, beach, travel services. AE, DC, MC, V.*

Baga Beach

8 km (5 mi) south of Vagator Beach

This small beach north of (and technically part of) Calangute Beach is a lively place known for its hopping "shack life." The many popular food and drink joints are headlined by St. Anthony's for seafood and Tito's Bar for nighttime revelry. The beach drops steeply to the shoreline, where fishing canoes make use of the easy boat-launching conditions to provide rides, often to the Wednesday market at Anjuna Beach just around the bend (the ride to Anjuna takes 15 minutes by sea, but significantly longer by road). Farther down the beach to the left of the entrance are more open, less crowded areas where you can spread out your towel and sunbathe. ⊠ *Bardez district.*

Dining and Lodging

$$$$ ✕ **St. Anthony's.** This simple restaurant–cum–beach shack serves an astonishing variety of fish dishes, and possibly the best sweet *lassi* (yogurt-and-milk drink) in India. The tuna steaks and pomfret dishes are particularly good. ⊠ *Baga, Bardez district. No credit cards.*

$ ⊞ **Hotel Baia Do Sol.** This modern hotel on Baga Beach provides the best accommodation in Baga; the only drawback is the 200-yard arrival walk along an earthen track. The rooms are average in size but cool and breezy, and some have good views of the sea and countryside. The staff is courteous, and in the monsoon season (late May–late September), rates are discounted by as much as 60%. ⊠ *Baga, Bardez 403516,* ☎ *832/ 276084 or 832/740323,* FAX *832/731415,* WEB *www.ndnaik.com. 22 rooms. Restaurant, beach, travel services. AE, DC, MC, V.*

Calangute Beach

16 km (10 mi) west of Panaji

Stretching some 16 km (10 mi) from Sinquerim Beach north through Vagator Beach, Calangute actually comprises several smaller beaches including Baga and Anjuna. The main part of Calangute Beach, about two thirds of the way down (just south of Baga Beach) is an open stretch of sand accessible by cement steps. Palm trees provide patchy shade. A sign warns that swimming is dangerous, as there's a fairly strong undertow. Calangute itself is bustling: the entrance area is crammed with stalls and shops. The government-run **Calangute Tourist Resort** (☎ 832/276024) has general information and changes currency and traveler's checks. ⊠ *Bardez district.*

Outdoor Activities and Sports

You can hop aboard a dolphin- or crocodile-spotting tour, which winds past thick mangroves along the Zuari and Mandovi rivers, or even take a ride on a banana boat. For information, stop into **Casa Goana Restaurant** (☎ 832/276362) or **Cats Cruise Boats** (☎ 832/ 277000). **Odyssey Tours** (☎ 832/276941) rents out a luxury yacht.

uerim Beach

5 km (3 mi) south of Calangute Beach

Along with Bogmalo Beach, Sinquerim is one of the few beaches where you can rent Windsurfers, water skis, and other aqua toys without having to be a guest at a hotel. Stretching in front of the three Taj resorts, this small sandy beach gets fairly crowded with tourists and vendors. The water is warm and clean, and its slightly higher waves make for good bodysurfing. ⊠ *Bardez district.*

Dining and Lodging

$$$$ ✕⚇ **Taj Holiday Village.** Designed as a sort of ritzy Goan village, this
  ★   delightful tropical resort consists of tile-roofed villas scattered around gardens and lawns that face Sinquerim Beach. All rooms have private terraces and are elegantly rustic. The staff is friendly, helpful, and efficient. For a great dining experience, head to the Banyan Tree restaurant, renowned for its Thai cuisine—specialties include *gaeng kiaw waan goong* (king prawns cooked in green curry) and *pad thai* (noodles tossed with bean sprouts and garnished with peanuts). Facilities at the adjoining Taj properties are shared by all three resorts. ⊠ *Sinquerim, Bardez 403519,* ☎ *832/276201 or 832/276210,* FAX *832/276045,* WEB *www.tajhotels.com. 144 rooms, 7 suites. 4 restaurants, bar, pool, hair salon, 5-hole golf course, tennis court, health club, Ping-Pong, squash, volleyball, beach, windsurfing, boating, jet skiing, parasailing, waterskiing, dance club, baby-sitting, dry cleaning, laundry service, business services, meeting room, travel services, airport shuttle. AE, DC, MC, V.*

$$$$ ⚇ **Aguada Hermitage.** If you crave seclusion and luxury—and can af-
  ★   ford them—by all means stay at this Taj property. Set on a hill overlooking Sinquerim Beach and the Arabian Sea, the units in these Goan-style villas are like separate, elegant homes. Each has a large terrace with upholstered garden furniture, one or two bedrooms, and several other rooms. A regular car service shuttles you down the hill to the nearby Taj Fort Aguada Beach Resort, with which the Aguada Hermitage shares reception and all facilities. You may also use the facilities at the Taj Holiday Village next door. ⊠ *Sinquerim, Bardez 403515,* ☎ *832/276201,* FAX *832/276044,* WEB *www.tajhotels.com. 15 villas. Access to all facilities at Taj Fort Aguada Beach Resort and Taj Holiday Village. AE, DC, MC, V.*

$$$$ ⚇ **Taj Fort Aguada Beach Resort.** The dark exterior of this hotel, set within the ramparts of a 17th-century fort, blends well with its dramatic surroundings. The chic, open-air lobby affords gorgeous views of the fort, sea, and beach. All rooms face the sea and are furnished with contemporary Goan-style dark wood and cane furniture; you can also stay in intimate, tile-roofed, two-unit cottages. All facilities at the resort's sister Taj properties next door are open for collective Taj use. ⊠ *Sinquerim, Bardez 403515,* ☎ *832/276201,* FAX *832/276044,* WEB *www.tajhotels.com. 64 rooms, 24 suites, 42 cottages. 3 restaurants, bar, pool, barbershop, hair salon, tennis court, health club, beach, windsurfing, boating, parasailing, waterskiing, baby-sitting, travel services, airport shuttle. AE, DC, MC, V.*

MARGAO AND THE SOUTH

Margao, within striking distance of several beaches and sights, makes a good base for exploring South Goa. The town itself, with a bustling market, is worth exploring, too.

Margao

33 km (20 mi) south of Panaji

Margao, a busy commercial center, is a jumping-off point for south Goa's beaches and one of the state's most exciting natural sights: Dudhsagar Waterfalls. Combine a trip to the beach with a taxi ride to nearby Collem one afternoon to see the falls.

★ With a name that means "Sea of Milk" in Konkani, the **Dudhsagar Waterfalls** are suitably spectacular and imposing, with water cascading almost 2,000 ft down a cliff to a rock-ribbed valley. The regular train here—which passes over the falls on a rocky viaduct—from Collem, in east Goa, has been temporarily suspended, but you can still access the foot of the falls via a rough, 10-km (6-mi) jeep ride (Rs. 300 per person round-trip). The journey traverses rugged rolling plains, lagoons, and narrow mud paths hemmed in by bushes. Pack refreshments and bath towels, and plan to spend a morning here. It isn't difficult to find a private nook, but watch your step—the rocks are slippery. Monkeys, birds, bees, butterflies, and thick foliage complete the wild experience. The ideal time for a trek here is early summer or just after the monsoon season; during monsoon season the approach road is often inaccessible. The Goa Tourism Development Corporation (GTDC) organizes day trips from Panaji for Rs. 400; you can also take a taxi from Margao to the town of Collem, then hire a private jeep (at the railway station or market) with driver to see the falls. ✉ *Sanguem district.*

Also known as the Ancestral Goa Museum, the **Big Foot Museum** recreates in miniature a 19th-century Goan village. Guides explain the utility and significance of every object and article on display; highlights are the fishermen's shack, a mock feni distillery, and the spice garden. Within the museum's sprawling confines is an enormous, canopied dance floor, used for open-air private parties. ✉ *Near Saviour of the World Church, Loutolim, 10 km (6 mi) north of Margao,* ☎ *834/777034 or 834/735064.* ⛁ *Rs. 5.* ☉ *Daily 9–6.*

A magnificent church (also a seminary) near the Zuari River houses the **Museum of Christian Art,** the only collection of its kind in Asia. When in Goa, the Portuguese recruited local talent—Hindus as well as Christians—to create their sacred images, so many of these paintings and sculptures are curious blends of European and traditional Indian styles. The church is in Rachol, 12 km (7 mi) from Margao. ✉ *Rachol, Salcette,* ⛁ *Rs. 5.* ☉ *Mon.–Sat. 9:30–5.*

Bogmalo Beach

24 km (15 mi) north of Margao

Picturesque and rarely overcrowded, this tiny crescent of fine sand is perfect for swimming and sunning. It's overlooked by a low, verdant hill topped by a few modern buildings on one side and the Bogmalo Beach Resort on the other. Two tiny islands look back at you from about 10 km (6 mi) out to sea. For the most privacy, walk down to the far right—fewer fishing boats, shacks, and people. Another of Bogmalo's assets is its boating and water-sports facilities. **Watersports Goa,** operating out of a shack on the beach, provides instruction in various sports and excursions to nearby islands. Trips to the islands are also run by the experienced young staff at the **Sandy Treat** snack shack (the first one jutting out on the right); reserve in advance. For a lunch break, try the **Seagull:** a simple, thatched-roof shack right on the beach serving some of the best prawn-curry rice in Goa. ✉ *Bardez district.*

Outdoor Activities and Sports

You can rent water-sports equipment from **Watersports Goa,** which operates out of a shack on the beach.

Colva Beach

16 km (10 mi) south of Bogmalo Beach

Colva Beach, about 6 km (4 mi) west of Margao, is the most crowded beach in south Goa. Its large parking and entrance areas are crowded with shacks selling snacks and souvenirs and young men offering their mopeds for rent. The first 1,000 ft of the beach feel hectic—they're stuffed with vendors, cows, and fishing boats—but the sand, backed by palm groves, stretches in both directions, promising plenty of quieter spots to settle down. The water is good for swimming, with only nominal waves. The row of restaurant and bar shacks is the focus of nightlife for the whole region. Colva Beach officially stretches nearly the entire length of the Salcete district, but it's broken up into smaller sections. The government-run **Tourist Cottages** (☎ 832/788047) doubles as an information center. ⊠ *Salcete district.*

Lodging

$$$$ 🏨 **The Leela Palace Goa.** You're greeted with a coconut drink and a map, and you'll need the latter to explore this 75-acre resort with a gorgeous secluded beach. The two-story, salmon-colored cement villas arranged along a winding artificial lagoon recall a South Florida condo colony. Inside, the rooms have cool tile floors, dark-wood furniture, well-appointed bathrooms, and private balconies. Rooms in the villas ("Pavilion" rooms) are better and only slightly more expensive than the standard rooms in larger buildings. Children are welcome, and there's even a play center, Just Kids, for them. ⊠ *Mobor Cavelossim, Salcete, Bardez 403731,* ☎ *832/871234,* FAX *832/871352,* WEB *www.theleela.com. 137 rooms, 83 suites. 3 restaurants, bar, pool, barbershop, hair salon, outdoor hot tub, sauna, spa, steam room, 9-hole golf course, 3 tennis courts, exercise room, windsurfing, boating, jet skiing, parasailing, waterskiing, fishing, bicycles, dance club, dry cleaning, laundry service, business services, meeting room, travel services, airport shuttle. AE, DC, MC, V.*

$$ 🏨 **Silver Sands Hotel.** A simple, minimalist building set slightly back from the road, this is the best hotel in Colva. It's low on atmosphere, but the rooms are good-sized and clean, and some have air-conditioning. In the evenings, an outdoor barbecue is served poolside and there's often live music, sometimes Western pop. ⊠ *Colva, Salcete 403708,* ☎ *832/ 788099 or 832/788100,* FAX *832/788102. 67 rooms. 2 restaurants, bar, pool, health club, hair salon, travel services, airport shuttle. AE, DC, MC, V.*

Shopping

For crafts and silk, check out the **Handicrafts and Silk Emporium** (⊠ Shopping Arcade, Silver Sands Hotel, ☎ 832/788100).

Palolem Beach

37 km (23 mi) southwest of Margao

For seclusion and idyllic scenery, Goa's southernmost sandy stretch—nicknamed "Paradise Beach"—is a dream. Palolem receives only those nature lovers and privacy-seekers willing to make the rugged, two-hour drive from the nearest resort (Leela Beach). Palm groves and low, green mountains back a long, curving stretch of white sand. Depending on the tides, you can wander past secluded coves and nooks sheltered by rocks. Far to the right, the beach ends in a rugged, rocky point teeming with crabs. The water is shallow and warm, with very little surf. Shacks sell refreshments near the main entrance; an occasional vendor dispenses pineapples and bananas from a weathered basket on his head; and local men entice people into wooden canoes to go and look for dolphins. ⊠ *Canacona district.*

GOA A TO Z

To research prices, get advice from other travelers, and book travel arrangements, visit www.fodors.com.

AIR TRAVEL

Air India makes international connections from Goa. Indian Airlines connects Goa to all major cities in India, including Bombay, Delhi, Madras, Ahmedabad, Calcutta, Cochin, and Hyderabad. Jet Airways flies between Goa and Bombay, Cochin, and Delhi. Check with your travel agent for the current schedules of other domestic airlines.
➤ AIRLINES AND CONTACTS: **Air India** (⊠ Hotel Fidalgo, Panaji, ☎ 832/431100 or 832/431101). **Indian Airlines** (⊠ Dempo House, Deyanand Bandodkar Marg, Panaji, ☎ 832/425525). **Jet Airways** (⊠ Sesa Ghor, near bus stand, Panaji, ☎ 832/431472 or 832/437497).

AIRPORTS AND TRANSFERS

Goa's airport is in Dabolim, 29 km (18 mi) from Panaji. Buses are infrequent, so it's usually best to take a taxi from here to your destination. You can arrange pre-paid taxi service at a counter inside the airport, or go straight outside and hire a private cab. Either way, the fare to Panaji should not exceed Rs. 300.
➤ AIRPORT INFORMATION: **Dabolim Airport** (☎ 832/540918).

BUS TRAVEL

The easiest way to reach Goa from Bombay over land is by bus, a 17-hour trip, which will take you to the bus station in Panaji. The most reliable and comfortable bus company is Quickways Travel, which makes the round-trip for Rs. 479.

Local buses are cheap and frequent, but they're terrifyingly over-crowded—be prepared to fight your way on and off.
➤ BUS INFORMATION: **Quickways Travel** (⊠ 1st Dhobitalao La., near Lalit Bar, Bombay, ☎ 22/209–1645; ⊠ 8 Gasalia Bldg., Margao, ☎ 832/715060).

CARS AND DRIVERS

To hire a car for sightseeing, contact local tour operators (☞ Tours).

EMERGENCIES

The Holy Spirit and Neha pharmacies are open 24 hours.
➤ EMERGENCY CONTACTS: **Ambulance** (☎ 102). **Fire** (☎ 101). **Police** (☎ 100).
➤ HOSPITAL: **Goa Medical College** (⊠ Bambolim, ☎ 832/225727).
➤ PHARMACIES: **Holy Spirit Medical Stores** (⊠ Old Market, Margao, ☎ 832/732553). **Neha Chemists and Druggists** (⊠ Mala, Near Bhandare Hospital, Panaji, ☎ 832/421313).

ENGLISH-LANGUAGE MEDIA

Singbal's Book House sells English-language newspapers and books; it's open Monday to Saturday, 9 to 4.
➤ CONTACT: **Singbal's Book House** (⊠ Opposite Mary Immaculate Conception Church, Panaji).

MAIL AND SHIPPING

The General Post Office in Panaji is open weekdays 9:30 to 5:30.
➤ POST OFFICES: **General Post Office** (✉ Patto Bridge, Panaji, ☎ 832/223706).

MONEY MATTERS

CURRENCY EXCHANGE

Most major hotels will change money for their guests. In Anjuna, go to the Oxford Money Exchange/Bureau de Change. In Colva, hotels run by the Goa Tourism Development Corporation (GTDC) have exchange desks.
➤ EXCHANGE SERVICES: **Oxford Money Exchange/Bureau de Change** (✉ 111/6, Mazal Vaddo, opposite chapel, ☎ 832/273251 or 832/273269). **State Bank of India** (✉ Near Municipal Garden, Margao, ☎ 832/721882 or 832/721889; 18th June Rd., Panaji, ☎ 832/224662 or 832/224566). **Thomas Cook** (✉ 8 Alcon Chambers, D. B. Marg, Panaji, ☎ 832/221312; roadside between Calangute and Baga, near Hotel Ofrill Bldg., ☎ 832/275693).

MOTORBIKES

You can rent motorbikes at bus stops, railway stations, markets, and beach resorts for about Rs. 300 per day. You'll need an international driver's license to drive anything larger than a 55-cc engine.

TAXIS

Try to negotiate a price before you set off. A six-hour day should cost about Rs. 600, but drivers will probably insist on your paying more. Many people rent motorbikes for the short trips between beaches.

TELEPHONES AND E-MAIL

There are many telephone kiosks in market areas. The best one in Margao is the Cyberlink Advertising and Communications Centre. You can send E-mail from the Cyber Inn in Margao.
➤ CONTACTS: **Cyber Inn** (✉ 105, Kalika Chambers, behind Grace Church, Varde Valaulikar Rd., Margao, ☎ 832/731531). **Cyberlink Advertising and Communications Centre** (✉ 9 Lower Ground Floor, Rangavi, opposite Municipal Bldg., ☎ 834/734414).

TOURS

There are literally dozens of private tour operators in Goa, most offering 10-hour tours of the state. Contact one of the agencies below for details.

For a private guide, contact a tourist office (☞ Visitor Information). The transport wing of the Goa Tourism Development Corporation runs day-long bus tours of both north and south Goa—departing from Panaji, Margao, and Colva Beach—as well as river cruises from the Santa Monica pier in Panaji.
➤ CONTACTS: **Coastal Tours and Travels** (✉ 31st January Rd., Panaji, ☎ 832/423072). **Goa Sea Travels Agency** (✉ opposite Tourist Hotel, Panaji, ☎ 832/425925). **Tourist Home** (✉ Patto Bridge, Panaji, ☎ 832/224483). **Trade Wings** (✉ 6 Mascarenhas Bldg., Mahatma Gandhi Rd., Panaji, ☎ 832/432430 or 832/432431). **Trans Orient** (✉ City Centre, 3rd floor, Panaji, ☎ 832/229724).

TRAIN TRAVEL

For train schedules and fares, contact the rail station in Margao or the Tourist Information Centre in Panaji. To arrive in Goa via the Konkan Scenic Railway from Karnataka, board in Mangalore at 7 AM and plan to reach Margao at 1:30 PM if all goes well. If you find the landscape arresting, get off at Karwar, just an hour and a half before Margao;

spend the afternoon in that picturesque town, then take a bus or taxi to Goa. If you're coming from Bombay, get schedule and fare information at the Tourist Information Centre in the Central Railway Station. Hop off at Margao.

➤ TRAIN INFORMATION: **Bombay Central Railway Station** (☎ 22/308–6288). **Tourist Information Centre, Kadamba Bus Stand, Panaji** (☎ 832/225620).

➤ TRAIN STATION: **Margao** (✉ 2 km from the main shopping area, ☎ 832/712790).

VISITOR INFORMATION

In Panaji, the Directorate of Tourism fields general inquiries. For assistance with reservations, including bus tours, contact the Goa Tourism Development Corporation (GTDC). Margao's Tourist Information Centre is a good source of information, including details on the Konkan Railway, and has maps of the state.

➤ TOURIST OFFICES: **Directorate of Tourism** (✉ Government of Goa, Tourist Home, Patto Bridge, Panaji, ☎ 832/228819). **Goa Tourism Development Corporation (GTDC)** (✉ Trionara Apartments, Dr. Alvares Costa Rd., Panaji, ☎ 832/226515, 832/226728, or 832/224132). **Margao Tourist Information Centre** (✉ Tourist Hostel, near Municipal Garden, Margao, ☎ 832/715204).

9 KARNATAKA

Outside Bangalore, Karnataka's high-tech tropical capital, village life transports you to an earlier time. Mysore is a city of palaces—the former maharaja's palace is an architectural tour de force. Near Mysore, the villages of Belur and Halebid have meticulously wrought 12th-century temples. The medieval city of Hampi is a hodgepodge of gorgeous ruins.

By Julie Tomasz

Updated by
Jayanth
Kodkani

KARNATAKA IS A MICROCOSM of the most colorful and fascinating aspects of India, presented at a comfort level that can be Oriental-sumptuous and Occidental-efficient. Roughly the size of New England, Karnataka has probably hosted human civilization as long as any place on earth. Scattered throughout the state, in such places as Belur, Halebid, and Hampi, are some of the greatest religious monuments in India. The climate is as varied as the culture, ranging from humid to dry and cool, the result of a geography that combines sea coast with tropical uplands and arid zones.

Karnataka's 46 million people—called Kannadigas after their language, Kannada—are sinewy and robust in build, humble in disposition. In villages, women wait patiently with their jugs at the well, which doubles as the social center. Men, often scantily dressed in *lungis* (colorful skirtlike wraps) or *dhotis* (white skirtlike wraps) work in the fields, walking slowly behind oxen dragging plows that have not changed much in 3,000 years. The climate makes it possible to live perpetually outdoors—village huts are often of rudimentary construction, and people frequently set up their beds outside.

The simplicity of Karnataka's countryside is balanced by the grand palaces and formal gardens of Mysore, the youthful cosmopolitanism of Bangalore, and the relics, both Hindu and Muslim, of centuries of royal living. Even the outdoors can impress if you spend a few days on safari in Nagarhole National Park.

Although Bangalore and Mysore are well connected by express trains and comfortable buses, there are advantages to traveling by car: the countryside along the way is lovely, verdant with palms and rice paddies and brightened by colorfully dressed women washing clothes in the roadside streams. Timid passengers and back-seat drivers, of course, may be put off by the Indian driver's way of roaring around curves marked with skull-and-crossbones signs that read "Accident Zone"—on roads crowded with giant buses, plodding oxcarts, and men pushing bicycles laden with bunches of coconuts.

Pleasures and Pastimes

Architecture
Karnataka is most famous for its astonishing Hindu temples and its Indo-Saracenic palaces: the Hoysala-dynasty temples of Belur and Halebid in the south, the enormous ruined town of Hampi in the center of the state, and the Maharaja's Palace in Mysore.

Dining
Karnataka is truly famed for its *thali*, a South Indian staple made up of rice surrounded by several bowls of vegetables and sauces, all mopped up with large helpings of *roti* (unleavened bread). The thali is cheap, filling, and usually fairly easy on a foreigner's stomach. Also, unlike most parts of India, Karnataka brews a fine cup of coffee.

Bangalore has an up-and-coming restaurant scene, but options for dining out in the rest of Karnataka are few, with good food but limited menus. You'll almost always find tasty, predominantly vegetarian southern favorites like *masala dosas* (stuffed crepes) and *idlis* (steamed rice cakes), both served with coconut chutney and other condiments. A popular rice dish is *bisi belebath*, spicy lentil curry and mixed vegetables topped with wafers.

Konkan Railway

For a scenic panorama of India's Western coast from Bombay clear down to Cochin, there's no topping the new Konkan Railway, which stretches 756 km (470 mi) across the states of Maharashtra, Goa, Karnataka, and Kerala. In its very first year, the train became the lifeline of this region, and a spectacular one at that, with more than 170 major bridges, 1,800 minor bridges, and 92 tunnels cutting through the imposing Western Ghats (a chain of highlands covered with tropical evergreen forests). To make the most of the Konkan Railway in Karnataka, take a ride on the Mangalore-Margao passenger train, which runs to and fro every day at a fare of just under Rs. 100. It isn't terribly plush, but the sights and sounds outside will absorb you. The train chugs across bridges—the longest on this route is the 2-km (1-mi) stretch over the river Sharavathi—and past rice paddies, sleepy villages, fishermen's backyards, hills, and marshy stretches where children play and cattle wander. Keeping you company inside is a mixed crowd: traders, nuns, students, laborers, fishermen, hawkers of snacks and beverages, and fellow travelers staring happily into the distance.

Lodging

Both Bangalore, the affluent state capital, and Mysore have sumptuous hotels set in verdant tropical gardens: since 1954, when the princely state of Mysore was incorporated into India, the maharaja's numerous summer palaces have been converted to luxury accommodations for travelers, including elegant restaurants in former grand ballrooms. Both cities also have some excellent hotels with very moderate rates. Options outside Bangalore and Mysore are few and far between.

Unless we indicate otherwise, hotels have central air-conditioning and bathrooms with tubs. In addition, many luxury hotels have exclusive floors with special privileges or facilities for the business traveler.

Performing Arts

Karnataka has a rich and ancient tradition of folk drama and dance, as well as a colorful contemporary scene featuring classical music and dance from throughout India. In Bangalore and Mysore, performances are frequent, sometimes daily, during the high tourist season (December through March) and major festivals; the rest of the year, there's usually something cultural brewing each weekend. Restaurants popular with foreigners sometimes have live music and even dance performances during dinner. Most events are free; if advance tickets are required, you can generally buy them at the venue for Rs. 50–Rs. 100.

Safaris

In southern Karnataka, thick forests—preserved from destruction by their status as national parks—are home to large elephant herds, tigers, wild bison and pigs, peacocks, and crocodiles. Ecotourism is taking off here, and some of the resorts (jointly sponsored by the government and private capital) are quite delightful. The Indian infrastructure here seems to run quite smoothly. If you're interested, inquire with **Jungle Lodges & Resorts Ltd.** (✉ Shrungar Shopping Centre, 2nd floor, M. G. Rd., Bangalore, ☎ 80/559–7021 or 80/559–7025, WEB www.junglelodges. com) about Nagarhole National Park, Ranganthittu Bird Sanctuary, Bhadra Wildlife Sanctuary, Bandipur, and Kabini.

Shopping

Karnakata's artisans flourish, creating exquisite hand-loomed silk fabrics, intricately inlaid rosewood furniture, and smooth sandalwood carvings. Sandalwood incense sticks, oils, and soaps make great, easy-to-carry gifts. Mysore is especially known for its incense and sandalwood, both of which are sold at the numerous spice-and-smell stalls lining the De-

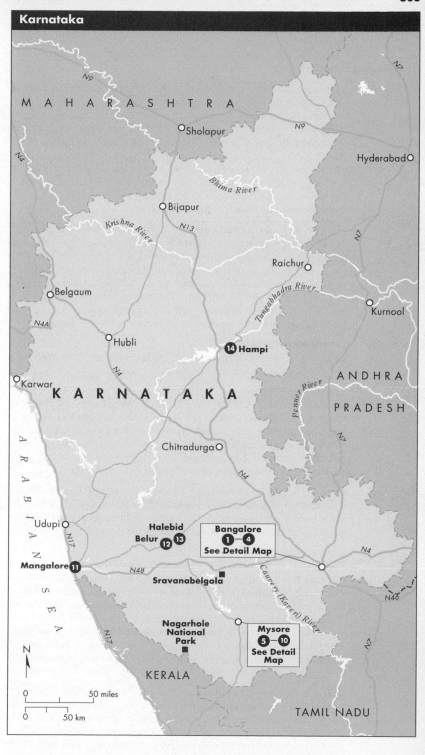

varaja Market. Bangalore also has curio shops. If you're not in a fixed-price government shop, bargain hard and remember that "old" often means 24 hours old.

Exploring Karnataka

Karnataka is a large state packed with fascinating places and historic sights. The main transport hub is Bangalore, so it's easiest to start your trip here. Both Bangalore, which considers itself the Silicon Valley of India, and Mysore (2½ hours away by train) are worth exploring in themselves. Bangalore is a boom town, with a population now in excess of five million; huge municipal gardens and a teeming old commercial district are interspersed with cybercafés. Mysore, in contrast, is an elegant old royal town, center of the princely state that existed from the mid-19th- to the mid-20th centuries. It's small in scale, tropical in appearance, and has India's finest zoo.

From Mysore, you can make two-day trips to Nagarhole National Park, on the Kerala border, home to elephants and tigers; or to the 11th- and 12th-century temples at Belur and Halebid, which between them hold more than 30,000 intricately carved sculptures; or to Sravanabelagola, with its awesome monolithic statue of the Jain saint Gomateshwara. For a refreshing outdoor stint, try the fishing camp on the banks of the Cauvery River. If you have time and stamina to spare, venture out from Bangalore to the spectacular abandoned city of Hampi.

Great Itineraries

Distances are long here, and road and rail transport are very slow. Don't try to see too much in a limited time.

IF YOU HAVE 2 DAYS

If you only have a few days in Karnataka, skip Bangalore and head straight to ⊡ **Mysore.** Spend the day exploring the Mysore Palace in the center of town and wandering the teeming Devaraja Market. In the afternoon, visit the sprawling zoo, where animals roam in open areas separated from onlookers by moats. Treat yourself to dinner at the Lalitha Mahal Palace Hotel, former home of the local maharaja.

For day two, hire a driver and leave Mysore early in the morning for a day trip to ⊡ **Belur** and ⊡ **Halebid,** 2½ hours away. Their temples are breathtaking, and if you're lucky, you might happen upon a Hindu wedding ceremony in the wedding temple at Belur.

IF YOU HAVE 5 DAYS

Spend your first day in ⊡ **Bangalore.** You can wander on your own or join a bus tour sponsored by the tourist office; just make sure you don't miss the Lal Bagh gardens or the fancy shopping arcades on Brigade and Mahatma Gandhi roads. After dinner, take the commuter train 2½–3 hours to ⊡ **Mysore** for your first night and second day. For day three, either book a safari in ⊡ **Nagarhole National Park,** with an overnight stay at the Kabini River Lodge, or take a car up to ⊡ **Belur** and ⊡ **Halebid** for the day, spending the night there (at nearby Hassan) or returning to Mysore in the evening.

Take a car back to Bangalore and then the overnight train to Hospet, arriving the morning of day four. Take a taxi or auto-rickshaw at Hospet and go straight to the astonishing ruins of ⊡ **Hampi,** 13 km (8 mi) outside town. Hire a guide at Hampi Bazaar and spend your last two days exploring the ruins. From Hospet you can make train connections to Guntakal, and from there to most major cities in India.

If you have time to spare, first follow the five-day itinerary above, making sure you see ⊞ **Nagarhole National Park.** Return to Bangalore and take the train to Hospet. Spend two days at **Hampi** and return by the same train to Bangalore or take a bus to Hassan. On day eight, explore ⊞ **Belur** and ⊞ **Halebid** and return to your hotel in Hassan. Take an early-morning bus to ⊞ **Mangalore,** about 4½ hours away. Spend the day roaming the beaches at Panambur, Malpe, or Ullal (by the Summer Sands Beach Resort) and the temple town of **Udupi.** The next morning, experience sustained coastal scenery with a trip on the scenic **Konkan Railway.** You can hop off at Karwar for lunch in the afternoon and take an evening train back to Mangalore, or take the train right out of Karnataka to Goa or Bombay.

When to Tour Karnataka

Like most of India, Karnataka is nicest between October and February, when the weather is sunny and dry but not unbearably hot. March through May is very hot, particularly in Hampi, and June through September is very wet, especially along the coast. If you can bear the heat, however, Karnataka's main attractions are much emptier in the hot months, and many hotels offer major discounts; just try to visit the Hampi ruins in the early morning or late afternoon to avoid the hot sun. Many towns hold long religious festivals just prior to the monsoon.

Numbers in the text correspond to numbers in the margin and on the Bangalore and Mysore maps.

BANGALORE

❶–❹ *1,040 km (645 mi) southeast of Bombay, 140 km (87 mi) northeast of Mysore, 290 km (180 mi) west of Madras*

Bangalore exudes modernity, albeit with touches of a long-standing culture clash. Brigade Road, St. Marks Road, Fraser Town, Cubbon Road, and Queen's Circle have all retained their names from the British days, and there's a divide between the cosmopolitan Cantonment area and the more traditional City area. The Cantonment's yuppies lead a Western lifestyle; at the other side of Cubbon Park, the City's more conventional inhabitants guard middle-class values and a section once ruled by the princely state of Mysore. M. G. Road and Brigade Road constitute the center of the garrison, where quaint old buildings sit next to latter-day shopping malls. Near the train station K. G. Road, also known as the Majestic area, abounds in offices, shops, cinemas, hawkers, and travelers.

There's an interesting anecdote about how Bangalore was named. King Ballala of the Hoysala dynasty once lost his way in the forest and chanced upon a poor old woman who could only offer him boiled beans. Pleased with her hospitality, the king christened the place as Bendakaluru, literally the "town of boiled beans." Over the centuries, the name became anglicized to Bangalore.

Kempegowda, a feudal lord, actually founded the city in AD 1537, and his son, Kempegowda II, developed it. After the fall of the Vijayanagar empire in 1638, the city came under the rule of the Sultan of Bijapur, Mohammed Adil Shah. Shah, who was pleased with the services of his trusted lieutenant Shahji Bhonsale (father of the Maratha King Shivaji), gave him the city as a gift. The Marathas ruled Bangalore for 49 years until they lost it to the Mughals who, in turn, handed it over to the Wodeyars of Mysore.

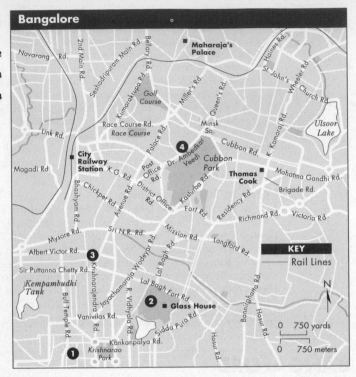

In 1759, the city was taken over by Hyder Ali, father of Tipu Sultan. Bangalore flourished during his reign and that of his son, Tipu, who was enthroned as the ruler of Mysore in 1783. Known as a brave warrior, Tipu fought against the British, and his exceptional military tactics and valiance earned him the title of the Tiger of Mysore. After Tipu died in battle, the British took over and modernized Bangalore. In 1881 the British returned much of it to the Wodeyars, who held great influence over the region until independence and the eventual abolition of princely rule.

Thanks to its salubrious climate and green environs, Bangalore is often called the "Pensioners' Paradise." In the 1980s it began to attract the telecommunications and technology industries, and it's now India's fastest-growing city. This boom has attracted multinational corporations and along with them have come such Western amenities as trendy boutiques, pizza parlors, cyber kiosks, and pubs. Indeed, beer is imbibed with gusto in nearly 200 establishments, though local authorities now enforce an 11 PM closing time. Despite all the growth, effective urban planning—rare in India—has given the city a serene, orderly feel.

A Good Walk

Bangalore's heart is the area near Mahatma Gandhi, Brigade, and Residency roads. The bustling streets around the train station and Race Course Road are also well worth getting lost in for a couple of hours. For a good tour, start with a taxi to the **Bull Temple** ①. A 20-minute walk east on B. P. Wadia Road brings you to the tropical **Lal Bagh Botanical Gardens** ②. Head north through the gardens and come out on the Lal Bagh Fort Road side; turn left onto this road and continue to a large intersection. On your left is Krishnarajendra Road; on your right, Avenue Road. Turn onto Avenue Road, and shortly, on your left, where Avenue Road is intersected by Albert Victor Road, you'll come to **Tipu's Palace** ③.

Outside the palace, the urban scenery is rather dull, so you might decide to cheat and take an auto-rickshaw. If you do, stop at Mysore Bank Circle and walk down K. G. Road for 10 minutes to get a feel for this crowded area. Alternately, follow the narrow, busy Avenue Road for about 2 km (1 mi) to reach Mysore Bank Circle and K. G. Road. From some point on K. G. Road, take an auto-rickshaw to **Vidhana Soudha** ④, on Dr. Ambedkar Veedi Road, the spectacular building that houses the state legislature. To your right is the redbrick High Court. Continue up Dr. Ambedkar Veedi Road until you come to the General Post Office building on your right. Turn right and walk toward Minsk Square (here, again, the scenery is insignificant, so you may want to take an auto-rickshaw). From Minsk Square you can walk left along the tree-lined Cubbon Road or straight toward Queen's Circle, with the cricket stadium on your left and Cubbon Park on your right. From either one, return to Queen's Circle, where M. G. Road—with its cybercafés, ritzy arcades, and craft and silk emporiums—starts.

TIMING

You'll need the best part of a day for this walk, though taking auto-rickshaws on the plainer stretches can save some time. The Lal Bagh Gardens deserve at least an hour, Tipu's Palace half an hour, and the Vidhana Soudha another half an hour. It's best to set off fairly early in the morning, as the gardens are most pleasant then (and in the early evening).

Sights to See

❶ Bull Temple. This small temple houses the enormous 1786 monolith of Nandi, the sacred Hindu bull, vehicle of Shiva. The temple's front yard bustles with activity: peddlers sell coconuts, bananas, and jasmine blossoms for offerings. Don't be alarmed if a woman sitting on the pavement suddenly yanks out a live cobra from a straw basket in front of her, taunting it to fan out its collar: for a few rupees, you can snap a photo of the angry creature from as close (or as far) as you wish. Inside, Nandi lies in his traditional position, leaning slightly to one side with his legs tucked beneath him. The bull's hefty black bulk is beautifully carved and ornamented with bells, and glistens with coconut oil that priests apply regularly to keep the stone moist. ✉ *Bull Temple Rd.* 🎫 *Free.* ☉ *Daily 6 AM–8 PM.*

❷ Lal Bagh Botanical Gardens. This 240-acre park, popular with young lovers, is one of the remaining reasons for Bangalore's increasingly obscure nickname, "The Garden City." Closed to auto traffic, the park is laced with pedestrian paths past more than 100 types of trees and thousands of varieties of plants and flowers from all over the world. Most of the flora are in fullest bloom between October and December. Some trees, like the venerable 200-year-old elephant tree near the western gate entrance, date from the time of Tipu Sultan, who continued to develop the park in the late 18th century after the death of his father, Hyder Ali, who designed the grounds in 1760. Marking the heart of Lal Bagh is the **Rose Garden,** a square, fenced-in plot blooming with some 150 different kinds of roses. Just beyond, near the north gate entrance, is the **Glass House,** a cross-shaped pavilion built in 1881 with London's Crystal Palace in mind. Twice a year, around Independence Day (August 15) and Republic Day (January 15), weeklong flower shows are held here. ✉ *Lal Bagh Fort Rd.,* ☎ *80/602231.* 🎫 *Free; Rs. 5 during flower shows.* ☉ *Daily sunrise–sunset.*

❸ Tipu's Palace. Tipu Sultan built this palace for himself in 1789. Made of wood, it's a replica of his summer palace on Srirangapatnam (a river island near Mysore), sans the elaborate fresco painting inside. The building now houses a modest photo exhibit about Tipu and his times. ⊠ *Albert Victor Rd.* 🎫 *$5.* ⊙ *Daily 8–5:30.*

❹ Vidhana Soudha. Bangalore's most beautiful building is a relatively recent addition to the city, built between 1954 and 1958 to house the state legislature and secretariat. The sprawling granite structure was designed in the Indo-Dravidian style, studded with pillars and carved ledges and topped with a central dome that's crowned, in turn, with a golden four-headed lion, emblem of the great 3rd-century BC Buddhist king Ashoka. The interior is not open to visitors. Facing the Vidhana Soudha head-on across the street is another of Bangalore's attractive public buildings, the pillared, redbrick High Court of Karnataka, built in 1885 as the seat of the then-British government. ⊠ *Dr. Ambedkar Veedhi Rd.*

NEED A BREAK?   Rs. 30 buys a cappuccino at the **Café Coffee Day** (⊠ Windsor House, Brigade Rd., ☎ 80/555–0949). The atmosphere is young and hip, the air-conditioning is a blessing, and another Rs. 60 buys you an hour of surfing the Web. Sandwiches and snacks are also available. **Barista's** (⊠ Commercial St.) offers exotic varieties of java at reasonable prices. Try a Brrrista, a popular cold concoction that's served with or without ice cream and is made of full-bodied espresso, milk-based granita, flavored syrup, and purified water. If you prefer dessert with your coffee, stop at one of the branches of the city's New Age café **Java City** (⊠ Cunningham Rd., ☎ 80/228–7746; ⊠ Lavelle Rd., ☎ 80/221–5779).

Dining and Lodging

Bangalore has an up-and-coming restaurant scene, growing more and more cosmopolitan by the month. Chinese restaurants abound, as do Italian, American, and other ethnic eateries. For the latest hot spots, consult your concierge, the city pages of the *Times of India*, the *Deccan Herald*, or the weekly, *City Reporter*, available in bookstores.

The city is also experiencing a lodging boom, with dozens of business-oriented hotels going up in the prime commercial areas. Competition is stiff, keeping the majority of hotels in the moderate price range.

$$$–$$$$ ✕ **The Royal Afghan.** This posh poolside barbecue restaurant in the Windsor Manor hotel is one of very few in India serving Afghan cuisine. Charcoal-grilled kebabs are popular, along with the finely minced mutton with *paratha* bread. ⊠ *Welcomgroup Windsor Manor, 25 Sankey Rd.,* ☎ *80/226–9898. AE, DC, MC, V. No lunch.*

$$–$$$$ ✕ **Ebony.** This popular rooftop restaurant sits unsuperstitiously on the 13th floor of a hotel. The tables on the two outdoor terraces have lovely views of Bangalore and are in high demand in the evening, when the South Indian sun cools down and the city lights come on. The excellent chef specializes in Parsi cuisine, unusual in Bangalore, and also cooks good North and South Indian and Continental fare. On Saturday you can sample unusual, spicy Balti food from the Indian-Afghan border. Note that the food is very spicy, and dinner reservations are essential. ⊠ *Ivory Tower Hotel, 13th floor, 84 M. G. Rd.,* ☎ *80/558–9333 or 80/560–001. AE, DC, MC, V.*

$$–$$$$ ✕ **Karavalli.** At this top restaurant you dine on a shady terrace walled in by hedges, or in an adjoining cottage. Waiters wear dhotis, and South Indian classical music sets the tone. The menu features coastal cuisines from Goa, Kerala, and Mangalore; two regional specialties are *kori gassi* (chicken pieces simmered in coconut gravy) served with *neer dosa* (a Karnataka-style crepe), and *kane bezule* (fish marinated in ground Mangalorean spices, then deep-fried). Save room for *bebinka*, the sin-

fully rich Goan dessert of egg yolk, butter, and coconut. ⊠ *Taj Gateway Hotel, 66 Residency Rd.,* ☎ *80/558–4545. AE, DC, MC, V.*

$$–$$$$ ✕ **Paradise Island.** India's very first Thai restaurant is set in a cross-
★ shape gazebo, surrounded by water and lush plants. The menu has
evolved to incorporate Chinese, Japanese, Singaporean, and other
Asian cuisines, but the emphasis remains on Thai food. Specialties in-
clude *som tam* (spicy-sweet raw-papaya salad tossed with peanut
sauce) and *hormok* (curried prawns or fish steamed and wrapped in
banana leaves). Try to save room for the coconut ice cream, or coconut
pancakes topped with orange sauce. ⊠ *Taj West End hotel, Race
Course Rd.,* ☎ *80/225–5055. AE, DC, MC, V.*

$$–$$$ ✕ **Nagarjuna Savoy.** Indian food from the state of Andhra Pradesh is
the focus of this smart modern restaurant, the upscale sister of the orig-
inal Nagarjuna eatery next door. Zesty-sweet chicken, mutton, and veg-
etable *biryani* are served on plates, not plantain leaves—not entirely
authentic, but fair enough if you're not used to eating with your hands.
The dining room is decorated with brass and copper masks and framed
prints of Indian folk art. ⊠ *45/3 Residency Rd.,* ☎ *80/558–7775. AE,
DC, MC, V.*

$$–$$$ ✕ **Tandoor.** The unusually long and sophisticated menu offers cuisine
★ from all over the subcontinent, with a focus on tandoori items that you
can watch being skewered and cooked by white-capped chefs behind
a large window into the kitchen. Particularly good are the chicken in
mint curry, chicken *seekh kabab* (think shish kebab), and fish *tikka*
(bite-size chunks). Gold-trimmed ivory walls and pillars, dimmed glass-
bead chandeliers, and single roses in small silver vases create a look of
traditional Indian splendor. One wall holds a beautiful mural of Afgha-
nis in the desert. The room fills nightly with a chic, professional crowd
and an amiable atmosphere. ⊠ *28 M. G. Rd.,* ☎ *80/558–4620. AE,
DC, MC, V.*

$$ ✕ **Angeethi.** Tucked away on the terrace of Museum Inn, this restaurant is fashioned after the many roadside eateries in the Punjab coun-
tryside: the decor includes a thatched roof, a water well, old Hindi film
posters, and a lamp post. Enjoy the kitsch atmosphere after you place
your order, since it'll be a while before your food arrives. It's worth
the wait, however. A moderately priced North Indian buffet is also available. ⊠ *Museum Inn, 1, Museum Rd.,* ☎ *80/559–4001 or 80/559–
5271. AE, DC, MC, V.*

$$ ✕ **Rice Bowl.** This spacious restaurant serves enormous helpings of Chi-
nese food. The soup and vegetable dishes are particularly good. The
decor is not enticing, but for Rs. 150 for an ample meal, who's look-
ing around? ⊠ *40/2 Lavelle Rd.,* ☎ *80/224–0216. AE, MC, V, DC.*

$–$$ ✕ **Chung Wah.** Modern East Asian decor—wooden latticework, Chinese fans and paintings on the wall, and hanging lanterns—defines this
cozy, popular restaurant, which offers most of China's several cuisines.
Two favorite dishes are *huli* chicken (sliced chicken simmered with soy
sauce and onions) and deboned pomfret with a choice of sauces from
mild to spicy. Expect crowds in the afternoon. ⊠ *45/1 Residency Rd.,*
☎ *80/558–2662. AE, MC, V.*

$–$$ ✕ **Koshy's.** For a coffee, beer, sandwich, or full-blown biriani, this old-
time café may be the quietest hideaway near busy M. G. Road. With
high ceilings, lots of smoke, and a dark, historic look, it has an air of
permanence, and the waiters won't blink an eye if you just want to
hang around for an hour sipping coffee and scribbling. Try the tender-
coconut soup. The separate dining section is called the Jewel Box. ⊠
35/2 Kasturba Rd., off Lavelle Rd., ☎ *80/221–3793 or 80/221–5030.
No credit cards.*

$–$$ ✕ **Mavalli Tiffin Rooms (MTR).** Come to this bustling Bangalore insti-
★ tution, established in 1924, for authentic vegetarian South Indian

food. Decor is decidedly not the point—some of the furniture is plastic—but you won't find better dosas in Bangalore, and you can't beat the prices. Desserts are also tasty, and the filter coffee is superb. You might have to wait for a table, but once the dhoti-clad bearer takes your order, food materializes quickly. ⊠ *Lalbagh Rd.,* ☎ *80/222–0022. No credit cards. Closed Mon.*

$–$$ ✕ **Nagarjuna Residency.** Justifiably popular, this large, noisy, casual emporium serves chicken, lamb, and vegetable *biriani* (rice casseroles) from Andhra Pradesh. In true South Indian style, the food is spooned onto a banana leaf, and you eat it with your fingers unless you request utensils. Don't order too much: *ghee* (clarified butter) makes the sauces incredibly rich. ⊠ *44/1, Residency Rd.,* ☎ *558–2233. No credit cards.*

$–$$ ✕ **Only Place.** Since its humble 1965 beginnings as a place where
★ American Peace Corps volunteers could get a wholesome taste of home and shoot the breeze with the kind and colorful owner, Haroon, the Only Place has become a Bangalore institution. Haroon still serves up what might well be the best American-style food in India. Best of all are his steaks—Haroon supplies beef to the American embassy and consulates, as well as other Western missions throughout India. The restaurant is conveniently located at the mouth of an ultramodern shopping mall. ⊠ *Mota Royal Arcade, 158 Brigade Rd.,* ☎ *80/558–8678. AE, DC, MC, V.*

$–$$ ✕ **Sunny's.** Small and elegant, Sunny's is best known for its French and Italian specialties—pizzas, pastas, and seasonal salads—along with deli items like hot dogs and sausages. It offers a grand dessert spread as well. Call ahead to reserve: lunchtime gets crowded. ⊠ *35/2, Kasturba Rd.,* ☎ *80/224–3642. AE, MC, V.*

$$$$ 🏨 **The Park Hotel.** India's first boutique hotel has been designed by Conran and Partners, U.K. The funky and vibrant colors of the building's exterior reflect the colors in India's vast and varied landscape. Each room has a different color scheme, and bright lighting makes things lively. The quality of service is in keeping with the spirit of the place—cheerful and fast. The 24-hour restaurant, Monsoon, offers a wide range of cuisine—from local, to Indonesian to Thai. ⊠ *14/7 M. G. Rd., 560001,* ☎ *80/559–4666,* FAX *80/559–4029,* WEB *www.theparkhotels. com. 110 rooms, 5 suites. Restaurant, bar, coffee shop, patisserie, pool, exercise room, baby-sitting, business services, meeting room, travel services. AE, DC, MC, V.*

$$$–$$$$ 🏨 **The Oberoi.** Slick, elegant, and well run, this young hotel has a stun-
★ ning lobby with a green marble floor, a central fountain, and a bank of windows overlooking the landscaped garden—which, in turn, is dominated by a gorgeous blossoming rain tree and a small waterfall cascading into a fish-filled lotus pond. The spacious rooms have polished green-marble entryways, private balconies, and handsome brass-and-teak furnishings. Each floor has a private butler. ⊠ *37/39 M. G. Rd., 560001,* ☎ *80/558–5858,* FAX *80/558–5966,* WEB *www.oberoihotels.com. 130 rooms, 9 suites. 2 restaurants, bar, pool, hair salon, health club, dry cleaning, laundry service, business services, meeting room, travel services, airport shuttle. AE, DC, MC, V.*

$$$–$$$$ 🏨 **Taj West End.** More than 100 years old, this hotel has a decidedly
★ Victorian look outside and in the public rooms. Most of the guest rooms are elegantly contemporary, with brass lamps and teak or solid cane furniture. The slightly more expensive "old world" rooms have a turn-of-the-20th-century look, with mahogany writing desks and brass four-poster beds. The best rooms in the main building are on the second floor; they open onto a veranda overlooking the pool. Suites have private verandas and sunlit alcoves. The setting is tropical, with 20 acres of lush gardens. ⊠ *23 Race Course Rd., 560001,* ☎ *80/225–9281 or 80/225–5055,* FAX *80/220–0010. 131 rooms, 9 suites. 3 restaurants, 2*

bars, patisserie, pool, sauna, 2 tennis courts, exercise room, baby-sitting, dry cleaning, laundry service, business services, travel services. AE, DC, MC, V.

$$$ ⛩ **Le Meridien.** The enormous atrium lobby of this modern high-rise sparkles with white marble and shiny brass carriage lamps. The hallways and rooms, in contrast, are surprisingly dark. The modern room decor includes burnt-orange carpeting, upholstered chairs and ottomans, and floral drapes and bedspreads. Windows are double-glazed. ✉ *28 Sankey Rd., 560052,* ☎ *80/226–2233,* FAX *80/226–7676. 196 rooms, 30 suites. Restaurant, bar, coffee shop, pool, hair salon, sauna, steam bath, tennis court, exercise room, baby-sitting, laundry service, business services, meeting room, travel services. AE, DC, MC, V.*

$$$ ⛩ **Welcomgroup Windsor Manor Sheraton and Towers.** Bangalore's prettiest hotel has a striking white exterior with arched windows and wrought-iron ornaments. In the lobby, a marble fountain sits beneath a domed skylight and massive teak pillars. The smaller, atrium lobby area in the Towers gleams with polished marble and brass, a suitable introduction to this opulent five-story wing geared toward business travelers. The handsome Manor rooms in the original wing have modern furnishings with endearing Victorian touches. ✉ *25 Sankey Rd., 560052,* ☎ *80/226–9898,* FAX *80/226–4941,* WEB *www.computan. on. ca/corp/sheraton/quickview/india.html. Manor 88 rooms, 12 suites; Towers 139 rooms, 1 suite. 2 restaurants, bar, coffee shop, pool, health club, dry cleaning, laundry service, business services, travel services. AE, DC, MC, V.*

$$ ⛩ **Ashok.** Built in 1971 in the park where Mahatma Gandhi once meditated, this hotel has a small memorial to Gandhi on the extensive grounds behind it. Guest rooms look fresh, with blue-gray and pale green decor and light-painted wood furnishings; the best rooms overlook the pool. The small marble lobby has low ceilings and comfortable wicker chairs. ✉ *Kumara Krupa, High Grounds, 560001,* ☎ *80/226–9462,* FAX *80/ 225–0033,* WEB *www.theashokgroup.com. 164 rooms, 17 suites. 2 restaurants, bar, coffee shop, pool, tennis court, hair salon, exercise room, dry cleaning, laundry service, meeting room, travel services. AE, DC, MC, V.*

$$ ⛩ **Central Park.** Tucked behind the Manipal Centre, a large commercial complex, this 10-story building is one of Bangalore's newer business hotels. Glass-backed elevators afford a view of the city en route to your room. Standard rooms are small, with standard modern furnishings and a few tartan-plaid details, but at almost the same price, the "park chamber" rooms on the executive floors are slightly larger, better-appointed, and include breakfast. ✉ *47 Dickenson Rd., 560042,* ☎ *80/558–4242,* FAX *80/558–8594. 126 rooms, 4 suites. Restaurant, bar, coffee shop, patisserie, bookstore, business services, meeting room, travel services. AE, DC, MC, V.*

$$ ⛩ **St. Mark's Hotel.** A short walk from the British Library and about 2 km (1 mi) from the center of town, this huge new hotel welcomes you with a marble-floored lobby. Rooms are carpeted in plush red, and come with coffee tables and flowery armchairs. The suites have separate living rooms and large wooden bars. ✉ *4/1 St. Mark's Rd., 560001,* ☎ *80/227–9090,* FAX *80/227–5700. 78 rooms, 18 suites. 2 restaurants, bar, café, business services, laundry service, travel services. AE, DC, MC, V.*

$$ ⛩ **Taj Gateway Hotel.** This Western-style Taj property offers cleaner and better-equipped rooms than its peers among the new, low- to mid-range business hotels, but it's on a very noisy street. The walls are adorned with framed abstract prints throughout; guest rooms have modern wood and wicker furniture and pale blue carpeting. Only the suites have bathtubs. ✉ *66 Residency Rd., 560025,* ☎ *80/558–4545,* FAX *80/558–*

4030. 94 rooms, 4 suites. 3 restaurants, bar, pool, exercise room, laundry service, business services, travel services. AE, DC, MC, V.

$$ **⊡ Taj Residency.** The large, white-marble lobby in this high-rise bustles with activity. Guest rooms are furnished with contemporary teak furniture and blue-and-green upholstery. Ask for a room on an upper floor with a lake view. ⊠ *41/3 M. G. Rd., 560001,* ☎ *80/558–4444,* FAX *80/558–4748,* WEB *residency.bangalore@tajhotels.com. 163 rooms, 5 suites. 2 restaurants, bar, coffee shop, patisserie, pool, exercise room, baby-sitting, business services, meeting room, travel services. AE, DC, MC, V.*

$–$$ **⊡ New Victoria.** Set back off the road and surrounded by palm trees and other tropical vegetation, this hotel is one of the best bargains in Bangalore. The airy rooms, with white walls sans embellishment, are average in size, and the atmosphere is friendly. Locals come by for snacks and drinks in the large courtyard bar-restaurant. ⊠ *47–48 Residency Rd., 560025,* ☎ *80/558–4076,* FAX *80/558–4945. Restaurant, bar, travel services. AE, DC, MC, V.*

Nightlife and the Arts

Nightlife

Bangalore is famous in India for its casual, upbeat pubs. Over the last 15 years, nearly 200 have sprung up throughout the city, providing a variety of hangouts where people of all types and trades can meet over a beer or other drink and listen to music (which is often loud) or watch TV. Most pubs are styled according to themes, such as a cricket stadium (New Night Watchman) or a subway station (The Underground). In an effort to curb local students' alcohol consumption, the government requires pubs to close for a few hours in the afternoon and shut down altogether by 11 PM; live bands must also call it a day at 11. Further regulations aimed at preventing prostitution and go-go club scenes have forbidden late-night dancing in clubs. A few major hotels, however, have special permits. All this may change, but it's at the whim of the government; check with your hotel for the latest on the entertainment scene.

Guzzlers' Inn (⊠ 48 Rest House Rd., off Brigade Rd., ☎ 80/558–7336) is a small and boisterous, often packed with young drinkers swaying to MTV. Don't let the posh, modern decor of the **I-Bar** (⊠ The Park Hotel, 14/7 M. G. Rd., ☎ 80/559–4666) fool you; the ambience is warm. At the **Jockey Club** (⊠ Taj Residency, 41/3 M. G. Rd., ☎ 80/558–4444) bar-restaurant white-gloved waiters serve silver steins of beer in a small room with richly carved teak walls, Belgian mirrors, and subdued lantern light. The **Megabowl** (⊠ Prestige Terminus II, Lower Ground Floor, Airport Rd., ☎ 80/527–0445) is a sports bar with pool tables, video games, *and* bowling lanes. **NASA** (⊠ 1/4 Church St., ☎ 80/558–6512) has the look and feel of a space shuttle; you duck through an oval door into two oval-shape rooms decorated in silver and black. The **New Night Watchman** (⊠ 46/1 Museum Rd., ☎ 80/558–8372), designed like a miniature cricket stadium, is popular with students.

At **180 Proof** (⊠ 40 St Marks Rd., Near British Council Library, ☎ 80/299–7290), a slightly upscale crowd relaxes inside an old stone building with psychedelic interiors. The **Polo Club**'s (⊠ Oberoi Hotel, 37–39 M. G. Rd., ☎ 80/558–5858) stained-glass windows afford views of lush gardens; a cascading waterfall adds to the serenity. Established in the 1980s, **Pub World** (⊠ 65 Residency Rd., Laxmi Plaza, ☎ 80/558–5206) may be the oldest pub in town, but it's still hip with its polished woods and shiny brass fixtures. On weekends, the **Purple Haze,**

(Opposite Konark Restaurant, Residency Rd., ☎ 80/221–3758) comes alive with hard rock and a throbbing dance floor, although it really isn't very quiet the rest of the week either. The **Royal Derby** (✉ Windsor Manor Sheraton, 25, Sankey Rd., ☎ 80/226–9898) is fashioned after a classic British pub and has a wide variety of cocktails and snacks. **Time and Again** (✉ Brigade Rd., ☎ 80/558–5845) is popular with a young set for dancing. **The Underground** (✉ 65 Blue Moon Complex, M. G. Rd., ☎ 80/558–9991) has one section designed after London's tube. Slightly cheesy but generally fun, this is a good place to end a night on the town.

The Arts

Your best sources for information on cultural happenings are the newspapers: the *Deccan Herald*'s column "In the City Today," usually on page 3, and the *Times of India*'s "Events" column in the city supplement. Other sources are posters, the Karnataka Department of Tourism (KDT), the *City Reporter* weekly magazine, and the staff at your hotel.

Bangalore has a number of venues for classical Indian music and dance and for plays, some in English. The violin-shape **Chowdiah Memorial Hall** (✉ Gayathri Devi Park Extension, Vyalikaval, ☎ 80/344–5810) hosts plays, dance and music performances, and film screenings. **Dr. H. Narasimaiah Kalakshetra** (✉ Jayanagar, 7th Block, ☎ 80/649684) is a popular destination for culture lovers in the southern part of the city. **Ravindra Kalakshetra** (✉ Jayachamarachendra Rd., ☎ 80/222–1271), built to commemorate the centenary of Nobel laureate Rabindranath Tagore's birth, houses a cultural academy and an auditorium where plays are held throughout the year. The Gothic-style **Sri Puttanachetty Town Hall** (✉ Sri Narasimharaja Circle, J. C. Rd., ☎ 80/222–1270) can seat more than 1,500 for its shows. The **Yavanika State Youth Center** (✉ Nrupathunga Rd., ☎ 80/221–4911) hosts free Indian classical music and dance performances and other cultural events most evenings.

On the outskirts of Bangalore, the **Nrityagram Dance Village** (✉ Nrityagram, Bangalore district, ☎ 80/558–5440) is a dance institution founded by the late Odissi dancer Protima Bedi. Here you can watch students at work while sampling aspects of Karnataka folk culture. The premises, which include a guest house, are modeled on a Karnataka village and designed for holistic living, with granite, stone, mud, and thatch the chief architectural ingredients. Nrityagram is the only village of its kind in India, devoted to the promotion and preservation of ancient classical-dance styles and two martial-art forms. For a taste of Indian mythology and cultural traditions, this is worth a visit.

Outdoor Activities and Sports

Bowling

If bowling strikes your fancy, head for **G's Alley** (✉ Mota Arcade, Brigade Rd., ☎ 80/558–8211). You can use the four-lane alley for Rs. 100 per game on weekdays, Rs. 125 on weekends and holidays. Tibetan and Chinese snacks are served.

Golf

The **Bangalore Golf Club** (✉ 2 Sankey Rd., ☎ 80/225–7121 or 80/226–6713), designed by the British in 1876, has a lovely 18-hole course open to the public. Call ahead to reserve your game. The restaurant serves some mouthwatering Chinese dishes, among other things.

Horse Racing

Thoroughbred racing is a major sport in Karnataka. The **Bangalore Turf Club** (✉ 1 Race Course Rd., ☎ 80/226–2391) goes into high gear from mid-May through the end of July and November through March, with races every Saturday and Sunday afternoon.

Shopping

Brigade Road is lined with flashy stores, foreign boutiques, and a number of multilevel shopping arcades. **Commercial Street** is a narrow, eclectic area packed with old and new shops selling everything from suitcase locks to Kashmiri hats to precious jewelry. **M. G. Road** is one of Bangalore's main shopping pockets, with government shops and some giant silk emporiums.

Antiques and Handicrafts

The state-run, fixed-price **Cauvery Emporium** (⊠ 49 M. G. Rd., ☎ 80/558–0317) sells all of Karnataka's craft products: sandalwood handicrafts, terra-cotta pots, carved rosewood furniture, silk, leather work, jute products, lacquered toys, *bidri* ware (decorative metal ware in black and silver tones), embossed bronze, soaps, perfumes, incense, and sachets. The **Central Cottage Industries Emporium** (⊠ 144 M. G. Rd., ☎ 80/558–4083 or 558–4084) is part of the nationwide government chain of fixed-price cottage-industry stores selling authentic crafts from all over India. It closes every day from 2 to 3. **Natesan's Antiqarts** (⊠ 76 M. G. Rd., ☎ 80/558–8344) sells an unusual collection of high-quality stone, bronze, and wood antiquities; old paintings; and exquisite new artifacts, plus silver jewelry and precious stones.

Books

Bangalore has about 10 large English-language bookstores. All have good bargains, but the best are on or near M. G. Road. **Gangaram's Book Bureau** (⊠ 72 M. G. Rd., ☎ 80/558–6783) is a four-story megastore selling books, CDs, cards, stationery, and toys. **Premier Bookshop** (⊠ 46/1 Church St., ☎ 80/558–8570), closed Sunday, is a small store crammed to the ceiling with books and owned by a friendly bibliophile named Shanbhag. At **Sankar's Book Stall** (⊠ 15/2, Madras Bank Rd., Off St Marks Rd., ☎ 80/558–6867) you can settle down on a sofa with your book. The **Strand Book Stall** (⊠ 113 Manipal Centre, Dickenson Rd., ☎ 80/558–0000), closed Sunday, has a wide selection of books.

Silks

A number of giant silk emporiums on M. G. Road sell top-quality Karnataka silk products, from solid-color material by the meter to bright, ornately hand-blocked saris and scarves. **Deepam Silk International** (⊠ M. G. Rd., ☎ 80/558–8760) has been in business for 25 years. **Karnataka Silk Industries Corporation Showroom** (⊠ Leo Complex, Residency Rd. Cross, off M. G. Rd., ☎ 80/582118; ⊠ Gupta Market, K. G. Rd., ☎ 80/262077), a fixed-price government shop, sells silks hot off the looms in Mysore. **Lakshmi Silk Creations** (⊠ 144 M. G. Rd., below Central Cottage Industries Emporium, ☎ 80/558–2129) has excellent silks. **Nalli Silks Arcade** (⊠ 21/24 M. G. Rd., ☎ 80/558–3178) sells silks of all kinds and some cotton clothing. **Salonee** (⊠ 8 Commercial St., ☎ 80/558–9637) has designer silks, chiffons, and cottons. **Vijayalakshmi Silks** (⊠ Blue Moon Complex, M. G. Rd., ☎ 80/558–7395) is another reliable option.

En Route   If you're driving to Mysore and would like an eyeful of Karnataka's folk traditions, stop at the **Janapada Loka Folk Arts Museum,** 53 km (33 mi) southwest of Bangalore. Displays showcase puppets, masks, agricultural implements, household articles, and some interesting color photographs of tribal life. There are also occasional live performances by drummers, snake-charmers, and gypsy dancers. A simple restaurant is on site. ✉ *Bangalore-Mysore Hwy., near Ramanagaram,* ☎ *913/ 71555 or 80/362768 to Karnataka Janapada Trust.* ✍ *Rs. 5.* ☉ *Wed.– Mon. 8–5.*

MYSORE

⑤–⑩ *140 km (87 mi) southwest of Bangalore, 1,177 km (730 mi) southeast of Bombay, 473 km (293 mi) north of Madras.*

No longer the capital of the princely state of Mysore, this palace-rich city survives as the principal residence of the former royal family. The maharajas accomplished much in the way of arts and culture, developing palaces, temples, and schools, and supporting the traditional Mysore school of painting, with its slightly cherubic Hindu images and abundance of gold leaf. When you witness the fruits of their patronage, you'll understand why Prince Jayachamaraja Wodeyar (father of the current prince, Srikandatta Wodeyar) was appointed the first actual governor of Karnataka. Mysore had been known for its progressivism during his reign.

Mysore has been called the City of Palaces. You can explore its main attraction, the Mysore Palace, in a few hours, and if you can manage a stay in the Lalitha Mahal Palace Hotel, the simple combination of the two will make your trip to Mysore worthwhile. An evening visit to Brindavan Gardens is a nice way to experience the Indian fascination with kitschy but charming colored musical fountains.

Despite its opulent past, there is nothing flashy or fancy about Mysore, at least not in the modern, commercial sense. There are relatively few places to wine and dine, and the streets are lined with far more dozing cows than boutiques. The congenial climate and small-town surroundings, replete with leafy avenues, make a trip to Mysore enchanting. Here you can admire (and buy) some of India's richest silks, woven with real gold, and other elements of an age-old spirit of elegance that endures even as it deteriorates over the years.

Palace Area

A Good Walk

Mysore is a small city, and its center is easy to walk around. Start your walk at the conveniently central **Mysore Palace** ⑤. Exit on the Albert Victor Road side and turn left; then, at the traffic circle with the clock tower, turn right. On the left you'll see the entrance to the Devaraja Market. When you've had your fill of shopping, return to the clock tower and go back along the Albert Victor Road past the palace. At Hardinge Circle, turn right onto Lok Ranjan Mahal Road. A few more minutes will bring you to the **Zoological Garden** ⑥. After strolling through the gardens, take a taxi to the top of **Chamundi Hill** ⑦ for a beautiful panorama of Mysore. Walk down the hill's 1,000 steps and catch a taxi, bus, or auto-rickshaw back to the city.

TIMING

You'll need at least five hours for this walk, and probably most of the day if you make it to Chamundi Hill. The distances are not long, but you'll probably want more than an hour or two at the palace, an hour at the market, and two or three hours at the zoo. Note that the zoo is closed on Tuesdays.

Sights to See

⑦ Chamundi Hill. Mysore looks its panoramic best from the top of this hill. The hill's 1,000 steps take you past a 16-ft stone **Nandi** (Shiva's holy bull), and the **Sri Chamundeswari Temple** on the summit is ded-

316

icated to the royal Wodeyar family's titular deity, the goddess Chamundi, an avatar of Parvati (Shiva's consort). The base of the temple dates from the 12th century; the ornately sculptured pyramidal *gopuram* (towering entrance) was built in the 1800s. Because it's still an active religious site, the entire area surrounding the structure teems with beggars and peddlers. The temple's inner entrances are staffed by aggressive priests hassling tourists into buying flower offerings and *bindis* (forehead dots), applied by a fat thumb right between your eyes. Tuesdays and Fridays, auspicious days, are the most crowded. In the middle of the parking lot stands a giant, colorfully painted **statue of Mahishasura**, the demon killed by the goddess Chamundi so that the region would be at peace; Mysore, originally called Mahishur, was named for him. The kitschy **Godly Museum** has gaudy paintings depicting eternal life and harmony. ⊠ *Southeast Mysore, 2½ km (1½ mi) south of Lalitha Mahal Palace Hotel.* ⊙ *Temple daily 6:30–12:30 and 4–8:30, Godly Museum daily 9–6.* ⊡ *Free.*

★ ❺ **Mysore Palace.** By far the most impressive structure in Mysore is the maharaja's palace, a massive edifice that took 15 years to rebuild (starting in 1897) after an earlier structure burned down. One of the largest palaces in India, it's set on 73 acres and designed in the Indo-Saracenic style—a synthesis of Hindu and Islamic architecture. The main rooms and halls are a profusion of domes, arches, turrets, and colonnades, all lavishly carved, etched, or painted, with few surfaces spared. The halls and pavilions glitter with unabashed opulence: giant brass gates for grand elephant entrances; silver-plated doors encrusted with patterns and figures; richly carved teak ceilings; ivory gods and goddesses; a 616-pound solid-gold howdah (in the first hallway you enter). The cavernous, octagonal **Kalyana Mantap** (Marriage Hall), where women sat behind screened balconies, exudes royal wealth, its turquoise- and gold-painted cast-iron pillars soaring up to a translucent dome of

Scottish stained glass with brilliantly colored peacocks and flowers. A massive brass chandelier from the former Czechoslovakia hangs far below, above a brilliantly multicolor tile floor. The **Durbar,** where public gatherings were held, is elegant and impressive, with a painted ceiling, turquoise Indo-Saracenic arches, and floors of white Italian marble inlaid, along the edges, with semi-precious stones. The smaller hall nearby, used for private gatherings, is rather gaudy, with sky-blue gold-leaf pillars, a stained-glass ceiling, a chandelier, and general Baroque excrescence; but there's some lovely carved wood on the ceiling, marquetry on the main doors, and inlaid ivory on the side doors.

The present-day maharaja (technically a prince—the last maharaja died in 1974) lives in a private wing at the rear of the palace. The **Residential Museum,** centered on a galleried courtyard, displays the prince's entire collection of Mysore paintings as well as artifacts illustrating royal life of the past.

On Sunday from 7 to 8 PM and on holidays, the palace is illuminated with thousands of tiny lights that turn it into a glittering statement of wealth. Negotiate the price for a guide: Rs. 50–Rs. 100 is optimal. For the ultimate palace experience, time your visit to coincide with the annual **Dussehra** festival in September or October, commemorating the victory of the goddess Durga (also known as Chamundi) over the demon Mahishasura. Mysore is known for its intensely colorful Dussehra celebrations: for 10 days palaces and temples are illuminated and cultural and sports events abound, culminating in a torchlight procession led by an elephant carrying an idol of the goddess herself in a howdah of pure gold. ⊠ *Mizra Rd.,* ☏ *821/22672.* ☜ *Palace Rs. 235; museum Rs. 235.* ☉ *Palace daily 10–5; museum daily 10:30–6:30. Shoes and cameras prohibited.*

⑥ Zoological Garden. This well-maintained 250-acre zoo is more than 100 years old (founded 1892). Today it's populated by lions, white tigers, giraffes, African elephants, hyenas, kangaroos, rhinos, and a variety of other animals from all over the world. One section is devoted to reptiles and snakes. A small museum has models of rare animals and birds. ⊠ *Indiranagar,* ☏ *821/520302.* ☜ *Rs. 235.* ☉ *Wed.–Mon. 8:30–5:30.*

Around Mysore: Art, Silk, and Gardens

A Good Tour

Hire a taxi for the whole day, or take auto-rickshaws from point to point. Start with a visit to the **Sri Jayachamarajendra Art Gallery** ⑧. After a tour of the **Government Silk Weaving Factory** ⑨, break for shopping and lunch. Finish with a trip to the **Brindavan Gardens** ⑩, 19 km (12 mi) northwest of Mysore, in time for the evening fountain show before returning to Mysore for a late dinner.

TIMING

This leisurely day trip gives you some free time in the afternoon to have a relaxed lunch and shop for silks and handicrafts. Plan to spend at least an hour at each attraction and some time traveling between them; the gardens are about half an hour's drive away.

Sights to See

⑩ Brindavan Gardens. Extending from the side of one of India's largest dams, this vast, terraced garden is the pride of Mysore and a magnet for Indian tourists, especially high-school and college groups. The park is rigidly laid out and carefully manicured, laced with long symmetrical paths and scores of fountains. Exposed metal pipes and concrete curbs betray its unnatural origins, but the profusion of fragrant flowers and the absence of cows and honking cars make it a comparatively peaceful place to stroll. At nightfall, people flock en masse to the far end of the gardens, a 30-minute long walk, to see water spout into the air only slightly out of sync with recorded pop-classical Indian music and pulsing colored lights. To get here, hire a taxi for the roughly 30-minute ride or take Bus 303/304 from the city bus station. ⊠ *Krishnaraja Sagar Rd., 19 km (12 mi) northwest of Mysore.* ☜ *Rs. 235; cameras Rs. 470.* ☉ *Gardens Mon.–Sat. 9–7:45, Sun. and holidays 9–8:30; fountain show fall–spring, weekdays 7–7:55 PM, weekends 8–8:55 PM; winter, daily 6:30–7:25 PM.*

❾ Government Silk Weaving Factory. The late maharaja created this factory in 1932, both to ensure the finest hand-loomed silks for himself and his royal family and to arrange for some profitable exportation. Now run by the Karnataka Silk Industries Corporation, the slightly dilapidated factory continues to produce Mysore silks coveted by women throughout India. From spinning and soaking to weaving and dyeing, it's all done here, resulting in simple cocoons, crêpe de Chine, chiffon, and other regal fabrics. Accompanied by a factory official, you can stroll through the numerous giant workrooms busy with whirring spooling machines and clanking mechanical looms, and witness the transformation of hundreds of hair-thin, colorless threads into a sari fit for a queen. Ask to see the work stations where threads of real gold are woven into elaborate *zari* borders. Bring your wallet for a post-tour pilgrimage to the factory showroom. The silks aren't as sumptuous as those in, say, Kanchipuram, but they make nice souvenirs, and the prices are good. ⊠ *Mananthody Rd.,* ☎ *821/21803.* ☜ *Free.* ☉ *Mon.–Sat. (except 2nd Sat. of month) 10:30–5. No cameras.*

❽ Sri Jayachamarajendra Art Gallery. Housed in the tired, 150-year-old Jaganmohan Palace, this slightly run-down museum displays paintings from various schools and periods of Indian art as well as beautiful antique inlaid wood, antique sandalwood and ivory carvings, and a variety of other decorative pieces. Some exhibits are truly esoteric, such as a set of carved-ivory vegetables and the amazing "rice paintings"—portraits painted on single grains of rice. The service of a guide is free, but most expect a tip. ⊠ *Jaganmohan Palace, Dewan's Rd., Devaraj Mohalla,* ☎ *821/23693.* ☜ *Rs. 470.* ☉ *Daily 8:30–6. No cameras.*

Dining and Lodging

Mysore has a relative dearth of sophisticated dining options. You can generally dine well in the hotels.

$$$ ✕ **Lalitha Mahal Palace Hotel.** Here you'll dine in the maharaja's cavernous former ballroom, a Baroque tour de force with stained-glass domes and sky-blue walls enhanced by ornate, white plaster moldings and pillars. Try the Mysore thali or the mutton *ulathiyathu* (mutton cooked with coconut, red chili, and curry). There's a flutist at lunch and a sitarist or vina player at dinner. You can even shoot some pool on your way out. ⊠ *T. Narsipur Rd.,* ☎ *821/571265. Reservations essential. AE, DC, MC, V.*

$$ ✕ **Gardenia.** The Quality Inn's restaurant has a contemporary Indian look, with upholstered rattan chairs and brass candle-lanterns on the tables at night. The menu features mostly North Indian fare, with some Chinese and Continental options. The tandoori items are delicious: try *malai murgh tikka* (tender, boneless chicken chunks seasoned with Mughlai masala spices) with some *paneer kulcha* (bread stuffed with cottage cheese and masala spices). ⊠ *Quality Inn Southern Star, 13–14 Vinoba Rd.,* ☎ *821/27217. AE, DC, MC, V.*

$$ ✕ **Green Hotel.** The restaurant at this novel hotel is superb. You dine outdoors in comfortable wicker chairs around tables dotted throughout the gardens, or in a sunny, white, high-ceiling, glass-enclosed terrace surrounded by plants indoors and out. Befitting the setting, service unfolds at a 19th-century pace, so don't come here in a hurry. The food is excellent pan-Indian, including spicy vegetable starters and some unusual chicken curries. This is also a quiet place to nurse a cool beer after dark. ✉ *2270 Vinoba Rd.,* ☎ *821/512536 or 821/512817. AE, DC, MC, V.*

$$ ✕ **Ilapur.** Specializing in spicy foods from Andhra Pradesh, this fresh, clean restaurant serves good biriani dishes—chicken, mutton, or vegetable—as well as various curries, North Indian tandoori items, and an economical vegetable thali. Avoid the attempts at Chinese cuisine. The decor is contemporary, with plastic plants and colorful paintings of Krishna. ✉ *2721/1 Sri Harsha Rd.,* ☎ *821/32878. AE, MC, V.*

$ ✕ **Jewel Rock.** Candlelight and colorful linens create a cozy, romantic atmosphere at this multicuisine restaurant. Chinese dishes, including nonspicy chicken in wine sauce (not on the menu) and sliced lamb with chilis, are the most popular entrées. ✉ *Hotel Maurya Palace, 2-3-7 Sri Harsha Rd.,* ☎ *821/35912. AE, DC, MC, V.*

$$$$ 🏨 **Lalitha Mahal Palace Hotel.** Just outside the city center, the gleam-
★ ing-white 1920s palace of the former maharaja—built to host his most important guest, the British Viceroy—is now a sumptuous hotel. The public areas are lavishly trimmed with ornate plaster moldings, huge pillars, and gorgeous domes; broad marble staircases rise and curve majestically up through the three floors. The best rooms are in the older section and have appealing, if not necessarily grand, Victorian furnishings. The suites are palatial, favored by film stars, Arabian sheiks, and honeymooners. The rooms in the new wing have a contemporary decor. Staying here is a delightful and unique experience, but not without occasional reminders of the palace's age: the hot water and air-conditioning are not entirely reliable. ✉ *T. Narsipur Rd., 570011,* ☎ *821/571265 or 821/571276,* 𝙵𝙰𝚇 *821/571770,* 𝚆𝙴𝙱 *www.ashokgroup.com. 45 rooms, 10 suites. Restaurant, bar, pool, hair salon, 2 tennis courts, health club, billiards, baby-sitting, meeting room, travel services, helipad. AE, DC, MC, V.*

$$ 🏨 **Quality Inn Southern Star.** Opened in 1985, India's first Quality Inn
★ property may also be its best. Some of the large guest rooms have floral drapes and bedspreads and coordinating pastel carpeting; other rooms are much darker and have dated 1980s decor. The cozy back lawn is surrounded by high hedges, removing it in spirit from the busy city road out front. Children love the cage of chattering parakeets and the tame white rabbits that hop lazily around the pool. ✉ *13–14 Vinoba Rd., 570005,* ☎ *821/438141 or 821/429686,* 𝙵𝙰𝚇 *821/421689,* 𝚆𝙴𝙱 *www. southernstarmysore.com. 72 rooms, 1 suite. 2 restaurants, bar, pool, hair salon, health club, laundry service, meeting room, travel services. AE, DC, MC, V.*

$ 🏨 **Green Hotel.** Once a palace, then a film studio, the Green Hotel is now run by a British charity whose profits fund environmental projects. Airy, charming, and largely sea green inside, it feels like a Raj-era lodge, its Edwardian drawing rooms equipped with chess boards. Guest rooms have dark-wood furnishings, high, wood-beam ceilings, and in some cases kitschy film memorabilia; on the other hand, rooms are not air-conditioned, and some have no closets or wardrobes. ✉ *2270 Vinoba Rd. (outside city center, past university), 570012,* ☎ *821/ 512536,* 𝙵𝙰𝚇 *821/516139. 12 rooms, 8 suites. Restaurant, bar, travel services. AE, DC, MC, V.*

$ 🏨 **Kings Kourt Hotel.** This three-story lodging is clean and new but lacks charm and historic appeal. The midsize rooms have modern furnishings in dark red and black, and small bathrooms. Those facing the back are quieter. A view of the greenery around town including the imposing Chamundi Hills is a plus. ⊠ *Jhansi Lakshmibai Rd., 570001,* ☎ *821/421142,* FAX *821/563131. 58 rooms, 2 suites. Restaurant, bar, laundry service, meeting room, business services, travel services. AE, DC, MC, V.*

Nightlife and the Arts

Your best bet for a drink is a hotel bar or lounge. The **Lalitha Mahal Palace Hotel** (⊠ T. Narsipur Rd., ☎ 821/571265 or 821/571276) has a good bar, with Victorian furnishings and a casual ambience; if you don't stay here, it's worth stopping in for a drink just to see the majestic building. **The Derby** (⊠ 13–14 Vinoba Rd., ☎ 821/438141 or 821/429686), at the Quality Inn, has an equestrian motif, complete with saddle-topped barstools and staff dressed as jockeys.

To find out what's happening in Mysore, check with the KDT and look for posters around town. **Kalamandir Auditorium** (⊠ Vinoba Rd., ☎ 821/28185) hosts theater, dance, ballet, folklore, and classical Indian music. Admission is usually free or nominal. Other performances are sometimes held in the **Jaganmohan Palace** (☎ 821/23693) or the Mysore Palace itself.

Outdoor Activities and Sports

Horse Racing

The **Mysore Race Club** (⊠ Race Course Rd., ☎ 821/521675) is a scene from August through October, with races about twice a week.

Shopping

Mysore is famous for its exquisite silks, fragrant jasmine, sandalwood products—oils, incense sticks, soaps, and carvings—and rosewood inlay work. The main shopping area is along **Sayaji Rao Road,** beginning at K. R. Circle in the center of town, with a plethora of silk emporiums, sweet stalls, and shops and hawkers of all kinds. Most shops are closed on Sunday.

Antiques and Handicrafts

Cauvery Art and Crafts Emporium (⊠ Sayaji Rao Rd., ☎ 821/21258) is the fixed-price government showroom for sandalwood carvings, rosewood figurines, brassware, and other Karnataka handicrafts. **Mysore Crafts Emporium** (⊠ 70-D Devaraja Urs Rd., ☎ 821/30294), the largest handicrafts showroom in Mysore, has a good selection of very reasonably priced local sandalwood and rosewood products, as well as crafts from other regions of India.

Markets

Devaraja Market (⊠ Devaraja Urs Rd.; ⊙ daily 6 AM–9 PM) is a bustling, old indoor fruit, vegetable, and flower market where you can immerse yourself in the vibrant colors and smells of Karnataka's bounteous produce.

Silks

Karnataka Silk Industries Corporation (⊠ Government Silk Weaving Factory Complex, Mananthody Rd., ☎ 821/21803; ⊠ Visveshwaraiah Bhavan, K. R. Circle, ☎ 821/22658; ⊠ Zoo Complex, Indiranagar, ☎ 821/25502), the state body that runs the Government Silk Weaving Factory, has several fixed-price showrooms where you can buy or just admire the profusion of silks created at the factory. The factory complex has a "seconds" showroom where a limited selection of silks with barely perceptible flaws are sold at up to 40% off. **Lakshmi Vilas** (✉ K. R. Circle, ☎ 821/420730) has a large selection of silks and other fabrics.

Side Trips

Cauvery River

Karnataka's rivers teem with fish and crocodiles, and fishing expeditions are becoming an important part of the state's tourist industry from December through March. The mammoth mahseer fish swim in the Cauvery River near Bhimeswari, about 100 km (60 mi) south of Bangalore and 75 km (46 mi) east of Mysore. Anglers fishing from *coracles* (round, basket-like boats) regularly hook mahseers weighing upwards of 50 pounds here, as well as smaller Carnatic carp, pink carp, and the good old catfish. The largest recorded catch was by an Englishman in 1992: 120 pounds. Catches can be weighed and photographed for proof but must be returned to the river.

LODGING

$$ ⊡ **Cauvery Fishing Camp.** This peaceful camp is on the bank of the Cauvery River. You sleep overlooking the river in basic, twin-bedded tents with attached bathrooms; simple, healthy meals, included in the room price, are served in an open-air dining area around a campfire. Trained guides take you to the prime angling spots in Jeeps or coracle boats, but fishing equipment is not provided. Reserve far in advance. ✉ *Bhimeswari, Karnataka. Reservations through Jungle Lodges & Resorts Ltd. Shrungar Shopping Centre, 2nd floor, M. G. Rd., Bangalore,* ☎ *80/559–7021 or 80/559–7025,* WEB *www.junglelodges.com. 6 tents. AE, DC, MC, V.*

Nagarhole National Park

The Karapur Forest of southwestern Karnataka has long provided India's now-defunct royalty—not to mention the world's zoos and circuses—with elephants. Many years ago, an infamous practice called *khedda* (wild-elephant roundup) was common, pitting swarms of skilled tribesmen against a herd of trumpeting elephants. Today, the kheddas have stopped, and instead of animals in terror you can watch wild elephants moving around the Nagarhole National Park (also known as Rajiv Gandhi Memorial Park), established in 1954.

From Kabini River Lodge you can join a fantastic game-viewing tour—from your Jeep you might spot dholes (wild dogs), a massively muscular Indian gaur (wild ox), barking deer, sambars (reddish-brown wild deer), sloth bears, crocodiles, and families of elephants (mothers, calves, "aunt" elephants, and tuskers), and, if you're lucky, an elusive leopard or tiger. You can also glide around in a coracle, a round, basket-shaped boat (lined with buffalo hide) that's so slow and quiet that you can draw very close to wild animals and the abundant birds (more than 225 different species) without disturbing them. The best viewing times are early morning and evening from October through March. The area surrounding Nagarhole is home to the Jenu Kurubas (traditionally beekeepers) and Betta Kurubas, two tribes currently fighting with the government over the rights to this land, which they consider their historical home. ✉ *Coorg region (between Kadagu and Mysore districts), 93 km (58 mi) southwest of Mysore, 08228,* ☎ *8228/334-1993.* ⊡ *Rs. 150.*

LODGING

$$$ ⊡ **Kabini River Lodge.** Once the hunting lodge of the viceroy and ma-
★ haraja, this resort within Nagarhole National Park is a charming combination of comfort and rusticity. The cabins are surrounded by colorful

trees, and monkeys roam through the grounds. The ambience is peaceful, with a languid daily routine: long Jeep safaris or coracle boating are broken up by morning and afternoon tea on the veranda and hearty open-air meals (included in the room rate; drinks are extra) with a variety of cuisines. At night, before dinner, guests can gather in the common room to watch a wildlife video. The rooms have overhead fans and stone floors; you can also stay in safari-style tents. ✉ *Karapur. Reservations through Jungle Lodges & Resorts Ltd., Shrungar Shopping Centre, 2nd floor, M. G. Rd., Bangalore 08228,* ☎ *80/559–7021 or 80/559–7025,* WEB *www.junglelodges.com. 14 rooms, 6 cottages. Restaurant, bar, travel services. AE, DC, MC, V.*

Sravanabelagola

If you have time en route between Mysore and Belur or Halebid, stop in the small town of Sravanabelagola to see the **colossal monolithic statue** of the Jain saint Gomateshwara, carved in AD 981 and alleged to be one of the largest monolithic statues in the world. Stark naked and towering 58 ft high, with 26-ft wide shoulders, 10-ft feet, and other similarly massive endowments, Gomateshwara is at once imposing and soothing. Once every 12 years, thousands of devotees congregate here for the Mahamastakabhishekha, a ceremony in which the 1,000-year-old statue is anointed with milk, ghee, curds, saffron, and gold coins. You have to climb 600 big steps to get there. Another site worth a visit is the Chandragupta Basti Jain temple, which has 600-year-old paintings. ✉ *84 km (52 mi) north of Mysore.*

MANGALORE

⑪   There's not much grand heritage in this coastal business center, but **Mangalore** is a mellow place to sample Karnataka's largely untouched beaches and jump on or off the deliciously scenic Konkan Railway. Once acclaimed as Karnataka's port city and pepper center, Mangalore has ceded the pepper honor to Cochin and now has the low-pressure feel of a breezy seaside town (with some bustling bazaars).

Upon arrival, take a taxi toward Malpe beach. En route, you'll pass the temple town of **Udupi,** once home of the ancient Sanskrit philosopher Madhwacharya. Udupi is known for both its **Lord Krishna temple,** trimmed with gold, and its vegetarian restaurants, so it's a nice place to break for a cup of coffee and a *masala dosa.* From the quiet yellow sands of Malpe beach you can hire a boat to the rocky **St. Mary's Island,** where Vasco da Gama is believed to have landed in the 15th century before he stopped at Calicut.

Back in Mangalore, snatch some time after dinner to watch some **Yakshagana,** an ancient folk form of dance-drama performed in colorful costumes and greasepaint. Usually a night-long program performed in open fields, the Yakshagana involves robust dancing and mime; an interpreter tells a story drawn customarily from mythology and sings to the accompaniment of drums and cymbals. Performances are now often held on stages.

Dining and Lodging

$$ ✕ **Hightide and Gallery** is the watering hole at the Taj Manjarun where you have access to some choice canapes. The wood paneling, cozy seating as well as efficient service can provide for a comfortable evening. If you wish to have dinner, walk across to the Galley, popular for its multicuisine fare, but particularly favored for the local delicacy: *kane bezule,* lady fish fried and curried. ✉ *Old Port Rd.,* ☎ *824/420585. Reservations essential. AE, DC, MC, V.*

$$ ✕ **Mangala Restaurant.** This cozy restaurant in the Moti Mahal hotel has brightly lit interiors and a quiet ambience. The teak furniture and the plain cream tablecloths lend a formal look, but bustles with activity on weekends when families troop in. The menu has a wide variety of Indian, Continental, and Chinese food, although you'd be advised to stick to the Indian fare. ✉ *Falnir Rd.,* ☎ *824/441411. Reservations essential. AE, DC, MC, V.*

$$ ⊞ **Summer Sands Beach Resort.** This budget hotel is an option if you want to be near the sea upon arrival. Only 24 of the rooms have air-conditioning, so request one when booking. The villas, set in coconut groves, are cool and detached, and the Ullal beach is a treat. Meals are included in the room rate. ✉ *Chota-Mangalore, Ullal,* ☎ *824/ 467690 or 467691,* ℻ *824/467693. 75 rooms. Restaurant, in-room safes, air-conditioning (some), billiards, playground, travel services. AE, DC, MC, V.*

$–$$ ⊞ **Taj Manjarun.** This is the best lodging in Mangalore, with a pleasant sea view and a lovely pool. The rooms, painted in light hues, are bright and cozy, and a bit breezy in the evening. The Galley restaurant offers both buffet and à la carte meals, and sometimes Indian and Western pop music. The Captain's Cabin pub is a nice, quiet corner for a quiet beer. ✉ *Old Port Rd., 575001,* ☎ *824/420420,* ℻ *824/420585. 100 rooms. Restaurant, coffee shop, pub, pool, beach, travel services. AE, DC, MC, V.*

$ ⊞ **Moti Mahal.** A large courtyard and a swimming pool, shopping arcade, spacious and airy rooms, barbecue and a discotheque—all combined with hospitable staff can make this a comfortable proposition. ✉ *Falnir Rd., 575001,* ☎ *824/441411 or 824/443143,* ℻ *824/441011. 75 rooms. Restaurant, coffee shop, pub, pool, beach, travel services. AE, DC, MC, V.*

BELUR AND HALEBID

Once flourishing cities of the 12th-century Hoysala dynasty, Belur and Halebid are now just fading rural villages. Both, however, hold some of the finest examples of stone carving in South India, called "the signs of a very confident Hindu culture" by writer V. S. Naipaul.

Hassan, an otherwise unexceptional town, is the gateway to the temples at Belur and Halebid—it's about 35 km (22 mi) away from each of the two, forming a triangle. Lodging options in Belur and Halebid are still few and far between, so you may want to base yourself in Hassan for a night or two.

To get the most out of the temples, hire a guide. You must remove your shoes before entering, so bring socks along on your visits; the stones can be painfully hot in the midday sun, particularly at Belur. If possible, bring a flashlight to see the temples' interior sculptures in full detail.

Belur

⑫ *192 km (120 mi) northwest of Mysore; 240 km (150 mi) west of Bangalore*

Set in a lush tropical landscape, the old city of Belur is dusty and rundown, with only one vestige of its splendid past. Still a functioning tem-
★ ple dedicated to a Vishnu incarnate, the **Temple of Lord Channakeshava** stands almost as pristine as it did the day it was completed in 1119— 103 years after it was begun by the Hoysala king Vishnuvardhana. Legend claims that when Muslim conquerors came to Belur to destroy the temple, they were so awed by its magnificence that they left it alone.

Carved of soapstone, the temple is shaped like a star to allow maximum surface area for carving: a total of 32 corners. Squat and flat on top, it sits on a platform of the same shape; to its left is a small prototype (without the ornate stonework), built just before the temple as a study. Inside, some 10,000 impossibly intricate sculptures ornament every possible surface, a profusion of gods and goddesses in all their varied aspects and incarnations—scenes from the great Hindu epic, the *Ramayana,* as well as hunters, dancers, musicians, and beautiful women dressing and adorning themselves.

In the center of the temple, the domed ceiling is supported by four pillars surmounted by sculptures of voluptuous women striking any number of graceful poses beneath the intricately pierced, scrolled, and scalloped stone canopies. The carving is so detailed that some of the stone bangles the women wear can be moved. ⊠ *Free, guide Rs. 50 for 2 people.* ⊙ *Daily 8 AM–8:30 PM; inner sanctums closed daily 1–3 and 5–6.*

South of the main temple, a smaller shrine, the **Channigaraya Temple,** is worth a good look. The other Hoysala temple, **Viranarayana,** has rows of very fine sculptures on its outer walls.

Lodging

$ 🏨 **Hotel Mayura Velapuri.** This is a standard, government-run tourist hotel, low on frills but fairly clean. The big advantage is that it's literally on the edge of the temple complex, the perfect vantage point for watching the sun rise and set over this sacred site. The kitchen serves vegetarian meals, particularly South Indian thalis. ⊠ *Outside temple entrance,* ☎ *8177/22209. Restaurant. No credit cards.*

Halebid

⑬ *35 km (22 mi) northeast of Belur; 35 km (22 mi) north of Hassan*

Halebid is a tiny rural village that was once the capital of the Hoysala
★ kingdom. Dedicated to the Hindu Lord Shiva, the **Hoysaleswara Temple** was begun by King Vishnuvardhana in 1121, after the one at Belur was complete. It was left unfinished after 190 years of labor because the Delhi sultanates' attacks on it leveled its pyramid-peaked roof. Like the temple at Belur, this one has a star-shaped plan, but as a double-shrine temple, it has two of everything—one for the king and one for the queen. Moreover, the sculptors' virtuosity reached its peak here, leaving some 20,000 statues. The figures are carved in such detail that they appear to have been etched. You can see the taut fibers of the cord from which a drum hangs, feel the weight of the jewel beads dangling from a dancer's neck, almost hear the swinging of the bells around the arms of the elephant god Ganesh. At one time the temple also had 84 statues hanging from the ceiling near pillars; all but 14 were seized by conquerors of one stripe or another.

The breathtaking friezes wrap all the way around the temple: first comes a row of elephants for stability, then a row of lordly lions for courage, then convoluting scrolls of swift horses, then a row of people in sexual poses. Indian philosophy has always merged the spiritual with the social and cultural. Consequently, religious monuments were also cultural centers. Temple sculptures from around the 8th century often depict images of musicians and dancers along with dieties; in about the 10th century, erotic themes were introduced as well. The inspiration for this was based on the the tantric thought of congeniality between spirituality and sexuality. Sensual well-being was deemed an essential ingredient of social life. Following the invasion of Islamic rulers, this tendency was curbed.

Above the erotic scenes is more scrollwork as well as scenes from the religious epics that present philosophical ideas and mirror the living conditions of the time. The largest frieze is also the most exuberant: here the *apsaras* (celestial maidens) are clothed in jewels, with bracelets on each of their several arms. Behind the queen's shrine (the one closest to the entrance) is a giant sculpture of Nandi the bull, Shiva's vehicle, with beautifully smooth features and a polished belly that almost seems to breathe. A small museum next to the temple displays various statues and brass and copper figures excavated from the surrounding area. 🖼 *Free.* ⊙ *Temple daily sunrise–sunset; museum Sat.–Thurs. 10–5.*

A few minutes down the road, the smaller **Kedareswara Temple** bears more exquisite carving. The lovely friezes are similar to those of the main temples at Belur and Halebid, and executed with equal finesse. Here also stand two relatively unadorned early **Jain temples,** their finely polished black pillars as reflective as mirrors. Set on a low hill next to a lake, this is an attractive, peaceful spot in its own right. 🖼 *Free.* ⊙ *Daily sunrise–sunset.*

Dining and Lodging

$$ ╳🖼 **Hotel Hassan Ashok.** The best lodging option in Hassan, this three-story modern hotel is about half an hour's drive from both Belur and Halebid. The rooms are reasonably priced and low on frills, with worn modern decor. Some are air-conditioned. The restaurant serves good Indian and Continental cuisine, and the staff is super-friendly. Try spicy South Indian thali or a milder Punjabi meal with or without meat. *Rasam,* a typical South Indian lentil soup, is a spicy way to start your meal. ✉ *Bangalore-Mangalore Rd., Hassan 673201,* ☎ *8172/68731 or 8172/68736,* 🅵🅰🆇 *08172/67154. 45 rooms, 1 suite. Restaurant, bar, laundry service, meeting room. AE, DC, MC, V.*

$ 🖼 **Hotel Mayura Shanthala.** The rooms are plain and uninspiring, and the food is no compensation (ordinary South Indian and North Indian vegetarian fare), but this government-run tourist accommodation is near the temple and serviceable for a short stay. ✉ *Temple Rd., Halebid,* ☎ *8177/3224. Restaurant, laundry service. No credit cards.*

HAMPI

★ ⑭ Located in the middle of Karnataka and difficult to reach, **Hampi** (also known as Vijayanagar) is the most awesome spectacle in the state. A ruined city of vast stone temples, elephant stables, barracks, and palaces, Hampi was the center of the largest Hindu empire in South India and a major point of confluence for both Hindu and Jain worshippers.

Legend has it that the city, which is spread over 180 square km (70 square mi) in a rocky valley surrounded by rugged mountains that wouldn't look out of place in the American Southwest, was founded by two brothers, Harihara and Bukka, in 1336. Some of the buildings, however, can be dated back 1,400 years. Hampi was a large and wealthy city of about 1 million people for more than two centuries, until Muslim invaders from the north conquered the empire in 1565, and in the process destroyed the faces of the thousands of statues and sculptures that adorn the numerous temples. To see Hampi in its entirety, you should spend two full days here. Most of the ruins are open free of charge, though some, seemingly chosen at random, charge Rs. 235 or Rs. 470.

Many people choose to explore the ruins by themselves, but you'll probably get more out of them if you hire one of the official guides who wait on the road leading into the still-thriving village of Hampi Bazaar. They charge about Rs. 450 for a full day.

The ruins are spread over two main areas: in the north, near Hampi Bazaar, they center on the enormous **Virupaksha Temple,** home to hundreds of monkeys and a hangout for dozens of children intrigued by the sight of foreigners.

In the south, in what's known as the Royal Enclosure area, a vast ruined **palace** overlooks a landscape of grandiose stone buildings every bit the equal of the major Maya and Aztec monuments. Particularly spectacular are the towering elephant stables, home to the eleven elephants of the royal guard.

The fairly good **Archaeological Museum** in the southern part of the ruins takes you through the (ongoing) excavation process and displays many of the weapons and cooking utensils found at Hampi, as well as some of the larger statues taken from the erstwhile Shiva and Vishnu temples. Snakes (some of them poisonous) hide in the museum's gardens, so be careful where you walk! The museum is open Saturday through Thursday from 10 to 5, and admission is free.

Dining and Lodging

Accommodations in Hampi itself are low-quality at best. There are several little rooming houses on the road leading into Hampi Bazaar, but for slightly more comfort, stay in Hospet, about 13 km (8 mi) from the ruins.

$ ✕ **Eagle Garden Restaurant.** There's a wide choice of chicken dishes, particularly Mughlai, at this restaurant near a canal, and the outdoor tables are fairly comfortable. ⊠ *Jambunatha Rd., Hospet,* ☎ *8394/ 28107. No credit cards.*

$ ✕ **Manasa/Naivedyam.** This pair of restaurants at the Hotel Priyadarshini covers a few bases: Manasa has cool outdoor tables, good chicken dishes, and a bar, while Naivedyam offers indoor dining and spicy vegetarian food prepared in South Indian and North Indian styles. The background music (which emanates from Manasa but is audible in both) is an eclectic mix of Hindi film music and Céline Dion. ⊠ *Hotel Priyadarshini, 45 Station Rd., Hospet,* ☎ *8394/28838. AE, DC, MC, V.*

$ ▥ **Malligi Tourist Home.** This is the best accommodation in Hospet, considering it's the only one with facilities like currency exchange and travel assistance. It's fairly clean for a small-town Indian hotel, and the vividly colored furnishings lift the spirits. A multicuisine restaurant and a bar add to the on-site perks. ⊠ *Jambunatha Rd., Hospet,* ☎ *8394/28101. 116 rooms. Restaurant, bar, pool, exercise room, coin laundry, travel services. AE, DC, MC, V.*

KARNATAKA A TO Z

To research prices, get advice from other travelers, and book travel arrangements, visit www.fodors.com.

AIR TRAVEL
All flights to Karnataka land in Bangalore, which is 140 km (90 mi) northeast of Mysore and 240 km (150 mi) from Nagarhole National Park (Kabini River Lodge). Bangalore has domestic flights to Bombay, Madras, Mangalore, Hyderabad, Delhi, Calcutta, Pune, Goa, and Ahmedabad, and international flights to Singapore, Sharjah (UAE), and Muscat (Oman). Connecting flights from Bombay serve New York, London, and Paris.

➤ AIRLINES AND CONTACTS: **Indian Airlines** (⊠ Cauvery Bhavan, K. G. Rd., Bangalore, ☎ 80/526–6333; 140 at airport for general inquiries;

141 at airport for reservations; ⊠ Lalbagh, Mangalore, ☎ 824/455669 or 824/442309, WEB www.indian-airlines.nic.in). **Jet Airways** (⊠ 1-Y. M. Block, Unity Buildings, J. C. Rd., Bangalore, ☎ 80/227–6620; 80/ 526–1926; 80/552–1898 at airport, WEB www.jetairways.com; ⊠ Ram Bhavan Complex, Mangalore, ☎ 824/440694 or 824/440596).

AIRPORTS

Two pre-paid taxi counters compete in Bangalore's arrivals hall. Rates offered by the state government outfit are slightly lower than those of its neighbor, but either one will charge you about Rs. 150 for the ride to a major hotel. There is a fleet of metered taxis in the parking lot at the arrivals-hall exit, and the same journey with one of them should cost about Rs. 100, but it's still best to agree on a price before you begin. An auto-rickshaw ride into the city costs about Rs. 80, but it only works well if you have very little luggage and are not in a hurry.

If you're skipping Bangalore altogether, you can book a car and driver at the Karnataka State Tourism Development Corporation (KSTDC) counter in Bangalore's airport and be straight off to Mysore or beyond. Taxis and car services will also take you long distances, but you're likely to be significantly overcharged.

➤ AIRPORT INFORMATION: **Bangalore Airport** (☎ 080/526–6233). **Mangalore Airport** (☎ 824/752433).

BUS TRAVEL

The KSTDC runs three-day bus tours from Bangalore to Hospet. From Bangalore's Subhash Nagar bus stop, Karnataka State Road Transport Corporation buses leave every 15 minutes to Mysore. The journey takes just under four hours, and the fare in a luxury vehicle is Rs. 75.

There's no easy way to reach Hassan, the gateway to Belur and Halebid. If you don't mind crowds, take the KSTDC-run bus from the Mysore bus station: the ride takes three hours, costs Rs. 40, and leaves every half hour throughout the day. Once in Hassan, hire a driver for the day and expect to pay more than Rs. 400. The KSTDC and various private companies also run tours of Belur and Halebid, and you can arrange a private car through Seagull Travels.

Local buses are frequent and cheap but decidedly not comfortable. Mornings and evenings see as many as eighty people stuffed into one bus.

➤ BUS INFORMATION: **Karnataka State Road Transport Corporation,** (⊠ Subhash Nagar, Bangalore, ☎ 080/2873377 or 080/2871261).

CARS AND DRIVERS

National highways connect Bangalore to Madras, the Kerala coast, Hyderabad, Bombay, and Goa. The best way to see Karnataka is to hire a car and driver. For journeys outside city limits, figure about Rs. 3.50 per km (the minimum distance is 250 km/155 mi), and for overnight trips a halt charge of Rs. 100 per night to feed and shelter the driver. Flat rates to get around within Bangalore or Mysore run approximately Rs. 450 for an eight-hour day, Rs. 30 for each additional hour. KSTDC's rates are slightly lower than those of private companies.

EMERGENCIES

In Bangalore, Al-Siddique Pharma Center and Janata Bazaar are open 24 hours.

➤ PHARMACIES: **Al-Siddique Pharma Center** (⊠ K. R. Rd., opposite Jamia Masjid, near City Market, Bangalore, ☎ 80/6504591). **Janata Bazaar** (⊠ in Victoria Hospital, Bangalore, ☎ 80/627471).

MAIL AND SHIPPING

➤ Post Office: **General Post Office** (✉ Raj Bhavan Rd., near Vidhana Soudha, Bangalore, ☎ 80/286–6772 or 80/286–7901).

MONEY MATTERS

ATMS

Cash machines in Bangalore are clustered mainly around M. G. Road and Brigade Road.

CURRENCY EXCHANGE

Most banks exchange foreign currency and cash traveler's checks. Most Western-style hotels will change money for guests. The main branches of the State Bank of India, generally open weekdays 10–1, change currency and usually cash traveler's checks as well. You can also try ANZ Grindlays Bank and the State Bank of Mysore, which has a branch in the airport arrivals area.

➤ Exchange Services: **ANZ Grindlays Bank** (✉ Raheja Towers 26/27, 1 M. G. Rd., ☎ 80/558–7684). **Synergy Financial Exchange LTD** (✉ 107 Raheja Plaza, 17 Commissariat Rd., D'Souza Circle, ☎ 80/558–7931). **Thomas Cook** (✉ 70 M. G. Rd., ☎ 80/558–1337). **Weizmann Limited** (✉ Center Point, 005-Ground Floor, 56, Residency Rd., ☎ 80/559–5379 or 80/558–2148).

TAXIS AND AUTO-RICKSHAWS

The three-wheel auto-rickshaw is a convenient, fast, and cheap way to travel short distances on congested streets. Note that the rides are bumpy, and you're exposed to the breezes, which often contain considerable exhaust fumes. Figure about Rs. 9 for the first km, Rs. 5 per additional km. From 10 PM to 5 AM the fare is 1½ times the meter reading—note that meters are sometimes faulty. Very often, you can hire an auto-rickshaw for the entire day (eight hours) for around Rs. 500: bargain with the driver, and don't pay until the day is done.

In major cities, regular taxis charge more or less according to their meters (usually more), with an initial charge of about Rs. 80 for the first 5 km (3 mi). As a tourist, you're vulnerable to being overcharged, so agree on a price with the driver before setting out.

There aren't many metered taxis on the streets in Bangalore—you'll find them mainly at train and bus stations and the airport. Have your hotel call one, or call a radio taxi from wherever you are. In Mysore, you can often flag down taxis on the street. If that doesn't work, pick one up at one of the taxi stands throughout the city, or ask your hotel to get one for you.

➤ Taxi Company: **Bangalore Radio Taxi** (☎ 80/332–0152 or 80/332–7589).

TOURS

In Bangalore, the KSTDC is widely used for its car-hire service and its full- and half-day bus tours of major sights in Karnataka. Most tours are inexpensive and low on frills—the buses are aging—but they provide a concise, well-rounded look at what's important. Jungle Lodges & Resorts Ltd., the outdoor-activity branch of the Karnataka Department of Tourism (KDT), has rustic facilities in the state's protected wild areas. Professional guides can take you on Jeep tours to wildlife-viewing spots or fish-rich rivers.

The Government of India Tourist Office trains and approves all official tour guides. Rates are low by Western standards (about Rs. 450 per eight-hour day, Rs. 900 for a trip outside the city), and the guides are informative and helpful. You can hire one directly or through most travel agents and tour operators.

Among the travel agents, Ambassador Travel Services has reliable cars and drivers at moderate rates. Clipper Holidays runs general-interest tours, special-interest tours, and treks of various lengths, and can arrange for a minimum of 15 people at a time to have dinner with the former prince of Mysore at his own palace. American Express Travel Services is represented in Bangalore by Marco Polo Travel and Tours. Sri Sathya Sai Tourists, out in a residential neighborhood, is open 24 hours a day, 365 days a year. The staff arranges general-interest tours, taxi and bus service, and currency exchange. In Mysore, Skyway and Siddharta arrange tours within Karnataka. Seagull Travels arranges tours and changes currency.

➤ CONTACTS: **Ambassador Travel Services** (✉ 76 Mission Rd., Kasturi Complex, 2nd floor, Bangalore, ☎ 80/224–1516 or 80/222–1342). **Clipper Holidays** (✉ Suite 406, Regency Enclave, Magrath Rd., Bangalore 560025, ☎ 80/559–9032). **Jungle Lodges & Resorts Ltd.** (✉ Shrungar Shopping Centre, 2nd floor, M. G. Rd., Bangalore, ☎ 80/559–7021 or 80/559–7025, WEB www.junglelodges.com). **Seagull Travels** (✉ Hotel Metropole, Mysore, ☎ 821/439732). **Siddharta Tours & Travels** (✉ Hotel Siddharta, 73/1 Guest House Rd., Nazarbad, Mysore, ☎ 821/34155 or 821/30555; ✉ Lalitha Mahal Palace Hotel, Mysore, ☎ 821/35702). **Skyway International Travels** (✉ 10 Madhu Nivas, Gandhi Square, Mysore ☎ 81/426642 or 81/426823). **Sri Sathya Sai Tourists** (✉ 433/30/1, 10th Main 28th A Cross, 4th Block, Jayanagar, Bangalore 560011, ☎ 80/664–1140, 80/634–6340, or 80/665–4410).

TRAIN TRAVEL

The reservations office at Bangalore City Railway Station is open Monday through Saturday 8 to 2 and 2:15 to 8, Sunday 8 to 2. Counter 14 on the ground floor is reserved exclusively for foreign tourists, senior citizens, and people with disabilities. Trains to Hospet (the jumping-off point for Hampi) run overnight from Bangalore, departing at 9:30 PM and arriving the next morning at 7:40. You can also reach Hospet directly from the north; trains run from Bombay to Guntakal, in Andhra Pradesh, and from there local connections run to Hospet. Note that trains in this part of the country are very slow.

Mangalore is linked by train to Bombay, Delhi, Kerala (Trivandrum and Ernakulam), and Madras. The scenic Konkan Railway leaves Mangalore early in the morning for its northbound trip along the Karnataka coast, reaching Karwar after 6 hours (Rs. 80), Margao (in Goa) after 7 hours (Rs. 100).

Several (air-conditioned) trains run between Bangalore and Mysore daily; the trip takes about 3 hours and the fare is about Rs. 200. The reservations office at Mysore Railway Station is open Monday through Saturday 8 to 2 and 2:15 to 8 and Sunday 8 to 2. The super-fast, air-conditioned, relatively expensive *Shatabdi Express* runs between Mysore and Madras via Bangalore (Rs. 400 round trip) every afternoon except Tuesday. There is also a 24-hour train to Bombay.

At this writing, the KSTDC plans to launch the Palace on Wheels service covering Mysore, Belur, Halebid, Hampi and Badami in a round trip from Bangalore to Bangalore. The service is expected to cost Rs. 7,050 to Rs. 9,400 and will feature a lounge car, a dining car, and an entertainment car. Jungle Lodges & Resorts Ltd. in Bangalore or any of the KSTDC offices will have information.

➤ TRAIN INFORMATION: **Konkan Railway** (in Mangalore ☎ 824/423137; for reservations ☎ 824/424002, WEB www.konkanrailway.com). **Southern Railway** (WEB www.srailway.com).

➤ TRAIN STATIONS: **Bangalore** (☎ 131 general inquiries; 132 reservations; 133 recorded information; 134 after-hours arrival and departure information). **Mysore** (☎ 821/520100 or 821/37300).

VISITOR INFORMATION

The KDT provides brochures, maps, and general information on Karnataka through two branches in Bangalore and one in Mysore. The offices are open Monday through Saturday (closed 2nd Saturday of month) 10 to 1:30 and 2:15 to 5:30.

The KSTDC based in Bangalore provides information and reservations for its state-run hotels, tours, and car-and-driver hire. Hours at the main office are Monday through Saturday 10 to 5:30 (closed 2nd Saturday of month). The Government of India Tourist Office has useful information on the region and arranges private guides; the office is open weekdays 10 to 5 and Saturday 10 to 1:30 (closed 2nd Saturday of month).

The KDT maintains an information office in Hassan Monday through Saturday from 10 to 5:30 (closed 2nd Saturday of month) offering advice on Belur and Halebid. In Belur, the small reception center inside the temple-yard entrance is open Monday through Saturday from 8:30 to 5:30, and sometimes on Sunday. The Tourist Information Center is a three-minute walk from the temple entrance and keeps the same hours as the reception center. Government-approved guides, available at the temple entrance, will take one or two people through the sights for about Rs.100.

The tourist office in Hampi Bazaar is pretty much empty, though it does have a few basic maps. There is, however, a Neha travel office on the one road through the village, as well as a sister bureau next door to Hotel Priyadarshini in Hospet. Theoretically, both are open Monday through Saturday 9 to 8, and both change currency.

➤ TOURIST OFFICES: **Belur Reception Center** (✉ Inside temple-yard entrance, ☎ 8177/22218). **Belur Tourist Information Center** (✉ Hotel Mayura Velapuri, Temple Rd., ☎ 8233/2209). **Government of India Tourist Office** (✉ KFC Bldg., 48 Church St., Bangalore, ☎ 80/558–5417). **KDT** (✉ K. G. Rd., Cauvery Bhavan, F Block, 1st floor, Bangalore, ☎ 80/221–5489; ✉ 9 St. Marks Rd., Bangalore, ☎ 80/223–6854; ✉ Old Exhibition Bldgs., Irwin Rd., Mysore, ☎ 821/22096 or 821/31061; ✉ Vartha Bhavan, B. M. Rd., Hassan, ☎ 8172/68862). **KSTDC** (✉ Yathrinivas Bldg., 10/4 Kasturba Rd., Bangalore, ☎ 80/221–2901 or 221–2902; ✉ Bangalore airport, ☎ 80/526–8012; ✉ Bangalore train station, ☎ 80/287–0068).

10 KERALA

Sea breezes brush Kerala's coconut palms,
and well-traveled waterways wind inland
to laid-back fishing villages. Ayurvedic
health programs invite you to relax, and the
colorful dance form, Kathakali, entices you
to learn more about India's performing arts.
The spice-trading city of Cochin—a pungent
center of commerce and cosmopolitanism—
contrasts sharply with all the nature to be
explored in the Lake Periyar Wildlife
Sanctuary. With all this on offer, Kerala
might be called elemental India.

By Vikram
Singh

Updated by
Shanti Menon

A CHARMING MYTH EXPLAINS THE CREATION OF KERALA, the narrow state running 560 km (350 mi) along India's western coast. Parashurama, an avatar of Vishnu, performed a series of penances to atone for a grievous sin, and the god of the sea rewarded his devotion by reclaiming Kerala from the deep.

In 1956 the Malayalam-speaking states of Cochin and Travancore joined with the district of Malabar to form Kerala. The new Indian state became the first place in the world to adopt a communist government in a free election, an event that caused global speculation. Today this tropical paradise, between the western mountains and the Arabian Sea, is one of India's most progressive states, with a literacy rate of well over 90%. Even in the shabbiest backwater toddy shop, where locals knock back glasses of potent coconut liquor, you'll find a copy of the day's newspaper.

The Malayalees make up India's most highly educated population; many are conversant in English, Hindi, and Tamil as well as Malayalam. In the nearly three millennia before the 1795 establishment of British rule, Phoenicians, Arabs, Jews, Chinese, and Europeans came in droves, attracted by the region's valuable cash crops: tea, rubber, cashews, teak, and spices—most notably black pepper and cardamom.

Since Independence, people have begun using the place names that were used prior to British colonization. The British had a strong presence in Kerala, so name changes are particularly germane here; hence Alleppey/Alappuzha, Calicut/Kozhikode, Cochin/Kochi, Quilon/Kollam, Trichur/Thrissur, and Trivandrum/Thiruvananthapuram. Official maps and tourist brochures reflect these changes but both the Anglicized and Malayalam names are still commonly used.

Pleasures and Pastimes

Ayurveda

A 2,000-year-old holistic medical science, Ayurveda has become linked with Kerala, thanks to the region's tropical climate, its rigorous standards of practice, and its wealth of medicinal herbs. Ayurveda's goal is to preserve a balance between the forces and principles thought to govern the body, mind, and soul. Doctors prescribe treatments based on your constitution, and remedies usually take the form of medicated oils and herbal concoctions that are ingested or massaged into or poured over the body. Resorts throughout Kerala offer Ayurvedic packages, from three-day general health and rejuvenation programs to longer treatments tailored to specific ailments. Ayurveda is thought to be especially effective for chronic arthritis, back pain, and repetitive strain injuries.

Beaches

Pristine beaches studded with coconut palms have long been Kerala's main attraction. Sadly, Kovalam, the state's best-known beach, has been all but ruined by overdevelopment. There are, however, still quiet places to relax a few kilometers north and south of Kovalam's main Lighthouse Beach. For serious pampering, wind down in a secluded cove on the Arabian Sea near Chowara, south of Kovalam, or Samudra Beach to the north. Indeed, some of the most pristine beaches are in the north, where facilities are practically nonexistent and the sight of a foreigner sunbathing still entertains locals. But come quick—a massive development project is underway near Bekal Fort in the Kasargode district.

Cruises

A slow ride on a traditional wooden houseboat is an exquisite way to experience central Kerala. Two- or three-hour cruises through inland waterways take you through sheltered villages; weeklong adventures run the length of the state. The town of Alleppey is flush with tour operators, and nearly every regional hotel now organizes backwater cruises of some sort.

Dining

The Kerala table is eclectic, savory, and adventuresome. Rice is the staple, coconut milk and coconut oil are the two most important ingredients, and seafood is the star. In Fort Cochin, in the city of Cochin, you can buy a fish—just caught in one of the Chinese-style nets used in the region—have it fried at a nearby stall, and enjoy it al fresco. *Karimeen,* or pearl spot, is the favorite fish of central Kerala, found only in the backwaters.

Kerala's Christian communities are famous for their beef dishes, while the *moppillah,* or Muslim cuisine of the north, features a variety of breads as well as distinctive meat and fish preparations. Vegetable dishes are plentiful, and a variety of bananas show up both cooked and raw, in entrées and desserts. Grated coconut and a type of sugar called *jaggery*—extracted from a native palm and not fully refined—are commonly used in sweets.

Kerala is known for *iddi appa,* or "string hoppers"—thin strands of dough formed into little nests that are steamed and served with coconut milk and sugar for breakfast or as an accompaniment to soups, stews, or curries. *Appam,* a slight variation on the theme, is a rice-flour pancake, thin and crispy on the edges with a spongy, raised center. Another specialty is *puttu,* a puddinglike dish made from fresh-grated coconut and rice flour, molded into a cylindrical shape and steamed.

Lodging

Nearly all the hotels in larger cities have air-conditioning; many resorts in less populated areas do not. In cool hill stations it's quite unnecessary, and beach properties rely on fan and sea breezes. In addition, some buildings have no window screens, so if a cool and/or bug-free sleep is part of your plan, ask about both. Many resorts, even upscale establishments, don't have TVs in their guest rooms. Outside of cities, power supply is tenuous. Most hotels have their own generators, but they take a few seconds to kick in. Don't be surprised if you're left in the darkness for a moment—it's unavoidable.

Most lodgings charge a 10% service fee, and the Indian government tacks on another 6–16%, depending on the facilities. In luxury places, count on paying a total of 25% in taxes. You may be able to offset such fees with off-season discounts—up to 75% during the monsoon season, from June to August. On the other hand, many hotels charge higher-than-usual rates in peak season, from mid-December to mid-January.

Performing Arts

The traditional Kathakali dance-drama is performed by many companies in Cochin and at Aranmula's Vijnana Kala Vedi Cultural Center. In addition, some 50 classical, folk, and tribal dances survive throughout Kerala, many unique to a particular caste or temple. The graceful, swaying movements of Mohiniyattam, a dance that lies somewhere between Kathakali and classical Bharata Natyam, are thought to mimic the movement of coconut palms. Kalaripayattu is Kerala's native martial art; some believe it was exported to China along with Buddhism. Many hotels in Kerala stage cultural performances in peak season.

Festivals

January's Tiruvatira is a celebration of folk dancing and singing by young Malayalee women. In Trichur (Thrissur), the Pooram and Vela festivals (March–April) are among Kerala's best-known events. Thrissur Pooram is an eight-day spectacle with parades of decked-up elephants, music, and fireworks. On the sixth day of the seven-day Arattapuzha Pooram, held at the Ayappa temple 14 km (9 mi) from Trichur, 61 elephants feature in the proceedings. In the north, Kannur and Kasargode are known for the extraordinary Theyyam (November to May), a religious dance of tribal origin in which participants in terrifying makeup and elaborate costumes are venerated by worshipers. The weeklong harvest festival, Onam (late August to early September), is celebrated with floral displays and snake-boat racing. In the Trichur and Palakaad districts, Onam brings Pulikali (or Kaduvakali)—men brightly painted as green-, yellow-, orange-, and red-striped tigers—to the streets.

Shopping

Crafts include cups, vases, spoons, and teapots carved from coconut shells; baskets, floor and table mats, and carpets hand-woven from coir, the fiber made from the husk of coconut fruit; and sleeping mats and handbags made of resilient, pliable kova grass. Brass lamps, rosewood elephants, and lacquered wooden boxes with brass fittings—traditionally used to store the family jewels—are also common. The craftsmen of Aranmula, northeast of Trivandrum, make mirrors out of metal. Spice shops abound in Cochin and near the hill plantations of Thekkady and Munnar. If you want to stock up on fresh pepper, cardamom, and cinnamon, Kerala is the place.

Exploring Kerala

Outside of Cochin, attractions are rustic: quiet beaches spiked with palm trees, fishing boats laden with the day's catch, and tranquil tea and spice plantations. Kerala is home to 12 wildlife sanctuaries and two national parks, including the renowned Lake Periyar Wildlife Sanctuary, near Thekkady, where you can observe creatures in their native habitat from the comfort of a riverboat. Rajamala National Park near Munnar is home to the endangered *nilgiri tahr,* a shy but sweet-tempered mountain goat. The hills surrounding Thekkady and Munnar are lovely for trekking, rich in waterfalls and bird song. Kerala's low-slung, wooden temples are modest and more restricted than those elsewhere in India: non-Hindus can't enter even the courtyards of most of them.

Great Itineraries

IF YOU HAVE 4 DAYS

Spend your first day and night in ⚄ **Cochin.** The next day, head to the resort town of ⚄ **Kumarakom** for a two-day stay. Spend a night pampering yourself with an Ayurvedic massage and great local food. The next day embark on an overnight houseboat cruise through inland waterways.

IF YOU HAVE 6 DAYS

Follow the four-day itinerary, and then hire a car for the beautiful drive inland to ⚄ **Thekkady** or **Munnar** for two nights and a full day in the hilly Idukki district. To view the wildlife in Thekkady's Lake Periyar Wildlife Sanctuary, take the 4 PM boat cruise or a more adventurous jungle trek. Scenic Munnar is Kerala's Switzerland, with the added attractions of wild elephants and the Rajamala sanctuary. Some travelers arrive in Kerala by car from Madurai, in Tamil Nadu; if that's your plan, visit Idukki on your way west toward the coast.

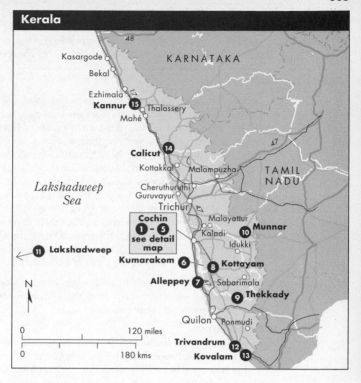

Kerala

KARNATAKA

Kasargode
Bekal
Ezhimala
Kannur 15 Thalassery
Mahé

Calicut 14
Kottakkal
Malampuzha

TAMIL
NADU

Cheruthuruthi
Guruvayur
Lakshadweep Sea
Trichur

Cochin
1 – 5
see detail map
Malayattur
Kaladi
Munnar 10
Idukki

11 Lakshadweep

Kumarakom 6
Kottayam 8

Alleppey 7 Sabarimala

9 Thekkady

Quilon Ponmudi

N

0 ———— 120 miles
0 ———— 180 kms

Trivandrum 12
Kovalam 13

IF YOU HAVE 9 DAYS

If beaches are your weakness, follow the six-day itinerary and swing back through Cochin to ⌘ **Lakshadweep.** Only about a third of these atolls off Kerala's coast are inhabited. A second option is to travel south from Thekkady to **Trivandrum,** Kerala's capital. Explore its sights and quiet lanes before heading for the mellow beaches, palm-fringed lagoons, and rocky coves near ⌘ **Kovalam.** A third option is to head for the rarely visited north to see the extraordinary Theyyam festivals of **Kannur** and the sweeping vistas of the fort at **Bekal,** near Kasargode.

When to Tour Kerala

Kerala's climate is sultry. For the best weather, come during the relatively cool season: between October and February. This is also a good time to see some of the more interesting festivals. March, April, and May are hot and humid, though the hill stations of Thekkady and Munnar are still pleasant. Heavy rains fall between June and mid-August, swallowing up most of the beaches and more than a few roads in low-lying areas, but crowds are at a minimum and hotel rates are slashed. Monsoon season is also supposed to be the best time for Ayurvedic treatments.

Numbers in the text correspond to numbers in the margin and on the Kerala and Cochin maps.

COCHIN

Cochin (Kochi) is one of the west coast's largest and oldest ports. The streets behind the docks of the historic Fort Cochin and Mattancherry districts are lined with old merchant houses, *godowns* (warehouses), and open courtyards heaped with betel nuts, ginger, peppercorns, and tea. Throughout the second millennium this ancient city exported spices, coffee, and coir, and imported culture and religion from Europe, China, and the Middle East. Today Cochin has a synagogue, several mosques, Portuguese Catholic churches, Hindu temples, and the United Church of South India (a collection of Protestant churches).

Exploring Cochin

The city is spread out over mainland, peninsula, and islands. Ernakulam, on the mainland 2 km (3 mi) from the harbor, is the commercial center and the one-time capital of the former state of Cochin. The fact that it was created by dredging the harbor makes Willingdon Island notable. The beautiful Bolghatty Island, north of Ernakulam, has a government-run hotel in a colonial structure that was once used by the Dutch governor and later by the British Resident. The historic Fort Cochin district, at the northern tip of the Mattancherry peninsula, is now home to many a coir magnate. Here houses often recall Tudor manors; some have been converted to hotels, others remain in the hands of the venerable tea and trading companies. The Mattancherry district is home to the city's dwindling Jewish community and is, along with Fort Cochin to the northwest, the city's historic center.

Traffic on land and the city's many bridges can be abominable. Private launches and small ferries zip through the waterways, making the journey as enjoyable as the destination.

A Good Tour

The sleepy, tree-lined streets of Fort Cochin are perfect for a leisurely stroll. Start at the **St. Francis Church** ①, where Portuguese explorer Vasco da Gama was once buried. Continue northeast along Church Street, passing colonial bungalows, to Vasco da Gama Square and the famed **Chinese fishing nets** ②. Take a right along the sea front past more colonial buildings, and another right down tiny Princess Street—one of the first streets built in Fort Cochin, it's crammed with shops and modest European residences. Complete the circle by heading south to Fosse Road. Take a right, walk one block and turn left on Pattalam Road. Follow it to Parade Road and turn left to reach the **Santa Cruz Cathedral** ③. From here, hop an autorickshaw to Mattancherry and visit the **Dutch Palace** ④ and the **Synagogue** ⑤. After leaving the synagogue, take a right and then a left onto Jew Town Road. Follow it for one block. On your left will be **Pepper Exchange;** step inside for a glimpse of local commerce in action. In the afternoon browse in antiques shops that line the streets near the synagogue or head back north to the jetty and catch a ferry to Ernakulam for shopping on Mahatma Gandhi (M. G.) Road.

TIMING

You can see Fort Cochin and Mattancherry in half a day. Remember that all houses of worship close for a few hours around lunchtime. The Dutch Palace is closed on Friday, the synagogue is closed to visitors on Saturday, and most shops are closed on Sunday.

Sights to See

❷ **Chinese Fishing Nets.** The precarious-looking bamboo and wood structures hovering like cranes over the waterfront are Cochin's famous Chinese fishing nets. Although they've become identified with the city, they're used throughout central Kerala. Thought to have been introduced by Chinese traders in the 14th century, the nets and their catch are easily accessible at Fort Cochin's Vasco da Gama Square. They're particularly picturesque at sunset or at any time when viewed from the deck of a boat.

Cochin

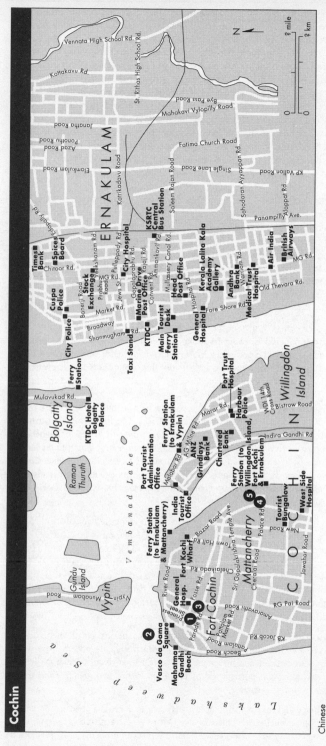

Chinese
Fishing Nets 2

Dutch Palace 4

St. Francis
Church 1

Santa Cruz
Cathedral 3

Synagogue 5

❹ Dutch Palace. Built by the Portuguese in the mid-16th century, this structure was taken over in 1663 by the Dutch, who made some additions before presenting it to the Rajas of Cochin. The rajas, in turn, added some of India's best mythological murals—the entire story of the *Ramayana* is told on the walls in a series of bedchambers, which also have inviting window seats. In the ladies' ground-floor chamber, you can see a colorful, mildly erotic depiction of Lord Krishna with his female devotees. The coronation hall near the entrance holds portraits and some of the rajas artifacts, including a fantastic palanquin covered in red wool. The palace has rare, traditional Keralite flooring, which looks like polished black marble but is actually a mix of burned coconut shells, charcoal, lime, plant juices, and egg whites. ⊠ *Palace Rd., Mattancherry,* ☏ *no phone.* ▦ *Free.* ⊙ *Sat.–Thurs. 10–5.*

OFF THE
BEATEN PATH

PEPPER EXCHANGE – The New York Stock Exchange it's not, but the Pepper Exchange does allow a glimpse into the world of spice trading. Monitors in a small room display the going rate of pepper, and men sit by phones in cubicles that line the walls. When a bid comes in, the yelling and finger-pointing starts. Then, just as suddenly, everyone goes back to reading the newspaper. You must obtain a visitor's pass from the secretary and remove your shoes before entering. ⊠ *Jew Town Rd., Mattancherry,* ☏ *no phone.* ▦ *Free.* ⊙ *Weekdays 9–4.*

NEED A
BREAK?

A favorite artists' hangout, Fort Cochin's **Kashi Art Cafe** (⊠ Burgher St., ☏ 484/769215) is about as funky as Kerala gets, displaying modern art on the walls and sculpture in the courtyard. Kashi serves light Continental fare and Western-style coffee–but the real treat is to experience the tiny pocket of Kerala subculture.

❶ St. Francis Church. The Portuguese flag first appeared in Fort Cochin in 1500, and Vasco da Gama arrived in 1502. The following year, Afonso de Albuquerque came with half a dozen ships full of settlers—he built the fort, and five friars in the crowd built India's first European church, St. Francis, in 1510. Da Gama returned in 1524 as Portuguese viceroy of the Indies, he died that same year, and was buried in this church. You can still visit his gravestone, but his remains were shipped back to Lisbon in 1538.

The church's history reflects the European struggle for colonial turf in India. It was a Catholic church until 1664, when it became a Dutch Reform church; it later became Anglican (1804 to 1947) and is now part of the Church of South India. Inside are beautifully engraved Dutch and Portuguese tombstones and the *doep boek*, a register of baptisms and marriages between 1751 and 1894 that you can view in photographic reproduction (the original is too fragile). ⊠ *Church St. between Parade Rd. and Bastion Rd.* ⊙ *Daily sunrise–sunset.*

❸ Santa Cruz Cathedral. The interior of this cathedral is full of turquoise and yellow tiles that some would call flamboyant, others downright gaudy. The cathedral's history dates from the 16th century, but the current structure was completed in 1904. ⊠ *Parade and K. B. Jacob Rds.* ⊙ *Daily sunrise–sunset.*

★ **❺ Synagogue.** The first migration of Jews to Kerala is thought to have taken place in the 6th century BC, followed by a much larger wave in the 1st century AD, when Jews fleeing Roman persecution in Jerusalem settled at Cranganore (on the coast about 26 km/16 mi north of Cochin). In the 4th century, the local king promised the Jews perpetual protection, and the colony flourished, serving as a haven for Jews from the Middle East and, in later centuries, Europe. When the Portuguese leader Afonso de Albuquerque discovered the Jews near Cochin in the 16th century, however, he destroyed their community, having received permission from his king to "exterminate them one by one." Muslim anti-Semitism flared up as well. The Jews rebuilt in Mattancherry but were able to live without fear only after the less-belligerent Dutch took control in 1663.

This peaceful synagogue was built in 1568 and was considerably embellished in the mid-18th century by a wealthy trader, Ezekiel Rahabi. He had the clock tower built and the floor paved with 1,100 hand-painted, blue-and-white Chinese tiles—each one different. Like the facade, the interior is white with blue trim, embellished with hanging glass lamps from Belgium and a chandelier from Italy; look up at the ladies' gallery for an eye-pleasing row of colored lamps. Ask to see the 200-year-old sheepskin Torah page, kept behind closed doors. The synagogue's most important relics—the impressive copper plates recording the 4th-century decree in which King Bhaskara Ravi Varma guaranteed the Jewish settlers domain over Cranganore—are no longer available for public viewing. You must remove your shoes before entering. ⊠ *Jew Town Rd., Mattancherry.* 🎫 *Rs. 2.* ☉ *Sun.–Fri. 10–noon and 3–5.*

Dining and Lodging

For a taste of delicious Keralite cuisine, seek out regional Malayalee restaurants or hotel restaurants that specialize in native fare. Many independent restaurants have grown so popular that it's advisable to call ahead for a table.

Most of the hotels and restaurants are in crowded Ernakulam. The handful of accommodations on the islands are quieter and more scenic; those on Willingdon Island also give you easy access to both Fort Cochin and the mainland Ernakulam district. Historic hotels are the specialty of Fort Cochin.

$$$ ✕ **Fort Cochin.** Bamboo and traditional furnishings give this outdoor
★ seafood restaurant the feel of a Keralite cottage. There's no menu: the day's catch is merely wheeled before you in a wooden cart, and your choice is cooked to order, whether you prefer it simply grilled or exquisitely curried. ⊠ *Casino Hotel, K. P. K. Menon Rd., Willingdon Island,* ☎ *484/668221. AE, DC, MC, V. No lunch.*

$$–$$$ ✕ **The History.** The food here is a testament to the myriad international influences on Cochin's history, drawing from the Middle East, Portugal, the local Jewish community, and the days of the British Raj. Some of the more historically relevant dishes are explained on the menu. The large, lofty space is capped with a gabled wooden roof that's supported by massive wood beams—it looks like a ship has been overturned to form the ceiling. The elegant dining room is lined with windows and warmly lit with chandeliers. ⊠ *Brunton Boatyard hotel, River Rd., Fort Cochin,* ☎ *484/215461. AE, DC, MC, V.*

$$–$$$ ✕ **Malabar Junction.** The mix of Keralite specialties and Mediterranean cuisine at this quirky restaurant isn't as crazy as it sounds—most dishes veer closer to one side or the other. A tasty red snapper fillet, for instance, is flavored with garlic and olives. Seafood is the specialty here, fresh and carefully prepared. ⊠ *Malabar House Residency, 1/268–1/269 Parade Rd., Fort Cochin,* ☎ *484/216666. AE.*

$$–$$$ ✕ **Rice Boats.** At this waterfront restaurant, you eat inside a traditional Keralite boat under a woven bamboo awning. The lighting is subdued, and oars and bamboo hats adorn the walls. The chef specializes in seafood, including *karimeen grandeur* (fresh local fish marinated in subtle spices then fried) and various lobster and prawn dishes. ⊠ *Taj Mal-*

abar Hotel, Malabar Rd., Willingdon Island, ☎ *484/666811. AE, DC, MC, V. No lunch.*

$$–$$$ ✕ **Thai Pavilion.** Don't be surprised if your waiter explains each dish to you upon presentation—this is, after all, Kerala's first Thai restaurant. The menu features plentiful seafood offerings and is reasonably authentic, though some dishes are on the sweet side. The *pla rad prik* is a very soft fish, nicely flavored with basil; the spicy classic *tom yam goong* soup doesn't disappoint. The dining room is done up in warm woods, with silver accents on the ceiling and chairs. Bevelled glass windows afford a glimpse of the sea. ✉ *Taj Malabar Hotel, Malabar Rd., Willingdon Island,* ☎ *484/666811. AE, DC, MC, V.*

$$ ✕ **The Renaissance.** The lunch buffet at the Avenue Regent's multicuisine restaurant is so popular that even visiting chefs pop in for a bite when they're in town. There's a variety of South Indian, North Indian, and Chinese specialties, but most people come for the hot, fresh, perfectly prepared appam—served with a mildly spicy coconut stew. ✉ *Avenue Regent hotel, 39/206 M. G. Rd., Ernakulam,* ☎ *484/372660, 484/ 372661, or 484/373537.*

$–$$ ✕ **Pandhal.** Surrounded by rough white-stucco walls, sheltered by a pine ceiling, and calmed by waterfall, you can partake of a variety of seafood, steak, Chinese, and Indian dishes. The restaurant gets crowded in the evening, making dinner reservations essential. ✉ *M. G. Rd., Ernakulam,* ☎ *484/367759. AE, DC, MC, V.*

$ ✕ **Fry's Village Restaurant.** Here four plain pavilions with bamboo curtains suffice to screen out the city's bustle. Lunch sees typical Kerala *thalis* (set combination meals), which incorporate such specialties as *molly* (fish fillet in a sweet green curry with coconuts) or the inexpensive *kadala* (Kerala plain curry) with *puttu* (steamed rice and coconut). Expect a crowd. ✉ *Chittoor Rd., Ernakulam,* ☎ *484/353983. No credit cards.*

$ ✕ **Pavilion.** In an out-of-the-way hotel south of Mattancherry, this extremely ordinary-looking restaurant is a well-kept secret. Ignore the multicultural cuisine and go straight for a fish dish like the prawn curry or the *meen pollichathu,* spiced fish steamed in a banana leaf; it's so hot even Malayalees break a sweat. If you'd like it toned down, tell the chef beforehand. ✉ *Hotel Abad, near intersection of Moulana Azad Rd. and Kochangadi Rd., Chullickal,* ☎ *484/228211. AE, DC, MC, V.*

$$$$ 🏨 **Brunton Boatyard.** Built in a combination of Dutch and Portuguese
★ colonial styles, this hotel is on the site of a former boatyard, facing Cochin harbor's Chinese fishing nets. *Pankhas* (manually operated wooden fans) dangle from the open-air lobby's lofty ceiling. A gracefully bowing tree shades the grassy courtyard, which is surrounded by whitewashed arcades lined with terra-cotta tile. In the guest rooms, the four-poster beds so high you need a footstool to climb in; the fixtures and furnishings are all antique in style, right down to the light switches. Most rooms have balconies from which to watch ships glide past in the harbor. ✉ *River Rd., Fort Cochin, 682001,* ☎ *484/215461,* ℻ *484/222562. 22 rooms, 4 suites. Restaurant, coffee shop, pool, massage, travel services. AE, DC, MC, V. BP.*

$$$ 🏨 **Malabar House Residency.** Luxurious yet homey, this 300-year-old villa once housed European traders and bankers. A dramatic swimming pool, graced with fallen frangipani, sits in the courtyard garden. Rooms are a mixture of traditional Keralite and contemporary: yellow and red walls are offset by antique wooden furnishings. Somehow, the curious combinations of elements work. Ayurvedic treatments are available on request. ✉ *1/268–1/269 Parade Rd., Fort Cochin, 682001,* ☎ *484/ 216666,* ℻ *484/217777,* 🌐 *www.malabarhouse.com. 17 rooms. 2 restaurants, bar, pool, travel services. AE. BP.*

\$\$\$ ⊞ **Taj Malabar.** At the tip of Willingdon Island, this hotel offers sea
★   views and free sunset boat rides through Cochin Harbor. Throughout,
modern tiles and brass details often complement dark woods and Ker-
ala-style furnishings. The lobby has a stunning carved-wood ceiling and
a similarly styled bar with a harbor view. In the Heritage Wing, refurbished wood floors have a warmer tone, but homage is paid to tradition in the ceiling over the sitting area. Elsewhere, hallways pick up
the dark woods yet again, along with carved door frames and attractive lanterns. Rooms in the newer wings are often modern, with blond-
wood furniture and lemon-yellow walls. Suites have terraces overlooking
the water. At this writing an Ayurvedic spa and an activity center were
in the works. ⊠ *Malabar Rd., Willingdon Island 682009,* ☎ *484/
666811,* FAX *484/668297,* WEB *www.tajhotels.com. 87 rooms, 9 suites.
3 restaurants, bar, pool, massage, Ping-Pong, travel services. AE, DC,
MC, V.*

\$\$–\$\$\$\$ ⊞ **Bolghatty Palace.** The Kerala Tourism Development Corporation
(KTDC) has transformed a 1744 Dutch trader's mansion on quiet
Bolghatty Island into a hotel, accessible only by public ferry from Ernakulam. A new annex blends beautifully with the original building.
Rooms are large, with high ceilings, wood furnishings, sea views, and
balconies. The fluorescent tube lighting and the curtains are less than
attractive, however. The four massive rooms in the original palace are
spectacular, with high wood-beamed ceilings, carved rosewood furniture, decadent couches and ottomans, modern bathrooms, and properly sumptuous draperies. There are also small, basic waterfront
cottages on stilts, complete with lovely views, and an Ayurvedic center. ⊠ *Bolghatty Island (Mulavukadu PO, Ernakulam 682504),* ☎ *484/
355003,* FAX *484/354879,* WEB *www.ktdc.com. 20 rooms, 6 cottages.
Restaurant, pub, golf course, pool, travel services. AE, MC, V.*

\$\$ ⊞ **Avenue Regent.** The spiffy marble lobby of this high-rise business
hotel has art deco red bands around the ceiling molding and in the floor
pattern. The carpeted rooms are spacious and contemporary. Request
a back-facing room for relative peace and quiet. ⊠ *39/2026 M. G. Rd.,
Ernakulam 682016,* ☎ FAX *484/372660,* WEB *www.avenueregent.com.
53 rooms. Restaurant, bar, coffee shop, business services, travel services. AE, DC, MC, V. BP.*

\$\$ ⊞ **Casino Hotel.** The cozy lobby of this casually handsome hotel has
cane furnishings; hallways are carpeted with locally made coir mats,
and the walls are dressed up with Tanjore glass paintings. Spacious,
wood-floored rooms also have coir mats and modern cane and wood
furniture; the master, bedside, and electrical control panels are nice
touches. All bathrooms are elegantly done in black marble, though not
all have tubs. At this writing, an Ayurvedic center was under construction.
⊠ *K. P. K. Menon Rd., Willingdon Island 682003,* ☎ *484/668221 or
484/668421,* FAX *484/668001. 67 rooms, 1 suite. 2 restaurants, bar, pool,
travel services. AE, DC, MC, V.*

\$\$ ⊞ **Fort Heritage.** Each room in this restored 17th-century Dutch mansion is slightly different from the next, though all are enormous and
have towering wooden ceilings and period reproduction furniture.
Ground floor rooms open, unfortunately, directly into the restaurant;
upstairs rooms surround a common area with a giant wooden swing;
a couple have balconies overlooking a courtyard. ⊠ *1/283 Napier St.,
Fort Cochin 682001,* ☎ FAX *484/215333 or 484/215455,* WEB
*www.fortheritage.com. 10 rooms. Restaurant, massage, laundry ser-
vice, tours. AE, DC, MC, V. CP.*

\$\$ ⊞ **Le Meridien.** On 15 landscaped acres in the outskirts of Ernakulam,
this imposing, green-tile-roofed building has all the amenities of both
a business hotel and a resort, including an impressive Ayurvedic center and a full-fledged fitness center. The enormous lobby is appointed

with colorful marble and massive bronze sculptures. Rooms are spacious, with light wood floors and modern furnishings. Views are often gorgeous, with manicured lawns in the foreground and beyond to the tiered pool and the Chinese fishing nets. ⊠ *Kundannur Junction, NH 47 Bypass, Maradu 682304,* ☎ *484/705777 or 484/705451,* FAX *484/705750,* WEB *www.lemeridien-hotels.com. 151 rooms. 2 restaurants, 2 bars, pool, hair salon, health club, jogging, tennis court, boating, business services, meeting rooms, travel services. AE, DC, MC, V.*

$$ 🏨 **Taj Residency.** Standard rooms in this beautifully maintained downtown hotel are on the small side, and their bathrooms have showers rather than tubs. Opt for one of the large, sea-facing rooms, which have spectacular views. The North Indian restaurant features classical music performances every night. ⊠ *Marine Dr., Ernakulam, 682031,* ☎ *484/371471,* FAX *484/371481. 96 rooms, 12 suites. Restaurant, bar, coffee shop, business services. AE, DC, MC, V.*

$$ 🏨 **The Trident.** Tasteful and stylish, this member of the Oberoi chain is outfitted for both business and leisure travelers. The low-rise, tile-roof building wraps around a central courtyard, so hallways are full of natural light. The bar area is separated from the lobby by a modernistic slab of black stone. In the rooms, which face the pool or the garden, sandy wood floors complement cream and teal color schemes. The staff is pleasant and helpful, and an Ayurvedic center is in the works. ⊠ *Bristow Rd., Willingdon Island, 682003,* ☎ *484/666816 or 484/669595,* FAX *484/668017 or 484/669393,* WEB *www.tridenthotels.com. 96 rooms. Restaurant, bar, pool, hair salon, exercise room, business services, travel services. AE, DC, MC, V.*

$ 🏨 **Woods Manor.** Thoughtful touches abound in this centrally located hotel, from the lobby's rock garden waterfall to the golden wrought elevator doors. Standard rooms are of average size, fitted with a window seat and a desk. Kerala Floor rooms have carved wooden ceilings and dark-wood and cane furniture. ⊠ *Woodlands Junction, M. G. Rd., Ernakulam 682011,* ☎ *484/382055 through 484/382059,* FAX *484/3820080. 68 rooms. Restaurant, pool, business services, travel services. AE, MC, V.*

The Arts

Art Gallery

The former home of the Parishith Thampuran Museum now houses the **Kerala Lalita Kala Akademi Gallery** (⊠ D. H. Rd., Ernakulam, ☎ 484/36907). There's not much here by way of explanation, but the traditional tile-roof building is cool and airy, and the interesting collection features contemporary works by Indian artists. Admission is Rs. 5, and the gallery is open Tuesday through Sunday 11 to 1 and 2 to 7.

Dance

In the 400-year-old Kathakali, a story—usually from an Indian epic—is told through dancing, pantomime, and music. Performances originally began at sundown and lasted all night; today they're often shortened to one or two hours. Many centers also offer the chance to watch dancers being made up.

Kathakali performances in the air-conditioned auditorium of the **Cochin Cultural Center** (⊠ Manikath Rd., off Ravipuram Rd., Ernakulam, ☎ 484/380366 or 484/373162) start at 6:30 PM, though you should arrive an hour before the show to see makeup being applied. **Kerala Kalamandalam** (⊠ Cheruthuruthy, 29 km/18 mi north of Trichur, ☎ 492/622418) provides training in Kathakali, Mohiniattam, and other native art forms. All-night Kathakali performances are staged here a few nights each year, and you're welcome to watch students in practice sessions that are held weekdays from 8:30 to noon and 3:30 to 5:30. The best Kathakali performances are at the **See India Foundation** (✉ Kalthil Parambil La., Ernakulam, ☎ 484/369471 or 484/371576), where the director provides lively explanations of the dance before every 6:45 PM show.

Martial Arts

Kerala's dramatic, high-flying martial art, Kalarippayattu, may be the oldest in Asia. Some scholars even believe that Buddhist monks from India introduced Kalarippayattu to China along with Buddhism. Participants learn both armed and unarmed combat techniques. One of the more unusual skills involves defending yourself against a knife-wielding attacker using only a piece of cloth. In peak season, many hotels stage performances. If you call in advance, you can watch Kalarippayattu practitioners at the **E. N. S. Kalari Centre** (✉ Nettoor, Ernakulam, ☎ 484/700810).

Shopping

The streets surrounding the synagogue in Mattancherry are crammed with stores that sell curios, and Fort Cochin's quiet Princess Street has a few small shops worth a browse. For saris, jewelry, handicrafts, and souvenirs, head to M. G. Road in Ernakulam. Be suspicious of the word "antique" in all stores.

The **Cochin Gallery** (✉ 6/116 Jew Town Rd., Mattancherry, ☎ no phone) carries jewelry, carpets, cushion covers, bronze figurines, and wooden boxes. Local hotels often get their antiques from **Crafter's** (✉ 6/141 Jew Town Rd., Mattancherry, ☎ 484/227652). It's crammed with stone and wood carvings, pillars, and doors as well as such portable items as painted tiles, navigational equipment, and wooden boxes. Cochin's upscale ladies buy the latest designer fineries at the pricey boutique, **Glada** (✉ Convent Rd., Ernakulam, ☎ 484/364952).

Whether you're looking for a little information on Kerala or a tome to while away the hours, stop by **Idiom Books** (✉ Jew Town Rd., Mattancherry, ☎ 484/224028), a small bookshop just opposite the synagogue. It has an intriguing collection of recent Western and Indian fiction, as well as books on history, culture, and religion. **Indian Arts and Curios** (✉ Jew Town Rd., Mattancherry, ☎ 484/228049) is one of Kerala's oldest and most-reliable curio shops.

Jayalakshmi (✉ M. G. Rd., near Rajaji Rd., Ernakulam, ☎ 484/373932, 484/381709, or 484/352850) houses a mind-blowing selection of saris, *lehangas* (long skirts with fitted blouses), and the like as well Indian and Western clothes for men and children. **Kairali** (✉ M. G. Rd., near Jose Junction, Ernakulam, ☎ 484/354507) is a fixed-price government shop with a good selection of Keralite handicrafts and curios. **Surabhi** (✉ M. G. Rd., Ernakulam, ☎ no phone) is run by the state's Handicrafts Cooperative Society. It has an impressive selection of local products.

Village Square (✉ 1/258 Napier St., Fort Cochin, ☎ 484/212132) is an expensive, though attractive, all-in-one shop with goods from all over India. You'll find brocade work, marble inlay boxes, and Kashmiri carpets in addition to local handicrafts and precious and semi-precious jewelry.

CENTRAL KERALA

★ Between Cochin and Quilon (Kollam), to the south, is the immense labyrinth of waterways called *kayals,* through which much of the life of the Malayalee has historically flowed. From the vastness of Vembanad Lake to quiet streams just large enough for a canoe, the backwaters have carried Kerala's largely coconut-based products from the village to the market for centuries.

A backwater cruise provides a window into traditional local life. You can take a two- or three-hour journey to a village or two or spend eight hours on the major waterway between Quilon and Alleppey (Allapuzha). Private travel agents and the Kerala Tourism Development Corporation (KTDC) can help you hire a private boat departing on just such a trip from Quilon, Alleppey, or Kumarakom.

Big ferries ply the Quilon—Alleppey route as if it were a highway, but houseboats wander at will through the fascinating small waterways. Shaded by a woven bamboo canopy and fanned by cool breezes, you'll drift past simple, tile-roof houses with canoes moored outside; tiny waterfront churches; and people washing themselves, their clothes, their dishes, and their children in the river. Women in bright pink and blue stroll past green paddy fields, their waist-length hair unbound and smelling of coconut oil. Graceful palms are everywhere, as are political slogans painted on walls, featuring the communist hammer and sickle in colors Lenin never intended.

Kumarakom

⑥ *80 km (50 mi) south of Cochin*

Some of Kerala's finest resorts are in this tiny, rapidly developing paradise on the shores of Vembanad Lake. Arundhati Roy's birthplace, Ayemenem, featured in her novel *The God of Small Things,* is close by. Birds abound in the backwaters, as well as in the sanctuary on the lake's eastern shore.

Lodging

$$$$ 🏨 **Coconut Lagoon.** The only way to reach this resort on Vembanad Lake is by boat from one of two pickup points along an adjoining river. The grounds are crisscrossed with canals and footbridges and dotted with white bungalows and two-story mansions that are a mixture of rustic and modern; the newer villa accommodations have their own plunge pools. The large, curving, main pool is a masterpiece, set near the lake under swaying palms. The open-air restaurant, reassembled from parts of a 300-year-old Keralite home, overlooks the water and serves dramatic buffets; a seafood restaurant was under construction at this writing. ⊠ *Vembanad Lake, Kumarakom 686563,* ☎ *481/524491 or 481/524373,* 🅵🅰🆇 *481/524495 or 481/525834. 28 bungalows, 14 mansions, 8 villas. 2 restaurants, pool, massage, spa, travel services. AE, DC, MC, V.*

$$$ 🏨 **Kumarakom Lake Resort.** The traditional villas (at this writing, 28 new ones were being built) are set around a network of canals. Rooms feature dark-wood ceilings and huge garden bathrooms. You can relax at the dramatic, lakeside infinity pool or at the Ayurvedic center. The restaurant is in a 200-year-old home with elaborate wood carvings. ⊠ *Kumarakom North PO, Kumarakom, 686563,* ☎ *481/524900, 481/524501, or 481/525020,* 🅵🅰🆇 *484/524987,* 🆆🅴🅱 *www.klresort.com. 22 villas. Restaurant, pool, health club, boating, fishing, billiards, business services, travel services. AE, DC, MC, V.*

$$$ 🏨 **Taj Garden Retreat.** The main building of this verdant resort is an 1891 plantation house, built by the son of an English missionary. Its large rooms open onto broad verandas, and it overlooks a small lagoon where you can canoe or pedal-boat. Guest quarters are in the main house, in freestanding cottages, or in stationary houseboats. The terrace is a lovely place to relax with a glass of lime juice. Vembanad Lake is a short boat ride away down a woodsy canal. ☒ *Kumarakom 686563,* ☎ *481/524377,* ℻ *481/524371,* 🌐 *www.tajhotels.com. 5 rooms, 10 cottages, 6 houseboat rooms. Restaurant, pool, massage, boating, travel services. AE, DC, MC, V.*

Alleppey

❼ *35 km (22 mi) southwest of Kumarakom*

This coir-manufacturing city was once known as the Venice of India, though most residents have abandoned their canoes for cars. Alleppey (Alappuzha) is an important gateway to the backwaters—tour operators abound here, and several resorts have sprung up nearby.

On the second Saturday in August, throngs of supporters line the shore to watch the annual Nehru Cup Snake Boat Race, which starts with a water procession and concludes dramatically as the boats (propelled by as many as 100 rowers) vie for the trophy. Several snake-boat races take place in the area from mid-July to mid-September. Check with the Alleppey Tourism Development Cooperative (ATDC) for exact times and locations.

Lodging

$$$$ 🏨 **Marari Beach.** With a palm-fringed beach, an excellent Ayurvedic center, and a setting 20 minutes from the backwaters and 15 km (9 mi) north of Alleppey, the Marari packs a lot of Kerala into one bundle. Nestled between two fishing villages, the 27-acre resort combines a warm, rustic feel with modern comforts. Brick paths lead through rows of deceptively modest thatch-roof villas, extremely spacious and comfortable, with open-air bathrooms. Private gardens and side entrances add an air of seclusion. The staff is friendly and professional, and the open-air restaurant features live music and fantastic food. ☒ *Mararikulam 688549,* ☎ *478/863801,* ℻ *478/863810. 49 cottages, 3 villas. Restaurant, bar, air-conditioning, pool, volleyball, beach, bicycles, shop, travel services. AE, DC, MC, V.*

$$$ 🏨 **Kayaloram Lake Resort.** A common veranda surrounds each of this unassuming resort's four buildings, and old wooden doors lead to the modestly furnished rooms. All 12 of them have baths with open-air showers; only 8 have air-conditioning. There's an on-site Ayurvedic center. The property is right on the lake; boats pick you up in Alleppey. ☒ *Punnamada (Alleppey 688011),* ☎ *477/260573 or 477/262931,* ℻ *477/252918,* 🌐 *www.kayaloram.com. 12 rooms. Restaurant, pool. AE, DC, MC, V.*

$ 🏨 **Palm Grove Lake Resort.** Simplicity rules the day at this coconut plantation hideaway overlooking the starting point of the Nehru Cup Snake Boat Race. It consists of just four cottages, made entirely of bamboo—walls, ceilings, doors, and windows. Furnishings are basic but comfortable; bathrooms are open air. The charm here is in the hammocks, the home-cooked food, the friendly staff, and the idyllic setting. ☒ *Punnamada (Alleppey 68006),* ☎ *477/245004 or 477/243474,* ℻ *477/251138. 4 cottages. Restaurant, massage, boating, fishing, travel services. No credit cards.*

Kottayam

❽ *50 km (31 mi) northeast of Alleppey*

Just inland from Alleppey, this pleasant town has several churches, established in the 1500s by missionaries. Cheriapally is the most interesting of these, still retaining much of its original blend of Portuguese and Kerala architecture. The interior features a wood-beamed roof and carved wooden ceilings; behind the altar are beautiful, faded murals. Today Kottayam is a center for rubber production, publishing, and transportation. From here there's bus service to the Lake Periyar Wildlife Sanctuary, ferry service to Alleppey, and train service on the the Cochin–Trivandrum route.

Lodging

$$$ 🏨 **Lake Village.** Don't be alarmed by the nondescript business hotel that fronts the main road—the Lake Village is behind it, a world apart. Its Ayurvedic center and its two-story cottages are on 5 garden acres. Each cottage has a balcony overlooking a canal, a downstairs sitting room, and upper-level bedrooms with wooden floors and ceilings and window seats. Unfortunately some have a rather jarring view of the business hotel as well as the backwater—choose your cottage carefully. ✉ *M. C. Rd., Kodimatha (Kottayam 686039),* ☎ *481/303623, 481/363638, 481/ 363639, or 481/36340,* FAX *481/363738,* WEB *www.thewindsorcastle.net. 17 cottages. 2 restaurants, pool, boating, fishing, business services, travel services. AE, MC, V.*

Thekkady

9 *116 km (72 mi) east of Kottayam*

Due east of Kumarakom and Kottayam, this mountain town sits at 3,000 ft above sea level in the Cardamom Hills, midway between Cochin and the temple city of Madurai in Tamil Nadu. Thekkady is the population center nearest the **Lake Periyar Wildlife Sanctuary,** one of India's best animal parks for spotting elephants, bison, wild boar, oxen, deer, and many species of birds. The best viewing period is October through May.

Lake Periyar, its many fingers winding around low-lying hills, is the heart of the 300-square-mi sanctuary. Forget exhausting treks or long safaris: here, you lounge in a motor launch as it drifts around bends and comes upon animals drinking at the shores. In dry season, when forest watering holes are empty, leopards and tigers also pad up to the water. A few words of advice: Indian children (and adults) love to scream and shout at wildlife sightings. To avoid losing the whole experience, hire a private launch (Rs. 1,500 for a 12-seater) through the KTDC. On a quiet trip, elephants hardly notice the intrusion, although younger pachyderms will peer at you out of curiosity and then run squealing back to their elders when your boat comes too close. If you're brave-hearted, you can spend a night in a jungle lodge (if you go on a forest trek, look out for leeches); if you're less adventurous you can commune with nature from the safety of a moated watchtower. Half-hour elephant rides are also available. For information about treks and the park, contact the KTDC. ✉ *KTDC, Shanmugham Rd., Ernakulam Cochin,* ☎ *484/353234.* 🎥 *Rs. 50, video cameras Rs. 100.*

Lodging

$$$$ 🏨 **Hotel Lake Palace.** A public ferry transports you to this former maharaja's hunting lodge on an island inside the Lake Periyar Wildlife Sanctuary. Six simple rooms, some with period furniture, look out through a palm-lined pathway and beyond to the lake and the preserve—you can spot animals from your balcony. Meals at the eclectic, fixed-menu restaurant are included. As the hotel is run by the state government, make reservations through the KTDC. ✉ *Lake Periyar Wildlife Sanctuary, Thekkady 685536,* ☎ *486/322023;* ✉ *KTDC, Shanmugham Rd., Ernakulam Cochin 682031,* ☎ *484/353234. 8 rooms. Restaurant, refrigerator, boating, travel services. AE, DC, MC, V. FAP.*

$$$$ ▥ **Spice Village.** Just outside the Lake Periyar Wildlife Sanctuary, this resort has well-maintained thatch-roof cottages built into a hillside. Lush plantings, including a spice garden, add fragrance and privacy. Interiors have knotty pine furnishings and trim, white walls, red-tile floors, and plaid upholstery and bedspreads. The restaurant serves Indian and Continental set meals. Jungle treks and Indian cooking classes are among the activities. ⊠ *Kummily Rd., Thekkady, 685536,* ☎ *486/ 322315,* FAX *486/322317. 52 cottages. Restaurant, bar, pool, massage, boating, meeting room, travel services. AE, DC, MC, V.*

$$$-$$$$ ▥ **Shalimar Spice Garden.** This rustic retreat is 20 bone-jarring minutes off the main road to Thekkady. Most guests come for the Ayurvedic-treatment packages and yoga classes; the emphasis is on serenity and relaxation. A wooden bridge over a duck pond leads to the main building—a whitewashed, thatch-roof affair that houses a restaurant specializing in authentic Italian and Keralite food. The small, spotlessly white cottages are spread out over a hillside. Decor is largely minimalist and perfectly executed, with only a colorful Rajasthani bedspread, a stained-glass window, or an ancient, dark-wood oar adding bits of contrast to each room. Bathrooms are lavish and large. ⊠ *Murikkady 685535,* ☎ FAX *486/322132,* WEB *www.shalimarkerala.com. 7 rooms, 7 cottages. Restaurant, pool, travel services. MC, V.*

$$$ ▥ **Taj Garden Retreat.** On a former coffee plantation, this woodsy Taj property offers concrete cottages raised on stilts; balconies are nice touches as is the thatch piled on the roofs, though it's more for effect than for function. Rooms are modern and reliable, and the restaurant, which serves a variety of cuisine, is excellent. ⊠ *Ambalambika Rd., Thekkady 685536,* ☎ *486/322273 and 486/322401 through 486/ 322407,* FAX *486/322106,* WEB *www.tajhotels.com. 32 rooms. Restaurant, bar, pool, massage, travel services. AE, DC, MC, V.*

$$ ▥ **Cardamom County.** Views from this steeply pitched resort are gorgeous. The mid-size rooms are in individual or double white-washed, red-tile-roof cottages with gabled ceilings. Each is appointed with dark-wood furniture and terra-cotta floors. There's an Ayurvedic center on the neatly manicured grounds as well as a fish pond where you can catch your own dinner. ⊠ *Thekkady Rd., Thekkady 685536,* ☎ *486/322866 or 486/322806,* FAX *486/322807,* WEB *www.cardamomcounty.com. 31 rooms. Restaurant, pool, health club, travel services. AE, MC, V.*

Munnar

❿ *100 km (62 mi) north of Thekkady, 130 km (80 mi) east of Cochin.*

On the drive from Thekkady to Munnar, a good road winds through lofty forests as well as spice and tea plantations. The town of Munnar itself is small and unattractive, but most of the land around it is owned by the Tata tea company and a few smaller concerns. The result is an unspoiled hill station, with hundreds of acres of tea, coffee, and cardamom plantations amid hills, lakes, streams, and waterfalls. During your visit you can tour these plantations; arrange trekking, rock-climbing, paragliding, and river trips; or just sit on your hotel balcony with a cup of tea, taking in the scenery.

Most lodgings can arrange a tea plantation tour, where you can walk through the steeply pitched, dense green hedges, and see how the leaf is processed. (The awful truth is that the dregs of the batch get shipped to America.) Cardamom plantations are just this side of heaven. The shade-loving spice needs plenty of forest cover, so a walk through a plantation feels like a stroll in the woods, complete with dappled sunlight, mountain streams, and birdsong.

The **Rajamala National Park,** 15 km (9 mi) northwest of Munnar, is home to the endangered nilgiri tahr. You can get close to this endearingly tame mountain goat, pushed to the brink of extinction by its utter lack of suspicion toward human beings. Half the world's remaining population live here. ☏ 486/530487. ⊠ *Rs. 50.* ⊙ *Daily 7–6; closed in monsoon season.*

Lodging

$$$ ⌂ **Club Mahindra.** Set between a mountain peak and a tea plantation—22 km (14 mi) east of Munnar—this large, family-oriented resort has guest quarters in the main building or in hillside cottages. Rooms are spacious, with wood floors and furnishings; deluxe rooms also have entrancing views. Cottages are large—a one-bedroom can sleep four—yet still homey. The activity center offers everything from video games to rappelling, and the restaurant serves excellent North Indian food as well as other types of cuisine. The Ayurvedic center is adequate. ⊠ *Kumily–Munnar Rd., Chinnakanal Village, 685618,* ☏ *486/849224,* FAX *486/849227,* WEB *www.clubmahindra.com. 38 rooms, 54 cottages. Restaurant, hair salon, boating, camping, children's programs, business services, travel services. AE, DC, MC, V.*

$$$ ⌂ **Tall Trees.** You can hardly spot the wood-and-stone structures of this hushed, breezy resort on a 66-acre cardamom plantation. Getting around the hilly property is a workout—especially the hike to the skylight-topped restaurant—but the setting is phenomenal. The views are of are trees, trees, trees. Standard double rooms are more pleasant than two-story deluxe rooms, which feel narrow and cramped. Luxury cottages have spacious upstairs living rooms and balconies; spiral staircases lead to two bedrooms and bathrooms downstairs. Furnishings are of rustic cane and rubber wood. At this writing, a library and a recreation room were under construction. ⊠ *Box 40, Bison Valley Rd., Munnar 685612,* ☏ *486/530641 or 486/530593,* FAX *484/370279,* WEB *www.thetalltreesmunnar.com. 16 rooms, 6 cottages. hiking, bicycles, recreation room, library. No credit cards. MAP.*

$$ ⌂ **Windermere Estate.** Plantation life is pretty darn good, especially when you're made to feel like the guest of a planter. Guest quarters here, just 2 km (1 mi) from Munnar, are in one of the five bedrooms of a stone cottage, which has a communal balcony and TV room. Service is warm and personalized. The hillside views are stunning, and the grounds are blessed with several streams and waterfalls, making for enchanting morning walks. ⊠ *Pothamedu (Box 21, Munnar 685612),* ☏ *486/530512, 486/530978 to estate, or 484/425237 for reservations,* FAX *484/427575,* WEB *www.winderemeremunnar.com. 5 rooms. Dining room, hiking. No credit cards. All-inclusive.*

$ ⌂ **Siena Village.** Some of the rooms at this hotel, 18 km (11 mi) east of Munnar, capture the country-lodge feeling perfectly. Ignore the single-story standard rooms and opt for a split-level deluxe one. Their lower-level sitting areas have timber floors, comfy couches, and working fireplaces; balcony views are of the Anayirankal Dam (its name means "where the elephants come"). The semicircular restaurant also has panoramic vistas. ⊠ *Chinnakanal 685618,* ☏ *486/849261, 486/ 849328, or 486/849461,* FAX *484/360254,* WEB *www.thesienavillage.com. 26 rooms. Restaurant, hiking, fishing, recreation room, business services, travel services. MC, V. CP.*

Lakshadweep

⑪ *250 km (160 mi) off the coast of Kerala*

Of the 36 or so coral atolls that make up the isolated paradise of Lakshadweep, only about 10 are inhabited, and their population is devoutly

Sunni Muslim. Tourism here is severely restricted to protect the fragile ecosystems and the traditional peoples. Your best bet is a stay on uninhabited Bangaram Island, where Casino Hotels operates a resort. On some Lakshadweep islands where tourism is allowed, accommodations are limited to simple tourist huts, and trips must be arranged through the **Society for the Promotion of Recreational Tourism and Sports** (SPORTS; ⊠ Harbour Rd., Willingdon Island, Cochin, ☎ 484/668387 or 484/668647). Flights leave Cochin six times a week; make all arrangements well in advance.

Lodging

$$$$ ⊞ **Bangaram Island Resort.** The emphasis is on preserving the envi-
★ ronment, making this resort seem like a true Eden. Accommodations are in simple, two- to four-bedroom, thatched cottages with terra-cotta floors and Western furnishings. Water sports are the order of the day: snorkeling, kayaking, scuba diving, windsurfing. Make reservations through the Casino Hotel in Cochin. ⊠ *Lakshadweep;* ⊠ *Casino Hotel, K. P. K. Menon Rd., Willingdon Island, Cochin 682003,* ☎ *484/ 668221,* ℻ *484/668001. 27 rooms, 3 bungalows. Restaurant, bar, dive shop, snorkeling, windsurfing, boating, fishing. AE, DC, MC, V. FAP.*

SOUTHERN KERALA

The beaches near Kovalam are southern Kerala's main attraction—in fact, they're what brought Western tourists to the state in the first place, as the hippie scene from Goa moved down the coast. Parts of Kovalam are overdeveloped and full of touts vending cheap tie-dye clothes. There are, however, still some pleasant spots to relax within a few miles of the main beach. Just a half hour from the Kovalam is Kerala's capital city of Trivandrum (Thiruvanandapuram), former home of the rajas of Travancore and now home to Kerala's primary international airport.

Trivandrum

 222 km (138 mi) south of Cochin, 253 km (157 mi) southwest of Thekkady

Built on seven low hills and cleansed by ocean breezes, Kerala's capital is surprisingly calm and pleasant. Trivandrum's few sights and quiet lanes outside the town center make it an enjoyable place to stop.

The handsome **Padmanabhaswamy Temple,** dedicated to Vishnu, has a seven-story *gopuram* (entrance tower). The date of its original construction has been placed at 3000 BC; legend has it that it was built by 4,000 masons, 6,000 laborers, and 100 elephants over the course of six months. In the main courtyard there's intricate granite sculpture, supplemented by more stonework on the nearly 400 pillars supporting the temple corridors. The complex is technically open only to Hindus and keeps erratic hours, so call ahead to be assured of at least a glimpse. ⊠ *M. G. Rd. at Chali Bazaar,* ☎ *471/450233.* ☉ *Sunrise– 12:30 and 4:30–9:30.*

The tiny entryway and haphazard sign might tempt you to pass on by, but do go in the **Kuthiramalika (Puthenmalika) Palace Museum.** The 18th-century Horse Palace has carved rosewood ceilings and treasures of the royal family, including an ivory throne, weapons, paintings, and gifts from foreign dignitaries. Lifesize Kathakali figures stand in the dance room. Carved horses for which the palace is named line the eaves of an inner courtyard. Only one-third of the enormous compound is open to visitors; the entrance fee includes a knowledgeable guide, who will politely demand a hefty tip at the end of the tour. Also note that you must remove your shoes upon entering. ☒ *Next to Padmanab-haswamy Temple, East Fort,* ☏ *no phone.* ☑ *Rs. 20, Rs. 1 shoe-stor-age charge.* ☉ *Tues.–Sun. 8:30–12:30 and 3:30–5:30.*

In an 80-acre park at the north end of M. G. Road are the many at-tractions of the **Museum and Art Gallery Complex.** Buy your ticket at the Natural History Museum, a musty collection of animal skeletons, dioramas, and stuffed birds. Head straight to the second floor to see an interesting model of a traditional *nalakettu* home, complete with costumed figurines and a full explanation. The Art Museum's collec-tion of local arts and crafts—including bronze and stone sculptures and musical instruments—is as noteworthy as the building itself, with its Cubist pattern of gables and its decorative interior. Memorabilia do-nated by the royal family, including a golden chariot used by the Ma-haraja of Travancore, is displayed in the tiny Sree Chitra Enclave. On the opposite side of the park, the Sree Chitra Art Gallery has an eclec-tic collection of paintings, including works of the Rajput, Mogul, and Tanjore schools; copies of the Ajanta and Sigirya frescoes; and works from China, Japan, Tibet, and Bali, along with canvases by modern Indian painters. ☒ *Museum Rd.,* ☏ *471/436275.* ☑ *Rs. 5.* ☉ *Thurs.–Tues. 10–5, Wed. 1–5.*

OFF THE BEATEN PATH About 50 km (32 mi) north of Trivandrum, the **Vijnana Kala Vedi Cultural Center** (☒ Tarayil Mukku Junction, Aranmula 689533, ☏ 4731/2552), established by a French woman in 1971, is dedicated to preserving the arts and heritage of Kerala. People from all over the world come to study everything from singing to cooking to language with experienced masters in a simple, village atmosphere. Space permitting, you can en-roll for as little as one week. The cost is $210, all-inclusive; there are discounts for longer stays.

Dining and Lodging

$$ ✕ **Orion.** Although it offers a variety of cuisines, this restaurant has acquired a reputation with locals for its traditional Indian dishes. The lunch-time South Indian buffet features such Kerala specialties as *elis-seri* (pumpkin with red beans) *avial* (mixed vegetables in a mild co-conut gravy), and fish curry. ☒ *The Residency Tower, Press Rd.,* ☏ *471/331661. AE, DC, MC, V.*

$$ ✕ **Swiss Bake House.** The graceful, two-story building—one-time home of the antiques-dealing Natesan family—is decorated with wood carvings and bronze artifacts. Come for the ambience as the food is only average. The attached café, however, serves lovely, Western-style pastries. ☒ *Vellyambalam Junction,* ☏ *471/311720. MC, V..*

$ ✕ **Amma.** There's nothing fancy here—just simple, tasty, vegetarian food like *amma* (mom) would make. The air-conditioned restaurant is comfortable and clean, and menu options range from soups and sal-ads to french fries. Opt for the traditional thali, a meal of unlimited rice served with small helpings of various vegetable preparations—a special thali comes with a whopping 18 dishes. ☒ *Subramaniam Rd.,* ☏ *471/338999. No credit cards.*

$ ✕ **Azad.** The ambience leaves much to be desired, but the food won't disappoint. Specialties include *biriani,* a flavorful rice cooked with chicken or mutton, and *kuthu paratha,* a Kerala Muslim delicacy of flat bread stuffed with minced fish. Azad has become a chain, but this, the orig-inal restaurant in East Fort, is reportedly the best. ☒ *M. G. Rd., East Fort, No credit cards.*

$$$ ▣ **South Park.** In one of Trivandrum's premier hotels, renovations were underway at this writing. Carpets in the large standard rooms were being replaced by wooden flooring, a foolproof way to get rid of the

mustiness that plagues most Kerala hotels. Street-facing rooms can be noisy; opt for one at the back. ✉ *Spencer Junction, M. G. Rd. 950346,* ☎ *471/333333,* FAX *471/331861,* WEB *www.thesouthpark.com. 83 rooms. Restaurant, coffee shop, bar, hair salon, massage, business center, travel services. AE, DC, MC, V.*

$$ ⊡ **Muthoot Plaza.** A roaring fountain encourages you to lounge ever deeper into the leather armchairs in the cream-tone marble lobby, where the Middle Eastern business clientele often gathers around the flat-screen TV or at the cyber-station. The carpeted rooms have high ceilings and bedside electric control panels. ✉ *Punnen Rd., 695039,* ☎ *471/337733,* FAX *471/337734,* WEB *www.sarovarparkplaza.com. 57 rooms. Restaurant, bar, coffee shop, exercise room, business services, travel services. AE, DC, MC, V.*

Shopping

For crafts from all over India, head to **Hastkala Exporters** (✉ G. A. K Rd., off M. G. Rd., ☎ 471/338462). Weavers for Travancore's royal family sell traditional Kerala saris at **Karalkada** (✉ Kaithamukku Junction, ☎ no phone). **Natesan's** (✉ M. G. Rd., ☎ 471/331594) is a respected art and antiques dealer. For Kerala handicrafts and souvenirs, hit the government emporium **SMSM** (✉ Statue Junction, off M. G. Rd., ☎ 471/330625).

Kovalam

⑬ *16 km (10 mi) south of Trivandrum*

Kovalam's sandy beaches are lined with palm-fringed lagoons and rocky coves. Fishermen in *lungis* (colorful cloth wraps) drag in nets filled with the day's catch, then push their slender wooden boats out again with a Malayalam "Heave ho." Here you can spend the day loafing on warm sand or rocky outcroppings, watch the sun set, then sit back as the dim lights of distant fishing boats come on. In peak season, outdoor eateries spring up right on the beach—just point to the fish of your choice and specify how you'd like it prepared.

Kovalam's irresistible beaches have given rise to tremendous development; the town itself and its main Lighthouse Beach have become overrun. There are still, however, a few beautiful, secluded beaches in villages to the north and south of Kovalam town.

Most area hotels offer Ayurvedic treatments, including complete health and revitalization packages (lasting anywhere from three days to one month) in which Ayurvedic doctors, masseurs, and yoga and meditation instructors team up to optimize your physical and spiritual well-being. If you don't want to commit to extended treatment, try an Ayurvedic oil massage: a vigorous rubdown involving copious amounts of oil, performed on a hard wooden table by a masseur with hands like driftwood. A postsession application of an herbal powder removes most of the unguent, leaving your skin feeling fresh. It's both invigorating and relaxing.

OFF THE
BEATEN PATH

PADMANABHAPURAM – Though it belongs to Kerala, this fantastic, 18th-century, carved-teak palace is actually across the border in neighboring Tamil Nadu, about a two-hour drive south of Kovalam on NH 47. Once home of the Travancore rajas, it's a rare example of wooden architecture in India.

Dining and Lodging

$ ✗ **Hotel Rockholm Restaurant.** You can eat indoors or on a terrace overlooking the ocean. Kovalam's best chef prepares excellent international and local dishes. Try the seasonal seafood dishes, such as fried mussels or prawns Kerala-style. ⊠ *Lighthouse Rd.,* ☎ *471/480607. AE, DC, MC, V.*

$$$$ 🏨 **Kovalam Ashok Beach Resort.** Although it's built in tiers on a bluff overlooking the Arabian Sea and it has a good beach, this resort resembles a housing project. Rooms in the main building and the sea-facing building have modern furnishings and private verandas; ask for an unobstructed sea view. Cottages, with tile floors and a cozier feel, have sea views and privacy. The Admiral Bar is a good spot for watching the sun set. ⊠ *Kovalam 695527,* ☎ *471/480101,* FAX *471/481522,* WEB *www.theashokgroup.com. 191 rooms, 8 suites. 3 restaurants, bar, 3 pools, massage, tennis court, health club, beach, travel services. AE, DC, MC, V.*

$$$$ 🏨 **Lagoona Davina.** U.K. native Davina Taylor has created an intimate guest house in a paradisiacal setting north of Kovalam. After a short drive from the airport, you're brought to a lagoon by boat. Small, thatched guest quarters line the beachfront. Warm yellow interiors are hand-painted with ethnic designs, carpeting is made from coir, beds have lavish canopies, and even the hot-water heater is swathed in sari material. If you don't feel like packing, just tell Davina your measurements and the colors you like, and she'll have clothes tailored for you. If that's not personalized enough, a room attendant is at your disposal throughout your stay. Ayurvedic massage, yoga, and reiki are available. ⊠ *Pachalloor 695527,* ☎ *471/380049 or 471/384857,* FAX *471/ 462935. 6 rooms, 1 cottage. Restaurant, pool, boating, travel services. No credit cards.*

$$$$ 🏨 **Nikki's Nest.** All rooms in this aerie south of Kovalam have commanding sea views. Set amid bougainvillea, coconut palms, banana trees, orchids, and acacia are thatch-roof, circular cottages and traditional wooden houses. The 13 cottage rooms are comfortable, spacious, and clean; some have air-conditioning. The traditional *nalakettu* homes are beautifully maintained, with wooden rafters and dark-wood windows that open out completely. A well-lit path leads down to the private, crescent-shape beach. There's an on-site Ayurvedic center and, at this writing, a swimming pool was under construction. ⊠ *Azhimala Shiva Temple Rd., Chowara 695591,* ☎ *471/481822, 471/483821, or 471/ 483822,* FAX *471/481182,* WEB *www.nikkisnest.com. 13 rooms, 3 houses. Restaurant, beach, business services, travel services. AE, DC, MC, V..*

$$$$ 🏨 **Surya Samudra Beach Garden.** Overlooking the sea 10 km (6 mi)
★ south of Kovalam, this rambling resort has an exquisite beach, lovely views, and a great deal of peace (loud noise isn't permitted). Most rooms are in restored Keralite wooden houses, each with an intricately carved facade, a domed wooden ceiling, open-air bathrooms, and understated decor. The handful of cottage rooms have interiors that blend modern and folk touches. Meals, prepared without preservatives, are served in an open-air restaurant. A new Ayurvedic spa complex was under construction at this writing. Note that the steep, rocky location isn't ideal for young children. Also, despite the high rates, this place is popular; reserve well in advance. ⊠ *Pulinkudi 695521,* ☎ *471/480413,* FAX *471/ 481124,* WEB *www.suryasamudra.com. 20 rooms. Restaurant, bar, pool, beach, travel services. DC, MC, V.*

$$$–$$$$ 🏨 **Somatheeram.** Stressed-out Westerners flock to this popular beach resort, equipped as it is with a fully staffed Ayurvedic hospital and a resident master. Lodging is in traditional houses or simple cottages along twisting paths on 15 lush acres above the sea. The grounds are a bit crowded, but the setting is still pleasant. None of the rooms is air-conditioned. ⊠ *Chowara 695501,* ☎ FAX *471/481600,* WEB *www. somatheeram.com. 55 rooms. Restaurant, beach, travel services. AE, DC, MC, V.*

$$$ ☷ **Coconut Bay.** In an undeveloped area just south of Kovalam, this 3-acre coconut-strewn property has a lovely private beach and an Ayurvedic center. The best views are actually from the wood-ceiling, non–air-conditioned rooms near the pool rather than the modern, red-brick, tile-roof villas that are closer to the sea. ✉ *Mulloor 695521,* ☎ *471/480566, 471/480668, or 471/484566,* FAX *471/343349,* WEB *www. coconutbay.com. 15 rooms. Restaurant, snorkeling, beach, boating, library, travel services. MC, V.*

$$$ ☷ **Poovar Island Resort.** A 20-minute ride through emerald backwaters south of Kovalam brings you to a palm-fringed island and its resort. The manicured grounds contain an Ayurvedic center and a large swimming pool. Tile-roof cottages, accessible via a boardwalk, hover on stilts above an artificial pond. Rooms are large, with wooden furnishings and high, wood-framed ceilings. A few unusual thatch-roof cottages float just off the beach (swimming isn't recommended); they're small, and they bob up and down quite a bit, but their balconies sit right over the water, affording a sparkling view. ✉ *Pozhiyoor 695513,* ☎ *471/212068, 471/212069, or 471/212073,* FAX *471/212092,* WEB *www.floatelsindia.com. 28 cottages. Restaurant, air-conditioning, beach, boating, business services, travel services. AE, DC, MC, V.*

$$ ☷ **Ideal Ayurvedic Resort.** This small, homey resort south of Kovalam has specialized in Ayurvedic treatment for the past eight years. Rooms in the marble-floor main building are simply furnished and spotless; some have balconies overlooking a coconut grove. There are also a few thatch-roof cottages, some with open-air bathrooms. The beach is a short walk away, but Ideal focuses more on Indian arts and culture than on fun in the sun; it offer study programs in yoga and Ayurveda, among other healing treatments. ✉ *Chowara 695501,* ☎ FAX *471/ 481632 or 471/482496,* WEB *www.idealayurvedicresort.com. 10 rooms, 5 cottages. Restaurant, travel services. AE, DC, MC, V.*

NORTHERN KERALA

If Kerala is unspoiled India, then Malabar, as the northern part of the state was once known, is unspoiled Kerala. Arab traders landed here long before Vasco da Gama, and many trading families converted to Islam. Various conquerors built forts along spectacular stretches of coastline, and some of Kerala's most unique and colorful religious festivals take place in this region. Tourism is in its infancy; facilities are few and far between, making a trip here highly rewarding.

Calicut

⑭ *146 km (91 miles) northwest of Cochin*

This city doesn't hold much excitement in itself, but Calicut (Kozhikode) has an airport and is a good base for exploring several interesting sights nearby, including the lushly forested Wyanad district to the northeast. The city's historical ties with the Middle East are clearly apparent in a strong Arab presence.

In the town of Beypore, 10 km (6 mi) south of Calicut on the Beypore Road, is the **Tasara Center for Creative Weaving** (✉ Beypore North, ☎ 495/414832), where you can see weavers working on giant hand looms. Tasara also hosts programs for artists-in-residence. Call ahead to arrange a visit.

A group of local fisherman started the **Theeram Nature Conservation Society** (☎ no phone) when they discovered the Olive Ridley turtles they'd been eating were an endangered species. The center and its small turtle hatchery are on the beach at Kolavippalam, near Payyoli, about 30 km (19 mi) north of Calicut and off NH 17. You can watch female turtles arrive on the beach in November and December to lay their eggs, which hatch in January and February.

Dining and Lodging

$ ✕ **Paragon.** It's not much to look at, but this Calicut stalwart serves up tasty food. The chicken biriani is excellent, as is the unusual fried shrimp dish that goes very well with parathas. ⊠ *Kannur Rd., Calicut,* ☎ *no phone. No credit cards.*

$$$$ 🏨 **Green Magic.** A true back-to-nature experience (there's not even a phone), this astonishing Wyanad district resort off the Wyanad Road 65 km (40 mi) northeast of Calicut has two extraordinary tree houses perched 90 ft above the forest floor. One is accessed by a water-powered, caged-in elevator, the other by a suspension bridge—to use either contraption requires a good deal of faith. If you suffer from vertigo, request one of the ground-level lodges, which have timber floors and stone walls. Everything here is constructed with indigenous materials, except for the modern bathrooms; but even they're stocked with herbal powders in place of soap, shampoo, and toothpaste. Lighting is restricted to kerosene lamps, traditional meals are served on banana leaves, and a resident elephant is available for treks. ⊠ *Vythiri,* ☎ *471/ 330437; 471/331507 for reservations through TourIndia,* FAX *471/ 331407,* WEB *www.richsoft.com/tourindia. 3 treehouse rooms, 8 lodges. No credit cards. All-inclusive.*

$$$$ 🏨 **Kadavu.** A swank riverside resort 18 km (11 mi) south of Calicut, Kadavu signals Malabar's foray into tourism. You enter the lobby under a traditional *mandapam,* a wood-framed canopy supported by pillars. A fountain cascades down a series of earthen pots; another spouts from the large lotus pool behind the lobby, which is flanked by the wings of the hotel. The courtyard opens onto an enormous swimming pool, from which steps descend to riverfront cottages. Rooms are large, with bay windows and modern or traditional brass-and-wood furnishings; cottages also have balconies screened by coconut palms. An array of water sports is offered, and you can relax with a treatment in the Ayurvedic center. ⊠ *Off N. H. Bypass, Azhinjilam, Feroke 673632,* ☎ *495/440570,* FAX *495/441475,* WEB *www.kadavu.com. 57 rooms, 17 cottages. 2 restaurants, coffee shop, pool, tennis court, boating, business services, travel services. AE, DC, MC, V.*

$$$ 🏨 **Taj Residency.** Calicut's premier hotel is frequented by airline crews and wealthy Omanis, who come for lengthy treatments at the well-regarded Ayurvedic center. A beautiful wooden ceiling with exposed beams caps the lobby, and rooms are large and carpeted, with a touches of wood trim. Some quarters have a leafy view; others overlook the pool. ⊠ *PT Usha Rd., Calicut 673032,* ☎ *495/765354,* FAX *495/ 766448,* WEB *www.tajhotels.com. 74 rooms. Restaurant, coffee shop, bar, business services, travel services. AE, DC, MC, V.*

$ 🏨 **Fortune Hotel.** Slim wooden pillars encircle the pleasant lobby of this modern business hotel, and there's a beautiful terra-cotta-tile atrium decorated with Kathakali figurines. Rooms are mid-size and comfortably furnished, with large bathrooms and small balconies. Nonsmokers must grin and bear it—there are no designated no-smoking rooms. The rooftop pool affords nice city views. and the room rate includes breakfast. ⊠ *Kannur Rd., Calicut 673006,* ☎ *495/768888,* FAX *495/768111,* WEB *www.fortunecalicut.com. 63 rooms. Restaurant, coffee shop, bar, pool, health club, massage, business services, travel services. AE, DC, MC, V. BP.*

Kannur

⑮ *92 km (57 mi) northwest of Calicut*

The Kannur district is the heartland of the Moppilahs, Kerala's Muslim community, and is a center for the hand-loom industry as well as the manufacture of *beedis,* potent Indian hand-rolled cigarettes. The town itself was for many years at the center of the maritime spice trade. The ruling Kolathiri rajas profited from it as did the European colonists. Today Kannur is a good hub for visiting several coastal sights—to the north and the south—including forts and undeveloped beaches. Come quick, though; a massive project in the works at Bekal could change everything.

Another regional draw is the spectacular religious dance called Theyyam. More than an art form, it's a type of worship—tribal in origin and thought to predate Hinduism in Kerala. Theyyams aren't held in traditional temples but rather in small shrines or family compounds. Dancers don elaborate costumes and terrifying makeup for the ritual dance, in which they're believed to become possessed by the spirit of the deity they represent. These divine powers are thought to allow them to perform feats such as dancing with a 30-ft headdress or a flaming costume or falling into a pile of burning embers. The ritual is accompanied by intense drumming, howling, and chanting. Theyyam season is from November to May.

The Portuguese built **Fort St. Angelo,** with the consent of the ruling Kolathiri Raja, in 1505 to protect their interests in the area. After passing into Dutch and then British hands, it's now maintained by the Archaeological Survey of India. There are still a few intact British cannons, and you get lovely views of the fishing activity in Moppillah Bay. ⊠ *Off NH 17, 3 km (2 mi) north of Kannur,* ☎ *no phone.* ⬚ *Free.* ⊙ *10–4:30.*

In 1839 Herman Gundert, a Protestant missionary from the Swiss Basel Mission, arrived in the town of Thalassery, south of Kannur. A prodigious scholar, Gundert published some 50 books on Malabar in the 20 years he lived here, including the first English–Malayalam dictionary. His bungalow is now part of a college campus. The small **Gundert Memorial Church** next to the campus is a pretty blend of Kerala and European architecture. The walls beside the altar are decorated with paintings of medicinal herbs—one of Gundert's many interests. ⊠ *National Hwy., 20 km (12 mi) south of Kannur,* ☎ *no phone.* ⬚ *Free.* ⊙ *Weekdays 10–4.*

The **Kanhirode Weaving Cooperative** is strewn with yarns of all colors, set out to dry after dyeing. You can watch the weavers at their giant, clackety-clacking looms, making bed sheets and upholstery for export as well as brightly colored saris. ⊠ *Off Kannur–Mysore Rd., 13 km (8 mi) east of Kannur, Kanhirode,* ☎ *497/851259.* ⬚ *Free.* ⊙ *Weekdays 9:30–4:30.*

The unusual **Sri Muthappan Temple** sits on the bank of the Valapattanam River at Parassini Kaduvu. It's devoted to Lord Shiva in the form of a tribal hunter, and it hosts Theyyam performances almost every day of the year. Though it's not as colorful as traditional outdoor festivals, you can at least get a taste of Theyyam. As Sri Muthappan is usually pictured with a hunting dog, friendly mutts roam the sanctuary, and offerings at the shrine take the form of bronze dog figurines. ⊠ *Off NH 17, 18 km (11 mi) north of Kannur, Parassini.* ⬚ *Free.* ⊙ *Theyyams usually held 5:30 AM–8 AM and 6:30 PM–8 PM.*

The drive north from Kannur to Bekal, in the Kasargode district, is a dreamy trip through sleepy towns with nothing but coconut and paddy fields in between. **Bekal Fort** is Kerala's largest, covering more than over 40 seafront acres. The 300-year-old structure rises from a green lawn, and affords views of the Arabian sea or distant coconut groves. You can easily spend a peaceful hour or two clambering around the ruins. The loudest noise you'll hear is the crashing of the waves against the ramparts. A massive resort development project is underway in the area, however, with grandiose plans to turn Bekal into a top Asian tourist destination. ⊠ *NH 17, 72 km (45 mi) north of Kannur, Bekal,* ☎ *499/ 772900.* ☜ *Rs. 240.* ⏱ *Daily 9–5.*

Dining and Lodging

$ ✗ **Coachman's Inn.** Local well-to-do families often dine here at tables made more private by small dividers. The food is top notch (the cooks supposedly served the royal family). The naan here is particularly good, garnished with black sesame seeds. Try also the fish *malabari* (a mild curry preparation) and the chicken *vattichathu* (a dry, spicy preparation with the chicken almost crumbled into small pieces). ⊠ *Kamala International, SM Rd., Kannur,* ☎ *497/766910. MC, V.*

$$$$ ▦ **Ayisha Manzil.** A stay in this 200-year-old clifftop home may be the best way to experience what north Kerala is all about. Your hosts are C. P. Moosa and his wife, Faiza, who cooks up fantastic nightly feasts featuring local specialties. Breakfast is served on the front terrace, overlooking the sea. The house manager can accompany you on excursions in the area, or you can just hang out by the gorgeous brick-tile pool. Rooms are palatial, with high wood-beam ceilings and antique teak and rosewood furnishings. Downstairs rooms have fully modern tiled bathrooms; rooms upstairs, though comfortable, are more rustic. ⊠ *Court Rd., Thalassery 670101,* ☎ 𝖥𝖠𝖷 *490/341590. 6 rooms. Dining room, pool, travel services. MC, V. All-inclusive.*

$ ▦ **Mascot.** This modest resort's hillcrest location affords fantastic sea views from every room. Standard rooms are clean and relatively spacious, with marble floors and plenty of windows; those with air-conditioning are a little smaller. Deluxe rooms are large and close to the water, with bay windows. A cliffside walkway leads to the large swimming pool and Ayurveda center. The closest beach has been taken over by the navy, but Payyambalam Beach is a 15-minute walk away. ⊠ *Near Baby Beach, Burnassery, Kannur 670013,* ☎ *497/708445, 497/ 708450, or 497/708455,* 𝖥𝖠𝖷 *497/705862,* 𝖶𝖤𝖡 *www.mascotresort.net. 25 rooms. Restaurant, pool, business services, travel services. AE, DC, MC, V.*

KERALA A TO Z

To research prices, get advice from other travelers, and book travel arrangements, visit www.fodors.com.

AIR TRAVEL

All flights to Kerala land at Cochin, Trivandrum, or Calicut. Air India, Silk Air, Gulf Air, and Air Lanka operate international flights to Trivandrum; Calicut and Cochin are linked to the Middle East by Air India and Indian Airlines. Indian Airlines and Jet Airways cover domestic routes. There are no flights within Kerala itself.

➤ AIRLINES AND CONTACTS: **Air India** (☎ 484/351295). **Air Lanka** (☎ 471/322309). **Gulf Air** (☎ 471/328003 or 471/501205). **Indian Airlines** (☎ 484/370242). **Jet Airways** (☎ 484/369423). **Silk Air** (☎ 484/ 367911).

AIRPORTS AND TRANSFERS

Cochin's international airport is about 40 km (25 mi) east of the city; abominable traffic can make it a two-hour trip. Some hotels offer free airport pickup; otherwise, a taxi will cost about Rs. 200. The small, confusing airport in Trivandrum is 6 km (4 mi) west of the city center; taxis charge about Rs. 50 to get to the city and Rs. 300–400 to reach Kovalam. Traffic can be heavy. Calicut's Karipur Airport is 23 km (14 mi) south of town; a cab will cost roughly Rs. 125.

➤ AIRPORT INFORMATION: **Karipur Airport** (☎ 495/712762). **Cochin International Airport** (☎ 484/610115). **Trivandrum International Airport** (☎ 471/501542 international information or 471/501537 domestic information).

BOAT AND FERRY TRAVEL

In Cochin, public ferries and private boats ply between Fort Cochin, Willingdon Island, and Ernakulam throughout the day. Ernakulam's main boat jetty is just south of the Taj Residency hotel. Boats leave for Fort Cochin roughly every half hour from 6 AM to 9 PM. There are three afternoon ferries to Mattancherry, and frequent ferries to Embarkation Jetty, on Willingdon Island's eastern tip. From this pleasant, uncrowded ferry station, there's frequent service to both Ernakulam and Fort Cochin. It's almost impossible to figure out which ferry is which— just ask. Ferry rides cost only a few rupees; from Ernakulam's High Court Jetty you can hire private boats, usually for about Rs. 70 per person.

The Kerala Tourism Development Corporation (KTDC) conducts two inexpensive boat tours of Cochin each day; the 3½-hour trips depart at 9 AM and 2 PM from the Sealord Jetty, opposite the Sealord Hotel, between the Main and High Court jetties. The Tourist Desk also conducts boat tours.

Kerala's backwaters are still used for some long-distance transport and commuting. There are an estimated 200–250 houseboats now operating in Kerala; most are based in the Alleppey district. When booking an overnight stay on a houseboat, make sure it comes equipped with solar panels and a fan, or you're in for a hot night. The going rate for a posh two-bedroom vessel is roughly Rs. 8,000; a one-bedroom will run about Rs. 5,000. Small boats feel cramped; 14 ft is a very comfortable width.

Private companies, the KTDC, and the Tourist Desk operate half-day backwater tours from Alleppey for around Rs. 100–Rs. 400. The Alleppey Tourism Development Cooperative (ATDC) runs daily trips between Alleppey and Quilon (8 hrs, Rs. 150). After Quilon, boats continue south to Trivandrum and Kovalam. Boats leave both Alleppey and Quilon at 10:30 AM. There's also an Alleppey–Kottayam round-trip excursion.

➤ BOAT AND FERRY INFORMATION: **ATDC** (✉ Komala Rd., Alleppey, ☎ 477/243462). **KTDC** (✉ Shanmugham Rd., Ernakulam, Cochin, ☎ 484/353234). **Tourist Desk** (✉ Main Boat Jetty, Ernakulam, Cochin, ☎ 484/371761).

CARS AND DRIVERS

Major roads are well maintained. If you're coming from Tamil Nadu, the drive from Madurai along the Madurai–Kottayam Road is stunning. National Highway (NH) 47 runs from Salem, in central Tamil Nadu, to Cochin through some lovely country before heading down the coast to Cape Comorin in Kanya Kumari. In 2001, NH 47 was repaved from Cochin to Trivandrum, making it a zippy highway, with

four lanes between Cochin and Alleppey. NH 17 runs along the coast
from Mangalore south to Cochin, though it gets a little rough north
of Calicut. Roads to the interior *ghats* (mountains) are often breathtaking, as the landscape changes from the brilliant lime green of the
paddy fields to the rich, dark green of the tea plantations and jungle.
The journey from Trivandrum to Cochin takes about six hours.

The most convenient way to get around Kerala is with a hired car and
driver. Figure about Rs. 5 per kilometer for a non–air-conditioned car
and a halt charge of Rs. 100 per night. An air-conditioned vehicle will
cost a bit more, but it can make the difference between a pleasant journey and an exhausting one. Shop around, and hire a car from a government-approved travel agency.

CYCLE-RICKSHAWS
Cycle-rickshaws aren't allowed in cities, but you might still see them
in smaller towns. They should be cheaper than auto-rickshaws; just
remember that the driver works hard for his money, and distances can
be considerable. Set your fare in advance.

EMERGENCIES
➤ CONTACTS: **Cosmopolitan Hospital** (✉ Maurinja Palayam, Trivan-
drum, ☎ 471/448182). **Lissy Hospital** (✉ Lissy Junction, Ernakulam,
Cochin, ☎ 484/352006).

MAIL AND SHIPPING
➤ POST OFFICES: **Calicut Main Post Office** (✉ Mananchira Rd., Calicut, ☎ 495/720164). **Ernakulam GPO** (✉ Hospital Rd., Ernakulam,
Cochin, ☎ 484/224661). **Trivandrum GPO** (✉ M. G. Rd., ☎ 471/
473071).

MONEY MATTERS
ATMS
ATMs are newly arrived to Kerala. A few machines in major cities will
allow you to advance rupees against your Visa or Master Card, provided your card is equipped with this feature. Check with your credit
card company before leaving home.

CURRENCY EXCHANGE
Most major hotels have exchange services. Thomas Cook offers good
rates. The Bank of India and ANZ Grindlays cash traveler's checks and
change money, as does any branch of the Bank of India. Traveler's checks
get marginally higher rates than cash.
➤ EXCHANGE SERVICES: **ANZ Grindlays** (✉ M. G. Rd., Ernakulam,
Cochin, ☎ 484/372086). **Bank of India** (✉ Shanmugham Rd., Ernakulam, Cochin, ☎ 484/360184). **Thomas Cook** (✉ M. G. Rd., Ernakulam, Cochin, ☎ 484/369729).

TAXIS AND AUTO-RICKSHAWS
Auto-rickshaws are a convenient and quick way to travel around town.
Figure Rs. 6 for the first kilometer and Rs. 2 per additional kilometer.
Don't be alarmed if your driver doesn't use the meter—it usually does-
n't work, and Kerala's rickshaws are generally honest; just be sure to
agree on a fare up front. Cabs are also a good option for destinations
in and around Cochin. Fares will run about Rs. 7 for the first kilometer
and Rs. 4 for each additional kilometer; most cabs have a Rs. 60 minimum. Ask at any tourist office about the latest legal rates. You can
hire taxis at your hotel, or pick them up at cab stands near the Sea Lord
Jetty or at the intersection of M. G. Road and Club Road.

TOURS

The KTDC has several tours, including wildlife-spotting excursions to the Lake Periyar Wildlife Sanctuary and one- to two-week trips that follow a pilgrim trail through Kerala's sacred shrines. Sita Travels can help with bookings and arrange a car and driver. The Great India Tour Company, one of Kerala's best travel agencies, has offices throughout South India. SATM Tours and Travel designs affordable packages around your interests. Trivandrum-based Tourindia created the houseboat phenomenon and offers unusual Kerala experiences. One intriguing two- to three-day trip—created by Tourindia and the forestry department—sends you deep into the jungle with a local guide, an armed escort, and a naturalist.

➤ CONTACTS: **Great India Tour Company** (✉ Mullassery Towers, Vanross Junction, Trivandrum, ☎ 471/331516; ✉ Pithuru Smarana, 1st floor, Srikandath Rd., Ravipuram, Cochin, ☎ 484/374109). **KTDC** (✉ Shanmugham Rd., Ernakulam, Cochin, ☎ 484/353234). **SATM Tours and Travel** (✉ Warriam Rd., Cochin, ☎ 484/365765). **Sita Travels** (✉ Tharakan Building, M. G. Rd. Ernakulam, Cochin, ☎ 484/361101). **Tourindia** (✉ PB 136 M. G. Rd., Trivandrum, ☎ 471/330437 or 471/331507).

TRAIN TRAVEL

Rail journeys in Kerala can be scenic, and more comfortable than traveling by car. The *KK Express*—which travels from Kanya Kumari, at India's southern tip, all the way up to New Delhi—is a good train to take between Trivandrum and Cochin. The *Rajdhani Express* stops in Trivandrum, Cochin, and Calicut on its way up to Delhi. Check with the KTDC for the latest schedules and fares.

➤ INFORMATION: **KTDC** (✉ Shanmugham Rd., Ernakulam, Cochin, ☎ 484/353234).

➤ TRAIN STATIONS: **Calicut Railway Station** (☎ 133). **Ernakulam Junction** (☎ 131). **Ernakulam Town Station** (☎ 484/353920). **Trivandrum Central Station** (☎ 132).

VISITOR INFORMATION

Excellent brochures, maps, and pamphlets on all of Kerala's districts are available at any KTDC office. In Cochin, the office is open daily 8 to 7. Trivandrum's two KTDC offices—one in town and one at the airport—are open weekdays 10 to 5.

In Cochin, an alternative source of information is the Tourist Desk, a private, nonprofit organization that conducts boat tours and provides clear, straightforward state information. In Kannur, the District Tourism Promotion Council is quite active. Central Kerala is well served by the ATDC. The Government of India Tourist Office—open weekdays 9 to 5:30 and Saturday 9 to 1—has its own vehicles, boats, lodgings, and tours.

➤ TOURIST INFORMATION: **ATDC** (✉ Komala Rd., Alleppey, ☎ 477/243462). **Government of India Tourist Office** (✉ Malabar Rd., Willingdon Island, Cochin, ☎ 484/668352). **Kannur District Tourism Promotion Council** (✉ Taluk Office Campus, Kannur, ☎ 497/706336). **KTDC** (✉ Shanmugham Rd.,, Ernakulam Cochin, ☎ 484/353234; ✉ Museum Rd., Trivandrum, ☎ 471/322279). **Tourist Desk** (✉ Main Boat Jetty, Ernakulam, Cochin, ☎ 484/371761).

11 TAMIL NADU

Madras, the capital of Tamil Nadu, encapsulates the spirit and culture of India's southernmost state. From the Bay of Bengal to the Nilgiri Hills, Tamil Nadu resonates with the history of the ancient Dravidians,India's original Hindu inhabitants. The soaring, brilliantly carved towers of South Indian's magnificent temples dominate the landscape, just as faith permeates Tamil life.

By Molly
Sholes and
Vikram Singh

Updated by
Kavita Milner

MORE THAN A FEW DEGREES of latitude and temperature separate India's Aryan north from its Dravidian south. Encompassing numerous cultures within them, North and South India have completely different climates, crops, cuisines, languages, architecture, and social customs. The state of Tamil Nadu—running about 805 km (500 mi) along the Bay of Bengal to India's southernmost tip, Cape Comorin—is the heartland of South India. From the Tamil coast, with its gorgeous, bright-green rice fields and coconut and banana trees, the land rises through the low-lying Eastern Ghats (mountains) up to tea, coffee, and spice plantations in the Nilgiri Hills, and finally to the higher Western Ghats.

Hinduism pervades the Tamils's lives, beliefs, philosophy, and behavior. A rich oral tradition, 2,000-year-old religious texts and literature, and Jain and Buddhist influences have made South Indian Hinduism a distinct, vibrant, evolving religion. The Tamils have survived incursions from North Indians and foreigners alike, but neither the Portuguese nor the French nor the British, who ruled Madras for 300 years, made more than a superficial dent in the soul of Tamil culture. Majestic South Indian temples with massive *gopurams* (entrance towers) and *vimanas* (towers over inner sanctums) dominate the Tamil landscape just as faith permeates Tamil life. A visit to at least one major temple is key to understanding this part of India.

About a third of Tamil Nadu is urban; many of the cities have more than 50,000 people. Even the smaller villages are not far from a city or town. A good bus system, frequent pilgrimages, a 70% literacy rate, and expanding and improving communications keep the Tamil villager reasonably well-informed, and far from isolated.

Pleasures and Pastimes

Dining
A traditional Tamil meal is a balance of the six tastes of Indian cuisine: sweet, sour, pungent, astringent, salty, and bitter. Rice is a basic ingredient, whether cooked or ground into flour. Tamil dishes can be hot or bland; those that are usually mild include *idlis,* cakes made of steamed rice and blackgram batter (rice and chick pea flour are soaked, ground into a batter, then steamed); plain *dosas,* crepes of rice and blackgram; *upma,* semolina and spices, often with vegetables; and curd-rice, yogurt mixed with rice at room temperature. The *thali,* available vegetarian or nonvegetarian, is a multi-course feast on one platter—a chance to sample various Indian dishes at once. Decoction, or "coffee by the yard," is strong filter coffee mixed with hot milk and poured back and forth between two metal tumblers until it is cool enough to drink, at which point it's also white with froth. It's delicious—the best cup of coffee you'll have in India.

Until recently, Tamils preferred to eat only in their homes for reasons of personal and religious purity. The best restaurants were confined to the larger hotels, which catered to foreign travelers. But Madras has become a cosmopolitan city, and fine restaurants are, increasingly, serving a variety of cuisines. The formerly ubiquitous Mughlai menus have been widely replaced with authentic ethnic food, including South Indian, Continental, Mediterranean, Chinese, Thai, Korean and even Tex-Mex. An 8% sales tax is often levied on food and drink.

Lodging
Many of the best hotels have plush decor, and unless otherwise noted, those that we list have air-conditioning. The state government runs

Tamil Nadu

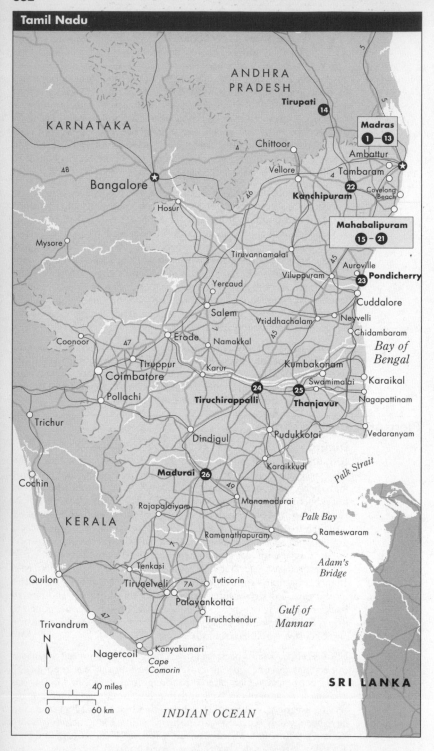

ANDHRA
PRADESH

KARNATAKA

Tirupati **14**

Madras **1** — **13**

Chittoor

Ambattur

Vellore

Tambaram

Bangalore

Kanchipuram **22**

Covelong
Beach

Hosur

Mahabalipuram

15 — **21**

Mysore

Tiruvannamalai

Auroville

Yercaud

Viluppuram

Pondicherry **23**

Salem

Vriddhachalam

Cuddalore

Coonoor

Erode

Namakkal

Neyveli

Chidambaram

*Bay of
Bengal*

Tiruppur

Karur

Kumbakonam

Coimbatore

Swamimalai

Karaikal

Pollachi

Tiruchirappalli **24**

Thanjavur **25**

Nagapattinam

Trichur

Dindigul

Pudukkotai

Vedaranyam

Palk Strait

Madurai **26**

Karaikkudi

Palk Bay

Cochin

Rajapalaiyam

Manamadurai

KERALA

Ramanathapuram

Rameswaram

*Adam's
Bridge*

Quilon

Tenkasi

Tuticorin

Tirunelveli

*Gulf of
Mannar*

Trivandrum

Palayankottai

Tiruchchendur

N

Nagercoil

Kanyakumari

*Cape
Comorin*

0   40 miles

0   60 km

SRI LANKA

INDIAN OCEAN

"Tamilnadu" hotels, which are modest, usually clean hotels with simple restaurants—modern versions of the *dak* bungalow, or rest house, of the British Raj. Some hotels in Madras have conference rooms, dedicated business-traveler floors and suites, secretarial services, and in-room fax machines. Due to increasing commercial travel, reservations for rooms in Madras are essential, especially between December and February. Tamil Nadu levies a 20% luxury tax on room rates, and a 10% hotel-expenditure tax on the total bill.

Performing Arts

Bharatanatyam, a feminine dance form (though some men have also begun to achieve proficiency in it), and Carnatic music are the best known of the traditional South Indian performing arts. Similar in composition to North Indian music, the Carnatic art is nonetheless distinguished by its instruments and its vocal style. Many Tamil film scores are written in the Carnatic style.

Shopping

Look for silver tribal jewelry, jute placemats, copies of Chola bronzes, Kanchipuram silks, *khadi* (hand-woven) shirts, carved wooden temple friezes, inlaid wooden boxes, contemporary artwork, and Thanjavur paintings. Bargaining isn't as prevalent as it once was, but almost everything here is a bargain anyway. Madras and Madurai have excellent shops, and nearly all major hotels have boutiques, most of which have fixed prices and take credit cards. Hotel stores tend to be expensive: shop around if you're buying a big-ticket item. Government-run craft emporiums have excellent selections, and surrounding most large temples are four streets of bazaars where bargaining is expected. In the past, bazaars were the *only* places to shop for groceries, household goods, jewelry, fruit, electronics, and paper products; over time, though, the supermarket concept has taken root.

Temples

With their lofty gopurams, vimanas, and majestic *mandapams* (pillared halls), temples are integral parts of Tamil culture. The gopurams are often brilliantly polychrome, and the mandapam friezes inside depict myths and legends of Hindu gods and goddesses, and sometimes tales of the temple's benefactor. South Indian temples throng daily with pilgrims and visitors; the larger, better-known temples are pilgrimage shrines or are visited mainly on special occasions, such as *Pongal* (harvest festival) and birthdays. The smaller temples are part of daily life.

South Indian Hinduism is a personal, ritualistic religion. Almost anything—a tree, a rock, a sculpture—can be an object of veneration. Hindus worship at their temples in a variety of ways. Some devotees withdraw to the inner sanctum for *puja*—acts of reverence—which consists of *darshan* ("spiritual seeing" or visual communication with the image of the deity), making a donation, and receiving blessings. Others worship a specific carved image in the mandapam frieze, and still others go to the sacred peepul tree and tie a ribbon around it. After puja, worshipers sit outside in the mandapam for a few minutes, absorbing the temple ambience. In a temple courtyard, you might even see priests blessing a brand-new car. Non-Hindus are usually free to explore these houses of worship, barring only the inner sanctum.

Exploring Tamil Nadu

Great Itineraries

Any doubling back on these routes is necessitated by heavy traffic and bad road conditions. On Tamil Nadu's main north-south artery, NH 45, speeds average 58 kph (35 mph) in the middle of the day. Thanjavur and Swamimalai are on secondary roads that can also be maddeningly slow.

Numbers in the text correspond to numbers in the margin and on the Tamil Nadu, Madras, and Mahabalipuram maps.

IF YOU HAVE 4 DAYS

Spend two days in historic ⌶ **Madras** to see its colorful bazaars and Hindu temples. On the third day drive south via the Shore Road to ⌶ **Mahabalipuram,** on the Bay of Bengal, to see the cave temples. The next morning leave early to explore **Kanchipuram,** a pilgrimage town with 200 temples and a thriving silk industry, on your way back to Madras.

IF YOU HAVE 7 DAYS

Spend two days and nights in ⌶ **Madras.** ①–⑬ On your third day, visit **Kanchipuram;** ㉒ continue south to ⌶ **Mahabalipuram** ⑮–㉑ for nights three and four. On day five, move on to ⌶ **Pondicherry** ㉓ to explore its French heritage and unwind a bit. On day six, drive to **Tiruchirappalli,** ㉔ then proceed late in the evening to ⌶ **Madurai.** ㉖ Devote day seven to the astonishing Meenakshi Temple before returning to Madras.

IF YOU HAVE 10 DAYS

After spending two days in ⌶ **Madras,** ①–⑬ travel to ⌶ **Mahabalipuram** ⑮–㉑ via the Shore Road, stopping at the **Crocodile Bank** or **DakshinaChitra** en route. Day-trip to **Kanchipuram** ㉒ and check out the migratory life in the **Vedanthangal Bird Sanctuary** on the way back to Mahabalipuram. Spend your fifth day in Mahabalipuram, exploring the cave temples and perhaps hitting the beach, before heading back to Madras. On day six, fly or take the train to ⌶ **Tiruchirappalli.** ㉔ Proceed to ⌶ **Thanjavur** ㉕ and Swamimalai on day seven to see the bronze foundry and the temples. On day eight, drive to ⌶ **Madurai** ㉖ and spend the night and the next day there before returning to Madras by plane or train.

When to Tour Tamil Nadu

The best time to visit is between November and February. True, the roads are in disrepair after the torrential rains of the monsoon season (which ends in September), but the sun is moderate in the winter months. This is the season for temple festivals and dance and music programs, and it's also the best time to observe migratory birds. Advance hotel and transport reservations are strongly recommended for this time of year. Note that Hindu temples close in the afternoon (noon–4). Most stores and museums are open all day.

MADRAS

Chennai is the new name for the old city of Madras, the garden gateway to South India. (The British named it after a fishing hamlet called Madraspatnam, supposedly offered to Francis Day, an East India Company trader, in 1639 by the Raja of Chandragiri, the last Vijayanagar ruler.) Madras is the fourth-largest city in India, but it still has room to expand. From the time the British first established Fort St. George on a sliver of beach, the city has grown by absorbing the surrounding villages. Each area has developed distinctly, often along caste lines, from the Chettiars (a South Indian caste of traders) of George Town to the civil servants and industrialists of Nungambakkam. Even today, municipal boundaries expand, multi-story apartment and office buildings replace bungalows, and new residential areas spring up along the Shore Road to Mahabalipuram. Growth has made traffic nearly unbearable here, with pollution and noise levels rising daily. Cars, buses, trucks, auto-rickshaws (or "autos," as they're popularly called), mopeds, bicycles, motorcycles, pedestrians, fish carts, and cows all compete for space in the streets; only yogic detachment keeps the frustration at a bearable level. (Traffic on the main avenues, like Anna Salai, is well regulated and moves along.) Generally speaking, be prepared for detours and delays.

In the early 1990s, a government committee called Vision 2000 launched a program intended to reverse years of inadequate urban planning; yet side roads are still full of potholes and bordered by picked-over garbage, and many destitute people camp on city streets. The water supply is woefully inadequate, even nonexistent in some areas. Tanker trucks bringing water into the city add to the congestion and pollution. The phone system is still insufficient, and the demand for electric power increases with population growth and business expansion.

The rapid arrival of multinational corporations has changed the placid pace of life in Madras, which in the old days was alive at 5 AM and asleep by 9 PM. Still, nothing seems to have shaken the city's spiritual essence. Madras is a fascinating place, its increasingly cosmopolitan face contrasting sharply with its resolutely religious soul.

Name Changes

Just as Madras has been renamed Chennai, so have many of the street names changed, very often to honor contemporary politicians. Some of the new names are not in colloquial usage, but here's a partial list, with the old name listed first (*salai* means street or road): Mount Road—Anna ("Elder Brother") Salai; Chamier's Road—Muthuramalinga Road; Mowbray's Road—T. T. K. (Krishnamachari) Road; Edward Eliot's Road—Dr. Radhakrishnan Salai; North Beach Road—Rajaji Salai; Nungambakkam High Road—Uttamar Gandhi Salai; Poonamallee High Road—Periyar E. V. R. High Road; South Beach Road—Kamarajar Road.

Northern Madras

A Good Tour

The best way to explore Madras is to follow the city's expansion south from Fort St. George. Some distances are short, but if the temperature is 100°F and the humidity 80%, you won't feel like walking; if oppressive heat threatens, hire a car. Start at **St. Mary's Church** ① in **Fort St. George.** Move on to the **Fort Museum** ②; then walk by the **Tamil Nadu State Legislature** ③. Return to St. Mary's Church, taking in the mixture of historic buildings and bureaucratic offices. Drive the ¼ mi to the **High Court** ④ via the road that tunnels through the fort's massive walls; park and walk to Armenian Street. Alternately, take a taxi or auto-rickshaw to N. S. C. Bose Road and get out at the junction of Armenian Street for a stroll through **George Town.** Walk down Armenian Street to the beautiful Armenian Church, which was built in 1629 and is no longer used for worship. As you wander on, look up and you'll see evidence of second-story residence—many merchants still live in George Town. On your way back to the High Court, pass the **Flower Bazaar** (⊠ N. S. C. Bose Rd.), a riot of color and fragrance, on your right. Just south of N. S. C. Bose Road and before Prakasam Road (formerly Pophams Broadway), check out the **Fruit Market,** where bananas ripen in enormous warehouses. Complete your tour of George Town back at the High Court.

TIMING

The ideal time to cover this route is Sunday morning, when the traffic and parking are most benign. The full tour should take five or six

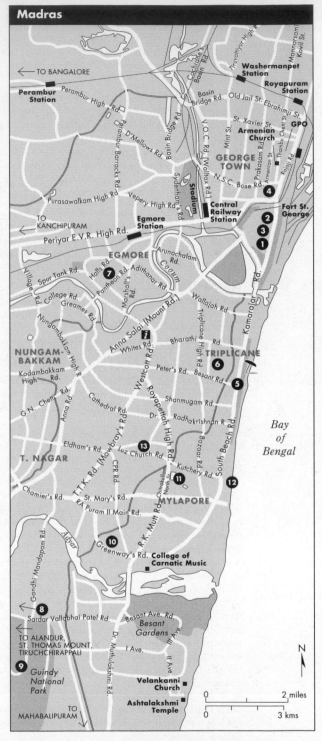

Madras

hours, including thorough tours of George Town and Fort St. George (two hours each) and half an hour in the High Court.

Sights to See

Fort St. George. The first British fort in India was founded by Francis Day on a thin strip of sand leased from the Raja of Chandragiri. Christened on St. George's Day in 1640, Fort St. George, complete with walls 20 ft thick, has remained the symbol of the Raj, its history intertwined with that of the rest of British India. The Indian army and civil service, Colin Mackenzie's land survey, and the British archaeological, botanical, and zoological surveys of India were all conceived on this site. Now the home of the Tamil Nadu State Legislature, it's quietest on Sunday. ✉ *Entrance on Kamarajar Rd.,* ☎ *no phone.*

❷ Fort Museum. Once an exchange used by East India Company merchants, this building is now a museum of Indian history. Everything from old uniforms and coins to palanquins and padlocks is on display, including some wonderful old prints. Study the exhibits closely, as they're not always well labeled. ✉ *Fort St. George,* ☎ *44/536–1127.* 🎫 *Indian citizens Rs. 5, others US$5.* ☉ *Sat.–Thurs. 10–5. No cameras, either still or video.*

George Town. If you tend toward agoraphobia, George Town is not the place for you, as walking—the only way to explore this teeming warren of congested streets—is often hard going. Before you venture into George Town, make sure you have a detailed map of this area so you can wander with confidence; many streets have similar names. For the full experience, come in the morning, when the bustle is at its peak.

Originally called Black Town, this 1½-by-2-mi area was first settled by lower-caste artisans who provided textiles to the British traders. After Black Town was burned in the British–French wars, the new town was laid out in a perfect grid pattern, each section housing a different group or caste with its own place of worship. The street names echo George Town's mercantile history, as each area bears the cultural characteristics of the group who migrated there in the course of doing business with (or for) the East India Company: Not only Indians but Portuguese, Scots, Armenians, and Jews settled here. Another prominent group are the Chettiars; you'll notice that many of the street names end in "chetti." Two competitive subcastes of the Chettiars long vied for mercantile power, first with the East India Company and then with the merchants of the Raj. ✉ *Bordered by Basin Bridge Rd., Old Jail St., Ebrahim Sabib St., and Rajaji Rd.*

★ ❹ High Court. This large judicial complex is a magnificent example of Indo-Saracenic architecture, built of red sandstone with intricate ornamentation on the walls and minarets. (The tallest minaret was used as a lighthouse until the 1970s.) Inside is a labyrinth of corridors and courts, most of which you can visit; court number 13 has the finest decorations inside. Within the compound is a tomb in the shape of pyramid; one of its two inscriptions is to the only son of Elihu Yale, governor of Fort St. George from 1687 to 1691. The child died in infancy and was buried in the High Court compound. ✉ *Just north of fort off N. S. C. Bose Rd., near intersection with Rajaji Salai.* 🎫 *Tour Rs. 10.* ☉ *Mon.–Sat. 10–5. Guided tours, Mon.–Sat. 10:30–1:45 and 2:30–4:30.*

★ ❶ St. Mary's Church. Consecrated in 1680, this church is the oldest masonry structure in Fort St. George and the oldest Anglican church east of Suez. The *punkahs* (pulley-operated ceiling fans) and some flags are gone, and the steeple has been replaced, but otherwise the building with its arcaded side aisles and bomb-proof roof has not changed. The marriage of governor Elihu Yale (of Yale University fame) was the first one performed here. Job Charnock, founder of Calcutta, had his three daughters baptized here before the family moved to Bengal, and St. Mary's congregation included, at one time or another, Thomas Pitt, Warren Hastings (later the first governor general of British India), Lord Cornwallis, and Arthur Wellesley, later the Duke of Wellington. ⊠ *Fort St. George.* 🎫 *Free.* ⊙ *Daily 9:30–5.*

❸ Tamil Nadu State Legislature. This crowded, active seat of the state government occupies most of the area between St. Mary's Church and the Fort Museum. The former house of Robert Clive (of the Battle of Plassey fame) is the "Pay Accounts" office. Other sections of the fort are under military control. This is a beautifully maintained area, but unfortunately you can't go in. ⊠ *Muthuswamy Iyer Rd.*

Central Madras

As Madras grew, the city moved south, expanding along the beach and inland to Egmore and Nungambakkam. The Chepauk district, home of Madras University and Chepauk Palace (now government offices), has some of India's best Indo-Saracenic buildings—a combination of Hindu, Muslim, and Victorian Gothic styles that makes a fitting display for a city with roots in all three cultures. Farther south along the beach is the Triplicane neighborhood, with the Parthasarathi Temple. Inland, toward the center of Madras is Anna Salai, a major shopping and business district. North of Anna Salai is Egmore, bordered by the curves of the Cooum River and home to the National Museum and Art Gallery. Farther south across the Cooum is Nungambakkam, traditionally a posh residential area of garden homes. It's now a mixture of expensive boutiques, hotels, and offices, but a few of the massive old houses with walled gardens remain. A new wave of small fast-food joints (as in hot dogs and pizza) and restaurants has hit Alwarpet, Egmore, and Nungambakkam.

A Good Tour

It's easiest to cover this ground by hiring a car and driver for the day, but you can also take auto-rickshaws from point to point. Early in the morning, drive south on Kamarajar Road from Fort St. George along the magnificent **Marina Beach** ⑤ and passing the Indo-Saracenic buildings of the government and university on your right. Note the brick Ice House near Presidency College: clipper ships from New England, which used ice as ballast, used to unload it here before it found its way into the drinks of the local nobility. Beyond the contemporary political structures and the public swimming pool on the ocean side is the marina promenade: have your driver stop at its north end (just south of the pool), and take a stroll. Rejoin your driver back in the promenade parking lot and drive to the **Parthasarathi Temple** ⑥. The **National Museum and Art Gallery** ⑦ punctuates your tour with a superb collection of South Indian bronzes.

TIMING

The marina walk and the temple will each take an hour, the cathedral about 45 minutes, and the museum two to three hours, for a total of between five and six hours.

Sights to See

★ **❺ Marina Beach.** This beach is a favorite early morning promenade and exercise spot. At 6 AM you can see fishing boats casting off and fit folks jogging and performing calisthenics or yoga. In the evening, strollers mix with women haggling with fishermen. During holidays the beach turns into a carnival, complete with vendors and hand-driven carousels, and everyone turns out to mingle and enjoy themselves. The undertow is strong here, so the beach is not used for swimming. ⊠ *Kamarajar Rd. between Edward Eliot's Rd. and Cathedral Rd.*

★ ❼ **National Museum and Art Gallery.** This museum is known for its superb collection of Pallava and Chola (8th- to 11th-century) bronze sculptures. The best-known work is probably the Chola Nataraj—a detailed 2-ft statue of the dancing Shiva, surrounded by the cosmic fire, that appears to be in constant motion. Many of the less spectacular bronzes are still worth studying for their detail and facial expressions. Other artworks from all over South India, including ancient Buddhist statues and Jain sculptures, are well represented. The museum also has an arms gallery, which is strong on weapons of the Raj period. ⊠ *Pantheon Rd., Egmore,* ☎ *44/826–9638.* ▧ *Rs. 3, still cameras Rs. 20, video cameras Rs. 100.* ☉ *Sat.–Thurs. 9–4:30.*

❻ **Parthasarathi Temple.** Built by the Pallavas in the 8th century and rebuilt by the Vijayanagar kings in the 11th century, this Vishnu temple is dedicated to Krishna, the *sarathi* (charioteer) of Partha (Arjuna), and is probably the oldest temple in Madras. Legend has it that on the eve of the great battle in the Pandava-Kaurava War, Krishna imparted to Arjuna the *Bhagavad Gita* (literally "Song of the Blessed Lord"), a religiophilosophic dialogue from the *Mahabharata* epic. After passing under the colorful gopuram, you'll enter the courtyard, which has several carved shrines. The four streets surrounding the temple have stalls selling flowers, small idols, and other puja articles; musical instruments; and jewelry. ⊠ *Off Triplicane High Rd.* ▧ *Free.* ☉ *Daily 6:30–noon and 4–8.*

Southern Madras

In the process of expanding ever southward, Madras incorporated old areas like Mylapore ("Town of Peacocks"), which has a 13th-century temple, and in the 1930s developed some new areas like Thyagaraja Nagar (T. Nagar). More recently, Besant Nagar and Kalakshetra Colony were incorporated, both residential areas with broad, tree-lined streets and excellent shopping areas where it's relatively easy to get around—except at rush hour. (At one busy intersection in Adyar there's an eatery called Hotel Traffic Jam.)

A Good Drive

In the morning, hire a car and go to the cantonment, a military base and officers' training academy, to see **St. Thomas Mount** ⑧. Drive back east to visit **Madras Snake Park** ⑨, in Guindy Park, and then J. Krishnamurti's home **The Study** ⑩. Follow R. K. Mutt Road north to the **Kapalishvara Temple** ⑪, then turn right and continue to the end of Kutchery Road to see the **Basilica of San Thome Cathedral** ⑫, noting the neo-Gothic architecture in contrast to that of St. George's Cathedral. End with **Luz Church** ⑬, the oldest church in the city.

TIMING

Allow five or six hours for this tour, as there's a lot of driving involved.

Sights to See

★ ⑫ **Basilica of San Thome Cathedral.** It's commonly held that Thomas the Apostle ("Doubting Thomas") lived his last years in South India, walking daily from his cave at Little Mount to the beach at Mylapore to preach. Before being captured by the French, Dutch, and English, San Thome was a Portuguese enclave, its name dating from the cathedral's inception in 1504. In the 1890s the cathedral was reconstructed as a neo-Gothic structure with a 180-ft-tall basilica. St. Thomas is thought to be entombed inside. ⊠ *San Thome High Rd.*

★ ⑪ **Kapalishvara Temple.** Dating from the 13th century, this crowded Shiva temple is one of the best examples of Dravidian architecture in India. During the Arupathumoovar festival (commemorating the 63 Saivite saints, who were devoted to Shiva, also known as Saiva in Sanskrit) in March, the temple streets are closed for 10 days to make room for processions of carts and idols around the complex. Kapalishvara Temple is not a rarefied pilgrimage site but a community gathering place for worship, very much a part of daily life.

Just inside the south entrance, under the gopuram, stands the shrine to Ganesh, a smooth black image of the monkey god that's grown shiny from so many offerings. Worshipers break coconuts in front of and on Ganesh to ask his blessing for a new venture or just for a good day. Sometimes in the late afternoon, a priest talks to groups of widows in the courtyard or mandapam. Farther on around the temple, to the left, you may see a man prostrate himself before the Nandi (the bull that is Shiva's vehicle) that guards the entrance to the inner sanctum. Continue around the building until you come to a mandapam with statues of the nine planets. It's auspicious to walk clockwise around these planets nine times, so join the procession. Several of the shrines set into the courtyard wall are accessible to non-Hindus. ⊠ *Between Chitrukullan North St. and Kutchery Rd., Mylapore.* ⊙ *Daily 4 AM–noon and 4 PM–8 PM.*

⑬ **Luz Church.** Built in 1516, this little, cream-color Portuguese church is the oldest church in the city. It has its own large courtyard, a welcome enclave amid the chaos of narrow pedestrian lanes around it. The interior is mostly whitewashed, with an altar that it seems to owe as much to Hindu as to Christian iconography. The ceiling above the altar bears a simple relief, and there's a small choir at the back. Legend surrounds the construction of the church: it is said to have been built by Portuguese sailors who claimed to see a mysterious light on the shore, which guided them safely to port. ⊠ *Luz Church Rd., Mylapore district.* ⊙ *Daily.*

⑨ **Madras Snake Park.** At the snake park you can see and photograph more than 40 species of the common snakes of India, as well as crocodiles, monitor lizards, chameleons, and tortoises. The park is at the edge of the Raj Bhavan (Government House). ⊠ *Raj Bhavan main post, Sardar Vallabbai Patel Rd.,* ☎ *44/235–3623.* 🎟 *Rs. 2, parking Rs. 2, cameras Rs. 5, video cameras Rs. 100.* ⊙ *Wed.–Mon. 8:30–5:30.*

⑧ **St. Thomas Mount.** Drive to the cantonment and take the road to the top of St. Thomas' Mount—a hillock with an old church—or climb the roughly 130 granite steps from the base below. After the cacophonous city traffic and the crush of crowded streets, the tiny, serene church of Senhora da Expectação (Our Lady of Expectation), built in 1523, offers an aerial view nearly 90 m (300 ft) above sea level. The interior, charmingly framed by a semicircular vaulted ceiling, is painted in bright, candy-colored hues. Legend has it that Thomas the Apostle was martyred while praying here. The stone cross set in the altar was excavated by the Portuguese—who built the church over it. ⊠ *St. Thomas Mount.* 🎟 *Free.* ⊙ *Daily.*

⑩ **The Study.** Shortly before his death in 1986, the thinker J. Krishnamurti directed that his home and gardens become a place of learning and contemplation, open to anyone who wished to study his teachings in quiet and tranquil surroundings. Called simply "The Study," the center contains a complete library of Krishnamurti's writings, and other books on religion, philosophy, psychology, literature, and the arts. ⊠ *Vasant*

Vihar, 64 Greenways Rd., ☏ *44/493–7803.* ▧ *Free; donations accepted.* ☉ *Tues.–Sun. 10–1 and 2–7; closed May 15–31.*

Dining and Lodging

$$-$$$$ ✕ **Golden Dragon.** Elegance sets the tone in this intimate Chinese restaurant: brass lanterns hang from the ceiling, and dragon murals decorate the walls. Try the panfried pomfret, Cantonese stir-fried shredded lamb, or the restaurant's crowning glory—smoked duck with pancakes. ⊠ *Taj Coromandel Hotel, 17 Nungambakkam High Rd.,* ☏ *44/827–2827. AE, DC, MC, V.*

$$-$$$ ✕ **Benjarong.** This Thai specialty restaurant serves excellent food: try the *Gai Hor* (deep-fried pieces of chicken marinated in herbs and spices), *Hormok Goong* (Thai-style prawn curry), and the *Tub Tim Siam* (water chestnuts in coconut milk). The setting is friendly and warm—the restaurant's small alcoves, in a renovated house, ensure plenty of privacy. ⊠ *146 T. T. K. Rd., Alwarpet,* ☏ *44/432–2640. AE, DC, MC, V.*

$$-$$$ ✕ **Dakshin.** Decorated with Thanjavur paintings, South Indian statues, and brass lanterns shaped like temple bells, this handsome restaurant serves exclusively South Indian cuisine. Meals are served on banana leaves and set on silver thali trays, and an Indian flutist plays nightly. One of the best entrées is Tamil Nadu's *daskshin yera* (fried prawns marinated in ginger, chili, and garlic), *nandu puttu* (steamed crab and rice flour; similar to couscous, but softer), or the spicy *mirupakaikodi* (sautéed chili chicken) from Andhra Pradesh. ⊠ *Welcomgroup Park Sheraton Hotel & Towers, 132 T. T. K. Rd., Alwarpret,* ☏ *44/499–4101. AE, DC, MC, V.*

$$-$$$ ✕ **Kyungbokgong** This quiet restaurant serves Korean and Japanese food. Try the set (fixed-price) Japanese seafood (including sushi) main course or the set "half" main course (excluding seafood)—both are excellent. ⊠ *18 Kasthuri Estate, 1st St., Alwarpet,* ☏ *44/467–1949. AE, DC, MC, V.*

$$-$$$ ✕ **Peshawari.** This place has an attractive Pathan (Indo-Iranian) decor, with rough stone walls and copper plates. Soft lighting sets a mellow tone. The Afghan cuisine emphasizes tandoori dishes. Try the tasty *murgh malai kabab* (boneless chicken kebabs marinated in cheese, cream, and lime juice) or *kadak seekh reshmi* (crisp rolled chicken cooked over a grill). ⊠ *Welcomgroup Chola Sheraton, 10 Cathedral Rd.,* ☏ *44/811–0101. AE, DC, MC, V.*

$$-$$$ ✕ **Raintree.** Set outdoors, amid trees garlanded with little white lights
★ that are lit up at night, this restaurant highlights a Bharatanatyam dance recital and/or an Indian flute performance with dinner (8–11 PM). Along with the show you'll enjoy fiery, pepper-laden Chettinad cuisine served on a banana leaf that's set in a copper plate. The *vathal kozhambu* (sun-ripened berries cooked in a spicy sauce) and *yera varuwal* (prawns marinated in masala, then deep-fried) are good choices. ⊠ *Taj Connemara, Binny Rd.,* ☏ *44/852–0123. AE, DC, MC, V. No lunch.*

$-$$ ✕ **Annalakshmi.** Named after the goddess of food, Annalakshmi is undoubtedly the best place in the city to enjoy a quiet, laid-back Indian vegetarian meal. Annalakshmi is run by a charitable trust; its genuine home-cooked food is prepared by volunteers, and then served, with silverware, in fairly regal settings. (Proceeds go to the trust, which gives money to medical, social, educational, and cultural causes). Try the amazing range of chutneys and the flavorful non-alcoholic health drink. The restaurant is closed on Mondays. ⊠ *804 Anna Salai,* ☏ *44/855–0296. AE, DC, MC, V.*

$-$$ ✕ **Cascade.** Chinese music accompanies tasty Chinese, Malaysian, Japanese, and Thai cuisine in this ever-busy restaurant. Come hungry—

portions are large. Popular items include Phuket fish (fried sailfish fillet with garlic and chili paste), chili crab, and Szechuan *sapo* (prawns, chicken, fish, or lamb marinated in five-spice powder, then cooked and served in a sapo dish). ⊠ *Kakani Towers, K. N. K. Rd., near Taj Coromandel Hotel,* ☎ *44/825–3836. AE, DC, MC, V.*

$–$$ ✕ **Don Pepe's Tex Mex.** At this popular Tex-Mex restaurant, try the chicken fajitas (with a non-alcoholic strawberry margarita to wash it down) or the burritos. The prawn dishes don't vary much one from to the other but are superlative nonetheless. The restaurant has a pleasant view of Cathedral Road. ⊠ *73 Cathedral Rd.,* ☎ *44/822–1461. AE, DC, MC, V.*

$ ✕ **Cakes and Bakes.** This cake shop is also a Western-style café that serves pizzas, sandwiches, milk shakes, and pastries. You can hunker down in the small, crowded eating area or take your food with you. ⊠ *Nungambakkam High Rd.,* ☎ *44/827–7075. No credit cards.*

$ ✕ **Saravana Bhavan.** This chain of South Indian vegetarian restaurants in Madras is notably clean. Some of the restaurants serve fast-food thalis, and others offer vegetarian entrées. Count on immaculate surroundings, great food, and exemplary service. ⊠ *Air-Conditioned Hall, Usman Rd., T. Nagar district,* ☎ *44/434–5577. Dr. Radhakrishnan Salai,* ☎ *44/811–5977. MC, V.*

$$$$ 🏨 **Taj Coromandel.** This central hotel emphasizes luxury and business
★ services. The giant lobby has a marble fountain, teak accents, Thanjavur paintings, and plenty of lounge space. Rooms throughout the building sport wonderful sketches by British artist Edward Orme. Many of the elegant, cream-color guest rooms—particularly those on the upper floors—have pleasant city views, including palm trees. Most rooms have personal fax machines, and suites have both shower stalls and tubs. There's also a high-quality pastry shop. ⊠ *37 M. G. Rd., 600034,* ☎ *44/827–2827 or 800/223–6800 in the U.S.,* 🆁🅰🆇 *44/827–7104,* 🆆🅴🅱 *www.tajhotels.com. 183 rooms, 22 suites. 4 restaurants, bar, patisserie, lobby lounge, in-room data ports, no-smoking floor, pool, barbershop, hair salon, hot tub, sauna, steam room, health club, business services, travel services. AE, DC, MC, V.*

$$$–$$$$ 🏨 **Welcomgroup Park Sheraton Hotel & Towers.** This modern hotel in
★ central Madras has everything the business traveler could possibly need. The Sheraton Towers suites are the ultimate in corporate luxury, with a conference room and such amenities as voice mail, in-room fax machines, and 24-hour business centers with Internet access. The hotel is notably trendy and has a courteous and efficient staff. The Gatsby 2000 disco, with a DJ and dancing, is one of the city's few nighttime entertainment venues. You get much better rates if you stay at the hotel rather than at the towers. ⊠ *132 T. T. K. Rd., Alwarpet 600018,* ☎ *44/499–4101,* 🆁🅰🆇 *44/499–7101,* 🆆🅴🅱 *www.welcomgroup.com. 283 rooms, 42 suites. 3 restaurants, bar, coffee shop, pool, sauna, health club, dance club, business services, travel services. AE, DC, MC, V.*

$$$ 🏨 **Fisherman's Cove.** The main building of this isolated Taj resort is colorful and whimsical: past the woodsy open-air lobby. The setting is luxurious: the large pool includes a swim-up bar, and there's a seafood restaurant outdoors, right on the edge of the sea. Also at the water's edge, the round seaside cottages have porches and garden showers (outdoors). Luxury cottages have spacious porches with hammocks where you can relax and catch a breeze plus air-conditioning and in-room data ports. The hotel is 28 km (17 mi) south of Madras on the Shore Road to Mahabalipuram. ⊠ *Covelong Beach, Kanchipuram 603112,* ☎ *4114/74304 through 4114/74310,* 🆁🅰🆇 *4114/74303. 50 rooms, 38 cottages. 2 restaurants, bar, in-room data ports, pool, tennis court, badminton, health club, Ping-Pong, windsurfing, jet skiing, waterskiing, baby-sitting, travel services. AE, DC, MC, V.*

$$$ 🏨 **Le Royal Meridien** This massive, lavishly tropical hotel is beautifully designed and extremely spacious. It has a magnificent lobby decorated in orange hues and a curvy outdoor pool ringed with palm trees. It's the city's newest five-star hotel. Close to the airport, and favored by business travelers and tourists alike, the hotel is set amid 3½ acres of tropical, landscaped gardens. Its multicuisine restaurant Cilantro is known for its live cooking stations and sushi bar. ✉ *1 G.S.T. Rd, St. Thomas Mount, 600016,* ☎ *44/2314343,* FAX *44/231–4344,* WEB *www. royalmeridien-chennai.com, 240 rooms. 3 restaurants, bar, pool, night club, business services, travel services. AE, DC, MC, V.*

$$$ 🏨 **Radisson.** This hotel—a white, neo-colonial building—has a charming garden and a wide porch on which you can lounge. Rooms are spacious, and furnished with classic, elegant wooden furniture. Service is extremely efficient. Golf (nearby) can be arranged. The hotel is a stone's throw from the airport. ✉ *355 G. S. T. Rd., St. Thomas Mount, 600016,* ☎ *44/231–0101,* FAX *44/231–0202,* WEB *www.radisson.com. 94 rooms, 8 suites. Restaurant, bar, coffee shop, pool, golf privileges, meeting room, health club, travel services. AE, DC, MC, V.*

$$$ 🏨 **Taj Connemara.** This historic luxury hotel—the only one in town,
★ offers excellent value. Built as a nawab's home in the 19th century, the building has generous hallways and is illuminated with lots of natural light. The old wing has been reconceived in art deco. Standard rooms are contemporary, but the pricier old-world rooms (in the old wing) are more exciting—each room, entered through a garden atrium, has a soaring ceiling, soft white lighting, blond wood, arched wooden room dividers, and a desk area that overlooks the outdoor pool. The lobby is flanked by Hindu statues, temple friezes, and palm trees in copper pots; the centerpiece is a lovely wrought-iron chandelier. The casual 24-hour coffee shop overlooks the pool, and the open-air Raintree restaurant offers classical Indian dance with dinner. ✉ *Binny Rd., 600002,* ☎ *44/852–0123,* FAX *44/852–3361,* WEB *www.tajhotels.com. 148 rooms, 12 suites. 3 restaurants, bar, pool, barbershop, hair salon, business services, meeting room, travel services. AE, DC, MC, V.*

$$$ 🏨 **The Trident.** This modern hotel has a small but attractive lobby with an interior garden and waterfall. An exquisite brass lotus pond is a welcoming sight for guests. Indian fabrics decorate the spacious and elegant rooms, the best of which overlook the pool. The hotel is near the airport, 10 km (6 mi) outside the city. ✉ *1/24 G. S. T. Rd., 600024,* ☎ *44/234–4747,* FAX *44/234–6699,* WEB *www.oberoihotels.com. 167 rooms. 2 restaurants, bar, pool, health club, business services, travel services, airport shuttle. AE, DC, MC, V.*

$$$ 🏨 **Welcomgroup Chola Sheraton.** The rooms in this modern hotel are comfortable and cozy, and guests on the Club floors get free airport transfers and champagne at check-in. The rooms are furnished with light-colored wood, and options for adjusting the lighting to different muted settings let you turn your room into a nice retreat from the bright sun outside. The hotel is in a central location, 2 km (1 mi) from downtown Madras. It's also close to several good restaurants and shopping areas. ✉ *10 Cathedral Rd., 600086,* ☎ *44/811–0101,* FAX *44/811–0202,* WEB *www.sheraton.com. 92 rooms. 2 restaurants, bar, coffee shop, pool, business services, meeting room, travel services. AE, DC, MC, V.*

$$–$$$ 🏨 **Ambassador Pallava.** This older hotel looks its age, but it has grand halls and a large lobby, and each guest room is decorated differently. Breakfast is included in the room rate. ✉ *53 Montieth Rd., 600008,* ☎ *44/855–4476 or 855–4068,* FAX *44/855–4492. 103 rooms, 12 suites. Restaurant, bar, coffee shop, pool, health club, dance club, business services, travel services. AE, DC, MC, V.*

$$–$$$ 🏨 **GRT Grand Days.** Soaring 31 m (100 ft) high, an atrium lobby sets the scene at this excellent hotel in the heart of Madras. Glass elevators take you up to rooms equipped with all the modern conveniences, such as minibars, coffeemakers, and personalized stationery. No-smoking rooms are available, and business travelers can make use of interview and meeting rooms, as well as Internet access and secretarial services. ✉ *120 Sir Thyagaraja Rd., T. Nagar district, 600017,* ☏ *44/822–0500,* FAX *44/823–0778,* WEB *www.grtgranddays.com. 135 rooms. 2 restaurants, bar, coffee shop, indoor pool, exercise room, business services, meeting room, travel services. AE, DC, MC, V.*

$$–$$$ 🏨 **Quality Inn Aruna.** All of the guest rooms at this modern hotel are large and tastefully decorated with contemporary furnishings. The best rooms overlook the outdoor pool—on the second story—and have nice views of Madras. The restaurant, Jewel in the Crown, serves excellent Indian meals at reasonable prices, and live classical Indian music accompanies dinner. Breakfast is included in the room rate. ✉ *144 Sterling Rd., 600034,* ☏ *44/825–9090,* FAX *44/825–8282. 82 rooms, 6 suites. Restaurant, coffee shop, bar, pool, health club. AE, DC, MC, V.*

$$ 🏨 **The Residency.** This nine-story hotel in T. Nagar makes no pretense to maharaja elegance: it's decorated with modest furnishings, in relatively austere style. However, service is courteous and prompt; that, combined with the hotel's location and room rates, make it very popular with Indian businessmen. Upper-floor corner rooms on two sides of the hotel have nice views of Madras. The 24-hour coffee shop serves both Indian and Continental food. ✉ *49 G. N. Chetty Rd., T. Nagar, 600017.* ☏ *44/825–3434,* FAX *44/825–0085,* WEB *www.theresidency.com. 112 rooms, 6 suites. Restaurant, bar, coffee shop, business services, travel services. AE, DC, MC, V.*

Nightlife and the Arts

Madras's nightlife mainly centers around dance and musical events. A national center of classical Indian dance and Carnatic music, Madras has been called the cultural capital of India. December is the peak month for recitals, though there are performances throughout the cooler months, too. For bars (normally open only until 11 PM) and discos, your best bets are large hotels.

Dance

Partially through the efforts of Western scholars, Tamil Nadu's folk music and dance have gotten renewed attention in recent years. Dances from all over India are performed at DakshinaChitra, south of Madras. Bharatanatyam, long-performed only by temple dancers, was revived in the 20th century by the famous classical Indian dancer Rukmini Devi. Widely performed in December, this is a highly stylized, dramatic dance featuring many of the *mudra* (meaningful hand gestures) that you see in Hindu statues.

The **Kalakshetra School** (✉ Tiruvanmiyur, ☏ 44/491–1169), founded by Rukmini Devi and now a government-run university, has music and dance classes that you can drop in and watch. **Kuchipudi Art Academy** (✉ 105 Greenways Rd., ☏ 44/493–7260, FAX 44/493–8473) has classes in Kuchipudi dance.

Music

The period from mid-December to mid-January is packed with hundreds of Carnatic music concerts and lectures. Concerts usually follow a set pattern: an initial melodic raga is followed by variations and improvisation by both the soloist and the accompanying instrumentalists. See the morning newspaper, *The Hindu,* for performance listings.

Outdoor Activities and Sports

Golf

The Madras exercise roomkhana Club has a 9-hole golf course in the center of the track at the **Madras Race Club** (⊠ Guindy Rd., Guindy district, ☎ 44/235–0774).

Horse Racing

The **Madras Race Club** (⊠ Guindy Rd., Guindy district, ☎ 44/235–0774) is a wonderful patch of greenery in industrial Guindy. Races are held two or more afternoons a week from November through March.

Shopping

Bazaars

The **Mylapore Temple Bazaar** (⊠ Off Bazaar Rd. near Kapalishvara Temple) specializes in silver jewelry. **Pondy Bazaar** (⊠ T. Nagar; bounded by Anna Salai, South Usman Rd., and Kodambakkam High Rd.) is a quintessential mixture of old- and new-style bazaars, with more than 30 stalls and stores selling everything from vegetables to silk saris and jewelry. **Spencer's Plaza** (⊠ 768–769 Anna Salai) has three floors of shops featuring leather goods, books, clothing, groceries, crockery, and handicrafts. You'll also find a Toys R Us, a Spencer's Super Store, and a good fast-food place here. The plaza's central fountain is surrounded by places to sit and rest your feet. The first floor has an American Express office with travel services. All of these bazaars are open daily.

Clothing

Alison's Exports (⊠ 43 College Rd., ☎ 44/826–2500) has an excellent collection of silks and cottons and an in-house tailor. **Fabindia** (⊠ Ilford House, 3 Woods Rd., off Anna Salai, ☎ 44/857–0365), in a beautifully restored heritage building, stocks ethnic prints for both men and women. The giant **Nalli Chinnasami Chetty** (⊠ 9 Nageswara Rd., Panagal Park, T. Nagar district ☎ 44/434–4115), better known as Nalli's, is famous for its Kanchipuram silk saris and overwhelming array of silk fabrics, not to mention casual cotton clothes. It's a zoo, in the best possible way, and service is excellent. **Radha Silks** (⊠ 1 Sannadhi St., Mylapore district, ☎ 44/494–1906 or 44/494–1909) has fine Kanchipuram silks. **Shilpi** (⊠ 29 Sir C. P. Ramaswamy Rd., Alwarpet, ☎ 44/499–0918 or 44/497–0503) is a very popular, chic boutique with well-designed ready-made clothes, including *salwars* (tunics), *kurtas* (shirts), skirts, and vests, as well as hand-loomed fabrics and household furnishings. **Shreenivas Silks and Saris** (⊠ 77 Sri Thyagaraya Rd., Pondy Bazaar, T. Nagar district, ☎ 44/828–4758) has fabulous Kanchipuram silks.

Jewelry

G. R. Thanga Maligai (⊠ 104 Usman Rd., T. Nagar district, ☎ 44/434–5052) has fine gold and silver jewelry.

Souvenirs

Aparna Art Gallery (⊠ 5 Bawa Rowther Rd.; Rayala Bldg., 781 Anna Salai) has old and new curios in wood and bronze, Thanjavur and Mysore paintings, and miniatures. The government-run **Central Cottage Industries Emporium** (⊠ Temple Tower, 476 Anna Salai, ☎ 44/433–0809) stocks clothes, handicrafts, bronzes, hand-loomed fabrics and rugs, and jewelry from all over India. **Victoria Technical Institute (VTI)** (⊠ 765 Anna Salai, ☎ 44/852–3141), in business for more than 100 years, has high-quality embroidery work, children's clothing, handicrafts, bronze and sandalwood items, metal lamps, wood carvings, and table linens.

Side Trips

Crocodile Bank
★ *34 km (21 mi) south of Madras.*

Founded by American conservationist Romulus Whittaker to protect India's dwindling crocodile population and to preserve the Irula (snake-catching) tribe's way of life, the Crocodile Bank has produced more than 6,000 crocodiles. They're even shipped to other countries to support croc populations worldwide. The reptiles—which also include muggers, gharials, and turtles—are housed in natural pens. Daily snake-venom extractions are not only an attraction, but have helped the Irulas maintain their culture. ✉ *Shore Rd., Vendanemeli,* ☎ *915–4833.* ☞ *Rs. 10, cameras Rs. 10, video cameras Rs. 75; snake-venom extraction Rs. 2, cameras Rs. 2, video cameras Rs. 20.* ☉ *Wed.–Mon. daily 10–4.*

DakshinaChitra
★ *29 km (18 mi) south of Madras.*

The heritage center at DakshinaChitra, a reconstructed village, is an exciting encapsulation of South Indian culture. In a pretty, almost rural setting, open-air displays embody domestic Indian architecture from the 19th and 20th centuries. Many of these buildings were painstakingly moved and reconstructed here. Along the 19th-century streets stand tradesmen's houses, each typical of its professional group. Artisans employ traditional techniques to make exquisite pottery, baskets, and carved stone items, some of which are for sale. Authenticity and attention to detail are the rule here. The 90-minute guided tour (for four to seven people at a time; prior booking required) is extraordinarily informative about Tamil history, language, and culture. Supported by a number of prominent Madras businesses, the center is expanding its displays to represent all four states of South India. The main hall of the Chettinad House hosts folk and classical dance performances, for which tickets can be reserved in advance. ✉ *Muttukadu, East Coast Rd., Chingelpet district, 603112,* ☎ *04114–45303. For brochure or reservations, contact the Madras Craft Foundation,* ✉ *G3, 6 Urur Olcott Rd., Besant Nagar neighborhood, Madras 600090,* ☎ *44/491–8943,* FAX *44/434–0149.* ☞ *Rs. 175.* ☉ *Wed.–Mon. 10–6.*

Tirupati
⑭ *152 km (94 mi) northwest of Madras.*

The town of Tirupati is renowned for the ancient **temple of Lord Venkateshwara** (an incarnation of Vishnu, also known as Balaji) on top of Tirumala Hill, 20 km (13 mi) outside town. This is one of the few temples in India that allow non-Hindus into the inner sanctum, where the holy of holies is kept—in this case, the 9-ft black idol of Balaji. Any wish made in front of the statue of Balaji is expected to be granted—as long as you're a true believer with a pure heart. Thousands of pilgrims from all over India flock here daily.

Buying a special tag that indicates a time you should join the special queue for darshan will reduce your waiting time to about two hours. (Pilgrims who pay Rs. 5 wait most of the day to get in.) The tag costs Rs. 50 and is available in Tirupati town; you don't necessarily have to go up to Tirumala Hill to buy it. When the time comes to enter the gold-painted gopuram, it won't take long: Telugu-speaking guards rush you through, hardly giving you enough time to glimpse the Dravidian-style Balaji, covered with gold jewelry and precious ornaments. This may all seem like a lot of effort for such a brief glimpse, but it's one of the few opportunities you'll have to mingle with Indian pilgrims, and it should help illustrate the power of Hindu spirituality.

Two roads, one for uphill traffic and the other for downhill traffic, help ease the flow of traffic to and from the temple, but you should still avoid going on weekends or public holidays, when the crowds can be truly daunting. Many pilgrims make the journey up the hill on foot, via a covered walkway. This is a strenuous climb, particularly in the heat of summer, and takes the better part of 3 hours. A taxi from the town costs between Rs. 400–500. Once darshan is over, you might consider walking a little farther up the hill to Sila Thoranam, a striking natural rock formation from antiquity.

LODGING

$$ ⊡ **Guestline Hotels and Resorts.** The more affluent pilgrims choose to stay here for relative luxury and quiet: The hotel is a good 2 mi from the train station, so milling crowds of devotees and hawkers can be temporarily left behind. The restaurants serve Indian fare. ⊠ *14-37 Karakambadi Rd., 517507,* ☎ *8574/80366,* FAX *8574/81774. 140 rooms. 2 restaurants, pool, health club. AE, DC, MC, V.*

$ ⊡ **Bhimas Residency Hotel.** This relatively new and luxurious hotel has spotless, spacious rooms that are an excellent value. Don't confuse it with the other hotels in the town containing the word "Bhimas" in their name. This one is conveniently located at the crossroads as you enter Tirupati town from the Madras road. The restaurant, Mohini, serves vegetarian South Indian and tandoori dishes. ⊠ *Renigunta Rd. near Railway Overbridge,* ☎ *8574/54541,* FAX *8574/54551,* WEB *www.bhimasresidency.com. 85 rooms. Restaurant, shop, business services. MC, V.*

$ ⊡ **Hotel Mayura.** Friendly and helpful staff make this an oasis from the ordeal of being one pilgrim among the 5,000 that visit Tirupati each day. Rooms have eclectic furnishings, but the beds are large and clean. The restaurant, Surya, serves good South Indian vegetarian dishes. ⊠ *209 T. P. Area, 517501,* ☎ *8574/25925,* FAX *8574/25911. 65 rooms. Restaurant. AE, DC, MC, V.*

MAHABALIPURAM, KANCHIPURAM, AND PONDICHERRY

Mahabalipuram and Kanchipuram reflect the glorious pasts of three great dynasties: Pallava, Chola, and Vijayanagar. The Pallava capital Kanchipuram, a town of learning, became fertile ground for a vast number of temples. From the port at Mahabalipuram, the Pallavas began to trade with China and Indonesia, a tradition expanded by succeeding empires. Together, the three dynasties laid the foundations of Tamil history, language, and religion, and with each dynasty the temples became larger and more elaborate. With the destruction of its port, Mahabalipuram became a deserted historical site, so that it's now largely a traveler's curiosity, while Kanchipuram is still a major pilgrimage destination. Pondicherry, with its strong French influence, is cherished for being refreshingly different from any other place in India.

Mahabalipuram

59 km (37 mi) south of Madras, 64 km (40 mi) southeast of Kanchipuram.

★ Mahabalipuram is a friendly old port city with four kinds of rock structures: monolithic rock temples (*rathas*), cave temples, temples constructed from a conglomeration of materials, and bas-relief sculptures carved on large rocks. In the 8th century, the Pallava dynasty conducted a thriving maritime trade here, sending emissaries to China, Southeast Asia, and Indonesia; carved stone is all that now remains of these dynamic businessmen, who ultimately ruled for 300 years.

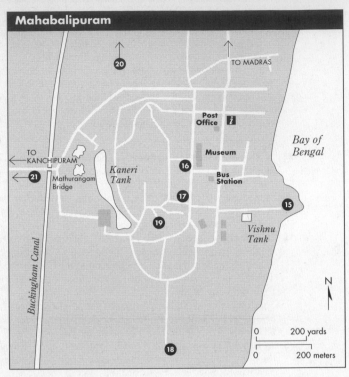

It's a wonderful place to visit, especially between December and February, as you can divide your time between exploring magnificent ancient temples and relaxing at a beach resort. In addition to the government shops and the museum, independent shops sell granite images and carvings reminiscent of the temples; many of these are remarkably well executed. The sights are open all day, but the best times to visit are early morning and late afternoon.

★ ⑮ Right on the Bay of Bengal, the **Shore Temple**—subject for centuries to the vicissitudes of sun, sea, and sand—is notable for the degree of detail that remains. You enter the temple from the back, through a courtyard surrounded by a massive wall topped by reclining bulls and two Shiva towers. Although ravaged by time, the calm image of Vishnu, lying in cosmic sleep on the sea with the serpent Sesha at his side, is juxtaposed with the clamor or waves pounding on the sea wall. The Shore Temple was built by the Pallava king Rajasimha in the early 8th century. ✉ *On ocean; follow signs.* ✉ *Temple and Five Rathas Rs. 5, video camera Rs. 25.*

⑯ The world's largest bas-relief—29 m (96 ft) long and 13 m (43 ft) high— the **Penance of Arjuna,** also called the Descent of the Ganges, is carved on two adjacent boulders. Created by the Pallava dynasty, the work dates from the 7th century. Among the many figures depicted, both mythical and real, is a figure of Shiva with an ascetic Arjuna to his left, standing on one leg. The rendering is thought to be a scene from the *Bhagavad Gita,* in which Arjuna asks Shiva for help defeating his enemies. An extensive but unfinished Pallava water canal system included a pool above the bas-relief; the idea was that water would cascade down a natural cleft in the rock from this pool, simulating the descent of the Ganges from the Himalayas. The entire, enormous project is a fascinating and vital combination of the mundane and the mythical. ✉ *On street leading to Five Rathas.*

More than a dozen cave temples are cut into the rock hill behind the Penance of Arjuna. Some are unfinished and some have been damaged, but many are quite remarkable. Most are atop the granite hill, so you have to take a short hike to reach them. The **Krishna Mandapam,** one of the later cave temples, has a naturalistic figure of a cow being milked. A sculpture on the back wall of this 12-column cave is a relief of Krishna holding up the Govardhan mountain to protect his people from floods ordered by the thunder god Indra.

★ ⑱ The **Five Rathas** are also called the Pancha Pandava Rathas for the Five Pandava sons in the Hindu epic *Mahabharata*. The Rathas, probably the most famous example of Pallava architecture, are carved out of five pieces of granite, each temple distinctive, with its own elevation, plan, and exquisite detail. From north to south, the individual Rathas are the **Draupadi** (named for the wife of the Pandavas), dedicated to the goddess Durga, a warrior wife of Shiva who rides a lion; the **Arjuna** (named for the charioteer of the *Bhagavad Gita,* part of the *Mahabharata*), dedicated to the thunder god Indra; the **Bhima** (named for a Pandava son), the largest temple; the **Sahadeva** (named for a Pandava prince), part of which represents a Buddhist chapel; and the **Dharmaraja,** dedicated to Shiva. Three animal sculptures—an elephant, a lion, and the Nandi bull (the vehicles of Indra, Durga, and Shiva)—complete the display. Because all the temples are unfinished, it's assumed that the animal carvings were meant to have been moved to the appropriate Ratha. The diversity of the images and their meanings reveals the complexity of South Indian Hinduism; studying them is a minicourse in the history of South Indian temple architecture.

★ ⑲ The **Mahishasuramardini Cave,** near the lighthouse on top of the hill, is probably the most outstanding of the mandapams. On the right wall is a carved panel depicting Durga riding a prancing lion and defeating the buffalo demon Mahishasura. On the opposite wall, in sharp contrast to this battle scene, is a deeply carved relief of Vishnu reclining on the great serpent Sesha. In this position, Vishnu is usually considered to be in a cosmic sleep, epitomizing his role as preserver of the universe. At the back of the cave are three cells containing statues of Shiva, his consort Uma, and their son Skanda—collectively known as Somaskanda, a common Pallava theme.

⑳ The **Tiger Cave,** which is actually two boulders set together, is in a shady grove near the ocean. It's a favorite picnic spot. Dedicated to Durga, the cave is distinguished by the crown of carved tiger heads around its temple. ⊠ *Village of Saluvankuppam, 5 km (3mi) north of Mahabalipuram.*

㉑ **Tirukkalikundram** (Sacred Hill of Kites) is the name of both a village and its temple, which has Dutch, English, and ancient Indian inscriptions. The ride here from Mahabalipuram takes you through paddy fields. Pilgrims come to climb the 500 steps to the temple on the hilltop at noon, in the hope that the two kites (hawks) will come to be fed by the Brahmin priests. ⊠ *15 km (9 mi) west of Mahabalipuram.*

Dining and Lodging

Lodging in Mahabalipuram varies widely, from inexpensive guest houses in town with weekly and monthly rates (that often include meals), to more costly resorts overlooking the ocean. There's an abundance of good, inexpensive restaurants serving mainly seafood.

$$–$$$ ✕ **Seafront Restaurant and Whispering Woods.** Set under a thatched roof on the beach, near a small outdoor dance floor, the Seafront has a lively atmosphere. Open flames light the romantic Whispering Woods, which has tables in a pine grove out of sight—but not sound—of the beach. Both places, part of the Silver Sands hotel, serve Chinese, Continental, and Indian dishes, including fresh seafood. Try the Gujarati and Rajasthani thali if you're in the mood for sweet-and-spicy fare. ⊠ *Silver Sands, East Coast Rd.,* ☎ *4114/42283. AE, DC, MC, V.*

$–$$ ✕ **Ideal Beach Resort.** Here you can eat in a garden or the simple indoor restaurant, where the murals, sculptures, and recommended dishes are all Sri Lankan. Try the rice with fish curry, or the excellent deviled fish; follow up with *vatil appam* (custard). Continental food is also available. ⊠ *East Coast Rd.,* ☎ *4114/42240 or 4114/42443. MC, V.*

$ ✕ **Moonraker.** The most popular of the shack restaurants, this is the perfect place to soak in the laid-back Mahabalipuram atmosphere. Dinner here is far more attractive than lunch and is cooked to suit Western tastes. However, a request for "Indian-style" food usually yields good results as well. Try the garlic prawns in butter sauce or the fried calamari—the restaurant serves exceptionally good seafood, European-style, at remarkably low prices. ⊠ *Othavadai St.,* ☎ *no phone. No credit cards.*

$$$ ⌂ **Temple Bay Ashok Beach Resort.** Overlooking the ocean, this government-owned complex has rooms in a main building and in cottages with two doubles per unit. The rooms and cottages vary widely in quality and character: the newer cottages are more sterile but have nicer facilities. Some rooms are quite elegant, even luxurious. The restaurant serves a variety of cuisines. ⊠ *East Coast Rd., 603104,* ☎ *4114/ 42251,* FAX *4114/42255. 7 rooms, 29 cottages. Restaurant, bar, pool, tennis court, beach, travel services. AE, DC, MC, V.*

$–$$ ⌂ **Ideal Beach Resort.** Run by Tamils from Sri Lanka, this relaxing resort has a tropical atmosphere, with lots of shrubs, trees, and sculptures. The best upstairs rooms have ocean views. ⊠ *East Coast Rd., 603104,* ☎ *4114/42240 or 4114/42443,* FAX *4114/42243,* WEB *www.idealresort. com. 5 rooms, 33 cottages. Restaurant, bar, pool, massage. MC, V.*

En Route   From October to March, thousands of waterbirds, egrets, pelicans, storks, and herons come to nest in the **Vedanthangal Bird Sanctuary,** the oldest bird haven in India. The best times to see them are late afternoon and early morning in December and January. ⊠ *35 km (22 mi) south of Chengalpattu, off NH 45 on road to Uttiramerur; for information contact the Wild Life Warden, DMS Compound, Anna Salai, Madras 600026,* ☎ *44/432–1471.* ⊙ *Daily 8–6.* ⊠ *Rs. 2.*

Kanchipuram

㉒   *76 km (47 mi) southwest of Madras, 65 km (40 mi) north of Mahabalipuram.*

The ride from Madras to Kanchipuram passes through paddy and sugarcane fields, and villages at very close range, with houses right on the roadside. You may have to stop for a goat crossing. Former capital of the ancient Pallavas, Kanchipuram holds the remains of three great dynasties—Pallava, Chola, and Vijayanagar—that for centuries weathered internal conflict and external trade but never northern invasion. The dynasties merely jostled each other, building ever greater shrines to their developing and intertwining sets of deities. Today, Kanchipuram, nicknamed the Golden City of 1,000 Temples (as well as "Kanchi"), is one of the seven holy pilgrimage sites for Hindus, with temples to both Shiva and Vishnu. Through the diversity of building styles here, you can trace the development of Dravidian temple architecture from the 8th century right up to the present.

The temples we cover below are some of the more famous, but there are plenty of others to explore. When you visit the pilgrimage temples, be prepared for rows of beggars and children beseeching you for candy and/or pens. Kanchipuram temples close from 12:30 to 4 PM, so do your sightseeing in the morning or early evening. Many of the temples have their own elephants (relating to the elephant-headed god Ganesh), who patiently stand by the main gopuram to bless anyone who makes a contribution. The elephants take the money in their trunks. It's an intriguing way to participate in a Hindu ritual.

The **Ekambaranathar Temple** was originally built before the mid-9th century by the Pallavas, but its most significant feature, a massive, 200-ft gopuram with more than 10 stories of intricate sculptures, was a 16th-century addition by the Vijayanagar kings. The temple is dedicated to Shiva, who appears in the form of earth, one of Hinduism's five sacred elements. Inside the courtyard is a mango tree thought to be 3,000 years old; each of its four main branches is said to bear fruit with a different taste, representing the four Hindu Vedas (sacred texts). The temple's name is quite possibly a modification of Eka Amra Nathar (Lord of the Mango Tree). Of the original 1,000 pillars that once stood in the mandapam, fewer than 600 remain. Alas, a visit to this temple can be marred by the machinations of touts, who may attach themselves to your side and insist on serving as guides, or even drag you down to the ablution tank and force you to perform a puja using puffed rice. You'll be billed for all such services, whether you want them or not. Try not to bring more cash than you're willing to part with.

The Ekambaranathar Temple is in the Saivite Brahmin section of Kanchipuram. On your way to the main entrance, notice the houses on either side of the rather dusty road, most augmented by open porches with raised sitting platforms. Some have *kolams* (rice-flour designs) in front of the entrance. These Brahmin houses epitomize the religious and cultural ambience of the temples; until fairly recently, Kanchipuram was a town segregated residentially by caste. ⊠ *Between W. and N. Mada Sts., northwest part of town.*

★ Built mainly during the reign of King Rajasimha (700–728), **Kailasanatha Temple**—named for Kailasa, Shiva's Himalayan paradise—carried the development of Pallava temple architecture one step beyond the monolithic Dharmaraja Ratha and Shore Temple at Mahabalipuram. From the dressed rock of the Shore Temple, the construction of Kailasanatha progressed to granite foundations and the more easily carved sandstone for the superstructure. The sculpted vimana—a tower over the inner sanctum—can trace its lineage in shape, design, and ornamentation to both the Shore Temple and the Dharmaraja Ratha. The cell-like structures surrounding the sanctum are similar in design to the Five Rathas; all have extensive sculptures of Shiva in various poses, symbolizing different aspects of his mythology. Lining the inner courtyard are 58 small meditation cells with remnants of multicolor 8th-century paintings on the wall. Removed from teeming hordes of pilgrims, this quiet temple is an exquisite place to contemplate the oral Hindu tradition preserved in stone. ⊠ *Putleri St., 1½ km (1 mi) west of town center.* ▩ *Rs. 200–Rs. 250 for English-speaking guides.*

In the heart of the old town, topped by a brilliant, gold-plated gopuram, **Sri Kamakshi Temple** hosts a famous winter car festival each February or March: deities from a number of temples are placed on wooden temple carts and pulled in a procession through the surrounding streets. Kamakshi is the wife of Shiva. ⊠ *Odai St.*

Built in the 8th century, **Vaikunthaperumal Temple** (Vishnu's paradise) is a single structure whose principal parts make an integrated whole. The four-story vimana is square, with three shrines, each depicting Vishnu in a different pose. The Vaikunthaperumal Temple is unusual for two components: its corridor for circumambulation of the shrines on the second and third floors, and its cloisters, with a colonnade of lion pillars and extensive sculptures bearing Pallava inscriptions. ☒ *1 km (½ mi) southwest of train station.*

Also known as the Devarajaswamy Temple, **Varadaraja Temple** (Bestower of Boons) is dedicated to Vishnu and is a favorite pilgrimage destination. Its exquisitely carved 100-pillar mandapam (with, in fact, 96 pillars) is one of the finest in India, and its decoration includes a massive chain carved from one stone. The temple was originally built in the 11th century, but the 100-ft gopuram was restored by the Vijayanagar kings 500 years later. ☒ *3 km (2 mi) southeast of town; follow Gandhi Rd. until you see the temple.* ☜ *Rs. 1, camera Rs. 5, video camera Rs. 50.*

Kanchipuram's silks and saris are famous throughout India for their brilliant colors and rich brocades of real gold and/or silver. More than 20,000 people work with silk alone in this city of weavers—entire families craft fabric in or near their homes, using age-old techniques. If you're curious about the process, stop into the **Weavers' Service Centre** (☒ 20 Railway Station Rd.), where several "demo" looms are usually in motion. Prices in the attached store are very reasonable.

Dining and Lodging
Accommodations in Kanchipuram are more for pilgrims than leisure travelers, and there are no "restaurants" in the Western sense.

$ ✕ **Hotel Saravana Bhavan.** Service is excellent in this hotel's immaculate, high-quality vegetarian restaurant that serves a basic thali, *puri* (deep-fried bread), and snacks, including masala dosas. It's a good place for a cup of South Indian coffee. One room is air-conditioned. ☒ *Center of town,* ☎ *4112/22505. MC, V.*

Shopping
Outside the Weavers' Service Centre, silk is often more expensive in Kanchi than in Madras. Buy from government-approved shops, many of which are on T. K. Nambi Street—**Shreenivas Silk House** (☒ 17-A, T. K. Nambi St.) is one of the best.

Pondicherry

㉓ *134 km (83 mi) south of Mahabalipuram, 160 km (100 mi) south of Madras.*

Small and quiet, Pondicherry is a lovely and unusual place—good if you want to take the pace of life down a few notches. A former French holding, Pondicherry still retains the flavor of its colonizers, who left only as recently as 1954. From the red *kepis* (caps) of the policemen to street names like Rue Romain Rolland, the French influence is deep-rooted and pervasive, and many of the local people still speak and study the language. This Union Territory, now also known as Puducheri, is a slice of France on Indian soil.

It is delightful to explore the grid of streets to the east of the canal that separated the French quarter from the rest of the town. On either side of the narrow streets rise tall white-washed villas swathed in bougainvillea, quaint churches and gardens, and little restaurants and cafés that serve French food and the best mineral water on the subcontinent. Even if you don't enter the heritage buildings in the area, the sense of living history is palpable.

A stroll down coastal **Goubert Avenue** (also known as Beach Road) is quiet and pleasant, with minimal traffic. You'll find plenty of people walking the beachfront in the evening, enjoying the feeling of holiday that manages to pervade Pondicherry throughout the year, even in the extreme heat of summer.

After your long and possibly hot walk—during which you might hear French being spoken on the street—there are plenty of places to quench your thirst and soak in the flavors of France. Almost all the restaurants in this area are housed in colonial-style buildings with gardens and old-world cane furniture. As for the genuine, reasonably priced French food—a visit to Pondicherry is definitely not complete without ordering bouillabaisse. The fish is local, but the soup is as good as any you've had in France.

About 10 km (6 mi) north of Pondicherry is **Auroville,** an international project—a group of villages—and "experiment in international living" conceived by The Mother, a companion of Sri Aurobindo. Once a freedom fighter, Sri Aurobindo moved to Pondicherry from Calcutta and founded an ashram here to propagate his ideas, a synthesis of yoga and modern science. Inaugurated in 1968, Auroville attracts those in search of enlightenment without the trappings of traditional religion. With more than 1,300 residents from all over the world, Auroville is meant to reflect the unity of the human spirit. Auroville is not a tourist attraction, and visitors need to spend a few days here at the least to understand the work being done.

A smart, interesting exhibition at the visitor's center explains the concept behind the Auroville project, and depicts how the Auroville community is involved in a variety of environment-friendly endeavours. They work with local villagers, introducing them to alternative technology and energy sources. Auroville has a handicrafts shop and a restaurant. The project has an informative Web site: WEB www.auroville-india.org.

Dining and Lodging

There are several hotels that offer good rooms and facilities in Pondicherry, and a smattering of guesthouses in the colonial quarter have preserved the French-Colonial ambience. The food is excellent in any of the small restaurants near the waterfront and within the grid of French-named streets.

$–$$ ✕ **Rendezvous.** A terrace restaurant that's very popular with tourists overlooks a charming sidestreet with whitewashed Mediterranean-style buildings. It's open for breakfast, lunch, and dinner, Rendezvous serves authentic bouillabaisse and excellent—fresh, delicately flavored—seafood overall. ✉ *30 Suffren St.,* ☎ *413/339132. No credit cards.*

$–$$ ✕ **Satsanga.** Here you'll get great French food with a little Italian thrown in. Try the owner/chef Pierre Elouard's green pepper steak or wood-fired pizza. The setting is charming: you can sit on the verandah or enjoy your meal in the restaurant's garden. ✉ *13 Lal Bahadur St.,* ☎ *413/225867. No credit cards. Closed Thurs.*

$$ 🏨 **Hotel Anandha Inn.** This towering white structure is one of Pondy's newest hotels. The rooms in the back, away from the main road, are the quietest. The hotel's restaurants serve Indian, Chinese, and Continental cuisines. ✉ *S. V. Patel Salai, 605001,* ☎ *413/330711,* FAX *413/331241,* WEB *www.anandhainn.com. 70 rooms. Restaurant, bar, business services, travel services. AE, DC, MC, V. CP.*

$ 🏨 **Hotel Mass.** The large, comfortable, and modern Hotel Mass is popular with business travelers. It's a good value with excellent service and hospitality. The bar is frequented by locals as well as guests. It is the only hotel in town with a swimming pool. The hotel is a little bit away—a few kilometers—from the French quarter. ✉ *M. M. Adigal Salai,*

605001, ☎ *413/204001,* FAX *413/203654. 111 rooms. Restaurant, bar, pool, business services, travel services. AE, DC, MC, V. CP.*

$ 🏨 **Park Guesthouse.** This quiet guest house is meant for ashram members and devotees, though tourists are allowed to stay if they observe the rather institutional rules regarding timing and abstinence from alcohol and smoking. The benefit: it has the best location in Pondicherry, right on the water at one end of Goubert Avenue. The drawback, besides the rules, is that there are no televisions, telephones, or room service. ⊠ *Goubert Ave.,* ☎ *413/34412. 85 rooms. Restaurant. No credit cards.*

Shopping

Shops are concentrated near the shore. Jawaharlal Nehru Street is particularly chockablock with stores selling everything from clothing to sweets. Pondy is known for its handmade paper, and arts and crafts products from Auroville and the Aurobindo ashram.

La Boutique d'Auroville (⊠ 38 J. N. St., ☎ 413/337264, ☉ Mon.–Sat. 9:30–1 and 3:30–8) is the official sales outlet for products from Auroville, which range from fine pottery to leather goods.

Splendour (⊠ 16 Goubert Ave., ☎ 413/336398, 413/334382, ☉ Thurs.–Tues. 9:30–1 and 4–8:30), is the sales outlet for Ashram products, from paper and candles to incense and potpourri.

TIRUCHIRAPPALLI, THANJAVUR, AND MADURAI

Stretching toward the south end of Tamil Nadu, these three cities were centers of dynastic activity for almost a thousand years. Between them, the Pallavas, Pandyas, Cholas, Vijayanagars, Nayaks, and Marathas left an architectural legacy of forts, palaces, and, of course, fantastic temples.

Tiruchirappalli

㉔ *325 km (202 mi) southwest of Madras.*

The temple city of Tiruchirappalli (City of the Three-Headed Demon) was a pawn in the feudal wars of the Pallavas, Pandyas, and Cholas, which continued until the 10th century, and from which point the Vijayanagar Empire reigned supreme. In the 18th century, Tiruchirappalli was at the center of the Carnatic wars between the British and French; and between these two violent periods, there were periodic Muslim incursions. All of this international activity had an influence on South India temple architecture, which reached its zenith in the Vijayanagar period under the Nayaks of Madurai (who built most of Tiruchirappalli) with the construction of one of the largest temples in South India: the Ranganathaswamy, on the island of Srirangam.

Tiruchirappalli—also known as Trichy—is spread-out, with hotels centered in the southern cantonment (the old Raj military area). If you don't hire a car, auto-rickshaws are probably the best transportation here. The flat landscape to the north is dominated by the Rock Fort, near the bridge to Srirangam, which lies between the Cauvery River and its tributary, the Kolidam.

★   The military and architectural heart of Tiruchirappalli is its startling **Rock Fort,** rising 272 ft above the city on the banks of the Cauvery River. Cut into the rock, 437 steps lead up to a temple dedicated to Lord Vinayaka (the mythical half-man, half-bird Garuda who is Vishnu's vehicle and who is prominent in *The Mahabharata*), then on to the summit. Along the way are various landings and shrines: an ancient temple dedicated to the elephant-headed god Ganesh, a Shiva temple, and cave temples cut into the rock. (Non-Hindus are not permitted into the temples). Finally, at the top, you're rewarded with a breathtaking view of Tiruchirappalli. To the north, the Srirangam temples rise dramatically out of fields and riverbeds.⊠ *2½ km (1½ mi) north of Trichy Cantonment.* ☎ *Rs.1., camera Rs.10, video camera Rs. 50 (no photography of deities or temple interior allowed).* ☉ *Daily 6–noon and 4–9.*

★ Covering more than 1 square km (¼ square mi) and dedicated to Vishnu, Srirangam's **Sri Ranganathaswamy Temple** (also known as the Great Temple), was built by various rulers of the Vijayanagar Empire between the 13th and 18th centuries, with a few 20th-century additions. The single-sanctum temple has seven concentric walls, 22 gopurams, and a north-to-south orientation rather than the usual east-to-west. Non-Hindus are not permitted into the inner sanctum.

Just as the Pallavas had rampant lions, the Vijayanagar dynasty had rearing horses, magnificently displayed here in the Horse Court, the fourth courtyard of the Seshadgiri mandapam. At the time of the Festival of Vaikuntha Ekadasi (in honor of Vishnu's paradise), pilgrims can see the idol of Ranganatha brought into the mandapam from the inner sanctum under the golden dome. During the January Car Festival, Srirangam's magnificent temple carts—exceptional in their artisanship—are taken out for a series of processions. The temple's extensive and beautiful collection of precious gems is included in the cart display. An island of temples, Srirangam was also a center of religious philosophy and learning. The great Vaishnava Acharya Ramanuja taught and wrote in the Srirangam school at the end of the 11th century. ⊠ *Srirangam Island, 8 km (5 mi) from Trichy by car.* ☎ *Entry free, Rs. 10 to climb wall for panoramic view, camera Rs. 20, video camera Rs. 75. No photography in sanctum.*

About 2½ km (1½ mi) east of the Great Temple, **Sri Jambukeswara Temple** (Shiva, Lord of the Mountain) is smaller, but its large central court is an excellent example of the Dravidian architecture from the final phase of the Madeira period (around 1600). The courtyard pillars are remarkable for their rampant dragons, elaborate foliated brackets, and royal Nayak portraits. ⊠ *Srirangam Island.* ☎ *Entry free, camera Rs. 10, video camera Rs. 125.* ☉ *Daily 6–noon and 4–9.*

Another shrine to Shiva is **Thiruvanaikkaval,** named for a legendary elephant that worshipped the linga (the phallic stone that is Shiva's primary abstract symbol). In the temple's Mambukeswaram pagoda, the linga is submerged in water—one of the five elements that Shiva represents. The architecture of this temple, with five walls and seven gopurams, is among the finest Dravidian work still in existence. ⊠ *3 km (2 mi) east of Srirangam.*

Dining and Lodging

Trichy's hotels are concentrated in the cantonment area, also called Junction (for the Tiruchirappalli Junction Railway Station).

$–$$ ✕ **Peaks of Kunlun** A Chinese restaurant at Jenney's Residency Hotel, Peaks of Kunlun is open only for dinner. Stick to the chicken and vegetable dishes and you'll be satisfied. ⊠ *3/14 McDonald's Rd,* ☎ *431/414414. AE, MC, V, DC.*

$ ✕ **Chembian.** This pleasant restaurant serves Indian, Chinese, and Continental cuisines. ⊠ *Hotel Sangam, Collector's Office Rd.,* ☎ *431/414700 or 431/414480. AE, DC, MC, V.*

$ ✕ **Woodlands.** Both Indian and Continental vegetarian cuisines go for reasonable prices here. Your best bet is the thali. ⊠ *Femina Hotel, 14-C Williams Rd., Cantonment,* ☎ *431/461551. AE, DC, MC, V.*

$$$$ ⊞ **Hotel Sangam.** This modern Western-style hotel is surrounded by a pleasant lawn. The best rooms overlook the pool, and are spacious, comfortable, and spotless. ⊠ *Collectors Office Rd., 620001,* ☎ *431/414700 or 431/414480,* ⅢX *431/415779. 56 rooms. Restaurant, bar, coffee shop, pool, health club, travel services. AE, DC, MC, V.*

$$ ⊞ **Jenneys Residency.** The best rooms in this high-rise hotel are spacious, with sturdy furniture and good upholstery, and they face the pool. The hotel has a Mexican theme bar—not exactly what you expect to find in a temple city in South India. Nonetheless, it's a popular nightspot, and it's much larger and more elaborate than its restaurant. ⊠ *3/14 McDonald's Rd., 620001,* ☎ *431/414414,* ⅢX *431/461451. 100 rooms, 23 suites. Restaurant, bar, coffee shop, pool, hair salon, health club, travel services. AE, DC, MC, V.*

$ ⊞ **Femina Hotel.** This central hotel has a bright, open marble lobby and clean and attractive rooms. The best rooms have small verandas and stunning views of the Great Temple and St. Joseph's Church. Beer is available through room service, but only for consumption in your room. ⊠ *14-C Williams Rd., Cantonment, 620001,* ☎ *431/414501,* ⅢX *431/410615. 157 rooms. Restaurant, room service, travel services. AE, DC, MC, V.*

Thanjavur

⑳ *55 km (34 mi) east of Tiruchirappalli.*

Nestled in the highly fertile delta of the Cauvery River, Thanjavur was the capital of the Cholas during their supremacy (907–1310). A fortuitous combination of flourishing agriculture, competent monarchs, and a long religious revival begun under the Pallavas in Kanchi, culminated in the building of the Thanjavur's Brihadiswara Temple. The two greatest Chola monarchs, Rajaraja I (985–1016) and his son Rajendra I (1012–1044), consolidated their South Indian empire from coast to coast, including Kerala, and added Ceylon, the Maldives, and Srivijaya, in what is now Indonesia, to their holdings. As a result, active trade developed with Southeast Asia and China, fostering a two-way cultural exchange: Thanjavur painting of the period shows some Chinese influence, and in Java, Indian influence led to universal appreciation of the epic poem *The Ramayana.*

★   Although this soaring monument to Rajaraja's spirituality is dedicated to Shiva, the sculptures on the gopuram of the **Brihadiswara Temple,** or Great Temple, depict Vishnu, and those inside are Buddhist. Until they were uncovered in 1970s, the more interesting Chola frescoes on the walls of the inner courtyard had been obscured by later Nayak paintings. Within a single courtyard, a giant Nandi bull (second-largest in India, next to the one in Mysore) and pillared halls point toward the 190-ft vimana, a pyramidal tower capped by a single 80-ton block of granite. This massive capstone was pulled to the top along an inclined plane that began in a village 6 km (4 mi) away. The delicate carving on the round granite cupola minimizes the capstone's size and provides a visual break from the massive pyramid. The temple's carefully planned and executed architecture make it a fine example of Dravidian artisanship; in fact, it's a UNESCO World Heritage Site. Visit the temple early in the morning before the crowds arrive. ⊠ *West Main Rd. at S. Rampart St.,* ☎ *no phone.* ☉ *6 AM–12:30 PM and 4–8:30.*

Thanjavur Palace is the central building in the great fort built by Nayak and Maratha kings. It's hard to find your way around this unbelievably dilapidated site, but visits to the **Art Gallery** (in Nayak Durbar Hall) and the **Royal Museum** are worth the effort. The art gallery has a magnificent collection of Chola bronzes. The Royal Museum displays clothing, arms, and other regal memorabilia. Near the art gallery is the **Saraswati Mahal Library,** a scholars' paradise with 46,000 rare palm-leaf and paper manuscripts in many languages. Cameras and video cameras are forbidden. ⊠ *Entrance on east wall, off East Main St.* ☉ *Daily, except national holidays; museum 9–6, art gallery 9–1 and 3–6, library Thurs.–Tues. 10–1 and 1:30–5:30.* 🎫 *Art Gallery Rs. 4, camera Rs. 30, video camera Rs. 200; Royal Museum Rs. 2, camera Rs. 15, video camera Rs. 100; library free.*

Dining and Lodging

Small vegetarian restaurants are easy to find in Thanjavur, especially along Gandhiji Road, in the center of town.

$–$$ ✕ **Les Repas.** A pleasant and clean restaurant at the Hotel Parisutham, Les Repas serves a wide range of Indian, Continental, and Chinese dishes. It's the only restaurant near the temple that offers spotless, air-conditioned comfort and Continental food. ⊠ *Hotel Parisutham, G.A. Rd.,* ☎ *4362/31801 or 4362/31844. AE, DC, MC, V.*

$$ 🏨 **Hotel Parisutham.** This modern hotel has a marvelous pool, pleasant canal views, and comfortable, well-equipped rooms. Without a doubt, this is the best place to stay if you're here for a quick trip, because it has an unbeatable location—a five-minute walk from the Great Temple. ⊠ *55 G. A. Canal Rd., 613001,* ☎ *4362/31801 or 4362/31844,* FAX *4362/30318. 50 rooms. Restaurant, bar, pool, business services, travel services. AE, DC, MC, V.*

$$ 🏨 **Hotel Sangam.** A quiet new hotel a little away from the town, on Trichy Road, Hotel Sangam is set in a tranquil garden. The rooms and service are fine. It's a good place to stay if you're driving to Tanjore by car. ⊠ *Trichy Rd. 620001,* ☎ *4362/25251,* FAX *4362/24895, 54 rooms. Restaurant, bar, travel services. AE, DC, MC, V.*

$ 🏨 **Ideal River View Resort.** Amid acres of paddy fields and semi-jungle, the Ideal River View Resort offers very comfortable and well-maintained air-conditioned cottages with balconies facing the Vennar River. Connected by road to Thanjavur, 4 km (2½ mi) away, it's a quiet, scenic place to unwind after sightseeing. The restaurant serves Indian, Continental, Chinese, and Sri Lankan cuisine. ⊠ *Vennar Bank, Palli Agraharam, 613003,* ☎ *4362/50533 or 4362/50633,* FAX *4362/51113. Restaurant, boating, fishing, travel services. MC, V.*

Shopping

R. Govindarajan (⊠ 31 Kuthiraikatti St., Karantha neighborhood, ☎ 4362/51282) has a large selection of Thanjavur paintings, brass and copper artifacts, wood carvings, and glass.

Madurai

㉖ *191 km (118 mi) southwest of Thanjavur, 142 km (88 mi) south of Tiruchirappalli.*

Once the capital of the Pandya dynasty, the second-largest city in Tamil Nadu supposedly got its name from the Tamil word for honey. According to legend, when King Kulasekhara Pandya first built Madurai—more than 2,500 years ago—Shiva shook nectar from his locks to purify and bless the new city. Known as the Temple City, Madurai's old city, south of the Vaigai River, was laid out in accordance with ancient temple custom, with the great Meenakshi Temple at the center. Shops and stalls surround the Meenakshi on three concentric squares of streets that are used for religious processions almost every day.

★ The **Meenakshi Temple,** also called the Great Temple, has two sanctuaries, one to Meenakshi (the fish-eyed goddess, consort of Shiva) and the other to Shiva in the form of Sundareswar. Legend has it that Shiva married the daughter of a Pandya chief in this form, and the temple's car festival celebrates this event each spring.

The temple's high point is the Hall of a Thousand Pillars, built in approximately 1560 and adorned with 985 elaborately carved pillars. The **Temple Art Museum,** also in the Hall of a Thousand Pillars, houses beautiful paintings and sculptures, although not all of these are accurately labeled. Among the many mandapams, the Kambattadi Mandapam is outstanding for its excellent sculptures depicting the manifestations of Shiva.

An excellent way to appreciate this awesome site is to wander slowly around the various crowded mandapams, observing the passionate worship that's going on. At 9:30 PM, return to the main temple to watch Shiva being carried to Meenakshi's bedroom, a procession that begins at the eastern gopuram. ⊠ *Between N., S., E., and W. Chithirai Sts.,* ☎ *452/744360.* 🔄 *Temple free; museum Rs. 2, camera Rs. 25, video camera not allowed.* ⊙ *Temple, daily 4:30 AM–12:30 PM and 4 PM–9:30 PM; museum, daily 7–5:30.*

Tirumala Nayak Mahal, an Indo-Saracenic palace, was built by Tirumala Nayak in 1636 and partially restored by Lord Napier, governor of Madras from 1866 to 1872. The palace is now largely in ruins, but its excellent sound-and-light show, nightly at 6:45 in English, dramatizes Madurai's past. ⊠ *1½ km (1 mi) north of Meenakshi Temple,* ☎ *452/732945.* 🔄 *Palace Rs. 2, sound-and-light show Rs. 2–Rs. 5.* ⊙ *Daily 9–1 and 2–5.*

Dining and Lodging

It's not hard to find a decent restaurant in sprawling Madurai, especially around the temple. There are plenty of places to stay on the west side of town, but the nicer hotels are across the river to the north.

$ ✕ **Surya.** A rooftop restaurant at the Hotel Supreme (don't stay here, rooms are seedy), Surya offers North and South Indian food for dinner, and thali lunches. Service is fast. ⊠ *110 W. Perumal Maistry St.,* ☎ *452/543151. MC, V.*

$$$ ☖ **Madura Park Inn.** This hotel, preferred by business travelers, boasts a unique contemporary design—for Madurai, that is. It has a large atrium and spacious rooms; it's a very comfortable hotel. The hotel is about 4 km (2½ mi) away from the bustle of the city center. ⊠ *38 Madakulam Main Rd., Palanganatham, 625003,* ☎ *452/771155,* ℻ *452/771888. 47 rooms. Restaurant, bar, health club, laundry service, business services. AE, DC, MC, V. BP.*

$$$ ☖ **Pandyan Hotel.** This unpretentious five-story hotel has lodged some famous personalities, including two former Indian Presidents and a King of Nepal. Most rooms are comfortable and have minimalist furnishings or floral bedspreads. The spacious suites are the nicest accommodations—they have king-size beds, a sitting area, and an extra table. The Queen's Room has large sliding doors and a view of the Meenakshi Temple. The restaurant serves South Indian, Chinese, and Continental food. Breakfast worth Rs. 100 is free for guests. The hotel is 20 minutes from the airport and 10 minutes from the train station and Madurai's shops. ⊠ *Race Course Rd., 625002,* ☎ *452/537090,* ℻ *452/533424,* 🌐 *www.pandyanhotel.com. 57 rooms. Restaurant, bar. AE, DC, MC, V.*

$$$ ☖ **Taj Garden Retreat.** Aptly named, this hilltop hotel in a verdant setting offers a view of Madurai from 6 km (4 mi) away. The rooms in

the period bungalow retain a British-colonial atmosphere, with vintage etchings on the walls, hardwood floors, and airy verandas with beautiful views. The other rooms are modern, villa-style. The restaurant serves excellent Indian and Continental cuisine and has a superb view of Madurai. ⊠ *Pasumalai Hill, 7 T. P. K. Rd., 625004,* ☎ *452/771601,* ℻ *452/771636. 50 rooms. Restaurant, bar, pool, tennis court. AE, DC, MC, V.*

$$ 🏨 **Germanus Days Inn.** This hotel has modern, comfortably furnished and upholstered rooms, and an attentive staff that offers warm and efficient service. ⊠ *28 Bypass Rd., 625010,* ☎ *452/782001,* ℻ *452/781478. 60 rooms, 4 suites. Restaurant, bar, laundry service, travel services. AE, DC, MC, V.*

Shopping
Shops full of carvings, textiles, and brasswork line the streets near Meenakshi Temple, particularly Town Hall Road and Masi Street. The **Handloom House** (⊠ E. Veli St.) has great hand-loomed cottons.

TAMIL NADU A TO Z

To research prices, get advice from other travelers, and book travel arrangements, visit www.fodors.com.

AIR TRAVEL
Madras's Meenambakkam Airport is served by several international flights (☞ Air Travel *in* Smart Travel Tips A to Z). Within India, Indian Airlines and Jet Airways connect Madras with Bombay, Delhi, Calcutta, Bangalore, Cochin, and Trivandrum, as well as Tiruchirappalli and Madurai. You can fly daily on Indian Airlines (only) from Madras to to Madurai, and five times a week from Madras to Trichy.
➤ AIRLINES AND CONTACTS: **Indian Airlines** (⊠ 19 Rukmani Lakshmipathi Rd./Marshalls Rd., Madras, ☎ 44/855–5200, 44/855–5204, or 44/140; ⊠ Dindigul Rd., Tiruchirapalli, ☎ 431/480233, 480930). **Jet Airways** (⊠ Thapar House, 43/44 Montieth Rd., Egmore, Madras, ☎ 44/841–4141).

AIRPORTS
Tamil Nadu's main airport is about 16 km (10 mi) from the center of Madras. A shuttle to any of the major hotels costs Rs. 50. Hired cars are available through prepaid booths just past the baggage claim areas; the ride will cost around Rs. 300.

Trichy's airport is 8 km (5 mi) from the city center. A cab, pre-paid at the airport, is your only option.
➤ AIRPORT INFORMATION: **Madras Meenambakkam Airport** (☎ 44/232–9971, 44/232–9972, or 140 for airport inquiries). **Trichy Airport** (☎ 431/481–633, 431/481–433, or 142 for airport inquiries).

BIKE TRAVEL
In temple cities and villages, cycle-rickshaws are a leisurely, pleasant, and cheap way to travel. Just remember that pedaling in the heat is strenuous: these men work hard. Set the fare in advance and be generous. Cycle-rickshaws in Kanchipuram cost about Rs. 70–Rs. 100 for the day. In most bigger cities they are not available—and also not advisable because they are very dangerous in city traffic.

BUS TRAVEL
Bus travel is not recommended. Buses are cheap, but they are slow, uncomfortable, unreliable, and very crowded—sometimes it's even difficult entering a bus. There are no toilet facilities.

CARS AND DRIVERS

Many travelers fly or take a train to Madurai or Tiruchirappalli, then hire a car and driver for the rest of their stay in Tamil Nadu. Drivers know the major routes, and as long as you're satisfied with your driver it can be both convenient and pleasant to have him with you for several days. Rates change, so get a price in advance and be sure it includes a halt charge if you're traveling overnight. Distances within Tamil Nadu are measured from mile 0 at Fort St. George in Madras. Hire a car from a government-licensed operator (☞ Travel Agencies) and figure about Rs. 3 to Rs. 7 per km, with a halt charge of Rs. 100 per night.
➤ RENTING CARS WITH DRIVERS: **Bala Tourist Service** (✉ 88A Kodambakkam High Rd., Madras, ☎ 44/822–4444, ℻ 44/822–3737, WEB www.balatouristservice.com).

CAR TRAVEL

Madras is linked to the north by National Highway 5 (NH 5), to the west by NH 4, and to the south by NH 45. Generally speaking, road and traffic conditions can make driving more time-consuming than the distance suggests; driving to Madras is most feasible from Bangalore, 334 km (207 mi) to the west. Car travel by night is not recommended—too many wild truck drivers. NH 7 (from Bangalore) and NH 45 (from Madras) are the state's major north–south arteries. East–west roads include NH 4 (Madras–Bangalore), NH 46 (Vellore–Bangalore), NH 47 (Salem–Coimbatore), and NH 49 (Madurai east to the coast and west into Kerala). From Madras, the drives south to Kanchipuram, Mahabalipuram, and Pondicherry are short and simple. The East Coast Road is more scenic than the NH 45 and gets you to Mahabalipuram in one hour. The drive from Tiruchirappalli to Thanjavur goes through beautiful, lush green paddy fields interspersed with canals. The day-long drive from Madras to Madurai on NH 5 takes you through several villages.

CONSULATES

The U.S. consulate is open weekdays 8:15–5. The U.K. consulate is open weekdays 8:30–4.
➤ UNITED KINGDOM: **Madras** (✉ 24 Anderson Rd., 600006, ☎ 44/827–3136). Consular Section (☎ 44/827–0658).
➤ UNITED STATES: **Madras** (✉ 220 Anna Salai, 600006, ☎ 44/827–3040).

EMERGENCIES

➤ CONTACTS: **Apollo Hospital** (✉ Graemes La., Madras, ☎ 44/829–3333).

MAIL AND SHIPPING

If you want to send mail from abroad, the Madras General Post Office (GPO) is the best place to do so; it's a hub for all of Madras.
➤ POST OFFICES: **Madras General Post Office (GPO)** (✉ Rajaji Salai, Madras, ☎ 44/526–7752).

MONEY MATTERS

ATMS

Banks in Tamil Nadu only accept ATM cards for their own machines. Make sure you have cash or traveler's checks.

CURRENCY EXCHANGE

In Madras, American Express is open 9:30–6:30; Thomas Cook has a foreign-exchange office that is open daily 9:30–6. In other cities it's best to cash traveler's checks at your hotel. The State Bank will cash them but it's a laborious process.

➤ EXCHANGE SERVICES: **American Express** (✉ G-17 Spencer Plaza, Anna Salai, Madras, ☏ 44/852–3638, FAX 44/852–3573). **Thomas Cook** (✉ Ceebros Centre, 45 Uttamar Gandhi Salai, Madras, ☏ 44/855–4600, FAX 44/858–8532).

TAXIS AND AUTO-RICKSHAWS

In congested towns and cities, where not all the streets are conducive to cars, auto-rickshaws can be the fastest and most economical way to get around. Often the meters don't work, so agree on a price before departure. The set rate is about Rs. 7 for the first kilometer, Rs. 2.25 for each additional kilometer. Be prepared to pay Rs. 10 over the meter reading.

Taxis are normally found only outside the big hotels. A taxi should cost about Rs. 7 for the first kilometer, Rs. 2 per additional kilometer. Make sure the driver uses his meter, or agree on the fare in advance.

With any kind of metered transit, it's wise to use a map to familiarize yourself with the shortest route to your destination. This is best done *before* you get into the taxi (or auto-rickshaw), but even with your driver staring at you in the rearview mirror, a little map work helps keep you from being taken advantage of. In smaller towns, which often have un-metered vehicles, *always* set the fare in advance.

TOURS

American Express shares an office with their money-changing services. Ashok Travel and Tours is open Monday through Saturday 10 to 5:30. The sales office of the Tamil Nadu Tourism Development Corporation is open weekdays 9:45 to 6. Welcome Tours and Travels provides extremely efficient service and is open 24 hours a day throughout the year. The Thomas Cook travel agency shares an office with its currency-exchange service and is open Monday through Saturday 9:30 to 6. Most major hotels also have travel desks where you can easily arrange a car and driver.
➤ CONTACTS: **American Express** (✉ G-17 Spencer Plaza, Anna Salai, Madras, ☏ 44/852–3592 or 44/852–3596). **Ashok Travel and Tours** (✉ 46 Pantheon Rd., Madras, ☏ 44/855–3203). **Tamil Nadu Tourism Development Corporation** (✉ 3 Periyar E. V. R. High Rd., Madras, ☏ 44/56–0294). **Thomas Cook** (✉ Ceebros Centre, 45 Uttamar Gandhi Salai, Madras, ☏ 44/855–4600, FAX 44/855–5090). **Welcome Tours and Travels** (✉ 150 Mount Rd., Madras, ☏ 44/852–1614, FAX 44/858–6655).

TRAIN TRAVEL

The Indian Railways booking service in Madras is in Besant Nagar on the ground floor of Rajaji Bhavan Complex. It's a bit more expensive than the Indrail office on the second floor of the Central Station (open 10 to 5), but it's much more convenient and efficient. Railway booking offices are open Monday through Saturday 8 to noon and 12:15 to 2, Sunday 8 to noon. There's also good train service to Bangalore both day and night. See the monthly *Hallo! Madras* for train schedules.

The air-conditioned chair-car service (Vaigai Express) from Madras to Tiruchirappalli (6 hours) and Madurai (7½ hours) is a relaxing way to see the countryside. Night trains to Madurai save you sightseeing time. The trains going south leave on the meter-gauge track from Egmore Station. See the monthly *Hallo! Madras* for schedules. Advance booking is necessary during the holiday months.

There are two daily trains from Madras to Tirupati, the *Tirupati–Madras Express* and the *Saptagiri Express*. Both take three hours. You can book a bus tour of Tirupati at the bus stand on Esplanade Road or at Central Station or Egmore Station.

➤ TRAIN INFORMATION: **Egmore Station** (☎ 44/535–3545).

VISITOR INFORMATION

The Government of India Tourist Office has offices opposite Spencer's and at the airport's domestic terminal, with knowledgeable staff and an astoundingly comprehensive computer database. The offices are open weekdays 9 to 5:45 and Saturday 9 to 1. *Hallo! Madras,* an informative monthly for the promotion of tourism, lists tours, music halls, cinemas, events, and airline and train schedules. It's available free at the Government of India Tourist Office and for Rs. 10 at bookstores. The "In the City" section of the Friday edition of *The Hindu* lists cultural events for the coming week.

Near the Government of India Tourist Office in town, the Tamil Nadu Tourism Development Corporation provides information and reserves cars and guided tours. The India Tourist Development Corporation arranges excursions throughout the state. If you plan to visit any restricted areas or need your visa extended, you should head for the Foreigners' Regional Registration Office.

Outside Madras: There's no tourist office in Kanchipuram, so you may want to contact the Tamil Nadu Tourism Development Corporation in Madras before your trip. The main tourist office in Madurai is open weekdays 10 to 5:45. There are branches at the airport and the train station. The Thanjavur tourist office is open Tuesday through Sunday from 10 to 1 and 2 to 5. In Tiruchirappalli, the tourist office is open every day from 10 to 5:45. In Pondicherry, the staff at the Tourist Information Bureau of the Directorate of Tourism is very helpful; the office is open Monday through Saturday from 10 to 5:30.

➤ TOURIST INFORMATION: **Foreigners' Regional Registration Office** (✉ Shastri Bhavan Annexe Bldg., Haddows Rd., ☎ 44/827–8210). **Government of India Tourist Office** (✉ 154 Anna Salai, Madras 600002, ☎ 44/852–4295 or 44/234–0386). **India Tourist Development Corporation** (ITDC, ✉ 29 Victoria Crescent at Commander in Chief [C-in-C] Rd., ☎ 44/827–8884). **Madurai** (✉ W. Veli St., ☎ 452/734757). **Pondicherry,** (✉ 40 Goubert Ave., ☎ 431/334575). **Tamil Nadu Tourism Development Corporation** (✉ 25 Dr. Radhakrishnan Salai, ☎ 44/854–6843). **Thanjavur** (✉ Hotel Tamilnadu complex, Gandhi Rd., ☎ 4362/21421). **Tiruchirappalli** (✉ Hotel Tamil Nadu complex, 1 Williams Rd., ☎ 431/460136; counters at train station and airport).

12 HYDERABAD

Capital of the southeastern state of
Andhra Pradesh, Hyderabad is relatively
undiscovered as a cultural destination,
but its rich Muslim heritage combines
intriguingly with its dynamic software
industry. The city is known for its fiery
cuisine, its shopping—especially for
pearls—and, increasingly, its success
in the global business of information
technology.

MOST PEOPLE VISIT HYDERABAD ON BUSINESS. Software and
telecommunications industries, as well as traditional textile
and jewelry trades, thrive here, and the city is beginning to
steal the limelight from Bangalore in the information-technology sector. It's too bad more leisure travelers don't visit, as they're missing an
Indian treasure. Set on rolling hills around the beautiful Hussain Sagar
Lake, the city's minarets pierce the clear blue sky. Here you can shop
for pearls and bangles, enjoy terrific food, and watch the colorful city
go by.

By Nigel Fisher

Updated by R.
Edwin Sudhir

Hyderabad is the capital of Andhra Pradesh, a large southeastern state
full of influences as varied as Buddhism in Ashoka's time and the
Mogul influx of the 16th century. No fewer than 16 languages (headed
by Telugu and Urdu) are spoken here. A long stretch of coast—dotted
with fishing villages and prone to flooding by monsoons—runs along
Bay of Bengal. Inland is the dry, even arid, Deccan Plateau.

Only 400 years old, Hyderabad reflects most dramatically its Mogul
and Telugu heritage. Quli Qutab Shah wrestled it from the Bahamani
kingdom in 1512 and built the fortress city of Golconda. Lack of water
and epidemics of plague and cholera convinced the fifth Quli to venture beyond his fortress and create a new city 10 km (6 mi) away on
the Musi River, with Charminar, an arch, as its center. Four great roads
fanned out from Charminar toward the four points of the compass.

The city's grandness and the wealth of the Qutab Shahi kingdom attracted the interest of Aurangzeb, the last great Mogul ruler. His armies
lay siege to Golconda and captured it in 1687. When the Mogul empire began to fragment, the viceroy, Asaf Jah I, proclaimed himself *nizam*
(ruler). The wealth of the nizams went beyond imagination. Stories of
the last nizam abound: he purportedly used a 260-carat diamond as a
paperweight, and during World War II he presented Britain's Royal Air
Force with a squadron of Hurricane fighters. When India was granted
independence from Great Britain, the nizam Usman Ali refused to join
the Union. He held out for a year until India marched in its army and
annexed the territory.

Today's city teems with approximately 5 million people who often appear to be on the streets en masse. If traffic is moving, prepare to hear
the crunch of an accident; if it's gridlocked, prepare to be all but overcome by exhaust fumes. But matters are improving. The city has constructed several overpasses to ease the congestion, and the state is
beginning road-widening projects. An army of cleaners toils through
the night, ensuring that Hyderabadis awake to a clean town. Note that
everyone uses the city name Hyderabad even when they're referring
to its twin city, Secunderabad, across the lake. Secunderabad is of note
only for its railway station, which receives many of Hyderabad's long-
distance trains.

Pleasures and Pastimes

Dining

Hyderabad is famous for food, including *haleem* (a slow-cooked treat
of pounded wheat, mutton, and spices), Hyderabadi *biriani* (a baked
meat and rice dish), and *bagare baingan* (eggplant in a spicy poppy–
sesame-seed sauce). Some of the best haleem is found in the Old Town
around the Mecca Masjid, though it's also available in classy restaurants. Chilies are grown on the plateau and among locals it's a point
of pride to shock the taste buds with fiery pain. The main hotels usually have a couple of restaurants, one Indian and one European, and,

except for one or two exceptions, these are the best (and safest) places to dine.

In 1994 the Andhra Pradesh government brought in prohibition. Only in leading hotels could alcohol be served and only then to out-of-state visitors who had to purchase a "drinking license" that permitted a couple of drinks a night at the hotel bar. In 1997 legislation was passed to end prohibition while imposing many restrictions on what, where, when, and to whom alcohol may be sold.

Lodging

Hyderabad has more hotel rooms than it can fill, and new construction is everywhere. New business hotels offer services and amenities of international caliber at prices half those of Delhi. These range from opulent to utilitarian. Inexpensive hotels with fairly primitive amenities are found around the train station in Secunderabad and in the center of Hyderabad.

Shopping

Hyderabad is a gathering center for the many handicrafts of Andhra Pradesh. Look for *nirmal* toys (delightfully colorful, lightweight wooden toys), *bidri* ware (a gunmetal-like alloy used for bangles, cufflinks, bowls, and other items), and ikat textiles (tie-dyed before they're woven). You'll also find silk, wool, and cotton carpets from the Warangal district. Hyderabad is the center of India's pearl trade: pearls from southeast Asia are sent here for polishing, sorting, and piercing. For pearls, the most exciting place is the Charminar Market, particularly just north of Charminar itself. The market bustles with everything you're likely to want, from textiles and handicrafts to bangles (west of Charminar). The omnipresent glass bangles worn throughout the country are produced in great quantities here.

EXPLORING HYDERABAD

Concentrate on Hyderabad if you're passing through Andhra Pradesh. Most of the city's interesting sights are in the Old Town, making it easy to walk around or take short auto-rickshaw trips. Don't bother with Hyderabad's twin city, Secunderabad, which, aside from its railway station, has little to offer the traveler. If you have the stamina and will be heading south to Madras, consider a detour to the temple town of Tirupati.

Great Itineraries

IF YOU HAVE 1 DAY

You could actually cover all of Hyderabad's major sights in one exhausting day. Try to spend at least two nights here, but if you can't, take an auto-rickshaw to the **Golconda Fort,** the original defensive settlement of Hyderabad, and the palatial tombs of the Muslim rulers, the **Qutab Shahi Tombs,** both several miles west of the city. Back in the Old Town, spend the rest of the day exploring **Charminar,** a four-story arched, minaret-topped gateway, and the area around it, which has good shopping.

IF YOU HAVE 2 DAYS

Follow the one-day itinerary your first day. The next day, visit the **Mecca Masjid,** India's second-largest mosque. Then head to the **Falaknuma Palace,** if it's open, and the eclectic **Salar Jung Museum.**

IF YOU HAVE 3 DAYS

Spend at least one day covering the sights mentioned above, then look outside the city. The most compelling attraction in Andhra Pradesh outside Hyderabad is the temple town of **Tirupati,** 732 km (454 mi) southeast of Hyderabad and accessible by tour bus in 12 hours. From there you can continue on by bus or train to Madras, four hours away.

When to Tour Hyderabad

Winter—mid-October through March—is the ideal time to visit, as the weather is dry and the temperature rarely climbs higher than 72°F (22°C). Evenings can even be chilly, requiring a sweater. In summer the temperature soars up to 104°F (40°C), cooling down just a little during the monsoon rains that fall from June through September.

Numbers in the text correspond to numbers in the margin and on the Hyderabad map.

A Good Tour

Make your first stop **Golconda Fort** ①, the original defensive settlement of Hyderabad. You can take an auto-rickshaw there, but to see it properly requires walking up a steep hill to its summer palace, and that is better done before the noonday sun beats down. From the fort go over to the nearby **Qutab Shahi Tombs** ②, the palatial tombs of the Muslim rulers, which are also better seen and photographed before the sun is overhead. From here it's a 7-km (4½-mi) auto-rickshaw ride to the center of the Old Town, whose landmark is **Charminar** ③, with its magnificent minarets. All around Charminar are bustling bazaars and close by is Laad Bazaar with rows of shops selling glass bangles, perfume, and lacquer. About 330 ft south of Charminar is India's second-largest mosque, the **Mecca Masjid** ④. The **Falaknuma Palace** ⑤ is another 2 km (1 mi) south. The **Salar Jung Museum** ⑥ is north of Charminar but still on the south side of the Musi River. In the evening, you may want to return to Golconda Fort to attend the sound-and-light show, especially if you're here on a Wednesday or Sunday, when the show is in English.

TIMING

This route can be covered in one extremely full day, but it's best split into two days. On account of Hyderabad's strong Muslim influence, the museums and some shops may be closed on Fridays. Non-Muslims are discouraged from visiting mosques on Fridays.

Sights to See

❸ **Charminar.** South of the Musi River, near the impressive Osmania Hospital and High Court buildings, you enter the Charkaman area in the heart of the Old City between four (*char*) great gates (*kaman*). Within these gates you'll find not only Hyderabad's famed pearl and bangle markets, but also the striking Charminar, an imposing granite edifice built by Mohammed Quli Qutab Shah in 1591 to appease the forces of evil and protect this new city from plague and epidemic. The arches, domes, and minarets show Islamic influence, while much of the ornamentation is Hindu in style. The no-traffic zone around the Charminar is a boon for pedestrians and protects the monuments from auto pollution. ⊠ *Charkaman center.* ☉ *Daily sunrise–sunset.*

❺ **Falaknuma Palace.** This stunning late 19th-century palace built by a Paigah noble is not open to the public, but it (along with its peaceful Japanese gardens) may one day be transformed into a luxury hotel by the Taj Group. People do often walk the 20 minutes south of Charminar, however, on the off chance that they'll be allowed to marvel at the stained-glass windows, carved ceilings, fine Italian marble staircases, and general 19th-century opulence that took nine years to create. Acquired by the sixth nizam in 1897, the palace has hosted both Indian and European royalty. Inquire at the tourist office or your hotel for more information. ⊠ *Tank Bund Rd.*

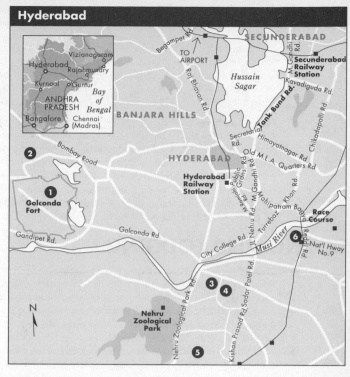

Hyderabad

❶ **Golconda Fort.** If you clap at the gate of this fort, it echoes clearly up to the summer palace, high on the hill just outside the city. These are the ruins of what was once the state capital: the fort often sheltered whole communities under siege for months, and though tremendously worn by time and war, it tells stories in crumbling stone. The fort only fell to one siege, but that siege was disastrous. In 1867, after eight months of bottling up the fort, Aurangzeb—with the assistance of a traitor who opened what is now called the Victory Gate—sent his troops storming in. In the belief that there was hidden gold here, Aurangzeb ordered the roofs of all palaces ripped off; so, 300 years later, only the walls stand amid the weeds and moss. The English version of the excellent, nightly sound-and-light show is performed every Wednesday and Sunday. ✉ *6 km (4 mi) west of the city (contact Andhra Pradesh Travel & Tourism Development Corporation in Hyderabad, ☎ 40/351–2401). ◉ Rs. 20 admission and light show. ☉ Daily sunrise–end of light show; light show, Nov.–Feb., daily 6:30; Mar.–Oct., daily 7.*

❹ **Mecca Masjid.** India's second-largest mosque, located in the Charkaman area in the center of the old part of town (south of Charminar), can hold 10,000 worshipers. Non-Muslims are welcome except at prayer time, which includes, of course, all day Friday. Some bricks here were made with earth brought from Mecca in 1618. The nizams' tombs line the left side of the courtyard. ✉ *Kishan Prasad Rd., southwest of Charminar, ☎ no phone. ◉ Free. ☉ Sat.–Thurs. except during services, which take place early morning.*

❷ **Qutab Shahi Tombs.** Each of the seven distinctive tombs of the Qutab Shahi dynasty has a square base surrounded by pointed arches. The seventh is unfinished because Shah Abdul Hassan was rudely interrupted in the building of his tomb by Aurangzeb, who defeated him and captured the Golconda Fort. ✉ *2 km (1 mi) north of Golconda Fort, ☎ 040/351–3410. ◉ Rs. 2. ☉ Sat.–Thurs. 9:30–5.*

❻ Salar Jung Museum. When you see the wealth of this collection, you might be astonished to learn that it all belonged to one man: Mir Yusuf Ali Khan Salar Jung III, who for a short time was prime minister. Thirty-five thousand items are crammed into 35 rooms. The fantastic Chola sculptures, European glass, Chinese jade, jeweled weapons, and modern Indian paintings are displayed with little information, but they're well worth a look anyway. ⊠ *C. L. Badari Malakpet (south of Musi River),* ☎ *040/452–3211.* ⊡ *Rs. 10.* ☉ *Sat.–Thurs., 10–5.*

Tank Bund Road. A showpiece of Hyderabad, Tank Bund is a promenade across the top of the dam that holds back the waters of Hussain Sagar Lake (4 mi by ½ mi), a dominant feature of the city. Many hotels are positioned so that their rooms overlook the lake, which is often used as a venue for sporting events. The road is lined with statues of the state's native sons, and a stunning sight from here is the 52-ft-high, 350-ton monolithic statue of Lord Buddha in the middle of the lake. ⊠ *East side of Hussain Sagar Lake.*

DINING AND LODGING

$$$ ✕ Dakhni. The setting is elegant, with dark wood pillars and and upholstered chairs and settees that are intimately placed around the room. The white walls are hung with handsome paintings. The chef serves good Andhra Pradesh and Deccan regional specialties. This is a good place to order haleem. ⊠ *Taj Banjara, Rd. No. 1, Banjara Hills,* ☎ *40/339–9999. AE, DC, MC, V.*

$$$ ✕ Firdaus. This restaurant evokes the elegance of the nizams, with *punka* (fans) gently swaying from the ceiling, waiters dressed in *sherwanis* (long Nehru-style jackets), and live *ghazal* (classical Indian vocal music) performances nightly, except Tuesday. The chef serves regal Hyderabadi cuisine. Try the *achar gosht* (lamb cooked in pickled tomato masala paste) and *nizami handi* (vegetable and cottage-cheese curry) or bagare baingan. ⊠ *Taj Krishna, Rd. No. 1, Banjara Hills,* ☎ *40/339–2323. AE, DC, MC, V.*

$$$ ✕ Kabab-E-Bahar. Outdoors on the edge of the lake, set on a lovely lawn, this restaurant serves excellent Hyderabadi cuisine buffet-style or à la carte. Try the very good kebabs and barbecue items. ⊠ *Taj Banjara, Rd. No. 1, Banjara Hills,* ☎ *40/339–9999. DC, MC, V. No lunch.*

$$$ ✕ Szechwan Garden. Overlooking beautiful waterfalls and surrounded by a Chinese rock garden, this restaurant offers tasty Szechuan cuisine. The honey spareribs, chicken in lotus leaves, and prawns in oyster sauce are all tasty choices. ⊠ *Taj Krishna, Rd. No. 1, Banjara Hills,* ☎ *40/339–3079. AE, DC, MC, V.*

$$$ ▥ ITC Kakatiya Sheraton. The imposing structure and grand lobby may
★ set a strong first impression but the warm hospitality and excellent service are what linger long after you leave this place. Rooms are tastefully laid out with an emphasis on comfort and you can surf to your heart's content on several international TV channels. Sip your favorite blend of tea at the Rani Rudrama's Court, a unique tea pavilion. ⊠ *Begumpet, 500016, Andhra Pradesh,* ☎ *40/340–0132,* ▥ *40/340–1045,* ▥ *www.welcomgroup.com. 167 rooms, 21 suites. 3 restaurants, coffee shop, tea shop, bar, pool, health club, business services, travel services. AE, DC, MC, V.*

$$$ ▥ Taj Krishna. Set on 9 acres overlooking Hussain Sagar Lake, the Taj
★ Krishna is a striking blend of modern architecture tempered by strong Mogul elements. Formal gardens grace the front lawn. Rooms have soft pastel decor and TVs with several international channels. Those facing the gardens and lake are the choicest. Service is exemplary.

✉ *Rd. No. 1, Banjara Hills, 500034, Andhra Pradesh,* ☎ *40/666–2323,* FAX *40/666–1313. 241 rooms, 16 suites. 2 restaurants, coffee shop, bar, pool, health club, business services, travel services. AE, DC, MC, V.*

$$$ 🏨 **Taj Residency.** Bold relief work adorns the high walls around the open lobby lounge, which is designed more to impress—with rambling sunken seating in a garishly colored pattern—than to enfold you in comfort. The rooms have thick carpets, writing desks, and couches. ✉ *Rd. No. 1, Banjara Hills, 500034,* ☎ *40/339–3939,* FAX *40/339–2684,* WEB *www.tajhotels.com. 135 rooms, 5 suites. 2 restaurants, bar, no-smoking rooms, pool, health club, business services, travel services. AE, DC, MC, V.*

$$ ✕ **Palace Heights.** This tasteful upper-floor restaurant in a modern high-rise has a great city view. Pictures of former nizams decorate the walls and antiques add a refined touch. Ask for a table by a window and choose from Continental, Chinese, and Indian cuisine. ✉ *Triveni Complex, Abids Rd.,* ☎ *40/475–4483. AE, DC, MC, V.*

$$ 🏨 **Ramada Hotel Manohar.** Just outside the airport—with soundproof rooms to eliminate aircraft noise—the Ramada is a good option for business travelers. It's got all the trappings of an international hotel, with service to match. ✉ *Near Airport Exit Rd., Begumpet, 500016,* ☎ *40/790–3333,* FAX *40/790–2222,* WEB *www.shreeshakti.com. 110 rooms, 25 suites. 2 restaurants, bar, coffee shop, pool, health club, business services, travel services. AE, DC, MC, V.*

$$ 🏨 **Taj Banjara.** This modern high-rise on Banjara Hills overlooks its own small lake. The spacious lobby is bedecked with marble, and the contemporary rooms are comfortable. Ask for a room with a lake view, on the upper floors. ✉ *Rd. No. 1, Banjara Hills, 500034,* ☎ *40/666–9999,* FAX *40/339–2218. 118 rooms, 9 suites. 3 restaurants, bar, coffee shop, pool, meeting room, travel services. AE, DC, MC, V.*

$ 🏨 **Green Park.** Near the airport, in the Greenlands area, this hotel is an excellent value for business travelers. The lobby is done in marble and the rooms are comfortable, with modern decor. The best rooms overlook the garden. ✉ *Begumpet Rd., 500016,* ☎ *40/375–7575,* FAX *40/375–7677,* WEB *www.hotelgreenpark.com. 133 rooms, 15 suites. Restaurant, bar, coffee shop, concierge floor, business services. AE, DC, MC, V.*

$ 🏨 **Viceroy.** This hotel stands conveniently between Hyderabad and Secunderabad and has stunning views over Hussain Sagar Lake. Glass elevators and terraced balconies overlook the open lobby; all the facilities are modern. Choice rooms have lake views, complete with spectacular sunsets. ✉ *Tank Bund Rd., 500380,* ☎ *40/753–8383,* FAX *40/753–8797. 178 rooms. Restaurant, coffee shop, pool, health club, business services, travel services. AE, DC, MC, V.*

SHOPPING

The **Lepakshi Handicrafts Emporium** (✉ 94 Minerva Complex, Gunfoundry, ☎ 40/323–5028) has a good variety of bidri ware, hand-loomed garments, and saris. **Mangatrai Pearls** (✉ 5-9-46, Basheerbagh, opposite Hotel Shanbagh, ☎ 40/323–5728; ✉ 22-6-191 Pathergatti, near Charminar, ☎ 040/457–7339) offers both high-quality pearls and good service. **Sanchay** (✉ Shops 21 and 22, Babukhan Estate, Basheerbagh, ☎ 40/329–9738) has a fine selection of high-quality hand-loomed silks.

HYDERABAD A TO Z

To research prices, get advice from other travelers, and book travel arrangements, visit www.fodors.com.

AIR TRAVEL TO AND FROM HYDERABAD

Hyderabad is served by frequent flights from all over India. Indian Air-lines has flights between Hyderabad and Bangalore, Bombay, Cal-cutta, Delhi, and Madras. Air India has service to Bombay and Singapore. Privately owned Jet Airways also serves Hyderabad; check with travel agents for current schedules of other domestic airlines. Air Sahara, another private airline which operates schedules in some sec-tors (thought not to Hyderabad), has an office here.

➤ AIRLINES AND CONTACTS: **Air India** (☎ 40/323–3319). **Air Sahara** (☎ 40/321–2767). **Indian Airlines** (☎ 40/329–9333 for reservations, 140 for inquiries). **Jet Airways** (☎ 40/330–1222).

AIRPORTS AND TRANSFERS

The airport is in Secunderabad, just north of Hussain Sagar Lake. You can book a prepaid taxi in the arrivals terminal; depending on your destination, the fare should fall between Rs. 50 and Rs. 300.

➤ AIRPORT INFORMATION: **Hyderabad airport** (✉ Sardar Patel Rd., Hy-derabad).

CARS AND DRIVERS

Air Travels and Cosy Cabs provide cars and drivers 24 hours a day.

➤ CONTACT: **Air Travels** (✉ 9 and 10 Ave. 7, Banjara Hills, ☎ 40/335–3099). **Cosy Cabs** (✉ Karan Apartments, Begumpet, ☎ 40/776–2023 or 40/776–0409).

EMERGENCIES

➤ CONTACTS: **Apollo Hospital** (✉ Jubilee Hills, ☎ 40/360–7777). **Fire** (☎ 101). **Police** (☎ 100).

MAIL AND SHIPPING

Blue Dart Express is associated with Federal Express and can get pack-ages just about anywhere.

➤ OVERNIGHT SERVICES: **Blue Dart Express** (✉ 1-2-61/62 Siddam Shetty Complex, Park La., ☎ 40/781–2746 or 40/781–2452).

➤ POST OFFICE: **General Post Office** (✉ Abid's Centre, ☎ 40/474–5978).

MONEY MATTERS

ATMS

The best neighborhood to find ATM machines is around the shopping area of Abid's.

CURRENCY EXCHANGE

All of the major hotels will change money for their guests. You can also visit Thomas Cook, open Monday through Saturday from 9:30 to 6.

➤ EXCHANGE SERVICE: **Thomas Cook** (✉ 6-1-57 Nasir Arcade, Saifabad, ☎ 40/323–1988).

TAXIS

Hyderabad is manageable on foot once you reach the district you want to explore. To get there, a metered auto-rickshaw or cycle rick-shaw is your best bet. Auto-rickshaws tend to go the long way to your destination unless you know—or pretend to know—where you're going. Unmetered taxis are overpriced and get you into more trouble in traffic, which becomes unbearable at rush hour. Only a cryptolo-gist can understand most addresses here, so landmarks and patience will serve you well.

TOURS

In addition to tourist offices and hotel-based travel agents, you can al-ways consult a travel agency for assistance. Ashok Travels runs deluxe buses to attractions within Andhra Pradesh such as Vijayawada, Tirupati, and Vishakapatnam.

➤ CONTACTS: **Ashok Travels** (✉ Lal Bahadur Stadium, ☎ 40/323–0766). **Jubilee Travels and Tours** (✉ 6-3-1090/B/A Somajiguda Raj Bhavan Rd., ☎ 40/331–2379). **Mercury Travels** (✉ 126, S.D. Road, Jaya Mansion, 1st floor, Secunderabad, ☎ 40/781–2712). **Sita World Travels** (✉ Sita House, 3-5-874, Hyderguda, ☎ 40/323–3628).

TRAIN TRAVEL

Hyderabad and Secunderabad are major rail centers. Some trains use either or both stations, but most long-distance trains use only Secunderabad. An auto-rickshaw to the center of Hyderabad costs Rs. 35. From Delhi, the *Rajdhani Express* takes 23 hours, while the less-expensive *A.P. Express* takes 26 hours, when it's running on time. From Bombay, the *Hyderabad–Bombay Express* takes 14 hours; from Madras, the *Charminar Express* takes 15 hours; and from Bhubaneswar, the *Falaknuma* takes 19 hours.

➤ TRAIN STATIONS: **Hyderabad Railway Station** (☎ 1345). **Secunderad Railway Station** (☎ 1345).

VISITOR INFORMATION

The Andhra Pradesh Travel & Tourism Development Corporation Ltd is open daily from 6:30 AM to 5:30 PM and has counters in both train stations. Its Tourism Information Centre is open daily from 6:30 AM to 7:30 PM. The Government of India Tourist Office is hard to find, has very little information on the region, and tends to be behind the times anyway. The monthly pamphlet "Channel 6" lists the latest urban goings-on; pick it up in a bookshop or major hotel.

➤ TOURIST OFFICES: **Andhra Pradesh Travel & Tourism Development Corporation Ltd** (APTTDC; ✉ Yatri Nivas, Sardar Patel Rd., ☎ 40/ 772–7100). **Government of India Tourist Office** (✉ Sandozi Bldg., Himayat Nagar, ☎ 40/763–0037). **Tourism Information Centre** (✉ Yatri Nivas, Sardar Patel Rd., Secunderabad, ☎ 40/781–6375).

13 BHUBANESWAR

Capital of the eastern coastal state of
Orissa, Bhubaneswar is an easy-going
temple city with 500 ancient shrines. Small
and reasonably peaceful, it's also a town of
artisans, as are the villages of Raghurajpur
and Pipli. Closer to the water, Konark is
famous for its half-ruined Sun Temple—
once a complete horse-drawn chariot
in stone, 225 ft tall—while Puri draws
crowds of pilgrims to its towering
Jagganath Temple.

O RISSA IS A TANGIBLY RELIGIOUS PLACE. The state was once a center of Buddhist learning, but changes in ruling dynasties brought changes in faith, moving away from Buddhism first to Jainism (circa 1st century BC) and then to Hinduism. It's now one of Hinduism's most active pilgrimage areas. The temple cities of Bhubaneswar, Puri, and Konark are showcases for Orissa's distinctive sacred architecture, with its unusual shapes and fabulous, often erotic, sculptures. Particularly in Bhubaneswar, the temples represent a coherent development of the Nagara style of Indo-Aryan design. Even beyond the hundreds of temples, you'll see signs of devotion everywhere: from village huts to taxis to hotels, the smiling face of Lord Jagannath, an avatar of Krishna and Orissa's main god, looks back at you.

By Nigel Fisher

Updated by Ami Trivedi

Orissa is also known as Utkala—"Land of Arts and Crafts." Striking crafts pop up everywhere, from the gaily colored appliqué umbrellas of Pipli to brass *dhokra,* animal and human figures of twisted wire. On palm-sheltered side streets, sculptors chisel statues from stone, and weavers create silk and cotton fabrics by hand.

Whether you're walking through Bhubaneswar's airport or a path in a tiny village, keep in mind that Orissa's infrastructure and facilities are very basic. Be patient, and prepare to settle into a slower pace.

Pleasures and Pastimes

Architecture

The temples of Bhubaneswar, Konark, and Puri, built between the 7th and 15th centuries, bear elaborate and fascinating detail. Canonical texts governed their structural forms and proportions. The Orissan temple consists almost entirely of a spire that vaults upward among much-lower turrets. Supporting the tower is the cube-shaped *deul* (shrine for the deity); next to the deul stands the *jagamohan* (porch), a meeting place for worshipers, usually square with a pyramidal roof. Sometimes one or two more halls—a *natmandir* (dancing hall) and a *bhogmandir* (hall of offerings)—are set in front of the porch. The architecture may seem heavy, but the sculptures on these temples are graceful, animated, often exuberantly erotic, and steeped in mythology. Most temples have a sacred tank in their yards, in which worshipers bathe themselves for religious cleansing.

Dining

In Bhubaneswar and Orissa's other towns and resort areas, expect good food at low prices in decidedly unassuming restaurants. You'll find fresh seafood—lobster, prawns, and fish called *bekti* and *rui*—and vegetables that benefit from Orissa's mineral-rich soils. A few restaurants offer a traditional Orissan item or two. Look for curries prepared with coconut milk, creamy gravies made with yogurt, and delicious *baigan* (eggplant) and *bhindi* (okra) dishes.

Lodging

You don't come to Orissa for the hotels. As a rule, they're utilitarian. Rates, however, are significantly lower than in more heavily traveled parts of India, and discounts are readily available. The pricier hotels offer air-conditioning and currency exchange, and their rooms have bathrooms with tubs.

Shopping

Orissa is renowned for its handicrafts. Look for *pata chitra* (exquisitely detailed, fine-lined religious paintings on cloth); *tala patra* (palm-leaf art); dhokra; *tarkashi* (exquisite silver-filigree jewelry and other items);

and appliqué work. Serious shopping entails side trips to the beautiful, largely hidden Orissan villages that are home to master craftspeople.

As in most of India, travelers are subject to grossly inflated prices, even in remote artisan hamlets. Start bargaining (it's expected) at half the original price and you may end up with a 30% to 40% "discount." In Pipli, competition drops the rate of initial inflation; here you'll only need to bargain down 5% to 10%. If you shy away from dickering, you can always buy good artifacts at fixed prices at the government emporiums.

EXPLORING BHUBANESWAR

Bhubaneswar's main temples are clustered in the Old Town within about 3 km (2 mi) of one another. It's entirely feasible to walk from one to the next, or you can hire a car and driver or a cycle-rickshaw.

The city is divided in two by the rail line. On the southeastern side is Old Town, with higgledy-piggledy streets, most of them unpaved, winding between residential areas and the temples. On the northwestern side is New Town, with wider streets and buildings spread out over a large area. There is no downtown, but the Station Square, just to the west of the railway station, is a gathering spot for auto-rickshaws and taxis. Two main streets, Janpath and Sachivalaya Marg, run north–south through New Town; these are crossed by the east-west road Raj Path, which goes west from Station Square out to National Highway 5, the trunk road heading north to Calcutta and south to Hyderabad.

Great Itineraries

Orissa's main destinations are Bhubaneswar, Konark, and Puri. If you're short on time, you can see this trio in two days, one devoted to Bhubaneswar and the other to Konark and Puri, with a possible stop at Pipli. With more time, you can spend another two or more days idling at Gopalpur-on-Sea, three hours south of Bhubaneswar by train.

Numbers in the margin correspond to points of interest on the Bhubaneswar and Environs map.

IF YOU HAVE 1 DAY
If you're on a flying visit, spend it exploring the ancient Hindu temples of ⊞ **Bhubaneswar.** Head directly to the Old Town to see Bindusagar; the Vaital, Parasurameswara, Mukteswar, Kedareswar, and Rajarani temples; and Brahmeswar. Hire transport to reach the Lingaraj Temple Complex and get back from there to the New Town. You'll also probably have time to visit the Tribal Museum, near the Baramunda Bus Station, west of New Town, to see the folk crafts of Orissa.

IF YOU HAVE 2 DAYS
Explore ⊞ **Bhubaneswar**'s Old Town on your first day. The next morning, leave early for the 90-minute journey to **Konark** and spend an hour or more at the Sun Temple. Have breakfast in Konark village and perhaps a swim at Konark's beach, Chandrabhapa, before going on to **Puri.** Spend an hour or two among the milling pilgrims and souvenir stalls; have lunch at the Mayfair; then head back for Bhubaneswar, stopping along the way at **Raghurajpur** to see the artisans, **Pipli** to inspect the appliqués, and **Dhauli,** the hill where Ashoka the Great slaughtered his enemies and then, in disgust, embraced Buddhism.

IF YOU HAVE 3 DAYS
Follow the two-day itinerary above. On your third day, take a three-hour train journey south to Berhampur and hop an auto-rickshaw to

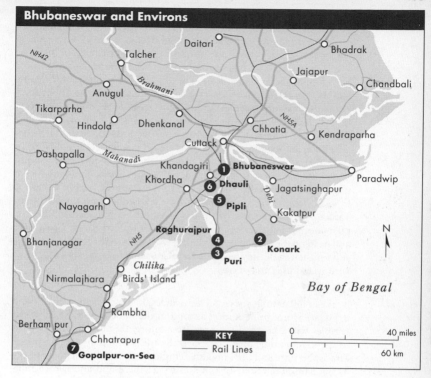

Bhubaneswar and Environs

Daitari
Bhadrak
NH42
Talcher
Jajapur
Chandbali
Brahmani
Anugul
Tikarparha
Hindola
Dhenkanal
Chhatia
NH5A
Kendraparha
Dashapalla
Mahanadi
Cuttack
Khandagiri
1 **Bhubaneswar**
Khordha
6 **Dhauli**
Jagatsinghapur
Paradwip
Debi
Nayagarh
5 **Pipli**
Kakatpur
N
Raghurajpur
Bhanjanagar
NH5
4
2 **Konark**
3 **Puri**
Chilika
Nirmalajhara
Birds' Island
Bay of Bengal
Rambha
Berham pur
Chhatrapur
KEY
0   40 miles
7 **Gopalpur-on-Sea**
— Rail Lines
0   60 km

🔲 **Gopalpur-on-Sea.** From here you can return to Bhubaneswar or continue south to Andhra Pradesh.

When to Tour Bhubaneswar

The ideal time to visit is from October to March, when the temperature is around 77°F (25°C) during the day and the air is relatively dry. After March the heat starts building up to 95°F (35°C) until the monsoon rains come in late May or early June. This cools things down a bit, but the rain can come down in buckets until mid-September.

Old Town Temples

❶ Bhubaneswar is known as India's city of temples, and once had some 7,000 religious shrines. Today only a fraction survive, but they still total around 500, in various stages of preservation. Unfortunately, the greatest Bhubaneswar temple, the Lingaraj, is off-limits to non-Hindus; you can see its huge tower from miles away, but the closest most foreign travelers will get to it is a viewing stand erected during the British Raj, when Lord Curzon, the British Viceroy, paid a visit.

Admission is technically free at all of Bhubaneswar's lovely temples. Upon entering any one of them, however, you may be harassed for money by the priest, who will follow you around, grumbling, with a dog-eared notebook (a phony donation register) scribbled with the names of foreign tourists and the amounts they've allegedly donated—with an extra zero tacked onto the end of each figure. The money is usually pocketed for the priest's own use rather than the preservation of the temple, but it's sometimes worth giving Rs. 10 or so just to avoid being tailed by a cranky priest.

The temples are open daily, from sunrise to sunset. Entrance into the inner sanctums of active temples may be restricted for half an hour or so during offering times (early morning, around noon, and late afternoon).

A Good Tour

The major temples are within an area of less than 3 mi by 1 mi, so you can walk among them if it's not too hot. If it is, make an arrangement with a taxi or auto-rickshaw; just negotiate the price first or you'll be overcharged. Start with **Bindusagar,** where early-morning bathers seek blessings. From here a walk west brings you to the 8th-century **Vaital Temple.** On the opposite (east) side of Bindusagar is the 7th-century **Parasurameswara Temple.** About 1 km (½ mi) to the west is the 10th-century **Mukteswar Temple;** on the same grounds is the whitewashed **Kedareswar Temple.** Continue east for 700 yards to see the 11th-century **Rajarani Temple,** standing pristine on manicured grounds. A little farther along the road going east are crossroads; turn right (south) and you'll come to wonderfully carved **Brahmeswar.** You might want transport to travel the 3 km (2 mi) to the **Lingaraj Temple Complex;** to walk here, retrace your steps to the crossroads and turn left onto Tankapai Road, back down the way you came, but before Rajarani take another left that will bring you down to Puri Road. Cross over and head up the small busy road lined with stalls to the temple. If there's still time left in the day, visit the **Tribal Museum** to learn about Orissa's various cultures and crafts.

TIMING

It takes a full morning to see all the temples. It's best to start early, around 8 AM, so as not to be hiking around in the midday sun. Most of the temples will take 15–20 minutes to explore, though you might want to spend more time browsing the stalls and soaking up the pilgrimage atmosphere around the Lingaraj Temple Complex. If you go on to the Tribal Museum, allow 15 minutes to get there and another 45 minutes inside.

Sights to See

Bindusagar. Surrounded by a stone embankment, the largest sacred tank in Bhubaneswar was the central point around which Bhubaneswar's multitude of temples was originally built. Believing that this tank is filled with water from every sacred stream and tank in India, and can therefore wash away sins, pilgrims come here to cleanse themselves.

Brahmeswar Temple. The outside of this 11th-century temple is sumptuously carved with scrolls of monkeys, swans, and deer, figures of gods and goddesses, and religious scenes. Over the entrance is a row of similar figures representing the nine planets. If you're lucky, you'll be shown around by a squat priest who will hold forth on the temple's carvings and their complicated symbolic significance. (He'll expect a tip.)

Lingaraj Temple Complex. This giant 11th-century shrine is considered the ultimate in Orissan temple architecture by Hindu devotees and art historians alike. A world in itself, with some 100 smaller votive shrines, the temple sits in a huge walled compound that teems with activity. The closest non-Hindus will get to this temple is the small, raised platform 100 yards away, from which you can strain to see the buildings' profuse exterior carvings, a high point of Hindu decorative art. Alas, unless you've brought binoculars, most of the details will elude you. Note that many enterprising locals post themselves at the foot of the platform stairs with a phony guest register and demand a donation for climbing the stairs. The money will not go to the temple, let alone the stairs, but into their pockets. Non-donors are likely to be harassed.

Dating from about 1050, the Lingaraj Temple originally consisted of only the porch and shrine; the dancing hall and the hall of offerings were added about 100 years later. The *vimana* (curvilinear tower), built without mortar, soars to a height of 147 ft.

★ **Mukteswar Temple.** Bhubaneswar's smallest temple was built in the 10th century. Its earthy-red sandstone body is encrusted with intricate carvings, from emaciated, crouching *sadhus* (Hindu holy men) to voluptuous, buxom women bedecked with jewels. On the left side of the entrance, the statues of bearers grimace under the temple's monumental weight. The Mukteswar's most distinctive feature is its *torana,* a thick-pillared, arched gateway draped with carved strings of beads and ornamented with statues of smiling women in languorous positions. Beyond the torana, set back in a shady yard, stands the **Kedareswar Temple,** with its 8-ft statue of Hanuman, the monkey god.

Parasurameswara Temple. Built in AD 650, this small temple is the oldest of those remaining in Bhubaneswar. It's a perfect example of the pre-10th-century Orissan style: a high spire curves up to a point over the sanctum, which houses the deity, and the pyramid-covered jagamohan, where people sit and pray. The facade is covered with carvings of Ganesh, the elephant god of wisdom and prosperity, and other deities and ornamentation.

★ **Rajarani Temple.** Standing by itself in green rice fields, far back from the road, this 11th-century structure is perhaps the most harmoniously proportioned temple in the city, and is definitely the most peaceful. The Orissan king who created the Rajarani died before its finishing touch—a deity—was installed, leaving its sanctum sanctorum eternally godless, yet filled with a lingering calm. There are no aggressive priests here. The temple's carvings are lovely, with dragons tucked into cracks, enchanting couples in erotic poses, and beautiful women smiling with a distinctly non-stony warmth. A small tip to the gardener-caretaker will get you inside.

Tribal Museum. This small, informal museum, run by the state's tribal-research institute, provides a glimpse of the traditions and daily lives of many of Orissa's 62 tribes. Set back in a garden, several thatched-roof huts in various styles house jewelry, ornaments, weapons, figurines, dresses, and other everyday objects. Many of the items are still in use, but some are being phased out as the modern world seeps in. ✉ *Tribal Research and Training Institute, National Hwy. No. 5, CRPF Sq.,* ☎ *674/403649.* ✆ *Free.* ☉ *Mon.–Sat. 10–5; closed 2nd Sat. of month.*

Vaital Temple. This 8th-century structure near the Bindusagar tank is one of the area's earlier temples. Unlike others in Bhubaneswar, it's devoted to tantric goddesses, and its two-story, barrel-shaped roof shows the influence of South Indian architecture. Bring a flashlight, if possible, to see the macabre carvings inside.

DINING AND LODGING

$$ ★ ✕ **Chandini.** The name means canopy, and in this elegant restaurant an antique *chandini* is suspended from the center of the ceiling. Paintings of Rajput heroes adorn the walls, along with old daggers and *jharokahs,* bay-window frames of carved stone. The kitchen serves delicious, somewhat small portions of Indian cuisine, from tangy, light tandoori dishes to richly gravied meats. Try the traditional Orissan *dahi machli,* Bay of Bengal fish cooked in creamy yogurt sauce. ✉ *The Oberoi, C.B. 1, Nayapalli,* ☎ *674/440890. AE, DC, MC, V. Closed Mon. No lunch.*

$$ ✕ **Executive–Swosti.** This cozy restaurant is a great place to sample traditional Orissan fare. With a few hours' advance notice, the chef will prepare specialties such as *santula* (mixed vegetables in coconut sauce) and dahi machli. For dessert, a rich square of *gajar ka halwa* (carrot halvah) is buttery, sweet, and divine. If you can't make advanced ar-

rangements for the Orissan *thali* (the traditional sample platter), try the *keema* vegetables (finely diced and served in a cashew gravy). Brown leather and mirrors create a dark, 1980s ambience, but it's brightened by green-and-white gingham linens and friendly service. The kitchen also serves Chinese and Continental food. ✉ *Hotel Swosti, 103 Janpath,* ☎ *674/404395. AE, DC, MC, V.*

$ ✕ **Aditya Park.** The wood-paneled dining area of this local favorite is warm, quiet, and dimly lit. Try the delectable *chilly* prawn (in a masala gravy) or vegetarian *chana masala* (chickpeas in a spicy onion and tomato sauce). The restaurant also serves tandoori dishes and Chinese cuisine. ✉ *Near Housing Board office, Bhoumanager Unit-IV,* ☎ *674/413702. No credit cards.*

$ ✕ **Cooks' Kitchen.** In the early 1990s, two young locals decided to open this very simple upstairs eatery based on the tremendous popularity of their tiny fast-food stand downstairs. The good selection of Indian and Chinese food includes *paneer pasanda* (chunks of curdled cheese with a zesty stuffing and a thick tomato sauce) and the Cooks' special *murg tikka nawabi* (boneless chicken prepared dry or with a masala sauce in a tandoori oven). ✉ *260 Bapuji Nagar or Market Bldg., 2nd floor, Alka Annex,* ☎ *674/530025, 674/530045, or 674/530065. No credit cards.*

$ ✕ **Dawat.** Once your eyes adjust to the darkness, you'll find yourself in a small dining room with white stucco walls and royal-blue tablecloths. Locals and travelers both like Dawat for its slightly more upscale (by Bhubaneswar standards) atmosphere and for its Chinese and good, reasonably priced Indian fare. Try the vegetable *dopiaza*, a spicy mix of fresh vegetables cooked *al dente*. ✉ *620 Sahid Nagar,* ☎ *674/ 507027. No credit cards.*

$ ✕ **Govinda.** After your temple tour, take a taxi or auto-rickshaw to the massively popular International Hare Krishna temple's in-house eatery, known for its simple, hygienic, strictly vegetarian meals served on metal thali trays that allow you to sample several dishes at once. Remember that this is a religious place, not a bona fide restaurant: leave your shoes at the entrance gate and prepare to eat with your hands. ✉ *Iskon Temple, National Hwy. No. 5, near The Oberoi,* ☎ *674/ 554283. No credit cards.*

$ ✕ **Venus Inn.** The menu in this age-old popular upstairs dining hall offers an endless variety of *dosas* (South Indian stuffed crepes) and *uttappams* (South Indian–style pizzas). Try the *rawa masala sada* dosa, stuffed with a slightly salty-and-sweet grain mixture, or the butter coconut uttappam, an Orissan specialty. A small, dark room filled with blue Formica-topped tables, this place is best suited for a quick, hearty lunch or snack rather than a lingering dinner. ✉ *217 Bapuji Nagar,* ☎ *674/532685. No credit cards.*

$$$$ 🏨 **Oberoi.** At this handsome two-story hotel, the most expensive in
★   town, the lobby's lights are tucked inside huge, brass temple bells, and the balcony is mounted on sandstone pillars and guarded by stone lions. Even at full occupancy, the common areas have a peaceful air. The rooms overlook either the pool or landscaped gardens, have attractive, modern teak furnishings complemented by Orissan hand-loomed fabrics, brass lamps, and framed prints of Bhubaneswar's temples. The only drawback is that the hotel is 10 km (6 mi) from the central part of New Town and even farther from the temples. ✉ *C.B. 1, Nayapalli, Bhubaneswar 751013,* ☎ *674/301010,* FAX *674/301302 or 674/300333,* WEB *www.oberoihotels.com/bhubm.htm. 64 rooms, 6 suites. 2 restaurants, bar, pool, 2 tennis courts, jogging, baby-sitting, dry cleaning, laundry service, business services, meeting room, travel services. AE, DC, MC, V.*

$$$ ☒ **Garden Inn.** This centrally located hotel is among the best in Bhubaneswar. Impressively designed to feel like an elegant garden, the three-story beige stucco building is fronted by stately pillars and a large terrace topped with a profusion of magenta bougainvillea. The window-lined lobby and hallways are sunny and filled with leafy plants in terra-cotta pots. The rooms, contemporary in style, are decorated with Orissan-print bedspreads in dark greens and maroons; deluxe rooms look out over the central courtyard. Friendly service ensures a comfortable stay. ☒ *A-112 Kharvel Nagar, Janpath, Bhubaneswar 751001,* ☎ *674/514120 through 674/514126,* FAX *674/504254. 61 rooms, 6 suites. Restaurant, bar, coffee shop, pool, hair salon, 2 tennis courts, sauna, exercise room, dry cleaning, laundry service, business services, meeting room, travel services. AE, DC, MC, V.*

$$$ ☒ **Mayfair Lagoon.** This tranquil resort is spread over 10 acres of land that incudes a 1½-acre lagoon. Guest quarters are spacious and bright with sandstone-tile floors and Orrisan-print bedspreads; they offer great views of the lagoon or garden areas and are well equipped with business facilities. Like the nearby Oberoi, the Lagoon is far from the region's major sights and railway station. *8-B Jaydev Vihar,751013,* ☎ *674/557701,* FAX *674/557702,* WEB *http://mayfair-resorts.com. 63 units. 3 restaurants, 2 bars, lounge, room service, pool, health club, shops, dry cleaning, laundry service, business services, meeting room, travel services, car rental. AE, DC, MC, V.*

$$$ ☒ **Quality Inn Crown** The lobby of this business hotel is decorated with ★   enormous 100-year-old wood carvings and a large crystal chandelier. The well-equipped guest rooms have sophisticated dark English furniture and deep-colored, hand-woven Orissan fabric bedspreads. *A1 (a), IRC Village, Nayapalli 751015,* ☎ *674/555500, 674/555551,* FAX *674/550001, www.qualityinncrown.com. 68 rooms. Restaurant, bar, coffee shop, pool, health club, business services. AE, DC, MC, V.*

$$$ ☒ **Swosti.** Friendly and well run, the Swosti offers efficient, courteous service and reasonable rates. The cozy lobby is decorated with Orissan pata chitra (highly detailed temple paintings). The building is on one of Bhubaneswar's main thoroughfares, close to the train station; for maximum quiet, ask for a room in the back. All of the rooms are a good size and clean, with plain, contemporary decor; most have bathtubs. ☒ *103 Janpath, Bhubaneswar 751001,* ☎ *674/404178 or 674/404397,* FAX *674/407524,* WEB *www.swosti.com. 53 rooms, 3 suites. 2 restaurants, bar, laundry service, meeting room, travel services. AE, DC, MC, V.*

$$$ ☒ **Swosti Plaza.** Also near the Oberoi, outside of the city center, this modern high-rise luxury hotel has fabulous views of the city. Rooms are centrally air-conditioned with marble floors and the Western luxury of a bathtub. *P-1 Jaydev Vihar, 751013,* ☎ *674/301936 through 674/301940,* FAX *674/301880,* WEB *www.swosti.com. 158 rooms. 3 restaurants, bar, pool, hot tub, massage, health club, bowling, billiards, recreation room, theater, meeting rooms, travel services. AE, DC, MC, V.*

$$ ☒ **Kalinga Ashok.** The lobby of this government-operated hotel is full of Orissan touches, including a miniature replica of Konark's chariot temple tucked in the corner and large hand-carved wooden temple doors leading to the restaurant. Room furnishings are slightly worn but comfortable, with dark carpeting and coordinating drapes and bedspreads with large floral designs. ☒ *Gautam Nagar, Bhubaneswar 751014,* ☎ *674/431055 or 674/431056,* FAX *674/432001,* WEB *www.ashokgroup.com. 58 rooms, 6 suites. 2 restaurants, bar, laundry service, meeting room, travel services. AE, DC, MC, V.*

$ ☒ **Bhubaneswar.** This budget hotel is simple and relatively clean, offering fan-cooled or air-conditioned rooms that have reddish carpeting and Indian toilets with private baths. The small dining room serves reasonable Indian fare and some European dishes. To get here from the train station, exit on the side opposite the town center (east) and walk south. Bhubaneswar Hotel is about 200 yards south on the right side. ⊠ *Cuttack Rd., Bhubaneswar 751001,* ☎ *674/416977. 46 rooms. Restaurant. No credit cards.*

$ 🏨 **The Marrion.** The modest rooms in this boxy, three-story hotel lack its lobby's Orissan touches, bearing instead a simple, slightly worn Western decor of dark-wood furniture and plain carpeting in pea green or orange-brown. The standard rooms tend to be stuffy; ask for a deluxe room overlooking the pool and for a bathroom with a tub. ⊠ *6 Janpath, Bhubaneswar 751001,* ☎ *674/502689, 674/502328, or 674/522472 through 674/522474,* ℻ *674/503287,* 🌐 *www.fhraindia/bhubaneswar/prachi. 55 rooms, 6 suites. 2 restaurants, pool, hair salon, health club, laundry service, meeting room, travel services. AE, DC, MC, V.*

$ 🏨 **Sishmo.** A giant replica of the wheel at the Sun Temple in Konark, reminds you that you're in the city of temples. Rooms have all the conveniences, from cable TV to minibar; ask for one on a higher floor so you get at least a glimpse of the many temples dotting the skyline. The large lobby is quiet and comfortable, setting the tone for a relaxing stay. ⊠ *86/A-1 Gautam Nagar, Bhubaneswar 751014,* ☎ *674/433600 or 674/433601,* ℻ *674/433351. 64 rooms, 8 suites. 2 restaurants, bar, coffee shop, laundry service, business services, travel services. AE, MC, V.*

NIGHTLIFE AND THE ARTS

The Arts

Odissi, the classical dance form native to Orissa, is perhaps the most lyrical style of Indian dance, flowing with graceful gestures and postures. In addition to classical Odissi, folk and tribal dances are still performed during festivals throughout the state; the **Konark Dance Festival,** in December, features the best of Odissi and other dance forms. Other than festivals, there are no regular cultural programs here. For information, contact the Orissa Department of Tourism or the College of Dance, Drama, and Music, near Rabindra Mandap.

Nightlife

For a local place with a mixed clientele in the evening, try the dimly lit bar in the **Hotel Pushpak** (⊠ Cuttack Rd., ☎ 675/408371).The **Hotel Swosti** (103 Janpath, ☎ 674/404178 or 674/404397) is a good informal option if you're in the center of town. The bar at the **Oberoi** (C.B. 1, Nayapalli, ☎ 674/301010) is a smart place to relax.

SHOPPING

Bhubaneswar's main shopping area is **Capital Market,** along the central stretch of Raj Path. Several good fabric and handicrafts shops, including the two government emporiums, are in the **Tower Market** shopping complex off the eastern side of Raj Path. All along Raj Path are stalls selling everything from bananas to bedcovers, mostly wares for locals; most are open daily from around 6 AM to 10 PM.

Kalamandir (⊠ 3 Western Tower Market Bldg., ☎ 674/530596) is one of the largest fabric and clothing shops in eastern India; it stocks traditional Orissan textiles as well as styles from all over India. **Kalinga Art Palace** (⊠ Plot 2132/4323, Nageswar Tangi, ☎ 674/51454) specializes in tribal artwork, with a notably large and high-quality collection of brass-wire dhokra, both new and antique. **Odissika** (⊠ 265 Lewis

Rd., ☎ 674/433314) has a host of stone carvings, terra-cotta objects, dhokra, and other authentic Orissan handicrafts. **Orissan State Handloom Weaver's Cooperative Society (Boyanika)** (✉ Western Tower Market Bldg., Hall 2, Ashok Nagar, ☎ no phone) has lovely saris, bedcovers, and fabrics in various Orissan styles and textures.

Sudarshan Arts and Crafts Village (✉ CB-5, Nayapalli, ☎ 674/402052) is a teaching center for stone-carving, where you can stroll through the small yard and watch young artisans squatting in the shade chiseling away at 10 different kinds of stone. **Utkalika** (✉ Orissa State Handicrafts Emporium, 1 Eastern Tower Market Bldg., Ashok Nagar, ☎ 674/530187), the government's fixed-price emporium, has a great selection of every type of Orissan handicraft.

SOUTH TO THE BAY OF BENGAL

The countryside around Bhubaneswar is lush with rice paddies so green they seem to glow, as well as coconut, mango, banana, and cashew trees. These verdant stretches are punctuated with tiny villages of mud huts with thatched roofs, their dry brown walls decorated with traditional white paintings. Konark, near the coast, is renowned for its extraordinary, half-ruined Sun Temple, and Puri's Jagannath Temple is one of Hinduism's holiest shrines. The villages of Raghurajpur and Pipli are known for their craftwork. Dhauli, the hill associated with Ashoka the Great, has a gentle Buddhist pagoda; Gopalpur-on-Sea is a beach destination.

Konark

❷ *64 km (40 mi) southeast of Bhubaneswar*

The sleepy town of Konark is home to one of India's most fabulous temples. The village exists for the temple, earning its income entirely from tourism via souvenir shops, food stalls, and basic restaurants.

★ Legend shrouds the **Sun Temple,** or "Black Pagoda," so called because of the dark patina that has covered it over the centuries. Built by King Narasimha in the 13th century in the shape of the sun god Surya's chariot—probably as much as a monument to Narasimha and his victory over the Muslims as to Surya—it is a wonder of architecture and engineering. Today, only half the main temple and the audience hall remain to suggest the Sun Temple's original shape, but the complex once had a dancing hall, an audience hall, and a tremendous tower that soared to 227 ft; by 1869 the tower had fallen to ruin, and the audience hall had to be filled with stone slabs and sealed off to prevent its collapse. The temple's location on coastal sand (it's not quite coastal; the sea has since receded 3 km [2 mi] from here) is majestic, but the briny air and the softness of the underlying dunes have taken their toll.

The Sun Temple was designed in the form of a chariot, with 24 wheels pulled by seven straining horses. Every last one of its surfaces is intricately carved with some of the most fantastic sculpture in India: platforms, horses, colossal mythical animals, whimsical depictions of daily life, images of war, erotic pairings. Every structural feature is significant; the chariot's seven horses represent the seven days of the week, the 24 wheels are the 24 fortnights of the Indian year, and the eight spokes of each wheel are the eight *pahars* into which the ancients divided day and night.

Try to arrive between 7 and 8 AM, before the busloads of pilgrims and other tourists show up. The Archaeological Survey of India provides guides, but ask to see an identification badge, as many less-informed freelance guides are also eager to take you around. The going rate is Rs. 20 per person. A tourist-information officer at the **Yatri Nivas** (☎ 6758/35820 or 6758/35821), an Orissa Tourism Development Corporation (OTDC) guest house just before the temple, is on duty Monday through Saturday from 10 to 5 (except the second Saturday of each month), and the guest-house staff can help travelers 24 hours a day.

Any of the tour operators and travel agencies in Bhubaneswar can arrange a day trip to Konark for you, but you can usually get a better price by simply cutting a deal with a local taxi driver. The trip takes about an hour and a half. ✉ *Off Puri Rd.* ✆ *Rs. 5.* ⊙ *Daily sunrise–sunset.*

Puri

❸ *60 km (36 mi) south of Bhubaneswar, 35 km (21 mi) south west of Konark*

The coastal town of Puri is heavily visited because it contains one of Hinduism's most sacred sites, the **Jagannath Temple.** Vast and beautiful, the temple is strictly off-limits to non-Hindus, who can glimpse it only from a distance; even the late Prime Minister Indira Gandhi was denied entrance, as she had married a non-Hindu. Still, it's fascinating to watch the pilgrims thrust their way to the temple through the crowds of vendors and vehicles that jam Puri's main street. Puri attracts even more crushing hordes during Rath Yatra (the midsummer festival, involving processions of deities on carts), one of the most spectacular of India's temple fairs.

Although Puri is touted as a beach getaway, it's gotten rather seedy. Locals sometimes use the beach as a cat does a sandbox. If you're looking for some clean, uncrowded sand in Orissa, hold out for Gopalpur-on-Sea.

Lodging

$$$–$$$$ ✗▥ **Toshali Sands.** On 30 acres along the still Nuanai river, this resort is an isolated and peaceful getaway. Lush cashew trees line the river, which empties into the Bay of Bengal, and the resort has a private beach. Rooms are tastefully decorated to provide a rustic Orissan atmosphere without sacrificing luxury. The restaurant, Phulpatna, serves a multi-cuisine menu which includes traditional Orissan cuisine, so hard to find in the restaurants of the state. Ask in advance for an Orissan *thali*, which includes *dahl ma* (dahl with local vegetables like yams, beans, pumpkin, eggplant, potatoes, and tomatoes), *ruhu* (sweet fish) curry, *khata* (sweet/sour condiment), *kheer* (rice with condensed milk), and curd with eggplant. ✉ *Ethnic Village Resort, Konark Marine Dr., 752002,* ☎ *6752/23571 through 6752/23573, or 6752/22888,* ☏ *6752/23899,* ▨ *www.toshaliresorts.com/set-sands.htm. 104 units. Restaurant, bar, pool, exercise room, health club, badminton, Ping-Pong, cinema, playground. AC, DC, MC, V.*

$$$ ▥ **Mayfair Beach Resort.** This vaguely New Mexico–style building with burnt-orange stucco walls is softened by lots of green vegetation. Most of the rooms have balconies that look over rooftops to the sea, just 300 ft away, and are cozily furnished with bric-a-brac. Meals are served on a patio, which is also a pleasant place to relax and have a beer. ✉ *Chakratirtha Rd., Puri 752002,* ☎ *6752/24041, 6752/24254, 674/24313,* ☏ *6752/24242. 34 rooms. 2 restaurants, pool, travel services. AE, MC, V.*

$ ▥ **South Eastern Railway Hotel.** Sometimes called the BNR Hotel, this is the only designated Heritage Hotel in Orissa. With its Raj ambience and relaxed pace (the SILENCE BETWEEN 2 AND 4 PM sign ensures you an undisturbed siesta), it harks back to an age gone by. High ceilings and sea breezes keep the place pleasantly cool; here, as at the Mayfair, you're about 300 ft from the beach. There's even a billiards room where you can shoot a few frames at leisure. Inquire about off-season discounts. ⊠ *Chakratirtha Rd., Puri 752002,* ☎ *6752/22063, 6752/ 23005, or 6752/23006,* ℻ *6752/23005. 34 rooms. Restaurant, billiards, laundry service, travel services. MC, V.*

Raghurajpur

★ ❹ *16 km (10 mi) north of Puri, 44 km (27 mi) south of Bhubaneswar*

Less than two hours' drive from Bhubaneswar, the artisans' village of Raghurajpur is a must-see. Every dwelling in this idyllic village set back from the main road is owned by a skilled artisan, and the art they produce—stone and wood carvings, pata chitra, tala patra (intricately etched and painted palm leaves)—is worth a trip in itself. If you're interested, the craftspeople will demonstrate their processes. The pata chitra artists, for example, do everything the old-fashioned way, from the preparatory rubbing of cloth with tamarind-seed gum and stones to executing razor-fine strokes of color with dyes made from plants and crushed stones. True, the prices are raised for travelers, but you can bargain them down to lower than you'd pay anywhere else; just expect to pay in rupees. Most artisans welcome customers daily from around 9 to 1 and 3 to 6.

Pipli

❺ *16 km (10 mi) southeast of Bhubaneswar, 28 km (17 mi) north of Puri*

The little village of Pipli is famous throughout India for its brightly colored appliqué work. Dozens of shops line both sides of the main street, each crammed with piles of cheery wall hangings, bedspreads, lamp shades, bags, beach umbrellas, and more in patchworks of bright greens, yellows, blues, and reds. You can watch the artisans sew in some of the shops.

Dhauli

★ ❻ *6 km (4 mi) southwest of Bhubaneswar*

It was from the top of this hill that India's legendary king, Ashoka the Great, looked down, in 272 BC, over the verdant countryside littered with bodies after his armies invaded what was then Kalinga. Overcome with horror, Ashoka underwent a transformation: He abandoned his drive to conquer, began to practice Buddhism, and went on to incite a moral and spiritual revolution throughout Orissa and the rest of India. The spot of **Ashoka's vantage point and conversion** is marked by the carving of an elephant emerging from a rock—said to be the oldest rock-cut sculpture in India (3rd century BC)—symbolizing the birth of Buddha and the emergence of Buddhism. Also carved into the stone are the Ashokan edicts in which the once-ruthless warrior declared that all men are his children.

A bit farther up the hill from Ashoka's vantage point and conversion is the **Shanti Stupa,** a Buddhist peace pagoda built jointly by Japanese and Indian groups in 1972. Visible from most points in Bhubaneswar, this striking, white-domed building, topped with several umbrella-like protrusions, resembles a massive alien crustacean from below; moving closer, you can sense how beautiful and peaceful it is. The view from here is lovely: the Daya River curving through the green rice paddies and cashew trees. ⊠ *Puri Rd.*

Gopalpur-on-Sea

❼ *178 km (110 mi) southwest of Bhubaneswar*

Gopalpur-on-Sea, Orissa's most popular beach resort is actually just a small fishing village with a few hotels scattered along the shore. The town itself has one street, which in turn has a few shops to satisfy the locals. The beach is long; you don't have to walk far to find solitude. To get here, take a three-hour train ride from Bhubaneswar to Berhampur (164 km, or 102 mi, south of the city), then transfer to an autorickshaw (Rs. 80) for the 14-km (9-mi) ride southeast.

Lodging

$$$ ▪ **Oberoi Palm Beach.** While the Oberoi is the best hotel in Gopalpur-on-Sea, don't expect the kind of Oberoi you experienced in Calcutta or Hyderabad. All is a bit worn here, and the staff may not be lickety-split. Rooms in this U-shaped building face the courtyard; those on the ground floor are susceptible to looks from passers-by. The dining room serves good Indian and Continental fare, but tends to smell like curry. A lawn, with games for children, separates the hotel from the beach. ✉ *Jagmohan Singh Rd., Gopalpur-on-Sea 761002,* ☎ *680/242021,* 𝖥𝖠𝖷 *680/282300. 18 rooms. Restaurant, pool. AE, DC, MC, V.*

$ ▪ **Holiday Home.** The location is excellent—just across the road from the beach and minutes from the center of town (such as it is). Rooms offer no more pampering than a bed and a table and chairs, but they're mopped down every day and—despite gaping holes, exposed pipes, and falling plaster—the bathrooms are functional. The overhead fans are hardly necessary with the constant sea breeze cooling the rooms. The staff is helpful and friendly. Meals can be served on request. ✉ *Gopalpur-on-Sea 761002,* ☎ *680/282049. 18 rooms. Restaurant. No credit cards.*

BHUBANESWAR A TO Z

To research prices, get advice from other travelers, and book travel arrangements, visit www.fodors.com.

AIR TRAVEL

Bhubaneswar Airport is about 5 km (3 mi) from the center of town. Indian Airlines flies to Bhubaneswar from Delhi, Calcutta, Madras, and Hyderabad. Jet Airways flies daily from Calcutta to Bhubaneswar.

CARRIERS
➤ CONTACTS: **Indian Airlines** (☎ 674/406472; 674/530593; 674/401084 at airport; 141 within airport). **Jet Airways** (☎ 674/535877 or 674/535308, 𝖶𝖤𝖡 asp.jetairways.com).

AIRPORTS AND TRANSFERS

The trip between the airport and city center takes about 15 to 20 minutes. Most hotels provide free shuttle service if you give them your flight information in advance. White Ambassador tourist taxis wait outside the terminal; fares are theoretically fixed, but be sure to agree on one before setting out. The fare to a central hotel should be around Rs. 75; to the Oberoi, slightly farther, about Rs. 110.

BUS TRAVEL TO AND FROM BHUBANESWAR

The new bus station, where you can catch an overnight bus to Calcutta, is 5 km (3 mi) from the city center on the main highway heading towards Calcutta. The old bus stand, also known as the old Capital bus stand, is near the Market Building shopping area in the city center.

BUS TRAVEL WITHIN ORISSA

Buses are the most inexpensive way to travel, but be prepared for extreme conditions: the buses are unreliable and the bus routes only go on main roads, leaving you to walk 2–4 km (1–2 mi) to get to villages. Car and driver is the best way to get around Orissa.

CARS AND DRIVERS

You can hire a car and driver from a travel agency, but taxis willingly rent themselves out for half or a full day. When negotiating with the driver, specify which places you plan to visit, as your itinerary, plus the length of time, will determine the fare. Four hours of local sightseeing should cost about Rs. 250 in a non-air-conditioned Ambassador car and around Rs. 700 with air-conditioning. For shorter excursions covering more than 10 km (6 mi) per hour, figure about Rs. 3 per km (Rs. 7 for a car with A/C), with a halt charge of Rs. 10 per hour.

EMERGENCIES

In the event of a medical or other emergency, your best bet is to speak with a hotel staffer.

MONEY

CURRENCY EXCHANGE

Most Western-style hotels will change money for their guests. You can also cash traveler's checks at the various national banks in Bhubaneswar; try the main branch of the State Bank of India. Banking hours are weekdays, 10 to 2, and sometimes Saturday 10 to noon.

➤ EXCHANGE SERVICE: **State Bank of India** (⊠ near Market Bldg., Raj Path).

TAXIS

Taxis in Orissa don't have meters, so you have to dicker for every ride. Ask your hotel for the appropriate taxi fare and then negotiate.

TOURS

The Orissa Tourism Development Corporation (OTDC) has reliable cars and drivers and conducts several good tours of Bhubaneswar and the whole region, all at reasonable rates. Swosti Travels is a well-established local company with strong experience in the region. You can also try Mercury Travels, which has cars and drivers at decent rates. Sita World Travels arranges trips in and around Bhubaneswar. Nabagunjara Travels Pvt. Ltd., in business since 1982, leads tours in Orissa.

A private tour guide can seriously enhance your sightseeing, especially with such artistically rich and potentially foreign monuments as Orissa's temples. The most knowledgeable and English-proficient guides are those trained by the Government of India Tourist Office; you can hire one through the OTDC or the Government of India Tourist Office for around Rs. 250 per half-day and Rs. 500 for a full day (eight hours). Overnight stays cost an additional Rs. 800 for the guide's food and accommodation.

➤ CONTACTS: **Mercury Travels** (⊠ The Oberoi, Nayapalli, ☎ 674/ 440890). **Nabagunjara Travels Pvt. Ltd.** (⊠ Balighar, 10 Rathandandra Rd., Bhubaneswar, ☎ 431659/759; ⊠ 9 S. N. Banerjee Rd., Calcutta, ☎ 33/244-0802). **Orissa Tourism Development Corporation (OTDC)** (⊠ Panthanivas, Old Block, Lewis Rd., Bhubaneswar, ☎ 674/ 431515). **Sita World Travels** (⊠ 14A Bapuji Nagar, Janpath, ☎ 674/ 531408). **Swosti Travels** (⊠ 103 Janpath, ☎ 674/518257, FAX 674/ 407524).

TRAIN TRAVEL

Bhubaneswar is on the Calcutta–Hyderabad/Madras line. The trip takes about eight hours from Calcutta on the overnight train, 20 hours from Hyderabad, and 25 hours from Madras. Suggestions from the staff at the train station's tourist-information center should be taken with a grain of salt; they'll push high-priced hotels from which they get commissions. Auto-rickshaws stand ready to meet all trains. The main exit, where the reservation office is located, is on the west side (on your right, coming from Calcutta). If you want to go directly to Cuttack Road, where the cheaper hotels are, take the east exit.

TRANSPORTATION WITHIN BHUBANESWAR

Hiring a car and driver for a half or full day is not expensive, and is the most convenient way to get around the city—you avoid having to haggle over fares with taxi or auto-rickshaw drivers.

Auto-rickshaws are cheaper though slower than taxis, but quicker through heavy traffic. Apply the same fare rules as you would for taxis. For short distances, cycle-rickshaws are easiest. A horde of them will await you at the train station; negotiate a fare with your pedaler before he pushes off.

VISITOR INFORMATION

The Orissa Department of Tourism is the best source of information on the state. The main office is open Monday through Saturday from 10 to 5 (closed second Sat. of month). The Government of India Tourist Office is also helpful; they're available weekdays from 10 to 5.

➤ TOURIST INFORMATION: **Government of India Tourist Office** (✉ B-21, B. J. B. Nagar, Kalpana Area, Bhubaneswar 751014, ☎ 674/432203; Bhubaneswar airport, ☎ no phone). **Orissa Department of Tourism** (✉ Paryatan Bhawan, Bhubaneswar 751014, ☎ 674/432177, WEB www. orissa-tourism.com; Bhubaneswar airport, ☎ 674/404006; Bhubaneswar train station, ☎ 674/530715).

14 CALCUTTA

Calcutta's streets tell stories. Old mansions dripping with moss and spotted with mildew recall both British influence and local affluence. Riches and poverty mingle here: upscale residential blocks border one-room tenements and shanties. Known at once for its Bengali heritage and cosmopolitan outlook, Calcutta is the creative capital of India, promoting art, music, and drama and drawing the best from performers and their fans. It will surprise you with its warmth and hospitality.

By Nigel Fisher

Updated by
Soumya
Bhattacharya

NOTHING CAN PREPARE YOU for Calcutta. As the birthplace of an empire and the home of the late Mother Teresa, as a playground for the rich and a haven for the destitute, as a wellspring of creative energy and a center for Marxist agitation, Calcutta dares people to make sense of it. Whether it shocks you or seduces you, Calcutta will impress itself upon you. To understand India today and learn from it, a trip to Calcutta is vital.

In 1690, Job Charnock, an agent for the British East India Company, leased the villages of Sutanati, Gobindpur, and Kalikutta and formed a trading post to supply his firm. Legend has it that Charnock had won the hearts of Bengalis when he married a local widow, thus saving her from *sati* (the custom that calls for a widow to throw herself on her husband's funeral pyre). Through Charnock's venture, the British gained a foothold in what had been the Sultanate of Delhi under the Moguls, and the directors of the East India Company became Indian *zamindars* (landowners) for the first time. It was here, as traders and landowners, that British entrepreneurs and adventurers began what would amount to the conquest of India and the establishment of the British Raj. More than any other city in India, Calcutta is tied to the evolution and disintegration of the British presence.

Calcutta is the capital of the state of West Bengal, which borders Bangladesh (formerly East Bengal). The Bengali people—animated, garrulous, intellectual, spirited, argumentative, anarchic, imaginative, and creative—have dominated this city and made it the soul of India for more than 150 years. Among the first to react to the intellectual and political stimuli of the West, they have produced many of India's most respected filmmakers, writers, scientists, musicians, dancers, and philosophers. Having embraced 19th-century European humanism, such Bengalis as the poet Rabindranath Tagore and others revived their indigenous culture and made the first organized efforts to oust the British. Emotions here ran high early on, and agitation in Bengal broke away from what would later be called Gandhian politics to choose terrorism—one reason the British moved their capital from Calcutta to Delhi in 1911.

Calcutta remained cosmopolitan and prosperous throughout the British period. But after Independence and Partition, in 1947, trouble began when the world's center of jute processing and distribution (Calcutta) was politically separated from its actual production center (the eastern Bengali hinterland). For Calcutta and the new East Pakistan, Partition was equivalent to separating the fingers of an industry from the thumb. Natural disasters—commonly cyclones and droughts but also, as in 1937, earthquakes—had long sent millions from East Bengal (which later became East Pakistan) to Calcutta in search of shelter and sustenance; after Partition a wave of 4 million political refugees from East Pakistan compounded and complicated the pressure. Conflict with China and Pakistan created millions more throughout the 1960s, and Pakistan's 1971 military crackdown alone sent 10 million temporary refugees into the city from what would soon become Bangladesh. By the mid-1970s, Calcutta was widely seen as the ultimate urban disaster. Riddled with disease and squalor, plagued by garbage and decay, the heart of the British Raj, the Paris of Asia, had quickly and dramatically collapsed.

Or had it? Calcutta's entire metropolitan district covers over 426 square km (264 square mi) and is home to over 12 million people. It comprises two municipal corporation areas (Calcutta and Howrah),

32 municipalities, 62 nonmunicipal urban centers, and more than 500 villages, and it hasn't really collapsed. What the city has learned, and has learned to accept, is that it's become marginalized in contemporary India's political and economic power structure. The people here have borne that acceptance with a slightly tired air of resignation and stoicism. A Marxist government has been ruling West Bengal for the last quarter of a century from the seat of power in Calcutta. But even they have adapted to the the new globalized economy, fusing Marx with market economics and talking less about agrarian reforms and more about the information technology revolution. As one local put it, "Calcutta is full of challenges, but there is hope and even fun in meeting those challenges." Today's traveler may actually notice more poverty in Bombay than in the city more often associated with human strife. Calcutta remains open, smiling, and thoughtful: amid the difficulties there is dignity, and amid the crises there are ideas.

Name Changes

In the last few decades, many of Calcutta's streets have been haphazardly renamed. Though some maps and street signs have only the new names, you're more likely to see just the old or both. Taxis and rickshaws use the names interchangeably, but old names are still favored, as most of the new names are ridiculously long and obscure. The most important name changes: Chowringhee Road is now Jawaharlal Nehru (J. L. Nehru) Road; Ballygunge Circular is now Pramathesh Barua Sarani; Bowbazar is now B. B. Ganguly Street; Harington Street is now Ho Chi Minh Sarani; Lansdowne Road is now Sarat Bose Road; Lower Circular Road is now A. J. C. Bose Road; Rippon Street is now Muzaffar Ahmed Street; and Theater Road is now Shakespeare Sarani. A complete list is available at the Government of India Tourist Office or in *Calcutta: Gateway to the East*. As if changing the names of streets was not confusing enough, the name of the city itself was officially recently changed. Calcutta, in all government records, is now called Kolkata, a transformation that's supposed to contribute to ridding this and other Indian cities of their colonial past. But as with the names of streets, the two names of the city are used interchangeably.

Pleasures and Pastimes

Dining

Like no other city in India, Calcutta has a tradition of dining out. Ironically, Bengali food itself was noticeably long absent from the city's restaurants, but this has changed in recent years. Bengali cuisine is highly varied in flavor and has both vegetarian and nonvegetarian strands, with fish figuring heavily. Prawns and shrimp are two favorites but because both are important exports, prices have risen and they are beyond the bounds of the average Bengali except as treats. Two popular Bengali dishes are *macher jhol* (fish curry) and *chingri malai* curry (prawns cooked in coconut milk and spices). Note that Thursday in Calcutta is meatless—no red meat is served in most establishments.

The unique cuisine that has developed in Calcutta since the influx of the Moguls in the 16th century is called Calcutta-Mughlai and remains the most common food in Calcutta today—it's what you'll see in carts and stalls throughout the city. Staples include *champ* (chicken or mutton cooked slowly in large, thick-cast open pans), *birianis* (rice-and-meat dishes), and tandoori items, none of which resembles dishes of the same name in places such as Oudh or Hyderabad. From roadside vendors, the most popular item is the Calcutta roll, in which seasoned meats and chutneys are wrapped in thick *parathas* (rich Indian breads) with onions and sometimes even eggs. Not to be missed are Bengali sweets, which fill the life of every native: sweet shops are everywhere, and the variety of their fare—from *payash* (fine-quality rice cooked in thickened milk) to *gokul pitha* (coconut and solidified milk balls, fried and dipped in sugar syrup) is beyond tempting. Two unsurpassed goodies are *rosogollas* (balls of cottage cheese soaked in sugar syrup), associated specifically with Calcutta, and the classic Bengali *misti doi* (sweetened yogurt).

Lodging

Calcutta's top few hotels are luxury establishments that meet international standards and then some. An exceptionally high luxury tax of 22% is added to your bill.

Shopping

All of India tempts the shopper here: a vast array of goods arrive in Calcutta from around the subcontinent, including crafts from Bangladesh and neighboring northeastern states. Prices are tantalizingly inexpensive. The irritants are touts, hustlers, and the instant friends who approach you claiming they have nothing to sell and later getting openly ticked off if you don't buy their goods. Learn to bargain, but be wary of where you do it. Although everything purchased from a roadside vendor is negotiable, government emporiums, shops that sell branded goods, or places with fixed-price tags will be affronted if you try to bargain.

Some of the most interesting crafts in West Bengal are brightly painted terra-cotta figurines and bas-reliefs, as well as other pottery items. *Dhokra* are cast figures made of clay and metal. Shells, bell metal, and soapstone are other media used in popular Bengali trinkets and figurines. Calcutta's bazaars and shops sell all kinds of textiles, including embroideries. With its longtime traditions of literacy and cosmopolitanism, Calcutta is also a good place to restock your English-language reading material.

Street Life

The vibrant interplay between survival and extinction is unusually manifest in Calcutta: the city throbs with a tenacious grasping for life. You feel it in the barrage on your senses of sound, smell, and sight. It is exhilarating, exhausting, and occasionally disquieting. Calcutta imposes culture shock—pedestrians scurry out of the way of horn-blaring vehicles swerving to avoid another beat-up vehicle and scraping past the rib-cage of a rickshaw-wallah (person who pulls a rickshaw). The frequent political processions can get old, but a walk through the old bookstalls on College Street will leave you rejuvenated.

EXPLORING CALCUTTA

Calcutta and Howrah (also written as Haora) straddle the Hooghly River with Calcutta on the east side, Howrah on the west. Across the Hooghly from Calcutta's old quarter, the Howrah district—which holds Calcutta's massive train station—is a constantly expanding suburb. On the eastern side of town is Salt Lake City, a planned, spotlessly clean, upscale residential community.

In Calcutta itself, the Howrah Bridge spills into Bara Bazaar, the vibrant wholesale market area that anchors the city's commerce. North Calcutta includes Bara Bazaar and Calcutta University and extends to the distant neighborhood of Chitpur and the Jain Temple in Tala. The heart of Central Calcutta remains B.B.D. Bagh (Binoy-Badel-Dinesh Bagh, formerly Dalhousie Square), where commerce and government have been concentrated since British times. Central Calcutta also holds the expansive Maidan park, the crowded bazaar at New Market, and the upmarket shops and restaurants on Park Street. At the south end of the Maidan are the Victoria Memorial and Calcutta's racecourse. South Calcutta has the Kali Temple and the late Mother Teresa's hospice in Kalighat and the National Library and zoo in Alipore. To the east is the Science City complex, which includes a huge auditorium and museum with scientific and educational exhibits.

Great Itineraries

At just over 300 years of age, Calcutta is a relatively new Indian city. You can breeze through its monuments, buildings, and temples in two or three days. Calcutta does offer something other than buildings, though—its teeming life and ambience. This can wear you down in two days or entice you to stay much longer than your schedule allows.

IF YOU HAVE 2 DAYS

If you have only one day in Calcutta, you'll have to be very selective. With two days, start by taking the pulse of the city's heart, **B.B.D. Bagh.** Take a taxi to the Jain **Paresnath Temple,** and from there continue to the eclectic **Marble Palace,** nearby **Nakhoda Mosque,** and **Rabindra Bharati University Museum.** At day's end, cross the **Howrah Bridge** by cab and drive south along the bank of the Hooghly River for a good look back at the city. (Cross back on the Second Hooghly Bridge, or Vivekananda Setu.) The next day, enter the **Maidan** and visit the **Victoria Memorial** and **St. Paul's Cathedral.** Back out on **Chowringhee** (J. L. Nehru Road), amble up to the **Indian Museum.** This plan should leave you time enough for shopping in the late afternoon and early evening in the fabulous, century-old New Market, where everything under the sun is for sale under one roof.

IF YOU HAVE 3 DAYS

You can see most of Calcutta's major sights comfortably in three days. Start by exploring **B.B.D. Bagh,** then take a taxi to **College Street** and walk around for a sense of the city's intellectual energy. Walk from College Street to the **Nakhoda Mosque,** European-style **Marble Palace,** and **Rabindra Bharati University Museum,** with its Bengali-school paintings and Tagore memorabilia. From here it's a short cab ride to the **Paresnath Temple.** Continue on to **Kumartuli** to see artists create clay icons by the river.

The next day, taxi up to the **Belur Math Shrine,** then cross back to the **Dakshineshwar Kali Temple** for a quick overview of Hinduism. Driving south on the east side of the river, cross the **Howrah Bridge** and drive south on Foreshore Road for the best view of Calcutta over the Hooghly. Cross back on the Second Hooghly Bridge. You can now enter the **Maidan** and breathe some fresh air before before visiting the **Victoria Memorial, Ft. William,** and the **Eden Gardens.** Finish by treating yourself to some shopping in **New Market.**

On day three, taxi down to **Nirmal Hirday** to visit the late Mother Teresa's first charitable home, then walk over to the famous **Kalighat Kali Temple.** You'll need a cab from here to **St. Paul's Cathedral,** but from the cathedral you can walk to **Chowringhee** and up to the **Indian Museum,** detouring a few blocks to Park Street to read colonial history from the headstones in **South Street Park Cemetery.**

When to Tour Calcutta

The hottest weather arrives in April and grows increasingly stifling through June, when the monsoon season begins. Monsoons run through mid-September and cool Calcutta down, though the occasional downpour means you can expect a soaking or two. The mild winter sets in

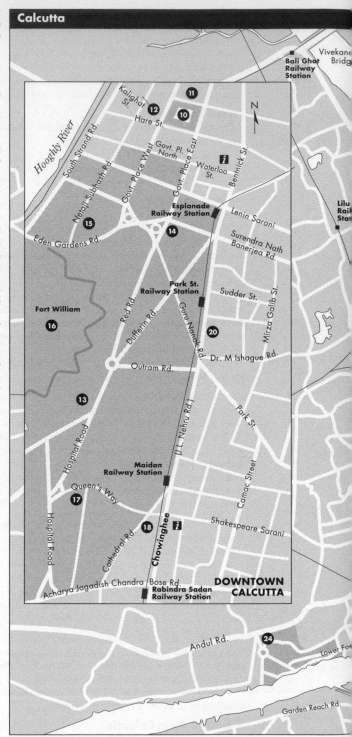

Calcutta

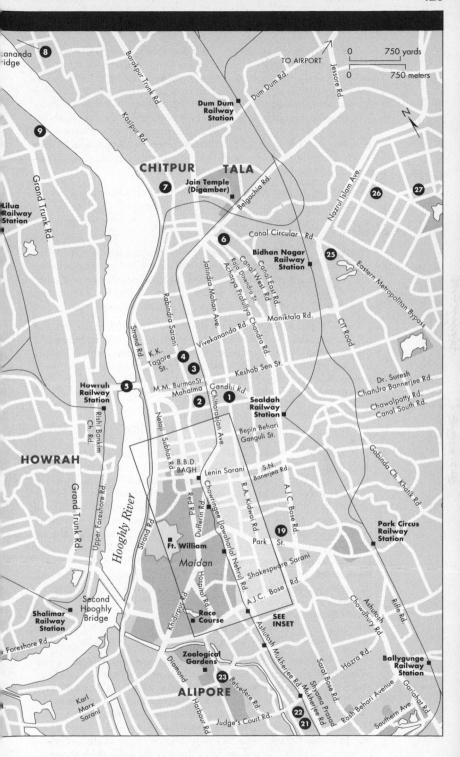

TO AIRPORT

0   750 yards
0   750 meters

8

ananda
ridge

9

Barakpur Trunk Rd.

Kasipur Rd.

**Dum Dum
Railway
Station**

Dum Dum Rd.

Jessore Rd.

26

27

CHITPUR   TALA

7   **Jain Temple
(Digamber)**

Belgachia Rd.

Nazrul Islam Ave.

**Lilua
Railway
Station**

Grand Trunk Rd.

Strand Rd.

6

Canal Circular   Rd.

**Bidhan Nagar
Railway
Station**

25

Eastern Metropolitan Bypass

Jatindra Mohan Ave.

Rabindra Sarani

Canal West Rd.

Raja Dinendra St.

Acharya Prafulya Chandra Rd.

Canal East Rd.

Maniktala Rd.

CIT Road

**Howrah
Railway
Station**   **5**

Vivekananda Rd.

K. K.
Tagore
St.

4
3

Keshab Sen St.

Dr. Suresh
Chandra Bannerjee Rd.

Chawalpatty Rd.
Canal South Rd.

M.M. Burman St.
Mahalma   Gandhi Rd.

2   **1**

Chitaranjan Ave.

**Sealdah
Railway
Station**

Rishi Bankim Ch. Rd.

Netaji Subhas Rd.

Bepin Behari
Ganguli St.

Gobinda Ch. Khatik Rd.

HOWRAH

Grand Trunk Rd.

Strand Rd.

Upper Foreshore Rd.

Hooghly River

**B.B.D.
BAGH**

Lenin Sarani

Red Rd.

Dufferin Rd.

Chowringee (Jawaharlal Nehru) Rd.

R.A. Kidwai Rd.

S.N.
Banerjea Rd.

A.J.C. Bose Rd.

**Park Circus
Railway
Station**

Ft. William

19

Park   St.

Shakespeare Sarani

Maidan

Hospital Rd.

A.J.C.   Bose   Rd.

Khidirpur Rd.

Ashutosh Chowdhury Rd.

Rifle Rd.

**Shalimar
Railway
Station**

Foreshore Rd.

Second
Hooghly
Bridge

**Race
Course**

**SEE
INSET**

Ashutosh Mukherjee Rd.

Sarat Bose Rd.

Hazra Rd.

**Ballygunge
Railway
Station**

Karl
Marx
Sarani

Diamond

**Zoological
Gardens**

Belvedere Rd.

23

Shyama Prasad Mukherjee Rd.

Rash Behari Avenue

Gariahat Rd.

ALIPORE

Harbour Rd.

Judge's Court Rd.

22

21

Southern Ave.

around December and lasts till March. This is the best time to visit. For an extraordinary visit, see Calcutta during the greatest Bengali fes

tival of the year, the Durga Puja (Durga is an incarnation of Kali, Calcutta's patron goddess). Colorful, handmade Hindu idols, sometimes in excess of 20 ft tall, are ceremoniously moved in large processions through the streets for several hours before reaching the river and being immersed in the Hooghly. The pujas (homage; literally, "worship") take place over several days in September or October; confirm the dates beforehand with the tourist office or an Indian travel agent. The rites and processions have an amazing vibrancy, often blending tradition with innovation; some idols even honor contemporary themes such as recent flood victims or the film star of the moment.

Numbers in the text correspond to numbers in the margin and on the Calcutta map.

North Calcutta

★ The streets in northern Calcutta are more crowded and narrower than those elsewhere in the city. This—the old village of Sutanuti—is where the Indians lived while the British spread their estates east and south of Ft. William and Dalhousie Square (B.B.D. Bagh). The architecture is charming, reflecting some Italian and Dutch influence.

North Calcutta's attractions are somewhat scattered. You'll need to take taxis at least sporadically. The bazaar areas surrounding Mahatama Gandhi Road are at once intensely commercial and residential; tourists are thin on the ground here, despite the fascinating sights and atmosphere. You may attract some curious stares, but anyone you stop and speak to is bound to be friendly and welcoming.

A Good Tour
Start with a morning coffee at the Indian Coffee House on **College Street** ①, then browse through the street's bookstalls. Walk west, crossing Chittaranjan Avenue, to the huge, sandstone **Nakhoda Mosque** ②, and climb to the top floor for a great view of the bustle in the streets below. Walk back to Chittaranjan Avenue, turn left (north), then left after a few blocks on Muktaram Basu Street—halfway down the block on the left you'll see the **Marble Palace** ③, a melange of international architecture, statues, and furnishings. From the palace it's a short walk north to Tagore Street, where you turn left for the **Rabindra Bharati University Museum** ④, in the poet's former home. Walking further west on Tagore Street brings you to the Hooghly River, with the **Howrah Bridge** ⑤ a block to the south. North and south of the Howrah Bridge along the waterfront is the wholesale flower market—before 7 AM. Also in this area is Strand Road, which heads south toward the Second Hooghly Bridge and, in the evening, makes for a delightful riverside stroll in that area. At sunset, both river and city look magical; Calcutta becomes a different town altogether.

A short taxi ride will bring you to the Jain **Paresnath Temple** ⑥, perhaps one of the cleanest buildings in Calcutta. A 30-minute walk or quick cab ride farther north, near the river, is an area called **Kumartuli** ⑦, where thousands of potters fashion clay images of gods and goddesses for Hindu festivals. The **Dakshineshwar Kali Temple** ⑧, a major Hindu pilgrimage site, requires another taxi ride north. Cross the Second Hooghly Bridge (again, it's best to take a cab) to the suburb of Howrah and head south along Belur Road to the **Belur Math Shrine** ⑨, headquarters of the Ramakrishna Mission. Return downtown by taxi.

TIMING

This tour takes the better part of a day and can be very tiring; pack a lunch before you set off. The Marble Palace, Rabindra Bharati museum, Paresnath Temple, and Dakshineshwar Kali Temple each take 30–60 minutes to absorb. Try to sandwich your touring between the rush hours, and remember that the Belur Math Shrine is closed from noon to 3:30 and the Nakhoda Mosque is off-limits for a spell on Friday morning.

Sights to See

9 Belur Math Shrine. This is the headquarters of the Ramakrishna Mission, a reform movement inspired by Ramakrishna Paramahansa, who died in 1886. Having forsaken his privileged Brahmin heritage, Ramakrishna preached the unity of religious faiths and an adherence to altruistic values for all people. His disciple, Swami Vivekananda, established the mission in 1898. The Belur Math Shrine resembles a church, a temple, or a mosque, depending on where you're standing. Somber *aarti* (chants and hymns) are sung in the immense prayer hall every evening; visitors are more than welcome. ✉ *Belur Rd., Howrah (2 km/1 mi south of Second Hooghly Bridge [Vivekananda Setu]).* ☉ *Daily 6:30– noon and 3:30–7:30.*

1 College Street. Part of the animated area around Calcutta University, the sidewalks of College Street are stuffed with bookstalls where you just might discover a treasure. The neighborhood establishments here, like the classic **Indian Coffee House** (✉ 15 Bankin Chatterjee St.), are crowded every night with students and intellectuals. Opposite the coffeehouse, a huge colonial building houses the university's **Presidency College**, arguably the most prestigious seat of learning in India.

★ **8 Dakshineshwar Kali Temple.** Far north along the Hooghly, this 19th-century complex with 13 temples is a major pilgrimage site for devotees of Shiva, Kali, Radha, and Krishna. The variety of temples makes this site a good introduction to the Hindu deities for the uninitiated. It was here that the 19th-century mystic Ramakrishna had the vision that led him to renounce his Brahmin caste and propound altruism and religious unity. His most famous disciple, Swami Vivekananda, went on to be a major force in the intellectual and spiritual growth of Calcutta and founded the Ramakrishna Mission, headquartered in the **Belur Math Shrine.** Ramakrishna's room here is a museum. ✉ *P. W. D. Rd., near Second Hooghly Bridge (Vivekananda Setu).* ☉ *Dawn–10 PM.* ✉ *Free.*

5 Howrah Bridge. The Howrah train station almost dumps you onto this structure, and the bridge in turn dumps you just north of Bara Bazaar in the heart of old Calcutta. Indeed, it seems more like a bazaar itself than a simple transport link between Howrah and Calcutta. Bordered by thin walkways, the bridge's eight lanes of chaotic traffic bear 2 million people each day in rickshaws, cars, scooters, bicycles, pushcarts, and animal-drawn carts. The web of girders stretches 1,500 ft over the Hooghly.

7 Kumartuli. In this area, countless potters create the millions of clay images that serve as idols during Calcutta's Hindu festival season. ✉ Chitpur Rd., between Bidhan Sarani and Jatindra Mohan.

★ **3 Marble Palace.** One of the strangest buildings in Calcutta was the inspiration of Raja Rajendra Mullick Bahadur, a member of Bengal's landed gentry. Mullick built the palace in 1855, making lavish use of Italian marble. It's set behind a lawn cluttered with sculptures of lions, the Buddha, Christopher Columbus, Jesus, the Virgin Mary, and Hindu gods. Near a small granite bungalow (where Mullick's descendants still live), a large pool is home to some exotic birds with large headdresses. The palace has an interior courtyard, complete with a throne room where a peacock often struts around the seat of honor. The upstairs rooms are downright Baroque: enormous mirrors and paintings cover the walls (including works by Reynolds, Rubens, and Murillo), gigantic chandeliers hang from the ceilings, and hundreds of statues and Far Eastern urns populate the rooms. The floors bear multicolored marble inlay on a giant scale, with a calico effect. Even the lamps are detailed creations, especially those on the staircases, where metal women are entwined in trees with a light bulb on each branch. Movie producers use the palace for Hindi films. ⊠ *46 Muktaram Basu St., off Chittaranjan Ave.* ⊠ *Free (technically you must obtain a pass from the West Bengal Tourist Office 24 hours in advance); tip your guide.* ⊘ *Tues., Wed., and Fri.–Sun. 10–4.*

★ ❷ **Nakhoda Mosque.** This massive red sandstone mosque, which can hold 10,000 worshipers, was built in 1926 as a copy of Akbar's tomb in Agra. Each floor has a prayer hall. The top floor has nice views of the streets below, which are crowded with stalls selling everything from paperback editions of the Koran to greasy kebabs. ⊠ *Mahatma Gandhi Rd. and Rabindra Sarani.* ⊠ *Free.* ⊘ *Daily sunrise–8 PM.*

★ ❻ **Paresnath Temple.** Built in 1867 and dedicated to Sitalnathji, the 10th of the 24 *tirthankaras* (perfect souls), this Jain temple is a flamboyant one, filled with inlaid-mirror pillars, stained-glass windows, floral-pattern marble floors, a gilded dome, and chandeliers from 19th-century Paris and Brussels. The garden holds blocks of glass mosaics depicting European figures, and statues covered with silver paint. Paresnath is an unusual place of honor for the typically ascetic Jains. ⊠ *Badridas Temple St., near Raja Dinendra St.* ⊘ *Daily sunrise–noon and 3–7.*

★ ❹ **Rabindra Bharati University Museum.** Within the walls of Rabindranath Tagore's cheerful, lemon-yellow home (which opens onto tree-lined galleries on the second floor), the university fosters cultural activities and maintains a display of paintings by artists of the Bengali school. The nerve center of Calcutta's intellectual activity around the turn of the 20th century, Tagore's abode now holds a wealth of memorabilia, including beautiful sepia photographs of the poet (quite fetching as a young man), his family, and his contemporaries. ⊠ *6/4 Dwarkanath Tagore La.,* ☎ *33/239–6601.* ⊠ *Free.* ⊘ *Weekdays 10–5, Sat. 10–1:30.*

Central Calcutta and the Maidan

The British first built Ft. William in the middle of a dense jungle. When disagreements led the local Bengali ruler, Siraj ud-Daula, to attack and destroy it, the British response was a quick and decisive battle led by Robert Clive. Following the Battle of Plassey (some 160 km/100 mi north of town), which transformed the British from traders into a ruling presence in 1757, the forest was cut down in order to provide a clear line for cannon fire in case of attack. It is really from the year 1757 that modern Calcutta traces its history, and from the new, impenetrable Ft. William (completed in 1773) that the city began its explosive growth.

Starting just north of the fort, central Calcutta became the commercial and political heart of the city. It was here that the British conducted business, and here that they built their stately homes. The immense area cleared for British cannons is now Calcutta's 3-square-km (2-square-mi) park, the Maidan, and central Calcutta now goes beyond the Maidan to B.B.D. Bagh square and most of the commercial and residential areas to the east of the giant park.

A Good Walk

Around **B.B.D. Bagh** ⑩ are some of the finest examples of Victorian architecture in Calcutta. Most of the buildings are still offices (government or otherwise) and are most interesting from the outside, even when admission is permitted. On the north side of the square is the **Writers' Building** ⑪; in the southeast corner is St. Andrew's Church, built in 1818. West and one block north is the **General Post Office** ⑫, and to its left is the redbrick Collectorate, Calcutta's oldest public building. Two blocks south is St. John's Church, which holds Job Charnock's mausoleum. (If the church is locked, you can call the vicar, ☎ 33/248–3439.) The High Court Building is on the next block south. Head east two blocks (until you're due south of B.B.D. Bagh) to see Raj Bhavan, home of the governor of West Bengal.

Cross Lenin Sarani and you're in the **Maidan** ⑬, a place to escape street traffic and diesel fumes and to enjoy green grass. Walk down Government Place East and you'll come to a traffic circle dominated by the **Ochterlony Monument** ⑭. Veer southwest and go down Eden Gardens Road to the **Eden Gardens** ⑮, which have a photogenic Burmese pagoda. If you walk along Strand Road toward the Hooghly from here, it's easy to arrange a brief, refreshing boat ride—boatmen are bound to approach you with offers of a "romantic" turn on the waters. Be careful, as the boats are often quite rickety; the going rate is about Rs. 50 for half an hour.

Continue a mile directly south of Eden Gardens to **Ft. William** ⑯, the East India Company's main strategic defense in Calcutta. Red Road cuts south through the Maidan to the **Victoria Memorial** ⑰, which serves (somewhat ironically) as a postcard image of Calcutta and houses a compelling museum of the city's history as well as some Raj memorabilia. Two hundred yards to the east along Queen's Way is **St. Paul's Cathedral** ⑱.

Queen's Way hits J. L. Nehru Road, colloquially known by its old name—**Chowringhee.** This is Calcutta's main drag—a wide boulevard bustling with pedestrians by day and a place for the homeless to stretch out by night. On the other side of Chowringhee, Queen's Road becomes Shakespeare Sarani, and after another 100 ft you'll see Calcutta's government tourist office on the right. Farther north on Chowringhee, Park Street comes in at an angle. Park Street shares with Chowringhee the prestige of having high rents for shops, hotels, and restaurants, and, in fact, if you're wandering around hungry in the evening, this is the best street to prowl for a good restaurant. About a mile down the street to the east is the **South Park Street Cemetery** ⑲, with the graves of many British who changed the course of India and never made it back to old Blighty. Back on Chowringhee, shortly after the intersection with Park Street is the **Indian Museum** ⑳, well worth dropping into for its collection of Indian antiquities. By now you will be in need of a little sophistication, which you can find at the Oberoi Grand hotel, a Victorian oasis just 200 yards farther up the thoroughfare.

TIMING

Two of the most interesting attractions on this route are the Victoria Memorial and the Indian Museum, for which you should allow 40 minutes apiece; the whole walk should take approximately four hours. If you are touring in the hot season, April–July, avoid walking during high noon.

Sights to See

★ ⑩ **B.B.D. Bagh.** The hub of all Calcutta, this square is still often referred to by its former name, Dalhousie Square. Once the administrative home of the East India Company, it later gave way to late-Victorian buildings used by the Colonial Civil Service and now houses the Indian government bureaucracy. Foot traffic is thick here. ⊠ *East of Hooghly River, just south of Howrah Bridge.*

★ **Chowringhee.** North Calcutta may be Calcutta's intellectual heart, but in an age of business-friendly communist governments, the slick commercial area east of the Maidan is the city's spinal cord. Now technically called Jawaharlal (or J. L.) Nehru Road, Chowringhee runs along the east side of the Maidan, with shops, hotels, and old Victorian buildings lining the other side of the wide pavement. In the evening, hawkers do their best with potential shoppers, and at night, the homeless bed down.

⑮ **Eden Gardens.** These flower-speckled gardens in the northwest corner of the Maidan are often crowded, but you can still find relief from the busy streets. Don't miss the picturesque Burmese pagoda. ⊠ *Eden Gardens Rd.* ▣ *Free.* ⊙ *24 hours.*

⑯ **Ft. William.** The irregular septagon south of the Eden Gardens is surrounded by a moat almost 50 ft wide. Begun in 1757 after Robert Clive's victory over Siraj ud-Daula at Plassey, Ft. William was designed to prevent any future attacks. The fort's walls, as well as its barracks, stables, and Church of St. Peter, have survived to this day chiefly because the fort has, in fact, never been attacked. The Indian government still uses the fort, but it's closed to the public. ⊠ *Strand Rd.*

⑫ **General Post Office** (GPO). This building's massive white Corinthian columns rest on the site of the original Ft. William, where the British were attacked in 1756 and many officers were imprisoned by Siraj ud-Daula in the infamous "Black Hole of Calcutta," a tiny space that caused most of the group to suffocate. ⊠ *Netaji Subhash Rd.*

⑳ **Indian Museum.** India's oldest museum has one of the largest and most comprehensive collections in Asia, including one of the best natural-history collections in the world. It's known locally as *Jadu Ghar,* the "House of Magic." The archaeology section has representative antiquities from prehistoric times to the Mogul period, including relics from Mohenjodaro and Harappa, the oldest excavated Indus Valley civilizations. The southern wing includes the Bharhut and Gandhara rooms (Indian art from the 2nd century BC to the 5th century AD), the Gupta and medieval galleries, and the Mogul gallery.

The Indian Museum also houses the world's largest collection of Indian coins; ask at the information desk for permission to see it. Gems and jewelry are on display. The art section on the first floor has a good collection of textiles, carpets, wood carving, papier-mâché figures, and terra-cotta pottery. A gallery on the third floor contains exquisite Persian and Indian miniature paintings, and banners from Tibetan monasteries. The anthropology section on the first floor is devoted to cultural anthropology, though the museum plans to establish India's first comprehensive exhibit on physical anthropology; some interesting specimens are an Egyptian mummy donated in 1880 by an English seaman, a fossilized 200-million-year-old tree trunk, the lower jaw of a 26-m (84-ft) whale, and meteorites dating back 50,000 years. ⊠ *27 J. L. Nehru Rd.,* ☏ *33/249–9853.* ▣ *Rs. 1 (free Fri.).* ⊙ *Sept.–Apr., Tues.–Sun. 10–4:30; May–Aug., Tues.–Sun. 11–5.*

★ ⑬ **Maidan.** Known as Calcutta's "green lung," the city's expansive park is dotted with some of its most significant attractions and is highly prized by its citizens, who turn out in the morning for sports and pony rides, and in the evening for snacks and carriage rides. The area came into existence when forests were cleared to give Ft. William a clear line of fire. ✉ *Just south of B.B.D. Bagh to just north of Alipore, and from the Hooghly River to J. L. Nehru Rd. and the shops of Park St.*

⑭ Ochterlony Monument. On the north end of the Maidan stands a 148-ft pillar commemorating Sir David Ochterlony's military victories over the Nepalese in the border war of 1814–16. Built in 1828, the impressive monument has a curious design: the base is Egyptian, the column is Syrian, and the cupola is Turkish. Now officially called the Shahid Minar (Martyr's Tower), it's been the site of many a political rally and student demonstration during Calcutta's turbulent post-Independence history. ✉ *J. L. Nehru Rd.*

⑱ St. Paul's Cathedral. Completed in 1847, the cathedral now has a steeple modeled after the one at Canterbury; previous steeples were destroyed by earthquakes in 1897 and 1934. Florentine frescoes, the stained-glass western window, and a gold communion plate presented by Queen Victoria are prize possessions. Interestingly, birds congregate in the interior eaves. ✉ *Cathedral Rd. east of Victoria Memorial,* ☎ *33/244–5756.* ⊙ *Daily 9–noon and 3–6.*

⑲ South Park Street Cemetery. The graves and memorials here form a repository of British imperial history. People who lived within the Raj from 1767 on are buried here, and in the records of their lives you can see the trials and triumphs of the building of an empire. ✉ *Park St. at Rawdon St.,* ☎ *no phone.* ⊙ *Sunrise–sunset.*

★ ⑰ Victoria Memorial. This massive, white marble monument was conceived in 1901 by Lord Curzon and built over a 20-year period. Designed in a mixture of Italian Renaissance and Saracenic styles, surrounded by extensive, carefully manicured gardens, and preceded by a typically sober statue of Victoria herself, it remains the single greatest symbol of the British Raj. Inside the building is an excellent museum of the history of Calcutta (there's a lot to read, but it will really sharpen your sense of the British-Bengali relationship) and various Raj-related exhibits including Queen Victoria's writing desk and piano, Indian miniature paintings, watercolors, and Persian books. Cameras and electronic equipment must be left at the entrance. ✉ *Queen's Way,* ☎ *33/248–5142.* ☞ *Rs. 2.* ⊙ *Tues.–Sun. 10–4:30; sound-and-light show Tues.–Sun. 7:15 and 8:15.*

⑪ Writers' Building. The original "writers" were the clerks of the British East India Company. Now a government office building, this dramatically Baroque edifice is closed to the public. ✉ *North side of B.B.D. Bagh.*

Southern Calcutta

Calcutta's rich and powerful moved consistently south as the city grew more and more crowded and unpleasant. Here you'll see an interesting mix of large colonial homes, modern hotels and businesses, open space, and crowded temple areas.

A Good Tour

You can reach **Kalighat Kali Temple** ㉑ by metro, getting off at Kalighat Station and walking north on Murkaharji Road for 10 minutes; or you can take a taxi, an interesting ride through a variety of neighborhoods. **Nirmal Hirday** ㉒, where Mother Teresa lived, work, and is buried, is just around the corner. The **National Library** ㉓ is a short taxi ride from either and puts you near the Taj Bengal hotel, a restful place for a coffee break. To reach the **Indian Botanical Gardens** ㉔, across the

Hooghly River in southern Howrah, take another taxi (about 15 minutes) across the Second Hooghly Bridge (Vivekananda Setu).

TIMING

Give yourself a full morning to cover this ground. Allow an hour and a half to arrive at and see Kalighat Kali Temple, another hour if you want to visit Nirmal Hirday. You many want to skip the National Library unless you want to bundle it with a high-class rest stop (or a stay) at the Taj Bengal, and go straight to the Indian Botanical Gardens.

Sights to See

★ ㉔ **Indian Botanical Gardens.** Across the Second Hooghly Bridge (Vivekananda Setu) in Howrah are the massive botanical gardens, first opened in 1786. Darjeeling and Assam teas were developed here. The gardens' banyan tree has one of the largest canopies in the world, covering a mind-boggling 1,300 square ft. The gardens are so huge that you can even find a place to relax on Sunday, when locals turn out in droves to enjoy their day off. ✉ *Between Andul Rd. and Kurz Ave., Shibpur, Howrah,* ☎ *33/660–3235.* ▧ *Free.* ☉ *Daily, 1 hr after sunrise–1 hr before sunset.*

★ ㉑ **Kalighat Kali Temple.** Built in 1809, the Kali is one of the most significant pilgrimage sites in India, with shrines to Shiva, Krishna, and Kali, the patron goddess of Calcutta. Human sacrifices were reputed to be common here during the 19th century, but only goats are slaughtered now, then offered to Kali with Ganges water and *bhang* (uncultivated hemp). The building, though surrounded by others, repays a close look with thin, multicolored layers of painted trim and swaths of tilework. Only Hindus are allowed in the inner sanctum, but the lanes and brilliant flower markets surrounding the temple have a lovely atmosphere in themselves. ✉ *Kalighat Rd.* ☉ *Daily sunrise–sunset.*

㉓ **National Library.** Once home to the lieutenant governor of Calcutta, this hefty neo-Renaissance building houses miles of books and pleasant reading rooms. The rare-book section holds some particularly significant works, adding to the importance of this 2-million-volume facility. There are no displays as such, but the grounds make for a pleasant short walk in scholarly company. ✉ *Belvedere Rd. (near Taj Bengal hotel), Alipore,* ☎ *33/223–5381.* ☉ *Weekdays 9–8, weekends 10–6.*

㉒ **Nirmal Hirday** (Pure Heart). Mother Teresa's first home for the dying is now one of 300 affiliated organizations worldwide that care for people in the most dire need. Learn more about Mother Teresa's work at the headquarters of the **Missionaries of Charity** (✉ 54A A. J. C. Bose Rd., ☎ 33/244–7115). It can be inspiring to see the joy among the people in one of the missionaries' homes or refuges. Mother Teresa is buried in this building—her home for 44 years—in what was formerly the cafeteria. ✉ *Next to Kali Temple.*

New Calcutta

A lot is said about Calcutta's history and traditions but with the winds of globalization sweeping across the country, a new generation—one that has grown up on international television and the internet—want their city to become a part of a global village. The old Calcutta is making way for the new. Travel along the Eastern Metropolitan (EM) Bypass for a taste of this contemporary city.

A Good Tour

Right on the EM Bypass is the **Swabhumi** ㉕, a sprawling complex that showcases the best of Indian arts and crafts. Just off and to the northeast of the bypass are **Nicco Park** ㉖, an amusement park, and **Aquatica** ㉗, a water park.

TIMING

Taking in all of these attractions will fill a very long day, so you might want to tackle only two of the three. Regardless, set out early by cab or a hired car. It's about 45 minutes from the heart of the city to the EM Bypass; the sights are all off the bypass and within 30 to 45 minutes of each other. Plan to spend two hours each at Swabhumi and Nicco Park; unless you're a real water park buff, an hour at Aquatica should suffice.

Sights to See

㉗ **Aquatica.** A nice place to chill—literally and figuratively—is this water park just off the Eastern Metropolitan Bypass. The rides are thrilling, and there's a huge pool in which youngsters do their own version of the MTV Grind. As you might expect, weekends are crowded. Admission includes access to all rides. ⊠ *Kochpukur, South 24 Parganas,* ☎ *33/ 221–3626.* ⌧ *Rs. 150.* ⊙ *Daily 10–5.*

㉖ **Nicco Park.** This amusement complex has acres of green space, numerous exciting rides, and many small restaurants in the complex. Even though ride tickets aren't included, admission is a steal at Rs. 25. ⊠ *Off EM Bypass,* ☎ *no phone.* ⌧ *Rs. 25.* ⊙ *Daily 10:30–8.*

㉕ **Swabhumi.** Opposite the Salt Lake Stadium, this heritage park complex is a mini-India. From traditional crafts to jugglers on stilts to a food court with ethnic cuisine—you'll find everything here. ⊠ *Off EM Bypass,* ☎ *no phone.* ⌧ *Rs. 10.* ⊙ *Daily 10–8.*

DINING

For breakfast or tea with sandwiches, try **Flury's Tea Room** (⊠ 18 Park St.), Calcutta's first Swiss confectioner and now an institution. A chicken or cheese omelette, beans on toast, and coffee would be within Rs. 125.

Bengali

$$ ✕ **Aheli.** This was Calcutta's first upscale Bengali restaurant, and it still draws a crowd. Traditional Bengali delicacies such as *macher sorse paturi* (fish cooked with mustard paste) and chingri malai curry are served in an intimate terra-cotta dining room. ⊠ *Peerless Inn, 12 J. L. Nehru Rd.,* ☎ *33/228–0301 or 33/228–0302. AE, DC, MC, V.*

$$ ✕ **Kewpies.** Quaint and exclusive, this restaurant is in high demand
★ at the moment. The delicious *thalis* (combination platters) are available both vegetarian and nonvegetarian, the latter with assorted meats or fish only, are served in a typically Bengali style: on cut banana leaves. You can also order the thali's vegetable or meat portions à la carte. ⊠ *2 Elgin La.,* ☎ *33/475–9880. Reservations essential. No credit cards.*

Eclectic

$$–$$$$ ✕ **The Hub.** This recently opened restaurant in the Taj Bengal hotel has
★ been dubbed Calcutta's "international food theater." The grand, spacious interior, with marble floors and a glass spiral staircase, matches that of the hotel lobby. You can see the chefs at work in the kitchen, and they prepare dishes to your taste, making a meal here somewhat interactive. Though the emphasis is on Italian food, you get a wide choice of cuisines. Try the homemade pasta or the rack of lamb in brown sauce.

✉ *Taj Bengal, 34B Belvedere Rd., Alipore,* ☎ *33/223–3939. Reservations essential. AE, DC, MC, V.*

$$ ✕ **The Sheriff.** Yes, it's Calcutta's only Wild West joint, and it's very popular with the smart crowd. The walls of this small space are bedecked with Stetsons, Colt revolvers, and lassos, and the waiters are dressed as cowboys. The Mexican food is fair enough if you need a little variety. ✉ *Sarat Bose Rd. at Elgin Rd.,* ☎ *33/280–6444. Reservations essential. AE.*

$–$$$ ✕ **Porto Rio.** Inside a white bungalow, helpful waitstaffers dart past whitewashed walls hung with elegant paintings and take orders from guests who are seated at tables adorned with red-check cloths. Although the menu has Continental items, it's the many dishes typical of India's eastern and western coasts that are the draw. The Goan fish curry and the roast crab are both excellent choices. ✉ *28 Circus Ave.,* ☎ *33/281–3921. No credit cards.*

$–$$ ✕ **Blue Fox.** Right in the thick of things and popular with a young, hip contingent, the large and spacious Blue Fox has high ceilings, an overhead loft with additional tables, and quiet modern-Indian decor. Among the various Indian and Continental dishes, the sizzlers and crab or lobster thermidor are good bets. ✉ *55 Park St.,* ☎ *33/249–7948. DC.*

$ ✕ **Taaja.** Taaja ("Fresh") is one of the best Continental restaurants in
★ Calcutta, serving Greek, French, Italian, Spanish, and Hungarian food, but it goes beyond this classification to offer dishes from the Caribbean and Far East as well. The menu gives new meaning to the word "eclectic." Paella, Cajun crab cakes, moussaka, and cannelloni are all memorable choices. ✉ *29/1A Ballygunge Circular Rd.,* ☎ *33/476–7334. Reservations essential. MC, V.*

Indian

$$–$$$$ ✕ **Sonargaon.** The name means "golden village," and this North In-
★ dian restaurant is a tasteful replica of a rural home, complete with a courtyard, a well, dark wood on taupe stone, copper curios, and metal light fixtures. Popular dishes include *kakori* kebab (minced lamb kebab), *murg Wajid Ali* (stuffed, pounded chicken breast marinated in saffron and cooked in a mildly spicy sauce), and chingri malai. ✉ *Taj Bengal, 34B Belvedere Rd., Alipore,* ☎ *33/223–3939. Reservations essential. AE, DC, MC, V.*

$–$$ ✕ **Zaranj.** Plush and well-decorated with a fountain and ornate furniture, this is a relaxing place for dinner: the staff doesn't rush you. Choose from a large à la carte menu with vegetarian and nonvegetarian options. The tasty *murgh nawabi* is a boneless chicken with yogurt and nuts roasted over a charcoal grill. ✉ *26 J. L. Nehru Rd.,* ☎ *33/249–5572. Reservations essential. AE, DC, V.*

$ ✕ **Peter Cat.** Peter Cat's so-called cello kebab—biriani-style rice with
★ egg, butter, two mutton kebabs, and one chicken kebab—is one of the most popular dishes in Calcutta. The dining room is intimate, with white stucco walls, Tiffany-style lamps, and soft lighting, and the menu is a mixture of good Continental and Indian dishes, especially tandoori fare. ✉ *18 Park St.,* ☎ *33/229–8841. DC, V.*

Pan-Asian

$$–$$$$ ✕ **Chinoiserie.** Consistently rated one of the best Chinese restaurants
★ in India (no mean honor these days), this specialty restaurant boasts pricey delicacies such as Peking duck and a highly unusual selection of corn dishes. One crunchy appetizer consists of deep-fried kernels of American corn; another dish features corn delicately flavored with garlic. Unsurpassed food, a calm green-and-beige color scheme accented

by old-world mirrors and paintings, and excellent Taj service make dining here an experience. Reservations are advised on weekdays and essential on weekends. ☒ *Taj Bengal, 34B Belvedere Rd., Alipore,* ☎ *33/223–3939. AE, DC, MC, V.*

$$–$$$$ ✕ **Mainland China.** Part of a national chain, this restaurant is popular with Calcutta's chic set. Though the dining room is large, grand mirrors give the illusion of even more space, and the furniture is minimalist though comfortable. The Szechuan menu is extensive. Opt for the seafood platter or the chicken in a hot garlic sauce. Attentive service and valet parking make for a posh evening. ☒ *3A Gurusaday Rd.,* ☎ *33/287–2006. Reservations essential. AE, DC, MC, V.*

$$–$$$$ ✕ **Zen.** Art Deco meets postmodern in the sleek lines of this Southeast Asian restaurant, which serves cuisines from all over the region. The Thai green curry and Indonesian specialties, such as *soto ayam* (glass noodles) and *nasi gorang* (mixed fried rice) are rare finds in India. The grilled lobster with sweet-and-sour dip is an indulgence worth the price. ☒ *Park Hotel, 17 Park St.,* ☎ *33/249–7336. Reservations essential. AE, DC, MC, V.*

$$–$$$ ✕ **China Valley.** Enormous statues of male and female Chinese figures dominate the decor, surrounded by a stunning array of vases and urns, and large aquariums filled with iridescent tropical fish spur the imagination. China Valley's food is top-grade; a popular dish is the hot, spicy prawn Shanghai with rice. ☒ *Ideal Plaza, 11/1 Sarat Bose Rd.,* ☎ *33/247–0294. Reservations essential. AE, DC, MC.*

$–$$ ✕ **Bar-B-Q.** This local favorite serves Cantonese and Szechuan dishes in a setting that innovatively mixes Chinese and German-chalet decor under a name that, of course, conjures neither of the two. Try the crisp fried chicken served with a mild "surprise" sauce or the boneless chili chicken. ☒ *43 Park St.,* ☎ *33/299916. Reservations essential on weekends. AE, DC, MC, V.*

$–$$ ✕ **Thai Tonight.** An alternative to the pricey, though more authentic, Thai food in luxury hotels' restaurants, this place offers a friendly ambience, great service, and even better prices. Try the standard chicken green curry or the bargain-priced glass noodles. ☒ *29/1A Ballygunge Circular Rd.,* ☎ *33/454–2036. Reservations essential. AE, DC, MC, V.*

$ ✕ **Momo Plaza.** Calcuttans love Tibetan food, and Momo Plaza is an ideal place for a Tibetan snack if you can forego physical ambience for the duration. The chicken-stuffed *momos*—dumplings which are also popular in Nepal—come steamed or fried, served with a very hot red-chili paste. They're accompanied by a light, watery spring-onion soup called *thukpa.* ☒ *2A Suburban Hospital Rd.,* ☎ *33/247–8250. No credit cards.*

LODGING

Unless otherwise noted, hotels have central air-conditioning and foreign-exchange facilities, and rooms have bathrooms with tubs. Some luxury hotels have exclusive floors with special privileges or facilities for the business traveler.

$$$ 🏨 **Ashok–Airport.** This modern high-rise with pleasant rooms is primarily for those whizzing through Calcutta in one night only. It's clean and fresh but offers little excitement and is far from Calcutta's attractions. ☒ *Calcutta Airport, 700052,* ☎ *33/552–9111,* FAX *33/552–9137. 144 rooms, 12 suites. 2 restaurants, bar, pool, hair salon, business services, travel services. AE, DC, MC, V.*

$$$ 🏨 **Hotel Hindustan International.** The HHI provides modern rooms within its plain white walls. Decor is neat and trim throughout, if not particularly inspiring. The best rooms overlook the pool, but many others have good views of Calcutta. ☒ *235/1 A. J. C. Bose Rd., 700020,* ☏ *33/247–2394,* FAX *33/247–2824. 212 rooms, 12 suites. 3 restaurants, bar, pool, spa, health club, nightclub, business services, travel services. AE, DC, MC, V.*

$$$ ⊞ **Oberoi Grand.** The height of elegance, this impeccably maintained
★ Victorian landmark in the center of town has a glowing white facade and a rich marble and dark-wood interior. The heritage is rich, service is top-notch, and the restaurants are excellent. Guest rooms lack any sense of antiquity, but they're spacious, with wall-to-wall carpeting and modern bathrooms. The best rooms overlook the interior courtyard and pool. ☒ *15 J. L. Nehru Rd., 700013,* ☏ *33/249–2323,* FAX *33/249– 1217,* WEB *www.oberoihotels.com. 213 rooms, 6 suites. 3 restaurants, bar, pool, sauna, health club, business services, travel services. AE, DC, MC, V.*

$$$ ⊞ **Park Hotel.** Inspired decoration has turned the Park into one of the
★ best hotels in Calcutta. Everything in this long, white building in the thick of things on Park Street has been designed with care: the lobby sparkles with mirrors and cut-glass chandeliers amid rich wood and marble; the restaurants and café are creative in everything from daring decor (black art deco meets Zen) to such simple touches as serving cappuccino. The rooms are comfortable, if small, and the staff is cheerful and helpful. The bar and nightclub are very popular with both Indians and expats. ☒ *17 Park St., 700016,* ☏ *33/249–7336,* FAX *33/ 249–7343,* WEB *www.theparkhotels.com. 155 rooms, 10 suites. 2 restaurants, bar, pool, nightclub, business services, travel services. AE, DC, MC, V.*

$$$ ⊞ **Taj Bengal.** Calcutta's Taj is a fusion of modern India and the na-
★ tion's cultural heritage. On the fringe of the city center, the hotel overlooks the Maidan and Victoria Memorial. The cavernous lobby is stylish and inviting, colored in tawny taupes and ice green, with running water and palm trees creating a sense of total calm. Modern Indian art, artifacts (including terra-cotta reliefs), and antiques are showcased throughout the building. Decor in the rooms, which you access via quiet triangular atriums, is essentially Western, with Eastern accents and Indian prints. Deluxe rooms have parquet floors, warm colors, and comfortable, often elaborately carved, Indian furniture. Service is truly outstanding here—familiar, smooth, and detail-oriented. ☒ *34B Belvedere Rd., Alipore, 700027,* ☏ *33/223–3939,* FAX *33/223–1766,* WEB *www.tajhotels.com. 216 rooms, 13 suites. 3 restaurants, bar, pool, health club, nightclub, business services, travel services. AE, DC, MC, V.*

$$ ⊞ **Fairlawn.** If you want old-fashioned charm and a taste of life in the
★ Raj, stay in this Calcutta landmark, built in 1801. A small hotel, the Fairlawn has memorabilia-cluttered walls, a winding staircase, and a great general ambience. Waiters wear gloves, a gong sounds during mealtimes, and rooms have chintz bedspreads and old-fashioned bathtubs. Ask for an air-conditioned room in the summer. All meals are included. ☒ *13A Sudder St., 700013,* ☏ *33/245–1510,* FAX *33/244– 1835. 22 rooms. Restaurant. AE, MC, V.*

$$ ⊞ **Kenilworth.** Popular with repeat visitors to Calcutta, this Best Western hotel has two attractive wings and pretty gardens. The common rooms are filled with marble and cheerfully furnished; guest rooms are comfortable and spacious, with standard, anonymous decor. Continental breakfast is included. ☒ *1–2 Little Russell St., 700071,* ☏ *33/242– 8394,* FAX *33/242–5136. 110 rooms. 2 restaurants, bar, bookstore, business services, travel services. AE, DC, MC, V.*

$$ ⊞ **Peerless Inn.** Situated on a crowded street near the Oberoi Grand and New Market, the Peerless has somewhat cramped rooms and decor in need of a facelift, but its location and price make it popular. The presence of the Bengali restaurant Aheli is a bonus. ⊠ *15 J. L. Nehru Rd., 700013,* ☎ *33/243–0301,* ℻ *33/248–6650. 123 rooms. 3 restaurants, bar, health club, business services. AE, DC, MC, V.*

$ ⊞ **Astor.** In this price category, the Astor is the least expensive and quite possibly the best in Calcutta. The staff is laid-back and friendly; the rooms are clean if somewhat small; and there are three restaurants, including a casual beer garden, ideal for whiling away a balmy evening. ⊠ *15 Shakespeare Sarani, 700071,* ☎ *33/282–9957,* ℻ *33/287–7430. 35 rooms. 3 restaurants. AE, MC, V.*

NIGHTLIFE AND THE ARTS

Nightlife

Nightlife became a Calcutta phenomenon in the 1990s—with the advent of discos, affluent young people began to hit the dance floors. Eating out, however, remains the nocturnal activity of choice, with 24-hour coffee shops at the top hotels doing a brisk business.

Bars and Lounges

The most attractive places to have a nightcap are the Oberoi Grand and the Taj Bengal. The pub at the Park Hotel is one of the few places with decent beer on tap, making it a pleasant afternoon watering hole. The bar at the Fairlawn Hotel draws an interesting group and is much more social than the others. Bars stay open until 11 PM or midnight and are closed on Thursday.

Discos

Calcutta's clubs are technically open only to members and hotel guests, but you can get in for either a cover charge or a smile, depending on the doorman. All clubs retain good DJs for a mixture of Indian pop and Western dance music.

Anticlock (⊠ Hotel Hindustan International, 235/1 A. J. C. Bose Rd., ☎ 33/247–2394) is a good choice, though the crowd gets rowdy as the evening wears on. **Big Ben** (⊠ Kenilworth Hotel, 1–2 Little Russell St. ☎ 33/282–8394) is an upscale pub where mid-career local professionals congregate. The barman is perhaps the best in town. Breathe freely at the spacious **Incognito** (⊠ Taj Bengal hotel, 34B Belvedere Rd., Alipore, ☎ 33/248–3939), where an upscale clientele relaxes around a glass-enclosed dance floor.

Play pool or dance into the wee hours at **London Pub** (⊠ Golden Park Hotel, 13 Ho Chi Minh Sarani, ☎ 33/288–3939). **Someplace Else** (⊠ Park Hotel, 17 Park St., ☎ 33/249–7336) may well be the best pub in town, though drinks are expensive. It has a small dance floor but great music with varying themes for almost each night of the week. The dance floor at **Tantra** (⊠ Park Hotel, 17 Park St., ☎ 33/249–7336) is hot and the decor is fantastic—cushions with embroidery and beadwork, jute items, dhurries, and silk hangings. Those over 30 may feel a bit out of place.

The Arts

Calcutta is India's deepest well of creative energy. Artists here live in the inspiring shadow of such pillars as Rabindranath Tagore and world-renowned film director Satyajit Ray; and, happily, the anxiety of influence has not intimidated contemporary artists. To find out what's happening, check *Calcutta This Fortnight,* available from the West Bengal Tourist Office and *CalCalling,* available in hotels. You can also check the listings pages of any English language daily newspaper. *Calcutta: Gateway to the East* has comprehensive listings.

Art Galleries

The **Academy of Fine Arts** (⊠ 2 Cathedral Rd., ☎ 33/223–4302) has a permanent collection of paintings (and manuscripts) by Rabindranath Tagore. The **Birla Academy of Art and Culture** (⊠ 108–109 Southern Ave., ☎ 33/466–2843) has interesting displays of art old and new. Modern Indian art is frequently shown at **Galerie 88** (⊠ 28B Shakespeare Sarani, ☎ 33/247–2274).

Film

Many movie theaters around New Market feature English-language films. Ask your hotel or the tourist office for information on current events; if they don't know what's on, they'll help you find out.

Performing Arts

Many auditoriums host regular performances of music, dance, and theater—the most Bengali of the performing arts.

English-language plays are regularly staged by the **British Council** (☎ 33/242–5478). Be sure to see what's happening at the **Academy of Fine Arts** (⊠ 2 Cathedral Rd., ☎ 33/242–1205), and don't be intimidated if the offerings are in Bengali—you can still see some fascinating dramatizations of familiar stories by the likes of Shakespeare and Goethe. Bengali productions are often staged at **Kalamandir** (⊠ 48 Shakespeare Sarani, ☎ 33/247–9086). Bengali dance and theater are often performed at **Rabindra Sadan** (⊠ Cathedral Rd., ☎ 33/248–9936).

OUTDOOR ACTIVITIES AND SPORTS

Calcutta still puts class first when it comes to sports, with the result that you need to be a member's guest to enter the golf and racing clubs. The **Royal Calcutta Golf Club** (⊠ 18 Golf Club Rd., ☎ 33/473–1288 or 33/473–1352) caters to the elite. For horse-racing enthusiasts, the **Royal Calcutta Turf Club** (RCTC, ⊠ 11 Russell St., ☎ 33/229–1104) has an old-world air of sophistication. Whether you want to watch or play, get cricket information from the **Calcutta Cricket and Football Club** (⊠ 19/1 Gurusaday Rd., ☎ 33/475–8721). The **Calcutta Polo Club** (⊠ 51 J. L. Nehru Rd., ☎ 33/242–2031) has the polo schedules.

SHOPPING

Shopping in Calcutta bazaars is an adventure, and a test of your ability to shake off touts. Part of the century-old **New Market** (officially Sir Stuart Hogg Market, ⊠ 19 Lindsay St., off J. L. Nehru Rd., behind Oberoi Grand) houses about 2,500 stores under one roof, selling cotton saris, Bankura clay horses, Malda brassware, leather from Shantiniketan, silk from Murshidabad, *khadi* cloth (handmade cotton), poultry, cheeses, nuts, and other foods.

Head up **Rabindra Sarani** from Lal Bazaar Road (near the West Bengal Tourist Office) and you'll soon enter an Islamic world. Women walk by in *burqas* (long, black, tent-shape robes), their eyes barely visible behind spiderlike veils. Men sit on elevated platforms selling Bengali *kurtas* (shirts) and pants, and colorful *lungis* and white *dhotis* (both wraps) for men. Other vendors sell vials of perfume created from flowers. Rabindra Sarani is interesting all the way to Chitpur Road.

On and around **Chitpur Road** you'll see a mixture of potters and shops that make musical instruments. East of Chitpur Road is **Bowbazar,** home to Calcutta's jewelers and an amazing array of good-quality gold and silver plus beautifully designed and crafted stone settings. Prices are reasonable, and each shop has an astrologer to help you find the most auspicious stone for your stars.

Auctions

Calcutta's Sunday auctions take place along Russell Street. A trip to the oldest auction house, the **Russell Exchange** (✉ 12C Russell St., ☎ 33/249–8974), or any of its neighbors is invariably entertaining. Goods auctioned range from antiques and period furniture to crockery and cutlery.

Bookstores

Landmark at Emami Shoppers' City (✉ 3 Lord Sinha Rd., ☎ 33/282–1174) is spacious and modern. It sells books and music under one roof. **Oxford Bookstore-Gallery** (✉ 17 Park St., ☎ 33/229–7662) has a wide array of books ranging from cookery, travel, and architecture to the very best fiction. Browse the net here or have an iced lemon tea at the tea bar. **Seagull** (✉ 31A SP Mukherjee Rd., ☎ 33/476–5865) has a wide range of titles but the selection is eclectic. Exhibitions and seminars add to the mix.

Clothing and Textiles

Dakshinapan (✉ near Dhakuria Bridge) houses government emporiums from all the states of India, making it an excellent place to eyeball a wide range of styles. Try the **Handloom House** (✉ 2 Lindsay St.) for crafted textiles, mostly cottons. **Manjusha** (✉ 7/1D Lindsay St.) sells all manner of textiles.

Monapali and Silk Route (✉ 15 Loudon St., ☎ 33/406103) are co-managed designer boutiques with lovely collections of women's saris and *salwar-kameez* (a two-piece outfit of long, loose-fitting tunic over loose pants tapered at the ankle) in cotton, satin, and silk. Designs are inspired by the Far East and enhanced with Indian motifs and artwork: batik, embroidery, and *zardozi* (gold threading).

Pantaloon (✉ 49/1 Gariahat Rd., ☎ 33/476–5307) sells everything from kids' clothes to shoes. The innovative **Weavers Studio** (✉ 5/1 Anil Moitra Rd., 2nd floor, Ballygunj Pl., ☎ 33/440–8937) sells high quality natural-dyed and embroidered textiles. **Westside** (✉ 22 Camac St., ☎ 33/281–7312) offers casual wear.

Crafts

For curios in a hurry, head to **Central Cottage Industries** (✉ 7 J. L. Nehru Rd.). Quaint little **Konark Collectables** (✉ Humayun Court, 20 Lindsay St., ☎ 33/247–7657) is stuffed with handicrafts.

SIDE TRIPS

Escape Calcutta's traffic and enrich your Bengali experience with a trip to either of two peaceful havens to the west. Vishnupur is characterized by its centuries-old terra-cotta temples, built from the local red clay and all but alive with the epic scenes carved into their panels. Shantiniketan is home to the university founded by Rabindranath Tagore, a center for art, music, and Bengali heritage. Nearby Sriniketan is a center of batik, embroidery, and terra-cotta craftsmanship.

Vishnupur

152 km (94 mi) west of Calcutta (8–10 hrs by road, overnight by train)

Set in a land of rich red soil, Vishnupur was the capital of the Hindu Malla kings from the 16th to 19th centuries, and saw fit to convert its surroundings into some mind-blowing terra-cotta temples. Between its intricate, lifelike temple panels and Old World charm, Vishnupur is exquisite, an integral part of Bengal. The clay pottery created here— particularly the Bankura horse, named for the district—attracts thousands for its sheer beauty and color. It's a long trip from Calcutta, but Vishnupur is worth a detour for its exceptional carvings and figurines, immortalizing old Bengal at its artistic best.

Built out of the local red laterite soil, the temple town is scattered with monuments to the Malla rulers. Sights are spread out, so the easiest way to explore is to hire a cycle-rickshaw and ride through the maze of narrow streets. Be sure to see the Madan Gopal, Madan Mohan, Radhagobinda, Rasmancha, and Shyamrai temples, all built around the 16th century; each has a story to tell through its intricately carved figurines. Dalmadol is a cannon of pure iron. Pathar Darwaza ("Doorway of Stone") marked the entrance to the Malla fort. Vishnupur is a great place to buy souvenirs, especially terra-cotta toys, conch-shell handicrafts, jewelry, and silk. In August or September, local snake charmers demonstrate their age-old prowess at a snake festival called the *jhapan,* at which, among other activities, men throw cobras at each other to test their respective mettle.

The only decent place to stay here is **Vishnupur Tourist Lodge** (✉ P.O. Vishnupur, Bankura, ☎ 03244/52013), which is modest and suburban. Don't expect anything beyond the very basic. It has a restaurant and 15 rooms, only one of which is air-conditioned; a double room costs Rs. 450. Reserve through the West Bengal Tourist Office in Calcutta.

Shantiniketan

★ *210 km (130 mi) northwest of Calcutta (four hours by train)*

Nobel Laureate Rabindranath Tagore's dream became reality here: a university dedicated to the liberal arts. Today the art and music schools at **Vishvabharati** are some of the best in the country. Designed in 1901 as a group of cottages in a green, idyllic setting, Shantiniketan embodies the Bengali artistic heritage. In accordance with Tagore's vision, some classes are still held outside, under the shade of huge trees, and stunning abstract sculptures reach toward the sky. A weekend retreat for many, Shantiniketan is almost a pilgrimage to Bengalis.

Within the university, Rabindra Bhavan is a museum full of photographs, Tagore's personal belongings, and the poet's much-coveted Nobel Prize. The art school, Kala Bhavan, is decorated with frescoes and murals outside, and you can watch students at work inside. Sangeet Bhavan is the music school. Uttarayan, where Tagore lived, is a charming complex of five houses, ranging from mud hut to mansion, in a variety of architectural styles.

A few minutes' drive outside Shantiniketan, **Sriniketan** is a rural-development center helping locals fend for themselves by creating stunning handicrafts—colorful batiks; intricate embroidery on saris, scarves, and bags; and terra-cotta items, including jewelry. This is a hidden shopper's paradise, with some of the most beautiful and exclusive craft items in Bengal. A great time to visit Shantiniketan is during the town's biggest festival, Poush Mela, which is usually held between December 22 and 25. The festival includes huge fairs where handicrafts and bric-a-brac are sold and performances of *bauls,* wandering minstrels who sing their unique variety of folk songs.

Lodging

$ ⊡ **Chhuti.** This sprawling hotel is the best in the vicinity, with a resort-like ambience and good food. Built with an eye for detail, it has all the amenities of a high-rise back in the metropolis. Guest rooms and the air-conditioned cottages are spacious, clean, and refreshing, and the caring, experienced staff looks after weary travelers' needs. ⊠ *241 Charupally, Jamboni, Bolpur,* ☎ *3463/52692. 20 rooms. Restaurant. No credit cards.*

$ ⊡ **Marks and Meadows.** More a resort than a mere rest stop, this is an ideal place to unwind. With its low room rates, this is a great value. Surrounded by greenery, it includes clean, tidy, nicely decorated rooms and some cottages as well. ⊠ *Sriniketan,* ☎ *33/245–8831, 33/245–0179, or 33/244–8254,* FAX *33/245–8831. 34 rooms. Restaurant, pool, badminton, Ping-Pong, recreation room, meeting room. No credit cards.*

CALCUTTA A TO Z

To research prices, get advice from other travelers, and book travel arrangements, visit www.fodors.com.

AIR TRAVEL

All international and domestic airlines use Dum Dum Airport, 15 km (9 mi) north of the city.

➤ AIRLINES AND CONTACTS: **Indian Airlines** (☎ 33/236–0810 or 33/236–0730). **Jet Airways** (☎ 33/229–2737 or 33/229–2660).

AIRPORT TRANSFERS

When you leave the baggage claim, you'll see counters where you can arrange free shuttle service if your hotel offers it. Outside the baggage claim/customs area, you can hire a taxi through the prepaid-taxi counter; the ride downtown takes about 40 minutes and costs around Rs. 100. Hire a taxi on your own through one of the hustlers outside the terminal and it will cost about Rs. 350. The airport coach (Rs. 50) goes to most of the upscale hotels and to the city center; its counter is also near the baggage-claim area.

BUS TRAVEL WITHIN CALCUTTA

Buses here are slow, creaking machines that belch fumes and are unbearably crowded during rush hours. They will cost you next to nothing but will set you back in terms of time and basic travelling comfort. They're best avoided.

CARS AND DRIVERS

You can hire a car and driver through one of the travel agencies listed below or the following rental agencies. Expect to pay Rs. 700 for half a day (four hours) and 80 km (50 mi), with an hourly and per-km rate beyond that. If you plan to do a lot in very little time, hiring a car can be useful, but hailing plain old taxis can be cheaper, and saves you from having to find parking or remember where you left your car and driver.

➤ CONTACTS: **Europcar Shaw Distributors** (⊠ 8/1 Sarat Bose Rd., ☎ 33/475–8916). **Hertz** (⊠ New Kenilworth Hotel, ½ Little Russel St., ☎ 33/242–8394). **Wenz** (⊠ Oberoi Grand, ☎ 33/249–2323 Ext. 6247).

CONSULATES

➤ CONTACTS: **British Consulate** (✉ 1 Ho Chi Minh Sarani, 700071, ☎ 33/33/282–5171). **Canadian Consulate** (✉ Duncan House, 31 NS Rd., 700001, ☎ 33/225–0163). **U.S. Consulate** (✉ 5/1 Ho Chi Minh Sarani, 700071, ☎ 33/282–3611).

EMERGENCIES

➤ GENERAL EMERGENCIES: **Fire** (☎ 101). **Police** (☎ 100).
➤ HOSPITAL: **Belle View Clinic** (✉ 9 U.N. Brahmachari St., ☎ 33/247–2321).

MAIL AND SHIPPING

➤ POST OFFICE: **General Post Office** (✉ BBD Bag, ☎ 33/242–1572).

MONEY MATTERS

ATMS

➤ CONTACTS: **HSBC** (✉ 31 BBD Bag or 15 Gariahat Rd. or 25A Shakespeare Sarani, ☎ 33/440–3930). **Standard Chartered Grindlays Bank** (✉ 19 Netaji Subhash Rd. or 41 Jawaharlal Nehru Rd., ☎ 33/246–5000).

CURRENCY EXCHANGE

Most of the legitimate currency exchange centers keep the same hours and offer the same services and rates. They give far better rates than the hotels. Steer clear of the many cubbyholes with slapdash signs outside touting rates that seem to good to be true (they are); these are particularly prevalent in the New Market area.

➤ EXCHANGE SERVICES: **American Express** (✉ 21 Old Court House St., ☎ 33/248–6281). **ANZ Grindlays Bank** (✉ 19 Netaji Subhash Rd., ☎ 33/220–8346). **Bank of America** (✉ 8 India Exchange Pl., ☎ 33/242–2042). **Citibank** (✉ Tata Center, 43 J. L. Nehru Rd., ☎ 33/292–9220). **State Bank of India** (✉ 33 J. L. Nehru Rd., ☎ 33/402430). **Thomas Cook** (✉ Chitrakoot Bldg., 230A A. J. C. Bose Rd., ☎ 33/247–5378).

RICKSHAWS

Calcutta is the last city on earth to use enormous Chinese-style rickshaws pulled by men on foot. At least 1 million people depend on the hard-earned wages of these men for what little daily sustenance and shelter they get. Many pullers say they wouldn't trade positions with cycle-rickshaw wallahs for anything. If you ever get the chance to pull a rickshaw, you will be horrified at how difficult it is, even when the rickshaw is empty. With that in mind, don't rush your driver, and tip generously—the driver deserves it. Rickshaw fares fluctuate depending on the distance to be traveled and the amount of traffic congestion; negotiate ahead of time, using Rs. 15 per 10 minutes as a guide.

SUBWAY TRAVEL

Calcutta's metro system, which has been evolving over the past few decades, is clean and efficient. Only the central part of the system is complete, from Tollygunge to Central Station in Tiretta; eventually (though not in the foreseeable future) it will connect Dum Dum Airport with downtown. Tickets cost Rs. 3–Rs. 7 and are available from machines and windows in every station. The metro runs daily until 9:30 PM and is crowded only at rush hour. Metro stations are marked on the government's tourist map, available free from tourist offices and most hotels.

TAXIS AND AUTO-RICKSHAWS

Most Calcuttans rely on buses, trams, and the spotless metro to get around, but you will probably rely on taxis, rickshaws, and your feet (the bus system is indecipherable, the rickety trams are good only for an early-morning ride, and the metro is somewhat limited). Calcutta is not a good city for driving; in response to the painful traffic situation, authorities have made many roads in Calcutta one-way, then the other way, then two ways at various times throughout the day and week. Take a cab to or from the area you're visiting, then walk or find a sturdy rickshaw.

The base fare in Calcutta is Rs. 10, and the meter should read about Rs. 25 after 3 km. The legal inflation factor, however, is 100%, and it changes periodically; so ask your hotel for the current inflation factor. If a driver refuses to turn the meter on, find another taxi. Traffic, unfortunately, plagues Calcutta, possibly bringing your cab to a full stop amid humid air and diesel exhaust, so at rush hour you may just want to find a sweet shop and wait until it's over.

Auto-rickshaws are cheaper than taxis, but they're not as easy to find in the city center. At rush hour they can be more efficient (albeit dirtier) alternatives; taxis are liable to get stuck in traffic.

TOURS
These agencies can arrange a car and driver for local sightseeing or help make long-distance travel arrangements.
➤ CONTACTS: **American Express** (✉ 21 Old Court House St., ☎ 33/248–4464). **Ashok Travel and Tours** (✉ Government of India Tourist Office, 4 Shakespeare Sarani, ☎ 33/440901 or 33/552–9111; Ashok Hotel, ☎ 33/440901 or 33/552–9111). **Mercury Travels** (✉ 46C J. L. Nehru Rd., ☎ 33/443555 or 33/249–2323; Oberoi Grand, ☎ 33/443555 or 33/249–2323). **Thomas Cook** (✉ Chitrakoot Bldg., 230A A. J. C. Bose Rd., ☎ 33/247–5378).

WALKING TOURS
The most interesting tours in Calcutta are the walks through various neighborhoods led by the Foundation for Conservation and Research of Urban Traditional Architecture (CRUTA).
➤ CONTACT: **Foundation for Conservation and Research of Urban Traditional Architecture** (✉ 67B Beadon St., 700006, ☎ 33/554–6127).

TELEPHONE NUMBERS
Phone numbers change with alarming frequency in Calcutta. Whenever you make a call and get a recorded message saying, "This telephone number does not exist," dial 1951 or 1952 to find out the new number. The service is good and computerized and you need only follow the instructions and punch the old digits to get hold of the new number.

TRAIN TRAVEL
Every day an incredible number of trains roll into and out of Howrah Junction, which is divided into the neighboring Old and New Howrah stations. A permanent population resides on the platforms among the ferocious crowds of travelers, vendors, and other locals; indeed, "platform children" attend school between the tracks here, taught to read and write by volunteers. The main reservation office has a foreign-tourist section upstairs, open daily 9–1 and 1:30–4; buying tickets here is a breeze with either foreign currency or a valid encashment certificate for rupees. There are also ticket offices on the first floor of Old Howrah Station, the second floor of New Howrah Station, and in Kalighat. Sealdah Station is used exclusively by trains to and from northern destinations such as Darjeeling. Tickets are sold on the platform level.

➤ TRAIN INFORMATION: **Howrah Junction** (✉ 1 block south of the west end of Howrah Bridge, ☎ 33/220–4025, or 1310). **Main Reservation Office** (✉ 6 Failie Pl., ☎ 33/660–3535) **Ticket Offices** (for first-class bookings; ✉ 14 Strand Rd., ☎ 33/220–3496). **Sealdah Station** (✉ east end of Bepin Behari Ganguly St., ☎ 33/350–3535 or 33/350–3496).

VISITOR INFORMATION

The West Bengal Tourist Office is open Monday through Saturday from 10 to 5. The regional Government of India Tourist Office is well equipped to help baffled travelers; it's open Monday through Saturday from 9 to 6. The Calcutta Information Centre is also helpful. Although the West Bengal Tourist Office is located in the heart of Calcutta's business hub, it will be able to give you information merely about destinations within the state. The Government of India Tourist Office, near the city center, gives more of an overall picture (including the state). The staff is friendly to boot.

➤ TOURIST OFFICES: **Calcutta Information Centre** (✉ 1/1 A. J. C. Bose Rd., ☎ 33/248–1451). **Government of India Tourist Office** (✉ 4 Shakespeare Sarani, Calcutta, ☎ 33/282–1472 or 33/282–5813). **West Bengal Tourist Office** (✉ 3/2 B.B.D. Bagh E, Calcutta 700001, ☎ 33/248–8271, 33/248–5917, or 33/248–5168).

15 PORTRAITS OF INDIA

India's Religions

Chronology

Books and Videos

Hindi Language

Dining Glossary

INDIA'S RELIGIONS

Hinduism, Buddhism, Jainism, and Sikhism all came into being in India, even though Buddhism is now mostly practiced elsewhere in Asia. Islam came from outside the country, yet India's large Muslim minority makes up the second-largest Muslim population in the world, after Indonesia's. India's calendar is crowded with festivals, and religion is evident everywhere in Indian life—from politics to art and architecture and the daily activities of millions of devotees.

Hinduism

Hinduism, with its literally countless gods and goddesses, extends back at least three millennia, to the hymns and ritual mantras of the ancient Sanskrit *Vedas*. It's almost impossible to define Hindu tradition in a way that would include all its major variants; the tradition's hallmark, perhaps, is its ability to adapt disparate elements—from local deities to rival philosophical systems—into a recognizably Hindu context. Perhaps the best way to start is with the *Bhagavad Gita*, a marvelous work of religious synthesis set in the midst of battle in the epic *Mahabharata*. Arjuna, one of five brothers who are the epic's heroes, falters on the battlefield, concerned that no good will come of defeating his enemies, who are also his cousins. Arjuna's charioteer, Krishna, an incarnation of the great god Vishnu, reminds him that Hindus believe in reincarnation and their ultimate goal is *moksha*, liberation from the endless cycle of rebirth. There are reasons, Krishna says, for the rivalry that led to the battle, and as a young warrior Arjuna must fulfill his particular duty (*dharma*) through action (*karma*) that is unconcerned with benefits or reward. Fulfilling one's assigned duty and moral obligation to society is a necessary step toward attaining higher religious knowledge (*jnana*) and the ultimate goal of union with God through devotion (*bhakti*). The *Gita*, as it is called, has a place in the homes of almost all modern Hindus. It does not have canonical authority above that of many other texts, yet it gives in outline a basic set of beliefs that are held in common.

Sacrifice is an essential part of dharma, and central to the practice of the earliest stage of Hinduism embodied in the *Vedas*. An offering to a god blesses the worshiper in return. Beginning with the *Upanishads*, appendixes to the *Vedas*, sacrifice has also been seen in metaphorical terms, as the sacrifice of the baser aspect of one's individuality, so that the individual soul, or spirit (*atman*), can merge with *brahman* (universal consciousness) and allow the realization of moksha.

Some Hindus also practice yoga, a combination of physical culture and meditation practice that is exemplified by the ascetics and sadhus in such places as Varanasi. Yoga (which literally means "yoke" or "union") uses mental and physical discipline to purify the body and rid the practitioner of conscious thought, so he or she can experience a sense of detachment from the realities of the physical world and a higher knowledge (jnana) similar in some ways to gnosis in the Western tradition. In the *Bhagavad Gita* many other forms of dedicated behavior, such as devotion or disinterested action, are described as forms of yoga.

Strictures underlying dharma and karma also help explain the thousands of castes that divide Hindus, which have been conceptualized in a framework of four segregated rankings: Brahmins (priests), Kshatriyas (nobles and warriors), Vaishyas (tradesmen), and Shudras (menial laborers). A fifth grouping, Panchama, falls outside this framework: the lowest rung of society. Once commonly known as "untouchables," the people in this class were named Harijans, or "Children of God," by Mahatma Gandhi and now prefer to be called Dalits, or the "oppressed."

To most Westerners, the caste system seems like cause for revolution, but it's been a complex and even flexible way of ordering society. In ancient India, unlike many other places, there was no all-powerful priestly class, and slavery was rare. There is evidence of considerable shifting in the status of various castes (though not of individuals) in Indian history. Still, historically, for those in the lowest categories, the system was doubtless cruel. While it is said that they accepted their fate, understanding it as a direct result of their karma in previous births, poetry by lower-caste Hindus from as early as the 12th century explicitly rejects caste. Centuries passed before the untouchables found their way out of exclusion; the catalysts were Mahatma Gandhi and Bhimrao Ramji Ambedkar, a Dalit leader who was one of the principle authors of the Indian Constitution. Despite their frequent disagreements, Gandhi's and Ambedkar's efforts changed the way modern India thinks about caste, and saw to it that discrimination based on caste was legally abolished in 1947. In practice, caste still regulates many aspects of Hindu behavior, such as marriage practices; and caste is emerging as a dominant element of Indian politics, much as ethnicity has done in the United States and other Western political systems.

Hindu Temples

The Hindu temple is filled with symbols. Before the structure is built, a priest traces a *mandala,* which represents the cosmos and determines the placement of all rooms and icons. The center of the temple, called the inner sanctum, represents the egg or womb from which all life originates; this is where the sacred deity resides. The *vimana* (spire) is directly over the inner sanctum, drawing devotees' attention to the heavenly realm and its connection with the sacred deity.

Many festivals take place in the temple's *mandapam,* a front porch that may be an elaborate pillared pavilion or a simple overhang. Water is the agent of purification. Ideally, a temple is constructed near a river or lake, but if no natural water source is available, a large tank is often built, with steps around it for ease of ablutions. Before the devout Hindu worships, he takes a ritual dip to rid himself of impurities. Daily *darshan,* or viewing of the idol—usually performed at sunrise, noon, sunset, and midnight—is imbued with sacred traditions. Ancient rituals combine in an elaborate pageantry that can include such personalized acts as feeding the deity or brushing its teeth, performed with a touching gentleness toward the god's idol. These rituals are often paralleled in worship at home shrines.

Before the priest enters the temple, he takes his sacred dip. The actual darshan takes place during a ceremony known as *arati* (moving flame), which begins with the clanging of a bell to ward off any evil presence and awaken the sleeping deity. Burning camphor sweetens the air as the priest recites mantras and blesses the idol with oils and sandalwood paste. The deity receives offerings of incense (an aroma favored by the gods), vermilion powder, flowers, and decorative platters of food. Lamps of *ghee* (clarified butter) and more camphor are waved before the idol; then the priest blesses the devotees, and often the door to the inner sanctum is closed to let the deity return to its sleeping state. Worshipers are given sweets and other food that has been offered to the deity; this food is known as *prasada* (translated by one scholar as "the edible form of God's grace") and can be taken home for distribution to friends and family members.

The Hindu Pantheon

It has been said that there are 330,000,000 gods in the Hindu pantheon. For the worshiper, this bewildering profusion can be simplified by dedication to a single god or goddess, or by the idea that many gods and goddesses are forms of a few great gods and goddesses. The celebrated German Indianist Max Muller has said that Hindus are not so much pantheists as xenotheists: supreme divinity can be invested serially in the deity being worshiped at any one moment by a particular person.

Through the mythology, iconography, and devotional song that surrounds them, Hindu gods and goddesses are remarkably personalized. This is in striking contrast to the abstract notion of ultimate reality, or brahman, found in the *Upanishads* and subscribed to by many Hindus even as they worship one or more specific anthropomorphized gods and goddesses. A well-known story about Krishna and the *gopis* (the pastoral maidens of Braj, near Agra) illustrates the delight Hindus take in the incarnation of their gods. Visited by a philosopher who expounded the higher truths of atman and brahman, which cannot be seen or described, one gopi said: "It's all very well to know brahman, but can the ultimate reality put its arms around you?"

Most important deities are clustered around the incarnations, families, and mythological associates of two great gods, Vishnu and Shiva, and their female consorts.

Brahma, creator of the world and progenitor of all living things, is the third member of the Hindu trinity. (Note that *Brahma,* the deity, is different from *brahman,* universal consciousness, and also from *Brahmin,* the priestly caste.) He is the keeper of cosmic time and a sort of master-of-ceremonies advancing story lines in myths, but he is not actively worshiped. In sculpture and painting, Brahma has four heads and four arms, each holding sway over a quarter of the universe and signifying one of the four *Vedas.* The rosary that he counts in one hand represents time, and his lotus seat represents the earth. Brahma's vehicle is the swan, symbol of the freedom that comes with knowledge. His consort is Saraswati, the goddess of learning.

Shiva is most famously depicted dancing the *tandava* dance of destruction, with which cosmic epochs come to an end so that new ones can be born. Shiva is the yogic ascetic par excellence, wearing snakes as garlands, ashes as ointment, and an animal-skin loincloth, and meditating in the Himalayas from one eon to the next. Paradoxically, however, he is married to Parvati, and his family and love life are celebrated in myth and art. Shiva's non-anthropomorphic form is the linga, a phallic symbol that rests in a *yoni,* which represents the womb. Worship of the linga is not explicitly phallic worship; the icon is as much an abstract representation of the axis mundi, the axis on which the world spins, or of how divine presence manifests itself on earth to Hindus.

Shiva's consorts take many forms, and are often considered aspects of one general goddess (Devi) or a female divine principle (*shakti*). Principle among these is Parvati, the daughter of Himalaya with whom Shiva had two sons: Ganesh, the elephant-headed god of wisdom and prosperity, and Kartikeya, known as Murugan in South India. Other shaktis include Durga, slayer of the buffalo demon, and Kali, sometimes called the goddess of death and depicted in terrible aspect, wearing a garland of skulls and dancing on Shiva's dead body. Shiva's mount, Nandi, the sacred bull, usually guards the entrance to a Shiva temple. Priests who pray to Shiva have three horizontal stripes painted on their foreheads.

The preserver of the universe, Vishnu, has nine known avatars, and a 10th is prophesied. Each successive avatar reflects a step up the evolutionary cycle, beginning with the fish and moving up to the ninth, Buddha, accepted by the all-embracing Hindus as a figure in their own pantheon. Vishnu's most popular incarnations are Rama and Krishna (the sixth and seventh, respectively), the two gods that embody humanity. Vishnu priests have three vertical stripes painted on their foreheads.

Vishnu appears with four arms to signify the four cardinal directions and his command over the realms they encompass. In one hand, he carries the lotus, symbol of the universe; in the other, a conch shell, which represents the evolutionary nature of all existence. The wheel in Vishnu's third hand refers to the rotation of the earth, with each spoke honoring a specific season of the year. In his fourth hand, Vishnu often holds a weapon to protect him from demons. A common image of Vishnu has him lying on a bed of coils formed by his serpent, Ananta, who symbolizes time; creation will begin when Vishnu wakes up. Vishnu has two consorts: Bhudevi, the goddess of Earth, and Lakshmi, the goddess of wealth and prosperity, who rose from the foam of the ocean like Venus. Lakshmi assumes a different name with each of Vishnu's avatars. When Vishnu is Rama, she's Sita; when he's Krishna, she's Radha.

Rama is the ideal king. As the hero of the Hindu epic *Ramayana,* he slew the 10-headed demon, Ravana, who had kidnapped Sita. This episode, including Sita's rescue by Hanuman, the monkey god and Rama's faithful servant, is celebrated during Dussehra, one of India's most festive holidays. There are three distinct phases in Krishna's mythology. (Some 19th-century Europeans saw this as the conflation of three different pre-Hindu gods into one Hindu one, but this concept is laughable to Krishna's devotees.) In the first phase, Krishna is a playful boy god, stealing butter from his mother's pantry. In the next, he is an amorous, flute-playing cowherd and the focus of a huge body of love poetry. Finally, he is the charioteer of the *Mahabharata,* interceding on behalf of the heroes and offering the wisdom of the *Bhagavad Gita.*

In addition to these major gods, there are countless village and regional gods, sometimes affiliated in myth with the great pan-Indian Hindu gods or goddesses. There are also many goddesses not paired off with male gods or celebrated in Sanskrit texts, such as Shitala Mata, the smallpox goddess (whose worship continues despite the eradication of smallpox). Since medieval times at least, great devotees from a wide range of castes and communities have also been venerated, and religious communities organized around their teachings.

Jainism

The origins of Jainism (the name comes from the word *jina,* or victor) go back more than 2,500 years. Jainism became a powerful sect during the time of Parsvanatha, who lived in the 8th century BC. At this time Hindu Brahmins dominated much of Indian religious life; like Buddhism, Jainism developed under the patronage of prosperous non-Brahmin communities. Jains revere 24 *tirthankaras* (perfect souls), men believed to have achieved spiritual victory and attained moksha.

Parsvanatha, the 23rd tirthankara, was a prince who renounced his wealth to become an ascetic. He advocated honesty, respect for all life (in the belief that every creature has a soul, and all souls are equal), and *ahimsa* (nonviolence); and he abhorred any form of theft and the ownership of property. The 24th tirthankara was Mahavira (Great Hero), who lived in the 6th century BC, around the time of the historic Buddha. Mahavira also became a monk, and eventually shed his clothes as a sign of devotion and absolute self-denial—to have no possessions. He advocated a life of denial, even though he realized his example would be difficult to follow.

In 300 BC, the original Jain scriptures were finally committed to writing. Jainism also split into two sects: Svetambaras, who wear white clothes, and Digambaras, who practice nudity and believe that women cannot achieve moksha until they are reborn as men. Women, according to Digambaras, are the greatest source of earthly temptation.

Rejecting the existence of a supreme being, Jains follow the model of the 24 tirthan-karas. They divide the universe into three worlds, which are divided in turn into numerous levels—devotees want to cross the metaphorical river of existence and obtain freedom for the soul from all three realms. The Jain cosmology is a common motif in religious paintings: the lower world, which normally looks like truncated pyramids, represents various infernos occupied by mortals who have sinned. The middle world, which resembles a disc, contains all non-living matter and life forms, including human beings who are struggling through the cycle of rebirth and striving for liberation. The upper world, often drum-shape with a bulging middle, is the realm of the gods (souls who have performed good deeds) and spirits. Some paintings also take the shape of the Cosmic Man: the truncated pyramids are turned into legs, the disc becomes the waist, and the upper world extends up from the abdomen. When devout beings who have done good deeds are depicted in the cosmos, their visible serenity increases—based on their good deeds—as they move up each level within the upper world.

The restrictions of Jainism are extensive. Because Jains are supposed to avoid all occupations that involve the destruction of any life form, many Jains are members of the trading community. Few are farmers. Jains are not permitted to eat meat or eggs, and many even shun vegetables and edible roots for fear of ingesting microscopic creatures in the process. They must also take 12 vows that include the practice of ahimsa and meditation, restrictions on the acquisition of wealth and unnecessary belongings, and the commitment to spend some time as a monk or nun.

An important Jain symbol is the swastika, with each appendage representing the four possible stages of birth: life in hell; life as an insect, animal, or bird; human life; and life as a god or demon. The three dots on top of the swastika stand for right faith, right knowledge, and right conduct. The half moon above the dots stands for moksha: the ultimate Jain goal.

Because one vow instructs devotees to contribute generously to the construction and maintenance of temples and animal hospitals, Jain temples are often exquisitely adorned. (The Charity Birds Hospital in Delhi is another remarkable response to this instruction.) Images of the 24 tirthankaras, depicted as ascetics with or without clothes, and usually made of white marble, embellish most Jain temples. Parsvanatha is blue or black, and usually appears with a snake; Mahavira is golden, and usually appears with a lion.

Islam

"There is no God but Allah, and Mohammed is His Prophet"—this is the *shahadah* (religious creed) and most important pillar of the Islamic faith. Islam originated with Mohammed (whose name means "highly praised"), who was born around AD 571 in the Arabian town of Mecca. A series of revelations from Allah, passed on through the Angel Gabriel, instructed Mohammed to preach against the paganism practiced by the Meccans. Mohammed saw himself as a social reformer, advocating a virtuous life in a city where virtue had vanished; but the Meccans saw him as a menace and a threat, and forced him to flee to Yathrib (now Medina).

This flight, in AD 622—which Muslims now call *hijra*—marks the beginning of the era in which Mohammed established the concept of Islam (which means "submission" and "peace") as a way of life. By the time Mohammed died in AD 632, the inhabitants of an expanse stretching from Samarkand (in Uzbekistan) to the Sahara had converted.

With the death of Mohammed, his father-in-law, Abu Bakr, one of the first converts to Islam, became the next ruler and was called caliph—"successor of the Prophet." In AD 656, during the reign of the fourth caliph, Ali (the Prophet's nephew and the husband of his daughter Fatima), civil war broke out. Ali moved his capital to Mesopotamia, where he was murdered by Muslim dissidents.

Ali's death signaled the beginning of a period of dissension between the traditionalists, Sunnis, who followed the orthodox teaching and example of the Prophet, and Ali's supporters, who claimed Ali's right to the caliphate based on his descent from the Prophet. In time, Ali's supporters broke away from the Sunnis and formed a sect known as the Shia, or Shiites.

Originally political in nature, the differences between the Sunnis and Shiites took on theological overtones. The Sunnis retained the doctrine of leadership by consensus. After Syrians massacred Hussain, Ali's son, at Karbala, in Iraq, the Shiites strengthened their resolution that only Mohammed's rightful heirs should rule. They modified the *shahadah:* "There is no god but Allah; Mohammed is the Prophet of God, and Ali is the Saint of God."

The concept of Islam means submission to Allah, or God—who is invisible yet omnipresent. To represent Allah in any form is a sin, thus the absence of icons in mosques and tombs. Every bit of decoration—often fashioned out of myriad tiny gems—is limited to inscriptions of the Koran, Muslims' holy scripture, and the names of Mohammed and the first four Caliphs, who were part of the first generation of followers.

Muslims believe that Allah has existed throughout time, but that humans had strayed from his true teaching until Mohammed set them straight. Islam has concepts similar to those of Judaism or Christianity: guardian angels, the day of judgment, the general resurrection, heaven and hell, and the eternal life of the soul. Muslims also follow a strict code of ethical conduct that encourages generosity, tolerance, and respect and forbids adultery, gambling, usury, and the consumption of pork and alcohol. Other Muslim duties are known as the five pillars of the faith: the recitation of the shahadah; *salat* (daily prayer); *zakat* (alms); *siyam* (fasting); and *haj* (pilgrimage). The believer must pray to Allah five times daily, preceding each occasion by performing ablutions. Men pray at a mosque under a prayer leader whenever possible, and are recommended to do so on Friday. Women are also recommended to attend public worship on Friday; men and women are segregated during prayer.

The ninth month of the Muslim calendar, Ramadan—in which Mohammed received his revelations—is a month of required fasting from sunrise to sunset for all but the weak, pregnant women, young children, and travelers (who make up the days of fasting later). In addition to food, drinking, smoking, and sexual intercourse are prohibited during daylight hours.

A Muslim is supposed to make the haj to the Great Mosque in Mecca once in his life to participate in 10 days of special rites, held during the 12th month of the lunar calendar. While on the haj, the pilgrim wears an *ihram* (seamless white robe) to symbolize equality and devotion to Allah and abstains from sexual relations, shaving, and cutting his hair and nails. Women are also supposed to go on haj; women on pilgrimage do not cover their hair. The returning pilgrim is entitled to the honorific "hajji" before his name and a turban carved on his tombstone.

The word mosque, or *masjid,* means "a place of prostration." Mosques are generally square in shape; built of stone, clay, or brick; and centered on an open courtyard surrounded with *madrasas* (schools) for students of the Koran. After the *muezzin* (crier) sings the call for prayer from the minaret (tower), the faithful line up in rows behind the *imam* (one who has studied the Koran). The imam stands in the sacred part of the masjid facing the *mihrab,* a niche in the wall that indicates the direction of Mecca. When the imam prays, the mihrab—an ingenious amplifier—bounces the imam's voice back to the devotees. In a mosque, only prayers are heard and prostrations made; ceremonies connected with birth, marriage, and death occur elsewhere.

Popular Islam in India involves not only prayer at home and in the mosque, but worship at the graves of great religious teachers of the past. On the anniversaries of the saints' deaths—the *urs,* or time of ascent to heaven—great fairs attract pilgrims, sometimes of many faiths, from all over the country.

Sikhism

The founder of Sikhism, Guru Nanak, was born into a Hindu family in 1469, at a time when the Lodi sultanate—a Muslim dynasty from Afghanistan—ruled his North Indian homeland. From an early age, he railed against the caste system, the corruption of Hindu priests, their superstitious beliefs, and their unwieldy family of gods. In his poems and teachings, Guru Nanak urged egalitarianism based on love and devotion to a single, non-incarnate divinity called the Wahi Guru, conceived as the embodiment of truth, goodness, and uniqueness. (These three words form the common Sikh greeting "Sat Sri Akal.")

Nanak's view of Sikhism, recorded in the *Adi Granth,* upheld the Islamic idea that the goal of religion was union with God, who dwelled within the soul. He believed that, through meditation and dharma (Hindu concepts), devotees could rid themselves of impurities, free themselves from the endless cycle of rebirth, and attain eternal bliss. For Hindus at the bottom of society, Sikhism offered equality and tolerance; they gladly converted, becoming Sikhs—disciples.

During the early years of the Mogul Empire, Sikhism flourished without interference until Emperor Jahangir assumed the throne. Resenting the Sikhs' rejection of Islam, Jahangir ultimately tortured and murdered the fifth guru. When Aurangzeb, the next emperor, revealed his own ruthless intolerance, Gobind Singh, the 10th and final guru, forged the Sikhs into a martial community that he called the *khalsa* ("pure"). Gobind Singh instructed every Sikh man to observe and wear the five *kakkari* (visible symbols): *kesh* (uncut hair and beard), *kachh* (boxer shorts), *kara* (a steel bangle), *kanga* (a wooden comb), and *kirpan* (a dagger). All Sikh men also assumed the surname Singh, meaning "lion" (though not all Singhs are Sikhs), and Sikh women adopted the name Kaur, meaning "lioness" or "princess." Members of the khalsa were to follow a strict code of conduct that forbade the use of alcohol and tobacco and advocated a life of meditation and courage.

Buddhism

Siddhartha Gautama was born into a princely family in Lumbini, near the India–Nepal border, around 563 BC. Upon encountering suffering during his first venture outside the palace as a young man, he renounced his privileged status—an act called the Great Renunciation—to live as an ascetic. He then entered a lengthy meditation that led to his Great Enlightenment, or nirvana.

Transformed, Siddhartha went to Sarnath, India (near Varanasi), and preached his revolutionary sermon on the *dharma* (truth), also called "The Setting in Motion of the Wheel of Truth or Law." His discourse set forth his Four Noble Truths, which define the essence of Buddhism: (1) Life is connected to suffering, (2) a suffering that arises from greed, insatiable desires, and the self-centered nature of humans; (3) once a person understands the cause of her suffering, she can overcome it by following (4) the Eightfold Path.

The Eightfold Path includes right views and right aspirations, which lead to wisdom. Right speech, right behavior, right means of livelihood, and right efforts to follow the path to salvation relate to proper and intelligent conduct. Right meditation and right contemplation bring nirvana (supreme bliss).

Siddhartha Gautama became the Buddha (Enlightened One), or Sakyamunni (Sage of the Sakya clan), and his faith became Theravada Buddhism, a religion of compassion and reason in which images were not worshiped, the existence of a permanent soul (*atman* to Hindus) was denied, and the authority of the Hindu *Vedas* was rejected. In the 1st century AD a second school, Mahayana Buddhism, was formed and introduced the concept of the *bodhisattva,* the enlightened being who postpones his own nirvana to help others. Unlike Theravadans—who prayed only before symbols, such as the Buddha's empty throne or his footprints—Mahayanists also worshiped before depictions of the various Buddhas, other gods and goddesses, and revered bodhisattvas. Over time, Mahayana Buddhism divided into subsects, based on differences in philosophical systems or ritual practices.

Ironically, Buddhism did not survive as a popular religion in India after its classical period. This is partly because of Hindu thinkers' response to the Buddhist challenge, embodied in works like the *Bhagavad Gita;* partly because increasingly sophisticated philosophy and esoteric ritual held little attraction for lay followers; and partly because major Buddhist institutions

were destroyed by Muslim iconoclasts. While Indian teachers brought Buddhism to Tibet and China—and it spread from there—Buddhist remnants in India are limited mainly to such monuments as the Great Stupa at Sanchi (Madhya Pradesh), the Ajanta caves, and sculptures in major museums. Nevertheless, Buddhist artworks are among India's great treasures, evolving over time from stupas holding relics of the Buddha to elaborate temple structures depicting scenes from the life of the Buddha and episodes in his past lives. Later tantric Buddhist art, which continued to flourish in Nepal and Tibet, includes a large pantheon of past and future Buddhas, goddesses, Bodhisattvas, and historical teachers of the faith.

Two major communities still practice Buddhism in India. Tibetans in India include those in Himalayan areas such as Ladakh, which were closely connected to Tibet, and some 100,000 refugees who fled Tibet after the Chinese took over in 1951 and are now dispersed in various parts of India. The Dalai Lama, head of the Gelugpas, the largest Tibetan Buddhist sect, now lives in Dharamsala, Himachal Pradesh, where a sizable Tibetan community works to preserve their traditions and the welfare of the refugee community. The other main Buddhist group, sometimes called neo-Buddhist, was founded by the Dalit leader Bhimrao Ramji Ambedkar, who urged fellow untouchables to abandon Hinduism in favor of Buddhism because the latter does not recognize caste.

— Kathleen Cox and Andy McCord

INDIA AT A GLANCE

ca. 2 million BC　First human occupation of area that is now India.

7000 BC　Earliest evidence of agricultural activity.

2500 BC　Indus Valley (also called Harappan) Civilization. Uniformly built cities were spread across several thousand miles of territory in a civilization that compared in size and accomplishment to ancient China or Mesopotamia. Its script, a series of symbols found of sets of clay seals, remains undeciphered.

1750 BC　Decline of Harappan civilization for which many theories have been advanced, including invasion and ecological disaster. The existence of this civilization was rediscovered in the 1920s.

1500–1200 BC　Composition of the Rigveda, early religious texts of Vedism—the precursor of all modern South Asian religions, including Hinduism, Buddhism, and Jainism.

ca. 1000 BC　Composition of other Vedas, including Sama Veda, Yajur Veda, and Atharva Veda.

ca. 1500–1000 BC　Evolution of caste (*varna*) system.

ca. 600 BC　Composition of the Upanishads, early Brahmanical religious texts.

ca. 600 BC　Life of Vardhamana, or Mahavira, the 24th *Tirthankara* and one of the most revered spiritual leaders of Jainism.

ca. 563–483 BC　Life of Siddhartha Gautama, the Buddha, founder of Buddhism. He was born in what is now Nepal, and did his teaching in what is now eastern India.

ca. 500 BC　Composition of the epic Ramayana had started by this date. This story of the perfect rulership of the King Rama, avatar of Lord Vishnu and of his quest to rescue his wife Sita from the demon king Ravana, is still considered by many to depict a model of governance and personal behavior for many Hindus.

ca. 400 BC　Composition of Panini's grammar of Sanskrit, which many still consider to be the most complete and accurate grammar of any language ever written.

ca. 300 BC　Earliest written records from southern India, including Tamil language collections.

326 BC　Invasion of Panjab by Alexander of Macedonia (Alexander the Great).

321–185 BC　Mauryan Empire extended over most of modern India and Pakistan and parts of Afghanistan. Emperors were Chandragupta, Bindusara, and, most famously, Ashoka, whose inscriptions on rocks and pillars encouraging Buddhist practice can still be seen throughout India. This was the largest territorial state in South Asia prior to the British Empire.

ca. 240 BC　Earliest surviving examples of Brahmi script, from which all indigenous writing systems of India are evolved.

ca. 100 BC–AD 400　Construction of Ajanta and Ellora cave temples in western India.

AD 319–467　Gupta Empire in North India. Coincides with what is considered the "Classical" period of Hindu civilization, with great achievements in the arts and literature.

ca. 400 The epic Mahabharata takes on its final form, although its composition was started almost 900 years earlier.

ca. 450 Life of Sanskrit poet and playwright Kalidasa, who wrote, among other works, Shakuntala and Meghaduta. He is considered the greatest writer of Sanskrit plays and poetry.

ca. 600 Earliest construction of sculptures and stone temples at Mahabilipuram in Tamil Nadu.

700 Muslim traders begin to visit the west coast of India.

ca. 711 Muhammad bin Qasim conquers Indus delta region, establishing first Muslim rule in South Asia.

900–1100 Construction of temples at Khajuraho.

997–1030 Raids from Afghanistan into India by Mahmud Ghazni, destroying Hindu temples and sowing the seeds of antipathy between members of the two faiths.

ca. 1206–1526 The Delhi Sultanate, the first modern era empire centered on Delhi.

ca. 1253–1325 Life of Amir Khusrau, preeminent Persian poet of India.

ca. 1440–1518 Life of Hindi syncretist poet Kabir of Varanasi.

ca. 1469–1539 Life of Guru Nanak, the founder of the Sikh religion.

1498 Arrival of Portuguese Vasco da Gama in Goa, the first direct sailing from Europe to India around the southern tip of Africa.

ca. 1498–after 1550 Life of Mirabai, poet of Rajasthan. Born into nobility, she left to become a mendicant and devotee of Krishna. Two hundred of her poems are verified as hers, but there may be as many as 1,300. They were originally written in Gujarati but were quickly translated into and sung in many languages.

1526 Battle of Panipat won by Babur, signaling the beginning of the Mughal Empire.

ca. 1532–1623 Life of Tulsidas, composer of the still most popular Hindi version of the epic Ramayana, the *Ramcharitmanas*.

1600 Charter of East India Company granted by Queen Elizabeth in London for it to execute trade in India, Southeast Asia, Japan, and China.

1608 First landing of an East India Company ship in India, in the western city of Surat, where they established a "factory," or trading post.

1632–1649 Taj Mahal built to fulfill a promise Mughal Emperor Shah Jahan made to his wife: to honor her by constructing a beautiful tomb for her. Craftsmen were brought in from around western Asia to execute the beautiful stonework of the structure.

ca. 1650 Construction of Red Fort in Delhi.

1707 Death of Aurangzeb, the last great Mughal Emperor, signaling the beginning of the demise of the Mughal Empire. It would not formally cease to exist until 1857.

1757 Battle of Plassey, at which a British East India Company-supported army defeated a Bengali general, and the Company directly controlled a part of India for the first time.

1765 Mughal Emperor grants the East India Company the right to collect tax revenue from Bengal, Bihar, and Orissa; this is the first Company administration of Indian territory.

ca. 1797– 1869 Life of Mirza Ghalib, preeminent Urdu poet of India, who was also renowned for his skill in Persian poetry and for his personal letters—still widely read.

1857 The Indian Mutiny. Indian troops of the British East India Copmany mutinied first, in the North Indian city of Meerut, and the revolt spread from there to most of the other cities of North India, although it centered on Delhi, the capital of the dying Mughal Empire. The immediate cause for the troops to revolt was their belief that the British were attempting to foist on them gun cartridges greased with pig and cow fat, which the troops were required to bite in preparation for their use. Such use would have violated the religious beliefs of both Hindus and Muslims. Long-term causes included East India Company misrule, including the annexation of the previously independent North Indian kingdom of Awadh (capital Lucknow) in 1856. It took a year for the British to reestablish their control over the territories.

1858 End of fighting between rebels and British army. The British took revenge on Indians, including blowing mutineers from cannons. There were also hangings and general looting of many cities.

1858 Abolition of the East India Company and imposition of direct British rule over India as a result of the hostilities of 1857–1858.

1869 Mohandas Karamchand (Mahatma) Gandhi born in Gujarat in western India.

ca. 1880– 1936 Life of Prem Chand, author of such novels as *Godan,* which deplored social inequalities in India. Prem Chand is considered the father of modern Hindi literature.

1885 Establishment of Indian National Congress. At the time it was devoted to improvement of British rule in India, it became the leading political party in India, through Independence in 1947 and until the mid-1990s.

ca. 1838– 1894 Life of Bankim Chandra Chatterjee, author whose works include early nationalist literature, such as *Anandamath,* which provided the lyrics for India's nationalist anthem before independence.

1876 Birth of Muhammad Ali Jinnah, founder of Pakistan.

1899–1950 Life of Bibhutibhushan Bandyopadhyay, author whose stories were made into film in the 1950s by Satyajit Ray.

1906 Establishment of Muslim League, the organization that would eventually lead the movement for the creation of Pakistan.

1913 Rabindranath Tagore awarded Nobel Prize for literature for his English transation of Gitanjali.

1913 First Indian feature film, *Raja Harishchandra,* by Dadasaheb Phalke. India currently has the world's largest film industry.

1915 Gandhi returns to great acclaim to India from South Africa.

1919 Jallianwalla Bagh massacre, in which a British army regiment killed hundreds of unarmed people gathered in a city park in the Panjabi city of Amritsar, leads to first significant calls for complete independence from Britain for India.

1920–22 First of Gandhi's *Satyagraha* ("Truth Force") campaigns.

1930 Gandhi courts arrest by leading the Salt March, defying British colonial rules against making untaxed salt.

1937 Indian National Congress sweeps elections for provincial legislatures, shuts out Muslim League from governing.

1940 Lahore Declaration of the Muslim League calls, for the first time, for the establishment of a separate state upon gaining independence from Britain for the Muslims of South Asia.

1947 Independence attained. Pakistan created. Jawaharlal Nehru becomes first Prime Minister of independent India, leading the country through the difficult process of establishing democratic rule in a post-colonial society. He had been a major figure in the Indian National Congress leading up to Independence. He served until his death in 1964. Muhammad Ali Jinnah became the first Prime Minister of independent Pakistan, until his death in 1948.

1948 Assassination of Gandhi on January 30 by a Hindu fanatic.

1948 Jinnah, Pakistan's first Prime Minister, dies on September 11.

1948 First Indo-Pakistan war over Kashmir.

1953 Promulgation of Indian Constitution, India declared a republic, celebrated on January 26 as Republic Day.

1955 Release of Pather Panchali, Satyajit Ray's first film. This is the first Indian "art" film to have success at home and abroad.

1956 Linguistic reorganization of states. The old colonial "presidency" of Madras is split up into the current Indian states of Tamil Nadu, Andhra Pradesh, Kerala, and Karnataka, according to language groupings. This establishes the pattern by which new states will be created, including Maharashtra, Gujarat, Punjab in the 1960s, and Uttaranchal, Jharkhand, and Chattisgarh in 2000.

1962 India-China war.

1964 Death of Jawaharlal Nehru.

1965 Second Indo-Pakistan war.

1966 Indira Gandhi becomes Prime Minister.

1971 Third Indo-Pakistan war, secession of Bangladesh from Pakistan.

ca. 1971 Indira sweeps national elections after success of Indian military in creation of Bangladesh.

1974 First Indian nuclear test.

1975–77 Emergency rule declared by Mrs. Gandhi—only national cessation of democratic government in independent India's history.

1977 Indira Gandhi calls elections, is resoundingly voted out of office.

1977–81 Government by Janata Party, the first non-Congress government in India's history. It falls apart due to inter-coalition squabbling. One of the members of the Janata coalition, the Bharatiya Jan Sangh, evolved into the Bharatiya Janata Party, the current ruling party as of 2001.

1981 Indira Gandhi elected Prime Minister.

June 1984 Raid on Sikh Golden Temple (called "Operation Bluestar" by the Indian Government) in Amritsar to move armed Sikh militants out of the temple complex. Many are killed, and Sikhs the world over are outraged at what they perceived to be a desecration of their holiest site.

October 1984   Assassination of Indira Gandhi by her Sikh bodyguards in retaliation for Operation Bluestar.

1987   Indian Peacekeeping Force (IPKF) becomes embroiled in conflict in Sri Lanka, earning the enmity of both sides, but especially of the Liberation Tigers of Tamil Eelam (LTTE).

1989   Rajiv Gandhi assassinated during election campaign by sympathizer of LTTE for actions of Indian military in Sri Lanka.

1991   Economic liberalization undertaken in face of balance of payments crisis caused by oil price rise.

1990s   Indian computer and software industry offers hope that India can change its economic status and follow its East Asian neighbors' model of prosperity. Still, this industry constitutes only a tiny percentage of economic activity and employment in the overwhelmingly agricultural economy.

1992   Destruction of Babri Masjid mosque in North Indian city of Aydohya after years of agitation by the Bharatiya Janata Party to have it turned into a Hindu Temple. Many claimed this mosque was built on the site of the birthplace of Lord Rama, hero of the Hindu epic *Ramayana,* and hence its destruction would allow restoration of a previously existing temple. Ensuing violence kills thousands nationwide.

Mid-1990s   Wave of English-language novels by Indian writers hits the literary world, including "God of Small Things" by Arundhati Roy.

1996   Election of Bharatiya Janata Party Prime Minister Atal Bihari Vajpayee, whose government lasts for 11 days. Coalition lead by Congress Party takes over until 1998.

1998   Election of Bharatiya Janata Party Prime Minister, government still in office.

1998   Indian and Pakistani nuclear tests. Economic sanctions instigated by United States against both nations.

May–July 1999   Fighting between India and Pakistan in Kargil. Pakistani "irregulars" cross the line of control between Indian- and Pakistan-controlled Kashmir, and take posts that were abandoned by Indian troops during the winter. Fighting lasts for almost three months, and eventually Pakistanis withdraw under pressure from the international community, particularly theUnited States.

1999   October Coup in Pakistan by Pervez Musharraf removes elected Prime Minister Nawaz Sharif.

2000   Bill Clinton makes first visit by U.S. President to India in 20 years, signaling new relationship between the world's largest democracies.

2001   July summit between Indian Prime Minister Atal Bihari Vajpayee and Pakistani leader Pervez Musharraf ends unsuccessfully after three days of talks. Skirmishes in Kashmir heat up during U.S. bombing of Afghanistan.

By Keith Snodgrass

BOOKS AND VIDEOS

Nonfiction

The classic work on early Indian history is A. L. Basham's *The Wonder that Was India*. Stanley Wolpert's *New History of India* (6th ed.) is a good survey. In *The Discovery of India*, Jawaharlal Nehru's sense of his country's history is passionate and poetic. *India Britannica,* by Geoffrey Moorhouse, is an entertaining and informative history of the British Raj. *Freedom at Midnight,* by Larry Collins and Dominique Lapierre, is a spellbinding account of India's break from Britain; *City of Joy,* by the same authors, is a powerful portrait of Calcutta. *India: A Million Mutinies Now,* by V. S. Naipaul, is an optimistic sequel to the author's brilliant but infuriating earlier books on India. Diana Eck's *Banaras: City of Light* is an engaging profile of the religious life of Varanasi, including an account of Hinduism as it has been lived over the centuries. Elisabeth Bumiller's balanced presentation of the lives of Indian women, *May You Be the Mother of a Hundred Sons,* stands out. Sunil Khilnani's *The Idea of India* is a brilliant essay on India's post-Nehru efforts to build an entity out of its challenging size, diversity, and economy. K. Ilaiah's *Why I am not a Hindu* stirred a far-reaching debate on caste in contemporary India. Nirad Chaudhuri's *Autobiography of an Unknown Indian* is a memoir of the Bengali author's early days in colonial India, including lively, insightful descriptions of Indian customs, castes, and relations with the British. *In Light of India* is a collection of learned essays by the Nobel Laureate and former Mexican ambassador Octavio Paz; one essay, "Feasts and Fasts," compares Indian and Mexican cuisines in such a way that both take on greater significance. Gita Mehta's *Snakes and Ladders* is a collection of short pieces on the state of modern India. James Cameron's *An Indian Summer* is a glib but loving memoir by a British journalist who lived in India both during and after the Raj.

Barbara Stoler Miller's *The Bhagavad-Gita: Krishna's Council in Time of War* is the best translation of the classic Hindu text. To understand the great Sanskrit epic *Mahabharata,* the most readable place to start is the screenplay to Peter Brook's film and stage version. Classical Hindu myths are retold in prose form in *Gods, Demons, and Others,* by the master writer R. K. Narayan, and more recently in the acclaimed volume *Ka,* by Roberto Calasso. A. K. Ramanujan's *Speaking of Shiva* is a stunningly beautiful translation of devotional poems from South India. *Myths and Symbols in Indian Art and Civilization,* by Heinrich Zimmer (completed and edited by Joseph Campbell), is essential for the art or mythology buff, and Stuart Cary Welch's *India: Art and Culture, 1300–1900* is a lavishly illustrated volume by a great connoisseur. The colorful mini-book *India and the Mughal Dynasty,* by Valérie Berinstain, makes a great pocket companion in much of North India. For ravishing photographs see *A Day in the Life of India,* people going about their business; *India Modern,* a contemporary treatment of traditional buildings and crafts; and the oversize retrospective *River of Colour: The India of Raghubir Singh.*

Traveler's India is a magazine designed to get your creative juices flowing as you plan your trip, with features on history, destinations, activities (horseback-riding in Rajasthan, say), and people (a short interview with Vikram Chandra; a profile of an American curator of Indian art). For an issue or a subscription contact Zeno Marketing Communications, Inc. (✉ 599 Edison Dr., East Windsor, NJ 08520, 609/426–0016, zenocom@aol.com).

Fiction

Rudyard Kipling's *Kim* is still the most intimate fictional account of India by a Westerner. In E. M. Forster's *A Passage to India,* the conflict between Indians and their British rulers is played out in the story of a man accused of rape. Bengali poet and Nobel Laureate Rabindranath Tagore wrote some enduring novels including *Gora* and *The Home and the World. Midnight's Children,* by Salman Rushdie, is the epic tale of a boy who was born the moment India gained independence. Rushdie's *The Moor's Last Sigh,* woven around a young man of mixed heritage, paints incomparably sensual portraits of Bombay and Cochin. Vikram Seth's mesmerizing *A Suitable Boy* portrays middle-class life in the 1950s through a timeless story of young love. Rohinton Mistry's *A Fine Balance* is an extraordinary study of the human condition, as experienced by a motley group of characters in 1970s Bombay; Mistry's *Such a Long Journey* weaves the poignant tale of a Parsi householder caught in a sudden whirl of tragedy. Arundhati Roy's *The God of Small Things,* set in 1960s Kerala, tells a disturbing story of brother-and-sister twins raised by a single mother. Bapsi Sidhwa's *Cracking India* sees the bloody partition of India and Pakistan through the eyes of a young girl in Lahore. Amit Chaudhuri's short novel *A Strange and Sublime Address* (published in the U.S. with Chaudhuri's *Freedom Song*) is a gorgeous story about a 10-year-old boy's stay with relatives in Calcutta. Anita Desai's *Fasting, Feasting* concerns a contemporary Indian family whose son goes off to college in the United States. *Hullabaloo in the Guava Orchard,* by Anita Desai's daughter Kiran Desai, is a hilarious look at family life in small-town India, centering on a young man's decision to go live in a guava tree. *Love and Longing in Bombay,* by Vikram Chandra, is a collection of short stories with a single narrator. Upamanyu Chatterjee's *English August* is a funny account of a contemporary rookie in the Indian Civil Service. Ahmed Ali's *Twilight in Delhi* gives a poignant account of Muslim urban society early in the 20th century. Khushwant Singh's *Delhi* is a bawdy and ultimately moving romp through Delhi's tumultuous history.

Not all good Indian writing has been published in the West. Once you're in India, look for English translations of Intizar Hussain's *Basti* and A. R. Ananthamurthy's *Samskara,* as well as new translated fiction from Macmillan India. Some of Tagore's poetry can be read in translation in such volumes as *Gitanjali* (1911) and *The Crescent Moon* (1913).

Film

The prolific Indian film industry has produced a wealth of historical and adventure movies, as well as some of the great international art films. India's premier filmmaker, Satyajit Ray, wrote and directed *Pather Panchali* (1955), *Aparajito* (1956), and *The World of Apu* (1959), a powerful trilogy depicting poverty and tragedy in the life of a Bengali boy. A prime example of Indian costume melodrama is *Aan* (1952), directed by Mehboob, a story of royalty tamed by peasants. *Shakespeare Wallah* (1965), written by Ruth Prawer Jhabvala and James Ivory and directed by Ivory, features a group of English actors on tour in India. *Heat and Dust* (1982), also written by Prawer Jhabvala and directed by Ivory, re-creates India's past through the discovery of a series of old letters. Deepa Mehta has made two major films: *Fire* (1996), in which two beautiful but neglected sisters-in-law turn to each other for affection, and *Earth* (1999), an adaptation of Bapsi Sidhwa's novel *Cracking India*. Both were highly controversial in India, as is Mehta's most recent film, *Water,* set in Varanasi.

Films set in India by Western directors are numerous. *Phantom India* (1969), directed by Louis Malle, is an epic documentary of Indian life. The award-winning *Gandhi* (1982), directed by Richard Attenborough, traces the adult life of the leader of India's independence movement. Based on E. M. Forster's novel, *A Passage to India* (1984) was directed by David Lean. *The Jewel in the Crown* (1984), a TV series based on part of Paul Scott's *Raj Quartet,* is an epic portrayal of Britain's last years of power in India, involving a romance between a British woman and an Indian man. *Salaam Bombay* (1988), directed by Mira Nair, is a heartbreaking fictionalized exposé of Bombay's homeless and slum children. *City of Joy* (1992), starring Patrick Swayze, is based on Dominique Lapierre's book about Calcutta.

THE HINDI LANGUAGE

Michael W.
Bollom

Among India's sixteen "official" languages, English and Hindi are the most commonly spoken. You can generally get by in English wherever you travel in India—and in the south you'll find more people speak English than Hindi. Nonetheless, a little Hindi will prove incredibly useful as you travel in the Hindi Belt—areas north of Maharashtra, east of Gujarat, west of Bengal, and south of Punjab. Outside the larger cities, where countless dialects are spoken, a few key Hindi words will improve your lot considerably. Even better, any attempt to speak Hindi will endear you to the Indians you encounter.

Hindi is a phonetic language. Once you learn the characters (30 consonants and 11 vowels), you can read and pronounce any Hindi word written in the traditional Devanagari script (recognizable by the line across the tops of the letters). This won't help you with the vocabulary, as Hindi and English share no cognates—you'll simply have to memorize the words and phrases below. One thing to remember is that people in India don't really say "please" and "thank you"; *kripeeya* is the term, but it's seldom used. "Please" is not listed down below, and the word for 'thank you' is not listed as 'kripeeya.' Other things to remember is that plenty of English words, such as minute, left, right, dentist, and doctors, as well as days of the week, that have been incorporated into the Hindi language. For food terms, see the dining glossary below.

One note on pronunciation: English speakers tend to heavily accent one syllable in a word at the expense of the others. Do not pronounce Hindi words this way or Indians will not understand you. Each syllable in a word should get equal treatment. Also, [n] is a nasalization of the preceding vowel, like the "n" in the French word garçon; you don't actually pronounce the [n].

English	Hindi	Pronunciation

Basics

English	Hindi	Pronunciation
Hello/goodbye (standard greeting in India)	namaste	nah-mas-tay
Hello/goodbye (Muslim greeting)	Salaam ale kum	sah-laam ah-lay come
Hello/goodbye (Sikh greeting)	sat sree akaal	sat sree ah kahl
My name is__.	Mera nam __.	may-rah nahm __.
What's your name?	Ap ka nam kya hai?	Ahp kah nahm kee-ya heh?
Yes	hah[n]	hah[n]
No	nahee[n]	nah-ee[n]
Thank you	dhanyavad	dhun-yuh-vahd (Hindu)
	shukreeya	shuk-ree-yah (Muslim)
Mr.	shree	shree (Hindu)
Mr. (preferred among Urdu speakers, and more commonly used in India)	sahib	sah-yeeb (Muslim)

Mrs.	shreemati	shree-mah-tee (Hindu)
Mrs. (preferred among Urdu speakers, and more commonly used in India)	memsahib	mem-sah-yeeb (Muslim)
Excuse me/sorry	maf kijeye	mahf kih-jee-yay
Forgive me	maf karo	mahf kah-ro
Get lost (also means "let's go" when said more benignly)	Chalo!	chah-lo!
What?	kya?	kee-yah?
Who?	kaun?	kow[n]?
Why?	kyo(n)?	kee-yoh[n]?
Water	panee	pah-nee
Food	khana	kah-nah

Time expressions

Today	aaj	ahj
Yesterday/tomorrow	kal	kull
Minute	minute	min-uht
Hour	ghanta	ghun-tah
Day	din	doyn
Week	hafta	huff-tah
Month	mahina	ma-heen-ah
Year	saal	sull
When	kab	kuhb
Morning	suube	soo-bay
(in the) afternoon	dopaher (ko)	doh-pah-herr koh
(in the) evening	shaam (ko)	shahm koh
(at) night	raat (ko)	raht koh

Health

I feel ill.	Mai[n] bimaar hu[n].	May bee-mahr hoo[n].
Pain	dard	dahrd
Stomach trouble	payt me gadbad	pah-yut may gud-bud
Indigestion	apacha	ah-pahch-ah
Headache	sir dard	sehr dahrd
Hospital	aspataal	ahs-pah-taal
Medicine	davaa	dah-vah

Numbers

1	ek	ache
2	do	doh
3	teen	teen
4	chaar	chahr
5	paanch	pahnch

6	che	chay
7	saat	saht
8	ath	aht
9	nau	now
10	das	duss
20	bees	bees
25	pachees	pah-chees
50	pachaas	pah-chahs
75	pachatar	pah-chah-tar
100	sau	sau (like ow with an s)
1,000	hazaar	hah-zaar
100,000	lakh	lahk
10,000,000	kror	kror (like roar with a k)

Shopping

Store	duukan	doo-kahn
Clothes/cloth (Use kapre to buy clothes, kapra to buy cloth.)	kapre/kapra	kuhp-ray/kuhp-rah
How much is this?	Ye kaise diya?	Yay kay-say dee-yah? (standard colloquial)
	Kitna	kit-nah (literally "How much?")
I want to buy ___.	Mai[n] ___ karidna chahaata hu[n].	May __ kah-reed-nah chah-haht-ah hoo[n].
Too much	zyaada	zeh-yah-dah
Reduce a bit	Kutch kam kijiye.	Kuhch calm kih-gee-yay.

Useful Phrases

Don't touch! (Important with unwanted attention)	Mat Chuo!	Maht-choo-oh!
I need ___.	Mujhe ___ chahiye.	Muh-jay __ chah-ee-yay.
How are you?	Aap kaise hai?	Ahp kay-say heh[n]?
Do you speak English?	Aap English bolte hai?	Ahp English bol-tay heh[n]?
I don't understand.	Samaj mai nahee aya.	Suh-mahj may na-hee[n] ah-yah.
I don't know.	Mujhe nahee pata.	Muh-jay na-hee[n] puh-tah.
I am lost.	Mai gum gaya.	May[n] gum gah-yah.
Just a moment.	Ek minute.	Ache min-uht.
What is this?	Ye kya hai?	Yay kee-yah heh[n]?

Where is the _____?	___ kaha hai?	_ kuh-hah[n] heh[n]?
A lot/very	bahut bara	bah-hoot bah-rah

DINING GLOSSARY

Aloo: potato
Baigan: eggplant
Barfi: milk-based sweet
Basmati rice: fragrant rice grown in the north
Besan: chickpea flour
Bhajia: vegetable fritters
Bhindi: okra
Biryani: rice dish
Chat: cold, spicy fruit or vegetable salad
Chai: tea
Chana: chickpeas
Chapati: unleavened whole wheat bread
Chawal: rice (generic)
Chutney: relish
Curd: yogurt
Dal: cooked lentils
Dosa: fried, crêpelike pancake (*masala dosa* is typical)
Dum pukht: stewlike, slow-cooked meals
Falooda: cellophane vermicelli
Feni: Goan cashew-nut liquor
Firni: sweet ground-rice pudding with pistachios
Garam masala: blend of roasted spices
Ghee: clarified butter
Gobi: cauliflower
Gosht: lamb or mutton
Gulab jamun: fried, syrupy milk balls
Haldi: tumeric
Idli: steamed rice cakes
Imli: tamarind
Jhingha: prawn; also called *chingra*
Jira: cumin
Kadhai: foods prepared in an iron pot similar to a wok
Katoris: small metal bowls placed on the *thali* (☞ *below*)
Kheer: cold, creamy rice pudding
Kichiri: rice-and-*dal* dish
Kofta: spicy meatballs
Kulcha: *naan* (☞ *below*) stuffed with herbs and onion
Kulfi: Indian ice cream
Ladoo: sugar balls roasted with *ghee*
Lassi: cold, sweet or salty yogurt drink
Machli: fish
Malai kofta: meatballs in creamy tomato sauce
Masala: spicy sauce (literally "mix")
Masala chai: spiced, sweet tea with milk
Mattar: peas
Methi paratha: bread stuffed with fenugreek leaves
Mirchi: chili
Murgh: chicken
Murgh reshmi: spicy minced chicken roll
Naan: leavened bread baked in *tandoor*
Namak: salt
Nimbu pani: lemonade

Paan: betel leaf stuffed with spices, nuts, or tobacco
Pakora: fritters
Paneer: compressed cheese
Papeeta: papaya
Pappadum: wafers
Pista: pistachio
Pomfret: fish similar to flounder
Poori: deep-fried puffed bread
Pullao: rice and meat dish
Pyaz: onion
Raita: spiced yogurt dish
Rasam: lentil broth served in the south
Rasmallai: sweet ricotta balls in creamy sauce
Roti: bread
Saag: spinach or mustard greens
Sabzi: vegetables
Sambar: South Indian dal, served with *dosas*
Samosa: deep-fried pastry stuffed with meat or vegetables
Seb: apple
Shaan-e-murgh: chicken breast stuffed with paneer
Shami kebab: deep-fried ground meat patty
Tandoor: clay oven
Thali: sampler of assorted dishes, served on a metal plate
Undhia: Gujarati mixed-vegetable dish

INDEX